A BIOGRAPHICAL DICTIONARY
OF DISSENTING ECONOMISTS

A Biographical Dictionary of Dissenting Economists

Edited by
Philip Arestis
Polytechnic of East London

and Malcolm Sawyer
University of Leeds

Edward Elgar

Published by
Edward Elgar Publishing Limited
Gower House
Croft Road
Aldershot
Hants GU11 3HR
England

Edward Elgar Publishing Limited
Distributed in the United States by
Ashgate Publishing Company
Old Post Road
Brookfield
Vermont 05036
USA

A CIP catalogue record for this book
is available from the British Library

Library of Congress Cataloguing in Publication Data
Arestis, Philip, 1941–
    A Biographical dictionary of dissenting economists/edited by
Philip Arestis and Malcolm Sawyer.
        p.   cm.
        1. Economists–Biography–Dictionaries. I. Sawyer, Malcolm C.
    HB76.B5 1991
    330'.0922–dc20
    [B]   91–16267
                                                                  CIP

ISBN 1 85278 331 1

Printed in Great Britain by
Billing & Sons Ltd, Worcester

Contents

Introduction

Many economists like to think of their discipline as a science where progress is made through the advancing of new theories and the careful empirical evaluation of such theories. Despite the criticism which this approach has received from philosophers of science, there is a strong belief amongst many economists that the central criterion of the adequacy of a theory is its predictive accuracy; the realism of its assumptions is not seen as an important issue and is thus ignored. Further, any economic analysis which does not provide predictions, even if it supplies explanation and insights, is dismissed. The economists that hold these views see themselves as ideologically neutral observers; as such the personalities, social backgrounds and political beliefs of their colleagues in the discipline are of little interest other than as gossip. Further, the economic system is viewed as harmonious with no essential conflicts between social classes.

The starting point of this dictionary is quite different. It is firmly based on the view that economics is *not* a neutral science, practised without thought being given to its social and political effects. The high priests of the economics profession decide what is published and who is to be appointed, thereby providing strong continuity for the prevailing orthodoxy. Despite this, many economists have dissented and sought to explore other avenues. Naturally, knowledge of their work and their lives is not as readily available as comparable knowledge about orthodox economists. This is precisely why we were persuaded that a dictionary of this kind may not only be welcome but long overdue. Consequently, we decided to emphasize two aspects in the dictionary. The first is to allow dissenters to describe the avenues which they have personally explored. The second is to see what social and political influences have been at work on individuals: why do they think they came to adopt the views they did? We have asked contributors to pay special attention in their analyses to these two aspects.

The dominant paradigm in economics is the neoclassical one. This has been particularly so in the United States and to a lesser degree in the native English-speaking world. In much of Continental Europe, neoclassical economics did not achieve the same dominance since Marxist economics had much more influence than in North America and Britain. The growing importance of the English language in economic discourse has been one of the forces spreading the influence of neoclassicism, particularly in, but not restricted to, Europe. But in the last 25 years the previously dominant neo-

Keynesianism (or to use Joan Robinson's expression 'bastard Keynesianism') has lost much of its influence and we have witnessed, perhaps as a reaction, an upsurge of work on a range of alternative approaches to economic analysis.

Neoclassical economics has been dominant in two major respects. The first is that the economists (including most Nobel prizewinners) and academic journals with the highest prestige operate predominantly within the neoclassical paradigm. The second is that the economic analysis to which students are systematically exposed is neoclassical. Systematic treatment of, say, post-Keynesian or Marxian economics is not often found in the teaching of the discipline, though textbooks on which such teaching can be based are now widely available. However, the disquiet which many economists feel over this orthodoxy has prompted some dissenting economics to be taught as a critique of that orthodoxy. More recently, and as a reaction to this disquiet, dissenting economics is quite often taught on compulsory courses. This is rather more the case in Europe than in the USA.

In neoclassical economic analysis, the focus is on the behaviour of the individual, who is viewed as a rational being with well-defined objectives which are ruthlessly pursued in an environment with good information. The interaction between individuals takes place through arms-length market relationships, and questions of power, class, race etc are ignored; moreover, as mentioned earlier, little attention is paid to social and political institutions. Society is viewed and analysed from the point of view of the individual rather than the individual in relation to society. Individual economic actors, whether households or firms, are seen as subordinated to a hypothetical market mechanism, relating to one another through this mechanism. This asocial element is not restricted to exchange but also covers production where factors are combined according to a technically determined relationship to produce the output.

The dissent indicated in the title of this dictionary is from neoclassical economics. Such dissenters are identified by a variety of labels (and sometimes no label at all) including institutionalist, post-Keynesian, Kaleckian, Marxian and neo-Marxian, Sraffian and radical political economists. The emergence of neoclassical economics can be dated from the 1870s and hence dissent from it some time later. This has led us to include only people who have made their main intellectual contribution in the twentieth century (causing the omission of some intellectual giants such as Marx). A few have disagreed with the title of the dictionary on the grounds that it is neoclassical economics which is the diversion from the classical tradition (from Ricardo and Marx): thus, it is argued, those we label as dissenters are the true descendants of the classical economists from whom the neoclassicists have diverged. This view may well be historically correct since the classical and surplus tradition clearly predates the neoclassical one. However, we have to recognize that the latter has been the dominant orthodoxy in the twentieth century, so that it is from that tradition that dissent occurs, a view accepted by most of our contributors.

A great deal of economic analysis is not specifically neoclassical, notably most of the study of industrial economics and much of (especially Keynesian) macroeconomics. These are areas of analysis which have sought to confront real-world problems, areas where neoclassical economics has been found wanting, though its advocates have sought increasingly to recapture them. Many who have felt uneasy with neoclassical economics have found a haven in, for example, industrial economics. There have been many who have made important contributions to these and other areas who could be included as non-neoclassical. Indeed the empirical work which has been carried out by such economists can often been used to underpin the analyses undertaken by dissenting economists. However, we have limited inclusion to those who have been explicit in their dissent from the neoclassical tradition.

The fact that dissenting economists have disagreements amongst themselves is reflected in this dictionary: some contributors are strongly critical of the work of other contributors. Indeed at times there have been sharp debates and a degree of intolerance amongst non-neoclassical economists. Nevertheless, it is possible to highlight some themes which a wide range of dissenting economists (though not all) would view as important. In methodological terms, there is an emphasis on *realism* in that theories should represent economic reality as accurately as possible. The construction of theory begins with 'realistic abstractions' rather than 'imaginary models' so that explanation, rather than prediction, is emphasized. When realism is highlighted in this way, it is inevitable that institutions and history become an integral part of economic analysis. However, this emphasis on realism does not rule out a concern with metaphysical questions such as the source of value.

Since the approach is organic, rather than atomistic, a more complex view of human nature and of individual behaviour has to be adopted than that found in neoclassical economics. Humans are viewed as social, rather than individual, animals. In this sense, the distribution aspects of economic theory and policy are particularly emphasized by dissenting economists; many would also focus on the antagonistic nature of the class conflict under capitalism and other social systems. The categories of value and surplus, however much they may be criticized for internal inconsistencies, encapsulate this antagonism directly (whereas the categories of profit and real wage in orthodox economics express the antagonism only by the imposition of external forces which are not fundamental to the theory). Although neoclassical economics has developed theories of growth, its primary concern is with the uses of existing resources. Dissenting economists, however, have made growth and accumulation central to their theorizing. These are important topics in their own right, but for many in the non-neoclassical tradition they permeate the whole of their economic analysis. For example, the determination of prices has significance for the distribution of income between profits and wages, while profits form a substantial part of the finance for accumulation.

The study of growth and accumulation, however, can only be undertaken satisfactorily in a specific historical context. The relevance of the emphasis on history is that the past of an economic system cannot be changed, whilst the future is uncertain. Uncertainty here means that the future is unknowable and unpredictable with the result that people's expectations can easily be frustrated. Yet expectations about the future must be formed to guide decision-making. Since market forces cannot deal with the unknowability and unpredictability of the future, other economic and social institutions must be used. This is one reason, amongst many, why most dissenting economists are critical of the consequences of unrestrained market forces.

It is this inherent uncertainty that leads to the existence of money, which provides liquidity and flexibility in the presence of lack of knowledge about the future. The importance of money is that it provides a link between the past and the present, and also between the present and the future. In this and other ways, banking and credit institutions assume paramount importance in the analyses advanced by many dissenting economists. Emphasis on them is only part of a general recognition of the many powerful institutions which mould much of economic life. Multinational corporations, for instance, have substantial power arising from their size and the international scale of their operations; their study has been central in the work of a number of dissenting economists. For them, it is clearly the case that the institutional arrangements of a society should be taken into account when the workings of an economy are analysed. These institutional factors are to be interpreted widely. They range from the size and control of firms, the extent of unionization amongst workers and the relationship between these (and other) groups to the legal framework within which these groups operate. The organization and control of the economic system are the issues here. The structure of power and conflict within that framework can be said to be of paramount importance in this analysis.

Underlying all these aspects is a strong belief that the subject matter of 'dissenting economists' is not economic analysis isolated from other social sciences. Such an approach to the study of economy and society is inevitably very much historical and political, as well as an antithesis to the notion of a value-free study as propagated by orthodox economists.

The major purpose of the dictionary is to provide a guide to the significant contributions of a number of important dissenting economists from around the world. We have sought to include names from a wide range of countries, not just the Anglo-Saxon ones, to give the dictionary a truly international character. But despite our efforts, a bias towards Anglo-Saxon economists remains. We hope to rectify this bias and other omissions in future editions and would welcome suggestions from our readers. Some previous biographical dictionaries of economists have included those whose work is most often cited by others ('citation count'). This approach was not available to us since the work of dissenters is seldom referred to in the major economics journals. Instead we drew up a provisional list on which comments were obtained from a wide range of colleagues, leading to a final list. The enthusiasm with which people have responded to our invitations to comment and to contribute have confirmed the potential usefulness of this dictionary.

People on the list for inclusion who are alive were invited to write their own contribution, and most of them have done so. In a few cases, they suggested someone else to write an entry on them, and we have duly invited the person named. Authors' names are omitted from the headings where the entries are autobiographical. Unfortunately, a small number of people have declined our invitation to contribute which largely explains the omissions which readers may notice.

We have not sought to impose a common pattern on entries, apart from the listing of major publications at the end of each and asking for a focus on their journeys through economics and how and by whom they have been influenced. We have not sought to achieve homogeneous entries. Although a certain amount of editing has been undertaken, we have not insisted on a single format or style. Thus in what follows, the reader will observe a variety of styles which are much more diverse than what might usually be expected in a dictionary of this type. By not imposing a common pattern the reader can gain some 'flavour' of the differences in approach and character of dissenting economists. Neither have we sought to vary the length of entries according to the 'importance' of the contributions made by the person concerned or any other criteria. All contributors were asked to write to the same length, though inevitably some were better at keeping to this restriction than others.

People writing about themselves decided whether they would use the first or third person, and most have chosen the former. A number of entries refer to early education: it should be noted here that for entries written by Americans, public schools are state-financed schools whilst for British entries public schools are private schools and grammar schools are selective state schools. In the text, publications by the various authors are referred to either by the title or by the year of publication. The full reference is provided at the end of the entry, as well as full details of other works which are referred to in the text.

Major political events (notably the rise of fascism in the 1930s, the Vietnam war and student protest in the late 1960s) have frequently had a significant impact on shaping the approach which individuals have adopted towards economic analysis. Others have highlighted the impact of their teachers, usually from the dissenting tradition. Still others have emphasized the iniquitous nature of the capitalist system in which they have been brought up. All have seen the purpose of economic analysis to be the understanding and improvement of the world in which we all live.

In compiling this dictionary we have received enthusiastic cooperation from many people. Some were already friends (and we hope that they remain so after our exploitation of them), and others have become so through contact over this project. Our friends, old and new, who have helped us are so many that any attempt to enumerate them here would not only be lengthy but run a serious risk of unintentional omissions. We do though allow ourselves three exceptions. We would like to thank by name Marion Tighe (from the Department of Applied Economics, Polytechnic of East London) and Sue Howard (from Edward Elgar Publishing Co) for their excellent secretarial and other assistance, and Edward Elgar for the initial suggestion for this dictionary and his subsequent support. We simply wish to express sincerely to all who have helped us, named and unnamed, our profound thanks. It can be truly said that without their assistance this dictionary would not have been possible.

Samir AMIN (born 1931)

Samir was born in Cairo in 1931 and was educated at the Lycée Français there. He gained a Ph.D. degree in Political Economy in Paris (1957) as well as degrees from the Institut de Statistiques and from the Institut d'Etudes Politiques. He then returned home where he was attached to the Planning bodies of Nasser's regime. He left Egypt in 1960 to work with the Ministry of Planning of the newly independent Mali (1960–63) and following this commenced an academic career. He has held the position of full Professor in France since 1966 and was for ten years (1970–80) the director of the UN African Institute for Economic Development and Planning (in Dakar). Since 1980 he has been directing the African Office of the Third World Forum, an international non-governmental association for research and debate.

The main contributions of Samir Amin can be classified under four headings: (i) a critique of the theory and experiences of development; (ii) an alternative proposal for the analysis of the global system which he calls 'really existing capitalism'; (iii) a re-reading of the history of social formations, and (iv) a reinterpretation of what he describes as 'post capitalist' societies.

Amin's critique of the theory of development goes back to his Ph.D. dissertation (1957) published later under the title *Accumulation on a World Scale*. Conventional theory presents a general view of the problem that might be summed up in the simple proposition that 'underdevelopment' is nothing more than delayed development. The emerging conclusions advocate 'development policies' focused on more thorough participation in the international division of labour. *Accumulation* was among the first texts to challenge this conventional wisdom. Bourgeois economics finds attractive only the study of contingent interconnections resulting from the play of such strictly economic phenomena as prices and incomes. Moreover, in this exercise it invariably posits a hypothetical system close to the 'ideal type' of capitalism. For that reason, an examination of bourgeois economic statements on 'underdevelopment' throws into exceedingly sharp relief the inadequacies and the narrow range of the conventional 'science' of economics. The limitations are most clearly visible in three areas of economic analysis: monetary problems, the conjunctural state of the economy, and international relations. That is hardly an accident. The ebb and flow of economic tides indicate that in proffering its hypotheses of spontaneous, ineluctable balance, bourgeois economics turns a blind eye to the contradictory dynamics inherent in capitalist accumulation. As for the theories it propounds on international exchanges, notably those of comparative advantage and the self-equilibrating balance of external payments, they rise no higher than a vapid ideology of universal harmony between nations operating as partners in the world capitalist system.

1

Such was the critical thrust developed in *Accumulation*. However, bourgeois economics aspires to the formulation of a social philosophy asserting a broader idea: that in its spread, the market of commodities and 'production factors' creates maximal conditions for the satisfaction of all, thus constituting a rational process transcending history. This claim stands on shaky ground. For the discipline of 'economics' itself is nothing more than a pseudo-science, a consequence of the economic alienation peculiar to capitalism. 'Economics' is the result of that peculiarly capitalist trait whereby phenomena generated by society seem to confront that same society as if they were natural laws external to it. Thus linked to the illusion of a rationality beyond history, bourgeois socio-economic philosophy is unable to deal with the real history of societies.

Beyond this critique Amin offers an alternative methodology to deal with the analysis of global capitalism in two books, *Imperialism and Unequal Development* and *The Law of Value and Historical Materialism*. According to him there are two ways of looking at the social reality of our modern world. The first stresses the fundamental relationship which defines the capitalist mode of production at its most abstract level and, from there, focuses on the allegedly fundamental class struggle between the proletariat and the bourgeoisie. The second stresses the other dimension of capitalist reality, its unequal development worldwide, and hence focuses its analysis on the consequences that polarization involves at every level, thus defining other issues in the political and social struggles that occupy the forefront of the historical stage. In this analytical framework, the development of the periphery has always been the history of a never-ending 'adjustment' to the demands and constraints of dominant capital. The centres 'restructure' themselves and the peripheries are 'adjusted' to these restructurings. Delinking is precisely reversing this relation; that is, subordinating external relations to the logic of internal development.

Polarization on a global level is thus the immanent product of the expansion of really existing capitalism. On the scale of the world capitalist system, the law of value operates on the basis of a truncated market which integrates the commerce of products and the movements of capital but excludes labour power from it. The worldwide law of value then tends to standardize the prices of merchandise but not the remunerations of labour since its range of world distribution is infinitely more open than that of the distribution of productivity. Even beyond the law of worldwide value, unequal access to natural resources, technological monopolies, extra-economic mechanisms of political and military domination – as well as the effects of the domination of life-styles, organization and consumption – have vastly increased this polarization in every dimension.

In fact, the polarization of wealth and power within the world capitalist system has passed through three stages. In the 17th and 18th centuries, thanks to the colonization of America and its effects on the acceleration of the mercantilist proto-capitalism of Atlantic Europe, that part of the world acquired for the first time a decisive superiority over the old civilizations of the Orient which it prepared to attack, thus bringing a halt to their own proto-capitalist evolution (and sometimes even precipitating regressive involution). In the 19th century the industrial revolution and then imperialism (in the classical Leninist sense of the term) accentuated this polarization of wealth and power which became expressed in the contrast between industrialized and non-industrialized countries. Amin proposes the thesis that the structural crisis of our own epoch, starting in 1970, begins a new stage in world domination (marked by new technologies, new forms of worldwide finance capital etc) which results not in a reduction but an aggravation of polarization. The peripheral industrialization of one part and the 'fourth-worldization' of another part constitute the new forms corresponding to this last stage of polarization.

This polarization has postponed the question of the eventual socialist transformation in the developed capitalist societies, while in the periphery it has required objectively envisaging a 'different development' from the one that would result – in these conditions – from its integration into the world capitalist system.

In this conceptual frame Amin has re-evaluated the various radical attempts at development which occurred throughout the 1960s and 1970s in the Third World (what he calls the 'Bandung Era 1955–75'). The Bandung project was defined by the following features: (i) a determination to develop productive forces and diversify production (notably to industrialize); (ii) a determination to ensure that the national state should lead and control the process; (iii) the belief that 'technical' models are 'neutral' and can simply be reproduced; (iv) the belief that this process does not involve a popular initiative as a starting point but simply popular support for state actions; (v) the belief that this process is not fundamentally in contradiction with participation in the international division of labour even if it involves temporary conflicts with the developed capitalist countries. Realization of this national bourgeois project involved the hegemonic national bourgeois class, through its state, acquiring control in a number of areas, at least of the following processes: (i) control of the reproduction of the labour force, which implies a relatively complete and balanced development so that local agriculture can be, *inter alia*, in a position to provide the basic ingredients of that reproduction in reasonable quantities and at reasonable prices to ensure the valorization of capital; (ii) control of national resources; (iii) control of local markets and the capacity to break through into the world market in competitive conditions; (iv) control of the financial circuits making it possible to centralize the surplus and direct it to productive uses; and (v) control of the technologies in use at the level of development of productive forces reached.

History has exposed the inadequacies and the fragility of the dream of the bourgeois nation-state in today's Third World. For after the initial period of post-war prosperity, the world economy slid into crisis in the early 1970s. Immediately the capitalist camp went on the offensive again and imposed the hard-nosed demands of the transnationalization process on Third World societies. It turned their shattered state machinery into simple transmission belts, and over the grave of the aborted bourgeois national-state, it erected the object of its own desire: the comprador state (1990b).

Amin also developed a reading of history consistent with his concept of unequal development (1980). In his opinion what separates capitalism from all the advanced societies preceding it is not only a quantitative difference of the degree of development of productive forces. The difference is also qualitative. In capitalism, surplus value is obtained through the economic mechanism of the law of value whereas in all earlier societies the extraction of the surplus took the form of a tribute imposed by non-economic means. The contrast between, on the one hand, the transparency of economic phenomena in pre-capitalist societies and, on the other, its opaqueness through the law of value in capitalism leads to a reversal of the hierarchy of authority. Whereas the economy directly commands the capitalist dynamic (which is then expressed through the play of economic laws which seem to impose themselves on society as laws of nature), a politico-ideological authority was dominant in earlier societies. Amin believes that Marx emphasized precisely this reversal of relations between structure and superstructure and therefore emphasized the essential character common to all advanced pre-capitalist forms (which Amin calls, for that reason, the 'tributary mode of production') in contrast to capitalism. Unfortunately, the dominant currents of Marxism refused to consider the superstructural dynamics (contenting themselves with a vague theory of the superstructure as a 'reflection' of the exigencies of the economic base), just as they refused to analyse the systems of pre-capitalist societies closely bound by multiple relations – political, cultural (religious among others) and economic. This reduction of Marxism did not predispose it to understand the transition to capitalism, while it inspired research in a false direction, namely that of the possible 'succession' of modes of production such as that of slavery-feudalism. Or by default, Marxism became trapped in the mythological contrast of the 'two roads': the open Occidental way (slavery-feudalism-capitalism) and the cul-de-sac of the 'Asiatic mode of production'. Amin has rejected these theses and has tried to demonstrate their Eurocentric character.

According to Amin, pre-capitalist societies are characterized by differentiation of the principal source or authority because of what he has called the 'central' or 'peripheral' nature of the tributary society under consideration. The 'central' or 'peripheral' character in pre-capitalism can be found in the area of the dominant authority, that is to say in the State (power) and in ideology (cultures, religions), whereas the 'central' or 'peripheral' character of a capitalist formation is located in the area of the economy. In this sense, Amin has defined feudalism not as a specific mode of production but as a specific – peripheral – form of tributary society. It was peripheral simply because the centralization of state power which defines central tributary society was embryonic: the absolute monarchies (close to the advanced tributary model) appeared relatively late in Europe, precisely in the proto-capitalist phase of the mercantilist transition. Amin has explained this peripheral character of feudalism by the proximity of the communal phase among the barbarians from which medieval Europe developed. But this lag in Europe – less advanced than the Oriental tributaries – did not seem to have been a handicap in the acceleration of later development, but on the contrary was an advantage because of the greater flexibility of the society which it encompassed.

Amin later developed his reflections on culture through a critique of Eurocentrism which he qualified as 'culturalism', meaning that it is based on the hypothesis that the different 'cultures' (European, Oriental) are charac-terized by transhistorical invariants which determine developments; these are not subject to the laws of general evolution. There he tried to show the mythological character of these invariants, artificially constructed both to legitimize the specific dynamic opened by European history (by the myths of Greek ancestry, by 'Christianophilia', by racism) and to legitimize by contrast the supposed impasse of other societies.

It is also in this overall framework that Amin discusses the issues of socialism (1983, 1989b, 1990a). In his opinion, Marx underestimated the centre-periphery polarization in the worldwide process of capitalist expan-sion. Marx thought that following industrial revolution, the capitalist system would take very little time to accomplish its universalizing mission. Reality worked out differently.

According to Amin, the challenging of the capitalist order from revolts in its periphery compels a rethink of the whole question of 'socialist transition' towards the abolition of classes. The Marxist tradition remains handicapped by its initial theoretical vision of 'workers' revolutions' opening up (on the basis of advanced productive forces) a rapid transition marked by popular democratic rule which should be considerably more democratic than the most democratic of bourgeois states. Nevertheless, all the revolutions of our time (Russia, China, Vietnam, Cuba, Yugoslavia etc) that were unmistakably socialist in intent have been the result of the unequal development in capitalist expansion. Global polarization has thus been the historical force behind these types of revolutions by the *peoples* of the periphery. They have been anti-capitalist in the sense of opposing existing capitalist development which has proved intolerable for the people. But that does not mean that these anti-capitalist revolutions are purely socialist. By the force of circumstance, they have a complex nature. The expression of their specific and new contradictions, which had not been imagined in the classical perspective of the socialist transition as conceived by Marx, gives post-capitalist regimes their real content, which is that of a *popular national construction* in which the socialist and capitalist forces and projects combine and conflict. This objective contradiction should be managed through political democracy and a mixed economy. Instead it has been managed through statism which negated its very existence, thus reflecting the reconstruction of privileged class interests.

Will the ongoing crisis of alleged socialist societies lead to the restoration of capitalism? Amin has stressed three main challenges that these societies face. First, the democratic issue: will they accept a pure and simple restoration of bourgeois political democracy or will they succeed in giving it a progressive content and thus move towards the social management of the economy? Second, the market issue: will these countries simply accept the law of market, which is bound to be operating savagely against them, or will they succeed in mastering the market through non-bureaucratic social planning? Third, the external issue: will these countries reintegrate into the world economy and so inevitably be peripheralized or will they succeed in mastering their opening of their economies? Amin argues that the answers to these questions will depend on the outcome of the ongoing social struggles. Will class interests override the popular dimension of the systems and opt openly for capitalism or, by contrast, will this dimension be reinforced through democracy?

For Amin the unilateral market solution can never put right unbearable social, political, internal and international contrasts. Critical thought is concerned precisely with identifying alternative social alliances which can provide escape routes from the vicious circles of the market. Different routes are required by the various regions of the world; specific individual policies cannot be derived from the unilateral rationality of the market. The imperatives of our time therefore imply the rebuilding of the world system on the basis of polycentrism. The various regions and countries should coordinate their visions and subordinate their external relations to the constraints of their internal development. They must not be tempted to adjust their internal development to the global expansion of capitalism.

The social alliances which define the content of the strategies for the various regions are necessarily different. In the West they will certainly keep a 'bourgeois' dimension, produced by a long history of advanced development. This reality does not preclude an evolution towards a socialization. In the East the alliances will call for a liberation of society from the exclusive rule of the state and will encourage a social dialectic which recognizes the conflict between capitalism and socialism. But in the Third World they will more often call for revolutionary change since here the bourgeois subalternization is unbearable. In all cases one can acknowledge a popular, national and regional content rather than a unilateral bourgeois vision of the market. This dramatic challenge is felt in the South stronger than in the West or in the East, but *Perestroika* is needed everywhere.

Amin suffers no illusions as to whether Marxism is going through a crisis. For him whoever approaches historical materialism as a method (not as a definitive theory forever sealed and delivered at the death of Marx, Lenin or Mao) knows that the changing realities of life present a dynamic Marxism with a continuing series of challenges to creative innovation. To renew its vitality, Marxism has to meet these challenges. The penalty for failure is atrophy. Only religious dogmatism, which is impervious to reality, is capable of seeing in an intellectual crisis nothing but threats to its own certainties.

Amin's Major Writings

(1974), *Accumulation on a World Scale*, two volumes, New York: Monthly Review Press.
(1976), *Unequal Development*, New York: Monthly Review Press.
(1977), *Imperialism and Unequal Development*, New York: Monthly Review Press.
(1978a), *The Arab Nation*, London: Zed.
(1978b), *The Law of Value and Historical Materialism*, New York: Monthly Review Press.
(1980), *Class and Nation, Historically and in the Current Crisis*, New York: Monthly Review Press.
(1983), *The Future of Maoism*, New York: Monthly Review Press.
(1989a), *Eurocentrism*, London: Zed; New York: Monthly Review Press.
(1989b), *After Capitalism, What ?* (in Arabic) Beyrout.
(1990a), *Delinking*, London: ZED.
(1990b), *Maldevelopment in Africa and in the Third World*, London: ZED.

Amin writes mainly in French and Arabic. A bibliography up to 1980, with commentary, is available in *The Arab Economy Today* (London: Zed) written by Aidan Foster-Carter, 'The Empirical Samir Amin: A Notice and Appreciation'.

Clarence Edwin AYRES (1891–1972)　　　　*Anne Mayhew*

Clarence Ayres, born and brought up in Massachusetts, received his B.A. and M.A. degrees from Brown University in 1912 and 1914 and his Ph.D. from the University of Chicago in 1917. At both institutions he combined the study of economics and philosophy, writing his dissertation on the 'The Nature of the Relationship Between Ethics and Economics'. After a brief period as an instructor in philosophy at the University of Chicago he was appointed associate professor of philosophy at Amherst in 1920.

Three themes of Ayres's career as a dissenting economist – his interest in current economic problems, Thorstein Veblen's influence on him, and his commitment to freedom of inquiry – became obvious during his brief career at Amherst where he associated closely with Walton Hamilton, a follower of

Veblen's approach. The programme that Hamilton had created was organized in a Veblenian manner as a study of two separate aspects of the economy: the pecuniary and the non-pecuniary. Everything that we know about Hamilton suggests that his programme was dominated by the application of this concept to the economic problems of the time, particularly to the control of industry in the interests of society. Ayres shared this interest.

Ayres's post-doctoral education with Hamilton ended in 1923. Alexander Meikeljohn, the innovative President of Amherst who had hired both Hamilton and Ayres, was fired by the Board of Trustees. Hamilton, Ayres, and a number of other faculty members resigned in protest. It was an episode that influenced Ayres's thinking about universities throughout his long career.

For Ayres there followed a brief appointment to the faculty at Reed College, a year as an Associate Editor at the *New Republic*, and another year as a teacher of philosophy at the Experimental College of the University of Wisconsin. Then, for a time Ayres lived on a ranch in New Mexico where he wrote his first two books: *Science: the False Messiah* and *Holier Than Thou: The Way of the Righteous*. As Ayres later noted, both of these were written when he still considered himself a philosopher rather than an economist; but both involved applications of Veblen's thought to the way in which science became intertwined with the human tendency to place faith in authority. By the end of the 1920s Ayres had returned to teaching, this time in economics. In 1930 he accepted a position in the Department of Economics at the University of Texas, where he remained until his retirement.

When Ayres assumed the role of academic economist he did so with a commitment to define 'institutional economics' more accurately and to develop the concept further. The name came from Walton Hamilton; the ideas which Ayres elaborated and espoused were originally developed by Veblen. Basic was the idea that all economies are systems made up of patterns of culturally specific human behaviour – of institutions. In turn, these institutions always involve two basic human tendencies: (i) to accept without question the mores, beliefs and legends that we learn through acculturation; and (ii) to use tools to acquire skills and new knowledge. The pecuniary aspects of the US economy stemmed largely from the first tendency; what Veblen called the non-pecuniary or industrial aspects largely from the second. From these apparently simple propositions Ayres mounted a full-scale assault upon conventional economics, offered suggestions as to how economists ought to proceed, and argued for informed economic reform.

Ayres's dissent from orthodox economics may be understood by taking the three propositions in turn.

1.   All economies are systems of patterned behaviour that are part of a specific human culture, a proposition in fundamental contradiction to

the idea that economies are manifestations of natural laws or natural human propensities. Adoption of the idea that patterns of economic behaviour are cultural meant that Ayres disagreed with orthodox economists at the most fundamental level. In an early article written in 1918 ('The Function and Problems of Economic Theory') Ayres denied J.B. Clark's conception of economic science as a search for 'natural' phenomenon, a theme to which he often returned. While Ayres has often been criticized for failing to understand later developments and improvements in microtheory, the truth is that as a responsible professional economist he *was* aware of refinements. However they had no effect on his own work; he dismissed them as efforts to find the hidden meaning of the natural order of things. What Ayres did accept was that the 'phenomena with which all the social sciences, including economics, are concerned are those of culture. ... Culture, the organized corpus of behavior of which economic activity is but a part, is a phenomenon *sui generis* ... it is not an epiphenomenon explicable in other and noncultural terms' (1944, p. 95).

2. People tend to accept without question the mores, beliefs and legends learned through the process of acculturation. Our social and economic organization derives from the past, is part of the culture that we acquire, and takes its force from the fact that it is difficult for humans to question that which they learn through the largely unselfconscious process of acculturation. Ayres used Veblen's term 'ceremonial' to describe that aspect of all institutions – of all patterns of human behaviour – that was 'past binding'. He noted that the term was inadequate because it fails to convey the central proposition that virtually all of what economists normally study is 'ceremonial'. The pecuniary organization of industrial processes – prices and their distributional consequences – is largely 'ceremonial' because it derives from inherited patterns of ownership and control, inherited power and status relationships, and inherited notions of value. These inherited notions are rarely questioned by economists who tend to accept the inherited order and justify it as part of a natural order.

3. The other aspect of human behaviour is the instrumental or technological which produces change and economic progress. By the use of tools people learn to do new things, solve problems and think in new ways. Novelty is thus introduced. The process of developing new tools does not depend upon individual inspiration or genius or upon pecuniary incentives (though those may be present) but occurs on the cultural level. Ayres called this the tool-combination principle. Invention (or discovery, or creation) is a consequence of 'the combination of previously existing devices' (1944, p. 116). New tools are created by com-

bining existing tools rather than by genius, need or a drive for profits, a fact which also explains the increased rapidity of technological change over time. Ayres used the mathematical theory of permutations as an analogy, for growth in the number of tools would progressively increase the number of possible combinations.

Unfortunately Ayres's arguments are subject to oversimplification and can easily be made to sound foolish. It has not been difficult for some to convert his arguments into an effort to classify economic behaviour as either ceremonial or technological, then to denounce the former and praise the latter. Ayres used the basic propositions of his institutional economics differently. Throughout his work he described all patterns of behaviour as a combination of the ceremonial and technological aspects – of faith and continuity combined with tool-using and learning. *The Theory of Economic Progress* offers Ayres's most closely reasoned theory of the economy. Combining tools leads to more and more tools and to an increased ability to manipulate the physical world. This technological change produces institutional change: 'technological development forces change upon the institutional structure by changing the material setting in which it operates' (1944, p. 187). Ayres did not accept the Marxian idea that class conflicts produce change. Nor did he accept the notion popular in sociology that, when institutions suitable to a particular technology are displaced by technological change, they are then replaced by a new set of appropriate institutions after a lag. 'There is no such thing as an institution that is "appropriate" to a given technology in any but a negative sense' (1944, p. 187).

The evolutionary process is carried forward by technological progress. To define progress, to use the term at all, required that Ayres deal with value, as he had been doing from his student days. According to Ayres, a dilemma exists when our realization that social beliefs are culturally determined, rather than reflecting some natural order, leads us to cultural relativism. From this relativism comes the proposition that there is no pancultural source of value. Ayres rejected this conclusion and argued that the 'technological continuum' through which mankind has learned to deal with nature was itself the locus of value. 'Better' has meaning when questions that derive from that continuum are asked and answered using the language of that continuum. Thus the question 'Does a steel knife cut meat better than a stone blade?' can sensibly be asked and answered.

Trouble arises from questions that do not derive from the technological continuum. 'The imagination of mankind is liable to that peculiar sort of stimulation which we have recently identified as "ceremonial". We become excited, and we begin to think in capital letters' (1944, p. 240). Ayres followed John Dewey in insisting that there were no ultimate 'ends' for mankind that would allow us to define PROGRESS (in capital letters) in any absolute sense. 'Ends' are 'means' and 'means' are 'ends', and it all depends upon where you start. Thus, it is exciting for humans who ask 'Does growing more hectares of rice serve the Greater Good of Mankind?' Questions about how many more hectares of rice can be grown, about the effect of this upon the ecology of the region, and about how many people can be fed with the rice can be answered. But asking whether growing additional rice serves a Greater Good cannot be answered as part of the technological continuum. This is frustrating to those who find it difficult to accept either that there are no 'ends' beyond those that we set for ourselves, or that many ends that we set are metaphysical and without pancultural meaning. It was, however, a limit that Ayres lived with quite comfortably.

This comfort may have come in part because of the optimism of the period in which he did much of his work. There did seem to be solutions to the economic ills of the time. In both *The Theory of Economic Progress* and, at much greater length, in *The Divine Right of Capital* Ayres argued strongly for reforms that would encourage the abundance that seemed possible. He insisted that confusing the two meanings of capital – capital as money and capital as industrial goods – stood in the way of industrial progress and full production. Ayres blamed this confusion partly on economists but mainly on the way in which Western economic institutions evolved. Because we confuse ourselves by using the same name for money and for industrial goods, we encourage saving which is the opposite of what is needed to encourage full production. Ayres suggested that if we redistributed income (he called it income diversion) through social security and public works, and especially through highly progressive taxation, it would be possible always to produce at capacity. The US would thus avoid the underproduction and unemployment created by the fiction that saving was necessary to create capital. Keynes is mentioned, but *The Divine Right of Capital* was not in the mould of the guides to Keynes and the new Keynesian macroeconomics that appeared in the US after 1945. Although Ayres's proposals for reform were like others put forth in the name of Keynes, Ayres justified his by differentiating between the ceremonially justified acquisition and ownership of capital through the use of money and the instrumentally justified recognition that it is machines – however 'owned' – that turn out the goods.

Ayres's view of institutional change is revealed in his belief that ownership of capital would not disappear following the reforms he advocated, but would be transformed. The institutions of US society would be altered, but the ceremonial and pecuniary would remain. He thought that both the individual economic power to manage and the vested right to income would continue. Ayres likened the probable transformation to the 'transfer of authority for the determination of legal identity and parentage from the church to the Bureau of Vital Statistics' noting that this transfer had 'not yet led to the disappearance of the sacrament of baptism' (1946, p. 194).

By the early 1960s, with the publication of *Toward a Reasonable Society*, Ayres had turned his attention from reforms needed to ensure more total production to the then common view that post-war affluence had not resulted in a better life. Ayres emphasized that people in the rich industrial societies *had achieved* a freedom, equality, security and abundance of goods not earlier available; these had been gained through the use of tools that evolved as part of the technological continuum.

Ayres did not live long enough to have to face the concerns of the 1970s and 1980s about the future of mankind on an overpopulated and polluted planet. Would he have accused those concerned with these issues of being 'excited and thinking in capital letters'? *Possibly.* But it is also conceivable that he would have argued that the same technological progress that allowed the use of DDT to control mosquitos and malaria also prompted us to learn that we had made a mistake in using a pesticide that polluted the food chain.

Ayres's most lasting contribution as a dissenting economist will be the elucidation of the work of Thorstein Veblen and the combination of it with that of John Dewey. By separating the industrial and non-pecuniary from the pecuniary, and by recognizing that the pecuniary is not essential to the operation of the industrial, Ayres was able to emphasize that many of our limits were self-imposed pecuniary ones. Our industrial economy was capable of more than we allowed. Our myth is that the pecuniary activities – saving money, buying financial assets – cause the industrial activities. To Ayres, however, the pecuniary organization was simply our culturally inherited way of organizing distribution; it was not the driving force of the economy. Our failure to recognize this stood in the way of the progress (written in small letters) that he believed possible.

Ayres's Major Writings

(1918), 'The Function and Problems of Economic Theory', *Journal of Political Economy*, **26**, 69–90.

(1944), *The Theory of Economic Progress*, Chapel Hill: University of North Carolina Press. 2nd ed, with 'Foreword – 1962', New York: Schocken Books.

(1946), *The Divine Right of Capital*, Boston: Houghton Mifflin Co.

(1952), *The Industrial Economy: Its Technological Basis and Institutional Destiny*, Boston: Houghton Mifflin Co.

(1961), *Toward a Reasonable Society: The Values of Industrial Civilization*, Austin: University of Texas Press.

(1963), 'The Legacy of Thorstein Veblen', in Joseph Dorfman et al, *Institutional Economics: Veblen, Commons and Mitchell Reconsidered*, Berkeley: University of California Press.

(1973), 'Prolegomenon to Institutionalism', Preface to the new edition of *Science: The False Messiah* and *Holier Than Thou: The Way of the Righteous*, New York: Augustus M. Kelley.

Other References

Chalk, A.F. (1976), 'Ayres's Views on Moral Relativism', in William Breit and William P. Culbertson, Jr (eds), *Science and Ceremony, The Institutional Economics of C.E. Ayres*, Austin: University of Texas Press.

Mayhew, A. (1981), 'Ayresian Technology, Technological Reasoning, and Doomsday', *Journal of Economic Issues*, **15**, 513–19.

Mayhew, A. (1987), 'The Beginnings of Institutionalism,' *Journal of Economic Issues*, **21**, 971–98.

Thomas BALOGH (1905–1985) BY *Paul Streeten*

Thomas Balogh, born in Budapest on 2 November 1905, died in London on 20 January 1985. He was one of that influential group of Hungarian exiled economists for whose ambitions and talents Hungary was too small and poor, but whose contribution always remained distinctly Hungarian. Experience of the power politics of the 1930s, as seen from Hungary dominated by Germany, equipped him well to understand the adjustments of a post-imperial Britain to a world in which power had ebbed away.

After studying law and economics at the Universities of Budapest and Berlin, he went in 1928 to America for two years as a Rockefeller Fellow. He had served as a guest apprentice in the research departments of the Banque de France, the Reichsbank and the Federal Reserve before he came to England. Schumpeter had given him a letter of introduction to Keynes, who was impressed by the young man's knowledge of the mechanism that led to persistent gold imports into France. Keynes published his memorandum in the *Economic Journal* and helped him to his first job in England with the banking firm O. T. Falk & Co. Balogh was elated by Keynes' interest, but it was O. T. Falk ('Foxy' Falk was a Churchillian Tory), the originator of many of Keynes' ideas, who started Balogh's conversion from the anti-inflationary creed in which he had grown up to his hostility to dear money and deflation. (One of his after-dinner reflections was to establish a link between an economist's attitude to inflation and his sex life: only a sado-masochist, unhappy in his private life and haunted by the fear that someone, somewhere might be happy, would want to make others suffer the pains of deflation and unemployment; a happy and fulfilled man is expansionist, wishing others also to have fun; and the outward test of his sex life was the attractiveness of the man's wife or mistress.) This conversion was aided by his experience as a member of the Secretariat of the League of Nations where he was shocked by the helplessness of what he came to view as orthodox platitudes in the face of the European crisis and collapse.

From 1934 to 1940 he was a Lecturer at University College London. At that time he wrote for the National Institute of Economic and Social Research his *Studies in Financial Organization*, in which a passion for rational reform was combined with a skilful command of intricate detail. In 1939 he went to Balliol College, Oxford, as a Lecturer, was elected to a Fellowship in 1945 and became university Reader in 1960. In Oxford he helped to establish the Institute of Statistics, which in the early days enabled refugee scholars to continue their work.

His Hungarian youth in the peripheral Balkan also provided a good vantage point from which to observe and understand the problems of the 'periphery' – of poor countries dominated by richer and more powerful ones. After the war his interests turned from banking to the developing countries.

He was economic adviser to the Indian Planning Board (1955 and 1960), to the governments of Malta (1955–57 and in the early 1970s) and Jamaica (1956), and to the Economic Commission for Latin America (1960). Mr Mintoff's demand for full integration into the United Kingdom appealed to Balogh's welfare imperialism, and he was heartbroken when the negotiations failed. He also advised the governments or central banks of Greece, Mauritius, Algeria and the Sudan.

Ever since his resignation from the Cabinet in 1951, Harold Wilson had been in close touch with Balogh, who was also an admirer of Bevan's. Wilson and Balogh worked together throughout the 1950s and early 1960s, in particular on the preparations for the 1964 election. One of Balogh's lines of argument was that a Labour government should be heavily committed to a policy of faster growth, sustained by a strong incomes policy and supported by more state intervention in industry. He thought that the Treasury would not be capable of carrying out such a policy and this led to the call for a separate Ministry of Expansion or Planning. These ideas were the origin of the Department of Economic Affairs.

After the Labour victory in 1964, Balogh was brought into the Cabinet Office as Adviser on Economic Affairs, with special reference to external economic policy. While he had previously been an opponent of the devaluation of sterling and may have influenced Wilson's decision against it in 1964, he had become convinced of its necessity by 1965. After three-and-a-half years in Number Ten he was made a life peer and returned to the University of Oxford. The defeat of the Wilson government in June 1970 was a great disappointment to him. Balogh retired from his Oxford readership in 1973 and continued to write, but was about to enter a new career. In 1974, after the return of the Labour government, he was made a Minister of State at the Department of Energy and, as a life peer, its spokesman in the Lords. He therefore played a key role in the creation of the British National Oil Corporation, becoming its deputy chairman between 1976 and 1978. Balogh's career in Whitehall might be considered as an opportunity to put his ideas to the practical test. But Labour policy hardly reflected the measures which he had advocated and the inference must be that he had little influence on economic policy.

Nevertheless Balogh was totally loyal to the Prime Minister, a fact which may explain why he swallowed a number of policies – the Common Market bid, the succession of deflationary measures and certain public expenditure cuts – to which he was utterly opposed. Several institutional changes were, however, due to Balogh's powers of persuasion, such as the setting up of the Department of Economic Affairs, the Ministry of Overseas Development and the Industrial Reconstruction Corporation; there was also his insistence on mergers and rationalization in industry, on the preparation of alternatives to entry into Europe, on an incomes policy and on the control of capital outflow. He also exercised considerable influence over the appointments of individuals.

Balogh had many insights long before the profession adopted them and before they had become accepted doctrine. And he realized the penalties suffered from being prematurely right. He had diagnosed the 1929 Stock Exchange boom and predicted the slump. He had predicted the deflationary effects of the 1931 depreciation of sterling against the mass of orthodox opinion and was severely taken to task for it by his superiors in the League of Nations. In his contribution to *The Economics of Full Employment*, published by the Oxford University Institute of Statistics, he explored brilliantly the connections between the exchange rate, the wage rate, the employment level and the balance of payments, an area neglected by Keynes himself in his *General Theory*. He saw the need for the international coordination of demand management. In emphasizing, against the prevailing Keynesian orthodoxy, the fact that people will anticipate and counteract government action he was a forerunner of the school of Rational Expectations which, however, he condemned as the reintroduction of perfect information and foresight. He and Kalecki elaborated a theory of the political business cycle in which policies of full employment and inflation alternate with those of unemployment, as the preferences of the electorate swing from one to the other. In development, he saw very early the need for linking rural reform to rural education, not through a drive to universal literacy with high dropout rates in primary schools, but through programmes aiming at whole rural families and relevant to the life and work of the farmers. He was an early advocate of rural public works that would combine laying the necessary infrastructure needed for development with remunerative, non-inflationary absorption of the underutilized labour in cooperatives, and at the same time mobilize the savings needed for this investment. He was a critic of the system of higher education set up by the British and the French in their ex-colonies in the image of their own universities. What were held up as 'centres of excellence' he condemned as 'centres of privilege'.

While others went in for calculating the returns on undifferentiated educational expenditure, he saw that some forms of education alienated the ruling groups in the developing countries and contributed to the problems of the educated unemployed in South Asia and the swollen ranks of aspiring clerks in the government services in Africa. They bred people more fit for rebellious than productive activities. He regarded the treatment of education as an input into the productive system as flawed. He saw clearly the defects in the specialized agencies of the United Nations and called for reforms that would reduce their technocratic biases, their heavy concentrations of staff in headquarters and the competitive piracy of their fiefdoms.

As adviser to S.R. Sen and the Food and Agriculture Organization of the UN he, together with Henry Ergas, used an afforestation study of the Mediterranean to design an integrated development plan for the countries of the region. He used trees almost literally as spearheads of a grand design. Together with S.R. Sen and Mordacai Ezekiel, he was one of the originators of food aid.

In these days of the adulation of free market forces, of pricism and of state minimalism, it is not fashionable to advocate planning and an active state, industrialization, import substitution, rapid capital accumulation or the conscious mobilization of underutilized labour. Yet it can be shown that these ideas have withstood the test of time and that countries following them have done better than others. Whatever the fashionable mythologists of the market may say, no country except Hong Kong has achieved development without protection and efficient government interventions, necessary not as alternatives to markets but as pre-conditions for the working of markets. Thomas Balogh's genius consisted not in applying doctrines, models or paradigms (as they say nowadays), but in a rapid intuitive grasp of complex situations.

Someone once said that there were three forms of conversation: monologue, dialogue and Balogh. There was indeed something unique about Thomas Balogh's discourse. He was witty, could spin imaginative theories from a few cues, blend acute characterization of individuals with the outline of great panoramas, mix gossip and history, illumination and humour, criticism and warmth. He had an uncanny knowledge of everything that was happening and a flamboyant way of telling it. Maynard Keynes once said that he could learn more of what was going on from Balogh in an hour or two than he himself could pick up during several days in London. This gift was a great asset in Number Ten, where he had hung a Picasso drawing of a horned and pipe-playing Pan on the wall of his room. His enemies called him a snooper, and it is true that he did not hesitate looking through other people's mail.

Superficially, his views appear full of contradictions. He advocated administrative controls and planning while denouncing administrators and planners for their incompetence and knavery. He wished to make the civil services of all countries more professional by introducing trained economists, while decrying the irrelevance of the economic doctrine in which they had been trained. His scorn for the dilettantes was matched only by his contempt for the professionals. He was an early advocate of an incomes policy for Britain through a 'social compact', but was the least compromising and consensus-seeking of men. He simultaneously preached higher production and praised the quiet life. He dismissed theoretical model-building as 'gadgeteering', but often put forward some simple (though ingenious) explanation of a phenomenon himself. He was passionately concerned with giving a fuller life and self-determination to the masses, and with protecting them from the sufferings inflicted by the impersonal play of market forces, while thinking that this could be done by a bureaucratic apparatus of central government.

But there was a unity of vision behind these paradoxes. The vision was more one of trained intuition, or what he called an open-ended approach, than based on rigorous analysis (which he dismissed as *rigor mortis*). And his intuition was often far ahead of his time. He had foreseen the need for exchange control during the war, had estimated German rearmament more accurately than the lower official estimates of the Treasury, and had predicted the rise of Germany when she was still a defeated power. He had written with insight on the dollar shortage before the rest of the profession had rushed in to analyse the phenomenon. When the ultimate, authoritative book on the subject appeared, the dollar shortage promptly disappeared. Yet his emphasis on technical progress, based on judicious government encouragement, has survived the test of time.

When the post-war battle over non-discriminatory trade and foreign exchange policies was at its height and when people condemned discrimination, Thomas Balogh would say, 'promiscuity is not usually regarded as a virtue and its opposite, discrimination, a vice. Why in economic policy-making?' Perhaps his greatest contribution lay in a continual questioning of the crystallized orthodoxies of economic doctrine.

Of course, he also made mistakes, although the germs of correcting them are often found in his own thinking. His opposition to the market (and to Dr Erhard's economic policy in Germany) and his predilection for direct quantitative controls have proved to be wrong, but at the same time nobody could have been more scathing about the deficiencies of bureaucrats and planners. He saw the dangers to price stability of full employment, but had excessive faith in an incomes policy. But again, he had no illusions about the trade unions, believing ultimately that some form of wage restraint could be the only means of combining full employment (and give workers, as well as consumers, a wider range of choice) with price stability. Finally, he wrote turbid and turgid prose, though he had a gift of occasionally hitting an apt phrase, especially in battle, such as the title of an essay on the British civil service, 'The Apotheosis of the Dilettante'.

Noel Annan, in a review of *Letters of Leonard Woolf* (*The New York Review of Books*, 29 March 1990), wrote that Leonard Woolf 'distrusted the new generation of socialist intellectuals, in particular Thomas Balogh' (who became Harold Wilson's economic adviser and whom Keynes contemptuously referred to as Oxballs). 'I mistrust everything he says', Woolf told [Kingsley] Martin (then editor of the *New Statesman*). Since at that time

Balogh was declaring that the 'dynamism' of the Soviet economy would give the Soviet Union in ten years 'an absolute preponderance economically over Western Europe', he had good cause. When I lived in Sussex as a neighbour of Leonard Woolf and Thomas Balogh visited me, I witnessed a very friendly and prolonged conversation between the two. (And I had met Noel Annan in Balogh's house.) It is true that Balogh successively cast the USA, Germany, the Soviet Union and the rich countries as a group in the role of the most 'dynamic' economy that inflicts damage on laggards, and that these roles were not justified, at least in the long run. He was the first to abandon no longer applicable prognoses. However, the economic analysis of the disequilibrating impulses propagated by a dynamic economy to the rest of the world remains a perceptive, dissenting insight against the prevailing view of equilibrating forces. Today it is as applicable to Japan as it was to the USA in the post-war period. He did, however, quarrel with Keynes (who, remember, had published his first paper in the *Economic Journal* and who had helped him to his first job in England) over the Bretton-Woods proposals and with Roy Harrod (who had brought him to Oxford) over post-war economic policy.

His contribution to Whitehall committee work, when he was Harold Wilson's chief economic adviser, was possibly not very effective. One could generally expect a spectacular and scintillating performance, but at the end of the meeting the draft of the paper would be much the same as at the beginning. This was so partly because he had only a very small staff and it was impossible to match the massive, detailed work that had gone into the preparation of a paper; partly because his manner was such that it put up people's backs; but perhaps most of all because his criticisms were too radical or too fundamental – he had really asked for an entirely different paper, written by different people or different departments – so that the civil servants simply did not know how to cope and so made no changes at all.

His path-breaking book *The Dollar Crisis* is dedicated to Lord Lindsay of Birker, Master of Balliol College, 'who never quite could convince me that Oxenstierna had the whole explanation...'. What does this mysterious dedication mean? Count Oxenstierna had written to his son in 1648, 'Dost thou not know, my son, with how little wisdom the world is governed?' Thomas Balogh disagreed with Lindsay, believing that knavery more than foolishness, cupidity more than stupidity, were responsible for the world's troubles. He was a fierce controversialist whose brain seemed to function best when his adrenalin was racing. As a result he made many enemies, and he enjoyed being beleaguered by opponents. He saw the world aligned in a battle between an army of black knights and a few white ones. He would like his motto to be, he once told me, *oderint, dum metuant* (let them hate, so long as they fear). And his hero was Don Giovanni, not mainly for his women, but because of the lack of regret with which he descended into the infernal regions.

Through his life he moved gradually to the left. In his youth he had been a follower of Admiral Horthy; later he became a liberal (in the Manchester, not the American, sense of the word), and did not become a socialist until the Second World War. He was only gradually converted from the anti-inflationary creed of the European bourgeoisie of the 1920s to a hostility to dear money and deflation. 'The palpable impotence of the respectable in the face of the rising crisis, their hopeless clinging to the oral magic of soothing platitudes when confronted with the collapse of the social framework and political stability of Central Europe, cured me of my childhood bogey of inflation.'

This kind of political evolution from right to left is regarded as exceptional, for the conventional view is that if anyone is not a socialist before the age of 30 there is something wrong with his heart, and if he is still a socialist after that age, there is something wrong with his head. Yet on reflection, one might recognize Balogh's evolution as unexceptional. For as people become established and secure in their professions, as they acquire tenure, they do not have to please their conservative superiors (assuming, for the sake of this argument, perhaps contradictorily, that they *are* conservative) in order to advance their careers. They can speak out frankly. Moreover, as they grow older, they accumulate wisdom and should 'see the light'. After all socialism, in Orwell's words, is 'elementary common sense', something no decent person can fail to support. Experience tends to belie this *a priori* expectation, but Thomas Balogh became more radical, always in the democratic mould, as he observed and analysed the unnecessary suffering imposed on people by conservative bankers, established civil servants, deflationist economists, monetarists and believers in fiscal rectitude. G.D.H. Cole, the Fabian socialist writer and Oxford professor, distinguished between 'A' and 'B' socialists. 'A' socialists were the anarchists; as a syndicalist, he counted himself among them. 'B' socialists were the bureaucrats, of whom Sidney and Beatrice Webb were outstanding examples. Balogh was a sceptical B-type. Sir Arthur Lewis, himself probably an A-type, once remarked that the difference between Balogh and himself was that Balogh fancied himself as the man behind the *guichet*, whereas Lewis saw himself as the man in front.

Although sometimes wrongly labelled an extreme left-wing economist and, in the early 1950s, described as the grey eminence of Bevanism, Balogh challenged many cherished socialist clichés. He was, in fact, quite moderate in the substance of the reforms he proposed, however passionate the form in which he advocated them and damned his opponents. His motto in this respect might have been *suaviter in re, fortiter in modo*. This contributed to his large number of enemies. It was indeed his passionate concerns which irritated and embarrassed the more conventional Englishman, who values detachment and restraint. To take economic problems so seriously, and on top of this to be prematurely right, is somehow regarded as ungentlemanly. Balogh once wrote, 'The worst fate is to be prematurely right. It is much better to be wrong at the right time, and then to recant with an air of apologetic candour.'

In his rooms in Balliol College three photographs stood on his chimneypiece: of Lord Lindsay, the Master of Balliol; of S.R. Sen, the Director-General of the UN Food and Agriculture Organization; and of Dom Mintoff, the Prime Minister of Malta. Each of these men combined a vision of a better world with considerable practical acumen. Each was both a thinker and a doer. Each married strong roots in his home community to a global vision and commitment.

Listening to Balogh was like wandering through a well-stocked department store. One never quite knew what wares would turn up next, but each department presented an array of beautiful and useful items. In whatever direction one moved, there were a myriad of unpredictable and delightful surprises.

Balogh was an inspiring teacher and an incredibly stimulating colleague. As a teacher, what some might consider a drawback can be an asset: the fact that he often spoke elliptically, that he made intuitive leaps and never presented pedantically, fully-worked-out chains of reasoning. His remarks were more in the nature of challenges, and one had to go home and work out their implications for oneself. Since his intuition was so often right, finding the analytical structure to support it was relatively easy. Thomas Balogh, though capable of great enjoyment and with a marvellous zest for life, was never content. He saw catastrophes and disasters ahead and, like Cassandra, felt no-one was listening to his warnings. He also suffered from a sense that his contributions were not properly acknowledged. He combined profound intuitive insights with the moral courage (or better, as the Austrians say, *Zivilcourage*) to advocate them in the face of the established consensus. What unperceptive critics considered his principal fault – the introduction of Central European ideas into the liberal Anglo-Saxon tradition – may well be his main intellectual contribution to his adopted country.

Balogh's Major Writings

(1947), *Studies in Financial Organization*, Cambridge: Cambridge University Press.
(1949), *The Dollar Crisis*, Oxford: Basil Blackwell.
(1963), *Unequal Partners*, Oxford: Basil Blackwell.
(1964), *The Economic Impact of Monetary and Commercial Institutions of a European Origin in Africa*, Cairo: National Bank of Egypt.
(1973), *Facts and Fancy in International Economic Relations*, Oxford: Pergamon.
(1983), *The Irrelevance of Conventional Economics*, London: Weidenfeld and Nicolson.

Paul Alexander BARAN (1910–1964)   BY *John Bellamy Foster*

Paul Baran, the internationally acclaimed Marxist economist, was born on 8 December 1910 into a Jewish family in Nikolaev, Russia, on the Black Sea. His father was a medical doctor with ties to the Menshevik branch of the Russian Social Democratic party. The chaos resulting from the First World War and the Russian Revolution made it impossible to find a suitable school for Baran to attend and his education up to age 11 was entirely under his father's tutelage. Dismayed by the continuing social disruption following the October Revolution, Baran's family left the USSR in 1921, stopping briefly at his father's ancestral home in Vilna, formerly part of Tsarist Russia and by that time part of Poland. Here his parents assumed Polish citizenship; as a minor entered on his mother's passport, Baran received automatic Polish nationality which he was to retain until naturalized as an American citizen during the Second World War. The family then proceeded to Germany where Baran's formal education began.

In 1925 Baran's father was offered a position in Moscow and his parents returned to the USSR while he stayed behind in Germany to complete his secondary education. Rejoining his family in 1926 Baran enrolled at the Plekhanov Institute of Economics at the University of Moscow. This was the era of the famous Soviet industrialization debates of the 1920s, which were to leave a deep and lasting imprint on Baran's thinking as an economist. However it was also a time of growing conflict within the Communist movement and Baran began to experience 'a strong nostalgia', as he later recalled, 'for the freedom and unfettered intellectual atmosphere of Germany'. In late 1928 he therefore accepted a research assignment at the Agricultural Academy of Berlin and, when this assignment ended, an assistantship with Friedrich Pollock at the famous Institute for Social Research in Frankfurt. There he was introduced to pioneering work in critical theory that had a considerable influence on his own development as a critical theorist in the field of economics.

After finishing his undergraduate studies Baran proceeded to Berlin where he completed a Ph.D. under Emil Lederer, a distinguished socialist economist who was later to found the famous 'university of exile' under the wing of the New School for Social Research in New York. In Berlin Baran met Rudolf Hilferding, author of *Finance Capital* and the most renowned economic theorist in the German and Austrian Social Democratic movements. Baran had by this time affiliated himself with the German Social Democratic party as the most hopeful force for combating Nazism. At Hilferding's urging, he wrote frequently for *Die Gesellschaft*, the official organ of the Social Democratic party edited by Hilferding, utilizing the penname of Alexander Gabriel in order to avoid causing trouble for his parents in Moscow.

After Hitler's rise to power Baran had no choice but to leave Germany, departing for Paris in 1933. In December 1934 he received a visa to visit his parents in the Soviet Union, where he was horrified by the conditions that he found in the midst of the Stalinist purges. Many of his friends and colleagues from his student days had been implicated in either the Trotsky or Bukharin oppositions. As an ex-Communist, Baran himself was highly suspect. Unable to get his visa extended in order to spend more time with his parents, Baran was forced to leave the USSR in January 1935. Returning to Vilna where his uncles had a timber business, he worked for a number of years as a business-man, and in 1938 was sent to London as the permanent representative of the Vilna interests.

Despite success in business, Baran continued to long for an academic career. Efforts to get an academic job in England failed and, seeing the Second World War coming, he took his savings and sailed for the US in October 1939. There he soon gained admittance as a graduate student in economics at Harvard. After completing his Harvard studies he accepted a fellowship at the Brookings Institution for the academic year 1941–42. He then turned to wartime Washington, where he worked successively in the Office of Price Administration, the Research and Development branch of the Office of Strategic Services, the United States' Strategic Bombing Survey in Germany, and finally as the head of the Economic Effects Division of the Survey's mission to Japan. After the war he took a job at the Department of Commerce and gave lectures at George Washington University, finally ac-cepting a position in the Research Department of the Federal Reserve Bank of New York. Baran accepted an offer to join the Stanford economics faculty in 1948, where he was promoted to full professor in 1951.

The hiring of Baran at Stanford occurred a few years before McCarthyism, which was still in its early stages, had cast its full shadow across the univer-sity campuses. As the witchhunt grew, Baran – who from the moment Stanford hired him until the time of his death was probably the only self-confessed Marxist economist teaching at a US university – became increasingly sub-ject to quasi-official harassment. Although tenure made it virtually impossible to fire him, he was required to carry heavier course loads than his colleagues and his salary was frozen – a fact that the Stanford administration took special pains to advertise to its potential donors. In his early articles for the independent socialist magazine *Monthly Review*, with which he was closely associated, Baran found it necessary to adopt the pseudonym of 'Historicus'. Nor did these difficulties ease appreciably with the end of McCarthyism itself. If anything, the political pressures on Baran intensified during the early 1960s as a result of his outspoken support of the Cuban revolution. Commenting in 1961 in a letter to a friend on the Stanford administration's persistent efforts to clamp down on him, this time over a recent visit to Cuba, he wrote, '[I]t burns me all up, plays havoc with my nervous sys-tem....' Three years later, in 1964, Baran died of a heart attack.

Although Baran was not a prolific writer throughout his career, the last decade of his life was extremely productive in this respect. It was during these years that he wrote his two major books, *The Political Economy of Growth* and (with Paul Sweezy) *Monopoly Capital,* each of which received widespread international recognition as belonging to the very best of the Marxian tradition in the post-war period. Moreover, it was in this last decade that Baran wrote most of the essays later included in *The Longer View* – a rich collection of writings, mainly covering economic topics, but also encompassing such subjects as 'Marxism and Psychoanalysis', 'The Commitment of the Intellectual' and 'The Nature of Marxism'.

The Political Economy of Growth analyses the patterns of development that characterize both the highly industrialized and underdeveloped economies of the modern world. Both a monumental work of scholarship, containing an intricately textured analysis of historical, social and economic events, and a powerful polemic against mainstream development theory, it is one of the classic studies underpinning contemporary monopoly-capital, dependency and world-system theories.

Baran's argument rests on his key analytical category of potential economic surplus. Derived from and presupposing Marx's surplus value, this category adapted Marx's earlier concept to the specific problem of development planning. Two long chapters apply the potential surplus concept to the circumstances of developed monopoly capitalist societies. This analysis was to be elaborated more fully in *Monopoly Capital.* Three further chapters, from which the fame of the work (particularly in the Third World) is largely derived, analyse underdevelopment in the periphery of the capitalist world economy.

Orthodox economics, according to Baran, usually treats the issue of the investment necessary for economic growth as if it were merely a question of the disposal of society's *actual* surplus (or actual savings), defined as 'the difference between society's actual current output and its actual current consumption'. Nevertheless, a complete understanding of the mobilization of economic resources requires the wider conceptual outlook offered by *potential* surplus, defined as 'the difference between the output that *could* be produced in a given natural and technological environment with the help of employable productive resources, and what might be regarded as essential consumption'. Potential surplus, in this sense, can be understood as including both actual surplus *plus* the following elements: (i) society's excess consumption, (ii) loss of output due to the existence of unproductive workers, (iii) loss of output due to irrational and wasteful organization of production, and (iv) loss of output due to open and disguised unemployment. Rapid growth, therefore, depends on successfully tapping those elements of potential surplus that are currently being wasted (and which therefore do not show up in actual surplus), as well as mobilizing surplus currently being siphoned off from abroad. But to address the issue of development in this way is to place under scrutiny the fundamental class relations and dependent international position of Third World capitalist societies.

The value of this conceptual approach was evident in the facility with which Baran was able to counter three of the most important postulates of mainstream development theory: (i) the notion that underdeveloped economies had always been underdeveloped, and were simply in the early stages of economic growth; (ii) the idea that the main obstacle to development is a 'vicious circle of poverty', requiring a diffusion of capital to the Third World; and (iii) the belief that the problems of underdeveloped societies can be traced to a dearth of capitalists or entrepreneurs embodying Western know-how and initiative.

Rather than following the common practice of assuming that the poorer economies of the periphery had always been relatively 'backward', Baran approached the issue historically. 'The question that immediately arises', he wrote, 'is why is it that in the backward countries there has been no advance along the lines of capitalist development that are familiar from the history of other capitalist countries, and why is it that forward movement there has been either slow or altogether absent?' The answer, he suggests, is to be found in the way in which capitalism was brought to these regions during the period of what Marx called 'primitive accumulation', characterized by 'undisguised looting, enslavement and murder', and in the way in which this very process served to 'smother fledgling industries' in the colonized societies. It was thus the European conquest and plundering of the rest of the globe that generated the great divide between core and periphery of the capitalist world economy that persists to this day. In illustrating this, Baran highlights the differing ways in which India and Japan were incorporated into the world capitalist economy, the first as a dependent social formation carrying the unfortunate legacy of what Andre Gunder Frank was later to call 'the development of underdevelopment'; the second representing the exceptional case of a society that was neither colonized nor subject to unequal treaties, and that, retaining control over its own economic surplus, was free to develop along the autocentric lines of the core European powers. The implication of this analysis was clear: incorporation on an unequal basis into the periphery of the capitalist world economy is itself the main cause of the plight of the underdeveloped economies.

The failure of development in the Third World, then, is not the result of 'original underdevelopment' – or a lack of capitalism. Nor, Baran went on to argue, could the failure to develop along European lines be traced to a 'vicious circle of poverty' – or a lack of capital. Even though the amount of actual surplus in such societies is typically small, the potential surplus –

given the extremely low levels of consumption – is such a large proportion of national income as 'to enable them to attain high, and indeed very high, rates of growth'. The key to underdevelopment, according to Baran, lies rather in the fact that the potential surplus that could be utilized for productive investment is to a large extent wasted away by the combined actions of the following class forces: (i) a semi-feudal landed oligarchy addicted to luxury consumption on the most extravagant scale imaginable; (ii) a large, parasitical strata of 'merchants, moneylenders and intermediaries of all kinds'; (iii) a small industrial bourgeoisie forced to subordinate itself to the interests of foreign capital; (iv) foreign multinationals geared mainly to the expatriation of profits; and (v) an overgrown state apparatus compelled to maintain a praetorian guard of hired mercenaries.

By focusing on the appropriation of potential surplus by various class forces in this way, Baran makes it clear that the problems of underdevelopment do not have to do primarily with a lack of capitalists (or entrepreneurs) any more than a lack of capitalism or capital. Rather the real difficulty lies in the existence of an imperialist structure of power in the world economy that places these societies in a situation of dependency, producing a disarticulated class structure which is itself predicated on the failure to mobilize the potential surplus in ways that would promote internal development. Under these circumstances, Baran argues, there is little chance that underdeveloped economies – with the possible exception of large Third World states with sizeable national bourgeoisies and strong anti-imperialist movements such as Egypt and India – will be able to channel surplus into productive areas that will spur development unless they first carry out full-scale, socialist-orientated revolutions aimed at delinking themselves to some degree from the capitalist world economy. In the periphery Baran's message was widely heard. Thus most subsequent Third World revolutionary movements, beginning with the Cuban revolution in 1959, were influenced directly or indirectly by ideas contained in *The Political Economy of Growth*.

Monopoly Capital by Baran and Sweezy was an attempt to elaborate more fully the interpretation of developed capitalism introduced in the relatively unsuccessful early chapters of *The Political Economy of Growth* as well as in Sweezy's *The Theory of Capitalist Development* (1942). It quickly gained a reputation as the most important attempt thus far to bring Marx's *Capital* up to date, modifying Marx's original analysis where necessary to account for the monopoly stage of development. It also represented an important critical departure from the prevailing Keynesian orthodoxy in macroeconomics – reflecting the alternative approach associated with such neo-Marxian (and post-Keynesian) thinkers as Michal Kalecki and Josef Steindl.

At the core of *Monopoly Capital* was the thesis that Marx's fundamental 'law of the tendency of the rate of profit to fall' associated with accumulation in the era of free competition, has been replaced, in the more restrictive competitive environment of monopoly capitalism (in which a handful of giant firms tend to dominate key industries), by a law of the tendency of the surplus to rise (defining surplus in terms similar to Baran's potential surplus). Under these circumstances, the critical problem is one of surplus absorption. Capitalist consumption accounts for a decreasing share of capitalist demand as income grows, while investment is hindered by the fact that it takes the form of new productive capacity, which cannot be expanded for long periods of time independently of final wage-based demand. Despite the ever-present possibility of new 'epoch-making innovations' emerging that could help absorb the potential surplus, such innovations – resembling the steam engine, the railroad and the automobile in their overall effect – are few and far between. Furthermore, 'foreign investment, far from being an outlet for domestically generated surplus, is a most efficient device for transferring surplus generated abroad to the investing country'. Hence, Baran and Sweezy conclude that the system has a powerful tendency towards stagnation, largely compensated for thus far through the rise of various countervailing factors divorced from the logic of accumulation itself, such as the growing sales effort, military spending and financial expansion. All such factors however are self-limiting and can be expected to lead to a doubling-over of economic contradictions in the not too distant future.

From the standpoint of its authors, the originality of *Monopoly Capital* lay not in its analysis of the stagnationist tendency itself (which had been thoroughly explored in the 1930s) but rather in its account of those countervailing factors that had allowed capitalism to prosper after the war. These included (to amplify on elements already mentioned above) such key historical eventualities as: (i) the epoch-making stimulus provided in the 1950s by the second great wave of 'automobilization' in the US (which should be understood as also encompassing the expansion of the steel, glass, rubber and petroleum industries, the building of the interstate highway system and the stimulus provided by the suburbanization of America); (ii) Cold War military spending, including two regional wars in Asia; (iii) the growing wasteful penetration of the sales effort into the production process; and (iv) the vast expansion of the credit-debt structure of the capitalist economy, to the extent that it eventually began to dwarf production itself. By analysing the way in which the surplus left its statistical trace in these and other areas, Baran and Sweezy enlarged the usual context of economics to take into account its wider historical setting.

The reemergence of conditions of economic stagnation in the 1970s, not long after *Monopoly Capital* was published, and the conjunctural response to this crisis by the dominant interests of the advanced capitalist world in the 1980s – involving a combination of global supply-side restructuring, huge military outlays and hyper-financial expansion – clearly pointed to the continuing relevance of this type of historical approach.

Baran and Sweezy thus made it clear that there was much more at stake in the analysis of the economy than the rate of growth, the rate of profit or the level of employment. The stupendous waste of society's surplus that had allowed capitalism to counter growing problems of surplus absorption should not be condoned, Baran was wont to point out, even when it does temporarily serve to prop up an economy that would otherwise visibly stagnate. The hunger of most of the world's population, the persistence of exploitation, poverty and alienation in the advanced capitalist world, and the squandering of precious intellectual, artistic and scientific achievements mean that the politicization of the way in which surplus is utilized will remain an urgent task for society and the key to rational, anti-capitalist struggle.

Given his background, it is perhaps not surprising that Baran was also an important analyst of the Soviet economy over the course of his career. While a devotee of national economic planning he remained a critic of what he called 'Stalinist terrorism' and hoped for the development of a 'free, socialist democracy' in the USSR. With respect to the Soviet, East German, Czechoslovakian, Hungarian and Polish economies he argued in 1962 that these had industrialized to the point that they must now necessarily abandon 'the "forced marches" characteristic...of the Stalin era; they *must* greatly liberalize the economic and social conditions prevailing in their societies if further economic, cultural and political advancement is to be assured. For here, as elsewhere, there is a powerful dialectic at work: the very system of extreme pressure on consumption, of unquestioned subordination to authority, and of rigidly dogmatic concentration on principal targets, which was imposed by Stalin and which enabled the Soviet Union to get over the "hump" of initial industrialization has turned, in the current phase of history, into a prohibitive obstacle to further economic and social growth' (1969).

It was this kind of unswerving commitment to what Baran himself called 'the confrontation of reality with reason' that no doubt partly explains John Kenneth Galbraith's remark in his memoirs that 'Baran was one of the most brilliant and, by a wide margin, the most interesting economist I have ever known'.

Baran's Major Writings

(1957), *The Political Economy of Growth*, New York: Monthly Review Press.
(1966), *Monopoly Capital* (co-authored by Paul M. Sweezy), New York: Monthly Review Press.
(1969), *The Longer View*, New York: Monthly Review Press.

Other References

Foster, J.B. (1986), *The Theory of Monopoly Capitalism*, New York: Monthly Review Press.

Foster, J.B. and Szlajfer, H. (eds)(1984), *The Faltering Economy*, New York: Monthly Review Press.

Galbraith, J.K. (1981), *A Life in Our Times*, Boston: Houghton Mifflin.

Huberman, L. and Sweezy, P.M. (eds)(1965), *Paul Baran: A Collective Portrait*, New York: Monthly Review Press.

Jacoby, R. (1987), *The Last Intellectuals*, New York: Basic Books.

Sweezy, P.M. (1987), 'Paul Alexander Baran', in *The New Palgrave Dictionary of Economics*, Vol 3, Macmillan Press.

Amit BHADURI (born 1938)

After finishing an elementary science degree from Presidency College, Calcutta – it used to be called Intermediate Science in India in those days – I joined the Economic Honours course in the same college in 1958. I had very little idea of Economics as an academic discipline. Looking back, it is not entirely clear to me why I decided to study Economics though I recall one personal reason: it was my disinclination to spend long afternoons doing experiments in the laboratories. The other more serious reason was the social milieu. The air was charged with a lot of left-wing political slogans in those days, and in middle-class Bengali homes it was not unusual to have frequent political discussions. The college union elections were also supposedly fought on 'ideological' grounds. In such an atmosphere, studying Economics was intellectually 'fashionable' and I also felt that it would give me a better grasp of political issues. I do not think at this stage that I was either serious or mature enough to distinguish between 'understanding' and scoring debating points among friends.

Teaching of Economics was of a high standard in Presidency College. In particular, Professor Bhabotosh Dutta who taught us mostly microeconomics, was one of the best teachers I have ever had. His lectures gave me an idea of the logical structure of the subject. But the academic programme in Presidency College, like elsewhere, hardly gave us any sense of social realism. Economics became largely a matter of understanding logical arguments without questioning their relevance. Even the teaching of Indian economics hardly helped matters in this respect. When I graduated from Presidency College in 1960 I had unknowingly accepted Economics as a subject where logical refinements of arguments, irrespective of their relevance, served as the governing principle.

After spending a few months at Calcutta University, I went to do the short (two-year) Economics Tripos at Cambridge where a number of well-known British Keynesians were teaching at that time. My first impression was that they lectured in a peculiarly unsystematic manner, each following his or her own line of thought. This was very different from the teaching I had been used to in India. Kaldor was an exciting lecturer and certainly brought a sense of relevance to economic theory which I had previous missed. Kahn I

simply could not understand. Joan Robinson was extremely erratic. However, even then I had a vague glimpse of her 'pictorial imagination'; at times
I got the impression that she visualized the economy as a picture before she
discussed its analytical interconnections. Dobb, discussing the history of
economic thought, did not rouse my interest. Goodwin lectured like an artist.
Pasinetti and Hahn were the clearest in their presentation and therefore
easiest to understand. Hahn represented mostly the mathematical fashions in
economics, lecturing on general equilibrium. Although his explanations were
clear and well-structured and he also supervised me, at no stage did I feel
that his subject had any relevance to the working of the capitalist economy.
Champernowne lectured on mathematical statistics, mostly probability theory,
with occasional digressions into mathematical models of economic growth
which were then being formulated by Kaldor.

Looking back, when I finished my Tripos in 1963 I had largely reinforced
my view of Economics as a subject of purely logical discourse, derived from
my earlier training in Calcutta. Economic theory was primarily a playground
for logical argument where little attention needed to be paid either to the
relevance of the assumptions or to the questions being asked. In the meantime, I had secured a scholarship to do postgraduate work at the Massachusetts
Institute of Technology. I went with the vague idea of working on the
Turnpike theorem, a fashionable topic in mathematical economics in those
days. The lectures in MIT were much more technique-orientated and the
year there was useful in a negative way. It made clear to me the kind of
economics I was not interested in doing. It was at this stage that, mostly as a
reaction, I carefully reread Keynes' *General Theory* and the first two volumes of Marx's *Capital*. I should admit that much of this reading was accomplished by not going to the regular lectures! In retrospect I think I was
more impressed by Keynes than by Marx, because Marx was too overwhelming with his powerful mixture of economics, philosophy and history
and it was difficult to identify the economic core on which he was building.
Keynes on the other hand was easier to understand, partly because his
canvas was far narrower. And also, we had been repeatedly exposed to his
ideas from different angles at Cambridge. My intellectual wavelength began
to diverge increasingly from those of most of my fellow graduate students at
MIT, not to speak of the teachers. I decided to return to Cambridge for my
Ph.D. or to try my hand at economic journalism, perhaps in the Bombay-
based Indian magazine *Economic & Political Weekly*. Since I had already
secured a studentship in Peterhouse, Cambridge, the soft option was to
complete my Ph.D. there. I returned in 1964 to work first with Richard Kahn
and then with Joan Robinson when she returned from one of her visits to
China. This was, I think, my period of transition towards becoming a professional economist. I still recall my puzzlement, when during the first few

supervisions, Joan Robinson insisted that I should be able to 'visualize' the economy first before deriving its characteristic features for theorizing. I read her *Accumulation of Capital* at this stage and vaguely understood her method of theorizing. I also read almost everything that Kalecki had written. He was easy to follow and combined precision and relevance in a way which I had not previously come across in any other economist. I found this combination especially exciting and Joan Robinson fully shared my enthusiasm for Kalecki during our discussions. My mind was more or less made up to do macroeconomics along similar lines, if possible relating it to the Indian economy. However, there was the pressure of finishing a Ph.D. thesis within 3 years and I chose to work on the problems posed by gestation-lags in investment planning. I found this to be a relatively unexplored area where one could easily use formal methods and get 'results' needed for a Ph.D. In the mid-1960s the capital theory controversy (with 'double switching' etc) was raging following the publication in 1960 of Sraffa's book *Production of Commodities by Means of Commodities*. As a young researcher it was difficult to remain indifferent to this intellectual excitement and, not very consciously, I also started following the debate, occasionally discussing it with Joan Robinson. This resulted in my first published paper in 1966. Although it was not related directly to my thesis, working on capital theory gave me the satisfaction of feeling that I was also contributing in my small way to the struggle against conventional neoclassical economic theory which I had begun to reject. I completed my Ph.D. work in 1967 on the 'Impact of Gestation Lags in Investment Planning'.

I decided to return to India immediately after my thesis. Instead of taking up a conventional teaching job, I decided to work on the economic aspects of primary education in India for a year in the Agro-Economic Research Centre in Delhi. The next year I joined the Delhi School of Economics. Since I continued to be interested in capital theory, I published occasional papers on this subject while teaching courses on planning and economic theory at the School. Around this time I wrote a paper on the significance of the controversies in capital theory from a Marxian view (1969); this was motivated by my interest to relate capital theory controversy to what I then understood to be Marx's methods in economics. It received some attention and was translated into several languages, possibly because many 'dissenting economists' wanted to draw on Marx to explain the significance of the capital theory debate which had become the logical focus of challenge to the neoclassical marginal productivity theory of profit. Around the same time, based on my earlier work on the thesis, I published two papers on the theory of project evaluation. I had never been satisfied with the dubious logical foundation of cost-benefit analysis and its subjectivist 'rate of time discount' concept. An approach developed by Kalecki on this issue had seemed more fruitful. Using Kalecki's method, I published a short paper on the subject (1968b). With the encouragement of Richard Goodwin, who was one of my thesis examiners, and Professor Lief Johansen of Oslo, I published another paper (1968a) emphasizing the role of foreign trade as a time-saving device in project planning. The only common theme of both these papers was my attempt to break away from the conventional mould of cost-benefit analysis.

I left the Delhi School of Economics to take up a job in the Ministry of Economic Planning in Sri Lanka in 1969. There I had my first practical experience with investment planning. However, I had plenty of spare time after office hours and continued with my interest in capital theory. During my Ph.D. work I had found a formula to show how different gestation lags associated with different techniques of production entailed different amounts of incremental 'locked-up' resources in a growing economy. This could provide a physical analogue to the reswitching of techniques. When this was written up and submitted for publication (1970), I received on the first draft some encouraging comment from Professor Hicks who had been working on similar problems. A few years later Hicks published his book *Capital and Time* (1973) where he explored the Austrian approach to capital theory in his usual original fashion. On reading this book, I realized that Hicks had assumed that I also came to my formulation through the same Austrian route. However, it was my thesis work on gestation lags and my interest in the on-going capital theory which had accidentally merged in that paper to create this impression. I was ashamed on my ignorance and tried to read Böhm Bawerk and Hayek on capital theory but, I must confess, without much benefit.

While in the Ministry of Planning in Sri Lanka I became familiar with some of the economic problems of small paddy cultivators in that country. I was particularly intrigued by the fact that traditional agriculture was so resistant to technological change. I gave up my job after a year in Sri Lanka where I had been working in a team to develop a computable, multisector, multiperiod planning model using Leontief's framework. The political atmosphere was electric at that time, the echoes of the Cultural Revolution in China reverberating all over South Asia. Maoist ideas were spreading rapidly. I returned to Calcutta, anticipating rapid political changes. Some of my former students and friends had joined the Maoist movement in India (called Naxalire) with various degrees of political involvement. I distinctly remember one of them who had gone to work among the peasants in the countryside coming back and telling me that he could not find real 'feudal' landlords anywhere in West Bengal. What he found instead were relatively small landowners who were also engaged in moneylending on an extensive scale. Although the Indian Maoists had already characterized Indian agriculture as 'semi-feudal', I presume they had little idea or time to discuss what it really meant. I was without a job and decided to travel in the countryside of West Bengal in 1970–71. During this time, I had the opportunity to talk to many peasants, sharecroppers and landless tribals in and around the province, especially about their perceptions of the nature of exploitation they suffered. Never having either the courage or the tenacity to enter serious politics, I decided to use my impressionistic knowledge of the West Bengal countryside to give content to the term 'semi-feudal agriculture'.

I left in the middle of 1971 with a one-year assignment with the UN in Vienna. The work was not very demanding leaving me time to formulate a model of semi-feudal agriculture. This was published in a left-wing Calcutta journal called *Frontier* and also as a more technical paper in the *Economic Journal* (1973), arousing both interest and hostility among many development economists. Since this paper was not based on anything I had read in economics books or articles, it probably had some sort of novelty of approach. My main interest was to show how moneylending and land rent – two different modes of surplus extraction – combined to result in agricultural stagnation. Predictably, academic economists of the mainstream reacted in a large number of theoretical papers largely trying to show why such interlocked transactions may not imply exploitation and may also be Pareto-optimal. Another paper on usurious interest rates, based on my impressions of the West Bengal countryside of that time, was published much later in 1977. This paper was written while in Hanoi in total isolation. It was an attempt to show that who bears the cost of default – the lender or the borrower – is a matter of economic power. Subsequently the *Cambridge Journal of Economics* published quite a few papers by others on this topic.

When I returned to India from Vienna, I first joined the Centre for Development Studies in Trivandrum. For personal reasons I had to give up this job soon and returned again to Delhi as professor at the newly-established Jawaharlal Nehru University in 1973. With most of my colleagues and especially with Professor Krishna Bharadwaj, I shared a good deal of common interest in economics. We thought it would be possible to build a relatively different kind of department where the M.A. course would not follow the usual pattern. Our initially small but enthusiastic group of colleagues were all serious about teaching and we launched an M.A. programme which, I still believe, had some freshness of approach and emphasis. I was responsible for teaching macroeconomic theory from 1973 to 1983, with a one-year break in North Vietnam in 1976. This is the longest job I have held to date. During this period I published my first book, *The Economic Structure of Backward Agriculture* (1983) which made extensive use of my earlier essays on the subject as well as of a relatively new idea: that of using biological analogies in a mathematical model to capture agrarian class relations (1981).

My attempts to teach the essentials of macroeconomics in a different and more relevant way resulted in accumulating lecture notes over the years. I never carried these to class, but spent more time each successive year deciding what to teach from the notes I had built up. My selection of material invariably revealed to me my own preference for the macroeconomic tradition of Marx, Kalecki and Keynes – the common themes running through their writings on capitalism. I left Nehru University in 1983 to teach in El Colégio de México where I had enough time to put together a book out of these lecture notes. This was published in the 'radical economics' series by Macmillan in 1986. Interestingly, I found the students in Mexico, like those in India, quite interested in these lectures. Some of them had actually encouraged me to complete the book by observing that macroeconomics taught this way made greater sense. However, I was soon to discover that this was a 'biased' view of macroeconomics – perhaps a Third World view? When I visited Stanford in 1986, I found many graduate students positively puzzled by my approach. They knew more about current fashions like game and agency theory, but relatively little about Keynes and almost nothing about Kalecki and Marx. Subsequently, I also taught as visiting professor in some universities in Europe, mostly in Austria, in Italy and in Norway. Students were considerably more receptive in these countries in general. My personal impression is that the pressure to conform to the current intellectual fashion is somewhat less in European universities; as a result, a significant minority of students are intellectually more open to non-orthodox ideas. Although the reward-system is biased heavily in favour of the conventional mainstream student, which is only to be expected, the 'punishment' for intellectual deviation is less severe than that meted out by the recruitment system of typical US economics departments. In the Italian, Spanish and (second) Indian editions of my book, I mention this explicitly in the Preface.

I had always been uncomfortable about the coexistence of apparently contradictory ideas in Marx and Keynes on the theory of effective demand, which also had serious implications for political ideology. Like Keynes, Marx seemed to suggest that a higher real wage was good for capitalism insofar as it alleviated the problem of 'underconsumption'. At the same time, his theory of 'periodic crisis' was based on the idea of profit squeeze brought about by militant workers receiving increased real wages in a boom; this also finds an echo in Kalecki's political trade cycles. Keynes' emphasis on effective demand indicates that, even in the absence of sufficient public investment, a higher real wage would help to relax the constraint of effective demand and thus make cooperation between capital and labour possible along social democratic lines. Marx's view of conflicting class interest, implied in his theory of periodic crisis and elegantly formulated by Goodwin (1967), was not easy to reconcile with his under-consumptionist arguments –

politically, it was the clash of ideas between radicals and social democrats. I recall discussing this problem with at least two prominent Keynesians, Kaldor and Joan Robinson, but was not convinced by their answers. In the traditional Keynesian framework (such as Kaldor's distribution theory) the Marxian distributive conflict starts only at or near full employment when output adjustment is supply-constrained. Thus one has to go to the aggregate supply side, beyond the theory of effective demand, to reconcile Marx or Kalecki with Keynes.

Fortunately, in recent years I have had the opportunity of working with economists from several continents in Helsinki at the World Institute of Development Economics Research (WIDER) on a research project on modern capitalism. I was reassured to find that Stephen Marglin of Harvard University had also been bothered by the same question for quite a long time. We worked together on this problem and published our joint research in several articles (1990a and b). I believe we have found a solution to this puzzle of reconciling Marx and Keynes within the Keynesian theory of effective demand in a way which does not rely on the aggregate supply constraint. This reformulation of Keynes's theory also indicates the conditions under which conflict and cooperation could emerge between the two classes in an advanced capitalist economy. This latest line of research excites me precisely because it clarifies political ideologies in terms of macroeconomic theory, rather than trying to formulate macroeconomic theory entirely in terms of preconceived political ideologies.

Bhaduri's Major Writings

(1966), 'The Concept of the Marginal Productivity of Capital and the Wicksell Effect', *Oxford Economic Papers*, **18**.
(1968a), 'Foreign Trade as a Time Saving Device in Project Planning', *Economics of Planning*, **8**.
(1968b), 'An Aspect of Project Selection: Durability versus Construction Period', *Economic Journal*, **78**.
(1969), 'On the Recent Controversy in Capital Theory: A Marxian View', *Economic Journal*, **79**.
(1970), 'A Physical Analogue of the Reswitching Problem', *Oxford Economic Papers*, **22**.
(1973), 'A Study in Agricultural Backwardness under Semi-feudalism', *Economic Journal*, **83**.
(1977), 'On the Formation of Usurious Interest Rates in Backward Agriculture', *Cambridge Journal of Economics*, **1**.
(1981), 'Class Relations and the Pattern of Accumulation in an Agrarian Economy', *Cambridge Journal of Economics*, **5**.
(1983), *The Economic Structure of Backward Agriculture*, Academic Press.
(1986), *Macroeconomics: The Dynamics of Commodity Production*, London: Macmillan.
(1990a), 'Profit Squeeze and Keynesian theory' (with S. Marglin) in S. Marglin and J. Schor (eds), *The Golden Age of Capitalism: Reinterpreting the Postwar Experience*, Oxford: Clarendon Press.
(1990b), 'Unemployment and Real Wage: The Economic Basis for Contesting Political Ideologies' (with S. Marglin), *Cambridge Journal of Economics*, **14**.

Krishna BHARADWAJ (born 1935)

I was born, the youngest of six children, on 21 August 1935 at Karwar, a small coastal town resting in the foothills of Sahyadri on the western coast of India. My father, Maruti Chandawarkar, was a highly motivated educationalist who actively supported the education of the deprived, particularly women and child-widows. When I was two, my family moved to Belgaum, a multilingual town, a place of confluence of north and south Indian cultural traditions known particularly for its music, dramatic arts and folk culture. It was also a politically alive place, a frontier town on the borders of the Portuguese colony of Goa. As part of the nationalist freedom movement, the young socialists were active in the town. One of the important achievements of Gandhi's strategy of nationalist struggle was the space it created for the active involvement in the liberation movement of women and children, of all ages and ranks. The movement had a profound impact during my youth in instilling an urge for social and economic action towards independent self-reliant development.

In 1951, I moved to Bombay for college education. Although fascinated by mathematics and sciences, it was mainly the mundane consideration of combining employment with study that prompted me towards the 'Arts'. After the death of my father in 1952, I began the study of economics specifically for the potentialities it held for employment. Once I took up the subject at the University of Bombay, however, I found it fascinating partly because of the lively social context it acquired just when independent India was launching upon the path of planned development.

In my graduate years, while the theory of value remained essentially a theory of competitive equilibrium with smatterings of monopolistic competition, what held our interest was macroeconomic theory, predominantly Keynesian (a little less of Kaleckian), together with the inter-industry studies which followed Leontief's pioneering work. Strategies of development and analytical techniques of planning dominated the professional debates. A general consensus among social scientists seemed to be that in order to accelerate the pace of development, transcending the protracted colonial interregnum, planned interventions of the state were imperative. This was the generally accepted view even among the big industrialists. Strong debates arose however on the diagnosis of backwardness and on the strategies of investment, particularly with the Second Five-Year Plan commencing in 1956, the planning policy having been launched in 1951.

My critical orientation towards economic theory began with my involvement in development theory as a doctoral student at the University of Bombay. Early attempts at theorizing on problems of development emerged mainly as an adaptation of the competitive equilibrium framework of resource allocation. This maintained that efficient resource utilization would occur in a competitive market economy composed of individual agents maximizing their return, given their endowment of primary resources, the technological possibilities of transformation and the set of preferences. The nature, source and hence the diagnosis of underdevelopment was thus attributed to limited availability of primary resources, adverse proportions of factor-supplies or their limited substitutability, biased preferences and imperfections or non-formation of markets which explained 'market failures' of various kinds. The state of underdevelopment was viewed as a departure from the competitive resource utilization model. A remedial policy widely discussed was the use of 'shadow' or implicit prices derived from the setting up of optimal programmes. A critique of this position was presented in my early paper 'The Logic of Implicit Prices' (1965).

The other strand in my early doctoral work emanated from the interdependent production models inspired by Leontief, on the basis of which consistency plan models were being constructed in India. My doctoral dissertation, submitted to University of Bombay in 1960, was on 'Techniques of Transportation Planning, with Special Reference to Railways'; in it I discussed the special problems of investment decisions relating to such a critical social-orientated sector in the context of the ongoing debates on plan strategies. I also used the first inter-industry transactions table constructed by the Indian Statistical Institute in Calcutta for projecting the rail-transport requirements of the plan.

The critique of neoclassical theory, particularly of distribution, was sharpened during my visit to Cambridge, Massachusetts. Accompanying my husband, Ranganath Bharadwaj, who was on a post-doctoral fellowship at Harvard, I joined the Center for International Studies at MIT. Then under the directorship of Professor Rosenstein Rodan, the Center was engaged in organizing research on developing countries, including India. I continued to consider problems of planning and development, but with greater critical perceptions. Apart from working on issues emerging from my doctoral dissertation, I examined the arguments emanating from Hirschman's strategy of development which stressed structural factors of 'backward' and 'forward' linkages to identify 'key' sectors. I was critical of the excessive emphasis placed on material linkages, with the relative neglect of the problem of effective demand. In 'Structural Linkages in the Indian Economy' (1962), I discussed Hirschman's notion of key sectors in planned development, pointing out the analytical weaknesses of the statistical measure of linkages. I also argued that the strategy based on structural interdependence was more workable with reference to choice between alternative programmes than for priority ranking of individual sectors.

During my stay at Cambridge, Professor Joan Robinson arrived on her famous trip to launch her attack on the aggregate production function and the neoclassical theory of distribution, and to debate with Professors Samuelson, Solow and other neoclassical theorists. At that time my approach to neoclassical theory was primarily formed in the context of the theory of development – siding against its static resource-allocative, individual-centred analysis. My interest in the distribution theory was rekindled by this controversy between the two Cambridges. As a critic of the marginal productivity theory of distribution, I became more pointedly aware of the capital-theoretic debate. I did not then know of the more fundamental critique of economic theory heralded by Piero Sraffa's work.

While finding that the input-output techniques gave an insight into the intersectoral material connections as transactions, I had two reservations about the predominantly production-based analysis as used in planning strategies. First, in plan models there was an excessive reliance on technologically-induced quantity relations. At the same time, the technological relations were presumed to operate under constant returns to scale so that the dynamic scale economies and 'externalities' that characterized the key sectors in history were left out of account. Secondly, the excessive – sometimes exclusive – emphasis on technological interdependence tended to ignore forces operating on income and demand formation. The use of inter-industry analysis needed to be supplemented by a theory of growth of output, consumption and investment, and also by appropriate characterization of exchange systems. The supreme importance given to technological linkages tended to neglect aspects of the formation of demand and the play of market forces. With entry into planning, the problem of development in India was perceived not merely as one of efficient allocation of given resources, but also as one of resource creation and market formation.

The Second Five-Year Plan adopted the Mahalanobis strategy of accelerating investment in heavy industry to lead eventually to a higher rate of income growth. Important debates on strategy ensued between the proponents of industrialization and those of 'agriculture first'. The Bombay School, where I was then a research student, supported the latter, advocating priority to agriculture (wage goods) in the interest of promoting capital formation through the use of surplus labour. The arguments drawn from the Lewis model of promoting industrialization in a dual economy on the basis of transferring surplus labour from agriculture to industry at a constant subsistence wage also appeared in the forefront of debates. A critique of these models was developed by me in 'Notes on Political Economy of Development: The Indian Case' (1972). By constructing a countercase I argued that even when the capitalist sector is supplied with labour at a constant subsistence wage, there could still be internal limitations on the growth of the capitalist industrial sector, due to the peculiar forces of differentiation (in production, exchange and distribution) that prevail in this non-competitive sector. This argument, appearing in 1965 and emphasizing the internal contradictions emerging from the industrial sector even when all constraints emanating from agriculture were held in abeyance, appeared counter-intuitive at that time. For the failure of agriculture to grow had created pressures on the government to review its earlier strategy of promoting investment in heavy industry and instead to sponsor the green revolution. When later in the 1970s the agriculture sector in the aggregate had shown remarkable buoyancy, industry experienced a deceleration and a different set of contradictions appeared to have emerged. I was to return to this theme again to deal explicitly with the question of differentiation in agriculture and industry within a political economy framework (see below).

During the interval there was a sea-change in my approach to the critique of economic theory. Although I had always opposed neoclassical theory, in this earlier phase my criticism was much more directed against its static, resource-allocational efficiency bias; against its symmetrical explanation of wages, profits, rent and interest as 'factor-prices' on the same principle as commodity prices; against the individual-centric perception of choice, and against the fallacy of composition involved in treating social welfare as a simple aggregation of individual welfares. It was not until I discovered through the Sraffian critique the structural contrasts between the two alternative theories – classical and demand-and-supply equilibrium (less appropriately termed neoclassical) – that my approach changed. Although I had been introduced to the capital theory debate through the Robinsonian onslaught, neither the full critical implications of the debate nor the reconstructive aspects of the controversy were clear to me until, on my return to Bombay from MIT, I came upon Piero Sraffa's *Production of Commodities*.

On my return to India in 1962, I joined the Department of Economics, Bombay University, as a lecturer. The turn in my research interests was quite dramatic. Sachin Chowdhury, the editor of *The Economic Weekly* who was a close friend of the Cambridge scholars Joan Robinson and Maurice Dobb and an admirer of Piero Sraffa, invited me to his office to extract – as was his style – a contribution to his *Weekly*. Knowing my interest in theory, he drew out of his drawer this slim volume: Sraffa's *Production of Commodities* and offered the book for review, suggesting it would be a feast for thought. Leafing through this, I agreed to review it in a month or so! Mr Chowdhury suggested – enigmatically, I thought then – that I could take my own time since the author had been writing it over decades and had published it even then only as a prelude to something more substantial. Thus I set upon reading the little book. My acquaintance with Marx was mainly from a cursory reading of *Capital* and with Smith and Ricardo mainly secondhand through history of thought compendiums. My interest in radical thought had been mainly nurtured on reading the left-Keynesians, Kalecki and the political arguments for state interventionist planning. Sraffa's book fascinated me and inspired me to read the originals in depth.

The review did not appear for two years (1964). It was a novice's effort to state in simple terms what appeared to me to be astonishingly and challengingly original. I was most taken by surprise when I received complimentary letters from Joan Robinson, Maurice Dobb, Ronald Meek and many other Indian and European scholars and from Piero Sraffa himself. It was through the efforts of Joan Robinson that Clare Hall generously offered me a fellowship to work at Cambridge in 1967. This gave me the unique opportunity to communicate with Piero Sraffa and with other scholars including Joan Robinson, Maurice Dobb, Richard Kahn, Nicholas Kaldor, Luigi Pasinetti, Pierangelo Garegnani and with a group of young economists from England and Europe interested in the revival of classical and Marxian theory. My association with Piero Sraffa until his death in 1983 radically altered my theoretical perspective in economics.

When I arrived in Cambridge, a major controversy had erupted over the neoclassical theory of profit. This followed Sraffa's demonstration of the possibility of reswitching of techniques and, more generally, the challenge to the existence of a normal demand function for capital (implying a monotonic inverse relation between capital intensity and the rate of profit). A major attack on the neoclassical theory of distribution appeared in the series of articles in the symposium on 'Paradoxes in Capital Theory' (*Quarterly Journal of Economics*, November 1966, pp. 503–83). I did not take part directly in the debate although I shared exciting discussions with its main participants and with the Sraffian scholars in Cambridge. I also wrote a paper (1970) to bring out the analytical significance of Sraffa's basic-non basic commodity distinction which (having been identified with the more familiar matrix-classification of decomposability and indecomposability) had led to misinterpretations of the Sraffian arguments.

The main task I undertook was to elaborate the Sraffian critique of economic theory which, as I understood it, brought out the distinctive differences in the theoretical approaches and the methodological frameworks of the two streams of economic theory. These were the classical or surplus-based theories (represented by Smith, Ricardo and Marx) and the currently dominating demand-and-supply equilibrium (DSE) theories spearheaded in the writings of Jevons, Menger and Walras. I saw Sraffa's work as achieving a two-fold task: reconstructing the long-submerged approach of the classical writers in economic theory and developing a critique of marginalist theory which had acquired dominance since the 1870s. Inspired by Sraffa's framework, I proceeded to take up certain debates in the history of political economy arising out of the works of Smith, Ricardo and Marx, and particularly concerning the questions of value and distribution. These revealed the particular framework that underlay the manner in which such problems were formulated, analysed and debated.

Some of the essays written over several years appear in *Themes in Value and Distribution: Classical Theory Reappraised* (1989) and share a certain thrust of analysis. The general critique of theory is advanced along three themes. One is the attempt to determine the basic common elements in the analytical approach of classical theory and to trace their development through the critical debates which resulted from the writings of Smith, Ricardo and Marx. Following Sraffa's unravelling of the classical approach in his masterly edition of Ricardo's works, I attempted to analyse the critical controversies in classical theory, to investigate the formation and evolution of the basic theoretical framework they shared and the specific concepts and categories they evolved. The attempt was to discover the explicit or implicit theoretical setting in which they analysed questions of value and distribution as basic to their theory of accumulation. Even when such explicit statements on the structure of theory are not available, it is possible, as Sraffa's analysis of Ricardo indicates, to discover the rational foundations of their propositions, for instance, by recognizing the peculiar framing of their theoretical questions, the specific forms in which logical difficulties are perceived and encountered, and their resolution attempted. Sraffa's reconstruction of Ricardo's system illustrates the method of enquiry. In parallel, I have also attempted to draw out the basic structure shared in neoclassical theory.

The second strand in my research is the unravelling of the differences in theoretical structure between classical and DSE theories in their explanation of prices, quantities and distribution. A general position of the methodological contrast between the two alternative schemes of theorizing was presented from a Sraffian perspective in my Dutt Memorial Lectures delivered in 1976 and published in 1978. In these, I laid out the structure of classical theory shared by Smith, Ricardo and Marx and compared it with the demand-and-supply based equilibrium theory. My central argument was that DSE theories resort to a method which is restrictive in its ability to incorporate the variety of conditions under which changes in output, methods of production, consumption and distribution take place, and that these limitations arise from the assumptions that are imposed for validating the theory. Secondly, the basis on which the well-behaved demand and supply functions are constructed throw up a number of logical difficulties such as the one raised in the capital theory debate.

The classical theory, on the other hand, allows openness for diverse factors to influence the determination of quantities (production, distribution and consumption). Moreover prices are treated as compatible with the required circular reproduction of the system consistent with the rules regarding the generation, appropriation and distribution of surplus. The two theories thus differ in their structures in explaining prices and quantities. It is the elaboration of this difference that explains, first, the relative openness of the classical theory to deal with historical change and, second, the restricted conception of change and choice presumed in the DSE theory (in order that it remain internally consistent with the theory of market equilibrium). By emphasizing the limitations of the DSE theory flowing from its logical structure and methodological approach, I have tried to lend accuracy and sharpness to earlier critiques directed against the utilitarian and subjective basis of DSE, the lack of realism of its assumptions etc. With the structural critique inspired by Sraffa, there is now an opportunity to give these criticisms a sounder logical basis.

The third strand in my studies is to focus on the different analytical structures of the two theories and to investigate attempts to assimilate and synthesize classical into DSE theory. I examine certain commonly adopted concepts like demand, supply and competition to show how concepts and notions placed in different theoretical frameworks acquire different connotations and roles. I use this argument to counter the 'continuity thesis' of unidirectional improvement of ideas that some DSE theorists hold in order to argue that the classical framework is at best only a partial scheme or a subsystem of the more general DSE theory. I have argued that original concepts like demand and supply, transplanted in a different theory, change not only their connotations but also their content. The danger is all the greater when abstract theoretical concepts like supply, demand and market are used unwarily in common parlance. A clear understanding of how the structures of various theories differ becomes essential for a careful interpretation of commonly used concepts and the theoretical propositions derived from them.

The viewpoint emerging in my work, greatly influenced by Sraffa, is the critique of theories on the basis of their structures, their logical coherence and their ability to give consistent answers to questions of social change. While these investigations mainly address questions of value and distribution, they can be extended to the theory of accumulation and change. While attempting to extend the Sraffian interpretation of the classical approach to the problem of effective demand, I have also tried to develop the surplus approach to problems of accumulation in developing countries like India. Thus my effort has been to provide a link between the resurgence of classical theory and the exploration of problems of development.

My first work to extend classical political economy into development theory attempted to analyse production conditions in Indian agriculture as reflected in the newly-published farm management studies. This was undertaken at the Department of Applied Economics, Cambridge, when I was a Senior Research Officer during 1968–69. The farm management surveys primarily recorded information about production and business conditions according to different centres, farm sizes and crops. Most economists used these data to discuss conventional equilibrium theoretic questions. I set out to explain the observed differences in production performance, input-utilization patterns and the differing terms of transactions on the basis of the differential involvement in markets of a differentiated peasantry. I proposed a classification of peasantry according to access to land, as well as to the nature of exchange involvement in the agrarian situation where competitive capitalist markets had not yet fully emerged. I attempted to stratify the peasants according to their status in production and their corresponding involvement in exchange under conditions of uneven commercialization. The output markets were more commercialized whereas those in labour, credit and land were not fully formed. In the paper I tried to relate the production status of the households to their involvement in different discriminatory exchange systems. In this work (completed in 1968 but published in 1974) the idea of interlinked markets and their consequences for the exploitative processes was offered for the first time.

It was after my return to Delhi to join the Jawaharlal Nehru University in 1971, however, that my endeavours to combine my work in the reconstruction of classical political economy with the problems of development took concrete shape. With the help of some other economists, the university offered me an opportunity to launch a programme in postgraduate studies for the newly constituted Centre for Economic Studies and Planning. Over these last years we have attempted to build postgraduate and research degree programmes that promoted critical thinking in economic theory, in development theory and policy. It is in my endeavours to combine theory and historical experience that I have found teaching and interactions with colleagues the most rewarding.

In the initial period I continued to work on the problems of agriculture. My idea of interlinked markets was taken over by game theorists who set up a variety of models of contractual markets. However, my main interest was in the differential dynamics that arise due to the coexistence of different exchange systems corresponding to a differentiated peasantry. In 'A View of Commercialization in Indian Agriculture' (1985), I extended these ideas on interlinked markets, emphasizing the varied dynamics generated by the different patterns of differentiation and the corresponding patterns of exchange involvements. A major difference in my analysis from the game-theoretic approach dominating formal analysis was that the latter continued to ask the standard neoclassical static efficiency questions and to explain the coexistence of different exchange systems rather than their transitions or their effects on the aggregate patterns of growth. My focus was on the macrodynamics that the processes of differentiation generated within the coexisting but interacting exchange systems. The differential patterns of accumulation generated in regions with different structures of production and exchange were discussed in the 1985 paper. I also reformulated my earlier essay on the political economy of development by proposing a differentiated production and exchange system in agriculture, adopting a wider differentiation of commodity sectors and introducing a wider categorization of income classes (1979).

What emerged out of my several studies on the production and exchange processes at work in the Indian economy was neither the simple scenario of dualism (reflected in an agriculture-industry dichotomy) nor the dynamic advance of capitalist accumulation drawn in the image of Britain as the home of capitalism. In my 1988 Daniel Thorner lecture, I discussed the genesis and consequences of the peculiar patterns of development experienced in India wherein, despite substantial changes in national product and its composition since the launching of planned development, no significant shift has occurred in the proportion of population depending on agriculture for bare survival or even in the numbers subsisting below the 'poverty line'.

In considering the dynamics of development in India, with its colonial past and within changing international conjunctures, I have found classical and Marxian theory much more open and flexible than neoclassical theory in dealing analytically with the processes of differentiation in production, distribution and exchange. I have thus attempted to combine my critique of economic theory and the reconstruction of the classical (including Marxian) approach with the analysis of historical change in the course of development. In a plenary address delivered at the Indian Economic Association's conference, I argued the methodological *superiority* of the classical approach over the neoclassical to deal with the problems of accumulation and change (1990). In other related publications (1988b and c), I have tried to draw upon the classical theory to derive conceptual frameworks for the handling of developmental problems, particularly in relating exchange conditions to production relations.

It is thus that my work in analysing the history of theory and in reconstructing classical and Marxian theory (inspired by the Sraffian perspective) has converged with my parallel interest in the problems of accumulation in developing countries.

Bharadwaj's Major Writings

(1962), 'Structural Linkages in the Indian Economy', *The Economic Week*, August. Reprinted as 'A Note on Structural Interdependence', *Kyklos*, **25**, 1972.

(1964), 'Value through Exogeneous Distribution', *Economic Weekly*, August. Reprinted in G.C. Harcourt and N.F. Laing (eds), *Capital and Growth*, Penguin, 1977.

(1965), 'The Logic of Implicit Prices', *Indian Economic Journal*, **12**.

(1970), 'On the Maximum Number of Switches between Two Production Systems', *Schweizerische Zeitschrift fur Volk Swistschaft und Statistik*, no 4.

(1974), *Production Conditions in Indian Agriculture as Reflected in the Farm Management Studies*, Cambridge University Press.

(1978), *Classical Political Economy and the Rise to Dominance of Supply and Demand Theories*, Orient Longmans; second revised edition, Calcutta: University Press India Ltd, 1986.

(1979), 'Towards a Macroeconomic Framework for a Developing Economy: The Indian Case', *Manchester School Journal*, 47.

(1985), 'A View of Commercialization in Indian Agriculture', *Journal of Peasant Studies*, 13.

(1988a), 'Dynamics of Development and the Formation of Labour Markets', Daniel Thorner Lecture submitted at Dhaka, December.

(1988b), 'Production and Exchange in Price Formation Economic Transition', in M. Baranzini and R. Scazzieri (eds), *Foundations of Economics*, Oxford: Basil Blackwell.

(1988c), 'The Analytics of Agriculture-Industry Relation', in K.J. Arrow (ed), *The Balance between Industry and Agriculture in Economic Development*, London: Macmillan.

(1989), *Themes in Value and Distribution: Classical Theory Reappraised*, London: Unwin Hyman.

(1990), 'Paradigms in Development Theory: Plea for a Labour-ist Approach, *Economic and Political Weekly*, 27 June.

Other References

Robinson, J., *Collected Economic Papers*, Oxford: Basil Blackwell, Vol IV, 1973; Vol V, 1979.

Sraffa, P. (ed) with M. Dobb (1951), *The Works and Correspondence of David Ricardo Vol I*, Cambridge: Cambridge University Press.

Sraffa, P. (1960), *Production of Commodities by Means of Commodities*, Cambridge: Cambridge University Press.

Kenneth E. BOULDING (born 1910)

I was born and grew up in Liverpool, which might almost be described as a dissenting city. On the downtown street where I grew up I think there were only one or two other Protestant English families. The rest were Irish, Jewish, even one black family, and some Belgian refugees from the First World War. I come from what might be called the Methodist upper working class. My father was a plumber with a small business of his own. My mother's father was a blacksmith. I think I was probably the first member of my family ever to go beyond the eighth grade. Nevertheless, my parents, grandparents, aunts and uncles were self-educated intelligent people. By this time Methodism had perhaps gone beyond dissent into a self-sufficient culture of its own, singularly devoid of envy of the rich and upper class which seemed remote and irrelevant. We did not think of ourselves as poor. Poor people were those who drank and went occasionally to the Salvation Army. By the time I was about ten years old, my father even had a small car for his business. And in the summer we would take brief trips either to see relations or the cathedrals of England. Overseas travel was unthinkable. Both my father and my grandfather were lay preachers, and I would go with them sometimes to hear them conduct Sunday services and give sermons. I was an only child and an only grandchild. I grew up in a very adult environment. As we lived right downtown, our house was the centre of a small extended family and constantly visited by travelling ministers. The conversation around the dining room table was diverse and stimulating. My father was an ardent Liberal and an admirer of William Ewart Gladstone (hence my middle name). I had one uncle who was a Conservative and another who was a Labour party man, the manager of a cooperative store. So political discussion was very interesting.

I was good at passing examinations, so I got a scholarship to the Liverpool Collegiate School, the local grammar school. My parents had a strong concern for my education and were very supportive. My grandfather, coming from a small country town in Somerset, thought education might corrupt me. He may have been right! At the Collegiate School I studied mostly mathematics, physics and chemistry my last three years, preparing for scholarship examinations for Oxford and Cambridge. I got a scholarship in chemistry to New College, Oxford. I read Chemistry my first year, but then persuaded the College to let me keep my scholarship and change to Politics, Philosophy and Economics. At the end of the summer term I went to the tutor in economics, Lionel Robbins, who was just about to leave to take up his professorship at the London School of Economics. I asked him what I should read during the summer. He suggested Marshall's *Principles of Economics*, Pigou's *The Economics of Welfare*, Cassel's *Theory of Social Economy* and Hawtrey's *The Economic Problem*. I got these books out of the library, took them home and read them during the summer, thus gaining my first foundation in economics. However as a Methodist from Liverpool who had just become a member of the Society of Friends (Quakers), I felt very much an alien at Oxford. The class lines between those who had been to boarding schools and those who had been to grammar schools were very sharply drawn. I found my friends among similar outcasts. I joined the Labour club, though I was never a very active member, and thought of myself as something of a Marxist until I had to read *Capital* which convinced me that Marx did not know much about the working class and its great diversity of subcultures.

While I was at Oxford I read Keynes' *Treatise on Money*, which had a great impact on me. I also read Irving Fisher. I thought he was a much better economist than Keynes, though not such a good philosopher. Two things about Keynes' *Treatise* had a great influence on my subsequent thinking. One was the 'widow's curse' theory of profit, which Keynes never went on to develop. The other was the idea of inflation and deflation as having a profound effect on human history in redistributing wealth and power structures, creating and destroying classes, and so on. After getting my 'First' in 1931, I stayed on for a year doing so-called graduate work. I even wrote a thesis, which I never submitted, on 'The Theory of International Capital Movements' which is my lost work.

Then in 1932 I got a Commonwealth Fellowship to the University of Chicago. Jacob Viner was my adviser. I took him my Oxford thesis. He turned over the pages, sniffed audibly, and said, 'Hmm ... Oxford ... no footnotes!' Then he suggested I take a Ph.D. I asked him what I would have to do. After he told me, I decided if I did that I would be a broken man. I had much better things to do with my life. At that time, of course, I had not realized that I would live the bulk of my life in the United States. And with my 'First' at Oxford, I already had my 'Good Housekeeping Seal of Approval' for academic life in Britain. So I had a wonderful time at Chicago, learned some econometrics from Henry Schultz, one of its founders, explored ideas with Frank Knight and found a wonderful circle of friends among the graduate students. During the summer of 1933 three of us took a vacation and travelled all round the US in a wonderful, old, open Buick. At the Grand Canyon I got the news that my father had died, so I went back to England to settle up his business, a difficult task as most of the needed information was in the head that was no longer there. I learned a lot of economics in those ten days, especially as he had died bankrupt.

In the autumn I went back to Harvard to work with Professor Schumpeter whom I had met on the boat going over to the US the year before. I wrote a paper for him on Bohm-Bawerk which I think persuaded me that equilibrium in economics was not much more than a useful fiction. I finished up with six months in Chicago, where my mother joined me, and then we went back to England in the summer of 1934, living with relations and with our savings running out fast. Fortunately I got a job at the end of the summer as a very humble assistant at the University of Edinburgh where the economics department, I thought, was still living in about the 1880s, although people were very kind to me personally. I became good friends with an accountant, William Baxter, who taught me what a balance sheet was, something that I had never learned at Oxford, and got me to read Paton's *Accounting Theory* which had a very profound effect on my economic thought. In those years I published a couple of articles on capital theory, looking at capital demographically as a population of goods, an idea which has been very fundamental in my thinking all my life. I also supplemented my meagre income by working for Lord Astor and Seebohm Rowntree on a study of British agriculture. I had never really been on a farm, yet I was fascinated by the geographical structure, particularly of livestock production, and again by the importance of the demography of livestock.

In 1936 Frank Knight published an article in *The Quarterly Journal of Economics* entitled 'The Theory of Investment Once More: Mr Boulding and the Austrians', which put me in such good company that I managed to get away with not having a Ph.D.

In August 1937, I went to a Quaker world conference in Philadelphia. While I was there one of my old Chicago friends got hold of me, saying that there was a job going at a little college in upstate New York, Colgate

University. After the conference I went up there, we looked each other over, I accepted the job and emigrated with one suitcase and an unused return ticket. The realization of how one's whole life can hang on a single telephone call perhaps aroused my interest in the extreme importance of improbable events.

While at Colgate University I wrote *Economic Analysis*, an intermediate textbook of great respectability, which actually went through four editions, lasting for more than 25 years. I have sometimes said that *Economic Analysis* was so respectable that I have been able to be disreputable ever since. The fourth edition in 1966 perhaps edged enough towards dissent to make it a failure.

I had read Keynes's *General Theory* before I wrote the first edition of *Economic Analysis*. It had not really penetrated my mind very much and the monetary theory in *Economic Analysis* in 1941 was essentially that of Irving Fisher. It is interesting perhaps that by 1948, when the second edition appeared, I had at least established my own image of what the *General Theory* was all about and included it.

In May 1941 I met Elise Bjorn-Hansen; we were engaged in 18 days, married in three months and continue to have a wonderful life together. The next year I was in Princeton, working for the League of Nations Economic and Financial Section on problems of economic adjustment after the First World War, particularly in European agriculture. Then there was a year at Fisk University, a black college in Nashville, Tennessee. In 1943 I went to Iowa State College at Ames where Theodore Schultz invited me to convert myself into a labour economist.

During this period I wrote a paper on 'A Liquidity Preference Theory of Market Prices' in which, going back again to capital theory, I argued that the relative price structure, especially in organized commodity and security markets, depended on the stocks of the commodities, money and other exchangeables in the hands of the marketers, and on what proportion of their assets the marketers wished to hold in the form of these various exchangeables. The formula is market price equals the quantity of money in the market multiplied by the commodity preference ratio, divided by the quantity of commodity in the market, multiplied by the liquidity preference ratio. The commodity preference ratio is the preferred level of the money value of the commodity held, divided by the money value of all assets including money. Similarly, the liquidity preference ratio is the preferred level of the quantity of money held, divided by the total value of all exchangeable assets held in the market. In the market it is assumed that there is no production or consumption of commodities or money. If there is no change in asset preferences, changes in the market price structure occur when there are changes in the quantity of exchangeables, including money, held in the market, which happens when any one item is more produced than consumed. This leads to the general statement that the relative price structure in a market is that at which people are willing to hold what is there to be held.

I regard this article as one of my most important contributions to economics and yet to my knowledge it has never received much attention, perhaps because it was published during the war and people's minds were busy with other things. This theory of market price also leads into the principle that there is an equilibrium structure of normal prices at any one time such that if the market price is less than the normal price for any commodity, its production will be relatively less advantageous and production will fall as resources move to the production of more advantageous goods. Consumption will also rise, so stocks of the commodity will fall. In the absence of changes in preferences, the market price will rise towards the normal price. This essentially is Adam Smith's theory. I am not sure it has been improved on much since.

The move to Ames was a very critical one in my intellectual development. The year that I spent studying the labour movement convinced me that if one were going to study any section of the real social world, one could not do this with just economics. One had to have political science, sociology, anthropology and psychology. This convinced me that all the social sciences were essentially studying the same thing, which was the total social system, from different vantage points. These considerations got me interested in the integration of the social sciences. When I went to the University of Michigan in 1949 I exercised a little bargaining power to be able to teach a seminar on the integration of the social sciences. I found that the social sciences did not want to be integrated very much, so the seminar turned into one on the integration of anybody I could integrate, which led into general systems.

Each year I would select a general topic, like conflict or growth, get together a group of people from the physical, biological and social sciences to see what each had to say about it. This led me into correspondence with Ludwig von Bertalanffy, the founder of general systems, and in the autumn of 1953, at the Center for Advanced Study in the Behavioral Sciences at Stanford, a little group of four of us around a lunch table founded what was then called the Society for the Advancement of General Systems, an organization which still flourishes under the title of the International Society for the Systems Sciences. With a few exceptions, general systems has not established itself in the role structures of universities, still less in high schools, where there is a great opportunity for it. Perhaps this is an idea whose time has not quite come. In the original 'manifesto' we defined a general system very broadly as any theoretical system which was relevant to more than one discipline.

The years in Ames also saw the writing of what I still feel is perhaps my major work in economics as such, my *Reconstruction of Economics* (1950). Following my early convictions that economics had suffered from a failure to distinguish stocks from flows and their relationships, I tried to reconstruct economics around the concept of the balance sheet rather than the income statement which I regard as a derivative – descriptive of changes in balance sheets. This applied both at the micro level in the theory of the firm and at the macro level in the theory of macrodistribution, which is what determines the distribution of national income, or something like it, as between profit, interest, rent and wages. At the micro level I argued that the simplest first approximation of the theory of the firm, or even of the household, is that of the homeostasis of the balance sheet or position statement, a process not dissimilar to that by which living organisms retain their health and vigour. Depreciation and consumption have to be offset by a corresponding production; money spent on inputs has to be offset by money received from the sale of outputs, and so on. Profit then emerges as the gross growth in net worth and arises from the ability to sell products for more than their costs, costs being the subtraction from net worth. Revenue, of course, can only be received from the sale of the product.

This view suggests that there is an element of truth in the Marxist concept of surplus value, though it is not necessarily or even usually derived from anything that could be called the 'exploitation of labour'. These considerations led into a macro theory of distribution which I have called the 'K Theory' (1985b). It was anticipated in some sense by Keynes in the 'widow's cruse' theory in the *Treatise on Money*, and by Kalecki in his famous remark, which seems to be part of oral tradition, that 'workers spend what they get and capitalists get what they spend'. It is implicit in some of Kaldor's models and, of course, has been propagated by myself. The central question is, how does the value of the product get to be greater than the money spent on costs? The answer here must be that it comes partly from household expenditures, out of income received in the form of profit if interest payments are regarded as a cost.

Another source of profit is investment itself in real capital or inventory. Initially this may simply appear as an increase in things like machines, buildings and inventories in the balance sheet, offset by a similar decrease in the money stock. The money stock, however, goes to households and comes back to the firm in the purchase of final goods or household goods at a price higher than their cost, thus creating profit. Another source of profit, somewhat related, is the shift in money stock from households into businesses, such as takes place at Christmas. This is a fluctuating shift. We see the money stock as a shifting cargo: sometimes it is shifting from households into businesses, sometimes from businesses into households.

It seems to me that some processes like these must be called into play in order to account for a phenomenon like the Great Depression of the 1930s. In 1932 and 1933 in the US and most of the capitalist world, profits were negative, interest as a proportion of national income had almost doubled since 1929, the proportion of national income going to labour had increased sharply and, of course, unemployment was 25 per cent. The conventional marginal productivity theory has to suppose that in 1932 and 1933 capital became fantastically plentiful and that labour was rather scarce, which seems implausible to the point of absurdity. This is not to say that marginal theory may not have some value in explaining shifts at the micro level within the capital structure, but at the macro level it simply breaks down. This is perhaps my major source of dissidence.

Another element in the situation which I developed rather later is that of the relation of unemployment to the gap between profit and interest rates. I have argued that when somebody is employed, the employer sacrifices the interest that could have been earned on the money spent on his wage in the hope of profit from the product of his work. In a situation like that of 1932 and 1933, it is almost literally true that anybody who hired anybody was either a philanthropist or a fool, or perhaps just a creature of habit. It is not surprising that unemployment was 25 per cent. The surprising thing is that it did not rise to 50 per cent and that the whole economy did not break down. Perhaps the only thing that kept us from total catastrophe was irrational expectations. Of all the factors that might affect unemployment, the most dramatic connection is that between unemployment and the ratio of profit to profit plus interest. This is, of course, particularly striking in the Great Depression and the recovery from it, but it is also evident in the years from 1950 onwards, with their mysteriously rising interest rates and increasing indebtedness. The present situation of the American economy is particularly threatening, with high interest rates, a continuing budget deficit and a private debt situation with the savings and loans banks that is almost getting out of hand. We have become a usurious society. Interest as a proportion of national income has gone from about 1 per cent in 1950 to about 9 per cent today. This is an intolerable burden which economists have completely neglected. There is a strange tendency in conventional economics to assume that profit and interest are much the same thing. Nothing could be further from the truth.

Another line of thought which came rather late in my life is the application of evolutionary theory to social systems, and especially to the economy. This interest can perhaps be traced to the year we spent in Japan at the International Christian University in 1963–64. My students were mostly Marxists, believing strongly in dialectics. I kept asking them, granted there are dialectical processes in history, but what about the non-dialectical ones?

At the end of my stay there I gave some lectures on 'Dialectical and Non-Dialectical Elements in the Interpretation of History', which became a book entitled *A Primer on Social Dynamics*, expanded later into *Ecodynamics*. In its simplest form the argument is that evolution, whether biological or social, is fundamentally a kind of learning process and that learning is not very dialectical, though it may sometimes have dialectical elements in it.

This led me to the view that economics had got the factors of production wrong – that land, labour and capital were hopelessly heterogeneous aggregates, about as useful as earth, air, fire and water for chemistry. All processes of production essentially involve getting from the genotype to the phenotype; that is, they originate in some genetic structure involving know-how, whether this is in the fertilized egg or in the plan for a building or an automobile. For the potential of this know-how to be realized it has to be able to capture energy in specific forms in order to select, transport and transform materials into the structure of the phenotype. My wisecrack on this is that the automobile is a species much like the horse – it just has a more complicated sex life. The genotypes of human artifacts are not contained in the artifacts themselves, as they are in biological species, but are contained in human minds, records, plans, computers and so on. Information in its complex forms – like know-how, know-what and know-whether – is then seen as the essential driving force behind both biological evolution and economic development. Capital is simply human know-how embodied in human artifacts. Then, of course, one sees the economy as an ecosystem of human artifacts, with a selective system based to a considerable extent on demand.

Land, labour and capital have some validity as categories of distribution, but what I have sometimes called the 'cookbook theory of production' – that we mix together land, labour and capital and out come potatoes – seems to me hopelessly inadequate. Production always starts with a genotype, whether of the fertilized egg or an idea. For the potential of the genotype to be realized, however, there must be access to what I have called the 'limiting factors' of energy, materials, space and time. Then it is the *most* limiting factor that is most significant, as when we are climbing a hill it is the first fence that stops us. In both biological and societal evolution this may be energy in some form, as on the tundra. Sometimes it is materials, as with the absence of water in the Sahara, or even trace elements in agriculture. Sometimes the limiting factor may be space, as it seems to be in tropical forests. Sometimes it may even be time, particularly when change in the environment is very rapid and there is no time to adjust to it. Both evolution in the biosphere and economic development are processes in the learning of complexity through genetic mutation and ecological selection. I suggest here the importance of the concept of the 'empty niche'; that is, a species that would have a niche in an ecosystem if it existed, the way Australia had an empty niche for rabbits. Once we discovered rather accidentally how to make gasoline from newly discovered oil wells, we created an empty niche for the internal combustion engine which had not existed previously.

Another aspect of my intellectual life, which I can only mention briefly here, is my concern for peace research as a very high intellectual priority in a world that is threatened with extinction by the institution of war. Peace I would almost define as the low-cost management of conflict. I wrote *Conflict and Defense* during a year spent in Jamaica (1959–60). There is a certain element in it of what I have sometimes called 'economics imperialism', an attempt to take the structures of economics, particularly in this case oligopoly theory, and apply them to the larger area of human conflict. My book on *Stable Peace*, written when I was the Tom Slick Distinguished Visiting Professor of World Peace at the LBJ School at the University of Texas in 1977, is also an attempt to look at what might be called 'development' in the field of conflict management. Even though my interest in general systems (*The World as a Total System*) and human betterment (*Human Betterment*) has carried me far beyond economics (*Beyond Economics*), a careful intellectual geneticist will spot genes in these activities that come from my training as an economist, just as they may detect the little boy from Liverpool inside the white-haired, not-very-retired professor who writes these sentences. I must confess I have enjoyed my life enormously. I may have a twinge of regret that my ideas have not been taken more seriously, but I am neither the first nor the last prophet to have had this experience.

Boulding's Major Writings

(1941), *Economic Analysis*, New York and London: Harper & Brothers; 2nd ed, 1948; 3rd ed, 1955; 4th ed, 1966.
(1944), 'A Liquidity Preference Theory of Market Prices', *Economica*, NS 11(42), 55–63.
(1950), *A Reconstruction of Economics*, New York: John Wiley & Sons.
(1962), *Conflict and Defense: A General Theory*, New York and London: Harper & Brothers.
(1968), *Beyond Economics: Essays on Society, Religion, and Ethics*, Ann Arbor: University of Michigan Press.
(1970), *A Primer on Social Dynamics: History as Dialectics and Development*, New York: The Free Press.
(1978a), *Ecodynamics: A New Theory of Societal Evolution*, London: Sage Publications.
(1978b), *Stable Peace*, Austin: University of Texas Press.
(1985a), *Human Betterment*, London: Sage Publications.
(1985b), 'Puzzles Over Distribution', *Challenge Magazine*, **28**(5), 4–10.
(1985c), *The World as a Total System*, London: Sage Publications.
(1985d), *Human Betterment*, London: Sage Publications.
(1989), *Three Faces of Power*, London: Sage Publications.

Other References

Kerman, C. (1974), *Creative Tension: The Life and Thought of Kenneth Boulding*, Ann Arbor: University of Michigan Press.

Pfaff, M. (ed) (1976), *Frontiers in Social Thought: Essays in Honor of Kenneth E. Boulding*, Amsterdam: North-Holland Publishing Company.

Silk, L. (1976), 'Kenneth E. Boulding', *The Economists*, New York: Basic Books.

Wright, R. (1988), 'Kenneth Boulding', *Three Scientists and Their Gods: Looking for Meaning in an Age of Information*, New York: Times Books.

Samuel BOWLES (born 1939)

The first year I taught introductory economics, one of my students asked me something like this: in view of the fact that scientific knowledge is freely available and people's biology is relatively similar around the world, why is it that some nations are so rich and others so poor? Another wanted to know whether this came about because 'they' were incompetent or because 'we' exploited 'them'. I had no answer; my training in neoclassical economics had left me totally unprepared to address these questions.

My students were surprised and mildly annoyed when I professed ignorance on issues which seemed to them exceptionally important and obviously economic in nature. They continued to press me, but they were leaning on an open door. It was 1965. With the civil rights movement in full swing, the Vietnam war escalating, and student power struggles erupting at schools and universities around the world, the chasm between the important issues of the day and what economists taught was simply too gaping for many of my generation to tolerate. I decided that I could not face my students unless I re-educated myself.

The problems of human agency, learning and the concentration of economic power and privilege became and have remained the primary foci of my research, from my early work on the economics of education in the mid-1960s to my current writing on agency theory and economic democracy. The resulting publications, most of them undertaken jointly with my colleague and friend Herbert Gintis, are united by a conviction that the concentration of power and privilege in the capitalist economy is an impediment to democracy: the authoritarian political structure of the enterprise, economic insecurity, as well as the unequal economic rewards characteristic of the capitalist economy make a mockery of political equality and obstruct the free and equal development of the individual. A major concern in this research has been to provide a coherent microeconomic foundation for a political economy committed to both democracy and economic justice. Gintis's and my recent research has developed an agency theoretic post-Walrasian value theory – which we term the 'theory of contested exchange' – an approach we have used to explore democratic alternatives to capitalism.

My political concerns have also led me to pursue research and popular writing on questions of macroeconomic theory, economic policy and the structure of the US economy. With David M. Gordon and Thomas E.

Weisskopf, I have sought to understand the underlying dynamic propelling the evolution of the post-World War II US economy, to explore the logic and consequences of right-wing economic policies, and to amend macroeconomic theory to take account of the role of class and other institutional relationships in the determination of productivity growth, profitability and investment. With Robert Boyer I have developed macroeconomic models of both Keynesian and Marxian inspiration to explore the relationship between the distribution of income, labour relations, class conflict, aggregate demand and the demand for labour.

With these and other co-authors I have sought to contribute to the development of democratic and egalitarian alternatives to right-wing economic policy and to identify steps leading towards distributive justice and popular participation in economic decision-making. These would enhance opportunities for human development, extend free time and provide a better quality of life through the elimination of the waste entailed by the enforcement of authoritarian and unfair social relationships.

This research has been essential to my political work which started with a modest project writing background papers for Dr Martin Luther King's poor people's march in 1968. More recent work has been with labour, peace, feminist and environmental activists through the Center for Popular Economics (which I helped to found in 1979), as well as involvement in Reverend Jesse Jackson's 1988 campaign for the Democratic party's presidential nomination. The relationship between my research and politics has been a two-way street: these political involvements, along with the questions of my students, have been the most important impetuses to the direction of my research and writing.

One cannot claim to understand fully the influences on one's political and professional trajectory, but for me the following stand out. My parents were exemplars of the democratic liberal political tradition – politically active, fair-minded and tolerant. They accepted unquestioningly the capitalist economy, while opposed to racism, sexism and great power domination of the Third World. Early in my university studies at Yale I began to suspect that their implicit support of capitalism might make their convictions contradictory.

My varied political education included an upbringing in rural New England as well as in India in the early 1950s. Thomas Paine and Mahatma Gandhi, not Marx or Lenin, were the political heroes of my early life; I worshipped Rosa Parks before I had even heard of Rosa Luxemburg. Though Marxism was not part of my childhood education, I rejected early on the Cold War politics of the 1950s, in part under the influence of friendships with Russians whom I met while touring the Soviet Union as a (not very good) musician in 1958 and 1959. Other lessons in my early political education included three years in Nigeria (teaching high school as a civil servant of the government of Northern Nigeria); involvement in the civil rights movement in the early 1960s; my firing from Harvard University (where I was a newly hired member of the economics faculty) for my refusal to sign an oath of loyalty to the US constitution, and the successful legal campaign to overturn both the firing and the oath; community organizing and other activism against the US intervention in Vietnam, and raising my children (for many years as a single parent).

Among the most important influences was my good fortune as a doctoral candidate and later as a faculty member at Harvard University to find as colleagues a remarkable group of leftist economists – among them Arthur MacEwan, Thomas Weisskopf, Richard Edwards, Michael Reich, Stephen Marglin, Herbert Gintis and Paddy Quick. Like others around the country who joined to found the Union for Radical Political Economics in 1968, we sought in seemingly endless seminars and conversations to develop an approach to economics which, unlike the dominant neoclassical paradigm, could illuminate rather than ignore or obfuscate our political concerns with racism, sexism, imperialism, injustice and the alienation of labour. Not surprisingly, Marxism was an important intellectual guidepost in this quest. Ironically, I was teaching at this time a thoroughly neoclassical course in advanced microeconomic theory to doctoral candidates at Harvard, the notes for which I published with David Kendrick as *Notes and Problems in Microeconomic Theory* (second edition with Peter Dixon, North Holland, 1980).

I began my collaboration with Herbert Gintis during the late 1960s, our first project being to fashion a neo-Marxian approach to the economics of education. Our research produced a series of econometric and other studies published singly and jointly (1972, 1974). This collaboration eventually resulted in the publication of *Schooling in Capitalist America* (1976), in which we explored the relationship between the evolution of capitalist class structure and the school system. In this work we empirically documented what we termed the 'correspondence principle': the tendency of the school system to adopt an hierarchical structure, class inequality and alienated systems of motivation characteristic of the capitalist economy. We also sought to understand the mechanisms underlying the correspondence principle through a reinterpretation of the history of US education. The correspondence principle became the basis for our critique of liberal educational philosophy: we argued, in short, that given the hierarchical and alienated nature of the labour process, the goals of free and equal human development and preparation for work were inconsistent in a capitalist society.

In 1973 I left Harvard, having been denied tenure (some thought on political grounds) and, with Herbert Gintis, Richard Edwards, Stephen Resnick and Richard Wolff, I relocated at the University of Massachusetts in Amherst.

With Leonard Rapping, James Crotty, Michael Best, Jane Humphries and our other new colleagues, we established an unusual doctoral programme offering students a variety of perspectives including post-Keynesian and Marxian economics, institutionalism and other variants of political economy in addition to neoclassical economics.

In 1979 I began working with David Gordon and Thomas Weisskopf, initially brought together at the request of a coalition of labour unions and progressive political groups to suggest a response by labour to the instability and stagnation of the US economy in the 1970s and to the drift to the right in public policy. Our first project, a theoretical and econometric explanation of the post-1965 productivity slowdown (using a microeconomic model of class relationships in the production process) appeared in 1983. Later studies built on the concept of a social structure of accumulation, earlier developed by Gordon in conjunction with Michael Reich and Richard Edwards, to model and econometrically explain long-term movements in the profit rate and the rate of accumulation, as well as trends in the cyclical variability of wages.

A central concept in this work was the cost of job loss – the income loss experienced by a worker as the result of the termination of his or her job. We used the cost of job loss as a measure of the effective threat exercised by employers over employees and, with Juliet Schor, documented its covariation over time with the rate of unemployment and the level of unemployment insurance and other income-replacing government transfers. In addition to being a robust predictor of movements in labour productivity and profitability, the cost of job loss also provided a compelling econometric account of the incidence of strikes (1987).

As well as a series of academic publications, Gordon, Weisskopf and I also developed for the US what might be described as a left-social democratic programme with a strong element of workplace democracy, published in two volumes entitled *Beyond the Waste Land* (1983b) and *After the Waste Land* (1991b).

After publication of *Schooling in Capitalist America*, Gintis and I turned to what became a decade-long study of the relationship between liberalism, Marxism and democratic theory, resulting in the publication of *Democracy and Capitalism* (1986). In this work we explored the difficulties of grounding democratic theory on either liberalism (due to its tendency to overlook power relations in the economy and the family, and its pre-social concept of the individual endowed with exogenously given wants and capacities) or Marxism (due to its tendency to underrate the despotic potential of the state, and its underdeveloped theory of individual choice). We proposed instead a grounding for democratic theory based on a political conception of markets and economic organizations and a model of individual action and human development in which both choice and social influences on individual development are given prominence. Our book may be considered a political critique of the capitalist economy and an argument for the radical potential of democratic (rather than specifically socialist) demands in a capitalist society.

Since the completion of this project, we have returned to the study of microeconomic theory more narrowly construed, building on Gintis' earlier work on the labour exchange and my research on the production process (1985) to propose a new microeconomic foundation for the political economy of capitalism. Crucial to this work is the notion that, contrary to the usual Walrasian assumption, contracts are not generally costlessly enforceable – notably those in labour markets and credit markets – and for this reason endogenous enforcement is ubiquitous in the capitalist economy. The result we show is that markets generally do not clear even in competitive equilibrium and that economic agents located on the short side of non-clearing markets – employers in the labour market, the wealthy in the credit market – exercise a well-defined type of power over their exchange partners, which we term 'short side power'. This model may be distinguished from recent theoretical developments in Marxian economics (such as the pioneering work of John Roemer) which rely on Walrasian market-clearing assumptions. We have used this model as the basis for a critique of the undemocratic and inefficient nature of the capitalist economy in two recent articles, 'Contested Exchange' (1990a) and 'The Democratic Firm' (1992). We have also investigated the commonalities and distinctions between contested exchange and other approaches to post-Walrasian economics such as transactions costs analysis, so-called efficiency wage theory, optimal contracting theory and principal agent theory in 'The Revenge of "Homo Economicus"' (1991a).

In the mid-1980s I began a collaboration with Robert Boyer. Integrating the insights of the French regulation school with those of the social structure of accumulation approach, we developed a macroeconomic approach which integrates the microeconomic modelling of the labour process by US radical economics with a treatment of aggregate demand derived from the work of Nicolas Kaldor and Michel Kalecki. In a series of recent theoretical papers we have analysed the high employment profit squeeze and its impact on employment and macroeconomic stability; the effect of egalitarian redistribution on equilibrium employment levels; the impact of state redistribution on growth and employment: and, finally, the relationship between labour market flexibility, employer collusion, union wage bargaining and equilibrium employment. An objective of this work is to explore the possibility that higher wages and more effective collective bargaining institutions may foster greater employment security (see 1988, 1990b and 1990c).

I am currently studying the relationship between economic institutions and the evolution of social norms using a variety of approaches including the theory of repeated games and to date have published 'Mandeville's Mistake' (1989).

Bowles's Major Writings

(1972), 'Schooling and Inequality from Generation to Generation', *Journal of Political Economy*, May/June.

(1974), 'The "Inheritance of IQ" and the Intergenerational Reproduction of Economic Inequality' (with Valerie Nelson), *Review of Economics and Statistics*, 61(1), February.

(1976), *Schooling in Capitalist America: Educational Reform and the Contradictions of Economic Life* (with H. Gintis), New York: Basic Books.

(1980), *Notes and Problems in Microeconomic Theory* (with David Kendrick), Chicago: Markham. Second edition (with Peter Dixon), Amsterdam: North Holland.

(1983a), 'Hearts and Minds: A Social Model of U.S. Productivity Growth' (with T. Weisskopf and D. Gordon), *Brookings Papers on Economic Activity*, 2.

(1983b), *Beyond the Waste Land: A Democratic Alternative to Economic Decline*, New York: Doubleday.

(1985), 'The Production Process in a Competitive Economy: Walrasian, Marxian and Neo-Hobbesian Models', *American Economic Review*, 76(1), March, 16–26.

(1986), *Democracy and Capitalism: Property, Community and the Contradictions of Modern Social Thought* (with H. Gintis), New York: Basic Books.

(1987), 'The Cost of Job Loss and the Incidence of Strikes' (with Juliet Schor), *Review of Economics and Statistics*, 69(4), November.

(1988), 'Labor Discipline and Aggregate Demand: A Macroeconomic Model' (with R. Boyer), *American Economic Review*, 78(2), May.

(1989), '"Mandeville's Mistake": The Moral Autonomy of the Self-Regulating Market Reconsidered', University of Massachusetts Discussion Papers in Economics.

(1990a), 'Contested Exchange: New Microfoundations for the Political Economy of Capitalism' (with H. Gintis), *Politics and Society*, 18(2).

(1990b), 'A Wage-Led Employment Regime: Income Distribution, Labour Discipline, and Aggregate Demand in Welfare Capitalism' in S. Marglin and J. Schor (eds), *The Golden Age of Capitalism: Reinterpreting the Postwar Experience*, Oxford: Clarendon.

(1990c), 'Labour Market Flexibility and Decentralization as Barriers to High Employment? Notes on Employer Collusion, Centralized Wage Bargaining and Aggregate Employment' in R. Brunette and C. Dell'Aringa (eds), *Labour Relations and Economic Performance*, Macmillan.

(1991a), 'The Revenge of Homo-Economicus: Post-Walrasian Economics and the Revival of Political Economy (with H. Gintis), *Journal of Economic Perspectives*, 5, Summer.

(1991b), *After the Waste Land: Towards a Democratic Economics for the Year 2000* (with T. Weisskopf and D. Gordon), M.E. Sharpe.

(1992), 'The Democratic Firm: An Agency Theoretic Evaluation' (with H. Gintis), in B. Gustafsson (ed), *Markets and Democracy: The Microeconomics of Participation and Efficiency*, Cambridge: Cambridge University Press.

Harry BRAVERMAN (1920–1976)   *Ugo Pagano*

Born in New York City into a working class family, Braverman was forced to terminate his college education after only one year. He worked in the Brooklyn Navy Yard for seven years primarily as a coppersmith. After the decline of the coppersmith trade due to the substitution of new processes and materials for traditional methods, Braverman worked in the steel industry, undertaking a wide range of skilled jobs; as he said, 'the trade of working copper provided the foundation in the elements of a number of other trades' (1974, p.5).

At the same time Braverman was deeply involved in trade union activities and in the socialist movement. He was co-editor of the *American Socialist* from its foundation in 1954. After this ceased publication in 1959, he started working as an editor at Grove Press where he became vice-president and general business manager. In 1967, he became managing director of *Monthly Review Press* where he worked until his death on the 2 August 1976 in Honesdale, Pennsylvania.

In some respects Braverman's book, *Labour and Monopoly Capital: The Degradation of Work in the Twentieth Century,* contains an autobiographic element which, according to Braverman himself, may make readers conclude that he has been influenced 'by a sentimental attachment to the outworn conditions, to now archaic modes of labour' (1974, p.6). Braverman's passionate rejection of this possibility reflects an admirable and rare attempt of finding a balance between life and science based on the awareness of the particular angle from which social reality has been observed.

The central place occupied in Braverman's creative work is immediately evident in the first chapter of *Labour and Monopoly Capitalism* where he restates the Marxian view that 'work as purposive action guided by intelligence is the special product of humankind' (1974, p.49). Unlike animals, men first conceive ideas and then execute them. Along with the greatness of humankind there is also the potential of being alienated and deprived of creativity. Since in humans conception and execution are autonomous, their unity in the activities of a single individual may be dissolved: an idea conceived by one person may be executed by another.

The possibility of dissolving the unity between conception and execution is exploited in the employment contract, which is the typical social relation of capitalism. By itself, the employment contract involves the sale of labour power or 'the power to labour over an agreed period of time' (1974, p.54). In other words, in the employment contract one agent accepts to execute, within certain limits, the actions conceived by another agent.

In the context of the employment relationship, the aim of management is to minimize the cost of labour power per unit of product. This has two aspects: the first is to pay as little as possible for the skills of the workers; the second is to make them work as hard as possible. Both aims are clearly evident in the principles according to which the division of labour is organized under capitalism.

The division of labour introduced in any capitalist firm destroys occupations and trades, subdividing them into meaningless and repetitive operations. This requires an explanation different from the maximization of 'learning by doing' involved in the Smithian principles of the division of labour. Such an explanation was given by Babbage and Taylor, and a great merit of Braverman has been to bring it to more general attention.

Whereas the Smithian principles of the division of labour rely on the maximization of 'learning acquired by doing', the Babbage principle is based on the idea that the division of labour should be organized to minimize the 'learning and the [strength] required for doing': the more detailed the division of labour, the lower is the skill requirement for each operation. Labour-power can be made cheaper by a comprehensive division of labour involving job de-skilling. According to Braverman, 'applied first to handicrafts and then to mechanical crafts, Babbage's principle eventually becomes the underlying force governing all forms of work in capitalist society, no matter in what setting or at what hierarchical level' (1974, pp.81–2).

As to Taylor, he realized that the traditional system of management was badly suited to increasing workers' efforts. It relied on the knowledge of the workers in the sense that the managers believed that the workers knew better than they did how to perform their jobs. Under traditional management, employees could work less than 'fairly' by exaggerating the time required to perform a certain job. The situation of 'asymmetric information' existing under traditional management implied that the managers had no means of challenging that sort of statement. Taylor's solution to this problem was straightforward: the managers and not the workers should know how the jobs could be best performed, plan how they should be carried out and give the workers detailed instructions about their execution. It was only by gaining the control of the labour process that the managers could invert the situation of asymmetric information and control the workers.

Braverman summarizes the content of Taylorism in three different principles:

1. dissociation of the labour process from the skills of the workers;
2. separation of conception from execution;
3. use of this monopoly over knowledge to control each step of the labour process and its mode of execution.

Observe that the principles of Babbage and Taylor lead to the same conclusion. *The dissociation of the labour process from the skills of the workers* not only allows for greater capitalist control but also, following Babbage, cheapens labour by decreasing learning time. In the same way, the *separation of conception and execution* implies greater capitalist control. It also means that fewer people should learn how to conceive and more should become cheap executors of others' decisions – this, again, being another implication of the Babbage principle. The same detailed division of labour cheapens labour-power and increases capitalists' control over labour and, consequently, workers' effort. For this double reason, according to Braverman, de-skilling jobs is a fundamental tendency of capitalism.

According to Braverman, the analysis of Taylorism is essential to the understanding of the real-life capitalist economy because in Taylor's work 'lies a theory which is nothing else than an explicit verbalization of the capitalist mode of production' (1974, p.86). This fundamental role of Taylorism is contrasted with the influence of schools of management which teach human relations and industrial psychology; according to Braverman, these have offered little more than cosmetic adjustments to the underlying principles of capitalist organization. Braverman observes how 'Taylorism dominates the world of production; the practitioners of "human relations" and "industrial psychology" are the maintenance crew for human machinery' (1974, p.87).

The state of 'human machinery' under capitalism is contrasted by Braverman with that of non-human machinery. He points out how capitalism is characterized 'by the incessant drive to enlarge and perfect machinery on the one hand, and to diminish the worker on the other' (1974, p.228).

The history of machinery is in striking contrast with the history of workers. Machines first acquire 'skills' specific to certain production processes. Then, especially after the electronic revolution, they tend also to acquire 'general purpose' abilities. By contrast the workers, deprived of traditional, craft-specific skills, become 'general purpose' not because their abilities are enlarged but because the scope of their jobs is narrowed. In other words, the worker becomes 'general purpose' because of job de-skilling: the tasks which he is required to perform have been divided into such detail and are so simple that each worker can be moved from one job to another without substantial training costs. In this sense, according to Braverman, the worker becomes 'a general-purpose machine operated by management' (1974, p.180). Machinery is also used to control the worker indirectly through the machine. By setting the pace of the machine the manager can control the effort and the tasks performed by the worker. Conception and execution even become physically separated: management makes machines execute tasks which require the execution of other tasks by the workers. De-skilled workers are increasingly controlled by means of 'skilled' machines.

According to Braverman, the drive of capitalists to cheapen labour and increase control over it is not limited to a particular sector or to a particular type of job. The job de-skilling consequences of the principles of Babbage and Taylor (as well as of the capitalist use of machinery) are also perfectly visible beyond the shop floor and outside industrial production. The service sector, the sales departments of industrial firms, secretarial work, the engineering profession and even the activity of management itself all come within the wide field of application of these principles. This field is not limited by the physical definitions of jobs and sectors. Its extension can go as far as capitalist property rights and can shape technology and the organization of work.

Because of the proletarization of large numbers of clerical and service sector workers, between two-thirds to three-quarters of all employees appear readily 'to conform to the dispossessed condition of a proletariat' (1974, p.403). However, Braverman admits that a considerable number of workers do not easily conform to this definition. Under modern monopoly capitalism we have a mass of people who do not fit into a polar conception of the class structure of society. The new 'middle class' of monopoly capitalism is qualitatively different from the petty bourgeoisie of pre-monopolist capitalism, which has largely disappeared. It was middle class in the sense that it was *outside* the process of capital accumulation: its members were neither capitalists nor workers. The new middle class of monopoly capitalism occupies a middle position within the process of capitalist accumulation in the sense that its members share characteristics of *both* capitalists and workers. 'Not only does it receive its petty share in the prerogatives and rewards of capital, but it also bears the mark of the proletarian conditions' (1974, p.406). The class structure of capitalism is continuously changing. New middle strata of employees emerge as a consequence of technological and organizational change. At a later stage, the same employees can be subjected to a process of 'rationalization' which implies cheapening of labour power and increasing control over workers on the lines suggested by Babbage and Taylor.

Braverman's work has been criticized for three interdependent reasons. First was his identification of Taylorism as the only typical form of organization under capitalism. Other authors have limited the field of application of Taylorism either to an historical phase of capitalism (Edwards, 1979; Gordon, Edwards and Reich, 1982), and/or to a certain country (Elbaum and Wilkinson, 1979; Littler, 1982), or to certain sections of the working class (for a survey see Sawyer, 1989, part 2). This point is strictly related to the second criticism: Braverman has ignored the fact that workers have successfully resisted Taylorism and that as a result, or even independently, of this resistance, capitalists themselves have found ways of controlling workers which are more efficient than Taylorism (Edwards, 1979; Friedman, 1977). Finally, Braverman has been criticized for his thesis that de-skilling has actually occurred in reality. It has been pointed out that, if some skills have disappeared, new skills have been created in the course of the development of capitalism. The sheer extension of formal training for the majority of workers seems to prove that re-skilling has occurred (Wood, 1982). I will start by considering this last objection and will return later to the first two criticisms.

It is an open issue whether de-skilling has occurred during the development of capitalism. Evidence for both de-skilling and re-skilling has been produced, but this is somewhat beside the point. Braverman's de-skilling hypothesis could be defended by saying that capitalism has a tendency to de-skill jobs. This tendency may be continuously operating even if technological change and other forces may act in the opposite direction (Sawyer, 1989, p.64).

This argument can be reinforced if one can show that capitalism has a tendency to de-skill jobs excessively in comparison with a society defined by a different system of property rights. The first step is to define this alternative society – a task which is implicitly attempted in Braverman's work. Although *Labour and Monopoly Capitalism* is about the development of capitalism and not about alternatives, it is largely inspired by the belief that it is possible (even if not easy) to create an alternative society where workers can develop their skills and where their needs as producers are taken into account. According to Braverman this requires something more than formal democracy at the workplace. 'Without the return of requisite technical knowledge to the mass of the workers and the reshaping of the organization of labour – without, in a word, a new and truly collective mode of production – balloting within factories and offices does not alter the fact the workers remain as dependent as before upon "experts" and can only choose among them, or vote for alternatives presented by them. Thus genuine workers' control has as its prerequisite the demystifying of technology and the reorganization of the mode of production. This does not mean, of course, that the seizure of power within industry through demands for workers' control is not a revolutionary act. It means rather that the true workers' democracy cannot subsist on a purely formal democratic scheme' (1974, p.445). Or, in other words, a different social system comes into being when the rights acquired by the workers can express themselves in a different technology and organization of work which takes into account their needs as human producers. Here is a fundamental reason for which Braverman must be considered a major dissenting economist.

Braverman's view of a 'good society' contrasts with the Pareto-optimal world described in orthodox welfare economics. Commenting upon the 'technical conditions' realized under capitalism, he observes that they are 'best adapted to everything but the needs of the people. These needs are, however, in the world of economists, "externalities" a notion that is absolutely incomprehensible from the human point of view, but from the capitalist point of view is perfectly clear and precise, since it simply means external to the balance sheet' (1974, pp.205–6). Under capitalism productivity becomes an end in itself: 'It is a measure of the manner in which capitalist standards have diverged from human standards that this situation is seen as representing a high degree of "economic efficiency"' (1974, p.206). Orthodox economics is not neutral. 'Only one who is the *master of the labour of others* will confuse labour power with any other agency for performing a task, because to him, steam, horse, water or human muscle which turns his mill are viewed as equivalents, as "factors of production". For *individuals who allocate their own labour power* (or a community which does the same) the difference between using labour power as against any other power is a difference upon which the entire "economy" turns' (1974, p.51).

Braverman's criticism can be developed by observing that in orthodox welfare economics, leisure – and not directly different uses of labour-power – enters the utility function of the individuals. It follows that individuals are implicitly assumed to be indifferent among different tasks and that their labour-power can be allocated in a way similar to that of steel and iron. If workers' preferences do not matter, then technological efficiency or maximum output per unit input is a necessary condition for maximizing social welfare. By contrast, if workers' preferences are taken into account, then less output may be preferable to more output if this is associated with more enjoyable work. Similarly, profit maximization is an optimal criterion for allocating work within the firm only if we assume that workers' preferences for their own work do not matter. Finally, if the workers are implicitly assumed to be indifferent to alternative allocations of their labour-power, it is even possible to show that job de-skilling is necessarily required to maximize social welfare (Pagano, 1985). In other words the optimal world of neoclassical economics is alien to Braverman's description of capitalism because it ignores workers' preferences for their own work; Braverman's ideal society is very far from both because it takes full account of these preferences. Still, the optimal world of neoclassical economics could be reformulated by the usual trick of introducing more markets; in particular, by assuming that there is a (possibly equilibrium) price for each use of labour. This solution is formally possible but it implies that firms, defined à la Coase (1937), or the employment contract, defined à la Simon (1957), do not exist. If firms exist in the sense that an internal allocation of labour is carried out within them, then they should internalize workers' preferences – an internalization which requires that workers have rights and, consequently, voice and power in the organization (Pagano, 1985).

Indeed recent mainstream economics, and in particular 'New Institutional Economics', justifies the efficiency of capitalism by the argument that, in a world of incomplete markets, capitalist ownership of firms can be optimal. Alchian and Demsetz (1972) maintain that in a market economy the property of the firm is efficiently acquired by the 'difficult-to-monitor factors' because it can save more on monitoring costs. Efficiency entitles difficult-to-monitor capital and managers to own and manage the firm. In a market economy the property of the firm is efficiently acquired by 'specific factors'. Unlike the owners of 'general purpose factors', the owners of 'firm-specific factors' can save more on costs which should otherwise be sustained to safeguard them, in an uncertain world, from the possible opportunism of the other partners. Managers and capitalists own and manage the firm because they own the relatively more specific factors. Workers will own and manage firms or, at least, will have some rights in the firm only when labour power is a 'difficult-to-monitor and/or specific factor'.

Harry Braverman's book contains a working hypothesis dissenting from that of New Institutional Economics. Whereas in the latter the workers have no rights in the firms where they work *because* they are 'easy to monitor' and/or 'general purpose' factors, in Braverman's book the workers *become* 'easy to monitor' and 'general purpose' factors because, under capitalism, they have no rights in the firm where they work. According to Braverman, it is because of capitalist property rights that the detailed division of labour on the lines suggested by Babbage and Taylor is implemented, with the result that the workers perform simple tasks which are easy to control and require only general purpose skills. Under capitalism the development of difficult-to-monitor human resources is inhibited by the fact that the workers have no rights in and attachment to the organization where they work. Similarly, the development of firm-specific skills, as well as the development of assets specific to the preferences of the present workers, are inhibited by the fact that, under capitalism, the rights to these assets are ill-defined. They belong neither to the employers (who can lose them if the workers quit) nor to the workers (who can lose them if fired).

It is no wonder that under the system of property rights of 'classical' capitalism the principle of minimizing the learning required for doing is over-applied, whereas the principles of maximizing the learning acquired by doing and of job satisfaction are under-applied. Unlike the latter two principles, the former decreases the cost of control and does not favour the development of human firm-specific resources. Under 'classical' capitalism, these resources are, in Braverman's words, externalities in the sense that they are external to the balance sheet, and the principles favouring their development are constrained by the appropriability conditions existing under the property rights of 'classical' capitalism (Pagano, 1988).

Finally let us now consider the objections to Braverman concerning the prominence he gives to Taylorism and the fact that he ignores workers' resistance. If workers can acquire new rights that entitle them to have greater control of their jobs, then we obtain a system of property rights different from that of 'classical capitalism'. Under this system of rights, the tendency to de-skill jobs excessively may well be reduced. For instance consider job security, which changes the worker from a simple seller of labour-power into a holder of a right in a particular job. The consequent absence of the threat of unemployment and attachment to the organization may mean that motivation can be increased by making the job more interesting – a task to which Taylorism is badly suited. Moreover, the existence of workers' rights in the firm implies that both workers and employers will not regard as an externality the development of firm-specific assets which enhance learning by doing and job satisfaction.

The fact that, in some important cases, workers have acquired rights different from the very limited ones which they have under the model of 'classical capitalism' considered by Braverman implies that his conclusions are less universal than they were intended to be. Still, this limit makes his message even more relevant. It is only by acquiring and/or defending rights at the workplace that workers can defend themselves against the tendency, built into 'classical capitalism', to expropriate them of their capacity for ideation and control and that they can acquire skills and a working environment consistent with their needs as workers.

Braverman's Major Publications
(1974), *Labour and Monopoly Capital*, New York: Monthly Review Press.

Other References
Coase, R.H. (1937), 'The Nature of the Firm', *Economica*, 4, 386–405.
Edwards, R. (1979), *Contested Terrain*, New York: Basic Books.
Elbaum, B. and Wilkinson, F. (1979), 'Industrial Relations and Uneven Development: a Comparative Study of the American and the British Steel Industries', *Cambridge Journal of Economics*, 3(3), 275–303.
Friedman, A.L. (1977), *Industry and Labour*, London: Macmillan.
Gordon, D.M., Edwards, R. and Reich, M. (1982), *Segmented Work, Divided Workers*, Cambridge: Cambridge University Press.
Littler, C.R. (1982), *The Development of the Labour Process in Capitalist Societies*, London: Heinemann.
Marx, K. (1967), *Capital*, New York: International Publishers.
Pagano, U. (1985), *Work and Welfare in Economic Theory*, Oxford: Basil Blackwell.
Pagano, U. (1988), 'Asset Specificity and the Labour Press Literature', Lecture notes for the I.S.E.R. Workshop and Economic and Institutions, *University of Siena-C. N. R.*, Siena
Sawyer, M. C. (1989), *The Challenge of Radical Political Economy*, Brighton: Harvester Wheatsheaf.
Simon, H.A. (1957), *Models of Man*, New York: John Wiley.
Woods, S. (ed.) (1982), *The Degradation of Work?: Skill, Deskilling and the Labour Process*, London: Hutchinson.

Nikolai Ivanovich BUKHARIN (1888–1938)   *John King*

Nikolai Bukharin was born into a middle-class family in Moscow, where he went to school. A student radical in 1905, he became a Bolshevik in the following year and worked as a propagandist and industrial organizer. Although he attended Moscow University between 1907 and 1910 he studied little, devoting most of his time to the political activities for which he was repeatedly arrested and eventually exiled. Bukharin fled to Germany in 1911, spending the next six years in a number of European countries and, finally, in the United States before returning to Russia in May 1917.

As an economist Bukharin was almost entirely self-educated, in the public libraries of various European capitals and of New York, though he did sit in on Böhm-Bawerk's lectures at the University of Vienna in 1913. For a Bolshevik, he took an unusually strong interest in contemporary non-Marxian social theory, and for a time inclined towards Bogdanov's heretical philosophical ideas. Bukharin began to write on economic theory while still in his early twenties, completing a major analysis of neoclassical value theory in 1914 and a path-breaking study of imperialism in the following year. Later writings included a lengthy critique of Rosa Luxemburg's and Otto Bauer's thinking on imperialism, and several important texts on the economics of communism and the transition to a post-capitalist society.

Bukharin was elected to the Bolshevik central committee in July 1917. He held no formal state office, but for a decade after the revolution was the party's leading theorist. In 1917 he became editor of *Pravda*, a post which he retained, almost without a break, for the next 12 years. With Zinoviev he was also in effective command of the Comintern during the 1920s. From his initial position on the left of the party, Bukharin supported Lenin's early maximalism, breaking with the official line over the Brest-Litovsk treaty and becoming, temporarily, the leader of the Left Communists. At first enthusiastic about War Communism, he had by 1922 rethought his position and became a defender of the New Economic Policy and the *smychka*, or worker-peasant alliance. He now advocated the gradual transition to communism which has become synonymous with Bukharinism.

His standing in the party was undermined at the end of the 1920s, first by the grain crisis which challenged the practicality of his economic strategy and then, fatally, by the onset of forced collectivization and Stalin's dictatorship. Forced to make a public recantation in November 1929, Bukharin remained a candidate member of the Central Committee and continued to work in minor state posts. For two years, in 1934–36, he even achieved partial rehabilitation as editor of the party newspaper *Izvestiia*. Bukharin eventually fell victim to Stalinist terror, being arrested in 1937 and executed in March 1938 after the most notorious of the show trials.

Bukharin's three principal contributions to economics were his critique of marginal utility theory, his analysis of imperialism, and his writings on the transition to communism in the Soviet Union. On the first of these issues he wrote a number of articles on the eve of the World War critical of Russian writers such as Struve and Tugan-Baranovsky. His most important work, however, was *The Economic Theory of the Leisure Class*, completed in 1914 but first published five years later. Here Bukharin draws heavily on the ideas of the Austro-Marxist Rudolf Hilferding, savaging first the methodology and then the substantive economic theory of the neoclassical school. Bourgeois economists adopt a subjective, unhistorical and static method which concentrates upon consumption, while Marxists are objectivists who recognize the historical specificity of political economy and focus their attention on the dynamics of capitalist production. Marginal utility cannot offer a satisfactory theory of price determination, Bukharin argues. It has no units of measurement; its principle of substitution is circular, taking for granted the market prices which are to be established; and, since it assumes supply to be given, it can say nothing about the determination of quantities. There is no subjective theory of the value of money, which is the most important of all commodities. If taken seriously, the supply and demand approach to price theory would in fact eliminate the need for any theory of value, including subjective ones.

Turning to the neoclassical theory of profit, Bukharin is equally severe. He rejects Böhm-Bawerk's mistaken definition of capital as a means of production rather than a social relation, and denies the significance attached by Austrian theorists to 'waiting', since all stages of production are undertaken simultaneously in any actual capitalist economy (Thomas Hodgkin had made this point almost a century earlier). Bukharin denied that either workers or capitalists systematically undervalue their future needs. Even if they were to do so, their subjective assessments of future as against present incomes do not exist in a vacuum, but are socially determined. The theory of waiting is apologetic, since it glosses over the differences in the economic position of the social classes which underpin their subjective rates of time preference. The entire subjective theory of value, Bukharin concludes, is 'a mere subterfuge' (p.156), undertaken solely in order to justify the status quo.

In an appendix reviewing Tugan-Baranovsky's *Foundations of Political Economy*, Bukharin makes a general critique of contemporary Marxists who advocated a synthesis of the labour theory of value and marginal utility analysis. Such attempts, he maintains, are necessarily invalid since the subjective and objective methods are in principle irreconcilable.

These arguments add little to those of Hilferding. Bukharin's most original contribution comes in the introduction to the *Economic Theory of the Leisure Class*, where he approaches the marginal utility school from a 'sociology of knowledge' perspective, and asserts that Austrian economics is 'the child of the bourgeoisie on its *last legs*' (p.23; original stress). It is the ideology of a rentier class divorced from production and interested only in consumption. Rentiers inevitably have an individualistic outlook on life, since they have no contact either with the proletariat or with industrial capitalists. Their fear of the future predisposes them to favour theories of static equilibrium. Hence, too, the stress in marginal utility analysis on consumption and the psychology of asocial individuals, and its rejection of historical specificity. In subjective value theory the 'declining bourgeois' has 'immortalised, in his fruitless theory ... the peculiarities of his failing psychology' (p.31).

This arresting hypothesis has never been adequately scrutinized, nor is it clear what sorts of evidence might legitimately be used to assess it. It runs into problems, as Bukharin himself acknowledged, when extended to what he terms the 'Anglo-American School', led by J.B. Clark, which evidently represented a progressive rather than a declining bourgeoisie. And its exact relationship to the 'conscious apologetics' hypothesis elaborated in the remainder of the book is not immediately obvious. Nevertheless, Bukharin's hypothesis remains an ambitious and strikingly original application of Marx's critical economic method to orthodox theory.

In *Imperialism and World Economy* Bukharin extended the existing Marxian analysis of imperialism in an equally bold manner. More than Hilferding or even Luxemburg, he pointed to the overriding importance of the world economy, which presupposed a world market for commodities and money capital that had set in motion forces tending to equalize the rate of profit and (eventually) wage rates across the globe, and had created a single world bourgeoisie and a world proletariat. This world economy was subject to no regulating agency, any more than the individual national economies had been in the nineteenth century. The anarchic nature of the world economy found its expression, Bukharin argued, in world economic crises and in wars; the recurrence of armed conflict between nation-states was 'an immanent law' of contemporary capitalism (p.54).

Within each country competition had been suppressed by the operation of monopolies, trusts and cartels. The processes of concentration and centralization of capital, which Marx was first to identify and Hilferding to elaborate upon, had now developed to the point where each national economy was virtually 'one gigantic combined enterprise under the tutelage of the financial kings and the capitalist state' (p.74). Bukharin claimed that government interference in economic life had progressed far enough that a new economic form had emerged which he termed 'state capitalism'. Secure in their control of the state, capitalists encouraged this process and invoked the active assistance of the state to promote their interests at the expense of their foreign competitors.

Here Bukharin reaches the crux of his argument. The acute contradictions of the world economy are the result of the overcoming of competitive anarchy within the individual nation-states. State capitalism involves the elimination of economic crises at the national level, only to transpose all the contradictions of the capitalist mode of production to the world economy. The conflict between nation-states which has replaced competition among individual capitalists is evidenced in tariff policy and in the struggle for the enlargement of national territory to protect markets, sources of raw materials, and outlets for surplus capital. Hence the massive expansion of armaments expenditures before 1914 and the onset of what Bukharin believed to be the first of a series of imperialist wars.

There was, he conceded, a counteracting tendency for the concentration and centralization of capital to overstep national boundaries, with the formation of international cartels and worldwide agreements between national monopolies. It was even conceivable that a single world trust might emerge, regulated by a world government and constituting a genuinely new economic form which would resemble slavery more closely than traditional capitalism. In practice, however, such a development was impossible, and Karl Kautsky's notion of a peaceful and monolithic 'ultra-imperialism' was merely a Utopian dream. The various national state capitalisms were unequal in both economic and military power; their stages of development and hence their costs of production differed, as did the strength of the armed forces at their disposal. This offered the stronger state capitalisms the prospect of defeating their rivals, making war inevitable. The human cost would be so immense, Bukharin concluded, that the proletariat would intervene to prevent imperialist war by the revolutionary overthrow of the capitalist world economy.

Many of these arguments would have been familiar to readers of Hilferding and Luxemburg. However, Bukharin was much less hesitant than Hilferding in asserting the unavoidability of war, and more confident than either writer that competition within the nation-state was at an end. Greatly influenced by the war economy measures of the belligerent powers, Bukharin was the first Marxist to emphasize the concept of state capitalism, which would feature prominently in subsequent Marxian analysis of capitalist evolution. His vision of a world divided between a few highly developed capitalist powers on one hand, and 'a periphery of undeveloped countries with a semi-agrarian or agrarian system on the other' (p.74), would find an echo in the work of later theorists of imperialism like Paul Baran. Bukharin's analysis of the world economy influenced the thinking of André Gunder Frank and Immanuel Wallerstein, while Lenin himself wrote an appreciative introduction to *Imperialism and World Economy* and – while remaining critical of Bukharin on several key points – borrowed heavily from him in his own, much more famous, pamphlet on imperialism.

As already noted, war was for Bukharin only one of the two contradictions of imperialism, the other being the occurrence of crises in the world economy. Few clues are given in *Imperialism and World Economy* as to the precise theory of economic crisis that he had in mind. Bukharin rectified the omission in 1926 in *Imperialism and the Accumulation of Capital*, an ill-tempered polemic against Luxemburg and Mikhail Tugan-Baranovsky. Repudiating all theories of capitalist breakdown, he argued instead for a model of cyclical crises based on the inability of the capitalist system to maintain the correct proportion between total output and total consumption. This was, in effect, an underconsumptionist theory of crisis thinly disguised in terms of disproportionality. Tugan-Baranovsky had been wrong, Bukharin alleged, to deny that growing consumption spending was at all relevant to profitable accumulation, while Luxemburg, for her part, was hopelessly confused in her analysis of the sources of increased demand during expanded reproduction.

Criticism of Tugan-Baranovsky also played a part in the third area of economics to which Bukharin contributed. At first his views on the transition from capitalism to communism were those of the Bolshevik left. In *The Economics of the Transformation Period*, which Cohen describes as 'his literary monument to the collective folly' of War Communism (p.87), Bukharin identified a 'process of decay' of the capitalist economy in which the social surplus was swallowed up by a regressive process of 'extended negative reproduction' (p.54). In such circumstances of disequilibrium and chaos, economic laws no longer applied. They must be replaced by extra-economic measures of revolutionary coercion under the dictatorship of the proletariat. A similar perspective is apparent in *The ABC of Communism*, written jointly with Evgeny Preobrazhensky, in which central planning is regarded as virtually synonymous with communist economic organization.

By 1923 it was Bukharin's ideas which had been transformed. In a series of articles (there is no single comprehensive text), he now argued that the transition to communism must be a gradual one, based on the continued acceptance of peasant agriculture (coupled with encouragement of cooperatives) and the maintenance of market relations.

At the political level, this was essential to preserve the alliance between the Russian peasantry and the working class, without which the Revolution itself was doomed. Economically, there was simply no alternative to a slower pace of industrial development than his former allies on the left were demanding. Bukharin became a vigorous critic of the programme of 'primitive socialist accumulation' proposed by Preobrazhensky, according to whom rapid industrialization was to be financed by the extraction from the peasants of their surplus product through systematically unequal exchange with state-owned industry.

For Bukharin, this was doubly mistaken. In the first place, the peasants would respond to a deterioration in their terms of trade by cutting back on the sale of their produce; fewer resources, not more, would be released to the socialist sector of the economy. Thus successful industrialization required that higher prices be paid for agricultural output, while the prices of manufactured goods must be reduced. Secondly, Preobrazhensky's ideas revealed the pernicious influence of Tugan-Baranovsky, who had mistakenly concluded that economic growth could proceed independently of increased consumption. To impoverish the peasants, Bukharin maintained, would simply retard development by restricting the expansion of demand for the output of Soviet industry.

Bukharin was never a 'market socialist', if by this is meant support for market relations as a permanent feature of a post-capitalist economy; the elimination of the market remained his ultimate goal. Nor can he be regarded as a democratic socialist, since he was opposed both to a multiparty system and to workers' self-management of industry. But Bukharin did offer a coherent alternative to what soon became infamous as the Stalinist road to Soviet industrialization. It is this, much more than his writings on value theory or even on imperialism, which make him relevant to the world economy of the 1990s.

Bukharin's Major Writings

(1917), in Russian. *Imperialism and World Economy*, London: Merlin 1972.

(1919a), in Russian. *The Economic Theory of the Leisure Class*, New York: Kelley, 1970. First English edition 1927.

(1919b), in Russian with E. Preobrazhensky. *The ABC of Communism*, Ann Arbor: University of Michigan Press, 1966. First English edition 1922.

(1920), in Russian. *Economics of the Transformation Period*, New York: Bergman, 1971.

(1926), in German. 'Imperialism and the Accumulation of Capital' (translated by Rudolf Wichmann), in K.J. Tarbuck (ed), *Rosa Luxemburg and Nikolai Bukharin, Imperialism and the Accumulation of Capital*, London: Allen Lane, 1972, 151–280.

(1982), *Selected Writings on the State and the Transition to Socialism*, Nottingham: Spokesman.

Other References

Cohen, S.F. (1974), *Bukharin and the Bolshevik Revolution: a Political Biography 1888–1938*, London: Wildwood House.

Haynes, M. (1985), *Nicholai Bukharin and the Transition from Capitalism to Socialism*, London: Croom Helm.

Howard, M.C. and King, J.E. (1989), *A History of Marxian Economics, Vol I. 1883–1929*. London: Macmillan, chapters 13, 15.

Lewin, M. (1974), *Political Undercurrents in Soviet Economic Debates*, London: Pluto.

Sukhamoy CHAKRAVARTY (born 1934)

It is perhaps best to begin this essay with a brief statement on how I look at the intellectual enterprise called economics.

Economics as a discipline appears to me to be located at the edge of 'history' and 'theory', a point that John Hicks used to stress with increasing frequency in the closing years of his life. I have no doubt that there are many eminent proponents of mainstream theorizing in economics who take the view that a knowledge of economic history is a necessary ingredient in the training of an economist. But they are quite clearly unable to accept the centrality of history to economic theorizing or, more importantly, to indicate precisely how history enters into economics. Clearly one could be a physicist or a theoretical chemist without being interested in the history of the earth or for that matter of the universe, although there are important points of contact between recent work in cosmology and elementary particle physics. Geologists and evolutionary biologists have, of course, maintained an interest in history. But it is rather uncommon these days to come across economic theorists who accept 'geology' as their model discipline. An exception is a recent pronouncement by Arrow (1986); however it would be difficult to discern any trace of historical thinking in his published work or, for that matter, in the work that he has so eminently inspired. Absence of evolutionary thinking in economics was strongly deplored by Veblen, but he has been outside the pale for most neoclassical economists who set the trend of research. Alfred Marshall was obviously very influential as a neoclassical theorist in his day. Although he noted in several places that economists would have to turn increasingly to biology to understand economic phenomena, he hardly provided any serious intellectual lead in this respect. Moreover the recognition of the essential role for an evolutionary viewpoint largely disappeared from the writings of his direct disciples, notably, A.C. Pigou.

It is only very recently that an evolutionary point of view has gained adherents amongst contemporary economists. It is not without reason that the *obiter dicta* of great minds, even when they happen to be suggestive, do not find much resonance with economists. It is true to say that the 'hard core' of modern neoclassical reasoning was profoundly shaped by the paradigm of 'classical mechanics', a point greatly stressed by Georgescu-Roegen in numerous places and taken to great lengths by Philip Mirowski in his recent book *More Heat than Light*. While few would deny that classical mechanics is a very powerful and elegant body of thought, and as an 'analytical simile' has its uses within economics, in my opinion, it would undoubtedly distort the nature and scope of economic theory if mechanics were to be held as the prototype for all significant theorizing. To a certain extent, this is because economists cannot be satisfied with conceptualizing 'time' and 'motion' in the way classical mechanics looks at these problems. This point was made by Joan Robinson when she distinguished between 'logical time' and 'historical time' and stressed the significance of the latter for economics. While I find her terminology infelicitous, I have always assumed that she wanted to point out the essential importance of irreversible phenomena for economists, not merely as a fact of life but also for defining their core concepts. It is worth mentioning here that there are no 'constants' in economics, remotely comparable with fundamental physical constants which could make predictions reliable exercises.

Historically, if we consider William Petty as the first modern economist, the genesis of classical economics and modern physics took place around the same time. Historians of ideas could easily discern some influence of Newton even on Smith's major work in economics since he was well versed in the history of astronomy. Nevertheless, while modern physics could be regarded as a fundamental rejection of Aristotle's concept of 'motion', the same could not be maintained of classical economics in relation to the Greek philosophers. In my opinion, an economist could still read with profit Aristotle's writings on politics and ethics although he would find that institutional differences between a Greek *Polis* and a modern nation-state would require a distinctly different articulation of certain basic economic categories. Also, the concept of a 'good life' was different for the ancient philosophers. However, Adam Smith himself was a philosopher first before he was an economist. So was his friend David Hume who made some notable contributions to economics. The greatness of Smith as an economist consisted in the way he conceptualized the historically emerging new socio-economic formation, the 'commercial society' as he called it. It would, however, be wrong to think that the rich texture of the institutional dimensions of Smith's reasoning, which profoundly shaped his thinking, can be seriously appreciated by looking at 'institutions' as solutions of suitably defined repeated games, a practice that is increasingly popular in presentday neoclassical economics (just as proving mathematical theorems regarding the efficacy of the invisible hand was a few decades ago). It is nonetheless interesting to observe that studying agrarian institutions in pre-industrial societies by using sophisticated arguments from 'principal-agent' theory and other similar related exercises has become the principal staple of the so-called microeconomics of development in mainstream economics. At the same time, insights of social anthropologists, background knowledge provided by ecologists, not to speak of cultural history, are often dismissed as little more than amusing stories, having little or no explanatory power.

The main reason for this widely shared practice would appear to lie in a highly restrictive concept of 'explanation'. An explanation in economics these days tends to be an explicit (preferably mathematical) deduction from an axiomatically specified set of assumptions, where time is treated as fully reversible, expectations are fairly stable (preferably 'rational') and human beings are disembodied 'agents' who optimize without incurring any costs of computation, be it in the classical set-up of constrained extrema or in terms of a rapidly growing language of game theoretic origin.

While I admire the logical ingenuity of some of these exercises, and would not be unwilling to use some of the techniques in well-specified contemporary contexts for understanding major problems facing us today (especially those that are most acute in developing countries), I cannot avoid feeling that these baroque constructions cannot take us far, regardless of how prestigious they may appear to moulders of current professional opinion.

How I arrived at this position is a matter that may need some explanation. But before that, I feel that certain basic facts about my training and experience as an economist may be told, more so because it is a biographical entry that I am presenting here.

I took to the study of economics when I was working for an undergraduate honours degree at the Presidency College, Calcutta. This was a fine teaching institution, where 'standard' (or mainstream) economics was taught with competence. There was, however, nothing much to distinguish economics as taught there from economics taught anywhere else in the Anglo-Saxon world, apart from the fact that we had to study a paper specially devoted to the analysis of Indian economic problems. The M.A. programme was in the same mould but included a course on the history of economic thought, taught straight from standard histories of the subject (prior to the appearance of Schumpeter's posthumous opus). Nevertheless, it provided one with an exposure to the thinking of classical economists, including Marx.

The major event of my student days was the publication of the First Five-Year Plan document in 1951, which stimulated all of us to look at Indian economic problems in a fresh perspective. The initial impact deepened when I personally came to know the late Professor P.C. Mahalanobis who was the main architect of the Second Five-Year Plan which started in the year I took my M.A. degree (1955). Prof. Mahalanobis was, of course, not an economist at all. By training he was a physicist, and by vocation a statistician. Methodologically he was a 'Kelvinist' in the sense that, like Lord Kelvin, he believed that science was measurement. The difference between Mahalanobis and the rest of our teachers was that he appreciated the importance of operationally meaningful models of economic relationships which could be filled in with the relevant Indian data. His primary interest was in influencing the formulation of economic policies. He motivated me strongly to look at Indian economic problems within a well-specified analytical frame. While I have never been able to accept his version of the Kelvinist dogma, I believe that in a basic sense, his influence on my thinking persisted through several decades.

Mahalanobis's influence deepened when I went to do my Ph.D. at the Netherlands School of Economics under the supervision of Professor Jan Tinbergen. Like Mahalanobis, Tinbergen was also a physicist by basic training and possessed the same quantitative orientation to economics. What also attracted me to both these men was their passionate commitment to economics as a discipline which could influence human conditions for the better. There was nothing of 'art for art's sake' in their work, nor did they believe that the 'market' left to itself would solve all pressing problems confronting society. Their approach may seem rather 'mechanistic', but it cannot be denied that they were always looking at concrete problems and searching for socially meaningful solutions.

Tinbergen's theory of economic policy had a powerful impact on my thinking during the late 1950s, as did some of the contemporaneous work of R. Frisch. My first book, *The Logic of Investment Planning* (first accepted as a Ph.D. thesis in 1958 and published a year later in a slightly expanded form) dealt with the classical issues of investment planning using a dynamic input-output framework with lags. It could be regarded as a multisectoral dynamic generalization of Mahalanobis's 'four-sector model' which formed the theoretical underpinning of India's Second Five-Year Plan. The policy analysis was cast in Tinbergen's 'fixed targets' framework. Apart from the discussion of gestation lags involved in capital formation, another notable feature of the book was the treatment of 'structural breaks', identified as a key problem in the context of planning for an underdeveloped country.

I followed up the initial research done under the supervision of Tinbergen with further work on planning at the Massachusetts Institute of Technology, where I developed a close working relationship with P.N. Rosenstein-Rodan. As early as 1943, Rosenstein-Rodan had written a brilliant essay which provided the analytical basis of development planning. At the time I knew him, his point of view could be described as 'structuralist'. Although initially trained at Vienna under F. Von Wieser, his approach had very little in common with many of the emigré Austrian economists such as Hayek. A close collaborator and friend of R. Prebisch in the 1950s, he delighted in emphasizing the importance of indivisibilities, various forms of threshold phenomenon – to the evident displeasure of his eminent Austrian contemporaries such as Gottfried Haberler.

My work at MIT proceeded along two lines. At one level, it extended my earlier research on disaggregated plan models into an optimizing framework. At a somewhat more abstract level, I tried to explore the logical foundations of Frank Ramsey's brilliant 1928 article on 'optimal savings', because I could not find a satisfactory answer to the question of how much a nation should save. My principal concern was with decision-making at the national level and not with explicating the savings behaviour of individuals in a utility-maximizing framework. In connection with the latter work, I had intellectual contacts with Paul A. Samuelson and Robert M. Solow, especially the former. One of the two papers I published at this time (1962a) dealt with the 'existence problem' in a Ramsey model, while the second (1962b) considered the characteristic features of optimal growth paths in finite horizon plan models. While the latter used different mathematical techniques and a somewhat more general formulation of social utility function, it was similar to a paper published by Richard Goodwin in 1961. It appeared that Goodwin and I had been pursuing somewhat similar lines of enquiry independently of each other. Not surprisingly, Goodwin was at that time greatly interested in planning questions and had also spent some time in India helping Mahalanobis prepare the nation's first input-output table.

It should be quite clear from this account that my principal motivation to pursue research work in economics came largely from a youthful impulse to do something relevant for the development of India. If the First Five-Year Plan had not been published in 1951, the year when I opted to study economics, I would probably have chosen philosophy. But I went in for economics as I believed that it combined practical relevance with rigour. I have always maintained an interest in philosophy, independent of its use in economics. During the 1960s I also made fairly extensive use of mathematics in my work. But towards the end of the decade, I began to feel that I required closer exposure to real-life situations if some relevance was to be breathed into the abstract planning models I was engaged in exploring. After completing my book *Capital and Development Planning* in 1969, I turned towards applied work which kept me occupied for nearly a decade. In 1971, the Indian Planning Commission was reconstituted and I was appointed a member, with wide-ranging responsibilities starting with Perspective Planning and ending with the preparation of annual budgets.

I spent a lot of time working on computable planning models as well as on various other policy-related issues. The work at the Planning Commission not merely deepened my understanding of the Indian economy, but also showed me that economic policy was only partly determined by economists. The work in the Planning Commission taught me some important lessons which are worth stating. First, that the proper sequence of decisions in time mattered a great deal, since movements in time were not like those in space, a point touched upon already. Second, it indicated the influence of social classes in shaping the outcome of policy decisions in an essential way, a point not obvious from abstract plan models. Third, it was apparent that 'optimization' was no more than an algorithmic device and not necessarily a very robust one in many situations. Finally, the importance of historical conjunctures became quite apparent in showing the appropriateness or otherwise of analytical constructs. (I have analysed Indian planning in my recent book *Development Planning: The Indian Experience*.)

In 1977, I went back to teaching at the Delhi School of Economics, a job I have maintained since 1963 except for occasional visits abroad, including the year 1984-85 which I spent at Cambridge (UK). I have also been engaged in recent years in debates about the teaching of economics in India, a subject of great importance in my opinion. In the area of international collaboration, I have served on the Executive Council of the Econometric Society, to which I was elected a Fellow in 1970, and more recently as Vice-President of the International Economic Association (1983–86). With occasional interruptions I have also been involved in a policy advisory capacity to the Government of India. Nevertheless, my principal occupations have been teaching and research, especially in the areas of development economics and in the history of economic theory.

I have stated in the first section my basic approach to economics which has no doubt been shaped in part by my exposure to planning and policy-making in real-life situations. It may be of some interest to state in this concluding section my current research endeavours.

I can describe myself primarily as a development economist. Issues in development theory that particularly interest me are best indicated by the work done by Allyn Young in the 1920s and by Nicholas Kaldor in the 1970s (especially his *Further Essays on Economic Theory and Policy*). I believe that the Young-Kaldor tradition of theorizing in economics is a very profound one, providing an indispensable guide to the understanding of development processes. By locating them in specific historical contexts, this line of thinking can yield substantial insights into why development has proceeded at such uneven rates amongst countries and regions.

Both for pursuing my researches into development problems and for providing a rich quarry of researchable ideas in economics, I have turned to classical economists including Marx, and in particular in recent years to Schumpeter (see my *Alternative Approaches to a Theory of Economic Growth*). Schumpeterian dynamics has engaged my attention especially over the last decade. More recently, my interest has linked up with the work done by Richard Goodwin (1989) on disaggregated models of cyclical growth under capitalism.

My principal source of disagreement with current trends of research in 'mainstream' economics rests on some methodological considerations. Methodological individualism, which constitutes the theoretical underpinning of mainstream economists, is in my opinion an insufficient and often misleading basis for understanding economic phenomena, as I believe that economy has always been embedded in 'society'. I would, of course, admit that the concept of embeddedness is a complex one and requires much further clarification. But I believe that earlier economists such as Smith, Marx and Keynes were basically correct in regarding economic behaviour as an aspect of social behaviour. Each had viewed capitalism in a distinctive way, which revealed a great deal more about its functioning than could be summed up in the bare logic of atomistic decision-making in a full competitive market economy. I also think that treatment of 'uncertainty' which is often used in contemporary theorizing has little more than tractability to commend it – a point that finds considerable support in Keynes' approach towards uncertainty.

I believe that those of us who object to methodological individualism as the basic credo of theorizing are not necessarily committed to a 'holistic' position in a mystical sense. Even in a subject like biology, highly fruitful research is currently taking place both on the molecular level and on the level of population as units of study. In a subject like economics, a simple reductionist position which treats the 'individual' as the ultimate unit can prove very misleading, since important patterns of economic behaviour arise on higher levels of organization. These get articulated through institutions which neoclassical analysis can at best handle in a very *ad hoc* way. History becomes essential to economists, primarily because it can provide us with important insights into the emergence of institutions over time. It is precisely because history is an open-ended process that the ambition of constructing an over-arching deductive system for economics appears to me a somewhat misplaced enterprise, even though it is regarded as the dominant research programme for those claiming to be active in the area of high theory.

Chakravarty's Major Writings

(1959), 'The Logic of Investment Planning' in *Contributions to Economic Analysis*, **18**, Amsterdam: North Holland.

(1962a), 'The Existence of Optimum Savings Programme', *Econometrica*, **30**.

(1962b), 'Optimal Savings with Finite Planning Horizon', *International Economic Review*, **3**.

(1982), *Alternative Approaches to a Theory of Economic Growth – Marx, Marshall, Schumpeter*, R.C. Dutt Memorial Lectures in Political Economy, Calcutta: Orient Longman Ltd.

(1987), *Development Planning: The Indian Experience*, Oxford: The Clarendon Press.

Other References

Arrow, K.J. (1986), in W.N. Parker, *Economic History and the Modern Economist*, Oxford: Basil Blackwell.

Goodwin, R.M. (1961), 'The Optimal Growth Path for an Underdeveloped Economy', *Economic Journal*, **71**.

Goodwin, R.M. (1989), *Essays in Nonlinear Economic Dynamics*, Frankfurt and New York: Peter Lang.

Kaldor, N. (1989), *Further Essays on Economic Theory and Pol' y*, London: Duckworth.

Mirowski, P. (1989), *More Heat Than Light*, Cambridge: Cambridge University Press.

Victoria CHICK (born 1936)

I was born in Berkeley, California. Berkeley is a wonderful place for an intelligent child to grow up. At the age of 14 I obtained reference privileges at the university library. My experience there gave me the feeling that I could always find out anything I really wanted to know: curiosity, backed up with a little effort, was always rewarded. I had learned intellectual independence at an early age, for my family, though well-educated, was conventional and did not really explore the reasons for things. In some sense all this just pushes the question of the origin of dissent one stage further back, for some children ask for reasons and others accept the conventions. I have to conclude that temperament is at the core of the matter.

My enquiring temperament was reinforced when I was 11 or so by a remarkable science teacher, a man who loved challenge, readily admitted when he was wrong and rewarded us for wit and humour. Making us partners in the game of learning, he was enormous fun and established in me a lifelong interest in science. In any case, science was what was happening in Berkeley at that time: E.O. Lawrence was a close neighbour, and in the local paper I read about the new elements, berkelium and californium, constructed in the cyclotron always visible at the top of the hills.

At 13 I went to the Anna Head School, a private girls' school a stone's throw from the university, run by a classicist and his archaeologist wife in a most humane and stimulating way. Academic excellence was at the centre of the school's values. Every girl was encouraged in her own particular strengths, and enthusiasm and eccentricity were regarded as evidence of character and treated as resources rather than attributes to be discouraged. Head's was a marvellous experience but it was, in a way, a rather bad preparation for life in the real world, particularly in those decidedly pre-feminist days.

After Anna Head, the first two years of undergraduate life at Berkeley were either not very exciting or, in the case of science courses, sexist in a way which would be actionable today (though I am told that the chemists are still pretty dreadful). Eventually the anti-feminism and my poor aptitude for mathematics led me out of science and into economics. When I entered postgraduate work, I felt at home again, as I had done at school. The department at Berkeley in those days was first rate. Amongst the staff were Irma Adelman, Dick Caves, Carlo Cipolla, Howard Ellis, Aaron Gordon, Dale Jorgenson, David Landis, Harvey Leibenstein, Abba Lerner, Roy Radner, Henry Rosovsky, Ben Ward and, most enduring in my life, Hyman Minsky. This eclectic band was held together (with difficulty I understand) by the iron hand in the velvet glove, Andreas Papandreou. June Flanders, Peter and Jean Grey, Joen Greenwood and Eugene Savin were fellow students. David Alhadeff from the business school, like Minsky and Cipolla, has remained a friend.

I specialized in international trade. Philip Bell, just returned from a year in England, gave us James Meade's *Geometry of International Trade* to cut our teeth on; I have been drawing fiendish diagrams ever since. At this stage I treated economics as an intellectual toy; the ideology and politics that lay behind it left me cold. (Politics still leaves me cold.)

After a while I had had enough of Berkeley, wrote a Master's thesis on Canada's experience with flexible exchange rates in the 1950s and, after a brief spell of 'real work', went to the London School of Economics to a similarly high-powered and eclectic department. Lionel Robbins was still head, and younger staff included Chris Archibald, Bernard Corry, Kelvin Lancaster, Dick Lipsey and Bill Phillips. David Laidler was there for one year as a temporary lecturer in the middle of his graduate studies. These people were the core of Economics Analytical and Descriptive ('A and D'), as the main economics department was called. I was attached to Richard Sayers's department of Monetary Economics.

It is a curious fact that the LSE, to this day, is structured along the lines of the neoclassical dichotomy. In those days, the early 1960s, which Bernard Corry calls the Keynesian Terror, anyone attached to 'A and D' believed that money did not matter and that it was *infra dig* to study it. I was studying the determinants of central bank holdings of international reserves, a topic which was becoming obsolete even as I worked on it.

One's education at LSE was watching economists at work – in the Robbins seminar and in the Three Tuns pub until closing time and beyond. What I had learned at Berkeley began to take shape, as the method of working from first principles, first introduced by David Alhadeff and Philip Bell, was reinforced.

Working from first principles, combined with an instinct to run results through time, led me gradually away from the neoclassical fastness of international trade to Keynes and post-Keynesian economics. It was a long and painstaking business for, despite my eclectic background, I had no training in or sensitivity to schools of thought in economics, except on the most superficial levels of pure technique (such as the quantity theory versus liquidity preference) or pure ideology (which beclouded the study of Marx). Amongst my teachers, only Minsky had made explicit the hidden agenda in economics, but his method of tossing out ideas as epigrams and leaving the student to fill in the gaps was too advanced for me at the time. Minsky had also tried to teach me *The General Theory* but, again, it was too early in my career.

In 1963 I went to University College London as an Assistant Lecturer, to teach monetary theory and macroeconomics. UCL has been my permanent home ever since. I was promoted to Lecturer the following year and to Reader in 1984.

I began to try to impose an order on monetary theory which, compared with international economics, was in great disarray at the time. It seemed obvious to me that all transactions in a money economy involve a transfer or creation of money as a counterpart. This fact, so central to international economics in the balance of payments, seemed completely lacking in macroeconomics. Money was just an element in a system of equations, 'a good like any other'. How odd that the mere insistence on double-entry bookkeeping could put one into the position of being a dissenting economist! But through it I was led to question the very foundations of macroeconomics as it then was – IS-LM, Patinkin's formulation of the real balance effect, and Tobin and Brainard's integration of portfolio theory with macro-flows. And thus I was forced to confront the problem of time in macroeconomics and the inadequacy of the neo-Walrasian method.

My attempts to raise these questions were formed into articles which met with incomprehension on the part of my colleagues and rejection from editors. I was persuaded that only a book would succeed. I published *The Theory of Monetary Policy (TMP)* in 1973, after thinking about its contents for about ten years. In it the Keynesian-monetarist debate was taken beyond the level of policy, even of theory, to the level of method, where I made the uncomfortable point that Tobin and Friedman stood together against the Radcliffe report, a document which had not been well received but in which I saw much virtue. The means by which money was generated, the connection between portfolios and flow decisions, and the link between money and the interest rate – especially through speculation – were singled out in *TMP* as key issues which have continued to occupy me. (I published two further pieces emphasizing method in the context of the monetary policy debate: 1978a and 1981.)

At the same time I found a home for one of my early papers attacking the structure of IS-LM analysis (1973). The sensation of finally getting into print on these issues was a strange one. It was one thing to dissent verbally in lectures and seminars, but I was now publicly committed. Had I still been working in a solitary way, the pressure by this time would have been hard to bear. But in 1968 or so I had been lucky in meeting Jan Kregel, then a graduate student in Cambridge, and through him other people of a similar persuasion. I had met Geoff Harcourt earlier, in 1962 or 1963, and liked him instantly, but my work was so underdeveloped then, and I was so diffident about it, that we hardly connected as fellow-dissenters until we met again in Australia in 1975. He has been a rock of support since then, and it is a delight to have him back in England.

With Jan's encouragement I went to the American Economic Association meetings in December 1971 at which Joan Robinson and Paul Davidson organized a gathering of non-mainstream economists to discuss bias in economic journals. Things were beginning to make sense, although it was unnerving to find that propositions which I had discovered by dint of considerable effort – for example that comparative statics cannot cope with change or that neoclassical economics used an exchange model to analyse production – had been known by Cambridge-trained economists for years.

Having thoroughly undermined conventional macroeconomics, at least to my own satisfaction, I returned to *The General Theory,* to which I had been introduced by Minsky at Berkeley. It had been our text for a whole term, but I had only grasped the basic ideas, rather like reading a novel simply for its plot. At the same time, browsing, I stumbled on Myrdal's *Monetary Equilibrium*, of which I had never heard, and Shackle's *Expectations, Investment and Income*. My education as a post-Keynesian economist was begun.

When Leijonhufvud's book (1968) was given to me as a birthday present, I felt I had been 'scooped'. It had been obvious to me from work I had done for *The Theory of Monetary Policy* that Keynes and Keynesians were worlds apart. But after some reflection I realized that even the critiques of Clower and Leijonhufvud, which are at the level of theory, were based on the neo-Walrasian method which was inappropriate for understanding Keynes. (For the profession at large, the 'Keynesian Revolution' represents a policy conclusion – a view of pathetic shallowness which the 'new Keynesians' perpetuate.) While on secondment at the Reserve Bank of Australia (1975–76), I finally succeeded in getting accepted for publication (1978b) my methodological critique of Clower's famous 1965 paper.

I predicted that the recession then beginning in Europe was the result of a long period of capital accumulation and was likely to be resistant to the fine-tuning and harmonization being widely prescribed. It was one of the few economic predictions I have ever made. It was right, but in the Bank I was the messenger that brings bad news, and although my view came straight from *The General Theory's* Chapter 17, it was controversial even to post-Keynesians (1978c). I also followed up my concern with speculative demand, shown in *TMP* to be so central to the monetarist debate, applying it to the international sphere ('Transnational Corporations', 1976).

Four further, briefer secondments followed, to the Universities of Southampton, California at Santa Cruz, Aarhus (Denmark) and McGill (Montreal) before my view of *The General Theory* was published (1983b). I portrayed the Keynesian Revolution as one of method, forced by taking money, time and uncertainty seriously. From the shift in method, the revolution in theory followed naturally – as Keynes himself said. (See also my 1985 article and forthcoming work on John Hicks' monetary theory.)

As one acquires a bit of history, one understands better that history shapes economic theory. Again this represents dissent, for mainstream theory prides itself on being 'institution free'. 'A Question of Relevance' (1983) shows the relation of *The General Theory* to the stylized facts of Keynes' time, while 'Monetary Increases' (1984) continues the task which Hicks began in

1967 of making explicit the interplay between monetary institutions and monetary theory. The work of 'Monetary Increases' was continued in 'The Evolution of the Banking System' (1986), which explores the connection between the stages of evolution of banking institutions and monetary and macro theory. To a point this idea was already present in *Macroeconomics after Keynes*, but it was taken further, to examine the significance of liability management. The article has had three 'offspring', the most promising of which was written with Sheila Dow, bringing the evolving banking system to bear on theories of regional development (1988). This work and the influence of a group of Brazilian graduate students and colleagues is drawing me into the underdeveloped area of finance and development.

The face of economics has changed enormously since I began in it. At one level, mainstream economics has closed ranks and defended itself far more vigorously. (That is a compliment in a way, as it indicates a perceived threat.) But the level of consciousness at which dissenters are working has been transformed by work on methodology, modes of thought and the philosophical underpinnings not only of economics but also of science, from which economics draws so much inspiration. The philosophy of science which informs mainstream economics is out of date by at least 60 years! (In 'Some Methodological Considerations in the Theory of Speculation', 1990, I drew analogies between changes in the philosophy of science and different approaches to the theory of speculation, claiming Keynes was the most modern.)

There is now a critical army of post-Keynesian economists, outside as well as within Cambridge. These economists are firmly setting their faces towards the future, to the task of building the positive alternative. The period of criticism and exegesis has served its purpose of establishing solid foundations on which we can build.

The launching of the *Journal of Post Keynesian Economics* by Paul Davidson and Sidney Weintraub marked a tremendous advance through which one discovered so many like-minded people, and work benefited from sympathetic (though rigorous) rather than hostile criticism. Philip Arestis and I established a Post Keynesian Economics Study Group two years ago with a similar effect, while the *Cambridge Journal of Economics* and the new *Review of Political Economy* have been additional favourable influences. Today few people could stumble into being dissenting economists as I did, simply by following arguments where they seemed to lead.

Chick's Major Writings

(1973a), *The Theory of Monetary Policy*, Gray-Mills; 2nd edn, Oxford: Basil Blackwell, 1977.

(1973b), 'Financial Counterparts of Saving and Investment and Inconsistency in Some Macro Models', *Weltwirtschaftliches Archiv*, **109**, Heft 4, 621–43.

(1976), 'Transnational Corporations and the Evolution of the International Monetary System', revised and reprinted in G.J. Crough (ed) (1979), *Transnational Banking and the World Economy*, Sydney: University of Sydney Press.

(1978a), 'Keynesians, Monetarists and Keynes: The End of the Debate – or a Beginning?', *Thames Papers in Political Economy*. Revised and reprinted in P. Arestis and A. Skouras (eds), *Post-Keynesian Economic Theory: A Challenge to Neo-Classical Economics*, Brighton: Harvester Wheatsheaf and New York: M.E. Sharpe, 1985.

(1978b), 'The Nature of the Keynesian Revolution: A Reassessment', *Australian Economic Papers*, **17**.

(1978c), 'Keynes' Theory, Keynesian Policy and the Post-War Inflation', *British Review of Economic Issues*, **1**.

(1981), 'On the Structure of the Theory of Monetary Policy', in D. Currie et al (eds), *Macroeconomic Analysis: Current Problems*, London: Croom Helm.

(1983a), 'A Question of Relevance: *The General Theory* in Keynes's Time and Ours', *South African Journal of Economics*, **5**, 388–406.

(1983b), *Macroeconomics After Keynes: A Reconsideration of The General Theory*, Massachusetts: MIT Press.

(1984), 'Monetary Increases and their Consequences: Streams, Backwaters and Floods', in A. Ingham and A.M. Ulph (eds), *Demand, Equilibrium and Trade: Essays in Honour of Ivor F. Pearce*, London: Macmillan.

(1985), 'Time and the Wage-Unit in Keynes's Method: History and Equilibrium', in T. Lawson and H. Pesaran (eds), *Keynes' Economics: Methodological Issues*, London: Croom Helm.

(1986), 'The Evolution of the Banking System and the Theory of Saving, Investment and Finance', *Economies et Sociétés*, Cahiers de l'ISMEA, série Monnaie et Production, no 3.

(1988), 'A Post Keynesian Perspective on the Relation between Banking and Regional Development' (with S.C. Dow), *Thames Papers in Political Economy*, 1–22. Reprinted in P. Arestis (ed), *Post-Keynesian Monetary Economics Theory: New Approaches to Financial Modelling*, Aldershot: Edward Elgar.

(1990), 'Some Methodological Considerations in the Theory of Speculation', in D.E. Moggridge (ed), *Perspectives on the History of Economic Thought, Vol IV: Keynes, Macroeconomics and Method*, Aldershot: Edward Elgar.

(Forthcoming), *On Money, Method and Keynes: Selected Essays by Victoria Chick*, P. Arestis and S. C. Dow (eds), London: Macmillan. (Most of the articles cited above will be reprinted in this volume.)

Other References

Clower, R.W. (1965), 'The Keynesian Counter-Revolution: A Theoretical Appraisal', in F.H. Hahn and F.P.R. Brechling (eds), *The Theory of Interest Rates*, London: Macmillan.

Hicks, J.R. (1967), 'Monetary Theory and History: an Attempt at Perspective', in J.R. Hicks, *Critical Essays in Monetary Theory*, Oxford: Clarendon Press.

Keynes, J.M. (1936), *The General Theory of Employment, Interest and Money*, London: Macmillan.

Leijonhufvud, A. (1968), *On Keynesian Economics and the Economics of Keynes*, Oxford: Oxford University Press.

Meade, J.E. (1956), *A Geometry of International Trade*, London: Allen and Unwin.

Myrdal, G. (1939), *Monetary Equilibrium*, London: William Hodge.

Shackle, G.L.S. (1968), *Expectations, Investment and Income*, 2nd edn, Oxford: Oxford University Press.

John Rogers COMMONS (1862–1945)   *Yngve Ramstad*

Founder of the 'Wisconsin School' of institutional economics, John R. Commons authored or co-authored 17 books and more than 50 articles on a broad range of practical and theoretical subjects and also served as a member of countless public bodies. A creative and original thinker, Commons took a unique approach both to issues of public policy and economic theory. Seeking to 'make Capitalism good', Commons, individually or through his students, was instrumental in designing most of the social legislation instituted in the United States during the New Deal era of the 1930s. Near the end of his career, while reflecting on the meaning of his own experiences, Commons concluded that the role of institutions – defined by him as 'collective action in control, liberation and expansion of individual action' – in the conduct of economic life has been both neglected and misunderstood by economic theorists. He devoted his final years to the task of working out a 'rounded-out theory of political economy' in which institutions are accorded their rightful place. The product of that effort – Commons's 'institutional economics' – reflects a philosophical and theoretical posture inconsistent with mainstream economics. Thus Commons may be said to have developed an alternative to the theoretical standpoint reflected in the classical and neoclassical tradition. Unfortunately, Commons's convoluted and idiosyncratic writing style, as well as his own repeated insistence that his ideas were not fundamentally in conflict with mainstream theory, obscured the radical 'gestalt shift' his 'volitional' reinterpretation of market processes in fact mandates. As a result, there are few who have comprehended the significance of Commons's thought or even that his work is an exercise in economic (meta?)theory.

Commons's early achievements gave little notice of the prominent place he was to carve out for himself within American society and the economics profession. Born in Indiana, Commons reported in his autobiography, *Myself* (1934), that he 'was brought up on Hoosierism, Republicanism, Presbyterianism and Spencerism'. After graduating, without distinction, from Oberlin College at the relatively advanced age of 26, Commons moved on to graduate work at Johns Hopkins University, where he took courses from, among others, Richard T. Ely. Performing poorly on his exams, he lost his fellowship after two years and left Johns Hopkins without the Ph.D. which he never obtained. From 1890 to 1899, Commons held a succession of teaching positions at Wesleyan, Oberlin, Indiana and Syracuse universities. After his first year of teaching, Commons concluded he was a complete failure as a lecturer on orthodox economic theory and adopted the practice, one he followed throughout his career, of using class time to discuss his own 'doubts' about economic theory and to explain the (substitute) insights he was gleaning from his own research.

During these early years, Commons published on a broad range of subjects. Having associated himself while at Johns Hopkins with the Social Gospel movement, Commons was particularly interested in issues relating to the amelioration of poverty and its attendant problems. Accordingly in his first work, *The Distribution of Wealth*, Commons attempted to explore issues relating to the 'imperfect' distribution of wealth he discerned to obtain in the American economy due to the rights enjoyed by various classes of property owners. Perhaps chastened by highly critical reviews, Commons judged the attempt to explore a concrete social problem through the lens provided by conventional theory – in this case, marginal productivity theory – a mistake. In fact, even though he took great pains to emphasize that he accepted as valid many of the insights worked into conventional theory, Commons never again used the 'orthodox' framework to structure his own analysis of a concrete issue. Commons argued forcefully in his collection of essays, *Social Reform and the Church*, that ministers and other Christians have a duty to promote the reforms needed to eliminate poverty and thereby to 'elevate the character' of the industrial worker. In his next book, *Proportional Representation*, Commons further argued that the required reforms would likely not be enacted unless a system of proportional representation for parties organized around the particular economic interests of different members of the body politic was substituted for the existing system of representation based on geographical boundaries (Commons later came to believe that industry-wide collective bargaining was a workable alternative to this drastic reform). Finally, in a series of seven articles under the title 'A Sociological View of Sovereignty', Commons sketched out a conjectural history of social evolution in which coercive 'institutions', enforced ultimately through the sanction of violence, were discerned to be the indispensable and pivotal elements of economic life. This insight later became a central tenet of Commons's 'institutional economics'.

Commons's academic career was suddenly disrupted when he lost his position at Syracuse for speaking at a rally in support of Sunday baseball for industrial workers (who at that time worked six days per week). Over the next five years (1899–1904) came a succession of temporary jobs. Commons first took on an assignment to construct what was apparently the first weekly index of wholesale prices in the US. He next undertook to write a report on immigration for the US Industrial Commission and ultimately produced a book based on his findings, *Races and Immigrants in America*. Upon finishing his work with the Industrial Commission, Commons took a position with the National Civic Federation, where he worked first on taxation and then on labour conciliation.

There is no evidence that Commons's published writings during these pre-Wisconsin years had any influence at all on practical affairs, yet it was during this stage of his career that four convictions took root which later jointly gave form to his unique approach to public policy issues. The first relates to the inherent tendencies of laissez-faire competition. Probably while still at Johns Hopkins, Commons came to accept unequivocally Henry Carter Adams's contention that unregulated competition degenerates inexorably into 'destructive competition' in which the 'least ethical competitors' are able to force 'down to their own low level' those who would prefer to be more ethical. He concluded that only by proscribing practices judged unacceptable can society ensure that the 'plane of competition' is maintained at an ethical level.

A second conviction pertains to the class nature of economic progress. Commons understood class dominance to be a conspicuous reality of economic life in the US. He further understood that in the turn-of-the-century American setting, property-owners were the dominant class and wage workers the 'excluded' class. Holding that 'class is the temporary means of bringing about the permanent welfare of all', Commons concluded that the economist who truly seeks to serve society as a whole must 'strive to give the excluded classes a larger and more just legal share in government and industry'. To be neutral, he maintained, meant in fact to assist the dominant class in the maintenance of the rules through which their dominance was effected. As Commons saw things, then, *in the specific historical setting confronting him*, it was the obligation of the economist seeking to serve the general welfare to associate himself with the strivings of the labour movement.

A third conviction relates to the role of so-called 'experts' in the determination of policy objectives. While carrying out his conciliation assignments for the National Civic Federation, Commons came to admire 'good' capitalists and to distrust intellectuals as leaders in the labour movement (on grounds similar to those outlined later by Selig Perlman, Commons's most famous student, in his *Theory of the Labor Movement*). Commons eventually generalized this distrust into a denunciation of all experts (such as economists) who seek to influence public policy by specifying for others the abstract objectives that they should be pursuing (such as economic efficiency or free trade). Commons ultimately concluded that 'reasonable' solutions to concrete problems emanating from 'scarcity' (what he referred to as 'reasonable practices') do not exist in the abstract and are in concrete circumstances whatever bargaining reveals to be – for now – an appropriate compromise between the conflicting purposes embraced by the principals. The bargaining should be between spokespersons possessing reasonably equal 'power to withhold' (what the other wants but cannot command) who have been collectively *self-selected* by the principals themselves. Market values consistent with such 'good practices' was clearly Commons's own normative desideratum.

A final conviction relates to the question of the most effective tactic for labour to use in pursuit of its class goals. While working on the immigration project, Commons travelled the country to investigate firsthand the conditions of labour experienced by immigrants and visited the headquarters of roughly half of the national trade unions. Based on his own experience and research, he concluded that the interests of the working class could be best advanced by collective bargaining, not socialism.

These four convictions help explain Commons's lifelong commitment to a strategy of 'practical idealism' in which he worked to further the class interests of workers through a stabilization of employment and a raising of the 'plane of competition' in the labour market. It was Commons's quest in other words, first, to discover policies that would stabilize employment and, second, to discover and implement practical institutional innovations through which the 'good practices' (practices favoured by workers themselves) already adopted by 'good employers' who nonetheless managed to remain competitive could be identified *and made mandatory for all*. Either that or innovations that would allow industrial wage workers to participate as equals in determining the 'working rules' through which the 'burdens and benefits of collective wealth production' are apportioned (that is, to participate as equals in 'rationing transactions' as explained below).

During Commons's lifetime, the resolution of conflicts through collective bargaining had not yet become a feature of the American landscape. The unavoidable task of making the necessary compromises between conflicting purposes went by default to the legislatures and courts and ultimately, with respect to the constitutionality of such compromises, to the Supreme Court. But the Supreme Court of Commons's time (as of now) was *not* constituted of individuals who in some meaningful way had been self-selected by competing economic interests or who were even 'of' the major competing interests. Commons thus always advocated institutional innovations that would substitute for Court adjudication administrative structures – the Wisconsin Industrial Commission is the best example – within which the aforementioned bargaining could take place and through which practices ensuring genuinely 'reasonable' values (outcomes), those closer to Commons's desideratum, could thereby be agreed upon.

In 1904, Commons, to use his own words, was 'born again' when Ely brought him to the University of Wisconsin to teach and take charge of a project to prepare a history of the American labour movement, the latter resulting ultimately in a ten-volume *A Documentary History of American Industrial Society* and a four-volume *History of Labor in the United States*. After arriving at Wisconsin, Commons's involvement in practical affairs only accelerated. He was requested almost immediately to draft a new civil service law for the state of Wisconsin. In 1905, he participated in a comparative study of municipal ownership in the US and Great Britain, after which he helped draft a new public utility law for the state. Next he participated in the Pittsburgh Survey, where he investigated labour conditions in the steel industry in the Pittsburgh area. In 1910, upon request by its recently elected socialist administration, he developed an elaborate scheme for administering the municipal affairs of Milwaukee. And in 1911, he drafted a Workmen's Compensation and Industrial Commission Act for Wisconsin. In

1913, he was appointed to the US Commission on Industrial Relations. After having become interested in monetary policy, due to his belief that stabilization of the wholesale price level is the precondition for the stabilization of employment, he was elected to the presidency of the National Monetary Association in 1922. The next year he helped develop the case against the US Steel Corporation in the famous Pittsburgh-Plus case. In 1924 he accepted an appointment from the Amalgamated Clothing Workers of America as administrator of a voluntary unemployment insurance scheme established in Chicago. Finally, in 1932, he assisted with the drafting of the nation's first unemployment insurance legislation, the Wisconsin Unemployment Compensation Act.

As this partial recapitulation shows, Commons's involvement with, and influence on, the formulation of public policy were clearly momentous. Yet somehow he continued to write, publishing an edited collection in 1905, *Trade Unionism and Labor Problems*; a collection of his articles in 1913 under the title *Labor and Administration*; a textbook in 1916, with John B. Andrews, outlining the details of labour law in various countries, *Principles of Labor Legislation* (revised in 1920 and 1927); a monograph in 1919, *Industrial Goodwill*, summarizing his own findings regarding the role of 'goodwill' in the workplace gleaned from his own investigations; and in 1921 another monograph, *Industrial Government* (with his students) about industry-wide collective bargaining.

Several of Commons's articles during this period also merit mention. In 'Tariff Revision and Protection for American Labor', Commons advocated protectionist measures to prevent deterioration of labour standards in the US. In 'American Shoemakers, 1648–1895: A Sketch of Industrial Evolution', Commons traced out how labour organization evolved in the US in response to changes in the organization of work precipitated by new forms of product competition. Commons obviously wrote this piece in part as a 'refutation' of what he understood, probably inaccurately, to be Marx's 'technological determinism' (relations of production as a consequence of changing forces of production). In 'Secular Trend and Business Cycles: A Classification of Theories', he described the leading business cycle theories of his day, explained their shortcomings and proposed as a replacement his own 'profit-margin theory' based on expectations about cyclical movements in the narrow per-unit gap between prices and costs of production (the 'profit-margin'). Based on this theory, Commons was an early advocate of discretionary monetary policy, actually drafting a bill in 1927 requiring the Federal Reserve to stabilize the wholesale price level (and hence the expected 'profit-margin').

As he grappled with the many problems he was investigating personally, Commons gradually came to believe that conventional economics embodied a distorted understanding of economic processes in a market system. He maintained, in particular, that economists had erred in apprehending economic life through mechanistic conceptions rooted in physical science and in embracing an excessively rationalistic and voluntaristic interpretation of behaviour. Held to be especially unfortunate was the practice of treating economic competition as a 'natural' means of economic interaction rooted in human nature. Equally objectionable was the presumption that, in the context of mutual dependence and in the face of conflicts of interest over the disposition of scarce things, order is obtained automatically through the workings of the 'price mechanism'.

In contrast, Commons understood unstructured competition – competition as a 'natural' process – to be inherently disorderly and degenerative (as reflected in the concept 'destructive competition'). In his view, it is only through the adoption and enforcement of mandatory 'working rules' and their adjustment by a sovereign-empowered authority (whenever concrete disputes threaten to undermine the security of expectations upon which forward-looking cooperative activity is dependent) that a reasonable degree of order can be maintained as individuals with conflicting interests compete with one another to obtain scarce things. It is of course a principal function of 'working rules' to specify how the burdens and benefits of cooperative activity are to be apportioned. In related fashion, Commons understood 'competition' to be nothing more than the set of behaviours prescribed or authorized by the set of working rules presently in effect. Since he perceived 'competition' to have no 'natural' character, Commons understood the further modification of those rules – that is, the further adjustment of 'competition' – to be solely a matter of human volition.

These insights gradually came into focus for Commons after he and his students had launched into a detailed and comprehensive study of the development of the concept of property in American law. In drafting new legislation restricting the activities of businesses, Commons recognized that ultimately the courts would have to decide whether or not those restrictions were constitutional; that is, whether they represented a 'reasonable' taking of 'property' in accordance with the constitutional requirement of 'due process'. In order to predict what the courts would do, Commons deemed it necessary to determine exactly what it meant by these legal terms. Tracing the manner in which the all-encompassing sovereignty of William the Conqueror had been transformed over many centuries into a system of diffused private holdings of 'property', Commons made the astonishing discovery that 'competition' and 'property rights' had been instituted in England through the same process of judicial resolution of disputes. In this process, moreover, he discovered that the judges had thus consecutively implanted into 'competition' their own purpose of trying to resolve the disputes by being as 'fair' as possible to all parties involved, thereby establishing the common law notion of 'reasonable value'.

Equally significant to Commons was his discovery that 'property' is entirely a socially-constructed concept whose content in fact boils down to whatever the state (through its agency, the courts) allows one person (or group) to withhold from another who needs or wants it. Alternatively, the term 'property rights' boils down to 'all those things a person can, may or must do or not do with respect to those things that are scarce'. 'Competition', in turn, is simply the behaviour produced by a given set of property rights (and correlative duties) *and has no meaning without those specific rights*. What Commons had discerned was that, contrary to the 'natural law' conceptions implicit in Adam Smith's *The Wealth of Nations* (as reflected in the 'invisible hand' metaphor) and in all succeeding theories of market behaviour, the 'market mechanism' is actually a product of Darwinian '*artificial* selection'. Through this 'competition' over centuries has been purposefully constructed by judges who, in their efforts to resolve conflicts of interest in a manner that would advance the public interest as effectively as possible, took over what they considered to be the 'good' practices of private parties and gave them the physical sanctions of sovereignty. In short, according to Commons, collective action lies at the heart of the 'market mechanism'. It is therefore in a knowledge of the actual 'working rules' of which that 'mechanism' is but the expression – not in a knowledge of abstract logic – that the principles of its operation can be discovered.

In beginning his study of the evolution of property rights, Commons was seeking to discover a way of effectuating the policy standpoint outlined earlier. This required that his concrete proposals infringing on the existing rights of employers be deemed by the Courts to be 'reasonable'; that is, to be found consistent with the Court's current stance toward 'property' and 'due process'. And here Commons saw an opening for, in 1890, the Supreme Court had substantively changed the constitutional meaning of the word property 'from physical things having only use-value to the exchange value of anything'. In a word, the legal meaning of property was extended to include 'intangible property', including the ownership of expected opportunities to earn income (via trademarks, copyrights, patents and so on). The assignment of ownership rights in jobs was obviously a possibility under this extended conception of property.

Commons's attempt to summarize his findings and to articulate the logic of his alternative understanding of market phenomena – what he referred to initially as a 'volitional theory of value' – is contained in the first of his two major theoretical treatises, *Legal Foundations of Capitalism*. In it, he undertook (i) to develop a genetic analysis of the principal 'working rules' (property rights) patterning 'competition' in the American economy; (ii) to show

how legal principles and other 'working rules', such as custom, can fit *into* the core of economic theory; and (iii) to indicate how the 'volitional theory of value' revealed in his genetic analysis of the US economy – a 'theory of reasonable value' – can be used to guide the ongoing process of authoritative institutional adjustment. In the second theoretical treatise, his magnum opus, *Institutional Economics: Its Place in Political Economy*, Commons sought to explain how his generalizations about the role of conflicts of interest and collective action (or 'institutions') in economic life – a standpoint he by now referred to simply as 'institutional economics' – can be synthesized with the 'magnificent insights' of earlier theorists so as to produce a truly comprehensive theory of political economy. Commons also attempted in this second work to delineate the (unconventional) methodological 'preconceptions' – an orientation subsequently characterized as 'holism' – through which he developed and sought to explain the structure of his 'institutional economics'. In a final, posthumous, theoretical work, *The Economics of Collective Action*, Commons attempted to reformulate his argument so that it could be more easily understood by the non-specialist. Unfortunately, this effort was not particularly successful.

Commons's theoretical reformulation of economic affairs grew out of his insight that economists had failed to grasp the significance of the dual nature of the term 'property' as materials (use-values or wealth) and as their ownership (exchange-values or assets). As he saw it, economists have focused exclusively on the first meaning of property and hence have emphasized the relationship between individual and materials (as in the theory of diminishing marginal utility) and ignored the fact that individuals must first acquire ownership before something can be used. Thus the fundamental relationship – acquiring and alienating rights of ownership – is one between individual and individual (or group). Accordingly, Commons argued that what is required of a valid economics is a 'negotiational psychology ... of persuasion, coercion, duress, command, obedience, fear [and] hope' relating to the exchange of ownership rights by individuals who are for the most part 'being[s] of stupidity, passion and ignorance'. Even more important, the 'fundamental unit of analysis' of such an economics must itself be a 'unit of transfer of legal control' through which the right is acquired to own or control the use of something currently owned by another. This 'fundamental unit', Commons maintained, is the 'transaction'.

Three quite distinct types of transactions were identified by Commons: the bargaining transaction between legal equals in which a voluntary transfer of the ownership of wealth is negotiated (as when people negotiate the exchange of title to a car); the managerial transaction between legal superior and inferior through which production is effected and thereby wealth created (as when a foreman commands that a particular task be undertaken); and the rationing transaction between legal superior and inferior through which the burdens and benefits of cooperative wealth-creating activity are apportioned (as when government commands that a minimum wage be paid). In addition, five interacting factors were isolated by Commons as 'running through all economic behaviour as a limiting and complementary interdependent relationship' and hence as fundamental to the explanation of every transaction: scarcity (availability relative to demand); efficiency (average productivity); working rule and custom ('collective action in control of individual action'); sovereignty ('the changing process of authorizing, prohibiting and regulating the use of physical force in human affairs'), and futurity (anticipation of the future).

Thus Commons brought in collective action (through working rules and custom) and the state (through sovereignty) as explanatory factors for each transaction. Indeed, the state can be seen to be an implicit participant in every transaction, for it is the only agency with the power to transfer property rights. Commons also emphasized that embodied in the transactions are the three fundamental 'social relations' revealed in economic activity: conflict of interests (in ownership rights), dependence (on the actions of others) and order (security of expectations). Recalling Commons's belief that 'competition' is a socially-constructed process of interaction in which the purposeful action of the courts has been decisive in determining its concrete character, it is significant that law (through the influence of 'working rules' and 'sovereignty'), economics (through the influence of 'scarcity', 'efficiency' and 'futurity') and ethics (through the purposes reflected in judicial decisions) are seen by him as joined into an inseparable whole in the transaction.

In spite of his theoretical and practical achievements, Commons has had virtually no impact on the subsequent development of economic theory. The reason is not difficult to discern. Setting out initially only to discover ways of 'making capitalism good', Commons ultimately pointed to a total reconstruction of economics. For despite Commons's own insistence that he sought only 'to give collective action, in all its varieties ... its due place in economic theory – not to create a different kind of economics divorced from preceding schools' – acceptance of Commons's 'institutional economics' does in fact require a concomitant repudiation of the belief structure underlying neoclassical (as well as Marxian) economics. Moreover, his framework does not lend itself to formalization. Without an 'invisible college' of dedicated disciples seeking to carry on his research programme (and he produced no such cadre), it was inevitable that Commons's 'institutional economics' would be stillborn. Yet it would seem that Commons's approach to 'raising the plane of competition' has been tested and validated in the 'negotiated economies' of the Scandinavian nations and Holland. Perhaps the European nations racing towards economic integration, as well as the former Warsaw

Pact nations presently endeavouring to institute market processes, would do well to reconsider the ideas of this neglected pragmatist.

Commons's Major Writings

(1893), *The Distribution of Wealth*, New York and London: Macmillan.

(1894), *Social Reform and the Church* (with an introduction by Richard T. Ely), New York and Boston: T. Y. Crowell.

(1896), *Proportional Representation*, New York and Boston: T. Y. Crowell.

(1899), 'A Sociological View of Sovereignty' in *American Journal of Sociology*, Vol V, pp. 1–15, 155–71, 347–66 (July–Nov 1899); Vol V, pp. 544–52, 683–95, 814–25 (Jan–May 1900); Vol VI, pp. 67–89 (July 1900). Reprinted as *A Sociological View of Sovereignty* (with an introductory essay by Joseph Dorfman), New York: Augustus M. Kelley, 1967.

(1905), *Trade Unionism and Labor Problems* (in collaboration with associates), New York and Boston: Ginn and Co.

(1907), *Races and Immigrants in America*, New York and London: Macmillan.

(1908), 'Tariff Revision and Protection for American Labor' in *Annals of the American Academy of Political and Social Science*, **32**, 315–20. Reprinted in *Labor and Administration* (see below).

(1909), 'American Shoemakers, 1648–1895: A Sketch of Industrial Evolution', in *Quarterly Journal of Economics*, **24**, 39–84. Reprinted in *Labor and Administration* (see below).

(1910–11), *A Documentary History of American Industrial Society*, 10 vols, in collaboration with associates. Cleveland: Arthur H. Clark.

(1913), *Labor and Administration*, New York: Macmillan. Reprint edition published by Augustus M. Kelley, 1964.

(1916), *Principles of Labor Legislation* (with J. B. Andrews), New York and London: Harper.

(1918), *History of Labor in the United States*, 4 vols, in collaboration with associates. New York: Macmillan, 1918 (vols 1 & 2); 1935 (vols 3 & 4).

(1919), *Industrial Goodwill*, New York: McGraw-Hill. Reprint published by Arno & The New York Times, 1969.

(1921), *Industrial Government* (in collaboration with associates), New York: Macmillan. Reprint published by Arno & The New York Times, 1969.

(1922), 'Secular Trend and Business Cycles: A Classification of Theories' (with H. L. McCracken and W. E. Zeuch) in *Review of Economic Statistics*, **4**, 244–63.

(1924), *Legal Foundations of Capitalism*, New York: Macmillan. Reprint edition published by The University of Wisconsin Press, 1968.

(1934a), *Institutional Economics: Its Place in Political Economy*, New York: Macmillan. Reprint edition published by The University of Wisconsin Press, 1961. Second reprint edition, with introductory essay by Malcolm Rutherford, published by Transaction Press, Brunswick, N.J., 1989.

(1934b), *Myself*, New York: Macmillan. Reprint edition published by The University of Wisconsin Press, 1964.

(1950), *The Economics of Collective Action* (with introductory and supplemental essays by Kenneth H. Parsons), New York: Macmillan.

Other References

Chamberlain, Neil W. (1963), 'The Institutional Economics of John R. Commons', in *Institutional Economics: Veblen, Commons and Mitchell Reconsidered*, Berkeley: University of California Press, 63–94.

Chasse, John Dennis (1986), 'John R. Commons and the Democratic State', *Journal of Economic Issues*, **20**, 759–84.

Harter, Lafayette G. (1962), *John R. Commons: His Assault on Laissez-Faire*, Corvallis: Oregon State University Press.

Parsons, Kenneth H. (1942), 'John R. Commons' Point of View', reprinted in John R. Commons, *The Economics of Collective Action*, New York: Macmillan, 1950, 341–75.

Ramstad, Yngve (1986), 'A Pragmatist's Quest for Holistic Knowledge: The Scientific Methodology of John R. Commons', *Journal of Economic Issues*, **20**, 1067–1105.

Ramstad, Yngve (1988), 'The Institutionalism of John R. Commons: Theoretical Foundations of a Volitional Economics', Mimeo. Forthcoming in *Research in the History of Economic Thought and Methodology*.

John CORNWALL (born 1928)

I was born in Spencer, Iowa, in 1928, the fifth child of Morgan and Inez Cornwall, and lived there until I finished secondary school. I was an avid reader but had little interest in school work, concentrating instead on sports. I attended the University of Iowa, as had my parents, with the expectation of taking a Bachelor of Arts degree followed by a law degree and then settling down as a small town Iowa lawyer like my father and both of my grandfathers.

During the 1930s and 1940s the president of the University of Iowa actively recruited European academics who had become political refugees. As a result I was fortunate to study with Kurt Schafer from Berlin and Gustav Bergman from Vienna. This was the turning point in my life. Through them I was introduced to the writings of social scientists such as Marx and Engels, Max Weber, Tawney and Keynes. As a result I developed a keen interest in the process of transformation of capitalist societies and the forces generating social and economic change, an interest that I have retained throughout my career. By the time I had completed my first degree I had definitely decided on an academic career. I was advised by my undergraduate mentors to temporarily escape from the American Middle West and take an advanced degree at a European university 'in order to gain self-confidence'. As my father was a man of means as well as a generous person, he willingly financed my two-year study at the London School of Economics.

I was accepted into the master's degree programme in economics under the supervision of Lionel Robbins in 1950. After attending classes for approximately one month, I concluded that most of economic theory as taught at the graduate level was rather silly and irrelevant, being largely static or comparative static microtheory devoid of a sense of history and the importance of institutions. As a result I attended few economics classes, instead finding much pleasure in the philosophy classes and seminars of Karl Popper, in A.W. Phillips's classes on difference and differential equations and in reading Chekhov at the School of Slavonic Studies (London University).

Even though I learned little in the way of conventional economic theory during this period, I was awarded the master's degree largely, I suspect, because I used the written and oral exams to point out to my chief examiner the shortcomings of some of his major works. I enrolled in the Ph.D. programme at Harvard in 1953 in spite of my conviction that conventional economic theory was of little value. Economic theory as taught at Harvard greatly reinforced this opinion and I found it very difficult to take my studies seriously. Fortunately at the time there was a Harvard economist with a strong interest in macrotheory, James Duesenberry, who convinced me that the proper endeavour for a serious economist is to search for that limited part of economic theory that is of value. Writing my thesis under his guidance was sheer delight. He was the first economist I had known who understood the need for economic theory to have explanatory power.

Following the completion of my Ph.D. programme in 1958 I took an appointment at Tufts University where I remained for 13 years. During the early years of this appointment I worked with Duesenberry on an econometric study of the flow of funds through commercial banks, but the intended book failed to materialize. Throughout this period I retained my interest in the historical transformation of capitalism and began what was to be a lengthy study of capitalist development. This was at the time of the ascendancy of neoclassical growth theory with its assumptions of full employment and balanced and steady growth tendencies, none of which were consistent with the historical record. I set as my task the discovery of the reasons why developed capitalist economies had (until then) experienced only one period of both prolonged and severe recession (a problem first posed by Duesenberry). An important part of my explanation considered how in the real world the supply-side of the economy adjusted to demand (in contrast to the mainstream view that supply is exogenously determined), a position that was to become a common theme in most of my writings. I had great difficulty in finding an American publisher for *Growth and Stability in a Mature Economy*, but was successful on my first try in Britain.

While at Tufts, I received post-doctoral fellowships allowing me to spend a year at Cambridge University in 1963–64 and a year at the Copenhagen School of Economics in 1966–67. The year in Denmark taught me that a capitalist system can modernize without large disparities in income, large-scale poverty or imperial ambitions. In fact my stay provided a practical demonstration that the benefits of capitalism can be harnessed for the common good. Humane capitalism is an attainable goal.

During the 1960s I was becoming increasingly concerned about the rising levels of violence and corruption under the American version of capitalism. As a result I accepted an offer to join the faculty at Southern Illinois University in 1970, hoping that a small university town in the American Middle West would be a more congenial place to work and raise a family. When this proved to be incorrect I accepted an offer from Dalhousie University and in 1976 moved to Canada.

By the second half of the 1970s my research efforts had shifted from the 'one paper – one idea' form of discourse to that of the longer treatise. What short papers I have published since settling in Canada have tended to be conference papers, usually outlining themes for books that I was in the process of writing. This change arose partly out of my long-term desire to develop theoretical models that would explain actual historical processes. Such a research agenda did not lend itself at all well to the production of 'snappy' journal articles. The feeling that conventional dynamic macrotheory could give only a partial explanation of historical developments reinforced the need to convey my ideas through books. With each successive research project I have undertaken, and especially with each book I have written, I found myself relying more and more on historical and institutional techniques to supplement the more conventional analytical ones. I have also felt an increasing need to work within a framework that incorporated other specialized fields in economics and other social sciences in order to develop fully my own ideas.

In my second book (*Modern Capitalism: Its Growth and Transformation*) I used a non-neoclassical model of growth to explain the high growth rates throughout the OECD economies in the post-World War II period up to the mid-1970s, as well as differences in growth rates across countries. I viewed institutional features of the labour and product markets as constraints on the way in which economic activities can be carried out, and as important forces accounting for differences in growth rates across countries and over time. The book also stressed that neoclassical growth theory was ill-suited to explain these differences, partly as it was in error in maintaining that differences in investment rates were an unimportant influence, and partly because of its balanced growth framework.

In the process of writing this book, I experienced a growing sense of guilt from studying the macrodynamics of output when the overriding macro problem of the time had become inflation. Rather than extend the study as I had originally planned, I published a shorter book and shifted my research interests to the conditions required for controlling inflation while maintaining full employment. By the mid-1970s it was clear to me that most governments had concluded that inflation could only be controlled by creating large-scale unemployment. My immediate interest was to explain the causes of the high and often accelerating rates of inflation of the late 1960s–early 1970s and to develop policies to contain inflation at full employment, allowing a return to the 'golden age'. The result was my third book (*The Conditions for Economic Recovery: A Post-Keynesian Analysis*). While building on the framework adopted in the first two books, in this study I emphasized not only the impact of institutions on performance but also the ability of economic performance to alter the institutions of a society. Although I was not aware of the expression at the time, it later became clear to me that I was groping with the idea of hysteresis and its importance in capitalist development. In a manner similar to my first book, I emphasized the endogenous nature of the (allegedly) exogenous supply constraints, this time by emphasizing the influence of economic performance on institutions. The multi-country approach of the study also made clear to me most dramatically another feature of capitalism; that it comes in many diverse forms, and that model building must take account of this diversity as well as of hysteresis.

Following the publication of my next book, jointly authored with Wendy Maclean (*Economic Recovery for Canada*), I returned to some of the themes first considered in *The Conditions for Economic Recovery*. I was now able to see more clearly how important was the role of hysteresis or path dependence in the development process of economies and how important the need to formalize this role explicitly. This was particularly true when hysteresis is formulated in terms of a causal chain. At any point in time a given institutional framework will constrain and therefore influence both performance and the policy options open to the authorities. Whichever option is chosen will, in turn, have a particular impact on the future institutional framework and therefore on future performance, including the future policy options available. Hence the importance of the choices made today. Instead of the economy moving towards some future predetermined by a set of institutions given from outside the system, in this formulation the future is indeterminate until past and current performances have been specified.

In addition I also began to recognize the importance of economic and political power and the way in which changes in the distribution of power will affect the policies adopted and therefore performance. This resulted in a book (*The Theory of Economic Breakdown: An Institutional-Analytical Approach*) in which the causal chain considered the full employment and welfare policies adopted following World War II as an induced policy response to the Great Depression of the 1930s. The 'Great Inflation' of the late 1960s–early 1970s was then interpreted as the result of changes in the labour market, themselves induced by the exceptional macro performances of the 1950s and 1960s. I concluded that the current restrictive aggregate demand policies, originally introduced in response to the Great Inflation, are even now inducing further (adverse) institutional changes.

My current research uses this framework of joint interaction between performances and institutions to explain macro developments over the past century in the developed capitalist economies.

Looking back over my career to my days as a graduate student, I can only conclude that my initial appraisal of economic theory was essentially correct. If anything the trend towards 'high tech' methods of analysis in macrotheory and the increased use of the competitive model lead me to conclude that the proportion of useful theory now taught in economic theory courses is even less than when I formed my original highly intuitive view in graduate school. Recent developments in my estimation have greatly increased the formalism in macrotheory and substantially reduced its economic content and explanatory value, developments that have now reached undergraduate texts. Like the more fashionable micro version, macrotheory is now also dominated by the static form of analysis, with little allowance for either institutional constraints on economic behaviour or structural change. Little interest is shown in model building along the lines of Marx and Schumpeter in which institutions both limit activities in the short run and evolve over time. Instead macro processes are modelled within an equilibrium framework in which performance over time is seen as interaction between economic variables which are constrained by a very limited unchanging set of forces given from outside the system. Equilibrium analysts then focus their attention on the convergence properties and equilibrium values of the economic variables, the latter being independent of the actual path the economy takes and uniquely determined once the unchanging exogenous forces are specified.

Neoclassical growth theory exemplifies this form of analysis perfectly. Assuming some exogenously given tastes and technology, summarized by a savings ratio and a production function, a long-run growth path for the economic variables is derived which, with 'well-behaved' functions, is uniquely determined by the exogenous and fixed rates of growth of the labour force and technical progress. Disturbances lead only to temporary deviations from the equilibrium path.

Leaving aside the importance of hysteresis effects in the real world, I have found the equilibrium framework inadequate for other reasons. As stated, economists who employ this framework often assume a frictionless world with few, if any, constraints on economic activity other than fixed tastes, technologies and endowments. Norms or conventions dictating acceptable behaviour, and, therefore constraining market activities, are simply ignored. Nor does equilibrium analysis deal with the relative speed with which the assumed exogenous forces change in the real world compared with the speed with which the economic variables converge on the equilibrium. Yet in modern capitalist economies changes in tastes, technologies and other institutional features are very rapid relative to the rate at which the economy can adjust, so much so that the convergence properties of the model take on much less interest and importance for me than the institutional changes themselves.

Recent developments in macrotheory are all the more difficult to comprehend given the events of the past two decades. Thus just as events since 1973 reveal that there is no self-correcting mechanism automatically bringing a capitalist system back towards some full-employment equilibrium with acceptable rates of inflation, developments in macrotheory spanning a similar period indicate that there is no feedback from real-world events to theory that could correct errors in the way macroeconomists have modelled these events. Unemployment may rise from approximately 10 million in 1973 to a predicted level of 29 million in 1990 in the OECD but this does not apparently require discarding the automatic full-employment assumption now built into so much of macrotheory. Rather it requires a recognition that 19 million more workers have decided to substitute leisure for work, as the currently popular new classical macroeconomics would have it.

This lack of a self-correcting mechanism within macrotheory, to bring our models more into line with reality, has been the biggest disappointment in my career. For if traumatic events such as those that have occurred over the past two decades or so do not lead to a recognition that capitalism is not self-regulating, then there is little guarantee that the economics profession will ever get it right on important macro issues.

My greatest satisfaction, looking at the period as a whole, has been personal friendships I have had with economists who 'got it right'. I feel quite fortunate to have known and worked with the Duesenberrys, Kaldors, Lundbergs and Sundrums of the profession.

Cornwall's Major Writings

(1972), *Growth and Stability in a Mature Economy*, London: Martin Robertson.
(1977), *Modern Capitalism: Its Growth and Transformation*, London: Martin Robertson.
(1983), *The Conditions for Economic Recovery: A Post-Keynesian Analysis*, Oxford: Basil Blackwell.
(1984), *Economic Recovery for Canada* (with Wendy Maclean), Toronto: James Lorimer.
(1990), *The Theory of Economic Breakdown: An Institutional-Analytical Approach*, Oxford: Basil Blackwell.

Keith COWLING (born 1936)

As a grammar schoolboy in Scunthorpe, Lincolnshire, I was quite clear what I wanted to do at university. Agriculture was my overwhelming interest and I duly proceeded to a degree in agricultural sciences at Wye College, University of London. (I remember, in my interview for admission, making an argument about relieving Third World poverty by introducing modern techniques of food production.) Whilst at Wye my interests shifted away from the physical sciences towards economics, and I moved on to the University of Illinois to do graduate work in agricultural economics. At Illinois I got a reasonably good grounding in economics – the agricultural economists did all the core graduate courses in the economics department and were generally well trained on the quantitative side. I went on to an Assistant Lectureship at Manchester (UK) where the focus of my research shifted from the estimation of agricultural supply functions (which had been the basis of my doctoral thesis) towards the factor markets serving agriculture. This had two important consequences for me; it led me into broader labour market issues and it got me interested in oligopolistic markets.

My first move out of agriculture was in the direction of the Phillips curve; it included some joint work with David Metcalf on the regional dimension of the curve and a monograph on Ireland written whilst visiting the Economic Research Institute in Dublin. As part of the latter work I discovered that industries in Ireland fell into two groups: one group where wage inflation was quite closely related to unemployment, and the second group where it appeared unaffected by unemployment, but was clearly influenced by price inflation and profitability. The first group of industries were characterized by rather open labour markets while the second appeared much more restricted. Being a monograph from Ireland, this research did not attract much attention in Britain and, on reflection, I feel I should have sought to publish the results in *Economica* which had printed Lipsey's much-quoted article on the subject. He compared the efficacy of the simplistic Phillips curve with the Kaldorian alternative based on profitability. What my work suggested was the existence of two sectors of the economy: one in which the simplistic curve may have some credibility and a second in which Kaldor's argument may hold sway. Of course it may have been significant that I was working in Ireland where rather more industries may have retained the relatively open-market characteristics required for the Phillips curve to work. I did not take my excursion into labour economics any further at that time, but my interest in Phillips curves resurfaced in the rather unlikely context of my book on *Monopoly Capitalism* where I developed the outlines of an inter-industry Phillips curve based on a varying degree of product market monopoly (Chapter 5).

My research on the factor markets serving agriculture also propelled me in the direction of oligopolistic markets; I already knew how the giants of the engineering and chemical industries dominated the markets for inputs into agriculture. My early research was concentrated on generating quality-adjusted price indexes – so called hedonic indexes – for use in demand estimation at the level of the aggregate market for the factor in question. However, I quickly became interested in the relevance of these indexes to disentangling the market power of the seller. The hedonic work provided estimates of quality-corrected prices for each firm which were used to generate estimates of the price elasticity of demand associated with specific firms. Generally this work on hedonic adjustment, done with Tony Rayner and John Cubbin, received considerable recognition, but its relevance for the assessment of market power was largely ignored.

It seemed quite natural that the above research should lead into an interest in advertising. Moving into markets for consumer goods, any attempt to capture firm elasticities of demand required some recognition of the role of advertising. By this time, 1969, I had progressed to the University of Warwick and was promoted to the new Chair in Industrial Economics – reflecting the shortage of candidates then in the field! In 1972 I organized a symposium on industrial economics at Warwick which was meant to be a launchpad for a new industrial economics in Britain – one constructed on a strong theoretical and econometric base. My own contribution to this symposium was a piece on advertising which aimed to test the Dorfman-Steiner theorem in an oligopoly context. Subsequently, the Department of Trade and Industry commissioned a report on advertising and a book, based on this report, was published in 1975. This had little impact in Britain and no coverage in the US. Nevertheless I believed then, and continue to believe now, that advertising is an important issue – a vital mechanism whereby power is accumulated and maintained. We had completed a systematic, econometric investigation of both its importance, and its multi-faceted role within the economy, but our conclusions were far too low key. Much more recently I had the opportunity of offering my views on advertising in the *Economic Review* (1985) where my conclusions show a rather sharper edge:

> I have suggested that advertising can best be understood in terms of producers attempting to influence or manipulate consumers' preferences. This view provides a criticism of the notion of consumer sovereignty which underpins most of standard microeconomic analysis, and also offers an explanation of the strong links between advertising and monopoly power (p.6).

At about the same time as *Advertising and Economic Behaviour* was published in 1975, the DTI approached John Cable, Paul Stoneman and me about a study of mergers in the UK. I was not very keen. I could not appreciate why examining a specific means by which power, size or control was achieved was particularly interesting. After all GM was powerful because of its size and dominance – what did it matter how it was created? Nevertheless I agreed and indeed I subsequently acknowledged that the subject does warrant some study. The book, *Mergers and Economic Performance*, certainly commanded more attention than our opus on advertising. More people were interested and it was seen as a significant contribution. On one thing I was quite clear: having analysed the results of our labours I was determined to avoid the sort of flabby conclusions we made in the case of advertising. The mergers in Britain in the late 1960s and early 1970s had been a national disaster and we said so.

Although some of the work mentioned above may have had radical overtones, nevertheless it was clearly nested within the neoclassical paradigm. Around 1974 or 1975, I happened to read Baran and Sweezy's *Monopoly Capital* and things were never quite the same again. Needless to say I did not agree with everything they said, and I could see huge gaps in some of their arguments, but it allowed me to view the field of industrial economics from a different and more revealing perspective. I was now better able to organize my thoughts, views, insights – and I could focus more clearly on what I already grasped. This was first, and imperfectly, reflected in a paper on 'Oligopoly and the Distribution of Income' which I wrote in 1975. Although an important paper for me, editors/reviewers considered it either not fully developed (a view with which I had to concur) or no advance on Cowling and Waterson's 'Price-Cost Margins and Market Structure' (*Economica*, 1976) or Cowling's 'On the Theoretical Specification of Industrial Structure-Performance Relationships' (*European Economic Review*, 1976). For me it was the first faltering step in moving from an old paradigm to a new one. However there was no stagnationist argument in the original version. I was still thinking of the early 1970s as being a cyclical downturn, and a stagnation thesis appeared irrelevant to earlier post-war Britain. Subsequently I added a stagnationist argument and a much revised version of the paper appeared in the *European Economic Review* (1981) just prior to the delayed publication of *Monopoly Capitalism*. The latter I felt was my most important contribution to date, and still do.

Obviously *Monopoly Capitalism* relied heavily on Kalecki and Baran and Sweezy. Writing this book helped me a lot – it allowed me to put things into perspective and to develop my view of the whole system. Before I was just dabbling in different facets of the whole and was failing to see the wood for the trees. Unfortunately, many people seemed to see the book's central contribution, if they saw any, as tying-down the Kaleckian model's link between structure and mark-up more rigorously, when in fact that contribution had already been made in Cowling and Waterson and in other places by other people. At the same time such a reaction is not all that surprising given my approach: I was emerging from an orthodoxy which most economists, inevitably, are affected by. The special contribution of the book, as I see it, was that it allowed the flows of two literatures to merge – rather than to stand apart, hardly recognizing each other, except briefly to shout abuse. There was a voluminous literature in more orthodox industrial economics/ organization which provided rich pickings for anyone seriously interested in developing the monopoly capitalist view of the world. My book offered some signposts and some preliminary reconnaissance. I thought the interesting parts were the more informal ideas scattered here and there, which reinforces the question as to why the whole approach was not more formalized.

My great concern with the profession as a whole has been its general move in the direction of formal aridity and emptiness. This is not only true of the neoclassical core but also of the development of classical Marxist analysis. Picking up the journals published in the 1940s, 1950s and 1960s was, and to some degree still is, to my mind, a much more rewarding and exciting experience than grappling with the more recent outflow. An elegant, or not so elegant, formality seems too often to be a disguise for a lack of ideas or insight. The conforming tendency of our profession, and its narrowing specializations, has led to a blinkered irrelevance. People seem not to have anything to say, or are too frightened, too repressed by the conventional wisdom, to say it. What I tried to do was to establish a relatively holistic and coherent framework, do some exploratory analysis and offer a few ideas about the way the economy appeared to be moving.

In developing the link between industrial structure, price-cost margins and thus distribution, the main thrust of the analysis was to show how the major corporations are able to control structure via their own strategic decision-making. On stagnation I tried to adapt Kalecki's framework to a modern context; in this task I was influenced by unpublished papers by Matthew Lambrinides who had been at Warwick during an earlier period. The question of investment remained problematic, as it had for Kalecki. My treatment of labour was incomplete but gave some pointers to important developments, like the vertical disintegration and fragmentation of production as a strategic corporate response to the growth of union power in the old industrial centres. The other part of the analysis of the position of labour which I felt was particularly interesting related to my attempt, with John Brack, to demonstrate how the underlying *supply* conditions within the labour market are significantly influenced by advertising in the product market. Finally the analysis of international trade continued the central theme of the strategic control by the giant corporations over structure. Since control over trade by the transnationals is now overwhelming, imports are no longer the competitive discipline within the product market they were once seen to be, although they are, of course, an increasingly effective discipline in terms of curbing the power of labour.

The analysis of the international dimension of monopoly capitalism was subsequently developed in a book with Roger Sugden on *Transnational Monopoly Capitalism*. Roger had completed his doctoral work in this area with me and we decided to join forces on a book which would be less parochial than *Monopoly Capitalism*. Rather than starting from a specific national economy, we began with the giant corporations and their global ambit and ambitions. We redefined the nature of the firm, leaving behind the Coasian concept which dominated the transnational literature and moving towards one which saw the firm essentially as a centre of strategic decision-making. This allowed the firm to extend itself through the market, for example, via subcontracting relations. We examined structure-performance links, the nature of rivalry and labour markets from this new perspective. In a final substantial section we offered a possible way forward for reconstructing the world order – recognizing the inefficiencies as well as the inequities and injustices of the system and proposing remedies. However, the book had little impact. To some extent this may have been due to a general petering-out of the debate, but I also feel that we failed to present our arguments in an attractive and interesting way – the very title of the book was enough to put most people off!

Since then my main concern has been with developing the case for community and national economic planning (within the context of a system described in the two books) and setting out what I see as the essential ingredients of such planning. The efficient allocation of resources is contingent on democratic choice, but efficiency is thwarted by concentrations of power which undermine that democratic choice. If powerful agents are allowed to make choices for communities, there is no reason to assume that those choices will correspond to the community's optimum and every reason to expect they will differ. This is the fundamental argument for imposing on market forces coherent, community-based, national and supranational planning systems within which they are allowed to operate. At the present time in modern economies the forces of transnationalism, centripetalism and short-termism – all interrelated and all connected to an underlying concentration of power, and therefore decision-making – provide the basic justification. These are not new factors, but they have currently assumed such significance that economic policy must now be fundamentally realigned to account fully for them.

Whilst transnationalism and short-termism will be broadly familiar, perhaps centripetalism needs a word of explanation, particularly as I now see it as the most fundamental force. It relates to the tendency for higher-level economic activities and their associated occupations to gravitate to the centre and to be lost to the periphery. At one and the same time the major corporations are internationalizing production (transnationalism) and drawing control of the use of an ever-increasing share of the world's economic resources into the ambit of the key cities of the world – the world's command cities. This process leads inevitably to the loss of a substantial degree of local, regional and national autonomy, Such a withdrawal of strategic decision-making from huge swathes of the world's surface and population will also mean that more and more of the world economy will be infected with short-termism. The growth of the forces of transnationalism and centripetalism implies an increasing failure to internalize various dynamic external economies within the decision-making of the increasingly dominant agents of the system. Thus to achieve efficiency in the allocation and utilization of economic resources requires national/community-based economic planning.

However, although planning can be seen as essential for efficiency, the nature of planning is all-important. Comprehensive, centralized planning is neither desirable nor feasible because it is too removed from the community. In recent papers I have been trying to isolate the central characteristics of an appropriate planning system and I feel we have much to learn from the Japanese approach. This requires the state to take a direct strategic decision-making role within the market economy to promote, nurture and guide key industries. But such a strategy for community economic development has to be informed with a vision of where we wish to go. This must, of necessity, come out of a wide democratic debate. As one way of beginning such a debate I have suggested recently that the creation of an extended system of flexible specialization might offer an attractive vision. Such a system could be seen as a modern recreation of many of the characteristics of traditional craft production, but now incorporating technologically sophisticated, highly flexible processes within a strategy of permanent innovation. Whilst many appear to expect that flexible specialization will crowd out the system of mass production operated by the giants, this will surely require a peculiarly supportive environment. To move towards a vision of thriving regional networks of small independent enterprises will require an industrial strategy which provides both a modern infrastructure and protection from the predations of the giants. My work in the immediate future will be orientated towards such visions and such strategies.

Cowling's Major Writings

(1965), *Determinants of Wage Inflation in Ireland*, Dublin: Economic Research Institute.

(1967), *Resource Structure of the Agricultural Industry: An Economic Analysis* (with D. Metcalf and A.J. Rayner), Oxford: Pergamon.

(1975), *Advertising and Economic Behaviour* (with John Cable, Michael Kelly and Tony McGuiness), London: Macmillan.

(1980), *Mergers and Economic Performance* (with others), Cambridge: Cambridge University Press.

(1982), *Monopoly Capitalism*, London: Macmillan. Revised, Japanese edition, 1988.

(1983), 'Advertising and Labour Supply: Work Week and Work Year in U.S. Manufacturing Industries, 1919–76' (with John Brack), *Kyklos*, **36**, 285–303.

(1987), *Transnational Monopoly Capitalism* (with Roger Sugden), Brighton: Harvester Wheatsheaf.

(1989), 'Exchange Rate Adjustment and Oligopoly Pricing Behaviour' (with Roger Sugden), *Cambridge Journal of Economics*, **13**, September.

(1990a), 'A New Industrial Strategy: Preparing Europe for the Turn of the Century', Presidential Address, Conference of the European Association for Research in Industrial Economics, Budapest, August 1989, published in *International Journal of Industrial Organisation*, **8**, June.

(1990b), *A New Economic Policy for Britain* (with Roger Sugden, eds), Manchester: Manchester University Press.

Paul DAVIDSON (born 1930)

Paul Davidson was born on 23 October 1930, a year less one day after the great Stock Market Crash of 1929. He grew up in a middle-class neighbourhood in Brooklyn, New York. His father was a general contractor who designed and remodelled store fronts. Despite the Great Depression and its obvious negative effects on investments and the retail trade, Davidson's father was able to eke out a living by working 12 to 14 hours a day – often six or seven days a week. Davidson's mother remained a traditional housewife although she kept the books for the family firm. At the beginning of the Second World War she entered the regular labour market and continued to work as a bookkeeper until she retired in the 1970s. As a teenager Davidson worked in his father's business during the summer when school was not in session.

Davidson's family put a great stress on education and wanted him to become a 'professional' – preferably a medical doctor. Davidson did attend Brooklyn College, where tuition and fees averaged less than $25 per year, graduating in 1950 with majors in Chemistry and Biology. From 1950 to 1952 he was a graduate student in biochemistry at the University of Pennsylvania, completing most of the course work for the Ph.D. degree while working as an instructor in biochemistry at the university's Medical and Dental Schools. He had decided to do a Ph.D. thesis regarding DNA (this was before the discovery of the 'double helix'). Although he enjoyed his teaching duties, he quickly lost interest in biochemical research and withdrew from the programme.

Not knowing what to 'do' for a living, he returned to New York and enrolled at City University for a business programme to prepare for the world of commerce. While there he was required to take a course in basic economics. As a biochemist trained in the questions of experimental design and statistical inference, he was appalled by the misuse of empirical data by economists. It was then that he decided how he could both make a mark for himself and a contribution to society and the economics profession.

Just before entering military service during the Korean war, Davidson married his wife, Louise, who became a lifelong partner in his professional economics activities. After military service (as an enlisted man on a biochemical research team), Davidson completed his graduate work for the M.B.A. degree. His Master's thesis was on 'The Statistical Analysis of Economic Times Series'.

Davidson applied to various graduate programmes at Harvard, MIT, Berkeley, Brown and the University of Pennsylvania. The programme at MIT particularly interested him, since it was based on a science background, but he finally chose the University of Pennsylvania, which offered him significantly greater financial support than the others. This higher income permitted Davidson and his wife to start a family. Their first son, Robert, was born in the spring of 1956. Davidson's decision to attend Pennsylvania, determined in large part by 'the invisible hand', shunted him from a programme of orthodox neoclassical training to one with more heretical components. At Pennsylvania, Davidson came under the influence of Sidney Weintraub who was just completing his masterpiece, *An Approach to the Theory of Income Distribution*. Weintraub became the dominating intellectual influence in Davidson's early career as he worked on his doctoral dissertation, 'Theories of Relative Shares'. This explains Davidson's early interest in Keynes' brand of macroeconomics, and also in the distribution of income. Although Weintraub had an important influence on his thinking over the years, they collaborated on only one published paper, 'Money as Cause and Effect' (1973b), and one unpublished paper, 'Theory of Monetary Policy under Wage Inflation'.

Davidson successfully defended his Ph.D. thesis in August 1958, only a few days after his second child, Diane, was born. His first job was as an Assistant Professor at Rutgers University. His first article, 'A Clarification of the Ricardian Rent Share' (1959), in the area of functional distribution was soon published. However, Davidson's salary at Rutgers did not keep up with the increasing demands of his growing family. Believing he could combine a non-academic job with his professional research interests, he joined Continental Oil Company, heading a small group of staff economists who were primarily involved in providing economic projections and evaluating investment projects for the Management Executive Committee of the corporation. The experience of participating in managerial decisions of a large corporation was invaluable in clarifying the fundamental flaws of the neoclassical theory of entrepreneurial expectation formation and decision-making.

Davidson was also able to bring his knowledge of Keynes's user cost analysis to bear on the economic problems of the oil industry. His 'Public Policy Problems of the Domestic Crude Oil Industry' (1963) was a result of his research and of interaction with management of the oil company.

Within a few months of joining the oil company, Davidson felt that his talents were not being fully employed. Furthermore, he and his wife felt uncomfortable with the conservative politics espoused by their newly-made friends and associates in Texas. Accordingly, Davidson resigned and accepted a position as Assistant Professor at the University of Pennsylvania. Returning to academic life permitted Davidson to switch his attention back to macroeconomics, as evidenced by his article 'Employment and Income Multipliers and the Price Level' (1962).

The connection between inflation, income distribution and money now became his central interest. It was not until Davidson 'cracked the nut' of

Keynes's Finance Motive analysis and showed his results to an enthusiastic Roy Harrod (who happened to be visiting Pennsylvania at the time) that he got a glimmer of the true role of money in the Keynesian Revolution. It was the publication of his 'Keynes's Finance Motive' article (1965) which provided Davidson with the confidence to strike out on his own in attempting to integrate monetary analysis into Keynes's revolutionary general theory.

'Money, Portfolio Balance, Capital Accumulation and Economic Growth', written in 1965, was a criticism of Tobin's article in *Econometrica* earlier that year on a 'money and growth' model; it also presented an alternative approach to money and capital accumulation more in tune with Keynes's *General Theory* and *Treatise on Money*. This alternative to Tobin's 1965 accumulation analysis involved utilizing the ratio of the spot market to the forward market price for capital (that is, the market price of existing real capital relative to the cost of producing new capital) as the relevant 'invisible hand' ratio directing the entrepreneurial determination of the rate of investment or disinvestment in real capital. This ratio is, of course, the equivalent of the famous q-ratio that Tobin was to discover in 1968.

The story of this paper's history from submission until its publication may have a moral for fledgling economists. Nine months after submission, on 6 January 1967, the editor of *Econometrica* sent back two referees' reports indicating that 'Both referees have found much in the paper of merit, but both feel that it falls short of being publishable in its present form ... [because it] is not precise enough in its analytic content.' Davidson duly revised the paper by merely introducing a simple algebraic equation in the text just before the verbal description of each supply or demand relationship that was discussed – a total of 14 equations added. Otherwise the textual exposition remained virtually unchanged. Three months later this revised version of the manuscript was accepted for publication!

Davidson hoped the paper would appear with a rejoinder from Tobin. He thought a response from such an eminent economist – even if very critical – would be extremely useful in promoting discussion of the Keynes's alternative developed by Davidson. The paper was published in the April 1968 issue without any comment from Tobin and it apparently failed to create any stir in the profession. It was then that Davidson decided that he must write a book which would tie all his thoughts on money and employment together in a bundle that could not be overlooked. That book, which was written during his stay at Cambridge University in 1970–71, was *Money and the Real World*.

Davidson's visit to Cambridge was one of the most productive investments of his life. He gained tremendously from the almost daily interactions with Basil Moore (who was also visiting) as well as from less frequent, but still fruitful, discussions with Nicholas Kaldor, Richard Kahn, Michael Posner and Ken Galbraith (also visiting). Most important was his relationship with

Joan Robinson. Davidson and Robinson immediately embarked on heated discussions regarding drafts of various chapters of his manuscript. She was clearly unhappy with his arguments regarding the Cambridge post-Keynesian approach and was particularly distressed with his criticisms of Kaldor's neo-Pasinetti theorem. After a few weeks of such discussions, she finally refused to speak to him about the book.

Nevertheless, almost every morning when Davidson arrived at the office he shared with Richard Kahn, he would find a blank sheet of paper with a handwritten question on the top. Robinson was setting him an essay to write. He would diligently compose his answer and when Joan Robinson went up for morning coffee, he would place the paper on her desk. After lunch Davidson would find the paper back on his desk with her easily recognizable scrawl indicating why the various points made were either wrong-headed or just plain wrong.

Davidson learned a tremendous amount from these daily essay exercises. In the years following his visit to Cambridge, he would often receive notes from Joan Robinson indicating when she especially liked something he'd published. For example, on 3 July 1978 she wrote about his paper 'Money and General Equilibrium': 'I much enjoyed your piece in ISMEA. I hope you will put the same points where they will be read in the USA.' And on 13 September 1978 regarding his paper 'Why Money Matters' Joan wrote: 'I like your piece about "crowding out". This ought to settle the matter.'

Davidson's friendship with John Hicks began after they met at the International Economics Association conference on 'The Microfoundations of Macroeconomics' in 1975 at S'Agora (Spain) where neoclassical Keynesians, monetarists, general equilibrium theorists and the emerging group of what was to be called post-Keynesians met. All the participants apparently agreed that the conference was a failure. Hicks recognized this in his introduction to the final session when he stated that 'our discussions had so far not done what we had set out to do. We had met to discuss a rather central issue in economics; but it had been shown that economists were not in a good state to discuss central issues... . We were each shooting off on our own paths, and we were lucky if we could keep in sight even our closest neighbor.' Nevertheless, after hearing his 'Discussion of Leijonhufuvd's "Social Consequences of Inflation"' Hicks told Davidson that he believed that their views on the microfoundations of macroeconomics were not dissimilar.

After this S'Agora conference, Hicks and Davidson kept in touch. Davidson believed he had some impact on Hicks changing his view regarding the importance of ISLM (see J. Hicks, 'ISLM: An Explanation', *Journal of Post Keynesian Economics*, **3**, 1980–81). In their continuing correspondence and at several meetings in London and at his home in Blockley during these years, Sir John provided Davidson with some very useful insights; though difficult to specify completely, these no doubt had an influence on his developing thought, especially with regard to time, liquidity, contracts and expectations. Hicks's influence is especially noticeable in Chapter 3 of Davidson's 1982 book *International Money and the Real World.*

On 13 February 1983, Hicks wrote regarding Davidson's 'Rational Expectations: A Fallacious Foundation' (1983) paper: 'I do like it very much. I have never been through that RE literature; you know that I don't have proper access to journals; but I had just enough to be put off by the smell of it. You have now *rationalized* my suspicions, and have shown me that I have missed my chance, of labelling my own point of view as *non-ergodic*. One needs a name like that to ram a point home.'

Davidson's interest in resource economics developed from the brief interlude mentioned above as an oil company economist. The 1963 article 'Public Policy Problems of the Domestic Crude Oil Industry' represented the distillation of analytical arguments that he developed in order to try to influence the decision-making of the Conoco management and the positions it should take relative to the new economic policy approach of President Kennedy. Although Davidson was not very successful in changing management's strategies, the President of the firm was apparently sufficiently impressed to ask Davidson to help him write his public speeches – which were, in those days, numerous.

This 'Domestic Crude' paper was apparently quite well regarded in the profession. Several well-known scholars in the field (A. F. Kahn, M. A. Adelman, R. H. Heflebower) initiated some further 'correspondence' discussion with him regarding resource economics. One of these persons recommended Davidson to Allen Kneese, of Resources For the Future, as a potential principal investigator on the demand for water recreational activities. Kneese and RFF provided a grant to study 'The Social Value of Water Recreational Facilities resulting from an Improvement in Water Quality in an Estuary: The Delare – A Case Study' (1966). The success of this initial water recreation study brought forth new invitations to take on additional 'resource' analysis, including 'Scenic Enhancement of Highways' (1967) and 'Recreational Use of TVA' (1968). A further massive study of two national recreation surveys for the US Bureau of Outdoor Recreation resulted in a book entitled *The Demand and Supply for Outdoor Recreation* (1969).

In 1973, with the OPEC embargo, the question of crude oil and energy was again on the nation's mind. Arthur Okun asked Davidson to do a study for Brookings regarding President Nixon's 'Project Independence'. At approximately the same time, people at the Ford Foundation's Energy Policy Project requested a study regarding incentives and the oil industry. These studies for Ford and Brookings emerged as 'The Relations of Economic Rent and Price Incentives to Oil and Gas Supplies' and 'Oil: Its Time Allocation and Project Independence'.

During the 1970s, the 'energy problem' was continually on the public's mind. Between 1973 and 1979, Davidson was asked to testify 19 times before various Congressional Committees on some aspect of this problem. He tried to carry his professional analysis over to the arena of actual policy decision-making.

In 1978, Davidson and Sidney Weintraub co-founded the *Journal of Post Keynesian Economics*. The 'Statement of Purposes' of this publication indicated that the journal's

> aim is to encourage evolving analysis and empirical study to contest the conformist orthodoxy that now suffuses economic journals in the United States. The *Journal of Post Keynesian Economics* will be committed to the principle that the cumulative development of economic theory is possible only when the theory is continuously subject to challenge, in terms of its ability both to explain the real world and to provide a reliable guide to public policy.

Here, then, was a journal created to encourage and provide a platform for 'dissenting economists' while trying to maintain a dialogue with those in the mainstream.

In the 1980s Davidson worked primarily in two areas: (i) expectations and non-probabilistic outcomes, and (ii) international financial relations. His 1983 article on 'Rational Expectations: A Fallacious Foundation for Studying Crucial Decision-Making Processes' linked the term non-ergodic processes with the earlier Keynes–Knight concept of uncertainty. The resulting discussion was capped by an article entitled 'Is Probability Theory Relevant?: A Post Keynesian Perspective'.

With his 1982 book *International Money and the Real World*, Davidson's attention turned to the financial relationships among open economies. He developed the concept of unionized monetary systems where all contracts were denominated in the same monetary unit, and non-unionized monetary systems where different contracts are denominated in different nominal units. This emphasis on contracts and the civil law led to the 1988 book *Economics for a Civilized Society* which Davidson co-authored with his third child, Greg Davidson. In recent years this has lead to policy-orientated papers dealing with international debt (1987 and 1990).

In 1986, after 28 years at Rutgers, Davidson accepted the J. F. Holly Chair of Excellence in Political Economy at the University of Tennessee in Knoxville. This has provided Davidson with additional resources to help him to continue as a productive 'dissenting economist'.

Davidson's Major Writings

Most of Davidson's papers have been published in two volumes entitled *Money and Employment* and *Inflation, Open Economies and Resources*, both published by Macmillan, 1991.

(1959), 'A Clarification of the Ricardian Rent Share', *Canadian Journal of Economics and Political Science*, **25**, May.

(1962), 'Employment and Income Multipliers and the Price Level', *American Economic Review*, **52**, September.

(1963), 'Public Policy Problems of the Domestic Crude Oil Industry', *American Economic Review*, **53**, March.

(1965), 'Keynes's Finance Motive', *Oxford Economic Papers*, **17**, March.

(1968), 'Money, Portfolio Balance, Capital Accumulation and Economic Growth', *Econometrica*, **36**, April.

(1969), *The Demand and Supply for Outdoor Recreation* (with C.J. Cicchetti and J.J. Seneca), Bureau of Economic Research.

(1973a), *Money and the Real World*, Macmillan and Halsted Press.

(1973b), 'Money as Cause and Effect' (with S. Weintraub), *Economic Journal*, **83**, December.

(1977), 'Money and General Equilibrium', *Economie Appliquée*, **4**.

(1978), 'Why Money Matters: Some Lessons of the Past Half Century of Monetary Theory', *Journal of Post Keynesian Economics*, **1**, Fall.

(1982), *International Money and the Real World*, Macmillan, Halsted Press, John Wiley.

(1983), 'Rational Expectations: A Fallacious Foundation for Studying Crucial Decision-Making Processes', *Journal of Post Keynesian Economics*, Winter.

(1987), 'A Modest Set of Proposals for Resolving the International Debt Problem', *Journal of Post Keynesian Economics*, **10**, Winter.

(1988), *Economics for a Civilized Society* (with G. Davidson), London: Macmillan, W.W. Norton.

(1990), 'Is Probability Theory Relevant?: a Post Keynesian Perspective', *Journal of Economic Perspectives*, **5**, Winter.

(1991), 'What International Payments System would Keynes have Recommended for the Twenty-First Century?' in P. Davidson and J. Kregel (eds), *Economic Problems of the 1990s: Europe, Less Developed Countries and the United States*, Aldershot: Edward Elgar.

Meghnad DESAI (born 1940)

I was born in Baroda in western India in 1940. Baroda was a 'native state'; that is, it was ruled by a King, the Gaekwar of Baroda. The town of Baroda was the capital of the state. It was well built with wide roads, good public sanitation and fine public buildings – all due to an enlightened King who had ruled for a long time and died just before 1940. But native states were passé and Baroda was absorbed into the Indian Republic in 1948. We moved to Bombay in 1950 where I went to school and later did my B.A. and M.A. degrees.

At school, I began to hate mathematics and although with my marks at the school-leaving examinations I could have opted for a Science degree leading to medicine or engineering, I chose an Arts degree as I could then avoid mathematics. But an Arts degree was a passport to unemployment except if you specialized in economics. My preferred desires were Sanskrit or history, but wisdom (the law of value?) prevailed and I chose economics.

Our education was liberal; libraries were good and you could spend a lot of the afternoon (after classes in the morning) in the library. Thus did I misspend my youth, in the Bombay University library round the year rather than just at exam time. I got by with reasonably good results and managed to be admitted as a Ph.D. candidate. While doing my M.A. I met Charles Whittlesey who was Professor of Money and Banking at the University of Pennsylvania and who was the Ford Foundation Visiting Professor. He encouraged me to take the Graduate Record Examination and apply to US universities. I applied only to Pennsylvania but luckily got a Ford Foundation Fellowship; thus I left Bombay in August 1961 to arrive in Philadelphia to do a Ph.D. There I was assigned as a Research Assistant to Lawrence Klein on the mistaken impression that, as an Indian, I must be good at Statistics. However Klein was very helpful and I was able to learn my econometrics in weekly individual sessions with him while working on 'An Econometric Model of the World Tin Economy' which became my Ph.D. thesis and was published in 1966.

My first job was in the Agricultural Economics Department at the University of California, Berkeley. It was as a Research Officer since I had decided that I did not fancy teaching. As my thesis had been on a commodity model I was assigned the task of finding out whether the price of milk in California was 'too high' as a result of producer capture of the market regulator. I did a massive micro simulation on an IBM 1620 and was able to answer 'yes' to the question and even derive alternative prices.

I could have stayed in the US, but it was 1965 and the Vietnam war. My Indian upbringing had made me somewhat radical anyway but the Free Speech Movement at Berkeley, which I supported financially and in other ways, strengthened this radicalism. (My previous reading of Marx put me in a rare category on the left – a leftist who had read Marx!) To stay on in the US meant applying for immigrant status (the Green Card) and that made me eligible for the draft. Being 25, single, non-white, and not a student anymore, I was prime meat. So I decided to go elsewhere and again, with fortune smiling, I landed a job at the LSE.

I arrived in London in September 1965. This was the beginning of the LSE's golden period of econometrics and mathematical economics. Denis Sargan was already there and Hahn and Gorman were expected soon. I was, however, only an applied econometrician and worried that the LSE only cared for econometric theorists. Bill Phillips and Denis Sargan put me at ease, but the pace was very hectic.

However, I had no wish to stay a commodity model builder. I wanted to be a general applied econometrician, if not an economist. At Penn, although I started my early career as a number cruncher, the influence of Klein and of Sidney Weintraub made me forever suspicious of neoclassical economics. Weintraub gave me a taste for Fundamental [Paleo] Keynesianism. He insisted we read *The General Theory* and Joan Robinson's *Accumulation of Capital*, but avoid Patinkin's *Money, Interest and Prices* like the plague and ignore most of the 'Recent Developments in Economic Theory' (the title of his graduate course which I took).

Earlier in Bombay, I had the benefit of access to a superb library; we were also encouraged to read the originals. Marx one could not but read growing up in India in those days; Schumpeter, Hayek and Keynes we also read. In lieu of Marshall, I read the entire value debate in the *Economic Journal* starting with Clapham's 'Empty Economic Boxes' up to 1932.

All this helped as I began to shape my professional life, teaching and working in applied econometrics. At that time cliometrics had just come into being; I made contact with economic historians and gave a seminar on quantitative economic history which started my longlasting interest in that area (1968). I was also trying to break into macroeconomics and began modelling the stop-go problem with Brian Henry (1970b and 1975a). When the student rebellion of 1968 led to demands to learn Marxist economics, I began teaching it informally. This led to my first published book *Marxian Economic Theory* (1974). The book is noteworthy for perhaps three innovations: the emphasis on values being unobservable due to fetishism and hence the centrality of price value transformation; the need to integrate the three circuits of capital, especially money capital; and the lack of a proper theory of accumulation as evidenced by the debacle of Marx's *Schemes of Reproduction*. I pursued the last as a research theme through the mid-1970s but was discouraged by the total incomprehension with which my efforts were greeted by Marxists, neoclassicals and post-Keynesians. Some of this did, however, get into *Marxian Economics* which was published in 1979.

The other theme that I pursued (with the encouragement of the late Prof. Sukhamoy Chakravarty) was the Goodwin model of the class struggle (1973). This led to the insight that the Phillips curve is misunderstood: it is not a short-run causal relationship but a long-run equilibrium removed from the time domain (1975b). I cannot say that much notice was taken of this then or subsequently, but I think this insight is quite profound. Some of this spilled over into applied econometrics and subliminally may have helped in the construction of the LSE's econometric methodology. The idea was developed in Chapter 7 of my *Applied Econometrics* (1976).

By the mid 1970s, I had therefore established my main academic interests – applied econometrics, Keynesian macroeconomics, Marxian economics and economic history. I could not avoid writing on Indian political economy either and contributed to the *New Left Review* a long analysis of the Indian political situation (1970a). I visited CORE in 1976–77. It was here that I had the time to pursue some writing on monetary theory. This work was avowedly non-neoclassical (influence of Sidney Weintraub) and although my papers on this area have not yet been published, I learnt a great deal about what I should like economics to be.

The homogeneity postulate is for me the central problem in economics – classical, Marxian, neoclassical or Keynesian. 'Real' variables can only be defined *ex post* in a monetary economy and are hence meaningless for a behavioural theory of capitalist economy. Chapter 4 of *The General Theory* and Chapter 19 are thus for me central. Myrdal's *Monetary Equilibrium* expresses this even better than Keynes does. Of recent authors only Minsky and Victoria Chick seem to me to have followed this difficult path. At the same time long-run equilibria and steady states are also snares in my view. Ricardo is thus one of my least favourite authors though I recognize his strength as the principal enemy. The world has to be modelled, if at all, as a dynamic, monetary disequilibrium.

Towards the middle of the 1970s I also became alarmed at the rise of monetarism. Starting with an attempt to test Jerome Stein's model of the choice between monetarism and Keynesianism, I wrote *Testing Monetarism* in 1981, in which my interests in econometrics, the history of thought and my commitment to paleo Keynesianism are combined. In the 1980s I pursued this further as part of anti-monetarism/anti-Thatcherist economics, concluding this phase with a paper jointly with Guglielmo Weber, entitled 'A Keynesian Econometric Model of the UK Economy' (1988a).

More recently my work has been on the issues of poverty, famine and human development, the major influence here being Amartya Sen. This ties in with my interests in political economy as well as economic history. It helps me develop operational non-neoclassical models, although I have not yet integrated this work with the monetary theory that I hope to develop.

The collapse of socialism in 1989–90 has coincided with a plan I had previously formulated to write a book on Hayek. I regard Hayek as a role-model for anyone who is serious about his/her political views. Hayek abandoned technical economics in 1945 and spent the next 30 years perfecting the philosophical foundations of liberalism. If we are serious about socialism, a similar effort is needed, although I am not sure that personally I have the self-denial to abandon economics and take up the task of investigating the foundations of socialism. I do, however, find myself much attracted by the utopian-socialists and by *real* dissenting economists such as John Ruskin.

The late Joan Robinson once said to me, not as a compliment, that I was a splittist. I now realize what she meant. I am Keynesian but not post-Keynesian, neo- or new-Keynesian; Marxist but not Leninist, neo-Ricardian, Sraffian or Trotskyist; anti-neoclassical but that means Marshall as well as, if not more than, Walras. I suppose I must like being out on my own.

Desai's Major Writings

(1966), 'An Econometric Model of the World Tin Economy', *Econometrica*, **34**.
(1968), 'Some Issues in Econometric History', *Economic History Review*, **21**.
(1970a), 'The Vortex in India', *New Left Review*, **61**.
(1970b), 'An Econometric Model of the UK Economy' (with S.G.B. Henry), in K. Hilton and D.F. Heathfield (eds), *Econometric Study of the UK*, London: Macmillan.

(1973), 'Growth Cycles and Inflation in a Model of the Class Struggle', *Journal of Economic Theory*, **6**.
(1974), *Marxian Economic Theory*, Gray-Mills.
(1975a), 'Fiscal Policy Simulations for the UK Economy' (with S.G.B. Henry), *Review of Economic Studies*, **42**.
(1975b), 'The Phillips Curve: a Revisionist Interpretation', *Economica*, **42**.
(1976), *Applied Econometrics*, Deddington: Philip Allan.
(1979), *Marxian Economics*, Oxford: Basil Blackwell.
(1981), *Testing Monetarism*, London: Frances Pinter.
(1988a), 'A Keynesian Econometric Model of the UK Economy' (with G. Weber), *Journal of Applied Econometrics*, **3**.
(1988b), 'An Econometric Approach to the Measurement of Poverty' (with Anup Shah), *Oxford Economic Papers*, **40**.

Carlos F. DIAZ-ALEJANDRO (1937–1985)   BY *J. Gabriel Palma*

Carlos Diaz-Alejandro was born on the 18 July 1937 in Havana and died one day short of his 48th birthday in New York City. He studied for one year at Leicester Junior College in Massachusetts before moving to Miami University in Oxford, Ohio, where he spent 3 years. In the autumn of 1957 he joined the doctorate programme at MIT and in 1961, at the age of 24, he finished his well-known Ph.D. thesis on Argentina's 1955–61 exchange-rate devaluation experience.

His first academic post was at Yale's Growth Centre. After three years he moved to Minnesota where he remained for 5 years. In 1969, at the age of 32, he went back to Yale, becoming the youngest Full Professor ever at the Faculty of Economics there. In 1983 he accepted a new position at Columbia University, and his sudden death in July 1985 found him in the process of moving to a new appointment at Harvard.

During his sabbatical leaves he visited many universities outside the US; he was a frequent guest in many Latin American research centres, and he also advised many institutions including CEPAL (ECLA), UNCTAD, ILO, the Group of 24 and the World Bank. Among many other numerous activities he was a (dissenting) member of the Kissinger Commission on Central America. He made his presence in this Commission famous by his strong and open criticism of US support for the 'Contras' in Nicaragua, and by his insistence that the best way in which the US could contribute to Central American economic development was by fully tying economic assistance to human rights and by allowing free and unlimited access of their exports into the US market. Needless to say, this and other quixotic attempts to influence US foreign policy in Central America were never among his greatest successes!

From a professional point of view I have always admired both his outstanding intellect and his capacity to relate professionally and personally to a wide variety of people. The former gave us powerful insights into Latin America's trade and development, her economic and financial history, including her many financial crises. The latter was a quality unique in a profession filled with political and personal differences. From a personal point of view I admired his sense of humour and wit, his approachability, his 'bridge-building' capacity, his aversion for positions of administrative power, his independence of mind and his common sense.

One general characteristic of all his work was his constant concern with the real world; he was continuously addressing, with an impeccable analytical rigour, some of the most important and controversial issues of Latin America's economic development. His contributions were also characterized by a rare capacity to weave together history and theory, abstract economic theory with Latin American socio-political life, reality and ideas, analytic and synthetic work. He certainly learnt from his mentors Kindleberger, Prebisch, Hirschman and Lewis. Finally, his work was also characterized by attempts to make contributions to subjects that had been virtually exhausted theoretically but which very much needed empirical research, and by his political economy approach to these subjects.

In his doctoral dissertation for MIT (finished in 1961 and published in 1965), Diaz-Alejandro analysed the controversy between the 'elasticity' and 'absorption' approaches relating to the Argentinian experience of devaluation between 1956 and 1961. According to him, on balance, this experience tended to support the first approach to the analysis of the balance of payments more than the second. Regarding the failure of the whole stabilization package, of which the policy of devaluation formed a part, he concluded that what the policy package completely failed to take into account was the transitional period. To one situation characterized by controls and regulations, the policy package attempted to superimpose mechanically a totally new framework where structural problems, more permanent disequilibria, spending habits of the capitalist class (in particular their low propensity to invest) and so on were to be radically transformed overnight.

At the same time, he discussed in detail how one of the main mechanisms by which devaluation influences both the balance of payments and economic growth is through its effects on income distribution. For him the apparent paradox of many devaluations, leading to an improvement in the trade balance *and* in a decrease in domestic output, can be explained by a redistributive effect caused by the devaluation. He even suggested that in the context of a semi-industrialized economy the latter may be more important than the effect of devaluation on relative prices. Therefore, devaluation can be seen as another instrument in the struggle between different sectors of society over their share in the national product. He later returned to this issue in his 1963 paper (see *Selected Essays*, 1988), where he argued that if devaluation redistributes income from workers to capitalists, and the latter have a lower propensity to consume than the former, then devaluation may turn out to be contractionary even if it leads to an improvement in the tradeable balance. This argument tended to contradict some aspects of the absorption approach and to support an intuitive view of many Latin American governments. In this work he also distinguished the short- and long-term effects of devaluation, being more sceptical about the latter.

As far as the likely success of a stabilization plan in a semi-industrialized economy, his research also convinced him that:

> In the long run, the success or failure of a stabilization effort will depend more on the capacity of governments to obtain a national consensus over the objectives and policy instruments [of the stabilization plan] than on the approval or help that they could receive from foreign investors or governments and international agencies. (Quoted in A. Bianchi et al, p. 201; my translation.)

A by-product of his early work on Argentina was his 1970 book where he studied some selected features of Argentina's economic development since 1860. Firstly, he discussed the country's remarkable pre-1930 achievements, a period in which per capita income was not only very high – according to some estimates, at the turn of the century it was about the same as those of Germany and Holland, and higher than those of Italy and Sweden – but its growth was also one of the highest in the world. Diaz-Alejandro placed this exceptional performance within the framework of a particularly successful integration of Argentina into the world economy. Secondly, he contrasted the pre-1930 period with post-1930, which he found characterized by low and unstable economic growth, stagnation – and even decline – in export quantum and a significantly dissimilar performance of the various sectors of the economy. He discussed whether this was the result of domestic policies or unfavourable exogenous circumstances, concluding that the Argentine experience during this period was a dramatic example of the dangers of ignoring the necessary balance between the production of exportables, importables and non-tradables: for him, the most important lesson of post-war Argentine experience was that if there had been less discrimination against exports, manufacturing expansion would have been greater.

He then studied in greater detail the performance of the rural and industrial sectors, attempting to explain the dissimilar performance of the economy before and after 1930. Regarding the manufacturing sector he concluded that the inefficiency of many Argentine manufacturing activities arose not so much because, according to optimal resource allocation, they should never have been set up in the first place; rather, their inefficiency was a result of a system of protection that failed either to encourage the quick maturing of infant activities or to promote what is usually called 'X-efficiency'. Finally, he discussed the history of tariffs between 1910 and 1940, the paradox of apparently high investment rates and low growth since World War II, and the stop-go cycles of recent years, as well as the sources and mechanism of Argentine inflation.

Not surprisingly, this book provoked a major controversy in Argentina by presenting the pre-Peron period as having a far better economic performance; the fact that his book was published shortly before Peron's 'Wagnerian' return to Argentina heightened adverse reactions. In his usual manner he did not dodge the controversy, and told his Peronist critics that:

> I doubt that lasting social reforms can be promoted while spreading incomplete or distorted notions of the past, or that such reforms need be accompanied by inefficient economic policies. Bizarre (and slightly paranoid) notions about economic history have helped to generate many exotic policies that have neither accelerated growth nor brought Argentina closer to realizing her social and political goals (1970, p. xv).

Diaz-Alejandro was always keenly interested in Latin American economic history, writing extensively on the 1930s and 1940s. His best known article on the subject is 'Latin America in the 1930s' (see *Essays*, 1988). In this he attempted to identify the causes of the very dissimilar performances of various Latin American countries during the Great Depression. He concluded that the basic difference lay in some being 'active' in fighting the effects of the world recession, while others kept faith with the traditional 'passive' mechanism of adjustment. The 'active' countries were mainly the large ones, but included Chile and Uruguay; they performed much better than the 'passive' ones – in fact, even better than most advanced countries during this period. The 'active' nature of their policy response included the early abandonment of the gold standard and some 'intuitive' pre-Keynesianisms such as flexible monetary and fiscal policies, real devaluations, moratoria on their foreign debt and massive public works programmes. For Diaz-Alejandro this heterodox reaction of some countries came about largely because the effect of the 1929 Depression on Latin America was not only an economic shock, but also an ideological one:

> The emergence of a protectionist and nationalistic Center was perhaps the greatest shock to Latin American economies during the early 1930s. The memory of this betrayal of Hume and Ricardo would last longer in the Periphery than in the Center (1981, p. 8).

For Diaz-Alejandro, the decade of the 1940s in Latin America was both the golden age of import-substituting industrialization and the age where the first seeds of decline were sown. Prosperity was widespread, but the 'easy phase' of import-substitution was quickly approaching and policies (like tariffs and controls) were not adjusting. At the same time, the opportunity cost of import-substitution was increasing due to the commodity boom of the Korean war (see *Essays*, 1988).

Among his articles on the general subject of 'trade and development', Diaz-Alejandro first discussed some key issues of Latin American import-substituting industrialization such as the high import intensity of import-substitution; he then considered the problems of the transition from import-substituting industrialization to export-led growth (see 1988). While providing a substantial growth in manufacturing activities, post-war import-substituting industrialization had usually failed to reduce foreign exchange shortages and recurrent balance of payment crises; this phenomenon was the result of the need for large quantities of imported intermediate and investment goods. Diaz-Alejandro concluded in his article that the import content of import-substituting industrialization becomes a problem only when an economy is attempting *to increase* the rate of growth of manufacturing; otherwise, 'the direct impact of this year's investment on the demand for imports should be more than offset by last year's investment in the import-substituting industry now coming to fruition' (1988, p. 20).

Regarding the transition towards export-led growth, he thought that import-substituting industrialization did provide an appropriate foundation for export expansion (a substantial industrial base, know-how, skills, experience etc), but he did not believe that the first part of the cycle actually required the flood of regulations and controls typical of the early 1970s in Latin America. Nor did he think it necessary to have dramatic changes in resource allocation (as in Chile after 1973) in order to switch from one strategy to the other. In fact, some of the distortions associated with the 'import-substitution syndrome' (such as quantitative restrictions on imports and credit rationing with subsidized rates) could be turned around and used to encourage and pressure established firms to export. Finally, on the issue of whether export-led growth would be able to achieve both more rapid and more equitable rates of growth simultaneously, Diaz-Alejandro was particularly sceptical; for him, on this issue, as in most others in economics, it was very difficult 'to kill two birds with one stone'.

He favoured export-led growth but never believed it could automatically result from 'getting the prices right', nor that it was a remedy for all economics ills. It could reduce foreign exchange constraints and improve resource allocation, but its effects on income distribution and employment were more doubtful; then again, in an uncertain international economic environment, it could actually increase the likelihood of 'stop-go' macroeconomic cycles. In summary, for him (writing in vintage Diaz-Alejandro) the benefits of trade 'depend (to the dismay of the lazy, the impatient or the seeker of mass-mobilizing slogans) on the circumstances in which trade takes place' (1988, p. 285). Sometimes these circumstances may not be very helpful for LDCs' export-led growth:

> The industrialized world, riddled with unpredictable tariffs and import quotas, could turn [LDCs'] export drives into disasters. ... Advice that Third World countries should design their trade policies as if the state of the world economy did not matter, or as if [LDCs] were small at all times, suggests evangelical fervour rather than scientific analysis (1980, p. 332).

Another issue of continuous interest within this subject of trade and development was that of economic integration in the periphery. Although a vigorous advocate of the need for such integration in Latin America, Diaz-Alejandro warned against 'too much of a good thing'; in this case it could lead towards excessive trade diversions and increasing distortions (1988).

Diaz-Alejandro re-examined all these issues and ideas relating to trade and development in his third book (1975a) – this time within the context of the Colombian economy – and also in an article written in the same period (1975b). He concentrated in depth on the analysis of the obvious proposition that the mere liberalization of imports does not necessarily, *per se*, produce an export expansion. There are problems relating to institutional constraints, distributive effects, unemployment, resource mobility, price flexibility in both product and factor markets, inefficiencies in the financial markets, slowness of multinational companies to react to new investment opportunities in Latin America, and market 'segmentations'. All these factors could at best produce a substantial time lag between import and export expansion (which the capital account could finance) and, at worst, economic disruptions of such magnitude that the whole experiment of opening up the economy could fail.

Diaz-Alejandro also wrote extensively on North–South relations. His best known articles are *North–South Relations* and those included in the *Selected Essays* (1988). Although a strong advocate of international trade, he was always quick to ground his views in the real world. For him, the more competitive the international market, the more the LDCs can benefit from it because the less the developed countries can manipulate it in their favour. On the other hand, exaggerated pessimism regarding international markets can lead to even less desirable situations like excessive inward-looking development, as in Argentina:

> With unfortunate frequency these excesses [those of import-substituting industrialization] harm Argentine consumers and benefit 'incipient' foreign industrialists whose power cannot be termed 'infant' (1965, p. 280).

In his opinion, LDCs should look (and fight) for international markets characterized by (i) unintrusiveness (do economic arrangements carry inevitable political burdens?); (ii) decomposibility (are the goods and services provided in packages that can be broken up if the buyer only wants a part?);

and (iii) reversibility (can transactions and other arrangements be ended as desired?) He discussed several concrete cases and concluded that LDCs exporting sophisticated manufactured goods could expose themselves to a great degree of vulnerability. He believed that foreign direct investment by transnationals and transactions in international capital markets should also meet the above conditions.

In this context, he was also a critic of the IMF's interventions in markets which were not within its competence:

> It is the business of the IMF to insist on balance of payments targets consistent with the repayment of its short-term loans. [...] It is not the business of the IMF to make loans conditional on policies whose connection to the balance of payments in the short run or even the medium run is tenuous, such as food subsidies, utility rates, controls over foreign corporations, or whether the banking system is public or private. It was a brilliant administrative stroke for the IMF staff to develop the 'monetary approach to the balance of payments' during the 1950s, allowing the translation of balance of payments targets into those involving domestic credit, but for many LDCs the assumptions needed to validate such translation, such as a stable demand for money, have become less and less convincing (1988, p. 169).

Latin American economics of the 1970s and 1980s provided Diaz-Alejandro with another major intellectual challenge which he accepted with vigour and pleasure. Not since the 1930s had Latin America witnessed such dramatic economic and political experiments as those undertaken during the 1970s and 1980s. The new military regimes of the Southern Cone applied their 'Chicago-orientated' policies with a degree of ferocity rivalled only by their treatment of political dissent.

As Velasco has said, Diaz-Alejandro's wisdom was twice as useful because it was delivered in a timely fashion. His papers of the late 1970s contain the basic ideas which later became accepted wisdom regarding both the policy mistakes of the pro-Chicago governments in Latin America, and the irrational behaviour of borrowers and lenders (both private and public) in the international capital markets. He particularly questioned the applicability of the monetary approach to the following: the balance of payments in semi-industrialized economies, the feasibility of simultaneous current and capital account liberalization, the growth and the size of voluntary private capital inflows, and the use of an exchange-rate policy to fight inflation.

Among his many articles of this period, his 'Southern Cone Stabilization Plans' stands out (written in 1979 and first published in 1981; included in 1988). Appearing just before the Mexican moratoria which triggered the general debt crisis, it ran completely against the tide of opinion in the North, both in the economics profession and in financial markets. Those were the days in which the *Wall Street Journal*, the *Financial Times* and *The Econo-*

mist were praising the 'Chilean economic miracle' of apparent liberalization, stabilization and growth and applauding all other similar experiments in Latin America. They seemed to forget that the missing link was a massive and unsustainable increase in foreign borrowing: capital flows into Chile in 1981 were two-and-a-half times larger than in 1979, and larger than total exports. The financial press of the North was not alone in getting it wrong however: in that year, shortly before the Mexican crisis, Paul Volker said that the recycling process had not yet pushed exposure of either borrowers or lenders to an unreasonable or unsustainable point in the aggregate, especially for US banks; the British Chancellor, Sir Geoffrey Howe, praised private banks for the success of their recycling process; a top executive of a leading British bank predicted that any slowdown in lending to LDCs in the 1980s would be due more to a fall in *demand* than to any general unwillingness to maintain the supply of finance; and the Director of the Western Hemisphere Department of the IMF claimed that overborrowing was very unlikely to happen in the LDCs' private sector (see Marcel and Palma, 1988).

A series of external shocks compounded the domestic policy mistakes in the early 1980s; these, together with the Centre's abrupt cessation of lending and drastic reduction in imports, were a recipe for disaster. A detailed analysis of the dynamics of this crisis was the last – and probably best known – of Diaz-Alejandro's contributions. The originality of the titles of these papers match the quality of their analysis, some examples being 'Latin American Debt: I Don't Think We are in Kansas Anymore', 'Open Economy, Closed Polity?' and 'Good-bye Financial Repression, Hello Financial Crash' (in 1988).

There can be little doubt that Carlos Diaz-Alejandro was the best Latin American economist of his generation and one of the best economists in the world on the subjects of trade and development. He was always intrigued to understand how the Latin American economies really worked. Most of his contributions originated in the examination of specific problems, invariably those which were the most important, controversial and often most difficult. His economics was always grounded in the real world. His work on economic history was permeated by the idea that history, no matter what history, is always of the present. As in the case of Prebisch, he basically belonged to the 'markets are good servants, but bad masters' Keynesian school of economic thought. By studying economic problems in their historical context, he avoided the sterility of pure formal theory that characterized so much of the economics of his own generation and the next.

He began his professional life in what must have been very difficult personal circumstances; he started his graduate programme at MIT when Fidel Castro landed clandestinely in Cuba and finished at the time of Bay of

Pigs. Those 4 years, the most dramatic of Cuba's troubled history, were very traumatic for him; in the most difficult decision of his life, he decided to remain as an academic in the US: courage does not always involve combat; 'they also serve who only stand and wait'.

It was not that he was unable to take a stand on difficult political issues. In 1975, for example, he told me that if the choice was Castro or Pinochet (which at that time looked increasingly like the only alternatives available to Latin America), he would not hesitate for a second in supporting Fidel Castro. What he longed for was a social democratic alternative with what he always called 'social-democratic economic policies'. These would include social-democratic stabilization policies where aggregate demand management remained essential, but where fairer income distribution and allocation of adjustment cost, incomes policies, export subsidies, capital controls, etc would all play a key role as well (see, for example, 'IMF Conditionality: What Kind?' in 1988).

After his decision to remain in the US, Cuba became such a sensitive issue that he could never write about her economy or history; it was only months before his sudden death that he decided to break this taboo and write a paper on Cuba for a project on Latin America's export-led growth before 1914 organized by Rosemary Thorp, myself and other friends. His death left us all feeling so empty that the project never took off.

We will never know whether he would have liked to be called a 'dissenting' economist. Nevertheless, as one of his colleagues once said about him, he was an economist who always 'respected history, used data carefully and theory selectively'. I think that, given the present state of our profession, one cannot be more 'dissenting' than that!

Diaz-Alejandro's Major Writings

(1965), *Exchange Rate Devaluation in a Semi-Industrialized Country: The Experience of Argentina 1955–1961*, Cambridge, Mass: MIT Press.

(1970), *Essays on the Economic History of the Argentine Republic*, New Haven: Yale University Press.

(1975a), *Foreign Trade Regimes and Economic Development: Colombia*, National Bureau of Economic Research.

(1975b), 'Trade Policy and Economic Development' in P. Kenan (ed), *International Trade and Finance*, CUP.

(1975c), 'North-South Relations: The Economic Component', *International Organization*, Winter.

(1980), 'Discussions', *American Economic Review*, **70**, Papers and Proceedings.

(1981), 'Stories of the 1930s for the 1980s', *NBER* Conference Paper No 130, November.

(1988), *Trade, Development and the World Economy: Selected Essays of Carlos Diaz-Alejandro* (ed by A. Velasco), Oxford: Blackwell.

Other References

Bianchi, A. (1985), Garcia, E., Ffrench-Davis, R. and Tockman, V., 'In Memoriam: Carlos Diaz-Alejandro (1937–1985)', *Colección estudios CIEPLAN*, **18**.

Calvo, G., Findlay, R., Kouri, P. and Braga de Macedo, J. (1989), *Debt, Stabilization and Development: Essays in Memory of Carlos Diaz-Alejandro*, Oxford: Basil Blackwell.

Marcel M. and Palma, J.G. (1988), 'Third World Debt and its Effects on the British Economy: A Southern View on Economic Mismanagement in the North', *Cambridge Journal of Economics*, 12, September.

Maurice Herbert DOBB (1900–1976)

BY *B.J. McFarlane and B.H. Pollitt*

Maurice H. Dobb was the foremost scholar of his day in Marxian political economy. Books such as *Political Economy and Capitalism* (1937), *Studies in the Development of Capitalism* (1946) and *Soviet Economic Development since 1917* (1948) were published in many editions and languages. Through these works and through subsequent writings on the theory and practice of planning and growth, as well as the economics of welfare, Dobb exercised an international influence over generations of readers. The versatility of Dobb's contributions to the arena of political economy and economic history was matched by the constancy of his interest in the historical foundation and evolution of economic and social ideas. This was the subject of his final major work, *Theories of Value and Distribution since Adam Smith* (1973).

Dobb was born on 24 July 1900 in London. He was educated at the Charterhouse School and at Pembroke College, Cambridge. His lively undergraduate career there was followed by research for his Ph.D. at the London School of Economics. He returned to Cambridge as a Lecturer in economics in 1924 and was a Fellow of Trinity College from 1948. He retired from his university post as Reader in economics in 1967.

Dobb's first book, *Capitalist Enterprise and Social Progress*, (1925), grew out of his doctoral research on 'The Entrepreneur'. While it laid a formal base for his academic career in the 1920s, as well as for a number of lecture courses, he later described this work as 'an unsuccessful and jejune attempt to combine the notion of surplus-value and exploitation with the theory of Marshall' (1978, p. 117).

Of far greater interest to him at that time was the fate of socialist development in Soviet Russia, and in the summer of 1925 he availed himself of an unusual opportunity to study Soviet political economy at first hand by living and working in Moscow. A substantial account of *Russian Economic Development since the Revolution* appeared under that title in 1928. Professional studies of the Soviet economy were then virtually unknown and the informative value of the book was widely appreciated, notably by economists such as J.M. Keynes and D.H. Robertson who had themselves made brief visits to Moscow at that time.

Throughout the 1920s and 1930s, Dobb made original contributions to institutional economics (such as his Cambridge economic handbook on *Wages*) and to Marxist discussions of theories of value, crisis and imperialism. Of these works, the best-known was *Political Economy and Capitalism* (1937). In retrospect, Dobb regarded this book as having been too hastily written (1978, p. 119); he felt its polemics did not adequately assimilate the challenge to orthodox economic theory then being mounted by Keynes and his followers. For several generations of Dobb's readers, however, it was the most trenchant critique of its day of the foundations of modern Western economic theory.

In the 1940s, Dobb's interest in economic history found expression in his seminal contribution to what were to become internationally influential debates on the transition from feudalism to capitalism. His ideas on this were initially shaped in the discussions of a group of British Marxist historians that included Dona Torr, Christopher Hill and Rodney Hilton. His own historical writing was distinguished by his deployment of the Marxist theory of surplus expropriation under different institutional and societal conditions, culminating with the publication of his *Studies in the Development of Capitalism* (1946). He was fond of quoting the historian Marc Bloch's assessment of the feudal system as one in which the medieval lord 'lived off the labour of other men'. For Dobb, such a description wrote on feudalism's face what its essential character really was. Capitalism, by contrast, was a commodity-producing, contractual society ruled by competition. The fact of exploitation was less obvious and had to be explained. In Dobb's view, Karl Marx had successfully reconciled the existence of surplus-value (as the new form of exploitation in capitalist society) with the rule of the market, the 'law of value' and the exchange relationships of universal 'commodity relations'.

By 1948, Dobb's work on the theme of value and price, including the transformation problem, had focused his attention upon Ricardo's notion of natural price and his 'exceptions' to the pure theory of value. In that same year he was invited to assist Piero Sraffa in the preparation of the Royal Economic Society's edition of Ricardo's *Works*. He came superbly equipped for what was to become a major task of intellectual midwifery: he was not only a longstanding personal friend of Sraffa's but was also one of the few individuals who could share with him a deep knowledge of and sympathy with the approach to economics of both Ricardo and Marx (Pollitt, 1988).

His interest in Ricardo's theory of economic growth (and in the fetters on that growth that could lead to a 'stationary state') was apparent during a lecture tour in India in 1950–51, most notably in lectures delivered to the Delhi School of Economics (1951). These discussed three major dynamic factors influencing economic growth: the division of labour, the accumulation of capital, and technical progress – these last two being regarded in reality as inseparable. He argued that new investment would generally stimulate qualitative improvements in the coefficients of production as well as quantitative increases in the stock of capital. A newly-developing economy must be assisted by policies that tapped investment-led productivity of both the 'widening' and the 'deepening' variety. To do this it must ward off those underlying trends towards a stationary state that had been pointed to by D. Ricardo and J.S. Mill; that is, a low growth of productivity in agriculture, financial bottlenecks and a low rate of profit in industry. In these lectures, Dobb drew out the strong similarities to be found in the approaches of Marx and Ricardo, and he corrected a number of misconceptions about Ricardo's analysis of growth and distribution. In all this the imprint of his recent joint labours with Sraffa was very evident.

With the main volumes of Ricardo's *Works* completed, Dobb turned to a detailed study of the planned economies of the USSR and Eastern Europe. This built on the expanded and updated treatment of the Soviet economy that he had published in 1948 as *Soviet Economic Development since 1917*. Two features of this work proved to be of special interest. Firstly, it demonstrated the close similarity between military strategy and the processes of central-ized economic planning when the objective pursued was a rapid emergence from industrial backwardness. Secondly, it provided an authoritative account of the 'Great Debate' in Soviet economics between the so-called 'teleological' and 'genetic' schools of planning. Dobb showed that the 'teleologists' adopted what was essentially an engineering approach, concentrating almost exclu-sively on the physical-technical properties of the economic system – an outlook that was attractive to the Party leadership of the day. The 'geneti-cists', by contrast, stressed the constraints upon growth imposed by structural bottlenecks and emphasized the need for inter-sectoral balance in the growth process. In the course of his exposition, Dobb introduced to his Western readership many of the great names of Soviet economic literature such as Strumilin, Sokolnikov, Feldman, Shanin and Kovalevsky, while his outline of the debates of the 1920s manifestly influenced the approach later of writers such as Alexander Erlich and Evsey Domar.

From the 1950s, Dobb's writings on planning in the socialist economies were concerned with pricing, investment planning, investment fluctuations and the advantages and disadvantages of central planning. In his *An Essay on Economic Growth and Planning*, Dobb gave quantitative precision to proposi-tions concerning the rate of investment, the distribution of investment between sectors, the choice of technique as well as methods of selecting investment projects in a centrally planned economy. He attacked the neoclassical pre-scription that an underdeveloped or socialist economy should choose a rate of investment according to some principle of time-discount. (At this time, the more extreme 'anti-planners' in the academic world and in the research secre-tariats of the UN were advocating that private markets should be the sole determinants of investment rates in society and in economic plans.) He was also concerned to combat an influential corollary, derived from doctrines of comparative cost and marginal productivity, according to which an underdeveloped country with surplus labour must always choose techniques of production which economize on capital. Dobb argued against the primacy of time-discount as a criterion of the rate of growth to be pursued, stressing the significance of other determinants of investment that were derived from the conditions of production. The key investment determinants developed in his own model were, firstly, the productive capacity of the capital goods sector and, secondly, the surplus of production of consumer goods over the self-consumption of the producers in the consumer goods sector. A number of academic economists not usually sympathetic to Dobb's outlook reviewed his *Essay* quite favourably and, unusually, (since the Soviet Academy had generally neglected Dobb's theoretical work), he was invited to outline his book to Gosplan in Moscow in 1962. But his advocacy of a choice of techniques that maximized economic surplus and growth rather than employment – a position reflecting his sympathy for prevailing socialist strategies of development – was a controversial one and it brought him into conflict with, among others, Michal Kalecki and Joan Robinson.

Dobb's interest in growth theory prompted him to revive, in 1955, the pioneering growth model first published in the Soviet Union by G.A. Feldman – a model more broadly publicized among Western economists by Evsey Domar (1957). During his frequent visits to Eastern Europe in the 1950s and 1960s, he was known to stress the richness of the Soviet literature of the 1920s on growth theory and to complain of its comparative neglect. In the West, American economists such as Erlich and Spulber had publicized much of this early work but had failed to evaluate it fittingly. Dobb did so, however, in some penetrating articles on the early Soviet discussions on economic growth (1967). In the process, he made a notable contribution of his own to the theory of growth of socialist economies, anticipating some of what later appeared in Michal Kalecki's classic work on this subject (1972).

After his formal retirement from Cambridge University in 1967, Dobb concerned himself primarily with three areas of teaching and research. The first was the revived interest in the British Classical school of political economy, most notably in the methods of Adam Smith, David Ricardo and Karl Marx. The second was a (related) preoccupation with the implications of Piero Sraffa's work (1960) for capital theory and for both Marxian and so-called 'neoclassical' economic theory. Finally, he maintained a continuing interest in the reform movement in Eastern Europe and the USSR.

Dobb's interest in classical economics, already evidenced in his earlier work on Ricardo, was given fresh impetus in the late 1960s and the 1970s. In 'Some Notes on Ricardo and his Thought', published in a *Festschrift* for

Jurgen Kuczynski in 1969, he drew attention to the close affinity of Ricardo and Marx on such issues as the significance of surplus, the uniform rate of profit, and the distinction between market and 'natural' prices. Dobb underlined the high respect in which Ricardo was held by Marx for his scientific honesty – his 'errors of genius'. This restated a message made more explicitly in Dobb's 1961 review of Sraffa's *Production of Commodities by Means of Commodities* to the effect that there was a distinctive 'line of thought' which stretched from Quesnay to Ricardo to Marx. In all their approaches, the common key question posed was: what is the origin of economic surplus? To this were added the complementary questions as to how the surplus was accumulated and which social classes shared in it.

Dobb's ideas on this 'line of development' in the history of economic thought featured prominently in the prestigious Marshall Lectures which he delivered at Cambridge in 1973. His view contrasted with the more generally received wisdom concerning a developing intellectual inheritance that had been handed down from Smith to J.S. Mill, and from Mill to Marshall and Jevons.

Equally prominent in these lectures was the role ascribed to ideology in the shaping of economic theory. The kernel of the argument was expressed to W. Brus in a letter of 25 July 1973: while it 'manages... to have some positive insights, and hence scientific elements (including of course purely technical aids)', economics, 'since it is a study of historically-developing society is *essentially* ideological, in the sense of an artifact of a particular social philosophy and outlook on society...'. This view was not held with the same force by other Marxist economists such as R.L. Meek, W. Brus and O. Lange, but Dobb's analysis of the writings and activities of figures like Senior and Jevons had given him a different perspective on the vexed issue of 'economics and ideology' – a perspective expounded more fully in his *Theories of Value and Distribution since Adam Smith* (1973).

The critique of so-called 'neoclassical' theory, notably stimulated by Sraffa's work of 1960, was a second, related, area of interest for Dobb in the final years of his life. In a paper delivered to a seminar at Manchester in 1969, and rewritten and published in 1970, Dobb made a vigorous entry into the so-called 'Cambridge Controversies' on capital theory. He argued that neoclassical theory was inadequate as a macroeconomic theory of production and distribution, and stressed that the connection between this theory and the classical school of economic thought was a spurious one. Dobb was later to warn against an 'ultra-left' approach to Ricardo that he thought to be too negative (see, for instance, 1976), and he urged younger Marxists to build on Sraffa's 'critique from within'.

Dobb did not live to see the collapse of the ruling regimes of the centrally-planned economies of Eastern Europe at the end of the 1980s, but from the early 1960s he had himself educated his Western readers in some of their structural economic defects. In *Socialist Planning: Some Problems*, for example, he stressed the significance of a shift from the 'extensive' phase of development, where growth is generated primarily by a larger workforce and forced savings, to an 'intensive' phase in which growth depended upon a modernization of the capital stock and an improved real product per man-hour. He drew most of his examples from Soviet and East European experience which pointed to the need for urgent reforms in the planning system. On the demand side, he showed that the growing complexity of the socialist economies required more serious attention to be paid to the structure of personal and social needs. This in turn pointed to the desirability of expanding the role for decentralized forms of management and decision-making. The case he advanced for decentralization and for an extension of democracy at the level of the factory floor was strengthened by his argument that many of the problems in socialist planning grew out of a conflict between pressures for operational speed, originating in 'planning from above', and the realities of shop-floor conditions.

In Dobb's view, the key obstacle to reform in the planned economies was an entrenched, conservative State bureaucracy. He suggested that such a bureaucracy had blocked reform in the Soviet economy from at least 1965; and had thwarted the efforts of economists such as Brus and Sik (both of whom Dobb supported) to advance reforms in the economies of Eastern Europe more generally.

Dobb's opinions on matters such as these did not square with the appraisals of some writers who portrayed him as an uncritical, lifelong apologist of the Soviet system (see Blaug and Storges, 1983). It was apparently not sufficiently well-known that, although a member of the British Communist party from 1922 until his death, his early writings, as epitomized by his booklet *On Marxism Today* (1932), had been vilified by Communist party spokesmen for their 'non-Marxist' character. Later, in 1956, he witnessed and was profoundly shocked by the suppression of a workers' demonstration in Poznan, Poland; he also publicly condemned his party's uncritical support for armed Soviet intervention in Hungary in the same year. In his support for the reform movement in Eastern Europe, he tended to be associated with a minority wing in his party from 1956; this changed only in 1968 when the British Communist party, with others in Western Europe, condemned the crushing by Soviet tanks of Dubcek's 'Prague spring' and 'Socialism with a human face'.

Dobb's dissidence, then, consisted primarily of a lifelong endeavour to combat Marshallian orthodoxy in economics. This was complemented by a quieter struggle, conducted from 1956, against Stalinism in the political economy of socialism. In his vision of the scope and method of political economy, he followed Ricardo and Marx. Perhaps less felicitously for some of his admirers, he also followed Marx in writing little about his own broader personal vision of socialist society.

Dobb's Major Writings

(1925), *Capitalist Enterprise and Social Progress*, London: Routledge.

(1928a), *Russian Economic Development since the Revolution*, London: Routledge.

(1928b), *Wages*, Cambridge: Cambridge University Press.

(1932), *On Marxism Today*, London: Hogarth Press.

(1937), *Political Economy and Capitalism*, London: Routledge.

(1939), Review of M. Kalecki's 'Essays on the Theory of Economic Fluctuations' in *Daily Worker*, London, 22 March.

(1946), *Studies in the Development of Capitalism*, London: Routledge.

(1948), *Soviet Economic Development since 1917*, London: Routledge and Kegan Paul.

(1951), *Some Aspects of Economic Development*, New Delhi: Ranjit.

(1955), 'Some Questions on Economic Growth', *Indian Journal of Economics*, July.

(1960), *An Essay on Economic Growth and Planning*, London: Routledge and Kegan Paul.

(1961), 'An Epoch-Making Book', *Labour Monthly*, London.

(1967), *Papers on Capitalism, Development and Planning*, London: Routledge and Kegan Paul.

(1969), *Welfare Economics and the Economics of Socialism*, Cambridge: Cambridge University Press.

(1970a), Some Reflections on the Sraffa System and the Critique of the so-called Neoclassical Theory of Value and Distribution', *De Economist*.

(1970b), *Socialist Planning: Some Problems*, London: Lawrence and Wishart.

(1973), *Theories of Value and Distribution since Adam Smith: Ideology and Economic Theory*, Cambridge: Cambridge University Press.

(1976), 'A Note on the Ricardo-Marx Discussion', *Science and Society*, **34**.

(1978), 'Random Biographical Notes', *Cambridge Journal of Economics* 2(2).

Other References

Blaug, M. and Sturges, P. (1983), *Who's Who in Economics*, Brighton: Harvester Wheatsheaf Books.

Domar, E. (1957), *Essays in Theory of Economic Growth*, Oxford: Oxford University Press.

Kalecki, M. (1972), *Selected Essays on the Economic Growth of the Socialist and Mixed Economy*, Cambridge: Cambridge University Press.

McFarlane, B.J. (1984), 'McFarlane on Dobb', in H.W. Spiegel and W.J. Samuels (eds), *Contemporary Economists in Perspective*, Vol 1, Greenwich, Conn. and London: JAI Press.

Pollitt, B.H. (1988), 'The Collaboration of Maurice Dobb in Sraffa's Edition of Ricardo', *Cambridge Journal of Economics*, **12**.

Sraffa, P. (1951–73), *Works and Correspondence of David Ricardo*, Cambridge: Cambridge University Press.

Sraffa, P. (1960), *Production of Commodities by Means of Commodities*, Cambridge: Cambridge University Press.

John EATWELL (born 1945) *Marina Colonna*

Born on the 2 February, 1945, John Eatwell was educated at Headlands Grammar School, Swindon, and at Queens' College, Cambridge, graduating in 1967 with a first-class degree in the Economics Tripos. He won a Kennedy Scholarship to Harvard University (1967–69), receiving the A.M. degree in 1969. He also received his Ph.D. from Harvard in 1975 for a thesis entitled 'Scarce and Produced Commodities: an Examination of Some Fundamentals in the Theory of Value from Ricardo to Walras'. In 1969 he had returned to Cambridge to take up a Research Fellowship at Queens' College, moving to a full teaching fellowship at Trinity College in 1970, a post he still holds. In 1975 Eatwell was appointed an Assistant Lecturer in the Faculty of Economics at Cambridge, being promoted to a Lectureship two years later. Since 1982 he has held a Visiting Professorship at the New School for Social Research, New York. He has also held Visiting Professorships at the universities of Columbia (1976), Massachusetts (1978) and Amsterdam (1982). In 1986 Eatwell became the Economic Adviser to Neil Kinnock, the Leader of the Labour party.

As an undergraduate Eatwell was greatly influenced by his supervisor, Ajit Singh, and by the lectures of Joan Robinson, Nicholas Kaldor and Luigi Pasinetti. Later his approach to economics was shaped by reading Pierangelo Garegnani's Cambridge Ph.D. dissertation (published in Italian in 1960 as *Il Capitale nelle Teorie della Distribuzione*) and by conversations at Trinity with Piero Sraffa. Throughout the 1970s he attempted both to develop the implications both of the critique of the neoclassical theory of capital (especially the implications for the Walrasian approach to neoclassical theory) and to assess the positive dimensions of Sraffa's rehabilitation of the classical analysis of value and distribution. In the early 1980s, his career took a new course. He had spent some time in Mexico in the late 1970s, working with Vladimir Brailovsky on applied policy problems. Now concern with the persistent problems of the British economy, and aversion to the damage being wrought by the policies of Margaret Thatcher's government, led him to the study of problems of economic policy in Britain, and in the West as a whole. His approach to these problems was influenced by the work of Wynne Godley and others at the Cambridge Department of Applied Economics. But his thinking evolved in a rather different direction. Study of economic policy in France and Germany suggested that sustainable long-run growth is associated with the application of measures which encourage and support long-term industrial investment in a context of macroeconomic stability, rather than with 'fine-tuning'. These ideas were first spelt out in a series for BBC television entitled 'Whatever Happened to Britain?' and in a book of the same title (1982). They were later developed in research work for the Labour party, providing some of the foundations for the reformulation of Labour party economic policy in the late 1980s.

Eatwell's work in economics is based on two complementary approaches to economic theory: on the one hand classical political economy and Sraffa's restatement of its theory of value and distribution, and on the other the particular approach to Keynesian economics dominant in Cambridge till the late 1970s, when a large group of economists was still working under the influence of Robinson, Kahn and Kaldor. His contributions cover a range of topics which can be grouped in three main classes: the critique of neoclassical theory in both its old and new versions; the restatement of a theoretical core alternative to neoclassical theory; and the use of that theoretical core in the interpretation of current economic problems. Since 1977, Eatwell has also been active in supporting and spreading the works of other economists following a similar path, both through collaborative writings, and through his editorial work. He helped found the *Cambridge Journal of Economics* (1977) and worked on its editorial board until 1985. Together with Murray Milgate and Giancarlo de Vivo, he established the journal *Contributions to Political Economy* (1982). He also edits the book series *Studies in Political Economy* for Academic Press (first 4 vols) and Macmillan (subsequent volumes).

Eatwell's rejection of neoclassical theory and policy rests on his original acceptance of the outcome of the debate, in the 1960s, concerning the logical foundations of the neoclassical theory of value and distribution and, in particular, concerning its treatment of capital as a factor of production. As Eatwell argued in 1990, 'capital theory is not a "branch" of economics, it is about the determination of prices in an economy with reproducible means of production ... simply the price theory of the economies in which we actually live'. The attempt to solve the problem of reproducible means of production via many markets (the endowment of capital goods being expressed as a vector, each capital good measured in its own 'technical units') has proved to be a 'solution' only at the cost of abandoning the concept of competitive long-run equilibrium. The traditional long-run equilibrium, with the associated uniform rate of profit and long-run prices, has been replaced by a new definition. In this new 'equilibrium' there is full mobility of all factors service between alternative uses and yet the prices of the services of capital goods are not generally compatible with a uniform rate of profit on the supply prices of the respective capital goods. This methodological and analytical shift, first pointed out by Garegnani (1976), raises a number of difficulties and involves far-reaching consequences which are commonly underestimated or ignored.

Eatwell examined these questions in an analysis of the relationship between the notion of competition and that of equilibrium (1982b). He argued that the new notion of equilibrium is a hybrid in which competition has its full effect on the markets for non-reproducible factor services, but in which the competitive adjustment of production to demand is limited in the case of capital goods. Consequently the new definition cannot be a 'centre of gravitation'; hence any short-term imperfections cannot be treated as deviations from equilibrium – instead they define a variety of new 'equilibria'.

In classical political economy, as well as in early neoclassical theory, the behaviour of a capitalist market economy was studied in terms of long-period competitive positions and the associated uniform rate of profit, which the persistent force of competition tends to establish. Competition is the central organizing concept which establishes the object of analysis, natural prices and the general rate of profit. It is a process which enforces and expresses the attempts of individual capitals to maximize profits (as in the case of classical political economy), or of individual agents to maximize utility, subject to the constraints of technology and endowment (as in the case of neoclassical theory). Eatwell pointed out that the assumption of price-taking behaviour, and hence of perfect competition, which are required in the neoclassical theory of value, led to a significant change in the notion of competition from that adopted by classical economists. The classical idea was dominated by the notion of mobility. But competition is now defined in terms of the infinity of infinitesimally small agents which generates the price-taking behaviour required by neoclassical theory. This latter proposition derives from the logical requirements of the neoclassical theory of value, and therefore makes the notion of competition a 'theory-generated concept'.

Eatwell also raised the question of how these 'short-period' general equilibria should be interpreted or, more precisely, in what sense they can be defined as 'competitive'. Their short-period character derives from the necessity of specifying the stock of producible means of production as a vector, with the result that the capital stock will not in general be appropriate to the structure of demand. But as Eatwell has argued, 'since the theory requires profit maximization as a basic behavioural postulate, the short period is a position from which, given the possibility of mobility, the economy would tend to move away'. Thus, some of the major factors (capital endowment) which general equilibrium theory regards as determining prices and quantities are themselves subject to change. According to Eatwell, this peculiarity, which in fact makes it difficult to distinguish the accidental from the persistent, has required a further change in the notion of competition: 'since the old definition [incorporating mobility] would expose this deficiency, the meaning of the term "competitive" has been redefined in terms of price-taking behaviour to make it consistent with changed method'.

On the other hand, Eatwell has also shown that Hicks's and Nuti's claim that the neo-Austrian approach to capital theory possesses all the analytical advantages of the von Neuman-Sraffa method – the uniqueness of the internal rate of return in a general model – may be valid only in a context of *partial* analysis (1975b).

Eatwell's approach to Keynesian economics has been expounded in several publications, most importantly in *Keynes's Economics and The Theory of Value and Distribution* (1983). His starting point is that a satisfactory theory of output must be associated with a theory of value and distribution. Given that coherent theories of output and distribution are long run, then the theory of output and employment must determine the normal or long-run positions of the system.

Keynes's analysis in the *General Theory* is couched in terms of the utilization of a given capital stock – a short-period position. Yet Eatwell argues that to sustain Keynes's case for an underemployment equilibrium, his analysis must be placed in a long-period setting, in which prices are at normal levels and the composition of production is adjusted to the composition of demand. Otherwise Keynes would have added little to the prevailing analysis of unemployment as a short-period rigidity. Eatwell's case for a long-period interpretation of the *General Theory* is reinforced by Keynes's assertion that his theory is designed 'to explain the outstanding features of our actual experience; namely, that we oscillate ... round an intermediate position appreciably below full employment and appreciably above the minimum employment a decline below which would endanger life' (Keynes, 1936, p. 254).

Eatwell's long-period interpretation of the *General Theory* contrasts sharply with the predominant identification of Keynes's analysis with 'short-period equilibrium'. However, he argues that confining Keynes's theory to a short period leads to its ready absorption into neoclassical analysis. Whilst in a long-period competitive equilibrium, a neoclassical model will display full employment, in the short-period there is no necessity for markets to clear. A variety of 'imperfections', social and institutional – such as sticky wages and prices, sticky interest rates, or the disruptive impact of uncertainty and expectations – can prevent the economy from reaching full employment. From this perspective, there is an underlying similarity in the large variety of such models of 'Keynesian' unemployment. In all of them, if the particular aspect of the economic system which gives rise to market failure were absent, then the system would tend towards the full employment of labour. None of these explanations is considered by Eatwell to deal with the central issue of the *General Theory* - the establishment of an 'under-employment equilibrium' by the normal working of the saving-investment relationship through the multiplier.

Eatwell argues, on both textual and logical ground, that Keynes rejected the idea that there is any tendency for a market economy to adjust towards full employment. While Keynes argued that the economy is self-adjusting in the sense that processes yield definite outcomes, he denied that the process of adjustment could be expressed in terms of orthodox price theory.

Following the argument first advanced by Garegnani (1964), Eatwell suggests that the absorption of Keynes's analysis into neoclassical theory and its consequent confinement to the short run can be traced to weaknesses in Keynes's theories of the rate of interest and of the determination of investment. Keynes's monetary theory of the rate of interest is seriously weakened by the fact that the speculative motive is based on the relationship between the current rate of interest and the normal or long-run rate. The possibility was therefore left open that in the long run the normal rate would be determined by the long-run relationship of the supply and demand for capital. Moreover, Keynes's use of the traditional marginal efficiency (productivity) of capital function forced him to defend his theory of unemployment on the basis of 'rigidities' in the interest rate (the failure of the interest rate to fall to a level associated with a full-employment rate of investment). Far better, suggests Eatwell, to reject the very notion of a well-behaved demand function for capital (investment) and link Keynes's principle of effective demand to the classical theory of value which does not rest on the proposition of the clearing of all factor markets.

Eatwell's Major Writings

(1973a), *An Introduction to Modern Economics* (with Joan Robinson), McGraw-Hill.

(1973b), 'Mr. Sraffa's Standard Commodity and the Rate of Exploitation', *Ekonomista*, 4 (in Polish); published in English, *Quarterly Journal of Economics*, 89.

(1974), 'Money Wage Inflation in Industrial Countries' (with J. Llewellyn and R. Tarling), *Review of Economic Studies*, 41.

(1975a), 'The Importance of Ricardo's "Essay on Profits"', *Economica*, 42.

(1975b), 'A Note on the Truncation Theorem', *Kyklos*, 28.

(1976), 'Irving Fisher's "Rate of Return over Cost" and the Rate of Profit in a Capitalistic Economy', in M. Brown, K. Sato, and P. Zarembka (eds), *Essays in Modern Capital Theory*, Amsterdam: North-Holland.

(1977), 'The Irrelevance of Returns to Scale in Sraffa's System', *Journal of Economic Literature*, 15.

(1982a), *Whatever Happened to Britain?*, London: Duckworth, American edition with additional chapter, New York: Oxford University Press, 1983.

(1982b), 'Competition', in I. Bradley and M. Howard (eds), *Classical and Marxian Political Economics*, Macmillan.

(1983a), *Keynes's Economics and the Theory of Value and Distribution* (edited with M. Milgate), London: Duckworth. American edition, New York: Oxford University Press, 1984.

(1983b), 'Between Two Worlds: Interest Groups, Class Structure and Capitalist Growth' (with S. Bowles), in D. Mueller (ed), The *Political Economy of Growth*, New Haven: Yale University Press.

(1983c), 'The Long-Period Theory of Unemployment', *Cambridge Journal of Economics*, 7.

(1984), 'Economic Theory and Political Power' (with R. Green), in B. Pimlott (ed), *Fabian Essays in Socialist Thought*, Aldershot: Gower.

(1985), 'Keynes, Keynesians, and British economic policy', in H. Wattel (ed), *The Policy Consequences of John Maynard Keynes*, New York: Sharpe.

(1987), *The New Palgrave. A Dictionary of Economics* (edited with M. Milgate and P. Newman), 4 Vols, London: Macmillan. Entries written by J. Eatwell: Absolute and exchangeable value (with M. Milgate and P. Newman); Competition: classical conceptions; Cost of production; Difficulty or facility of production; Imperfectionist models; Import substitution and export-led growth; Keynesianism; Marginal efficiency of capital; Natural and

normal conditions; Offer; Own rates of interest; Propensity to consume; Return to scale; Socially necessary technique; Standard commodity; Walras's theory of capital; Zero-profit condition; Sraffa, Piero (with C. Panico).
(1990), Introduction to J. Eatwell, M. Milgate and P. Newman (eds), *The New Palgrave: Capital Theory*, London: Macmillan.

Other References

Garegnani, P. (1976), 'On a change in the notion of equilibrium in recent work on value and distribution: a comment on Samuelson', in M. Brown, K. Sato and P. Zarembka (eds), *Essays in Modern Capital Theory*, Amsterdam: North-Holland.
Keynes, J.M. (1936), *The General Theory of Employment, Interest and Money*, London: Macmillan.

Alfred EICHNER (1937–1988) *Philip Arestis*

Alfred Eichner was a leading figure of the post-Keynesian/institutionalist school of thought in economics. Most of his academic life was devoted singlemindedly to the formulation, construction, estimation and dissemination of a comprehensive theoretical framework which, he hoped, would be encompassing enough to encapsulate most, if not all, theoretical strands within the post-Keynesian/institutionalist tradition of economic thought.

Eichner was born in Washington, D.C. in 1937. He spent his undergraduate years at Columbia University under the guidance of Professor Eli Ginsberg, who became his mentor. This was an important ingredient in Eichner's intellectual development since Ginsberg had been a student of Wesley C. Mitchell and John Maurice Clark, influential institutionalists. Eichner was, therefore, introduced to non-conventional thinking at a very early stage in his academic career. Ginsberg's influence must have been deeply ingrained in Alfred, for he remained a staunch 'dissenting' economist for the rest of his short life. He received his A.B. in 1958 and his Ph.D. in 1966, also from Columbia. His training was not just in institutional economics, but also in economic history; during these years he collaborated with Ginsberg on economic history of black Americans in a book entitled *The Troublesome Presence: The American Democracy and the Negro* (1964).

Eichner was first appointed as Senior Research Associate at Columbia but later, in 1961, became Professor of Human Resources. For the next ten years he was heavily involved in a research project on the Conservation of Human Resources. This involvement and collaboration continued even after he had left Columbia, lasting until 1979. In 1971 he moved to the State University of New York at Purchase as Professor of Economics and Chair of the Department. Very active still with both teaching and research, he initiated and helped to form the Centre for Economic and Anthopogenic Research (CEAR) which he directed from 1979. In 1980 he was appointed Professor of Economics at Rutgers University, a position he held until his death on 10 February 1988.

It is very important to note at this juncture the remarkable rapport Eichner managed to develop and nourish with his students. Unassuming and supportive, he was always available to see them, advise them, comment on their essays and most important of all, invite and respect their criticisms. Eichner was a very gifted, articulate and thoughtful teacher, always deeply and genuinely concerned with the intellectual welfare of his students. This is an aspect of his academic work that cannot be overemphasized.

His major works include *The Emergence of Oligopoly: Sugar Refining as a Case Study* (1969); *The Megacorp and Oligopoly: Micro Foundations of Macro Dynamics* (1976); *Controlling Social Expenditures: The Search for Output Measures*, with Charles Brecher, (1979); and his most comprehensive work, albeit unfinished in parts, *The Macrodynamics of Advanced Market Economies* (1988). Furthermore, *A Guide to Post-Keynesian Economics* (1978) and *Why Economics is Not Yet a Science* (1983) are two volumes of essays by institutionalists and post-Keynesians which he edited. *Towards a New Economics* (1985), another volume which he edited, comprised essays both published and unpublished. His essay with J. Kregel in the *Journal of Economic Literature* (1975) is an important contribution to the development of post-Keynesian economics.

Professor Eichner was a member of the editorial board of the *Journal of Post Keynesian Economics* and my co-editor of the *Thames Papers in Political Economy*, a position he cherished and worked on very hard, not just in terms of the routine tasks of an editor but, more importantly, in terms of promoting this journal throughout the world.

Eichner's early exposure to institutional economics must have helped him enormously to formulate his post-Keynesian ideas for he believed that the latter was a constructive outcome of the institutionalist critique against mainstream neoclassical economics. There is absolutely no doubt that Eichner was one of the protagonists of the 'younger' generation of post-Keynesians. But unlike many, if not all, of his contemporaries, the type of post-Keynesianism he worked so hard for was encompassing. He strived, especially later in his life, to demonstrate that not only was it desirable, but indeed possible, to orchestrate the possibility of what Geoff Harcourt and Omar Hamouda describe in a paper in the *Bulletin of Economic Research* (1989), 'From Critique to Coherence': that post-Keynesian economics had passed the state of critique and entered the stage of coherence. Before he attempted to demonstrate this all-important aspect of post-Keynesian economics, Eichner's work had involved two other no less important ingredients. The first chronologically was the microeconomic core of post-Keynesian economics, and the second a methodological attack on neoclassical economics along with a study of the methodological foundations of post-Keynesianism.

Eichner firmly believed and supported the view that, to use his own words, 'it is possible to place economics on a solid empirical foundation'. Not surprisingly one of his first major contributions, *The Megacorp and Oligopoly: Micro Foundations of Macro Dynamics*, demonstrated that industrial capitalist economies are characterized by 'megacorps' whose behaviour is distinctly different from that of the atomistic firms of the neoclassical paradigm. In particular, the pricing decisions of oligopolistic firms are firmly based on the notion of mark-up over unit costs. This particular contribution was supplemented by the further hypothesis that the size of the mark-up is predominantly determined by the financial needs of firms to finance investment. Clearly, the objective of the mark-up is the creation of a discretionary investible surplus, a proposition which follows from the empirical observation that megacorps generally finance a high proportion of their investment programmes from undistributed profits.

Eichner utilized the novel concept of 'corporate levy' (the amount of funds megacorps are able to generate from internal sources to finance investment expenditure) as determined by the demand for and supply of additional investment funds. The manipulation of the corporate levy by oligopolists is constrained by three factors: the substitution factor (possible loss in the oligopolists' share of the market to competing goods); the entry factor (potential loss to new entrants in the market); and the threat of governmental intervention (such as nationalization, price controls etc). In this way the possibility of both internal and external financing was alluded to. A determinate solution to pricing was then established which was firmly linked to distribution and capital accumulation.

The other important implication of this analysis was that it provided a firm theoretical microfoundation to macroeconomics. This was done in a way which precluded the necessity of having to distinguish sharply between microeconomics and macroeconomics. By contrast, in the mainstream of the discipline, the two are governed by different sets of principles – neoclassical microeconomic theory clothed with macro-Keynesian theoretical principles – from which ensued the very well-known theoretical incompatibility of traditional economics. This was referred to by Eichner as the 'fallacy of composition' – the fallacy here being that *wholes* can be considered as the sum of *parts*. More concretely, the neoclassical aggregation of microunits to arrive at macrorelationships implies the erroneous conclusion that propositions postulated at the macrolevel necessarily conform with the assumptions made at the microlevel.

The methodological part of Eichner's contribution to post-Keynesian economics begins with a critique of the reliance of neoclassical economics on the mechanistic view of the universe inspired by Newton's *Principia*. In neoclassical economics the *individual economic actor* is the analogue of the *atom* of Newtonian mechanics. 'Reality' is perceived as the interaction of individual economic agents whose natures are invariable and permanent, the implication being that society can be explained in terms of individual economic agents and not the other way round (as it should be in Eichner's view). When economics is viewed in this *atomistic* way it becomes the study of how to satisfy an unlimited number of needs through a limited number of resources. From this the logical proposition follows that *effects* can be distinguished from *causes* and that the causal link runs from the latter to the former.

Eichner totally rejected this methodological approach to the study of real economic phenomena and proposed instead the cybernetic or systems approach to the understanding of real economic life. This philosophical framework, which incidentally encompasses *Newtonian mechanics* and *Hegelian dialectics* as special cases, is the most general approach available to economists and other social scientists. The economy is composed of subsystems which respond to impacts from the environment but also influence it dynamically. The subject matter of economics in this view is the study of how an economic system expands over time, not only by reproducing itself but also by creating and distributing a social surplus. When the economic system is viewed in this dynamic way and as part of several major societal systems, a truly 'social sciences' approach to the study of economics is possible. But even when the economic system is looked at in isolation, the principle of the cybernetics methodology is still applicable in that it is analysed in terms of *input*, *output* and *feedback*. Eichner argued that when the study of economics is couched in this particular way, it really is very close to the classical paradigm. This is so, in his view, because of the emphasis placed upon social relations, the distribution of income and the dynamics embedded in the analysis of an economy that grows, and changes, over time.

Eichner utilized this methodological framework to show that neoclassical economics cannot be said to be a science. For it fails to pass the usual epistemological tests: the test of coherence (whether there is internal consistency in terms of the theory's conclusions and assumptions); that of correspondence (which tests whether the conclusions arrived at in the theoretical framework under scrutiny conform with actual economic phenomena); of comprehensiveness (whether the theory takes on board and deals with all the available facts pertaining to the phenomenon under consideration); and the test of parsimony (which attempts to establish whether the theory contains superfluous elements which could be dropped without damaging the credibility of the theory). To demonstrate, Eichner identifies the key features of neoclassical economics as being indifference curves, isoquants, positively sloped supply curves, marginal physical product curves, the IS/LM model and the Phillips curve. These features, the cornerstone of neoclassical economics, have yet to be empirically validated by economists in Eichner's view. In addition, they fail the criteria just referred to. Indifference curves and isoquants cannot be derived empirically; they thus fail the correspondence and parsimony tests. Supply curves do not slope positively since constant or increasing returns to scale prevail, and also industrial firms are price setters, not price takers. Consequently, the contention that supply curves slope upwards fails the coherence and comprehensiveness tests. Marginal physical product curves assume variable technical coefficients when the evidence points to fixed technical coefficients. Furthermore, given the proposition that the 'marginal productivity of capital' is indeterminate, it follows that this theoretical construct fails the correspondence test. Similarly for the IS/LM framework and the Phillips curve, which do not appear to have much empirical substance.

Eichner's post-Keynesianism purports to avoid the methodological problems of traditional economics. In doing so, he aims to base economics firmly on reality and thus complete the aborted revolution as initiated by Keynes. His economic theory, therefore, attempts to explain how a real economic system with advanced institutions operates. Clearly, if economics is to be viewed in this way, there are certain prerequisites which must be met. First, variables must be observable. Second, the theory that applies to the microlevel should be consistent with the theory that is more relevant to the macrolevel. Third, the theoretical framework must be comprehensive and coherent enough to encompass all the essential features of the economic system and also represent the behaviour of the institutions that characterize modern advanced market economies. These institutions are, first and foremost, the megacorps referred to above. There is also the neoclassical proprietorship which is the representative firm of the non-oligopolistic sectors of the economy. Both the megacorp and the neoclassical firm constitute the production subsystem of the economy. There exist strong trade unions who bargain on behalf of their members with employers over wages and working conditions. A government sector that is committed to counter-cyclical economic policies to stabilize an essentially unstable economic system. In performing this function the government through the Central Bank is able to create money, although total money supply is largely credit money created by the actions of private economic agents including the banking system.

Finally, the operation of the international economy is also taken on board with all its concomitant institutional paraphernalia. All these ingredients were very important to the theme which Eichner was working on just before his death, epitomized in his most comprehensive work (though unfinished in parts) *The Macrodynamics of Advanced Market Economies*. In this work, Eichner is concerned with cyclical fluctuations or deviations from empirically estimated secular trends. Cyclical behaviour and secular growth must proceed hand-in-hand; they are interdependent and, indeed, the two together constitute the economy's macrodynamic behaviour. Essentially he attempts to encompass both short-run and long-run analysis in a coherent macroeconomic model. Since short-term and long-term issues are viewed as dominant, both should he taken on board in any serious study of the economy. At the stage of the model's development where Eichner left it, it was the short-run analysis which had received more attention, with the long-run developments derived by fitting a trend line to the data on relevant economic variables.

Thus, along with all other post-Keynesian and institutionalist economists, Eichner adopted the view that cycles are an endogenous process in an economic environment characterized by instabilities; random shocks exacerbate cycles but they are never the cause of them. The future is *uncertain* with production needing and taking *time*, while the financial system is continually subjected to speculative excesses. These characteristics cannot be accounted for unless the institutional and structural developments of economies are encapsulated in any serious attempt to model economic phenomena. Epitomizing this approach, therefore, is its emphasis on institutions as they evolve through time and as they differ from economy to economy, and its detailed analysis of structural changes to modern capitalism.

Eichner's model is based on a number of theories: a theory of aggregate demand; a theory of production; a theory of growth and distribution; and theory of prices, pricing and wage inflation; and a theory of money, credit and finance. Furthermore, the model is conveniently divided into five interacting blocks.

Block I explains the rate of growth of discretionary expenditures (expenditure on durables plus investment expenditure) for each of the sectors in the economy, both in real terms and in nominal terms. Discretionary expenditure in real terms is related to disposable income, the ratio of discretionary expenditure to discretionary funds, the rate of interest, and a number of exogenous and policy variables. This block reflects the theory of aggregate demand behaviour encapsulating both household and investment attitudes.

Block II determines the rate of growth of output and employment. The analysis here is based on the Leontief model where the assumption of fixed technical coefficients is alluded to. Two implications follow. First, the rate of growth of output is influenced by discretionary expenditure in real terms, and the ratio of discretionary expenditure to discretionary funds. The second implication is that employment is essentially a function of output growth and an exogenously-determined rate of growth of government-supported employment.

Block III explains the ratio of discretionary expenditure to discretionary funds. With discretionary expenditure identified in Block I, this block is essentially concerned with the determination of discretionary funds of each sector in the economy – in effect, encapsulating the theory of income distribution. It ought to be emphasized that central to the analysis thus far is the role of capital accumulation which determines not just the cyclical behaviour of the economy but also the secular growth of the economy and distribution. The greater the rate of capital accumulation, the more intense the pace of economic growth and the higher the relative share of income going to profits (given the rate of capacity utilization). In this block, the cyclical movement of discretionary funds of the various sectors is hypothesized to depend on income, prices, nominal wages and taxes. The latter two are taken as exogenously determined: taxes as set by the government, and nominal wages by socio-political factors such as collective bargaining.

The price-variable is determined in Block IV. A mark-up pricing model is postulated, where the growth of prices is made a function of unit labour cost, unit material cost and taxes. With taxes and unit material costs being treated as exogenous, unit labour costs are viewed as the difference between the exogenously determined wages and labour productively (itself related to discretionary expenditure).

Finally, there is a comprehensive credit sector in the model – Block V. The degree of liquidity pressure and interest rates are the strategic credit sector variables. The degree of liquidity pressure variable is governed by the demand for short-term loans (namely bank lending to the public) relative to the lending capacity of commercial banks (namely bank deposits). They are both endogenous variables determined by income, rate of interest and the discretionary expenditure/discretionary funds ratio. 'Market' interest rates are fundamentally determined by the degree of liquidity pressure variable, the discount rate and other exogenous variables (such as open market operations, for example). The degree of liquidity pressure is, in fact, the supreme financial determinant of discretionary expenditures, and thus real output and employment. It also partially influences interest rates, which are also expected to have some influence on discretionary expenditure. The availability effect is thus expected to be considerably greater than that of interest rates.

This way of modelling the economy does have certain crucial policy implications. Most importantly, monetary and fiscal policies cannot be trusted to cure inflation; when combined for that purpose they lead to *stagflation*. It is *incomes policy* instead that should be adopted and implemented to sustain healthy and non-inflationary growth paths. But it is not the kind of incomes policy implemented in the 1960s and 1970s, in the UK for example, which is designed to hold down money wages. That was unacceptable to Eichner. An incomes policy should not be imposed. It should gain acceptance by all economic classes (workers and capitalists) and should apply to all forms of income, dividends, rents as well as money wages. It ought to be a 'Social Contract' more in the Swedish mould rather than the type adopted by any other western social-democratic government.

This type of analysis cannot be sustained without appropriate empirical backing. Eichner did provide substantial evidence on all five blocks summarized above. What he sadly did not have time to do, though, was to bring all five empirically estimated blocks together to provide a full post-Keynesian/institutionalist model of the US economy.

Eichner's Major Writings

(1964), *The Troublesome Presence: The American Democracy and the Negro* (with Eli Ginsberg), New York: Free Press.

(1969), *The Emergence of Oligopoly: Sugar Refining as a Case Study*, Cambridge: Cambridge University Press.

(1975), 'An Essay on Post-Keynesian Theory: A New Paradigm in Economics' (with J. Kregel), *Journal of Economic Literature*, **13**, December.

(1976), *The Megacorp and Oligopoly: Micro Foundations of Macro Dynamics*, Cambridge: Cambridge University Press.

(1978), *A Guide to Post-Keynesian Economics*, New York: M.E. Sharpe Inc.

(1979a), 'A Post-Keynesian Short-Period Model', *Journal of Post Keynesian Economics*, **1**, Summer.

(1979b), *Controlling Social Expenditures: The Search for Output Measures* (with Charles Brecker), New York: Allenheld Osmun.

(1983), *Why Economics is not yet a Science*, New York: M.E. Sharpe Inc.

(1985), *Towards a New Economics: Essays in Post-Keynesian and Institutionalist Theory*, New York: M.E. Sharpe Inc.

(1988a), *The Macrodynamics of Advanced Market Economies*, New York: M.E. Sharpe Inc.

(1988b), 'The Post-Keynesian and Institutionalist Theory of Money and Credit' (with Philip Arestis), *Journal of Economic Issues*, **22**(4).

Other References

Arestis, P. (1989), 'Pricing, Distribution, Investment and Growth: The Economics of A.S. Eichner', *Review of Political Economy*, **1**(1).

Eichner, A.S. (1973), 'A Theory of the Determination of the Mark-up Under Oligopoly', *Economic Journal*, **83**, December.

Eichner, A.S. (1977), 'The Geometry of Macrodynamic Balance', *Australian Economic Papers*, **16**, June.

Groves, M., Lee, F. and Milberg, W. (1989), 'The Power of Ideas and the Impact of One Man: Alfred Eichner, 1937–1988', *Journal of Post Keynesian Economics*, **11**(3).

Milberg, W. (ed)(1991), *The Megacorp and Macrodynamics: Essays in Memory of Alfred Eichner*, New York: M.E. Sharpe Inc.

Street, J., Arestis, P. and Tool, M.R. (1988), 'In Memoriam: Alfred S. Eichner, 1937 to 1988', *Journal of Economic Issues*, **22**(4).

Duncan K. FOLEY (born 1942)

I was born in Columbus, Ohio, in 1942 and grew up living in and near Philadelphia where I attended public grade schools, Central High School, and Swarthmore College. When I was 12 years old my family began to attend Quaker meetings. Quaker concerns for social justice and pacifism had a deep effect on me, and I joined the Society of Friends, of which I am still a member, as an adolescent.

I chose to major in mathematics at Swarthmore College, where I also had my first contact with economics. William Brown's exposition of Keynes' cross in the first semester of introductory economics ignited my interest in the possibility of using mathematical models to explain aggregate social phenomena. The second semester of the course on microeconomics appealed less to my imagination. In general my reaction to the neoclassical theories of the household and firm was critical and unconvinced (like that of many of my own undergraduate students to this day). Joseph Conard, who taught me Economic Theory, responded to my complaint that the theory of consumer choice could not explain how people decided to buy candy from a candy machine by suggesting that I learn neoclassical theory thoroughly before I ventured to criticize it. This remark made a big impression on me.

When I graduated from Swarthmore in 1964 my only well-formed opinion about my future was that I knew I did not want to be a college teacher. I was interested in politics and foreign affairs, and applied to enter the US foreign service, which contemplated accepting me despite the difficulties posed by my pacifism. Personal considerations prompted me to delay entering the foreign service for a year, and I elected to spend the time studying economics at Yale University.

I reacted negatively to much of the graduate programme in economics at Yale. Herbert Scarf's lucid and elegant lectures on mathematical economics, however, made a lasting impression and constituted the bulk of my imperfect education (or processing) in economics, since I had been exempted from the first year of theory courses on the basis of my work at Swarthmore. I considered centring my thesis research on turnpike models with consumption or on equilibrium with incomplete forward markets, but a paper I wrote for Scarf's course on equilibrium theory with public goods luckily developed rapidly into a viable topic ('Resource Allocation and the Public Sector'). In my thesis I pointed out that the purely ordinal nature of preferences did not (as was sometimes implied in the teaching of welfare economics) prevent the comparison of the well-being of different individuals. I proposed comparing two individuals' well-being by asking each to rank two consumption bundles in her own ordering. If both insisted that her own bundle was superior, it seemed sensible to say that the individual with the superior bundle was better off. If no individual envied another's bundle, an allocation might be regarded as not unequal. Since this test depended only on ordinal comparisons, it was not subject to the criticisms levelled at attempts to compare cardinal utilities.

I left Yale for a teaching job at MIT in 1966. I still had no serious intention of pursuing a career as an academic economist. Yale had given me a Ph.D. and revealed the power of modern mathematical methods in economics, but had made little progress in imbuing me with the norms and values of the US economics profession. For example, I did not have (and still do not have) a proper field of interest, like public finance or money, as an economist.

MIT and its Economics department struck me as exciting but anxious institutions. The faculty valued its excellent graduate students and instructed and advised them with serious attention. Paul Samuelson and his protégé Robert Solow had achieved enormous intellectual visibility and political influence, setting a formidable and discouraging standard for us juniors. Enormous pressure for rapid publication constantly threatened to reduce the scope for risky, reflective or critical thought.

My intellectual project was then (and still is) to find firm foundations for the economic theories of money and macroeconomic stability. I had the great good fortune to collaborate with Miguel Sidrauski in the early stages of this project. Our book, *Monetary and Fiscal Policy in a Growing Economy*, addressed the issue of the determination of investment in the then-dominant IS-LM framework. We showed that the IS-LM structure is incompatible with a rigorous conception of an independent demand for investment. Our consistent analysis of dynamic economic models with the methods of nonlinear differential equations clarified the relations between stock and flow equilibrium in macroeconomic models; it also helped to prepare the way for the later use of state-space modelling concepts in economic dynamics. This work revealed difficulties in the project of basing a theory of macroeconomic fluctuations on rigorous neoclassical foundations. We were able to introduce money and financial assets only in an *ad hoc* manner, and our rigorous treatment of stock-flow equilibrium seemed to rule out an autonomous role for firms and firm investment decisions in this type of model.

My work over the next five years explored in more depth the problems of time, uncertainty and money in the context of the neoclassical general equilibrium model. 'Economic Equilibrium with Costly Marketing' considered the problem of transaction costs and the existence of markets in the general equilibrium model. Transaction costs rule out the existence of futures markets necessary to handle intertemporal decisions in the Arrow-Debreu framework, without, unhappily, generating a concept of money or finance within the theory. 'Asset Management under Trading Uncertainty' (with Martin Hellwig) began to explore the mathematics of dynamic economic models of consumer choice, breaking away from the full insurance implicit in the Arrow-Debreu framework. These lines of work seemed to me to point to a fundamental inability of the Walrasian general equilibrium paradigm to address problems of dynamics, stability and finance. I also came to feel that these theoretical weaknesses were at the root of the unsatisfactory connection between theory and measurement in economics. Econometric practice (at that time) too often consisted of testing weak implications of neoclassical models against even weaker alternatives. I found lacking any close connection between theoretical concept and operational measurement that informs the physical sciences, as well as any confrontation of real alternative hypotheses in empirical tests. These problems could be explained by basic structural flaws in the Walrasian theory itself.

The years I spent at MIT pondering these problems were filled with the turmoil of the war in Vietnam and political movements against the war, for civil rights, and for social justice. These issues were particularly poignant for a young economist like myself. Many brilliantly successful economists of the previous generation had combined scholarly research with government service and political consultation. From 1966 on it became increasingly difficult to persuade oneself that public service in the US would have any positive effect on issues of poverty, social justice, civil rights or peace. A mainstream career combining government service, political influence and scholarship seemed instead likely to end up in support of repressive and violent policies in poor foreign countries, and in the sale of these policies to the US electorate. Efforts to transform society through government policy – the heritage of the New Deal that heartened and motivated many economists of the previous generation – were failing. Fierce opposition to economic and racial equality limited the financial resources of these programmes, and political conflict together with bureaucratic methods undercut their goals. I found myself more often disagreeing with my colleagues about the educational direction of both the department and the institution, and even about details of administration involving hierarchy and gender. In an effort to reduce anxieties and achieve a more open intellectual dialogue, I experimented with hierarchy by promising the same 'A' grade to all the students in one first-year economic theory class. But the anxieties reappeared because students knew that the purpose of first-year courses was to sort them out and were sure that this would take place some other way if there were no grade differences. I asked my department chairman how large a reduction in pay I would have to take if I discharged all my other duties except for grading the students. He explained to me that grading was inseparable from the overall mission of the department, so that the pay cut would have to be 100%.

These years also made me dissatisfied with the substance of my teaching. An economics that concentrated exclusively on the mathematics of individual optimization and market interaction seemed disastrously cut off from the debates of history, politics and philosophy. Problems of social organization tended to be dealt with by economists through cost-benefit analysis, an application of the Pareto criterion. This discourse was narrow and reductionist, ignoring the role of institutions in human affairs, and of growth and change in human beings themselves. When I reported my conclusion that the Pareto criterion was irrelevant to real political debate to a senior colleague, he said that if I really believed that I should get out of economics. (I later published these opinions in 'Problems vs Conflicts: Economic Theory and Ideology'. Unfortunately the method of comparison of individual well-being I had proposed in my thesis depended on the same static model of individual choice and social interaction as the Pareto comparison, and was subject to the same criticisms.) It was becoming increasingly apparent to me that the pressures at MIT to occupy professional space (publishing in competitive journals, going to conferences, influencing appointments at other institutions, getting grants, giving grants, administering professional organizations and so forth) were not conducive to a quiet and reflective resolution of these intellectual issues.

In 1973 my wife took a job teaching Classics at Stanford University and I followed her there as an Associate Professor without tenure in the Economics department.

At Stanford I continued my work on stock-flow problems in macroeconomics (published as 'On Two Specifications of Asset Equilibrium in Macroeconomic Models'). This paper posed the question of whether equilibrium is fundamentally to be thought of as a willingness of economic agents to hold their wealth in the form of available existing assets, or as a material balance between flow supplies of and demands for produced commodities. With perfect foresight (or what was then coming to be called 'rational expectations') these conceptions are equivalent, but in the absence of good information about the future, the conceptions differ and lead to different models.

One legacy of the political turmoil of the 1960s in the Stanford Economics department was a group of able graduate students who were passionately committed to the revival of Marxian economics in the curriculum. These students had formed an unofficial seminar and were requesting that it be recognized by the department and that a senior scholar be appointed to teach Marxian and Sraffian economic theory. The level of intellectual discussion of Marx in this seminar was high, due not least to the influence of Donald Harris, then a Visiting Professor in the department, and of Bridget O'Laughlin, an anthropologist interested in problems of economic development. This seminar was one of the most interesting things to happen at Stanford at the time, offering me the chance to learn something about Marxist and (as I discovered) more broadly classical (Smithian, Ricardian and Sraffian) alternatives to Walrasian economics. I undertook a study of Marx to see whether he offered a coherent alternative approach to economics, and whether this approach could address the problems of money and macroeconomic stability that had gripped me.

It is very difficult for someone trained in modern Walrasian economics to read Marx. His language is confusing, not so much because of entirely new concepts, which one could learn afresh, but because of the appearance of familiar concepts in a different theoretical and methodological structure. Many Marxian formulations contain the treacherous possibility of being interpreted consistently within a Walrasian framework, a context in which they appear to be wrong or have a significance very different from what Marx meant.

My study of Marx took several years, and was an important extension of my education as an economist. (I later summarized it in *Money, Accumulation and Crisis*, and *Understanding Capital: Marx's Economic Theory*, books based on courses I subsequently taught at Barnard College and Columbia University.) Neoclassical economics makes more sense seen as a reaction to the Classical tradition Marx criticized, corrected and shaped to the needs of his class-based politics. I concluded that there was a coherent and consistent economic theory in Marx. The Marxian conception of the circuit of capital is an alternative to Walrasian equilibrium as a conception of the economic system as a whole, and addresses some important weaknesses of the Walrasian paradigm. The circuit of capital is at root a dynamic, rather than static, conception of economic interaction. Marx correctly accounts for the emergence of money simultaneously with the development of exchange and the commodity system, rather than inserting money and finance into a barter economy, as many monetary theorists do. Marx's critique of Ricardo's vision of the stationary state (on the ground that the nature of capitalism is to overcome resource limitations through technological change) establishes a rational basis for the theory of growth. The Marxian theory of labour-power also correctly places demography on an economic foundation. But there is in Marx no complete solution to my problems of money and macroeconomic stability. Marx addresses only tentatively and incompletely the problem of the articulation of the microeconomic and macroeconomic aspects of the economy. The monetary theory of a commodity standard money that he developed on the basis of Tooke's work needs fundamental revision to address modern financial institutions and problems. His accounts of the relation between credit and aggregate demand and of the dynamics of capitalist crisis are suggestive of several lines of explanation, but do not completely set out any one.

In 1975 the Stanford Economics department offered me reappointment on terms (without tenure) that I judged were incompatible with carrying out my research. During the discussions that followed the department's decision, I found myself under pressure to define myself either as a Marxist or as a neoclassical economist. I am afraid I was unable to satisfy either side. There are many fundamental ideas in Marx that I agree with: the general approach of historical materialism to the study of human societies; the insistence on the importance of class divisions and exploitation in analysing social dynamics; the links between money and social labour-time enunciated by Marx's theory of value; the circuit of capital; the centrality of technological change to capitalist economic development; the critique of the commodity form as a social organizing principle, and the analysis of social theory in terms of ideological context, for example. But other parts of Marx's discourse seem off the track to me: his explanation of the evolution of workers' standards of living in capitalist development is self-contradictory; his account of revolutionary change based in class conflict is inconsistent; and his presumptions about the institutions of socialist economies seem naive to the point of irresponsibility. I am a wholehearted advocate of abstraction and mathematization as methods in economics (and I think Marx would have agreed with me, for what that is worth). I would not find it any more appropriate to exclude Walrasian ideas from economics than to exclude classical ones (as US economists came perilously close to doing in this period).

I moved from Stanford to Barnard College of Columbia University (where my wife is now Professor of Classics) in 1977. At Barnard, to my delight, I found in the Economics department shaped by Deborah Milenkovitch a supportive atmosphere that allows me to pursue my research. After publishing the books on Marx mentioned above, I have returned to the project of examining the problems of money, prices and macroeconomic stability, with the idea of bringing the insights of the classical and Marxian traditions to bear on these issues. I have worked recently on the dynamical stability of the circuit of capital model with finance (for example, 'Liquidity-Profit Rate Cycles in a Capitalist Economy' and 'Endogenous Financial-Production Cycles in a Macroeconomic Model'). These models follow in the tradition of Kaldor, Hicks and Goodwin, in viewing the macroeconomy as locally unstable because of accelerator effects on investment. This local instability is limited by financial and liquidity effects, giving rise to limit cycle behaviour. I am also currently (1990) interested in the classical and Marxian concepts of prices of production ('On Prices of Production in a General Model of Production'), and the structure of rational expectations equilibria in classical economies with stochastic technical change.

To be a dissenting economist, I suppose, is to criticize the dominant economic theories of a time and place. I do not believe that neoclassical economic theory is a mature science established on firm philosophical and methodological principles. As a result I believe that it is necessary for economics education and scholarly discourse to be more diverse than the dominant opinion among US economists allows. When I see narrowness of theoretical and methodological viewpoint and intolerance of critical positions threatening the intellectual integrity of economics, I dissent. But to project scientific understanding of economic interactions, to the questions of economics, I say yes.

Foley's Major Writings

(1967), 'Resource Allocation and the Public Sector', *Yale Economic Essays*, **7**(1), 43–98.

(1970), 'Economic Equilibrium with Costly Marketing', *Journal of Economic Theory*, **2**(3), 276–91.

(1971), *Monetary and Fiscal Policy in a Growing Economy* (with Miguel Sidrauski), New York: Macmillan.

(1975a), 'Asset Management under Trading Uncertainty' (with M. Hellwig), *Review of Economic Studies*, **42**(3), 327–46.

(1975b), 'On Two Specifications of Asset Equilibrium in Macroeconomic Models', *Journal of Political Economy*, **83**(2), 303–24; Correction: 1977, **85**(2), 401–2.

(1975c), 'Problems vs Conflicts: Economic Theory and Ideology', *American Economic Review*, **45**(2), 231–6.

(1985), 'On Prices of Production in a General Model of Production', *Contributions to Political Economy*, **4**, 25–36.

(1986a), *Understanding Capital: Marx's Economic Theory*, Cambridge: Harvard University Press.

(1986b), *Money, Accumulation and Crisis*, Harwood Academic.

(1986c), 'Stabilization Policy in a Nonlinear Business Cycle Model', in W. Semmler (ed), *Competition, Instability, and Nonlinear Cycles*, Berlin: Springer-Verlag.

(1986d), 'Liquidity-Profit Rate Cycles in a Capitalist Economy', *Journal of Economic Behavior and Organization*, **8**, 363–76.

(Forthcoming), 'Endogenous Financial-Production Cycles in a Macroeconomic Model'.

Andre Gunder FRANK (born 1929)

I was born in 1929 in Berlin. My pacifist novelist father took me out of Nazi Germany to Switzerland when I was four years old. In the 1950s, he wrote his autobiography under the title *Links wo das Herz Ist* (translated as *Heart on the Left*). We had gone on to the United States in 1940–41, where I went to Ann Arbor High School and then to Swarthmore College. There, in part under my father's influence, I studied economics and became a Keynesian. In 1950, not knowing what I was letting myself in for, I started a Ph.D. in economics at the University of Chicago. I took Milton Friedman's economic theory course and passed my Ph.D. exams in economic theory and public finance with flying colours. Despite that, I received a letter from the Chicago Economics department advising me to leave because of my unsuitability or our 'incompatibility'.

I went on to the University of Michigan and studied for a semester with Kenneth Boulding and Richard Musgrave. I presented a paper on welfare economics for Boulding, which proved that it is impossible to separate efficiency in resource allocation from equity in income distribution. Boulding gave me an 'A+'. For my M.A. at Chicago, they had made me cut out the heart of the argument and then gave me a 'C'. Then I dropped out altogether. I became a beatnic at the Vesuvius cafe in San Francisco's North Beach before Jack Keruac arrived there *On the Road*.

I was introduced to 'development' and at the same time re-entered the University of Chicago through the back door. This was the availability of a research assistantship in Bert Hoselitz's Research Center in Economic Development and Cultural Change. In Bert's absence on leave, the planner and acting director Harvey Perloff hired me only to admit, to his dismay, that I was 'the most philosophical person' he had ever met. He asked me critically to evaluate the early World Bank reports on Ceylon, Nicaragua and Turkey, which were sadly lacking, in my opinion.

For reasons of financial circumstance, I then spent an interval at Chicago working on the Soviet economy (in a research project whose final client was the US Army Psychological Warfare Division!) As a result, I subsequently wrote my Chicago economics Ph.D. dissertation on a comparison of productivity growth between agriculture and industry in the Soviet Ukraine (1958a). In this thesis, I independently worked out the concepts and measures of general productivity – later to be known as total productivity – and the contribution of human capital and organization to economic growth. According to H.W. Arndt (1987, p. 62), the idea of human capital was 'almost single-handedly introduced into economics' by the then chairman of the Chicago Economics department, T.W. Schultz, who was subsequently awarded the Nobel Prize.

It was this work of mine to which John Toye referred (1987, p. 104) when he wrote: 'the archetypical Western radicalized intellectual who at that time [1970s] dominated development thinking was Andre Gunder Frank, the orthodox Chicago economist who abruptly became a Latin American revolutionary figure' (cf. Frank, 1958b and 1972). My ex-colleague and friend at Michigan State, Paul Strassman, would later call me a 'renegade' from Chicago economics.

Yet already at the University of Chicago, I spent more and more of my time studying and associating with anthropologists. This helped me come to the same conclusion as my friend Bert Hoselitz (but, I thought, independently of him) that the determinant factors in economic development were really *social*. Social change, therefore, seemed the key to both social and economic development. I wrote about social conflict and favourably reviewed Albert Hirschman's *Strategy of Economic Development* in Bert Hoselitz's journal.

A paper I presented at an anthropology conference was subsequently reprinted in the business management text *Studies in Managerial Process and Organizational Behavior* (Turner et al, 1972). I also said the same and more at a State Department training seminar for visiting Third World technicians. From this idea about social change it was but a short step (for me, if not for others) to reach the conclusion that the most important real factors in development are political. Since political change seemed difficult if not impossible to achieve through reform, the obvious answer seemed to be political revolution. It became increasingly clear to me that all American (including my own) development studies and thinking could not solve development problems. Instead they were themselves really part of the problem, since they sought to deny and obscure both the real problem and the real solution, which lay in politics.

To find out more, I went to Cuba in 1960, soon after the revolution. I also briefly looked at political change in Kwame Nkrumah's Ghana (where I was disappointed to find little) and in Seku Toure's Guinea (where I mistakenly thought that I had found more and better). Then I decided to be consequential: I quit my assistant professorship at Michigan State University (where I had led an interdisciplinary development seminar and already complained about MSU training police forces in South Vietnam – many years before this CIA project would become a public scandal). I went to find out for myself – from the 'inside' in the underdeveloped Third World. Since I decided I could never become an African, I went to Latin America where acculturation seemed less daunting.

In 1962, I left the US and went to Mexico, which led to my writing about the 'Janus faces' of Mexican inequality. I saw internal colonialism there instead of separate sectors in a 'dual' economy or society. In Venezuela, my friend Hector Silva Michelena told me that I had written a Hamlet without the Prince of Denmark of American imperialism. Then, via Peru and Bolivia, I arrived in Chile. There, Marta Fuentes and I met, shared our concern for social justice and married. We had two children with whom, as with each other, we still speak Spanish. Upon marriage, we set off into the unknown, beginning in Brazil.

This was the time of the Cuban revolution and President Kennedy's response through the reformist Alliance for Progress. At its Punta del Este meeting, Che Guevara called the Alliance 'the latrinization' of Latin America. These political issues of development put ECLA/CEPAL-type structuralism on the political-economic agenda. They called for some land, tax, administrative, educational, health (including latrines) and other reforms and/or social development. However, this agenda was more theoretical than practical. I welcomed any proposed reforms, but considered them insufficient if not altogether unworkable. Moreover, many of the proposals were not designed to overcome the political obstacles to reform, but to maintain them. So was the military and police repression of popular demands, which I condemned. I put my confidence in the Cuban way and socialism instead.

After the 1962–63 Sino-Soviet split and their lengthy document debates, I also accepted the Chinese line on socialism, because it appeared more revolutionary. The line and practice of the Soviet and Soviet-aligned Latin American Communist parties were too reformist. In several publications, I argued that in practice these 'Communist' policies were hardly distinguishable from 'national bourgeois' and ECLA/CEPAL reformism. The only substantial difference was that the former did, and the latter did not, refer to American imperialism as an obstacle to development in Latin America and elsewhere in the Third World.

In Brazil I wrote several 'political' articles which were critical of received economic doctrine and even of reformist policy. One countered the claim of the American ambassador in Brazil that US aid helped much, and of the Brazilian ambassador in the US, that this aid helped little. I argued that the aid was really exploitation. The article, published in the *Jornal do Brasil*, made a big political splash and brought me sudden fame. Another article on foreign investment, 'Mechanisms of Imperialism', countered the gospel according to which the Third World needed foreign investment and capital aid because the principal obstacle to its development was its shortage of capital. I countered this universally accepted supply-side theory with the essentially Keynesian demand-side argument that the real economic obstacle was insufficient market demand for productive national investment. The same kind of Keynesian and structuralist argument also underlay the policies of Brazilian and other nationalists, like Celso Furtado, the founder of SUDENE who was then Minister of Planning. I argued that his and others' policies of structural reform were insufficient to expand the internal market and generate development.

I worked on my first three theoretical works in Brasilia and later in Rio, where our first son was born in 1963. They were directed comprehensively against development theory and policy derived from (or camouflaged by) neoclassical and monetarist development theory; against Keynesian and structuralist explanations; and against CEPAL/ECLA, Alliance for Progress, *and* orthodox Marxist and Communist party theory, policy and praxis. I put them all in the same sack. The reason was that, whatever their differences, they *all* shared the view that underdevelopment was original or traditional. They all posited that development would result from gradual reforms in dual economies/societies, in which the modern sector would expand and eliminate the traditional one. In a word, I quarrelled with them more about their vision of underdevelopment than about development itself. I did *not* then find it remarkable that all also shared an essentially similar vision of capital accumulation through industrial growth equals development. Because, so did I! One of the subsequent critiques of my 'paradigm change from Rostow to Gunder Frank' (as Aidan Foster-Carter called my writings on dependence) was that I only turned orthodoxy on its head. Doing so evaded and rendered impossible any *other* fundamental sideways critique and reformulation, which I now regard as necessary.

The first of the three works argued against dualism. It went into battle especially against the then left-right-and-centre dominant version according to which Brazilian and Latin American (traditional) agriculture is feudal and that therefore capitalist reform was in order. The second theoretical work in 1963 was a much farther ranging critique of received theories. It was revised in 1965–66. After a dozen rejections, it was finally published in 1967 in the student magazine *Catalyst* under the title 'The Sociology of Development and Underdevelopment'. The critique targeted the theories of all my former friends at Chicago, like Bert Hoselitz and Manning Nash, as well as acquaintances or not at MIT, like Rostow and McClelland. In particular, I rejected the notion of 'original' underdevelopment, 'traditional' society and subsequent 'stages of growth', as well as development through neo-Parsonian social pattern variables and neo-Weberian cultural and psychological change. I found this new sociology of development to be 'empirically invalid when confronted with reality, theoretically inadequate in terms of its own classical social scientific standards, and policy-wise ineffective for pursuing its supposed intention of promoting the development of underdeveloped countries' (reprinted in 1969, p. 21).

The third work in 1963 was an extension from the second in the same manuscript. I sought to develop an *alternative* reading, interpretation and theory of *the development of underdevelopment*. I saw it as the result of *dependence* and, as the opposite side of the coin (turning things on their head), of development within a *single world capitalist system*. All of these ideas and terms were in the original 1963 manuscript, which was not published until 1975 by Oxford University Press in India under the title *On Capitalist Underdevelopment*. The 1963 manuscript began:

> Underdevelopment is not just the lack of development. Before there was development there was no underdevelopment. ... [They] are also related, both through the common historical process that they have shared during the past several centuries and through their mutual, that is reciprocal, influence that they have had, still have, and will continue to have, on each other throughout history (1975, p. 1).

For me, the upshot of all these theoretical and political reflections – and maybe of the unpleasant experiences in and with reformist institutions – was that continued participation in the same world capitalist system could only mean continued development of underdevelopment. That is, there would be neither equity, nor efficiency, nor economic development. The political conclusions, therefore, were to de-link from the system externally and to transit to self-reliant socialism internally (or some undefined international socialist cooperation) in order to make in- or non-dependent economic development possible. I hardly considered and left for crossing-that-bridge-when-we-came-to-it how such post-revolutionary economic and social development would then be promoted and organized, not to mention guaranteed. I also gave short shrift to how the necessarily not so democratic (pre)revolutionary means might or might not promote or even preclude the desirable post-revolutionary end.

These early general ideas on dependent underdevelopment in the world as a whole were my guides to a more specific analyses: 'The Development of Underdevelopment in Chile' was written in that country in 1964. On a one-month consultancy for the UN ECLA/CEPAL, I also discovered the urban 'informal' sector, which I called the 'unstable sector' (reprinted in 1969). My wife and I then went to Mexico where, in 1965, our second son, Miguel, was born; I also wrote the second essay on 'The Development of Underdevelopment in Brazil'. The next year I wrote the more general 'The Development of Underdevelopment', whose original title continued '... and the Underdevelopment of Development'. The essays on Chile and Brazil, along with some others, became my first book *Capitalism and Underdevelopment in Latin America* (1967). However, I had to pass literally untold trials and tribulations before I was finally able to get it published in English in 1967, in French in 1968, and in Spanish only in 1970. The preface argued that 'it will be necessary instead scientifically to study the real process of world capitalist development and underdevelopment' and that '*social* science must be *political* science'.

In Mexico also, I initiated three new departures. I was the first professor at the National School of Economics of the National Autonomous University of Mexico to dream up and teach a course on the economic (under)development of Latin America. I was the first person (after persuading the editors of *Comercio Exterior*, who had first rejected my 'unorthodox' accounting procedures) to publish an accounting statement of Latin America's external payments and receipts. This distinguished between services and goods in order to demonstrate that the Latin American current account deficit was due to a large *deficit on service account, especially from financial service payments*. My 'unorthodox' novelty was subsequently transformed into a new orthodoxy, which became particularly important in the now standard calculations of the ratio of debt service to export earnings. My third initiative was to organize prominent progressive Latin American economists to sign a statement on 'The Need for New Teaching and Research of Economics in Latin America' based on its dependence. These are reprinted in *Latin America: Underdevelopment or Revolution* (1969). I also argued the then outrageous, now standard, thesis about how local Mexican history was influenced by the world economic system, which was finally published in 1979 as *Mexican Agriculture 1521–1630: Transformation of the Mode of Production.*

In 1966, we went to Canada, where with Said Shah I developed a long reader which, in jigsaw puzzle fashion, put together a theory and analysis of dependence in Asia, Africa and Latin America. This was my magnum opus, but nobody has ever wanted to publish it. In 1968, we returned to Chile via 'May 1968' in Paris. I prepared a detailed critique of the then ECLA/CEPAL analysis and reformist policy, as well as an answer to criticisms of my earlier writings on dependence, which was published as *Lumpenbourgeoisie: Lumpendevelopment.*

I then wrote several drafts of a 'theoretical introduction' to the ill-fated reader. Once I lost all hope for its publication, I made its 'introduction' into another ever longer manuscript until the 1973 military coup in Chile stopped my work. The manuscript was divided into two parts, which were later published separately as *World Accumulation 1492–1789* and *Dependent Accumulation and Underdevelopment.* Both books analysed the development of a single capitalist world economy and world system since 1492. The first laid great stress on the role of both long, world economic cycles and of crises of capital accumulation in shaping world development as a whole; the second focused on their roles in shaping dependence and underdevelopment. As always, I experienced much trouble and delay in getting them finally published in 1978. Before I left Chile, I received a draft of the first volume of Wallerstein's (1974) *Modern World System.* The publisher asked me to write a blurb for its dust jacket in which I said the book would become an instant classic. It did. My books, sadly, were never heard of again.

I then began work on the economic and social history of the world system, starting with the contemporary world economic crisis and intending to work backwards. As it turned out for the next 17 years, I only foresaw and accompanied the development of this crisis. Not until 1989 did I start to go back to unravel the development of the present world (economic) system over the last 5,000 years (Frank, 1990).

As early as 1972, at a September conference in Rome, I said that the world had entered a new Kondratieff B period of crisis, which would spell terrible economic exploitation and political oppression in much of the Third World, especially in Latin America. I repeated an earlier 1972 judgement that 'dependence [theory] is dead, long live dependence and the class struggle' and suggested that, not dependence theory, but the analysis of the world crisis of capital accumulation should be on the analytical and theoretical agenda (reprinted in *Reflection on the Economic Crisis*, 1981b).

I would spend the next 19 years full time on this agenda, writing several books, among them *Crisis: In the World Economy* and *Crisis: In the Third*

World, and countless articles. My analysis countered the universally received wisdom that another crisis was impossible. Samuelson and others, for instance, claimed that business cycle analysts had supposedly done their work so well as to have analysed and policy prescribed the business cycle out of existence. Then, when the stubborn facts (not my writings) hit them on the nose, the OECD and the McCracken Report, for instance, blamed stagflation on the 'external' 'oil shocks' which I argued was also contrary to fact. Alas, all to no avail.

A few aspects of this (for me) all-consuming work on 'the crisis' perhaps deserve special mention here. In Chile, the midwife for the subsequent economic and social transformation was Pinochet's military coup in 1973 and the monetarism carried to Chile personally by my ex-professors at Chicago, Milton Friedman, Arnold Harberger and their 'Chicago Boys', as their other disciples are called in Chile. The new policies were imposed by General Pinochet as 'equilibrium on the point of a bayonet'. That was the subtitle of my *Economic Genocide in Chile*, which started as two open letters to my former professors at Chicago. My letters also recalled the arrival of the first Chilean students to be taught by Harberger at Chicago while I tried and failed to write a dissertation under his direction in the mid 1950s. In his militarized Chile, Pinochet gave the Chicago Boys free reign over economic policy. Therefore it was only natural for Friedman and Harberger to come down and recommend their shock treatment therapy. 'Free to Chose' Friedman argued that the magic of the market (efficiency?) comes first and (equity?) freedom later, and he was awarded the Nobel Prize (only for economics, not for peace, thank God). It was also only natural that I would dissent in a strongly-worded economic, political and moral critique.

In 1972 I had also predicted, and in 1976 I analysed, the reincorporation of the socialist countries into the capitalist world economy (1977 and 1980, Chapter 4). However, it was not then so evident that the 'import-led growth' in the East European socialist NICs (Newly Industrializing Countries) was essentially the same as 'export-led growth' in the capitalist NICs. The former export to import and the latter import to export. I said that both types of growth bring the world economic crisis into the East Asian, East European and South American NICs, the difference being that NIC growth in Eastern Europe has been less successful than in East Asia. Countries in the latter region now outcompete the East Europeans in the world market and want to invade their own domestic ones too. Export-led growth has been about equally unsuccessful in South America. But all things considered, the East European model was politically less repressive and inequitable (except partially in Romania) than in both capitalist NIC areas. Proposals, including mine, to resolve the Third World debt crisis abound. However, hardly anyone ever asks how to make the South American and East European NICs competitive against the East Asian ones and others after their debt service has made the former lose out so much in the technological and other competitions on the world market.

Beyond the discussion of these 'details', my main argument was that the socialist countries had no alternative but to compete in the world economy, albeit badly. Therefore, also, in 1983 I published a book on *The European Challenge: From Atlantic Alliance to Pan-European Entente for Peace and Jobs*, which argued for the realistic and preferable prospects of an East-West political-economic regional alternative in all of Europe. In 1986 and since, I extended the argument to prospective Japanese- and American-led regionalization and possible political-economic bloc formation. As usual, my arguments found no takers. The events of 1989, however, particularly in Eastern Europe (analysed in 1990c), made the prospects I had outlined visible to all.

All these and other developments obliged the whole world, and even development thinkers, to rethink. As for myself, I began a 1980 article with the words: 'The events of 1979 in and between Kampuchea, Vietnam and China oblige socialists to undertake an agonizing reappraisal' (reprinted in my *Critique and Anti-Critique*, 1984). They certainly obliged my wife and me to revise our own thinking about socialism, development and democracy, as reflected in our 'Ten Theses on Social Movements' (1989).

Gunder Frank's Major Writings

(1958a), 'General Productivity in Soviet Agriculture and Industry: The Ukraine 1928–53', *Journal of Political Economy*, **66**, December.

(1958b), 'Goal Ambiguity and Conflicting Standards: An Approach to the Study of Organization', *Human Organization*, **17**(1), Winter.

(1967), *Capitalism and Underdevelopment in Latin America*, New York: Monthly Review Press.

(1969), *Latin America: Underdevelopment or Revolution*, New York: Monthly Review Press.

(1972), *Lumpenbourgeoisie: Lumpendevelopment*, New York: Monthly Review Press.

(1975), *On Capitalist Underdevelopment*, Bombay: Oxford University Press.

(1976), *Economic Genocide in Chile: Equilibrium on the Point of a Bayonet*, Nottingham: Spokesman Books.

(1977), 'Long Live Transideological Enterprise: The Socialist Economies in the Capitalist International Division of Labor', *Review*, 1(1), Summer.

(1978a), *World Accumulation 1492–1789*, Monthly Review Press and Macmillan Press.

(1978b), *Dependent Accumulation and Underdevelopment*, Monthly Review Press and Macmillan Press.

(1979), *Mexican Agriculture 1521–1630: Transformation of the Mode of Production*, Cambridge University Press.

(1980), *Crisis: In the World Economy*, New York: Holmes and Meier and Heinemann.

(1981a), *Crisis: In the Third World*, New York: Homes and Meier and Heinemann.

(1981b), *Reflections on the Economic Crisis*, New York: Monthly Review Press and London: Hutchinson.

(1982), *Dynamics of Global Crisis* (with S. Amin, G. Arrighi and I. Wallerstein), Monthly Review Press and Macmillan Press.

(1983), *The European Challenge*, Nottingham: Spokesman Press. Also Westbury, Conn: Lawrence Hill Publishers, 1984.

(1984), *Critique and Anti-Critique*, New York: Praeger Publishers and London: Macmillan Press.

(1989), 'Ten Theses on Social Movements', *World Development*, **17**(2), February.

(1990a), 'A Theoretical Introduction to Five Thousand Years of World System History', *Review*, **13**.

(1990b), 'Civil Democracy Social Movements in World History' (with M. Fuentes), in S. Amin, G. Arrighi, A.G. Frank & I. Wallerstein, *Transforming the Revolution; Social Movements and the World-System*, New York: Monthly Review Press.

(1990c), 'Revolution in Eastern Europe: Lessons for Democratic Socialist Movements (and Socialists)' in *The Future of Socialism: Perspectives from the Left*, William K. Tabb (ed) New York: Monthly Review Press, 87–105. Also in *Third World Quarterly* (London) **XII** (2), April, 1990, 36–52.

(Forthcoming), 'The Underdevelopment of Development' (with Marta Fuentes Frank) in *Equity and Efficiency in Economic Development: Essays in Honor of Benjamin Higgins*, Donald J. Savoie (ed) Montreal: McGill Queens University Press. Published in expanded form as a book in Spanish, *El Subdesarrollo del Desarrollo: Ensayo Autobiografico con una Bibliografia de sus Publicaciones*, Caracas: Editorial Nueva Sociedad, 1991. (The present autobiographical note is a brief excerpt therefrom.)

Other References

Arndt, H.W. (1957), *Economic Development: The History of an Idea*, University of Chicago Press.

Toye, J. (1987), *Dilemmas of Development*, Oxford: Basil Blackwell.

Turner, J.H. et al (1972), *Studies in Managerial Process and Organizational Behaviour*, Glenview, Ill: Scott and Foreman.

John Kenneth GALBRAITH (born 1908)   *Steven Pressman*

John Kenneth Galbraith was born in 1908 in Iona Station, a small town on the northern shore of Lake Erie. He grew up in rural Southern Ontario, part of Scotch Canada. By his own account, his schooling was interrupted several times by farm work and his academic record undistinguished.

In the autumn of 1926, Galbraith enrolled at Ontario Agricultural College (OAC) in nearby Guelph. He was rather unimpressed with his fellow students. 'Leadership in the student body was solidly in the hands of those who combined an outgoing anti-intellectualism with a sound interest in livestock.' Faculty members were not any better. Practical instruction in the agricultural sciences, Galbraith thought, lacked content. In addition, 'anyone who questioned the established agricultural truths, many of which were wildly wrong, was sharply rebuked and ... marked down as a troublemaker' (1971, p. 261).

During his senior year at OAC, Galbraith noticed an advertisement for research assistantships in agricultural economics at Berkeley, with an annual stipend of $720. Attracted, Galbraith copied down the details, applied and was selected. Thus in 1931 Galbraith set out for California.

Galbraith was very happy in Berkeley. In contrast to OAC, he encountered professors who knew their subjects and who invited debate, as well as bright and thoughtful students. At Berkeley, Galbraith was influenced primarily by the economics of Alfred Marshall and Thorstein Veblen. It was not until later that he was drawn to the economics of John Maynard Keynes.

In his third year at Berkeley, Galbraith commuted to Davis, where he was paid $1800 to teach economics, agricultural economics, farm management and accounting. He also wrote a Ph.D. thesis on the expenditures of California counties. Later, Galbraith was to admit that this dissertation 'was without distinction. ... The purpose was to get the degree' (1981, p. 22).

While putting the finishing touches on his thesis in the spring of 1933, Galbraith received a $2400 job offer from Harvard. Advised that one advanced in academia by flashing job offers from other institutions, Galbraith let his Dean at Berkeley know that Harvard was after him. The Dean warmly congratulated Galbraith and advised him to accept the generous offer at once. 'In a moment I realized to my horror I had no choice. I couldn't now plead to stay at two-thirds the price. The great love of my life was over' (1971, p. 270).

Galbraith has been based at Harvard ever since, with time off to pursue political, diplomatic and writing interests. In 1941 he went to Washington to become deputy administrator of the Office of Price Administration, a position which made him price czar of the US until 1943. In that year he joined the editorial board of *Fortune*. Galbraith credits Henry Luce, then editor of the magazine, with helping to develop his famed writing style. In the spring of 1945 he became a director of the US Strategic Bombing Survey.

164

During the 1950s and 1960s Galbraith was especially active in politics. He was an adviser and speechwriter in the presidential campaigns of Adlai Stevenson and John Kennedy. In 1961, President Kennedy appointed Galbraith Ambassador to India, a position he held until 1963 (see 1969b). In 1968 he worked for Senator Eugene McCarthy's Presidential campaign, and in 1972 for Senator George McGovern's.

A Theory of Price Control, Galbraith's first major book, was published in 1952. It argues that controls on wages and prices are a necessary ingredient (along with traditional fiscal and monetary policies) of any anti-inflation policy. Controls are required because inflation is caused primarily by the pressure of higher incomes on prices and higher prices on incomes. The only practical solution is for the government to prevent the market power of labour unions and large businesses from causing a spiralling inflation.

Many economists argue that the most efficient way to allocate goods and services is to let the free market set prices and wages. In their view, government administered pricing and government interference in the labour market only misallocates resources. They also contend that controls create a needless bureaucracy to monitor compliance and that they would require rationing of goods. In contrast, Galbraith argues in his *Theory of Price Control* that oligopolistic firms do not take prices that are set in the market. Firms in the oligopolistic sector of the economy are price makers rather than price takers, and 'it is relatively easy to fix prices that are already fixed' (p. 17).

In imperfect markets there is a strong element of convention, with prices habitually set by a mark-up on costs of production. Moreover, the markup itself is conventional. As a result, controls on prices become government attempts to change conventions so that they have less costly outcomes. Monitoring of controls is made easier, according to Galbraith, by the fact that prices need to be controlled only in the oligopolistic sector of the economy, since market power exists only in this sector. Consequently, only a thousand or so firms need to be monitored. And enforcement is assisted by the fact that large oligopolistic firms are all in the public eye.

Finally, Galbraith notes that sellers control demand in imperfect markets. Therefore large firms control sales when they control prices. This is done by allocating supplies to specific sellers – the effective equivalent of rationing. Consequently, 'when the government fixes prices, it delegates to sellers in imperfect markets the responsibility of rationing their customers which they, in turn, have the power to undertake' (p. 11).

Also published in 1952 was *American Capitalism*. This work attempts to explain the satisfactory performance of the US economy in the post-war years. This success, according to Galbraith, was not the result of adhering to the tenets of neoclassical economics – free markets and greater competition.

Rather, the US economy thrived because it violated these tenets by allowing economic power to develop.

Economic success requires technological advance. This, in turn, requires capital to finance research. It also requires organization to undertake the development of technological breakthroughs and to use their fruits. Since only large firms have such capabilities, only they can invest in technology. Finally, technological advance requires large firms because 'unless a firm has a substantial share of the market it has no strong incentive to undertake a large expenditure on development' (p. 87).

The problem with allowing economic power to develop is that this power may be abused by the large firm. Traditionally, competition among firms prevents price gouging and underpaying employees. According to Galbraith, the power of oligopolies gets mitigated by countervailing power. The restraint on the power of the firm comes from the other side of the market – from suppliers and customers and labour unions. If a seller has some degree of monopoly power, there will be a financial inducement for others to co-opt some of that market power and partake in the monopoly profits. Thus unions develop in response to the power of the large corporation, and large retail chains develop in response to the large and powerful manufacturing firms.

The policy implication of this analysis is that government should not attack market power through antitrust laws, but should help develop countervailing power. This it can do by supporting those who lack market power. For example, minimum wages support non-unionized workers; federal legislation, such as the Wagner Act, protects unionized workers. In the past, agricultural price supports assisted the small farmer.

The *Affluent Society*, published in 1958, did much to make the name 'Galbraith' a household word. Written at a time when classical economic principles were experiencing a resurgence, the book sought to counter this trend. It did so by going after the heart and soul of the traditional view of the economy – the doctrine of consumer sovereignty. This view holds that consumers know what they want, and that businesses produce what the consumer desires.

Galbraith attacks the theory of consumer demand by attacking its fundamental presupposition that tastes and demand originate within the consumer. This, Galbraith argues, runs counter to common sense and counter to what we know occurs all the time in the real world. Demand does *not* originate with the consumer; it is contrived *for* the consumer by the firm through advertising.

If consumers wanted goods of their own volition, this would indicate some primacy for the goods that business produce. Since demand is contrived, rather than originating in the individual, there is no primacy for goods produced by the business sector of the economy. Public goods are to be viewed as at least equally important. In addition, our demand for the goods produced by business is a demand for goods which we all recognize as frivolous and not of paramount importance. Even the economic principle of diminishing marginal utility recognizes that this will be the case: as we consume more and more, what we consume is less and less important.

Years of favouring private production and neglecting public goods has created a situation of private affluence and public squalor. In a much-quoted passage from *The Affluent Society*, Galbraith describes this contrast:

> The family which takes its mauve and cerise, air-conditioned, power-steered and power-braked automobile out for a tour passes through cities that are badly paved, made hideous by litter, blighted buildings, billboards, and posts for wires that should long since have been put underground. ... They picnic on exquisitely packaged food from a portable icebox by a polluted stream and go on to spend the night at a park which is a menace to public health and morals. Just before dozing off on an air mattress, beneath a nylon tent, amid the stench of decaying refuse, they may reflect vaguely on the curious unevenness of their blessings (p. 198–99).

The policy solution here is to redress this imbalance by having the state provide more public goods. This requires higher taxes to divert funds from private hands, where they will purchase less needed commodities, to the public treasury, where they will satisfy public needs. Galbraith thus resists tax reduction, even if it favours the poor. He advocates increasing sales taxes as well as increasing income taxes and closing tax loopholes.

One important area where Galbraith has challenged traditional economics is the theory of the firm. In *The New Industrial State* Galbraith argues that the industrial sector of the economy is not what economics textbooks teach us. We do not have competitive markets with a large number of firms subject to the will of the people. Rather, we have non-competitive markets and large firms controlling the market. These firms do not attempt to maximize the profits of shareholders; rather, they attempt to control the market and make it more reliable.

Large firms plan because they must plan. The market is too uncertain for the firm. Investment in technology is very costly; hence the firm cannot risk that, after expensive investment, there will be no demand for the goods they produce. They must therefore seek to eliminate market forces wherever they arise.

The large corporation frees itself from the market in several ways. Through vertical integration it takes over suppliers and outlet sources. By developing many diverse products, the firm can absorb the consequences of a drastic change in consumer tastes or aversion of consumers to a particular product. Finally, through long-term contracts between producers and suppliers the uncertainty of changes in the market is eliminated.

Traditional economic theory holds that the firm is run by the owner. This view, according to Galbraith, is severely antiquated. The firms that produce most of the goods and services we buy are run by professional managers. Those managers who partake in the decision-making for the firm Galbraith calls the 'technostructure'. It is here that corporate power lies. The technostructure has usurped power from the entrepreneur and the owner because the important decisions of the large modern firm must rely on the technical and scientific knowledge of many individuals. One person cannot be familiar with all the aspects of engineering, procurement, quality control, labour relations and marketing which are a necessary part of doing business. Group decision-making and technical expertise is important, and power therefore passes to the group.

Unlike owners, who have a vested interest in maximizing profits, the technostructure gains little from profit maximization. Rather, the interest of the technostructure is to make the market more reliable and predictable. Its goals are survival, growth and technical virtuosity. Survival means a minimum amount of earnings so that the independence of the decision-makers is maintained. Growth is important because it assures the minimum level of profits necessary and prevents the discharge of members of the technostructure as a cost-saving measure. Growth also serves the psychological needs of the technostructure – the prestige from working for a large well-known firm. Finally, technical virtuosity means more jobs and promotions for members of the technostructure.

Problems arise with this new industrial structure because, unlike the competitive market structure, there is no assurance that the technostructure will make decisions in the public interest. This opens the door for government economic policies to redress the balance between the large corporation and the public interest.

In 1972 Galbraith was made President of the American Economic Association – the highest accolade economists can give one of their own. Few dissenting economists have received such a tribute. At the end of every year, the President addresses his/her peers at the annual AEA convention. Galbraith's address ('Power and the Useful Economist', reprinted in Sharpe, 1973) criticized the economics profession for ignoring power and thereby employing irrelevant theories.

Mainstream economic thinking removes power from the realm of discourse by denying its existence and by assuming that the market will mitigate the power of the firm. As a result, economic analysis ignores the most serious problems of modern society – war, economic inequality and environmental decay. These problems stem from power struggles between corporations wanting growth and profits on the one hand, and public concern about economic security, the environment and the arms race on the other.

When these issues are viewed as conflicts between two competing powers, the state comes to acquire an additional role in economic affairs. The state must side with the public purpose in order to countervail the power of the large corporations. This is the theme of *Economics and the Public Purpose*, which was published in 1973.

This work begins by arguing that the US economy has become bifurcated. Large firms, part of what Galbraith calls the 'planning system', have acquired enormous economic power. They have power to control prices. They have resources at their disposal which allows them to mould public opinion. Advertising by the large firm equates happiness with goods produced by the private sector of the economy. It can also urge the public that environmental damage is imaginary, benign or being eliminated. Finally, large firms have great ability to influence the political process to their advantage.

In contrast, small firms are subject to the dictates of the market. They have acquired little economic power and have little ability to sway public opinion or the political process. They are thus at a competitive disadvantage relative to the planning system. The result is unequal economic development – too many goods produced by the planning system and an inadequate supply of goods produced by the market system. Likewise, important public goods may get neglected due to the political influence of the planning system.

The first step towards solving these problems is what Galbraith calls 'the emancipation of belief'. The public must recognize the conflict between the purposes of the planning system and the public purpose. Educators must ensure that education is not a form of social conditioning in the interests of the large firm. This necessitates the divorce of the university from large corporate donors. The emancipation of belief also requires that economic pedagogy stop denying the existence of economic power. Such denials serve to protect the planning system from scrutiny and control. In addition, the State must be emancipated from the influence of the large corporation. Public financing of elections is necessary to protect Congress from large corporate contributors seeking to buy influence.

After belief is freed from the convenient truths perpetrated by the planning system, the state must work to equalize power between the planning and the market systems. There must be a redistribution of income from the planning system to the market system. In particular, policies are required such as agricultural price fixing, action to stabilize prices, minimum wage legislation, guaranteed minimum incomes, protective tariffs and support for small businesses. We must also redress the imbalance between the supply of private goods and the supply of public services.

Several themes stand out from the more than 20 books that Galbraith has written over the years. First, large firms have acquired substantial economic power. Second, this power encourages technological development and thus contributes importantly to economic well-being. Hence it is better to counter the power of the large firm than to eliminate that power through antitrust action. Governments must therefore support and assist the development of countervailing power in the private sector of the economy. Third, the government must itself counter the power of the large corporation. It must ensure that an adequate supply of public goods are provided. It must keep the large corporation from doing irreversible damage to the environment or pushing madly to stockpile and supply arms. Finally, the government must countervail the power of the large corporations through the imposition of wage and price controls.

Over the past half century, then, the heterodox vision of Galbraith has been one of government power used, first, for the public good and, second, to prevent the power of the large corporation from being put to negative ends.

Galbraith's Major Writings
(1952a), *American Capitalism*, Boston: Houghton Mifflin.
(1952b), *A Theory of Price Control*, Cambridge: Harvard University Press.
(1954), *The Great Crash 1929*, Boston: Houghton Mifflin.
(1967), *The New Industrial State*, New York: New American Library.
(1969a), *The Affluent Society*, New York: New American Library.
(1969b), *Ambassador's Journal*, New York: New American Library.
(1971), *Economics, Peace and Laughter*, New York: New American Library.
(1973), *Economics and the Public Purpose*, New York: New American Library.
(1979), *Annals of an Abiding Liberal*, Boston: Houghton Mifflin.
(1981), *A Life in Our Times*, Boston: Houghton Mifflin.

Other References
Hession, C. (1972), *John Kenneth Galbraith and his Critics*, New York: New American Library.
Reisman, D. (1980), *Galbraith and Market Capitalism*, New York: New York University Press.
Sharpe, M.E. (1973), *John Kenneth Galbraith and the Lower Economics*, White Plains: International Arts and Sciences Press.
Solow, R. (1967), 'Son of Affluence', *The Public Interest*, Fall 1967, 100–8; and Galbraith's reply, 'Review of a Review', *The Public Interest*, Fall 1967, 109–18.

Pierangelo GAREGNANI (born 1930)   *Fabio Petri*

Pierangelo Garegnani, born in Milan, Italy in 1930, studied 'scienze politiche' (politics and economics) at the University of Pavia. His Laurea (M.A.) thesis on Ricardo's theory of value, stimulated by Sraffa's 1951 *Introduction* to Ricardo, won him a Trinity College grant for graduate study abroad, which allowed him to go to Cambridge in 1954, where he obtained a Ph.D. in Economics. He lived in the same college (Trinity) as Sraffa; his supervisor was Maurice Dobb. The dissertation, 'A Problem in the Theory of Capital from Ricardo to Wicksell', submitted in 1958, is still unpublished. However, a revised version was published in Italian in 1960, and many of its basic results on the classical approach became available in English in 1987 and those on the marginalist approach in 1990(b). In 1960 he became assistant to the chair of Volrico Travaglini in Rome. He also worked at SVIMEZ, a state-financed Research Institute for the development of the Italian south, where in 1962 he wrote an internal publication (for private circulation only) on the causes of unemployment. The first part of this was to become 'Notes on Consumption' (originally published in Italian in 1964–65); the remainder, still unpublished, will be summarized later. In 1961–62 he was at MIT with a Rockefeller Foundation Fellowship (on that occasion he pointed out to Samuelson the limitations of 'surrogate production functions', see 1970). After two years spent as lecturer at the University of Sassari, in 1964 he became full professor, first at Sassari, then in 1966 at Pavia, in 1970 at Florence, and from 1974 at Rome, where he still teaches. From 1980 to 1986 he co-directed, with Sergio Parrinello and Jan Kregel, the Trieste International School of Advanced Economic Studies, an annual two-week gathering of 'dissenting' economists, with seminars and lectures for advanced students. Having been appointed Sraffa's literary executor by the latter's will, he is currently working on editing Sraffa's unpublished writings.

Garegnani is the theorist who – after Sraffa – has perhaps contributed most to the reappraisal of the 'surplus' approach of the classical economists and Marx, as well as to the criticism of the marginalist or 'neoclassical' approach to value and distribution, in particular its conception of capital.

He has clarified, defended and developed Sraffa's interpretation of the classical authors, and its implications for the appraisal of Marx. He contrasts the marginalists' simultaneous determination of prices, distribution and quantities with the attitude of classical economists. When determining the rate of profits, the latter took as given (i.e. as determined in other parts of their overall analysis): (i) the real wage, (ii) the quantities produced, and (iii) the conditions of production. Behind the most glaring difference – the given real wage (in which institutional and customary elements play a central role) – one can trace, Garegnani (1987, 1990) argues, a deeper analytical difference: the absence of the marginalists' conception of production as the combination of factors of production substitutable (directly, or, through consumer choice, indirectly) one for another. Upon this conception rests the derivation of decreasing demand curves for factors which is the foundation of the entire marginalist edifice, justifying the determination of the rate of profits simultaneously with the real wage and with outputs. Then a real wage fixed by institutional factors – a possibility occasionally admitted by marginalist authors – *impedes* the full working of the competitive mechanism; it endogenously determines the level of labour employment (and of output), a higher real wage implying less employment and less output.

In the classical authors, on the contrary, one finds no decreasing demand curves for labour or capital. Then an 'institutional' determination of the real wage is *indispensable* (the marginalist mechanism of supply and demand for labour would make the real wage zero or indeterminate), and is accordingly seen as part of the nature of capitalism itself. As a result, classical authors saw competition on labour markets as tending to equalize wages for similar types of work, *not* as tending to decrease wages indefinitely so long as there was labour unemployment. High unemployment would only exert a pressure slowly to revise downwards the accepted notions of 'fair wage' which regulate competition among workers. Nor, in the classical authors, is there any univocal connection between rate of profits, or real wage, and output levels (hence the separate determination of these too). For instance, in Marx the effect of a rise in real wages on employment may be positive or negative (the stimulus to investment deriving from an increase in demand for wage goods may or may not be stronger than the disincentive deriving from the lower rate of profits), depending on the magnitude of the wage rise and the specific historical situation.

It is then only natural that in classical analyses one should find a separate part, a 'core' (Garegnani, 1987, 1990a), where the rate of profits is determined on the basis of a real wage and of conditions of production considered as given, or as independently varying parameters, while in the 'core' the variables are connected by necessary relations: if the real wage increases, the rate of profits *must* decrease as dictated by technology. But in the other parts (the analyses of the real wage, of employment and accumulation, of technical change, of the composition of output, and of their interactions), there is room – which the classical authors admitted – for multiplicity and variability according to the circumstances of the relevant influences. This makes it impossible to establish the effects of changes in one variable on other variables with sufficient univocity and generality, thus preventing a simultaneous general determination (for instance, of changes in distribution, quantities produced and technology). It suggests instead an analysis in separate successive stages, if necessary with iterations to take account of feedbacks. Thus the effect of a change in real wages on the rate of profits may be first determined in the 'core' on the basis of the given conditions of production, and then modified in a second stage if the changes in quantities produced (to be determined according to the specific situation) affect the conditions of production, owing to changes of no-rent land or to non-constant returns to scale. This method endows the classical approach with great flexibility, making it compatible with different theories of investment or of distribution.

Garegnani clarifies the development of classical value theory as resulting from the problem with the treatment of capital which arises in this approach when, in the 'core', the determination of the rate of profits is attempted. While the determination of the surplus as a physical aggregate of heterogeneous commodities (the difference between net social product and total real wages) posed no great difficulties, in the determination of the rate of profits an apparent *danger of circularity* arose. Abstracting (for simplicity) from rents, the rate of profits is determined as the ratio between the value of the surplus product (that is, profits) and the value of anticipated capital. Thus, the relative values of commodities must be known. Classical economists realized that, in general, commodities exchange at ratios which depend on the rate of profits: hence the danger of circularity of a rate of profits depending on a ratio not determinable before the rate of profits is known.

Taking his clue from Sraffa's *Introduction* to Ricardo, Garegnani argues that the role of the 'corn' sector in Ricardo's 1815 *Essay on Corn*, and of the labour theory of value in Ricardo's *Principles* and in Marx, were ways out of that danger of circularity, in the only imperfect ways concretely possible at the time. In the *Essay on Corn* the hypothesis that, in the agricultural sector, product and capital are physically sufficiently homogeneous makes the rate of profits a ratio of physical quantities. If commodities exchange at labour values, the aggregates determining the rate of profits can be calculated without knowing the latter. Ricardo was conscious that relative prices change with the rate of profits, and all his life searched for a way to overcome this problem. Marx started from Ricardo and, on the basis of his analytical advances, concluded that the divergences of prices from labour values, being due to 'organic compositions' diverging from the average, must cancel out in the economy as a whole. Marx was mistaken here. But the mistake is not an irreparable one.

A non-circular determination of the rate of profits *is* possible, either via Sraffa's simultaneous equations or his standard commodity, or in the way found by Garegnani (1960; see 1987). He determines the rate of profits as the ratio of surplus to capital in the vertically integrated wage sector, with prices measured in labour commanded (the value of the surplus product of the sector, which consists of wages, is then a quantity of labour), and with capital represented as dated quantities of labour, each multiplied by the unknown rate of profits for the corresponding time period (the rate of profits, although entering the aggregates, remains the only unknown variable).

The strict analytical continuity between Ricardo and Marx shows that the role of the labour theory of value in Marx is the same as in Ricardo – to determine the rate of profits. Against additional or alternative roles often attributed to Marx's labour theory of value, Garegnani makes two points (1981). First, that the apparently aprioristic exposition of Volume I of *Capital* was due to Marx's conclusion (reached earlier) that the general rate of profits is the same as if commodities exchanged at labour values. This authorized him initially to assume exchanges at labour values – the assumption easiest to follow for his readers – it made no difference for the problems discussed in that first volume. Second, that the differences from Ricardo, often considered in the Marxist tradition to indicate other roles of labour values in Marx (e.g. the labour/labour-power distinction or the abstract-labour/concrete-labour distinction), have strictly analytical motivations. Marx attributes Smith's mistake on prices resolving into wages, profits and rents (forgetting about 'constant capital') to the absence of the distinction between concrete and abstract labour. Therefore the correct determination of the rate of profits and of prices of production, far from weakening Marx's general approach, confirms its soundness. It verifies that the rate of profits *can* be determined on the basis of the same data from which Marx begins to calculate labour's embodied and surplus value – the physically specified wage and the conditions of production.

Nor does exploitation need the labour theory of value to be confirmed (1981): what it needs is the correctness of the classical approach, which sees the positivity of profits as due simply to the power given to the owners of capital (by the institutional structure of capitalism) to appropriate part of the labourers' product solely by virtue of their collective monopoly of the conditions of production. This view makes it possible to refute the accusation of the bourgeoisie that the revenue of feudal lords was the fruit of exploitation, being due to their monopoly of land which obliged the serfs to accept performing *corvées* .

Garegnani's original criticisms of the marginalist approach address both its long- and short-period versions. Written in 1960, before Sraffa's results on reswitching, the criticism concentrates on the contradiction between the requirement that the capital endowment be a datum independent of prices and hence of distribution, and the requirement – as old as Adam Smith and accepted by all founders of marginalist economics including Walras – of a uniform rate of profits (or rate of interest on the produced means of production evaluated at supply prices). Garegnani proves (see 1990b, p. 19) that the second requirement is incompatible with taking as given (as Walras does) the *vector* of the several endowments of the different capital goods. The resulting system of equations is generally devoid of a solution. The economic reason is simple: in order to operate, the tendency to a uniform rate of return on supply price must alter the remunerations of the several capital goods. To that end, it must alter their relative supplies, what is not allowed in Walras. Therefore the proportions between the endowments of the several capital goods must be endogenously determined. Marginalist theorists must then conceive the several capital goods as embodying different amounts of a single factor of production 'capital' – capable of changing 'form' (i.e. composition) without changing in 'quantity' – and must take as given the endowment of this single factor 'capital'. This is in fact the conception of capital to be found in the generality of marginalist authors (with the single exception of Walras) up to very recent times.

However, 'capital' should be measured in units independent of distribution, and yet univocally connected with production and – at given prices – with costs, otherwise it would be impossible to derive the demand for it from cost minimization (therefore physical measures such as weight will not do). No such measure exists. Böhm-Bawerk's 'average period of production', the only attempt at finding such a measure, is shown (see 1990b, pp. 23–7) to require three unacceptable conditions for its validity: only one non-produced factor, only circulating capital, and simple (instead of compound) interest. Which is why Wicksell, after initially adopting the period-of-production approach to 'capital', later abandons it and, like everybody else (apart from Walras), measures the endowment of 'capital' as an amount of *value*. But since the value of capital goods is not independent of distribution, there is no way out of the contradiction.

One escape route increasingly attempted by neoclassical value theorists in recent decades has been temporary or intertemporal equilibria; these maintain Walras's given vector of endowments of the several capital goods but drop the uniform rate of return on supply price. Garegnani responds critically (1976, 1990b, Section V), arguing that this shift to notions of very-short-period equilibrium entailing as it does the abandonment of the *method* – which had remained the same across the change in *theory* from the classical to the marginalist approach. This method explains market prices and quantities as gravitating around and towards normal or 'long-period' positions characterized by a uniform rate of profits. Its abandonment introduces grave new difficulties:

- a lack of sufficient persistence of the equilibrium. The several capital endowments (and also, in temporary equilibria, the shape of expectation functions) can change so quickly as to deprive the equilibrium of its traditional role of a position around and towards which market variables gravitate, making its significance unclear (the analysis of change through comparative statics becomes impossible);
- a dilemma between the absurd assumption (in intertemporal equilibria) of perfect foresight or complete futures markets over an infinite future, and the assumption (in temporary equilibria) of exogenously given expectation functions (with a risk of indefiniteness of results, which come to depend on largely arbitrary assumptions on expectations);
- a lack of sufficient substitutability between factors once different capital goods are treated as different factors. Changes in methods of production generally entail, not just different proportions among the same capital

goods or between them and labour, but rather the employment of different capital goods. Thus almost certainly in these short-period equilibria, a very high proportion of equilibrium factor prices would be zero (1990b, Section VI), including perhaps the price of labour.

In his 1976 essay, Garegnani (with proof from Hicks's case) shows that the shift appears due, not to any intrinsic shortcomings of the traditional notion of long-period positions, but instead to the desire to avoid measuring capital as an amount of value – a problem arising in the determination of long-period positions *in the marginalist approach* only. And yet the avoidance of the notion of value capital as a factor of production is only illusory (1990b): *the traditional marginalist conception of 'capital' as a single factor is still implicit* in the assumed stability of the savings-investment market. This stability requires a decreasing investment schedule; but marginalist authors always derived and only can derive the downward-sloping investment schedule from the downward-sloping demand function for 'capital', investment representing the demand for 'free' capital: this derivation becomes impossible if, as 'reverse capital deepening' shows, the demand for capital can have nearly any shape. The result is 'reverse capital deepening' which destroys the entire *factual basis* (1990b) of the marginalist approach by showing the falsity of the logical deduction (from technical and consumer choice) of well-behaved substitution between on labour and on (value) 'capital' (1970). 'Reverse capital deepening' undermines not only aggregate production functions, but also the right to assume that the rate of interest is the price capable of bringing investment into equality with full-employment savings. The very-short-period versions of marginalist theory then appear *even weaker* than the traditional ones, because the difficulties with value 'capital' are not eliminated, and to them new difficulties are added. The conclusion is clear: the marginalist approach is indefensible in all its versions.

Garegnani has also brought the criticism of marginalist investment theory to bear on Keynesian economics. In his 'Notes' (1978–79, Part II), he argues that the reason why the debates on Keynes are so inconclusive is the presence in Keynes of fundamentally incompatible elements: the principle of effective demand – that savings are adjusted to investment by variations of national income – and the negation of a spontaneous tendency to full employment coexist uneasily with marginalist notions (the decreasing demand schedule for labour and, above all, the decreasing investment schedule), leading to 'neoclassical synthesis' counter-arguments. A situation of uncertainty has continued to this day on whether the marginalist long-run equilibrating mechanisms would be strong enough to counter the disequilibrating influences coming from vagaries of expectations, multiplier-accelerator interactions or financial instabilities etc. The uncertainty extends to the internal consistency of Keynes's own analysis. Real wage and normal rate of return on capital are necessarily tied by an inverse relation, whereas in Keynes a decrease in the interest rate decreases the real wage. Also, even on marginalist grounds, the decreasing marginal efficiency of investment is not easily reconcilable with persistent unemployment, since employment can then increase in proportion with the capital stock. (As to the short-period rising supply price of capital goods – an implausible assumption anyway – Keynes himself admits that it is only a transitory element whose influence becomes irrelevant over longer periods.) But the now-evident deficiencies of marginalist capital theory permit one to cut through these uncertainties. Keynes's conclusion as to the absence of a tendency to full employment does not need volatility of expectations or monetary 'complications' to 'keep at bay' the marginalist 'real' forces making for full employment, which Keynes himself had not rejected. Rather, these 'real' forces appear not to exist (also see 1989).

Garegnani advocates the reconstruction of political economy on the basis of a modernized surplus approach incorporating Keynes's principle of effective demand. He argues that since the imperfections of Ricardo's (and Marx's) theory of value – which were the main *scientific* reason why the surplus approach was abandoned – *can* be corrected to make the surplus approach solid. At the same time insurmountable deficiencies have emerged in the *marginalist* approach. Since the surplus approach appears to have been abandoned prematurely, it seems natural to revert to it as the basis for a reconstruction of economic theory. After Sraffa and the work stimulated by him on the 'core', what is required for a reconstruction is, essentially, a theory of distribution, and a theory of output; theories for which solid starting points are provided by the classical analysis of distribution and accumulation and by Keynes's principle of effective demand.

On the forces determining distribution, Garegnani has noticed (1990a) that recent research on wage differentials and discrimination confirms the importance of institutional and customary elements. Expanding upon Sraffa's remark that the rate of profits is susceptible of being determined by monetary policy, Garegnani has suggested exploring the possibility that monetary authorities could affect distribution by influencing the real rate of interest and thus the (somewhat higher) minimum rate of profit which investment must earn, a minimum towards which the actual rate of profit should tend owing to competition. 'This does not entail maintaining afresh that the wage bargain has no power to change real wages: the policy of the monetary authorities is not conducted in a vacuum and the movement of prices and of the money wages determined in the wage bargain will be amongst the most important considerations in the formulation of the policy' (1978–79, p.63).

However, Garegnani expresses scepticism about the 'Cambridge' theories of distribution (Joan Robinson, Kaldor) which argue that investment generates the corresponding amount of savings by altering the share of profits. These theories appear to ignore the adaptability of output to demand without changes in distribution, in the short run by variations of the degree of utilization of capacity, and in the longer run by adapting productive capacity (1982).

On the explanation of output and employment, Garegnani argues that what is basically needed is a theory of investment; to determine employment once investment is given we now have Keynes's principle of effective demand. 'Say's law' (investment supposedly determined by full-capacity savings) must be rejected, having no solid justification in Ricardo, nor in marginalist theory. Neither is it supported by the observation of a fairly full utilization of productive capacity on average over decades, most probably because productive capacity adapts to demand (1990b). The actual determinants of investment, Garegnani argues (1962), can be reduced to two – expected demand and technical progress – although neither can guarantee the full utilization of capacity. (Particularly interesting is his denial that the rate of profits may be a direct influence on investment. Only if an increase in demand is foreseen will investors expect to sell an increased amount of product at prices not below normal, thus gaining at least the ruling rate of profits; otherwise they will not invest and this whatever the rate of profits. Changes in the rate of profits can only affect investment indirectly, for instance by altering the multiplier.) Thus investment will normally fall short of full-capacity savings; the resulting waste is not well appreciated because, contrary to unemployment, it is largely invisible. One does not see the lost production of consumption goods, even more the cumulative loss of potential productive capacity. Thus Garegnani demonstrates (1962) that in the years 1955–60 Italy's growth rate was limited, not by any supply-side or balance-of-payments constraint, but simply by insufficient investment. In each one of those years Italy (a structural-unemployment country) might have afforded, without any need to reduce consumption, a production of investment goods 15% greater than the observed one, with a resulting increase of productive capacity at the end of the six years sufficient to eliminate structural unemployment. The general implication is that social control of the accumulation process is necessary because capitalism wastes potential savings and has no tendency spontaneously to absorb unemployment. The absence, historically observed in the industrial countries, of very great and persisting differences between the supply of labour and the demand for it results from adaptations of the *supply* of labour to demand. In the past various 'reserve armies' have provided this supply, including pre-capitalist sectors, agricultural underemployment and housewives, as well as frequent and controlled migration flows (1990a, 16).

Garegnani's Major Writings

(1960), *Il capitale nelle teorie della distribuzione*, Milan: Giuffré.

(1962), *Il problema della domanda effettiva nello sviluppo economico italiano*, Rome: Srimez.

(1970), 'Heterogeneous Capital, the Production Function and the Theory of Distribution', *Review of Economic Studies*, **37**.

(1976), 'On a Change in the Notion of Equilibrium in Recent Work on Value and Distribution', in M. Brown, K. Sato and P. Zarembka (eds), *Essays in Modern Capital Theory*, Amsterdam: North-Holland. Reprinted in J. Eatwell and M. Milgate (eds), *Keynes's Economics and the Theory of Value and Distribution*, Oxford University Press and Duckworth, 1983.

(1978–79), 'Notes on Consumption, Investment and Effective Demand: Parts I and II', *Cambridge Journal of Economics*, **2** and **3**. Reprinted in J. Eatwell and M. Milgate (1983).

(1981), *Marx e gli economisti classici*, Turin: Einaudi.

(1982), 'Summary of the paper "Some Notes for an Analysis of Accumulation"', manuscript distributed at the Trieste International School of Economics.

(1984), 'On Some Illusory Instances of "Marginal Products"', *Metroeconomica*.

(1987), 'Surplus Approach to Value and Distribution', in *The New Palgrave Dictionary of Economics*, Macmillan.

(1989), 'Some Notes on Capital, Expectations and the Analysis of Changes' in G. Feiwel (ed), *Joan Robinson and Modern Economic Theory*, London: Macmillan.

(1990a), 'Sraffa: Classical versus Marginalist Analysis' in K. Bharadwaj and B. Schefold (eds), *Essays on Sraffa*, London: Unwin and Hyman.

(1990b), 'Quantity of Capital', in *The New Palgrave Dictionary of Economics: Capital Theory*, Macmillan.

Nicholas GEORGESCU-ROEGEN (born 1906)

Eighty-four years ago I was the first born of a family whose ancestry could not serve as an ingratiating introduction. I knew none of my grandparents. My mother came from a truly modest family of six children, three of whom were completely illiterate. She was a teacher at a professional girls school. At the time of my birth my father was an army captain. A couple of years later he came upon a major slipping away with some meat from the soldiers' foodstock. During the ensuing altercation my father struck the culprit. For striking a superior he should have been court-martialled but in view of the nastiness of the episode he was just pressed to resign. I can offer no proof, but I believe that learning at a very young age about that tragic event in my family fostered my idiosyncratic repugnance against trespass. In the society of scientists one could deplore the unavowed shams in education – the now corrupt title of Master of Arts, once Alfred Marshall's qualification, or the idle Ph.D. requirement for foreign language efficiency. (A deeper dissection is in 1976a.) And I should not fail to decry the plagiarisms towards which the intelligentsia shows no disgust. Quasi-plagiarism is committed by many an author who refers only to very recent works although the primary contributions to that field go back several decades. The manifest intent is for such an author to appear as belonging to a tidal wave of a new discovery.

A second influence on my development came from the town of Constantza where I was born and raised; having been an important trading centre for centuries, this was a truly cosmopolitan town. Occupations followed roughly national lines and so did marriages, but there were no conflicts whatsoever in this regard. Growing up in such an atmosphere I reached the faith that, although people are not identical, each can contribute to the happiness of society (if other things do not impinge upon it). Any restrictions imposed without imperative reason against particular groups of humans have always given me goose pimples, as in the US in mid-1930s where hotels still had brass plaques outside to advise that only Caucasians were accepted, and where the town of Brookline (Mass) was at one time bedecked with immense placards painted with anti-Semitic slogans. During the madness that plagued Europe since the 1930s I could not possibly escape from being terrorized in Romania by the entire gamut of extremists against whom I protested loudly enough to put my life in danger, a risk that almost materialized twice.

The foregoing sentiments are so obviously beyond question that they do not constitute dissent. Yet one of them is germane to dissent. As I have argued in several places, first in 'The Steady State and Ecological Salvation', the commandment 'love thy neighbour as thyself' cannot sustain an entropic salvation. A new one, 'love thy species as thyself', must be accepted. This is the strongest dissent to the vulgar question used by many economists, 'What has posterity ever done for us?' From a first hint of bioeconomics I observed that societies of other species, which take care of their offspring in unimaginable ways, could teach us some very good lessons. True, some standard economists have ultimately succumbed to the idea that concern with the welfare of future generations is a *sine qua non* for the survival of the species and come out with a characteristic observation: certainly, they say, the welfare of all future human generations is fully ensured by the common fact that every family cares about its children, those children in turn care about their own children, and so on down the line. But as in many other cases the desire of getting out of a tight professional spot has got the best of standard economists' logic. None has stopped to ask whether the relation 'to take care of' is transitive for, if it were, our present welfare should have been warranted by Adam and Eve.

The first fateful influence on my development was that of my father. Under his kind incitements, by the time I was four I could dance with the three Rs. I kept writing the numbers from 1 to 99 on any piece of paper I could get hold of. Probably to spare the paper in the house my father kept from me the secret of how to write the number 'one hundred', which was to be my discovery by all kinds of R&D. When I was seven I lost not only a father but also a mind who could have prepared me to cope with the kind of world that began with the 1914 war.

In the elementary school my love for arithmetic was first enhanced by a teacher who taught us how to solve, by elementary means, problems that belong to college algebra. Guided by other devoted teachers, by the age of

14 I saw my name in print in *Gazeta Matematica*, a didactical periodical then in its fiftieth year. While in the lycée I participated in a strenuous national competition for mathematics in which I once came second and once first. Naturally, I enrolled at the Faculty of Mathematics of the University of Bucharest where I listened to some of the world renowned masters and got my *licence ès mathémathiques* in 1926.

Ever since my first contact with the mysteries of mathematics I dreamed of becoming a teacher of that discipline. Now, with the licence in my pocket, that dream seemed fulfilled. However, as I was soon to discover, some fulfilled dreams are metastable. Of course, my spirits were lifted up when on the recommendation of the Faculty of Mathematics I was awarded a scholarship to study at the Sorbonne which, together with Gottingen, then formed the two mathematical 'navels' of the world. One of my professors, Traian Lalescu, frustrated by the lack of data relevant to Romania's economic problems, advised me: 'In Paris, study mathematical statistics. We urgently need statisticians, rather than pure mathematicians.' I felt this as a call to intellectual arms and, ignoring my old dream, I switched to statistics. My dissertation was so well received that members of the committee wrote on my diploma *'félicitations du jury'*. Emile Borel presented a resumé of it to the *Académie des Sciences* and the entire October 1930 issue of *Journal de la Société de Statistique de Paris* was devoted to its discussion.

The dissertation began with an analysis of the general stochastical scatter in which *all* variables are affected by random errors – a total novelty because even now the theory just covers the simplified case in which only one variable is affected by error. On that result I based a special method for discovering the latent cyclical components of time series, a result especially important at that time when business cycles were the focus of great attention. I still wonder to this day why this important (as I think) method has never been noticed in any way although Schumpeter used it in his *Business Cycles* and a detailed English summary appeared in *Proceedings of the International Statistical Conference* (1947), in *Econometrica* (1948) and in Chapter 10 of my *Essays* (1976b). One plausible explanation is that Herman Wold, who had excellent public relations, proposed an almost identical model in 1938; Wold attracted all attention.

I took two economics courses, one with Jacques Rueff, the other magisterially taught by Albert Aftalion. From those courses and from my own intellectual torments I reached the idea that economic phenomena cannot be described by a mathematical system, a faith that I have never renounced. So although studies of business cycles were then in great vogue, I decided to apply my method of discovering cyclical components, not to economic data, but to the rainfall in Paris (which, curiously, showed the same periodicities as those recognized in economics by Schumpeter).

The Paris interlude was the first switch on my life tracks. I came as a mathematician and left as a statistician. I then yearned to do some research under Karl Pearson whose contributions had been highly praised by Georges Darmois, the chairman of my dissertation. There were two obstacles though: the cost of living in England was then far higher than the usual Romanian stipend, and I did not even know what 'good bye' meant. The solution came from the family of a Master of French, Leonard Hurst, whom I had befriended in Paris. With things getting hard because of the depression, they – a working-class family – took me in as a paying guest for 17 $^1/_2$ shillings per week! An extension of my Romanian scholarship thus permitted me to go to London and also to learn English (as a child does) from the wonderful lady of the house, a marvellous retired schoolteacher.

The contribution closest to Karl Pearson's heart was the method of moments, a formidable idea that has unfortunately been completely shelved by the peculiar undercurrents of the society of scientists. I said unfortunately because Pearson's method is superior in research to the maximum likelihood, as now tends to be admitted. It was from that field that I chose the topic of a paper of more than 40 pages published in *Biometrika* (1932). My direct, simple contacts with Pearson for almost two years, together with the study of his magnificent *Grammar of Science*, convinced me that a scholar must also do some philosophy in order continuously to control the verisimilitude of his own scientific endeavours. Pearson was a Machian, a disciple of a philosophy that has been downgraded like no other but is still endorsed, even by some pundits of physics. In a subdued way I became a Machian too. In fact, this peculiar philosophy is the root of my most irritating dissents. I profess an epistemology concerned mainly with the analytical representations of observed phenomena. Satisfactory representation is the primary issue in any scientific endeavour. The controversies about the use of mathematics in economics would clear up if the antagonists saw that mathematics is irreproachable; the fault rests with the economist who applies it to flawed representations. *Analytical Economics* was the title I coined for my first English monograph (1966).

Having heard from Aftalion's course of the so-called 'Harvard Economic Barometer' of Warren and Pearson, based on three periodic series, and of the fantasized manipulations of economic data by Karl Karsten, I kept wondering whether some connection might exist between those activities and my period analysis. Naturally, I was elated when the Rockefeller Foundation granted me a fellowship to visit Harvard University. It was there that the second switch on my life tracks was waiting for me. By the time I arrived there (1934) the Economic Barometer had closed shop. Failing to establish an amiable relation with Professor W.L. Crum, who directed research in periodograms, in utter despair I decided to contact the person in charge of the course of Business Cycles. This is how by mere chance I met the man who was to have the most decisive influence on my further thinking, Joseph A. Schumpeter, whose name I did not even know at first how to pronounce correctly.

From the small group of young Rockefeller Fellows – Nicholas Kaldor, Oscar Lange, August Losch, Fritz Machlup, Gerhard Tintner – who met weekly under Schumpeter's guidance as well as from the private luncheons I often had with him, I turned into an economist with a degree from 'Universitas Schumpeteriana'. I naturally plunged first into the mathematical theory of utility. My first economics paper (*Quarterly Journal of Economics*, 1935) was on a mathematical slip of Pareto, not a great feat since Pareto, although a truly great economist, was not an accomplished mathematician. But I was rather out of step for mathematical economics which was still esoteric.

My most significant work of that period was a long essay on 'The Pure Theory of Consumers' Behavior' in which, through the prism of my epistemology, I constructed new analytical issues of the utility concept. I began with a logical dissection of indifference and ended with a theory of satiety and of stochastic choice; ever since, these have served as the trade articles for contributions to utility theory. My salient finding concerned a time-honoured paradox of why the differential elements derived from consumer demand are integrable if the economy consists of only two commodities. Dissenting from an assertion by Vito Volterra that in two dimensions the differential elements *are always integrable so as to provide an ordinal map for utility*, I pointed out that the issue is not hanging on the number of dimensions, that *even in two dimensions demand elements are not necessarily so integrable*. I have repeatedly returned to this point, the last time in a 1973 paper reprinted as Chapter 13 of my *Essays* (1976b) where I proved a stronger theorem: even if the differential elements are integrable into an ophelimity map, *that map does not necessarily reveal an ophelimity order*. It is curious, nonetheless, that this result has not been incorporated into the utility theory, not mentioned even in the works critical of revealed preference. I presume that the exceptional popularity of Paul Samuelson's construction, which requires complete integrability, is alone responsible for it.

Schumpeter wanted to write a theory volume with me; this led to an offer to join that department. It is next to impossible for me to conceive *now* why I turned him down, if it was not the memory of Lalescu's call. I returned to Bucharest where I had several jobs rather unrelated to my mathematical economic armamentarium. I went back to teach statistical methods while living through four dictatorships, the last brought in by the Soviet tanks. And it was my hard fate, later, to get the onerous job as Secretary General of the Romanian Armistice Commission which, however, did allow me to learn more about how the great powers implement their written treaties. During my 12-year 'exile' in my own country until fleeing from the Communist terror, I also learned two invaluable economic lessons that were to represent the third and a very important switch on my life tracks.

I had entered into a wonderful friendship with Andrew Edson, the Secretary of the US Legation in Bucharest and a Ph.D. candidate in economics at Harvard. One day Andy softly said, 'Romania is a deficient economy because her institutions are inept. The man who just sits outside the office of every high functionary, public or private, does nothing to deserve a slice of the national cake.' The fundamental principle of standard theory – marginal pricing – was violated by my own economic world. The answer to this anomaly, when it finally dawned upon me, was that in an overpopulated country marginal pricing is the worst economic policy. In a country of dearth, people must work as much as they can in order to maximize the national product, to the point where their marginal productivity may even approach zero.

The internal logic of the Agrarians who insisted on the merits of family farms (where there are no wages) was thus justified. I presented this idea at a 1948 after-dinner chat at the University of Chicago, which was followed by a general silence: the group did not want to expose me as an economic ignoramus. Hating to have the paper refused I sat on a draft until the day when George Richardson, after listening to a lecture of mine, immediately committed me to prepare a version to be published as a leading article in *Oxford Economic Papers* (1960). In spite of the lack of attention for the political implications of my agrarian theory, after more than 40 years I still think it to be highly valuable, particularly my belief in the efficiency of the family farm (see Chapter 6 of 1976b).

In my essay in *Oxford Economic Papers* I pointed out, first, that there are endless types of economies and that each one requires a different theory; *no single theory could describe them all* – an idea which is anathema for the standard school. Second, that the famous Arrow-Debreu proof of the existence of a solution of the Walrasian system rested on an absurd premise: namely, that all individuals are *ab initio* endowed with an adequate income forever. That exposure must have so appalled the econometric establishment that at the 1969 conference of the American Economic Association, they scheduled their business meeting at the same hour as my Richard T. Ely Lecture! But other signs over the years have revealed that those with vested interests in extolling standard economics have striven to obstruct the publication of my works and to support even flawed attacks against them (see 'My Life Philosophy', forthcoming).

The second lesson I learned in Romania happened as the Communists, still encountering resistance, thought of using wild inflation to stop the peasants from bringing food to the recalcitrant towns. Since there was virtually nothing the peasants could find to buy, I thought the strategy would surely succeed. To my public shame, the peasants kept selling food even for almost worthless bills because, for them, any form of money was the *summum bonum*. They just kept filling their mattresses with paper money. That monetary disappearing act of 1947 strengthened my awareness of the danger that resides in money manipulations.

Having learned this truth from my personal experience, not from theoretical books, I was unable to accept Keynes's thesis in which planned inflation – a euphemism for government spending – is the unique prescription for universal economic growth. The process of economic development cannot be reduced to the simple Keynesian tool, the diagram with a line at 45°. Because of this simplification Keynes's approach became the darling of a whole generation of economists, while the idea that government spending makes everybody happier supplied politicians with a new 'invisible hand', the Keynesian one which picks the pockets of the taxpayers as if under anesthesia. If the bottom line is drawn, government spending does not pickpocket only the contemporary generation; it pickpockets future generations in a quite swift manner which must in the end come to account. The present formidable struggle in the US with the crushing amount of public interest repayable on public debt – created by past government spending – proves that the issue of intergenerational distribution pertains not only to natural resources (1971), but to money as well. Turning to underdeveloped countries, inflation is a means by which virtually all economic growth benefits the privileged classes (Chapter 7 in 1976b).

My objection to the neoclassical production function (Chapters 4, 5 and 10 of 1976b) and the 'factors' comprising it led me into a dialectical discussion of that common but never properly defined concept: process. I argued first that a process is identified by a tempo-spatial boundary and described only by the elements that cross it. Input and output can then be defined analytically rather than linguistically. For an adequate analytical representation of a material process I introduced the essentially different concepts of 'fund' – the agents – and 'flow' – the elements transformed by the agents (Chapter 9 in 1971 and 4 and 5 in 1976b). Like any analytical domain, that of analytical production processes had to have a proper unit. For it I proposed the elementary process, which brings forth a fact hard to accept at first: that idleness of agents is a physical predicament of production. In this predicament lies the scarcity of time in our productive activity, a scarcity that may be reduced primarily by the special arrangements of the elementary processes illustrated by the factory system.

In a 1970 pamphlet (Chapter 3 in 1976b) I pointed out for the first time the important role of the entropy law for the existence of our species. As I argued then, the entropy law is the root of economic scarcity: it states that the natural resources on which our existence depends are continuously and irrevocably turned into waste. For us this is the most important of all the laws of the relatively new science – thermodynamics – which in essence is the physics not only of economic value, but of biological phenomena as well. Some, to oppose my idea, argue that the entropy law, like many other laws in history, will be refuted. But history is on the opposite side: few planks now count on the eventual refutation of the entropy law.

I have grown tired of trying to convince the champions of 'sustainable development' that this plank is even more foolhardy than 'steady state'; that even a steady state needs a constant flow of resources that are continuously and irrevocably degraded into waste as the entropy law requires. Even Malthus (as I said in Chapter 1 of 1976b) was not Malthusian enough when he accepted as possible an eternal steady state.

To oppose my ideas a series of so-called alternative technologies have been publicized with deafening din: solar technology, in the first place, followed by gasohol and a few others. Fusion is no longer the great hope of the old, and fission may prove to be good only for bombs and wrecks (as I said at a symposium where the Nobelites present did not chop off my head).

For some 20 years I have struggled with the vital problem of the long-run future of our exosomatic species. My results must stand up, for otherwise anyone eager of literary success would have put me down with loud criticism. However, no recognized scholar has wanted to cross intellectual swords with me. My staunch claims are for two entirely novel thoughts. The first is the Fourth Law of Thermodynamics (1977), which states that a closed system – that is, a system that can exchange only energy with its environment, as the Earth approximately is – cannot produce mechanical work forever at a *constant rate*.

My second finding concerns the fact that alternative techniques have been exalted blindly, without anyone realizing how special must be that which could sustain a viable technology. Surprisingly, among the immense number of feasible techniques (or recipes) known to humans throughout history, only a few can sustain a viable technology; that is, a technology that can go on as long as its proper type of energy is forthcoming. (Certainly, no recipe can produce energy or matter; it can only use them.) I have proposed to call these special recipes Promethean for the good reason that fire best illustrates their peculiar properties. To wit, fire changes energy of one form (chemical) into one of another form (heat) and may also generate a chain reaction: with just the flame of a match we can burn a whole forest, nay, all forests. Our first mineral technology was based on fire from wood. Before long we reached a crisis as forests were being depleted. In essence that crisis was identical to the present one. Prometheus II – two mortals, Thomas Savary and Thomas Newcomen – saved the day with the invention of another

Promethean recipe: the steam engine which changes heat energy into motor energy and which has thereby triggered a chain reaction because, as in the case of fire, with a little coal we can mine more coal and metals to make more machines. A legion of ecological tyros exists who, through luxurious leaflets and magniloquent global forums, seek to convince us all that one of their favourite alternative technologies is just around the corner. They are set on terribly dangerous propaganda for if that promise were true, why should everyone not have a car that accelerates to 100 miles per hour before the cigarette lighter gets hot? No thought about the future of our species can be more disastrous than wishful thinking and decrying the realists as doomsayers.

From what I have said so far it is clear that the only true hope for our species, fully exosomatic as it has evolved, is whether Prometheus III will come soon. When? The nature of this question is bioeconomic because, as I explained (Chapter 1 of 1976b), it concerns the intimate relation between our biological existence and our economic activity. Indeed, these two domains have many features in common.

The promise of sustainable development is the most saleable snake oil ever contrived. Members of the academe now sell it in global forums amply subsidized by enterprises of the highest rank. The participants who exult in mutually convincing themselves that the future can be one of continuous sustainable development remind one of those who in earlier times gathered to get delight from *panem et circenses.*

It is in the opposition to this way of preparing to face the entropic menace that hovers over our species that resides my sharpest and tragic dissent.

Georgescu-Roegen's Major Writings

(1930), 'Le problème de la recherche des composantes cycliques d'un phénomène, *Journal de la Société Statistique de Paris*, October.

(1947), 'Further Contributions to the Scatter Analysis', *Proceedings of the International Statistical Conference*, **5**.

(1951), 'The Aggregate Linear Production Function and its Application to von Neumann's Economic Model', in T.C. Koopmans et al (eds), *Activity Analysis of Production and Allocation*, Wiley and Sons.

(1960), 'Economic Theory and Agrarian Economics', *Oxford Economic Papers*, **12**.

(1966), *Analytical Economics: Issues and Problems*, Cambridge: Harvard University Press.

(1971), *The Entropy Law and the Economic Process*, Cambridge: Harvard University Press.

(1976a), 'Economics and Educational Development', *Journal of Education Finance*, **2**.

(1976b), *Energy and Economic Myths: Institutional and Analytical Economic Essays*, Oxford: Pergamon Press.

(1977), 'The Steady State and Ecological Salvation', *BioScience*, **27**.

(1983), 'The Promethean Condition of Viable Technologies', *Materials and Society*, **7**.

(Forthcoming), 'My Life Philosophy', in M. Szensberg (ed), *The Life Philosophies of Eminent Economists*, Cambridge University Press.

Herbert GINTIS (born 1939)

I began graduate school in Mathematics at Harvard University in 1961. I received my Ph.D. in Economics from Harvard eight years later, and continued as a faculty member there until 1974. My career as a graduate student and young academic thus coincided with four momentous twentieth-century political movements in the United States: the anti-war movement, the counter-culture movement, the Civil Rights movement and the feminist movement. These political events profoundly affected my career and the contents of my work.

I realized at the time of John F. Kennedy's assassination that mathematics was not sufficiently in tune with the events of our times and, despite my love for the subject, I abandoned writing my dissertation to begin anew in economics. I had never taken a course in economics, but a friend who had studied Marx told me it was a good field because 'economics determines everything else'.

As a graduate student, I came to believe that there were three great issues in political economy that could not be put right by traditional economics: inequality and discrimination, alienation and overly materialistic cultural values, and the unaccountability of economic power. I eventually identified two major problems with neoclassical economics that prevented it from dealing with these issues: the assumption that preferences are exogenous, and the assumption that contracts could be costlessly enforced by the state. The first of these became the subject of my Ph.D. dissertation, 'Alienation and Inequality' (1969), parts of which were published as 'A Radical Analysis of Welfare Economics and Individual Development' and parts as 'Welfare Criteria with Endogenous Preferences: The Economics of Education'. Discussion of the second assumption appeared in 'The Nature of the Labor Exchange of the Theory of Capitalist Production'.

The basic arguments here were quite straightforward. Since economic theory takes preferences as given, it has a materialistic bias: people can improve only by getting *things*, rather than becoming better *persons*. A radical welfare economics must consider personal development as much as the growth of material wealth in order to deal with the major issues of advanced societies. Moreover, since economic theory takes contracts as exogenously enforced, it has no need for a notion of *economic power*. But the most basic of all economic relationships, that between boss and worker, is 'incomplete' in that the state can enforce no *quid pro quo* from a worker. The firm must act as a system of power to extract labour from labour power.

These analytical insights led me to write a number of articles that attempted to link countercultural themes to political themes in the early 1970s. These included 'New Working Class and Revolutionary Youth', *Socialist Revolution* (May, 1970); 'Power and Alienation', *Review of Radical Political Economics*, 4 (Fall, 1972); and 'Activism and Counterculture: The Dialectics of Consciousness in the Corporate State', *Telos*, **12** (Summer, 1972). They also led me to the first of many fruitful collaborations with my colleague Samuel Bowles in *Schooling in Capitalist Society* (1976b).

Attempting to understand education flowed naturally from my twin concerns with inequality and alienation, since the schools were supposed to create, first, equality (and did not) and, second, fully developed human beings (and did not). Rather than bemoan this fact, Bowles and I argued that schools reinforced inequality and produced submissive, rather than mature self-actualizing adults. My first work in this area (in my dissertation) was to show that personality rather than cognitive traits accounted for the contribution of schooling to income. This led to several articles, including 'Education, Technology, and the Characteristics of Worker Productivity', *American Economic Review* (May, 1971); and 'Towards a Political Economy of Education', *Harvard Educational Review*, **42**(1), (February, 1972), as well as my contribution to Christopher Jencks' book, *Inequality: A Reassessment of the Effect of Family and Schooling in America* (Basic Books, 1972).

Bowles and I combined our expertises and developed a common theoretical approach by jointly addressing the themes of inequality and personal development in education, both statistically and historically in *Schooling in Capitalist America*, as well as in our critique of the neoclassical theory of schooling in 'The Problems with Human Capital Theory', *American Economic Review* (May, 1975). Our basic argument was that the undemocratic and hierarchical character of the capitalist firm required that individuals develop submissive and non-assertive personality traits, and at the same time ensured a great degree of economic inequality. At a time when there was great demand for educational reform to solve problems of inequality and alienation, we argued for a certain 'principle of correspondence': the current degree of inequality and the lack of personal development in schools corresponded to the positions in the economic system that students had to assume after they left school. Hence only the *transformation of the economy* towards worker control and democratic economic accountability could set the stage for such a broad educational reform.

In 1975, with several colleagues, I moved to the University of Massachusetts, where we set up a new graduate programme reflecting research efforts into what was then known as 'radical economics'. In this period Bowles and I were engaged in an ambitious attempt to reformulate Marxian political economy in such a way as to make it relevant to the modern world. Central to this endeavour was the renovation of the Marxian theory of value, which we attempted in several articles, including 'The Marxian Theory of Value and Heterogeneous Labor: A Critique and Reformulation', *Cambridge Journal of Economics*, **1**(2), (1977), and 'Structure and Practice in the Labor Theory of Value' (1981).

By the time this last article was published, however, we had already realized that the Marxian theory of value failed to illuminate the main problems of modern economic theory, and in addition was politically irrelevant in the context of contemporary social issues. Even before this, we had begun an extensive reassessment of Marxian social theory, and became more and more critical of its general principles. My first published work in this area was 'Theory, Practice and the Tools of Communicative Discourse', *Socialist Review*, **50–51** (March–June, 1980), which dealt with the general Marxist theory of social struggle. I also wrote, with Samuel Bowles, 'Education as a Site of Contradiction in Reproduction of the Capital-Labor Relationship', *Journal of Economic and Industrial Democracy* (1981), and 'Contradiction and Reproduction in Educational Theory', in Len Barton (ed), *Schooling, Ideology, and Curriculum* (Falmer Press, 1981). These articles, while strongly defending our book *Schooling in Capitalist America*, argued that we had made too close a functional connection between schools and the economy. In particular, we now argued that the educational system in liberal democratic societies, by virtue of its attachment to a public sphere that prizes liberty and democracy, instilled values that often conflict with the hierarchical capitalist enterprise. It is this contradiction, we argued, that accounts for the importance of student movements and the generally progressive contribution of schools to social change.

My fundamental views on political economy, one outgrowth of which was the above, had begun to change in the mid-1970s as a result of the wave of authoritarian revolutions in Latin America and elsewhere in the Third World, as well as in sharp recoil against the Trilateral Commission – a group of American, European, and Japanese intellectuals who argued that democracies were increasingly 'ungovernable'. I began to think that liberal political philosophy and the individual rights associated with it were not the 'bourgeois values' that Marx so scathingly attacked, but rather were both the product of, and the major support of, exploited groups in society. Marx's mistake, Bowles and I began to think, was to see power as homogeneous, and the state as a mere reflection of society. In place of this, we argued that power was irreducibly heterogeneous, and there were always structural contradictions between the various spheres of social life.

This led us to begin a full-scale critique of Marxian theory, with an aim towards improving it. While we wrote much on the topic, we published little except for an article in German 'Die Heterogeneitat von Macht', *Das Argument*, **140** (Juli-August, 1983). Rather, we began an in-depth review of economic history with an eye towards integrating a theory of state and class exploitation. One important result was 'State and Class in European Feudalism' (1984); this reinterpreted the so-called 'transition from feudalism to capitalism' in light of the provocative works of Perry Anderson and Maurice Dobb.

In this paper we argued that the 16th and 17th centuries in Europe were a unique social formation, in which expanding despotic states made strategic alliances with weak but growing commercial classes to form a 'state-commercial alliance' that guided the movement to modern capitalism. In this alliance, the major European states attempted to consolidate power but could not. A series of revolutions in the period led to constitutional government and the pacification of absolutism.

At the same time, we began to revise our conception of the history of capitalism itself, writing 'The Crisis of Liberal Democratic Capitalism', *Politics and Society*, **11** (1982); and 'The Welfare State and Long-Term Economic Growth: Marxian, Neoclassical, and Keynesian Approaches', *American Economic Review*, (May, 1982). These explained the economic downturn and political transformation of the advanced countries in the post-Vietnam era, which we interpreted in terms of confrontation between 'person rights' and 'property rights' rather than in traditional Marxian terms. The history of American capitalism, we wrote, involved a series of 'accords' or 'class compromises' that allowed the smooth accumulation of capital in very different economic periods.

To pursue these studies, I had taken a year in 1978 to work at the Institute for Advanced Studies in Princeton (New Jersey) under the auspices of Albert Hirschman. Several of my colleagues there, including the historian William Sewell Jr, the political scientist Alesandro Pizzorno, the sociologist Claus Offe and Hirschman himself, were exploring issues closely related to my own. The Institute was an excellent place to work because there was a general acceptance of diversity, a willingness to put up with temporarily 'half -baked ideas' and yet a unremittingly critical stance towards imperfection.

During the next two years at the University of Massachusetts, Samuel Bowles and I combined our research results, coordinated our ideas (they had never been far apart, since we always communicated and worked together, albeit at a distance), and charted the major ideas that would occupy us for the next six years. In this period we wrote an article that clearly registered our new concerns with democratic accountability and the theory of economic power: 'The Power of Capital: On the Inadequacy of the Conception of the Capitalist Economy as "Private"', *Philosophical Forum*, **14**(3–4), (Spring–Summer, 1983). This article, which used a new kind of microeconomic argument in place of the Marxian theory of value to propose a democratic workplace, seemed to show the fruitfulness of pursuing a theory of economic power in a wider context.

I returned to Harvard University as a Visiting Professor in 1982 and 1983, where I presented these 'new ideas' in both the Sociology and Economics departments. The result of Bowles's and my joint work was our book *De-*

mocracy and Capitalism: Property, Theory, and the Contradictions of Modern Social Theory which foreshadowed many of the major themes that have surfaced in the human rights and democratic movements of the past few years.

In 1986, having completed *Democracy and Capitalism*, I began to envisage the possibility of developing a fully consistent alternative to the Walrasian model, in which precisely one assumption is dropped: that of costless third-party contract enforcement. In an Appendix to Bowles's and my 1981 article 'Structure and Practice in the Labor Theory of Value', we included a little model of endogenous contract enforcement in the labour market. While I was at Harvard, I began an article with my colleague Tsuneo Ishikawa; these ideas were fully developed in 'Wages, Work Discipline, and Unemployment', *Journal of Japanese and International Economies*, 1 (1987). In the late 1980s many economists, including Joseph Stiglitz as well as Samuel Bowles and myself, began thinking of endogenous enforcement in the labour market as a very powerful mode of organizing our models of labour market behaviour.

My notions of developing a complete alternative microfoundation of political economy, taking the major outlines of the Walrasian model but dropping the assumption of exogenous enforcement, began to take shape while Bowles and I were completing *Democracy and Capitalism;* these notions were well advanced by 1987. In this period I wrote two pieces attempting to apply the idea of endogenous enforcement to understanding why competitive markets are hostile to democratic firms. The major reason, I argued, is that however competitive from the point of view of productive efficiency, democratic firms would not have adequate access to capital markets. The article 'The Principle of External Accountability in Financial Markets', in M. Aoki, B. Gustafsson, and O. Williamson (eds) *The Firm as a Nexus of Treaties* (Russell Sage, 1989) argued that it is easier for outside owners to discipline a single manager than a large number of workers. Similarly, in 'Financial Markets and the Political Structure of the Enterprise', *Journal of Economic Behavior and Organization*, 1 (1989), I argued that the risk-taking behaviour of democratically constituted firms would not be satisfactory to banks or equity markets.

In 1987 I began extending this vision from labour and capital to consumer goods and international financial markets. In the political economy of consumption, I argued that competitive markets favour consumers over producers in the same way they favour bosses over workers and lenders over borrowers: they give consumers the 'power to switch'. This was the theme of 'The Power to Switch: On the Political Economy of Consumer Sovereignty', in S. Bowles, R. C. Edwards and W. G. Shepherd (eds), *Unconventional Wisdom: Essays in Honor of John Kenneth Galbraith* (Houghton-Mifflin, 1989).

In a similar line of analysis, my colleague Gerald Epstein and I began a study of international capital markets, with the overriding idea that, since there is no third-party enforcement of lending and borrowing agreements, credit rationing should be the norm. Patterns of lending and borrowing should also be explicable in terms of the lender's capacity to enforce repayment and the borrower's reluctance to become subject to a lender's threats not to renew lending relationships. We published this research, which included empirically quite compelling evidence, in our article 'International Capital Markets and the Limits of National Economic Policy', in T. Banuri and J. B. Schor, *Financial Openness and National Autonomy* (Oxford: Clarendon, 1990).

In my view, there remains a major area to be completed before the project comes to fruition: the theory of monetary equilibrium. This has been my preoccupation for the past year. I now believe I have a handle on the integration of monetary theory into the framework of endogenous contract enforcement (or 'contested exchange', as Samuel Bowles and I have come to call it). However to achieve this, I have had to bring into question an additional aspect of the Walrasian model: the assumption that agents in a market economy trade with the market as a whole (in the person of the 'auctioneer'). Rather, I have pursued the strategy of developing models of face-to-face exchange, in which a medium of exchange emerges as a least-cost instrument of endogenous enforcement of certain types of exchange relationships.

Gintis's Major Writings

(1972), 'A Radical Analysis of Welfare Economics and Individual Development', *Quarterly Journal of Economics*, **86**, November.
(1974), 'Welfare Criteria with Endogenous Preferences: The Economics of Education', *International Economic Review*, **15**(2).
(1976a), The Nature of the Labor Exchange of the Theory of Capitalist Production', *Review of Radical Political Economics*, **8**(2).
(1976b), *Schooling in Capitalist Society; Educational Reform and the Contradictions of Economic Life* (with S. Bowles), New York: Basic Books.
(1981), 'Structure and Practice in the Labour Theory of Value' (with S. Bowles), *Review of Radical Political Economics*, **12**(1).
(1984), 'State and Class in European Feudalism' (with S. Bowles) in C. Bright and S. Harding (eds), *Statemaking and Social Movements: Essays in History and Theory*, Ann Arbor: University of Michigan Press.
(1986), *Democracy and Capitalism: Property, Theory and the Contradictions of Modern Social Theory*, New York: Basic Books.

Wynne GODLEY (born 1926)

I was born in 1926 and went to school at Rugby. I owe my undergraduate education, which was completed in 1947, to two great teachers – Isaiah Berlin and P.W.S Andrews. For the next few years I pursued a career as an oboe player, first studying at the Paris Conservatoire, then earning my living as a performer. In 1954, through the good offices of P.W.S Andrews, I obtained a position as an economic assistant in the Metal Box Co. and in 1956 I joined the economic section of the Treasury which was then under the inspiring leadership of Sir Robert Hall. I owe my training as a 'general purpose' Treasury economist to my senior colleagues, Jack Downie and Bryan Hopkin.

It is not easy to remember that in the late 1950s the system of compiling national income statistics had only been operating for a few years and that quarterly figures were only just coming into existence. Little econometric work on time series had been done, and there existed little in the way of a body of knowledge which could be directly used to inform our work. Public discussion was led by journalists.

In 1958 I wrote the first paper (subsequently published in 1976), to which I now attach any importance – an empirical study of mark-up pricing. In formulating the mark-up hypothesis, I was of course influenced by my associations with Andrews and Hall, who had both done work of fundamental importance on this subject. Yet at the time I had no appreciation of the theoretical implications of my conclusions, being then only concerned to piece together bits of a macroeconomic model which would yield reliable forecasts.

In 1962 I was seconded for two years to the National Institute where, with the help of technically better qualified colleagues (particularly James Shepherd), I produced a number of econometric studies in which I tried to summarize and formalize some key relationships. However, my subsequent attempts to use these relationships to make forecasts led me to form a sceptical view as to the ability of econometrics to advance empirical knowledge about time series – a scepticism I have since found no reason to qualify.

By the mid-1960s I was anyone's equal as a *conjoncturiste*, with a detailed knowledge of the provenance and meaning of most economic statistics and of the quarter-by-quarter history of the economy over the post-war period. In addition to being in operational charge of short-term economic forecasting in the Treasury, I created the statistical system on which (Kaldor's) Selective Employment Tax was based and undertook the calculations which underlay the devaluation of sterling in 1967.

As a result of this apprenticeship at the 'sharp end' of economic policy-making, I had formed by the late 1960s a system of views about how the economy works which corresponded roughly to what people now call 'crude' Keynesianism. That is, I thought real output and employment were determined by the exogenous variables of the model – government expenditure and exports – interacting sequentially through the combined effects of the multiplier and accelerator, while inflation was a largely contingent process (which, as stated by the OED, 'may or may not happen') only weakly related to the pressure of demand (1974a). But I recognized early on that performance in foreign trade was an abiding constraint on growth. In no sense did this set of views make me into a 'dissenting' economist. The same opinions were held by virtually all my colleagues in the Civil Service and, so far as I could discern, in comparable institutions in foreign countries. I had, for instance, no sense of any difference in *Weltanschauung* when discussing any aspect of economics with Arthur Okun.

In the second half of the 1960s I developed an increasingly close working relationship, and friendship, with Nicholas Kaldor who was working at the Treasury during most of that time. It was basically at his instance that I decided, in 1970, to leave the Treasury to become Director of the Department of Applied Economics at Cambridge. My principle objective in making this move was to carry out in public the same work that I had carried out, perforce in secrecy, in the Treasury and hopefully thereby to raise the level of the public discussion of economic policy. (Even as late as 1970 not much policy-orientated work was being done outside the Civil Service.) I had no interest whatever in economic theory unless, and to the extent that, it was directly concerned with real life economies and would be relevant for policy determination.

I now consider that my work in the 1970s, in particular the formation of the Cambridge Economic Policy Group (CEPG) in partnership with Francis Cripps and the publication of a series of reviews between 1971 and 1982, was on the whole a success. It certainly did contribute to the public discussion of economic policy, as can be gauged by the amount of response and 'coverage' we received. Although some forecasting errors were made, we also had some notable 'coups', for instance our steadfast view (in contrast to that taken by other forecasting bodies as well as by W. Rees Mogg and Professors Ball and Matthews) that the Heath-Barber boom would crash because it was based on a consumer boom without regard for the growth of net export demand; also that the Thatcher-Howe policies of 1979–81 would generate by far the biggest slump of the post-war period from which no recovery could occur without a 'U-turn'.

However, far and away our most important contribution to the discussion of economic policy resided in the insistence of the CEPG on the (basically Kaldorian) point that it was the success or failure of manufacturing industry in selling goods in world markets which would determine the growth (or decline) of the economy as a whole. In view of the endemic weakness of British manufacturing, we took a consistently very gloomy view about the long-term prospects of the British economy – at least unless, by hook or by crook, the extremely adverse trends in foreign trade could be reversed. This view has been fully justified by events up to the time of writing.

There are two aspects (in particular) of the work of the CEPG which put its members into a category which may be termed 'dissenting'. The first – a matter mainly of concern to the modelling fraternity and academic econometricians – was the unconventional view we took about how to construct and use an econometric model. Thus we attached prime importance to what may be termed 'model architecture' by which I mean that the underlying accounting was coherent, without any 'dustbin' equations or sectors; everything came from somewhere and went somewhere. Our view, by which I still stand, was that model architecture in this sense takes priority over parameter estimation; I am even prepared to conjecture that a properly 'architected' model will deliver much the same results over a wide range of parameter estimates, particularly if the model is used for the simulation of medium- or long-term scenarios. Furthermore our use of the model was unconventional in that we treated it, not as something which would generate accurate forecasts of what would actually happen, but as a tool that informed our minds as to a great many possible outcomes conditional on a wide range of alternative assumptions both about exogenous variables and about parameter values. In using our model in this way we were greatly assisted by Cripps's programming expertise, which permitted us to work with a speed and flexibility not generally available at that time. I should add that econometrics, as usually defined, played (advisedly) a relatively minor role in our work.

The second, and more egregious, respect in which we became a 'dissident' group was that, as a result of trying to think through the possible ways in which Britain's net export demand might be improved, we entertained the possibility that international trade should be, in some sense, 'managed'. There might, we argued, be no way in which the adverse trends could be reversed other than some form of control of imports. Our argument (see for instance Cripps, 1978; Cripps and Godley, 1978) was never one in favour of protectionism as normally understood – that is, the selective and unilateral protection of relatively failing industries under conditions of general stagnation. On the contrary, we were most careful to lay down conditions under which the management of trade would benefit not only our own country (without making its industry less efficient) but would also increase the level of trade and output in the rest of the world. The two basic principles were, first, that trade management should reduce import propensities without ever reducing imports themselves (in total) below what they otherwise would have been; and, second, that 'protection' should be as minimally selective as possible (for example, through the use of market mechanisms such as auction quotas) so that industrial inefficiency would not be sponsored.

I was surprised by the hostility with which our ideas about trade were received. It seemed to me at the time, and still seems to me, that the arguments actually used against us (at their most coherent by Maurice Scott et al, 1980) did not, in practice, rest on a well-articulated theoretical position but on very special assumptions about behavioural relationships and international political responses. (I have, to the best of my ability, answered these particular points in Christodoulakis and Godley, 1987.)

In 1982 the ESRC decided to withdraw all substantial support from the CEPG, making it impossible for us to continue to function as a group. It apparently made this decision on the grounds of our lack of competence, although no significant discussion had taken place and no site visit ever made.

The controversy about free trade forced me to rely (personally) far less on Kaldor where theoretical matters were concerned and to become a better scholar myself. However, I found nothing in the literature to make me change my mind. My initial problem with the academic subject was straightforwardly one of comprehension. For instance, I spent long hours staring at Edgeworth box diagrams in the opening chapters of textbooks which showed the usual price lines and indifference curves. The trouble turned out to be that it was nowhere explained in the textbooks I read that resource endowments were assumed to be given and fully utilized, and that the proof of the gains from trade took these assumptions as axiomatic. This was not, for me, a promising model on which to build since the precise point at issue was whether or not free trade would have the effect of reducing national production. Further investigation caused me ever-increasing astonishment that the standard theory of international trade, in much more sophisticated versions, depended on comparably special, and empirically contra-factual, assumptions.

The 'dissident' argument in favour of managed trade is well summarized in Kaldor (1980), where he points out that the modern theory of international trade is based on the assumption that all production takes place according to the conditions described by the neoclassical production function, with constant returns to scale. Kaldor postulated instead, and he was surely right to do so, that the principle of circular and cumulative causation leads (through dynamically increasing returns) to a process, not of convergence, but of polarization between successful and unsuccessful economies in which success in competitive performance feeds on itself and losers become immiserated by trade.

I never believed that the events of the 1970s confuted the basic system of ideas on which I had been nurtured in the Treasury. In particular I had always seen (and still, on the whole, see) inflation as a process which is contingent in terms of economic theory. Certainly I did not feel confuted by the fact that the rise in commodity prices in 1973 and the 'threshold' scheme which effectively indexed wages to prices (too often forgotten in econometric studies) caused retail price inflation to reach 20 per cent in 1974; indeed, in Cripps and Godley (1974a) inflation of this order was predicted.

Nevertheless I did find myself badly outflanked by the rise in the influence of monetarism which really became important at the beginning of the 1970s. It was not, as I now see it, that the monetarists won any argument in the sense that they made propositions which I was forced to concede, on reflection, were correct. They won it for a different reason which I now admit with some shame and frustration – namely because in my own thinking I was only just beginning to incorporate balance sheet concepts systematically and therefore found myself unable, at the elementary level of accountancy, to give convincing answers to perfectly simple questions about where money 'was' in my model.

When I was forced into retrenchment, admittedly rather late in the day, I encountered the same problem that I have already described in mastering conventional trade theory: I had extraordinary difficulty in understanding, not the sentences, but what real life state of affairs mainstream 'neoclassical' macroeconomics could possibly be held to be describing. I went through the standard textbooks on macroeconomics and then back to the underlying professional literature (the *locus classicus* being, as I now see it, Modigliani, 1944 and 1963). I taught myself how to draw the diagrams and solve the equation systems, but for years could not make any connection between these and the real world as I knew it.

My breakthrough started as a result of yet another rereading of Patinkin (1965) at the beginning of which he brings his introductory theory to life by asking readers to imagine that all goods arrive randomly in parcels on Mondays (there is no production in his elementary model), while sums of 'money' (a financial asset which has no counterpart liability) are discovered to be randomly distributed among agents. 'Trading' takes place on Monday afternoons only, the outcome of which is that the price of all goods individually and of goods in general relative to the predetermined stock of 'money' are somehow determined such as to eliminate all excess demands including that for real money balances. Here was a story which, however improbable, I could at least understand. And it was this fable which enabled me to construct my own story in terms of which the model of the neoclassical macroeconomic synthesis – the AD-AS analysis of the textbooks – could fairly readily be understood as characterizing some imaginary world.

The story in question is not different in spirit from the Patinkin one (even if it is far more complicated) because in essence it reinstates the notion of an *exchange* economy. Thus the role of the neoclassical production function is not to characterize real life production in the way that, for instance, Pasinetti (1977) characterizes it, but to enable labour to be instantaneously converted into a profit maximizing supply of goods so that 'goods' and labour can be traded against one another. Then instead of having 'auctions' at which all that happens is that the price of goods is determined, we have auctions at which prices for 'product' (a single good), labour and 'money' are found such that the 'markets' for product, labour, money and bonds are all simultaneously cleared.

There is obviously not room here for a proper critique of this elaborate and ingenious but utterly absurd story, but I cannot resist the following observations. In general, the pretence in virtually every modern textbook that the single good which constitutes 'real product' in this abstract and timeless model may be identified with the dear old GDP is worse than ridiculous – it is fraudulent. There is nothing illogical about the notion that every 'agent' engages in a series of disjunct trading episodes in which he or she in the capacity of a worker responds to alternative configurations of the three relevant 'prices' with an offer of labour (seven hours today?); in the capacity of an entrepreneur with an offer to supply product and to purchase investment goods; in the capacity of a household to purchase consumption goods as well as to hold money balances and bonds. There is nothing illogical about it but it is perfectly obvious that nothing like this ever happens. And it is not just a case of parts of the system not quite working because of the existence of time lags or rigidities. No! I declare the entire notion of a macroeconomic general equilibrium (in which agents grope, in trading episodes that can never be satisfactorily located in real time, towards market clearing prices simultaneously for product, labour, money and bonds) to be a chimera.

Yet it is a chimera which can apparently paralyse part of the mind of anyone who has been inhabited by it. For I do believe that studying this system of ideas can explain why monetarism had the day it did, why its day is not yet done and why it succeeded in putting nearly everyone, but most unexpectedly American Keynesians, on the defensive. It could do this because the basic model of mainstream macroeconomics is one in which 'money' is exogenous in the sense that it does not even have an accounting relationship with anything else, and in which firms, all sitting on their production frontiers and operating under conditions of perfect competition, are maximizing profits. It then only requires relatively weak assumptions, in particular that money wages are flexible, to reach the conclusion that output and employment are determined by supply conditions alone, while changes in the 'money supply' affect the price level and nothing else.

To this statement of dissent I add that my strong objection to mainstream macroeconomics does not derive only from my perception that it does not describe modern industrial economies well. It derives as much, or more, from the perception, which I have indicated *seriatim*, that it is highly tendentious politically.

In conclusion I sketch, in very hazy terms, the alternative in which I believe.

I insist, to begin with, that the world to be studied is one in which institutions, in particular industrial corporations and banks, have a distinct existence and motivation. Next, the production process must be seen as taking time, hence the need for credit.

A realistic model of such an economy must start out with a comprehensive system of national and sectoral balance sheets with which all flow concepts are coherently related. As the (hypothetical) equilibrium conditions should be conceived in terms of real stock-flow ratios, the entire system of accounts needs to be inflation accounted, leading to unconventional definitions of real GNP, real personal income and the current balance of payments.

To capture the main processes without too complicated a model, I think it best to start by characterizing the determination of output and the distribution of income in a single region of a modern industrial economy, since this can feature realistically the importance of trade with the 'outside' world (in this case the other regions) without having to be concerned with exchange rates or the balance of payments. The objective (I hypothesize) of industrial firms is to maximize, not profits, but their own market shares, while that of banks is to maximize their balance sheets. Firms operate under conditions of imperfect competition and increasing returns; the implementation of their growth-maximizing strategy requires a set of related decisions to invest and set prices at levels relative to costs which generate adequate finance (given various other constraints as set out in Adrian Wood, 1975). The growth of output in the region depends on the success firms have in selling 'abroad'. The success or failure of the region will, however, be modified by the fact that the central government will be providing transfers as well as public services to some known standard. The government may also help backward or failing regions with some kind of regional development policy – the analogue of 'trade management' in an international setting.

I aim to show, in work which I now have well in hand, how this model can be expanded to describe the behaviour of households and banks, how inflation may be generated out of a struggle for shares of the real national income, how government policy can affect the various outcomes and what difference is made by assuming a multi-currency and multi-government world.

Godley's Major Writings

(1974a), 'Demand, Inflation and Economic Policy' (with T.F. Cripps), *London and Cambridge Economic Bulletin*, January.

(1974b), 'Inflation in the United Kingdom', in *Worldwide Inflation: Theory and Recent Experience*, Washington: Brookings Institution.

(1976), 'Costs Prices and Demand in the Short Run', in M.J.C. Surrey (ed), *Macroeconomic Themes*, Oxford: Oxford University Press.

(1978), 'Control of Imports as a means to Full Employment: The UK's Case' (with T.F. Cripps), *Cambridge Journal of Economics*, **2**, September.

(1983), Macroeconomics (with T.F. Cripps), Oxford: Oxford University Press and London: Fontana.

(1987), 'A Dynamic Model for the Analysis of Trade Policy Options' (with N. Christodoulakis), *Journal of Policy Modelling*, **9**.

Other References

Cripps, T.F. (1978), 'Causes of Growth and Recession in World Trade', *Cambridge Economic Policy Review*, No 4.

Kaldor, N. (1980), 'The Foundations of Free Trade Theory and Recent Experiences', in E. Malinvaud, E. and J.P. Fitoussi (eds), *Unemployment in Western Countries*, London: Macmillan.

Modigliani, F. (1944), 'Liquidity Preference and the Theory of Interest and Money', *Econometrica*, **12.**

Modigliani, F. (1963), 'The Monetary Mechanism and its Interaction with Real Phenomena, *Review of Economics and Statistics*, **45**, Supplement.

Pasinetti, L. (1977), *Lectures on the Theory of Production*, London: Macmillan.

Patinkin, D. (1965), *Money, Interest and Prices*, Harper and Row.

Scott, M., Corden, W.M. and Little, I.M.D. (1980), *The Case Against Import Controls* (Thames Essay No 24), Trade Policy Research Center.

Wood, A. (1975), *A Theory of Profits*, Cambridge: Cambridge University Press.

Richard Murphey GOODWIN (born 1913)   *Massimo di Matteo*

Richard (Dick for friends) Goodwin's life may be viewed from three different angles reflecting his multifaceted personality. Throughout his life he has been simultaneously an artist, a political spirit and an economist.

Born in Newcastle (Indiana) in 1913, the son of a lawyer turned banker, his love of the arts was fostered by his aunts, one of whom had lived in Paris and breathed the exciting atmosphere of the artistic vanguard. He decided not to become a professional artist because of what he regarded as lack of talent, but has continued painting all his life. A catalogue of his paintings is now being published.

He won a scholarship to Harvard where he read Political Science and graduated in 1934 with a dissertation entitled 'A Critique of Marxism'. While a student he took an active part in university life, writing political and cultural pieces for the student magazine, *The Harvard Critic*, of which he was an editor. His love of politics and curiosity about the big developments of the 1930s (Fascism and Nazism) have continued up to the present time, developing when he went to Oxford (St John's) as a Rhodes Scholar in 1934 for three years. There he read Philosophy, Politics and Economics but paid frequent visits to Italy and Germany to study Nazi-Fascism at first hand. He was a member of the Communist party until the Molotov-von Ribbentrop pact.

The tragic events of the Great Depression (including his father and his grandfather both going bankrupt) and his experiences in Europe shifted his interests towards political economy and he enrolled as a Ph.D. student at Harvard. His thesis, initiated under H. Phelps Brown's supervision in Oxford, was 'Studies in Money in England and Wales: 1919 to 1938' and its main results were soon published (reprinted in 1982). Here we find a first attempt at building a statistics of the money supply and velocity in the UK (needless to say he did it without a computer and this permanently put him off empirical work). He became convinced that trade cycles are not the result of mismanagement by the monetary authorities (a common opinion then, as it is again now) simply because money supply responds endogenously to business conditions rather than vice versa.

During the late 1930s, overcoming his initial distrust due to the Austrian economist's right-wing ideas, he was increasingly influenced by the teaching and personality of Schumpeter. When Goodwin was appointed at Harvard, as an assistant to the unorthodox J.H. Williams, Schumpeter and Gottfried Haberler attended the first course he ever gave on linear cycle theory. His interest in cycle theory was stimulated by attending Jacob Marschak's seminar and Roy Harrod's tutorials in Oxford. There he also became infected by Keynes's ideas. This was always a major point of discussion with Schumpeter who never came to accept the central message of the *General Theory* despite Goodwin's repeated efforts of persuasion.

Already before the war, then, the fundamental elements of Dick Goodwin's vision were in place, ready to be refined into what was later called the m-k-s (Marx-Keynes-Schumpeter) system by Goodwin himself. One of his first papers, 'Innovations and Irregularity in Business Cycles' (reprinted in 1989), is full of Schumpeterian and Keynesian inspirations. In its simplest version it is a lagged multiplier model in which investments, instead of being driven by expectations, are modelled as a sinusoidal function of time in accordance with Schumpeter's swarms of innovations, with the intention of bringing in historical events. This leads to cycles in income that reflect the oscillations contained in the investment waves. So even if the inner mechanism of the economic system is stable (that is it does not amplify the impulse), the latter nevertheless keeps the oscillation in income alive. This interpretation of the impulse seems to Goodwin more satisfactory than that of Frisch which resorts to random shocks. The model can be complicated in various ways. One of the most interesting is to assume that the waves in innovative investment are irregular oscillations so that they can be approximated by sums of sinusoidal functions: in this way the resulting fluctuations in income will be irregular as well, resembling actual statistics:

> An explanation of the reality of a tendency to periodicity is obtained without any strict periodicity ever existing. The historical individuality of each cycle is introduced into the rigidity of mathematical business cycle theory. The complex wave form follows. The ever changing severity of fluctuation can be explained. So long as capitalism is not stationary so long as there is any exciting expenditure the oscillations may temporarily become less severe or more severe, but they will not tend to die out. This results in spite of the fact that the mechanism itself has damping (1989, pp. 183–4).

A few points can be made. First the subject of Goodwin's theorizing is the evolution in time of the capitalist system. As far as methodology is concerned, no attention is paid to individuals; the idea is to build aggregative models consistent with what is shown in time series. Lastly Frisch's conceptual framework of impulse and response for analysing cycles is accepted.

The final ingredient needed to produce the most famous paper on cycle theory of the Harvard period was provided by chance. During the war Goodwin taught physics to the army and became acquainted with the applied maths used by physicists. When he went back to economics he knew the limitations of linear analysis for explaining persistent oscillations. He had fruitful discussions with Le Corbeiller (a physicist at Harvard) and subsequently produced 'The Nonlinear Accelerator and the Business Cycle', read in December 1948 at a meeting of the Econometric Society in Cleveland (reprinted in 1982). The central hypothesis concerns the behaviour of investment when there is a difference between actual and desired capital, with firms trying to fill the gap as quickly as possible. When actual stock is lower than desired, investment is kept at the maximum rate allowed by productive capacity; when the opposite occurs disinvestment is at the maximum rate allowed by not replacing capital goods that are scrapped (in other words, gross investment is zero). Finally if desired capital equals actual capital, net investment is zero (only replacement takes place) and capital remains unchanged. The peculiarity of the model is that whenever the system is not in equilibrium – namely desired stock is different from actual stock – it undergoes a cyclical pattern that is neither damped nor explosive. Suppose that actual stock is less than desired stock: net investment is determined according to the behavioural hypothesis described above. Therefore income is determined via the multiplier mechanism and consequently desired capital is determined as well, being closely related to the value of output. Capital will go on increasing until it reaches the desired level; at this point investment falls to zero. Income falls as well, via the multiplier; a new level of desired capital is determined. The stock of capital goes on decreasing until it reaches the desired value. Here net investment (which was negative) rises to zero: income rises too and desired capital with it, so that net investment again becomes positive. Thus the cyclical movement repeats itself again and again. This case is later dealt with by catastrophe theory, but was anticipated by Goodwin.

A few noteworthy features of this paper can be identified. First, Goodwin rejects Frisch's approach by assuming that the cycle can be wholly endogenous and that no external forces are necessary to keep it alive. Second, the values of the parameters are no longer crucial for an oscillatory solution, as for example in Samuelson's accelerator–multiplier model. Third, as long as the (absolute value of) depreciation (assumed constant) and the maximum rate of production of capital goods are different, the upswing and the downswing will be of different duration; presumably the latter will be longer.

Important generalizations can be made by including technical progress, lags in the multiplier process, and finally lags between investment decisions and actual expenditures in capital goods. What finally emerges is a nonlinear model that admits a (unique) limit cycle. The latter designates a stable movement (all trajectories tend to it from wherever they start) and can be seen as a generalization of the concept of stable equilibrium (since the latter can be regarded as a stable movement so small as to degenerate to a point). Of particular interest is the introduction of technical progress in the form of a constant rate of growth of capital. In this way the desired capital is a function of both income and time. In later papers explaining growth (1982), much emphasis is given to the Duesenberry (ratchet) effect that induces an asymmetry in the consumption, and therefore income, pattern.

Before leaving the Harvard period, mention should be made of Goodwin's work on multi-sectoral theory. 'The Multiplier as Matrix' and 'Does the Matrix Multiplier Oscillate?' (1983) were inspired by Leontief's input-output analysis. It is worth noting that these were the first economics articles to use the Frobenius theorems on positive matrices (although I have recently been informed by Prof. Morishima that in his 'Dynamic Economic Theory' published in 1950 in Japanese, he also applied Perron-Frobenius theorems). The papers' main finding was that, barring exceptional cases, in a suitably modified Leontief open model with a simple lag, national income will oscillate in response to changes in injections before reaching a new equilibrium level. To show this interesting result Goodwin relies on a device he often used again. This consists in transforming the coefficient matrix in order to solve the problem more simply. Goodwin has always been of the opinion that economics is a hopelessly difficult subject due to the complexity of the relationships between its parts: 'There is just *one* problem', he is always saying. Therefore ingenious simplifications are welcome.

The starting point of the transformation is that, generically, any empirical matrix has *n* distinct latent roots (for example, see section 5 of A4 in the Mathematical Appendix to 1987). A modal matrix exists that will transform the system matrix into a diagonal matrix with its n distinct roots along the main diagonal. Putting the matrix in canonical form and redefining variables accordingly, the system of *n* interconnected equations can be reduced to *n* decoupled equations that are easily solvable. In this way the system can be seen as the sum of its parts.

From this superb work two directions can be taken, both of which were subsequently pursued by Goodwin. One is to apply the multi-sectoral scheme and the impulse-response framework to problems of demand and cost inflation, as well as to international trade and policy (see 'A Note on the Theory of Inflationary Process' and 'The World Matrix Multiplier', 1983). The other is the extensive use of the diagonalization procedure to gain insights into the dynamics of general linear equilibrium (see his 'Static and Dynamic Linear General Equilibrium Models' published in 1953, but conceptually derived from the 'Multiplier as Matrix' paper).

The other innovative paper that cannot escape our attention is 'Iteration, Automatic Computers, and Economic Dynamics' (1982), read in Varese in 1950 at a meeting of the Econometric Society. In it the old problem of how to solve the Walrasian equations of general equilibrium is given a novel treatment. The device of tatonnement is interpreted as a practical method, namely an algorithm for solving the system: then a constructive proof of equilibrium is outlined. This interpretation was ignored until the 1960s and 1970s when Uzawa and Morishima took it up again. The iteration procedure that Goodwin envisaged includes price, quantity and mixed (price-quantity) adjustments.

This concludes what Goodwin himself calls his 'first life', namely the Harvard period. At the end of 1949, with the dissent of only Schumpeter and Haberler, Harvard decided that Goodwin had no future there as an economist. He took a Rockfeller scholarship and went to work with Richard Stone at the Department of Applied Economics, Cambridge (UK). When his year was up the Keynesians (mainly Richard Kahn) offered him a Lectureship. He accepted the offer and settled into his second home. At this time McCarthyism was making life unpleasant for left-wing supporters in the US. He remained in Cambridge, at Peterhouse, until his retirement nearly 30 years later.

By far the most important and influential piece in the field of cycles and growth produced during this second period was his superb 'A Growth Cycle' (1982), read at the first World Congress of the Econometric Society in Rome in 1965. The model is elegant and simple. Capitalists invest all they save; workers consume all their wages; the rate of change of the real wage depends on the unemployment rate; no money illusion is involved. There are fixed coefficients and two factors only – capital and labour. The labour force and labour productivity grow at a constant rate. As has been noted, the model is an interpretation of Marx's contradictory process of accumulation, as the following quotation shows:

> When profit is greatest employment is average and the high growth rate pushes employment to its maximum which squeezes the profit rate to its average value. The deceleration in growth lowers employment relative to its average value again, where profit and growth are again at their nadir. This low growth rate leads to a fall in output and employment to well below full employment, thus restoring profitability to its average value because productivity is now rising faster than wage rates. ... The improved profitability carries the seeds of its own destruction by engendering a too vigorous expansion of output and employment thus destroying the reserve army of labour and strengthening labour's bargaining power (1982, p. 171).

The cyclical process and therefore the crisis are not caused by a Keynesian lack of effective demand, but by the operation of the labour market through competition between workers that squeezes profits. The result is that income grows at a rate fluctuating around the Harrodian natural rate which can be attained only if initial conditions are appropriate. Fluctuations will be wider the farther the distance from the natural rate at time 0. In other words, the amplitude depends crucially on the initial conditions (past history). However, it is true that for each cycle the average values of the unemployment rate and the wage share are constant and equal to the coordinates at the centre of the fluctuation. This is a feature of the mathematical structure of the model which is formally identical to the predator-prey model originally elaborated by Lotka and greatly expanded by Volterra. In particular the (non-zero) stationary solution is a centre of the fluctuations. This means that the solution is dynamically stable (though not asymptotically stable) and structurally unstable. However, this feature is not a drawback since the model has been interpreted to be 'suitable either as the ideal type at a high level of abstraction or as a general frame of reference for average and long-term intercyclical comparisons' (Vercelli, 1982, p.186). The model has been generalized in a number of directions (by the introduction of financial and monetary variables, effective demand, government expenditure and taxation etc) producing a relevant literature, but in only a few cases have its qualitative features been preserved.

During the Cambridge period, Goodwin applied the strand of thought expressed in 'Multiplier as Matrix' – the diagonalization procedure – variously to the problems of the labour theory of value and the transformation problem, to the dual dynamic theory of value and output, to the Wicksell theory of capital and to the problem of reswitching (1983); the last application has been termed impossible in a purely circulating capital model where wages are paid in advance.

Finally we cannot overlook Goodwin's brilliant paper on 'The Optimal Growth Path for an Underdeveloped Economy' (1982), inspired during his period with the Indian Planning Commission under the direction of Mahalanobis. Within nine months he managed to build the first input-output table (12 sectors) for India despite the paucity of reliable data. For an underdeveloped country moving from a traditional low-productive economy to a more advanced (high-productive) one, Goodwin argues that it is optimal, under simplified hypotheses, to compress consumption in the early phases of the transition so as to raise the rate of growth and enable a rise in consumption later. This policy can be shown to maximize the utility of consumption per capita over the whole period. Various numerical examples also demonstrate that the results are rather robust with respect to changes in labour force growth, value of the capital/output ratio etc. From the mathematical point of view the problem is one of calculus of variations where an integral (representing the overall value of future consumption) is maximized over a finite interval, given technical conditions and labour force growth. The problem then becomes one of feasibility, namely how planners can induce the high and rising propensity to save necessary to build machines that will permit a rise in consumption per capita only much later. There are also ethical problems involved since the sacrifice of today's generations will be required to benefit later generations. However the task of the economist is to present the problem and to indicate a range of solutions from which governments can choose.

The Cambridge period ended with Goodwin's retirement in 1980. In the autumn of the same year the Department of Political Economy of the University of Siena, taking advantage of a new bill that allowed foreigners to become professors in Italian universities, invited Dick Goodwin to apply for a chair in Siena. This marked the beginning of the third period of his life which, under the stimulus provided by young department members, has been both productive and happy. Already towards the end of the 1970s and increasingly in the Siennese period, Goodwin had come across exciting new developments in mathematics that he thought could be usefully employed in solving problems faced by economists in their analysis of the evolution of capitalism. I am referring especially to the catastrophe theory of Thom and Zeeman, the chaos theory and finally the bifurcation theory.

Goodwin has emphasized time and again that, to explain persistent cycles, nonlinear models are necessary since otherwise one has to rely on random shocks to keep the cycle alive. The maintenance of the cycle would be the result of chance or at best exogenous events. In Goodwin's vision the role of random events is confined to rendering more irregular the perfect cycle that results from a deterministic model. However the existence of chaotic motions is regarded by Goodwin as a new source (in addition to random shocks) of irregularity of fluctuations occurring in time series. In this respect the economy is like the weather: both are highly irregular so that predictions are unreliable or even impossible. The existence of chaos undermines the simple dichotomy between deterministic models (whose trajectories, given the laws of motion and initial conditions, can be predicted) and stochastic models. Prediction becomes faulty since an arbitrarily small change in initial conditions may lead to trajectories that diverge from one another as time goes on. This is especially relevant in economics since initial conditions cannot be measured exactly. Goodwin built several models that display chaotic trajectories which he described in a book *Chaotic Economic Dynamics* (1990). This includes essays on the (Ricardian) corn economy, the von Neumann model and an integrated model of Kitchin and Juglar cycles based on multiplier-accelerator interaction.

The other major and new development in Goodwin's thought in Siena has been his interest in long waves. These were popularized by Schumpeter in his 'Business Cycles' but were relegated to oblivion until the mid-1970s (at least in English-speaking countries). Since his participation in a Conference on Long Waves in Weimar in 1985, Goodwin has produced several models attempting to formalize the Schumpeterian idea that capitalism evolves in an unsteady fashion through short, medium and long cycles. In 'Towards a Theory of Long Waves' (1989), he formulates a model in which in addition to induced investment (via the accelerator), there is also innovative investment which follows a logistic pattern. He assumes that inventions grow more or less at a constant rate, but innovative investment goes up and down. Such investment is positively affected by the level of output since innovations are less risky to introduce when demand is high. By means of simulations he is able to show that within the time span of the logistic (approximately 45 years), the economy exhibits a complete long wave accompanied by shorter fluctuations similar to trade cycles. Here is what lies behind the upper turning point:

> ... there is a positive feedback from investment in the innovative concepts through a multiplier effect to output levels and growth rates, leading to rising effective demand and hence accelerating innovative investment. ... However as innovation accelerates it gradually reduces the gap between potentially feasible conceptions and their embodiment (1989, p.58).

These words contain an unusual justification of the logistic which is therefore not only an empirical representation of the innovative process, but has a theoretical foundation. Again his approach combines Keynesian and Schumpeterian ideas, the two theories always being regarded as complementary. The pattern that results is broadly in accordance with observed facts as recently reviewed by Kleinknecht (1987).

Before turning to a general assessment of Goodwin's scientific work, it is important to include a short review of a representative paper on multi-sectoral analysis, 'The Use of Gradient Dynamics in Linear General Disequilibrium Theory' (1989), in which he summarizes his lifelong study. He examines the stability problem of a general equilibrium linear model of Walras-von Neumann type. The question one wishes to answer within the model is not 'does an equilibrium exist'? but 'can a freely functioning, competitive economy achieve a given equilibrium solution'? If not, the equilibrium is devoid of meaning. Goodwin formalizes two pairs of adjustment processes. The first is that, in each sector, price change depends on the difference between price and unit cost, whereas output change depends on the difference between supply and demand: in this case the system is asymptotically stable and no fluctuations occur. The second hypothesis is that price variation depends on the difference between demand and supply whereas output variation depends on the difference between price and cost: in this situation there will be 2n (n being the sectors) centres exhibiting simple harmonic motion. Considering pairs of motions there are almost certain to be one or more irrational ratios between periodicities, so that the shape of the resultant waves will never repeat and there will be no strict periodicity. If there are many irrational ratios the resulting time series may appear chaotic. This picture is made even more complicated by considerations about stocks and inventories that give rise to further reasons for instability.

In the field of political economy Goodwin devoted his efforts to the study of the evolution of capitalism, taking inspiration from Marx, Keynes and Schumpeter. He rejected neoclassical analysis mainly because, being essentially a static theory, it leaves out precisely what matters most; moreover its greatest achievement, namely welfare prescriptions, is crucially based on the untenable hypothesis of full employment. From Marx he did not take the labour theory of value and its conundrums, but rather his insights into the laws of movement of the capitalist system (in particular the industrial reserve army mechanism and the idea that in the long run labour is never in short supply). Coupled with the view of capitalists as an organ of accumulation, this is the core of the Marxist vision. From Keynes he took the rejection of Say's law that output depends on demand. This in general will entail a positive level of unemployment so that the powerful analytical concept of the multiplier can be profitably used. In addition prices are determined basically by costs, especially labour (and raw materials) costs. This duality between prices and output is perhaps his most longstanding idea. From Schumpeter he took the idea that cycle and development are not only linked, but must be explained within a unified mechanism centred on the innovation process. The profits squeeze due to the working of the labour market is periodically relaxed by innovation swarms. He shares with Schumpeter the belief that Walrasian theory describes an ideal state never actually reached by the economy. He finds that von Neumann's model is not inconsistent with Schumpeter's vision since the rate of profits is positive only when the rate of growth is positive.

Coming now to some of Goodwin's more personal features, we first stress his lifelong attention to sciences like physics, biology and applied mathematics with a view to capturing methods or instruments to help conceptualize the complicated world of the economy. Secondly, we notice his faith in nonlinear models of the cycle that can only provide explanations for self-perpetuating oscillations. Thirdly, in his multi-sectoral models he employs a framework based on the impulse-response (or injection and diffusion) mechanism as a way of analysing the response of an economy to an external force. Hence long-run tendencies are described by a nonlinear mechanism whereas the diffusion of injections within the system in the medium run is analysed by linear multi-sectoral models. To see how this enormously difficult task is accomplished, the reader is referred to the first part of (1987). This is a revised version of his Siennese lectures to undergraduates, co-authored with R.M. Punzo. It marks a complete departure from the 'Treatise on Nonlinear Business Cycles' (more properly called 'Mathematical Methods in Dynamical Economics') which, in his Preface to *The Dynamics to a Capitalist Economy*, Samuelson recalls having been in preparation around 1950. But as Samuelson himself writes:

> Good Burgundy is worth waiting for. Vintage produce from the Goodwin workshop repays us with compound interest for our long abstinence.

Goodwin's Major Writings
Goodwin's original unpublished documents are kept in the Goodwin Fund at the Faculty of Economics and Banking Library in the University of Siena. The material is currently being catalogued.

(1982), *Essays in Economic Dynamics*, London: Macmillan.
(1983), *Essays in Linear Economic Structures*, London: Macmillan.
(1987), *The Dynamics of a Capitalist Economy* (with R.M. Punzo), Cambridge: Polity Press.
(1989), *Essays in Nonlinear Economic Dynamics*, Frankfurt am Main: P. Lang.
(1990), *Chaotic Economic Dynamics*, Oxford: Clarendon Press.

Other References
Kleinknecht, A. (1987), *Innovation Patterns in Crisis and Prosperity*, London: Macmillan.
Vercelli, A. (1982), 'Is Instability Enough to Discredit a Model', *Economic Notes*.

David M. GORDON (born 1944)
I was born in Washington, D.C. in 1944. I come from a family of economists: my father, the late Robert Aaron Gordon, was a noted macroeconomist and a president of the American Economics Association; my mother, Margaret S. Gordon, is well-known for her contributions on social welfare policy, international trade and employment policy; and my brother, Robert J. Gordon, is a leading 'new Keynesian' macroeconomist. There are no other members of our immediate family. Given that density of economists among us, we acquired in the early 1970s the nickname of 'the Flying Wallendas of Economics'.

Despite these origins, I thought throughout college that I would avoid economics. Circumstances nonetheless intervened in the year after college – largely driven by the problem of the draft and the Vietnam war – and despite myself I entered the graduate programme in economics at Harvard University. I completed my Ph.D. in 1971 and in 1973 began teaching at the New School for Social Research, where I have remained to this day.

My general concerns as a political economist have concentrated both on helping to forge a coherent left analytic framework within economics and on contributing to the formation of a progressive and hopefully socialist political movement in the United States. As part of that effort, I and many of my colleagues have devoted considerable energy to building small but hopefully stable institutions. These include the Union for Radical Political Economics, the left professional grouping of political economists in the US; economics departments with strength in left political economy, such as the New School and the University of Massachusetts at Amherst; and institutions committed to outreach economic education, such as my own Center for Democratic Alternatives in New York and the Center for Popular Economics in Amherst. Throughout, many of us on the left in economics in the US have tried both to develop our own internal discussions and approach and to engage in critical debate and dialogue with the mainstream.

In turn, my own work as a political economist has emphasized both critique and constructive analysis. It may be useful to review that work as involving six main strands.

One general concern has involved methodology. Many of us in the US, building primarily upon the Marxian analytic tradition, have aimed to establish the central importance for economic analysis of attention to power relationships, conflicts and institutional transformation. I first stressed some of these themes, in a comparative context, in my *Theories of Poverty* and *Underemployment* (1972). The same kinds of concerns have continued throughout subsequent work on the structure of the labour process, urban transformation, stages of accumulation, the determination of profitability in advanced capitalist economies, and the internal contradictions of the accumulation process. My most recent effort to clarify methodological issues of central importance for a left (and 'materialist') analysis comes in a long and ambitious manuscript nearing completion, tentatively titled *Remaking History: A Critical Reconstruction of the Transition from Feudalism to Capitalist in Western Europe*, which I hope will be in print by the end of 1992. In this volume, I try to engage with and move beyond many of the longstanding methodological debates about historical transformation, using the time-honoured 'Transition' in Western Europe as a case study for that argument.

A second strand of work has involved my effort to conceptualize an intermediate level of analysis within Marxian economics which can provide the basis for a 'stage-theoretic' analysis of capitalism. Closely related methodologically to some parallel analysis independently developed by the French 'regulation' school, my own work – both individually and with several collaborators – has built upon the concept of a 'social structure of accumulation' (SSA), a coherent and determinate constellation of institutions which permits rapid and stable capital accumulation. I first introduced this concept in 1978 and then formalized it in a 1980 article. This framework has been developed further in joint work with Richard Edwards and Michael Reich (1982, especially Chapter 2), and with Samuel Bowles and Thomas E. Weisskopf (see, for example, 1989). Although most of our work has concentrated on the US, and particularly on the post-World War II period, I have tried to build connections with recent debates about changing structures of the global economy (1988) and to more general debates about the character and determinants of long swings in capitalist economies (see, for a review of that work, 1990). (See also my own analysis of stages in the development of cities in 1974.) Throughout this work, I and my collaborators have consistently sought to persuade neoclassical economists that power and institutions 'matter'.

A third strand has focused more specifically on the labour process and labour markets. Many of us in what has sometimes been called the 'social relations school' in the US have since the early 1970s sought to argue that the capitalist labour process is shaped not merely by technology – by engineering requirements – but also by the logic and contradictions of capital-labour conflict. My own contributions to this effort have taken three forms.

1. I have tried to contribute to the theoretical conceptualization of such conflicts and to clarify their implications for the organization of production. (Some of my earliest efforts are presented in 1972, Chapter 5.)
2. Along with many others, I have tried to contribute to the more specific analysis of the *segmentation* of the labour process and labour markets arguing, at least in the case of the US, that institutionalized divisions across firms and production processes have created enduring differentiation among types of jobs. This work has aimed both at trying to understand some of the sources of economic inequality and political divisions among workers in advanced capitalist economies, and at critiquing neoclassical views of the labour market as a single competitive market in which differences among *workers*, rather than those among *jobs,* dominate the determination of market outcomes. Early efforts in these directions, including my own dissertation, are summarized in *Theories of Poverty and Underemployment* (Chapters 5–7), while a full historical, institutional and analytic summary of this perspective is provided in the joint work with Richard Edwards and Michael Reich, *Segmented Work, Divided Workers.*
3. This work had obvious implications for the determination of labour productivity. Some of us have contrasted a 'technical model' of productivity, characteristic of both neoclassical economics and traditional Marxian analyses, with a 'social model' of productivity in which social relations, particularly those affecting the determination of variable labour intensity,

also play a central role. My own contributions to this analysis have been developed primarily with Samuel Bowles and Thomas E. Weisskopf (see both 1983a and 1983b).

A fourth and increasingly important strand of my work has turned towards what may best be characterized as 'left applied macroeconomics'. One part of this effort, developed jointly with Bowles and Weisskopf, has concentrated on elaborating the implications of a neo-Marxian attention to power, conflict and institutions for the determination of core macroeconomic interactions among profitability and investment. In a series of both theoretical and econometric explorations, we have developed a quantitative representation of the post-war social structure of accumulation in the US; deployed that model of 'power relations' to explain the determinants of profitability; and built from that power-profits nexus to what we have called an 'SSA model of investment' in which power relations partly determine investment through the channel of their influence on profitability. (See 1989 for a summary of much of this work.)

Another recent part of this effort has involved my own long-term project to create a fairly large-scale left applied macroeconometric model of the post-war US economy. The model builds theoretically upon both neo-Marxian and post-Keynesian foundations and incorporates the core macro relationships explored with Bowles and Weisskopf at both the abstract and stage-theoretic levels. It goes beyond that work to try further to model the interrelationships among the full array of endogenous variables traditionally incorporated into macroeconometric models. My purpose in this effort is hardly to enter forecasting contests; rather, I hope to demonstrate that a left perspective can be moulded into a complete and internally consistent model of an advanced capitalist macroeconomy, and to use that model in order to clarify the most important analytic differences among neoclassical, post-Keynesian and traditional Marxian approaches and my own synthetic left perspective. This work is still very much in progress, but I hope to begin publishing essays and ultimately one or two books based on the project within another two to four years.

My fifth professional concern as a political economist has focused on policy debates. In the absence of a strong social democratic or labour party in the US, those of us on the economics left have been forced to seek influence on economic policy more through our writing than through consulting or direct policy-making. Numbers of us have tried to craft a 'democratic' policy alternative to both right-wing and centrist policy perspectives. Bowles, Weisskopf and I have presented our own versions of that democratic economics in our two joint books (1983a and 1991). Building on that foundation, for example, I also worked closely with the Jesse Jackson 1988 presidential campaign, drafting many of its policy papers on economic and budget policy.

A final strand of my work has involved what many of us call 'popular economics'. Again faced with a political vacuum on the left in the US, many of us have concentrated our political efforts at outreach educational work aimed at providing information and analysis about the economy for grass-roots activists in labour, women's, peace, community and environmental movements. This work has in general sought to stress the importance of power in the political economy and to underscore the potential impact of popular mobilization for a more democratic economy. In my own case, I have worked through an educational outreach institute which I founded in 1975, originally called the Institute for Labor Education and Research and then renamed in 1981 as the Center for Democratic Alternatives. Most recently as part of that effort, I edited and published a 'participatory' newsletter called *Progressive Agenda* from 1986 to 1989.

How does it feel to have worked for 20 years on the fringes of the economics profession and the political system in the United States? My feelings seem to remain relatively constant: I feel pleased with the choices that I and many of my collaborators have made and the work we have produced; frustrated by the condescending complacency of mainstream economists; angered by the greed and irrationality which dominate the US political economy; and still hopeful for the prospects of a significant progressive mobilization towards a more just and humane society as we turn towards the 21st century.

Gordon's Major Writings

(1972), *Theories of Poverty and Underemployment*, Lexington: Lexington Books.

(1974), 'Capitalist Development and the History of American Cities', in W. Tabb and L. Sawers (eds), *Marxism and the Metropolis*, Oxford University Press. Revised edition 1984.

(1980), 'Stages of Accumulation and Long Economic Cycles', in T. Hopkins and I. Wallerstein (eds), *Processes of the World-System*, London: Sage Publications.

(1982), *Segmented Work, Divided Workers: The Historical Transformation of Labor in the United States* (with Richard Edwards and Michael Reich), Cambridge University Press.

(1983a), *Beyond the Waste Land: A Democratic Alternative to Economic Decline* (with Samuel Bowles and Thomas E. Weisskopf), New York: Anchor Press/Doubleday.

(1983b), 'Heart and Minds: A Social Model of U.S. Productivity Growth' (with Samuel Bowles and Thomas E. Weisskopf), *Brookings Papers on Economic Activity*, **2**.

(1988), 'The Global Economy: New Edifice or Crumbling Foundations', *New Left Review*, No 168, March-April.

(1989), 'Business Ascendancy and Economic Impasse: A Structural Retrospective on Conservative Economics, 1979–87' (with Samuel Bowles and Thomas E. Weisskopf), *Journal of Economic Perspectives*, Winter.

(1990), 'Inside and Outside the Long Swing: The Endogeneity Debate and the Social Structures of Accumulation Approach', *Review*, **13**.

(1991), *After the Waste Land: A Democratic Economics for the year 2000* (with Samuel Bowles and Thomas E. Weisskopf), New York: M.E. Sharpe.

Augusto GRAZIANI (born 1933)

Graziani was born in Naples (Italy) in 1933. After graduating from the University of Naples, he undertook post-graduate work in Great Britain at the LSE and in the US at Harvard University. He began his teaching career in the University of Catania in 1959, subsequently moving to the University of Naples and finally to Rome.

Graziani parted company with neoclassical theory very early in that he never considered consumers' preferences and technology as being exogeneous variables, or money as being neutral. Graziani's main theoretical postulates are that the power of producers originates from the fact of having access to credit; that producers impose their own choices upon consumers; and that technological progress is part and parcel of the profit-maximizing behaviour of firms. In Graziani's view, the sovereignty of producers only holds if we consider producers as a group. The strategies of single producers, or of groups belonging to one single industry or nation, face limitations which may appear as demand constraints, but are in fact the result of conflicts among rival groups.

Graziani's thought has undeniably been strongly influenced by the Marxian tradition. Graziani has never discussed explicitly and in detail such crucial aspects of Marxian theory as the labour theory of value, but he clearly conceives society as being formed by conflicting classes. On the other hand, the influence of Schumpeter is equally clear so far as the role of credit is concerned, as is that of the post-Keynesian school, in that Graziani fully accepts the Kaldorian (or Kaleckian) theory of income distribution.

What follows is an illustration of Graziani's work in the field of macroeconomics. His attention to development and to regional disparities, being mainly centred on specific problems of the Italian economy, will be dealt with only briefly.

The first organic work in which Graziani clearly appeared as a dissident economist is the book, *The Development of an Open Economy* (Italian text, 1969). This is largely devoted to an analysis of Italian economic development of the 1950s and early 1960s although the initial chapters, containing a theoretical model, have more general implications.

Graziani starts by criticizing the traditional Theory of Comparative Costs according to which each country should specialize in the production of those commodities in which, given its factor endowments, it enjoys a comparative advantage. Graziani emphasizes the fact that, even in the absence of advantages connected to relative factor endowments, if producers want to enter the world market, the required degree of competitiveness can be reached provided appropriate technologies are chosen. The neoclassical model is thus reversed because, according to it, factor endowments determine the productivity of resources and therefore the degree of competitiveness of the national industry. In Graziani's thought, once the decision to enter the world market has been taken, international competition determines the level of productivity to be attained, the technologies required and therefore the level of employment in the exporting sector. In this sector, advanced technologies, high productivity and high wage rates will prevail. The remaining labour force must then find employment in the non-tradables sector, where the reverse mechanism is at work: employment is fixed, while the relative endowments of capital and labour determine labour productivity and the rate of wages. The dualistic structure which is the outcome of this process tends to perpetuate itself. Because of the pressure coming from the low-wage sector, the increase in wage rates in the exporting sector lags behind the increase in labour productivity. The price level thus tends to be stable, which helps to reinforce the competitiveness of exports. At the same time, the resulting increase in profits stimulates investment and insures further increases in productivity. The higher level of wage rates in the dynamic sector as compared to the rest of the economy gives rise to a domestic demand for high-income commodities. The exporting sectors are then able to couple domestic and foreign demand, thereby reducing the danger of fluctuations as well as of demand failures.

When Graziani produced his interpretation of an export-led economy, the dominant model of a dual economy was that elaborated by Vera Lutz (1962). In her model, dualism was mainly ascribed to the action of trade unions, which would induce high wage-rates in big firms, with the consequence of altering relative prices in favour of capital-intensive technologies and of reducing employment. In Graziani's model, instead, the starting point in the process is the decision of producers to enter the world market, while the stronger position of trade unions in the exporting sector comes only as a consequence.

The rejection of the neoclassical model of general equilibrium, already implicit in Graziani's work on dualism, was further pursued on strictly theoretical grounds in an essay published in *General Equilibrium and Macroeconomic Equilibrium* (1965). Here, after reviewing criticisms regarding the internal consistency of the model of general equilibrium, Graziani puts forward the suggestion that an overall equilibrium position is in itself inconsistent with the typical features of a capitalist economy. In a changing economy, in which by definition the rates of growth of single sectors differ, rates of profit must also differ, in order to draw resources out of declining sectors and into expanding ones. While a short-period equilibrium, in which positive and negative quasi-rents are present, affords a reasonably realistic picture, a position of full equilibrium has little to do with the actual working of a market economy.

Graziani's subsequent theoretical work was developed in the field of money, his basic idea being that, in a monetary economy, the power of producers depends on their having a privileged access to bank credit and financial markets.

Graziani devoted attention very early to the problems of the circulation of money. His first work dealing with the monetary circuit (even if the term was not used) goes back to 1956. From the very beginning Graziani followed the debates concerning the priority of the Stockholm school over the Keynesian school (he reviewed Landgren's book immediately after its publication in 1960). More recently, he has re-examined the Marxian theory of money (1986) and given a personal systematization of the French theory of the monetary circuit. A more exhaustive statement of his monetary theory can be found in his essay in *The Theory of the Monetary Circuit* (1989b).

The basic questions raised by Graziani in his monetary works can be summarized as follows: (i) As to the origins of money, has there been a gradual evolution from commodity money to credit money, or has money been in the nature of credit ever since its first appearance? (ii) Is the role of money one of making exchanges easier or less costly, or one of making it possible for producers to earn profits? (iii) Does money perform its most relevant roles when it is spent or when it is kept as an idle balance?

The very possibility of the existence of a commodity money is denied by way of an initial definition, in that an economy using a commodity as money would in fact be a barter economy. A truly monetary economy must therefore make use of some form of *credit money*, something which must have been true ever since the inception of monetary economies. The next step is a rejection of any model in which the stock of money has a given magnitude. To consider money stock as being totally determined by the government deficit is also rejected in favour of a broader definition, according to which the stock of money may also originate from credit granted by the banking system to agents, typically firms. (In an open economy, a third source of variation in the money stock would, of course, be the surplus or deficit of the balance of payments.) In fact, in contrast to most macro models, Graziani often considers the money stock as being totally determined by bank credit, something which makes his model very similar to the Wicksellian one of a 'pure credit' economy.

In order to make clear the role of money, Graziani gives a full description of the process of money circulation, starting with the creation of money (which takes place when bank credit is initially granted to an agent) and ending with the final destruction of money (which takes place the moment the initial credit is paid back to the bank). The basic phases of money circulation in a closed economy can be synthesized as follows:

1. *Credit creation.* The banking system grants credit to firms in order to enable them to meet their running costs. The moment a firm makes its first payment (for instance, the payment of wages), money is created as the simultaneous debt of the firm towards the bank (bank loan) and credit of the wage-earner towards the bank (bank deposit). Typically, a monetary payment gives rise to a triangular debt and credit relationship among agents (the bank, the payer and the payee), while it does not create any direct debt-credit relationship between the two non-banking agents. The essence of a monetary payment is that it allows the payer to settle his debt to the payee thanks to the presence of a third party (the bank), whereas in a credit economy the payer would only make a promise of payment and would still be a debtor to his counterpart. The opening phase shows clearly that the role of banks is one of creating credit. It also shows that the decision of a bank to grant a loan gives rise to the simultaneous appearance of a deposit. Banks as a whole create deposits the same moment they grant loans. They do not, and could not, collect deposits without having previously granted loans.

2. *The goods market.* Wage-earners spend a part of their money income on the goods market. To the same extent, firms get back their money outlays and are able to repay their debt to the banks. Wage-earners can only buy on the commodity market what firms have decided to produce in the form of consumer goods, or anyhow what firms have decided to put on sale. They are unable to acquire what has been produced in the form of capital goods, or what firms have decided to keep for themselves.

3. *Financial saving.* Wage-earners may place a portion of their savings on securities issued by firms on the financial market. To the same extent, firms get back a second portion of their money outlays and are able to make a further repayment of their bank debt. Clearly at this point the role of the financial market is not one of collecting savings in order to finance investment, but rather one of making it possible for firms to repay their bank debts.

4. *Money balances.* To the extent that wage-earners decide to increase their money balances, firms will be unable to repay their bank debt and will be forced to ask the banks to increase the amount of their loans just to keep their activity at a constant level. It is the decision of savers to keep part of their savings in money form that forces firms to ask for bank credit. In other words, the demand for deposits gives rise to a demand for loans. This result contrasts with the conventional presentation according to which deposits do not act on the demand side, but rather increase the potential supply of loans on the part of the banks.

5. *Income distribution.* At the end of the production cycle, wage-earners get the portion of output they have consumed plus the property of the

financial wealth they have accumulated as securities or bank deposits. The question now arises whether financial wealth owned by individual wage-earners can be considered as actual wealth for wage-earners taken as a group. In principle, securities are representative of capital goods, and bank deposits can be converted into real goods at any time. Therefore both should be regarded as actual wealth (this is why Keynes in his *Treatise on Money* defined a firm's profits as being equal not to the whole of investment but only to the difference between investment and savings of households). Graziani, however, follows the post-Keynesian tradition and argues that wage-earners would never be able to convert financial wealth into real wealth, even if they wanted to. If wage-earners decided to sell their securities or to spend out their bank deposits, they would only cause money prices to go up, but would not succeed in increasing the actual level of their real consumption which is limited anyhow by the amount of commodities firms have decided to bring to the market. In Graziani's view financial wealth is only fictitious wealth to wage-earners as a class. Real income of wage-earners is equal to the amount of real goods they can buy, and total profits equal total invest-ment. This does not mean that financial wealth is totally meaningless. In fact, it allows single wage-earners to modify the time-shape of their own consumption by having recourse to reciprocal loans which leave the time-shape of total consumption unchanged.

The model of a pure credit economy used by Graziani brings him to a number of heterodox conclusions, some of which deserve mention. All of them depend on the specific features of the model, namely that bank credit is the only source of liquidity and that banks and firms are considered as separate entities.

The first point concerns the problem of *real and monetary interest* (1983a, 1985a). According to the received doctrine, inflation in itself reduces the burden of debt in that it reduces the level of real interest (of course this does not happen if nominal interest rates are revised with inflation). In a pure credit economy this is no longer true. Here the stock of money in existence is a debt of firms to the banks. If the velocity of circulation is assumed constant, any increase in prices brings about a proportional increase in the stock of money, and therefore in the debt of firms to the banking system. In consequence, the nominal financial burden of the firms goes up with inflation. Therefore even if, with constant nominal rates, the real *rate* of interest goes down with inflation, the *total real financial burden* remains constant. On the other hand, if interest rates follow the Fisher rule and are revised with inflation, the real financial burden of firms will go up. Therefore the Fisher rule only applies to an economy in which the money stock is totally created by the government deficit.

Another consequence drawn from the pure credit model concerns the so-called *inflation tax*. According to received doctrine, any government expenditure financed by money creation brings about an increase in the price level, causes disposable income of the non-government sector to decrease, and is therefore the equivalent of a tax. Graziani shows that, if the government spends on transfers and not on commodities, not only is the tax no longer levied, but the financial burden of firms is reduced in that the government deficit freely supplies an amount of liquidity that firms would otherwise have borrowed at interest from the banks (1985).

A third point concerns the *limits of monetary policy*. Since the real cost of production to firms is only calculated by the output of consumption goods (or anyhow by the amount of commodities available for sale), the monetary costs of output are irrelevant to total profits. This implies that interest payments made by firms to savers are also irrelevant. A higher level of interest rates on securities (analogous to what happens with a higher level of money wages) can be a source of inflation but does not act as a brake on the level of investment (1983a).

The above presentation may generate the impression that Graziani totally rejects the Keynesian theory of money, in that he makes no mention of money as a stock of wealth and never deals with demand failures, liquidity traps or other typical categories of the Keynesian model. A similar impression can be raised especially by some of his writings (such as 1983b). In fact, Graziani draws a clear distinction between two roles of money.

So far as the *distribution of income* is concerned, what matters is money as *purchasing power*. Producers can hire labour, run the production process and earn profits because bank credit endows them with the necessary purchasing power. What allows producers to acquire real resources (labour force and finished goods) and earn real profits is bank credit. Wage-earners instead can only make use of their labour force by selling it against a money wage, namely against scraps of paper which they will only be able to turn into real goods to the extent that producers have decided to bring to the market a corresponding supply of commodities (1984a, 1985b).

Money as a form of wealth becomes relevant when the *determination of aggregate demand* is considered. Here Keynesian analysis is crucial in that any accumulation of idle balances, by increasing the debt of firms towards the banks, may cause a decline in demand. As a consequence, Graziani, far from rejecting the *General Theory*, would consider it as only partially representative of Keynes's thought and would emphasize the need, in order to get a full picture of Keynes's contribution, of taking equally into account the whole of his monetary writings.

The consideration of money as an endogeneous variable is strictly connected to Graziani's re-examination of the main trends in the history of economic analysis. Most historical reconstructions are made in terms of a chronological succession, progressing from superficial and imprecise to more refined analytical models. In the dominant version, the succession is from classical thought to the crucial turning point of 1870, when marginal theory made its appearance, followed by the Keynesian revolution, soon revised as a special case of the more general neoclassical model. Against this official reconstruction, the neo-Ricardian school considers that the high-level results reached by the classical school with Ricardo and Marx were followed by a long period of decline, dominated by the neoclassical approach and by its symmetrical analysis of demand and supply. Such an approach dominated the scene until new light was brought by Keynes in the 1930s and Sraffa in the 1960s.

Against similar reconstructions made in terms of one single chronological process, Graziani views the history of economic analysis as being formed by two parallel and conflicting lines of thought. The first views the economic process as the result of individual actions, mainly interpreted in terms of the maximizing behaviour of individuals. Its main representatives are A. Smith, W.N. Senior, J.B. Say, A. Marshall, L. Walras, C. Menger, up to present-day neo-neoclassical economists. The second line views the economic process as determined by the actions of conflicting social classes or groups. Much of Graziani's work in this field has been devoted to showing how not only Ricardo and Marx, but also authors like T.R. Malthus, K. Wicksell, J.A. Schumpeter and J.M. Keynes, belong to this group.

Although usually considered a neoclassical author, Graziani believes that Wicksell should be re-examined in the light of his theory of money and credit (Wicksell, 1898). The relevant point in Wicksell's model is not his definition of money as an endogenous variable; rather it is his conception of the economic process as resulting from the conflicting actions of social groups (banks, firms, capitalists, wage-earners), in which single agents lose their identity and autonomy of decision-making (Wicksell, 1898, Chapter 9, Section B).

In Graziani's judgement, J.A. Schumpeter deserves similar treatment thanks to the theory of money and credit contained in his works on development and fluctuations (Schumpeter, 1912, 1939). After giving a clear definition of banking as an activity of credit creation, Schumpeter also shows how bankers and firms, by means of their joint decisions, can impose their choices upon consumers who play a merely passive role in the economic process. The rejection of consumers' sovereignty and the leading role assigned to bankers and entrepreneurs make Schumpeter a heterodox economist.

Something has already been said concerning Graziani's interpretation of Keynesian theory (this point has been analysed in Graziani, 1981, 1984b and

1989c). His starting point is that the *General Theory* should not be considered an exhaustive presentation of Keynes' thought. Along with Schumpeter (1954, p.1176), Graziani believes that taking money stock as a given magnitude (at least in the first part of the book) is a weak point in the Keynesian model. It prevents Keynes from analysing the role of the banking system and the relationship between banks and firms. Graziani recognizes that it was Keynes's intention in the *General Theory* to present an equilibrium analysis, for which purpose money had to be analysed as an observable magnitude and therefore defined as a stock. In any case, he thinks that a complete picture of Keynes's thought can only emerge from a simultaneous consideration of the *Treatise*, the *General Theory,* and his articles on the 'finance motive' (1937). Here Keynes defines money as purchasing power created by the banks and placed in the hands of firms; he also gives a full description of what he himself calls 'the power of the banks'.

Graziani's Major Writings

(1961), Review of K.-G. Landgren, *Den Nya Economien i Sverige*, Bollettino dell'Università di Napoli, n.1.

(1965), *Equilibrio generale ed equilibrio macroeconomico* (General Equilibrium and Macroeconomic Equilibrium), Naples: ESI.

(1969), *Lo sviluppo di un' economia aperta* (The Development in an Open Economy), Naples: ESI.

(1977), 'Il processo capitalistico di J.A. Schumpeter' (Introduction to the Italian edition of J.A. Schumpeter, *Business Cycles*), Turin: Boringhieri.

(1981), 'Keynes e il Trattato sulla moneta' (Keynes and the Treatis on Money), in B. Jossa (ed), *Studi di economia keynesiana*, Naples: Liguori.

(1983a), 'Interesse monetario e interesse reale' (Nominal Interest and Real Interest), *Studi economici*, n.20.

(1983b), 'Aspetti della dottrina monetaria di Keynes' (Some Aspects of Keynes' Monetary Theory), in T. Cozzi (ed), *Keynes*, Turin.

(1984a), 'Moneta senza crisi' (Money with no Crises), *Studi economici*, n.24.

(1984b), 'The Debate on Keynes' Finance Motive', *Economic Notes*, n.1.

(1985a), 'Intérêt monétaire et intérêt réel', in R. Arena (ed), *Production, circulation et monnaie*, Paris: PUF.

(1985b), 'Monnaie, intérêt, dépense publique', Économie et Sociétés, *Série Monnaie et Production*, n.2, Paris: Ismea.

(1986), 'La teoria marxiana della moneta' (Marx's Theory of Money), in C. Mancina (ed), *Marx e il mondo contemporaneo*, Rome: Editori Riuniti.

(1989a), 'J.A. Schumpeter and Italian Economic Thought', *Studi economici*, n.1.

(1989b), 'The Theory of the Monetary Circuit', *Thames Papers in Political Economy*, Spring.

(1989c), 'Nuove interpretazioni nell'analisi monetaria di Keynes' (New Interpretations in Keynes' Monetary Analysis), Report at the annual meeting of the Italian Economic Society, Rome, October.

Other References

Keynes, J.M. (1930), *A Treatise on Money*, London: Macmillan. (*Collected Writings*, vols V and VI, 1971.)

Keynes, J.M. (1936), *The General Theory of Employment, Interest and Money*, London: Macmillan. (C.W., VII, 1973.)

Keynes, J.M. (1937), 'Alternative Theories of the Rate of Interest', *Economic Journal*, June. (C.W., XIV, 1973.)

Lutz, V.C. (1962), *Italy: A Study in Economic Development*, Oxford University Press.

Schumpeter, J.A. (1934), *The Theory of Economic Development*, Harvard University Press. (Original German edition, München, 1912.)

Schumpeter, J.A. (1939), *Business Cycles*, New York: Macmillan.

Schumpeter, J.A. (1954), *History of Economic Analysis*, Oxford University Press.

Wicksell, K. (1934), *Interest and Prices*, London: Macmillan. (Original German edition, Jena, 1898.)

Keith B. GRIFFIN (born 1938)   *James K. Boyce*

Born in 1938 in Colon (Panama), Keith Griffin spent part of his childhood in Latin America, including a year in Bogota in 1948 when a political assassination followed by mass urban rioting led to Colombia's *violencia*. His concern with economic development and income distribution grew from this early experience.

In 1960, upon graduation from Williams College in western Massachusetts, Griffin went to Oxford University as a Marshall scholar, studying at Balliol under the supervision of Paul Streeten and the late Thomas Balogh. After completing his doctorate, teaching at the University of Chile in Santiago, and serving as an agricultural adviser to the government in newly independent Algeria, Griffin was appointed in 1965 to a teaching fellowship at Magdalen College, Oxford. His association with Magdalen continued until 1988 when, having served as the College's President for nine years, he left Oxford to become Chair of the Department of Economics at the University of California, Riverside.

Griffin's book, *Underdevelopment in Spanish America: An Interpretation* (1969), addressed a number of issues in development economics, including agrarian problems, foreign trade, the role of capital imports, inflation and regional integration. A major theme here, as in Griffin's subsequent work, was the negative effects of international economic relations upon Third World countries, in particular upon their poor majorities. Unlike some contributors to the emerging 'dependency school', however, Griffin gave equal weight to internal class structures and institutions as barriers to development.

In *Planning Development* (1970a), Griffin addressed such nuts-and-bolts matters as plan formulation, input-output analysis, benefit-cost analysis, and sectoral development policies. The resulting handbook for development practitioners demonstrated that unorthodox economic analysis need not, and should not, remain confined to the armchairs of academia.

In the early 1970s Griffin was commissioned by the UN Research Institute for Social Development to carry out a study of the economic and social implications of the introduction of highly fertilizer-responsive varieties of wheat and rice in Asia, Latin America and to a lesser extent Africa. *The Political Economy of Agrarian Change* (1974), an outcome of this research, advanced a radical critique of this 'green revolution' development strategy. Griffin's central argument is that in settings marked by great inequalities of land ownership, such a production-orientated strategy exacerbates distributional inequity. As a result the position of the rural poor may deteriorate not only relatively, but also absolutely. Griffin does not argue that growth in food production is unnecessary, rather that production increases are insufficient to reduce hunger and malnutrition significantly. 'The reason lies not so much in inadequate technology,' Griffin concludes, 'as in inappropriate institutions and policy. The explanation for the latter, in turn, lies not in the ignorance of those who govern but in the powerlessness of most of those who are governed.'

In the mid-1970s Griffin served as Chief of the Rural and Urban Employment Policies Branch of the International Labour Organization, in which capacity he organized a set of detailed studies on trends in rural poverty in seven Asian countries and four Indian states. The resulting volume, *Poverty and Landlessness in Rural Asia* (1977), presented strong evidence that a significant proportion of low-income families in rural Asia had experienced absolute declines in their real incomes in the preceding two decades. In all but one case, this occurred despite rising average real incomes and rising food output per capita. The exception was Bangladesh, where an interesting variant of this pattern emerged: despite falling average incomes, the rural rich in that country secured rising real incomes, while the incomes of the poor fell faster than average.

In an introductory chapter, Griffin summarized this evidence and offered a powerful critique of the technocratic agricultural strategy. 'When the poor starve,' he observed, 'it is not mainly because there is no food but because they do not have the wherewithal to acquire food. In other words, the problem of world hunger cannot be solved merely by attempting to increase production.'

When confronted with evidence of persistent or deepening rural poverty, defenders of the green revolution strategy often lay the blame on rapid population growth. In the opening chapter of *Poverty and Landlessness*, Griffin anticipates this argument, again stressing the institutional framework within which growth occurs: '[R]apid population growth is certainly not the only cause of the increasing poverty of some sections of the rural population in Asia,' he wrote. 'Equally important causes seem to be the unequal ownership of land and other productive assets, allocative mechanisms which discriminate in favour of the owners of wealth, and a pattern of investment and technical change which is biased against labour.'

A central theme in Griffin's writings on agrarian issues is the critique of the unidimensionality of the conventional analysis. The notion that rising land productivity can solve the problem of rural poverty, and the claim that if it fails to do so the culprit must be population growth, are both woefully incomplete. In particular, they do not examine the institutions governing the distribution of wealth and power. For Griffin these are crucial. '[T]he only way to alter substantially the distribution of income is by altering the distribution of wealth', he concludes in *Poverty and Landlessness*. 'In agrarian countries this implies above all the need for land reform.'

In the late 1970s and 1980s, Griffin's interest in institutional change and land reform took him to China. He travelled widely in the Chinese countryside and, with a team of colleagues, carried out scholarly investigations into the country's organization of production and distribution, resulting in *Growth and Equality in Rural China* (1981). Griffin also edited and contributed to the volume *Institutional Reform and Economic Development in the Chinese Countryside* (1984); further essays on China appear in Griffin's *World Hunger and the World Economy* (1987). A distinctive feature of Griffin's writings on China is that he combines a sympathetic understanding of the recent process of economic reform with a deep respect for the country's economic achievements since the 1949 Revolution. Unlike many observers of contemporary China, he interprets the post-Mao reforms not as the triumph of capitalism, but rather as innovations within an ongoing and open-ended socialist development strategy.

In 1982 Griffin was able to study another ostensibly socialist development strategy, when he headed the International Labour Organization's Employment Advisory Mission to Ethiopia. The mission's report was suppressed at the insistence of the Ethiopian government and has never been published. Griffin's own conclusions can be glimpsed, however, in his two essays on Ethiopia in *World Hunger and the World Economy*. One examines the 'horrendous consequences of wrong priorities', notably the government's decision to pursue a military solution to ethnic separatism. A second essay, co-authored with Roger Hay, argues that grassroots producer cooperatives could play an important role in rural development in Ethiopia, particularly in mobilizing labour for investment, but have yet to do so.

Griffin's essay on communal land tenure systems in the same volume takes the distinctly unfashionable position that communal agricultural systems can (and frequently do) outperform individual tenure systems in terms of both efficiency and equity. This does not imply that Griffin sees no role for markets or private agricultural production; on the contrary, both can complement a well-organized communal system. In China, for example, Griffin found in the late 1970s that private animal production not only coexisted with communal grain production, but also contributed to a more equal inter-household distribution of income.

Griffin's concerns have by no means been limited to agriculture. In 'Financing Development Plans in Pakistan' (1965), Griffin argued that despite fairly substantial increases in per capita income, the Pakistani growth strategy so exacerbated inequalities that the 'vast majority of the Pakistani population probably has a lower standard of living today than when the country achieved its independence in 1947'. In particular, Griffin documented the massive transfer of resources from agriculture to industry, a transfer with a pronounced regional dimension due to the overwhelming importance of agriculture in East Pakistan and the concentration of industrial investment in West Pakistan. This economic disparity fuelled the political tensions which culminated in civil war and the birth of Bangladesh in 1971.

In the same article, Griffin drew upon Pakistan's experience to attack the conventional wisdom that foreign 'aid' (that is, inflows of external capital at below-market interest rates) necessarily promotes more rapid economic growth. He generalized this critique in 'Foreign Capital, Domestic Savings and Economic Development' (1970b) arguing that aid inflows could result in lower domestic savings and higher incremental capital-output ratios in the recipient countries, which called into question not only the magnitude but also the sign of the net impact upon growth.

'Foreign Assistance: Objectives and Consequences' (1970c) further developed the radical critique of foreign aid. Griffin and Enos observe that economic aid is an instrument of foreign policy through which strong countries engage in symbolic as opposed to military battles. With more than a touch of irony they write: 'Perhaps the world should be grateful to the politicians and economists who have created a means by which resources devoted to conflicts can be destroyed without physical injury'. They add, however, that this conclusion may be 'too optimistic' given the deleterious effects of aid upon people in recipient countries. In addition to the savings and efficiency impacts mentioned above, Griffin and Enos argue that the most important reason why foreign assistance frequently hinders growth is that it strengthens the political status quo, thereby preventing needed institutional changes such as land reform.

Griffin reaffirms this critique in a more recent essay entitled 'Doubts about Aid', in the volume *World Hunger and the World Economy*. Unlike right-wing critics of aid, Griffin endorses in principle international redistribution of income and the use of government taxation to bring this about. His criticisms derive instead from observation of the actual results of existing aid programmes. 'In practice foreign aid is doing little to promote growth in the Third World,' he concludes, 'and even less to alleviate poverty. In the end it appears to be doing little more than sustaining corrupt and often vicious regimes in power, sometimes deliberately and sometimes perhaps not.'

Griffin's analysis of the international debt crisis of the 1980s has been equally forthright. At a seminar held in Mexico City in July 1984, Griffin called upon debtor countries such as Mexico and Brazil to 'get together and form a cartel' or, failing that, to band together informally with one member acting as a 'default leader' analogous to the price leader in an oligopolistic industry. Griffin told his audience that 'default – disguised, partial but more than marginal, done in a polite, quiet and gentlemanly way, but default none the less – is the name of the game.' His remarks (subsequently published in *World Hunger and the World Economy*) received prominent coverage in the Mexican press, prompting an official disclaimer from the Mexican government. In retrospect, however, his conclusion appears controversial not so much for its substance as for the openness with which it was expressed.

In June 1988 Griffin advocated this approach in the pages of the International Monetary Fund/World Bank quarterly, *Finance and Development*, in a guest article entitled 'Towards a Cooperative Settlement of the Debt Problem'. While recognizing that the governments of many debtor countries spent borrowed capital unwisely and adopted inappropriate policies, notably exchange rate overvaluation, Griffin argues that the root of the debt crisis lies in the economic policies of the major industrial countries. He again calls for collective action or default leadership by debtor countries. Furthermore, he points to the conflict of interest between the financial and industrial sectors within the creditor countries: the negative net transfer from the Third World benefits the former at the expense of markets for the latter. Hence 'a potential alliance in favor of debt alleviation exists between the governments and people of debtor countries and the industrialists and foreign traders of the creditor countries'. Here Griffin sees a political basis for a negotiated settlement.

The elimination of the negative net transfer from heavily indebted Third World countries will of course not solve all their economic problems. The 'developing' countries will continue to face an international playing field tilted in favour of those already 'developed'. In 'The International Transmission of Inequality' (published in his *International Inequality and National Poverty*, 1978), Griffin argues that the concentration of technical advance in the rich countries, together with the allocation of resources on the basis of profit maximization, tend to result in the structural impoverishment of Third World countries as their resources are extracted through trade, migration and finance capital flows.

In *The Transition to Egalitarian Development* (1981b), Griffin considers the practical problems confronting any Third World country which attempts a radical shift in development priorities towards poverty reduction. Although Griffin and James claim that their analysis could apply to capitalist as well as socialist development strategies, they note that in practice 'egalitarian development is more likely to occur after a revolution has established a socialist economy'. Their book provides a manual for economic policy makers grappling with such a transition.

Beginning with the premise of a government committed to the rapid elimination of absolute poverty, Griffin and James trace a series of necessary steps, the first of which is a rapid redistribution of assets. Such a redistribution is likely to result in excess demand for wage goods such as food, clothing, and housing. Griffin and James argue that international trade can provide at best only a partial solution to this problem. Hence they outline a number of transitional supply and demand management measures: these include rationing, price controls and market mechanisms on the supply side, coupled with demand-side measures designed to ward off the disincentive effects of supply management. A review of the experiences of Cuba, China and Chile under Allende provides lessons on the importance of achieving the right policy mix, including the mix between market and administrative interventions.

Griffin's latest book, *Alternative Strategies for Economic Development* (1989) draws together a number of the recurrent strands in his work, in the framework of an analysis of the diverse development strategies pursued in various Third World countries during the past three decades. Griffin distinguishes six broad strategies which he terms monetarism, the open economy, industrialization, the green revolution, redistribution and socialism. Comparing these in terms of resource utilization, savings and investment, growth, human capital formation, poverty and inequality, the role of the state and democratic participation, he finds trade-offs as well as complementarities. Here as elsewhere, Griffin poses hard questions and eschews easy answers.

Griffin's Major Writings

(1965), 'Financing Development Plans in Pakistan', *Pakistan Development Review*. Reprinted in K. Griffin and A.R. Khan (eds), *Growth and Inequality in Pakistan*, London: Macmillan, 1972.

(1969), *Underdevelopment in Spanish America: An Interpretation*, London: Allen and Unwin.

(1970a), *Planning Development* (with J. Enos), London: Addison-Wesley.

(1970b), 'Foreign Capital, Domestic Savings and Economic Development', *Bulletin of the Oxford Institute of Economics and Statistics*, **32**.

(1970c), 'Foreign Assistance: Objectives and Consequences' (with J. Enos), *Economic Development and Cultural Change*, **18**.

(1974), *The Political Economy of Agrarian Change*, Macmillan and Harvard University Press; 2nd edn, 1979.

(1977), *Poverty and Landlessness in Rural Asia* (with A.R. Khan), ILO.

(1978), *International Inequality and National Poverty*, London: Macmillan.

(1981a), *Growth and Equality in Rural China* (with A. Saith), Bangkok: Maruzen.

(1981b), *The Transition to Egalitarian Development* (with J. James), London: Macmillan and New York: St Martin's.

(1984), *Institutional Reform and Economic Development in the Chinese Countryside*, London: Macmillan. Chinese edn, Hong Kong: Chinese University Press, 1987.

(1987), *World Hunger and the World Economy*, London: Macmillan.

(1988), 'Towards a Cooperative Settlement of the Debt Problem', *Finance and Development*, **25**, June.

(1989), *Alternative Strategies for Economic Development*, London: Macmillan for the OECD Development Centre.

Peter GROENEWEGEN (born 1939)

Peter Groenewegen was born in 1939 in Kerkrade (Limburg, the Netherlands). He migrated with his family to Australia in 1952 and in his secondary
studies concentrated on history. His realization that an understanding of
modern history required a knowledge of economics made him decide in
1957 to pursue that subject at the University of Sydney rather than Arts, the
traditional family field of study. Sydney's Economics faculty during the
1950s had a number of unusual features in its syllabus. For example, its
courses included a very systematic study of the work of Schumpeter, while
Kalecki's *Economic Dynamics* was a text for macroeconomics. The final
honours year syllabus contained a compulsory course on the history of
economic thought, and lecture courses dealing with topics such as the economics of socialism and critiques of capitalism, the last being taught by
Bruce McFarlane and Ted Wheelwright respectively.

Groenewegen joined the staff of the Economics faculty in 1962 as a
Teaching Fellow, completed his doctoral dissertation at the LSE under Bernard
Corry (1963–65) and then returned to the University of Sydney as a lecturer
(1965). He was appointed to a full Chair in Economics in 1980. He had
joined the Labor party as a student, but resigned from membership in 1966
because of opposition to its then stance on Australia's involvement in the
Vietnam war. In 1989 he became Foundation Director of the Centre for the
Study of the History of Economic Thought at Sydney University, designed
to encourage such studies partly by the production of reprints of economic
classics; he commenced in 1982 with reprinting the 1738 classic, *Some
Thoughts on the Interest of Money in General*.

Early influences on his economics came less from his Sydney teachers
(exceptions being Jim Wilson and Bruce McFarlane) than from a study
circle organized by an economist-librarian, Frank Dunn. This heightened his
interest in the history of economics and enabled intensive critical study of
Ricardo, Wicksell, Marx and Cantillon as well as of Viner's monumental
study on international trade. Critical faculties were likewise sharpened by
his association with the Sydney Libertarians, an anarchist group strongly
influenced by the Sydney academic philosopher, John Anderson. Historical
work on the development of agriculture and technology in Europe loomed
large in his original research, concentrating as it did on the history of
economic thought. Publications on Turgot (1977, 1987), based on his Masters thesis, were a major product of this research. This work also gave him a
thorough grasp of classical political economy in Marx's meaning of that
term, which made him very receptive to the surplus approach to economic
thinking then being developed on Sraffian lines. As is the case with many
other historians of economics in academic teaching positions, he selected
public finance as an additional research area. Like the history of economic

thought, this subject permits a broad perspective on the discipline and, moreover, enables an active participation in practical policy discussion.

No theoretician, but strongly in support of the need for theoretical analysis provided its limitations are fully understood (1982, p.17), his public finance work has a strong institutionalist flavour. This is clear both from his text on public finance, which is specifically tied to an Australian institutional setting (1979a), and in his material on fiscal federalism, which describes the traditional theory as inspired by US practice, hence failing to explain satisfactorily alternative experience in federalism (1983). His text stresses different perspectives on theory; for example, his discussion of incidence theory juxtaposes Harberger's general equilibrium analysis and Kaleckian incidence theory. Likewise, it is highly critical of the current anti-public sector fashion, stressing the inherent need for adequate public spending growth essential to maintaining living standards as the population increases, and criticizing neutrality as an overriding tax criteria because governments actively need to encourage productive, and to discourage unproductive, activities (1988).

This last stance relates to Groenewegen's affiliation with Sraffian economists, to the extent that he strongly advocates a serious rehabilitation of classical economics as a more fruitful approach to the solution of many economic problems than is provided by marginalist economics. He actively taught the critique of neoclassical capital theory during the late 1960s and early 1970s. He also assisted in establishing a course of post-Keynesian economics at the University of Sydney in 1977, a course which since then has disseminated its alternative theoretical perspective to many senior students. Aspects of these developments are covered in his survey of 'Radical Economics' in Australia (1979b), his 1986 Newcastle Lecture defending post-Keynesian economics and his *History of Australian Economics* (with Bruce McFarlane, 1990). Emphasis on the value of an institutionalist approach, combined with critical scepticism of the dominant theory and an emphasis on the importance of history for economic understanding characterize much of his published work.

Groenewegen's Major Writings

(1977), *The Economics of A.R.J. Turgot*, The Hague: Martinus Nyhoff.

(1979a), *Public Finance in Australia: Theory and Practice*, Sydney: Prentice Hall.

(1979b), 'Radical Economics', in F.H. Green (ed), *Surveys of Australian Economics*, Sydney: Allen and Unwin, Vol. II, 172–223.

(1982), 'History and Political Economy: Smith, Marx and Marshall', *Australian Economic Papers*, **21**(38), June, 1–17.

(1983), 'Tax Assignment and Revenue Sharing in Australia', in C.E. McLure Jr (ed), *Tax Assignment in Federal Countries*, Canberra: ANU Press, 293–316.

(1986), 'In Defence of Post-Keynesian Economics', 1986 Newcastle Lecture on Political Economy, University of Newcastle Occasional Paper No 131.

(1987), 'Turgot 1727–1781', in J. Eatwell, M. Milgate and P. Newman (eds), *The New Palgrave*, London: Macmillan, Vol IV, 707–12.

(1988), 'Rehabilitating the Classical Notions of Productive and Unproductive Labour with Special Reference to their Relevance to Taxation', in G.H. Brennan, B.S. Grewal and P. Groenewegen (eds), *Taxation and Fiscal Federalism: Essays in Honour of Russell Mathews*, Canberra: ANU Press, 83–102.

(1990), *A History of Australian Economics* (with B. McFarlane), London: Routledge.

G. C. HARCOURT (born 1931)

To understand how I came to my 'dissenting' views I need to be autobiographical. I like to say that I am an Australian patriot and a Cambridge economist. I was born in Melbourne in 1931 into a middle-class assimilationist, agnostic Jewish household with right-wing political views. Melbourne then was a stuffy, snobby place, marked by sectarian battles between Catholics and Protestants, who were nevertheless united in their unthinking anti-Semitism towards a large Jewish community. Political and especially religious problems were, from very early on, stark and frightening experiences for me. So, when I went to the University of Melbourne in 1950, itself a veritable paradise of enlightenment and tolerance after my schooldays, it was no accident that I became absorbed in the search for a political philosophy and a religious creed, as well as in economics (which I loved).

I found a political philosophy more quickly than a religious creed. I abandoned the right-wing views of my parents six months or so into my first year and became a socialist, convinced by the lectures on economic geography that private enterprise competitive institutions were neither the most rational nor efficient means to develop society's basic resources, especially when the needs of future generations had to be taken into account.

It was a much longer journey to religious belief, puzzled as I was by the divergence between the beliefs and professed moral values of Christians (in particular) on the one hand, and their actions on the other. By my fourth year though, helped by discussions with a number of theologians in my College (Queen's) and by the Student Christian Movement, I had adopted a working hypothesis of belief in God. Basically I argued that *personal* morality could safely be left to a personal relationship with God; that it was a useless and misguided, indeed unhealthy, struggle to tackle on your own, and that Christian principles provided the basic blueprint for the just and equitable society that I wanted to see established, through institutions that would allow compassion, cooperation and justice to flourish. My religious and political beliefs merged at this juncture, fending off what I saw as the unhealthy absorption with self of the evangelicals, by diverting energies outwards towards community objectives and the care of other people. I differed from socialist humanists only in that I did not believe that these ends could be attained, unaided, by persons alone. I joined the Australian Labor Party (ALP) in 1953, the year that I was baptised, and when I took up my first lecturing post at Adelaide in 1958, I began to say that I was the only Jewish Methodist in Adelaide.

The Commerce Faculty at the University of Melbourne was Cambridge-orientated. We were brought up on Keynes's works, reading the *Tract* in our first year and *The General Theory* in our second. Piero Sraffa, Dennis Robertson, Austin and Joan Robinson, Richard Kahn and Nicholas Kaldor soon became everyday names to us. Wilfred Prest's dog-eared copy of

Marshall's *Principles* was a familiar sight too. There was also a strong neoclassical influence so that Wicksteed's *Common Sense*, along with the *Tract*, were the first two great works I read. Boulding's *Economic Analysis* was our advanced theory book and I can still remember – now I wonder why – how excited I was when I realized that the formal structure of consumer theory was exactly the same as that of production theory. We were exposed to Kalecki's writings too. Economic history and history of thought were also prominent; as an undergraduate I read virtually all the great books from *The Wealth of Nations* to *The General Theory*. I was defeated by Volume I of *Capital*, turning in desperation to Sweezy's *Theory of Capitalist Development* in order to try to understand Marx's concepts. I read a lot of Dobb's work, *Political Economy and Capitalism* having a lasting impact on me. We read *Value and Capital* (including the mathematical appendices), the *Foundations* and, currently topical, Trygve Haavelmo's *Econometrica* supplement, as well as many of the then classic papers of mathematical economics. I also read Hayek's *Pure Theory of Capital*.

For my undergraduate dissertation (30,000 words) I tried to integrate the analysis of Kurt Rothschild's seminal 1947 *Economic Journal* paper on price theory and oligopoly with the macroeconomic system of *The General Theory* in order to study the reserve policy of Australian companies during the Great Depression. I used accounting data – explicitly applying what I had learned, in a first-year one-off course on profit and loss accounts, balance sheets and funds statements – in the empirical work. I did not get far with the synthesis, but it does illustrate that I have always been interested in micro foundations and that I did not, even then, accept the artificial distinction between micro and macro which does so much harm to the way we teach economic theory.

I graduated in 1953 and worked for the next 18 months on a Pilot Survey of Income and Saving in Melbourne. In August 1955, I left Melbourne, as it turned out permanently, for King's College, Cambridge – where else? – to do a Ph.D., initially with Nicky Kaldor as my supervisor (a disaster for both of us) and then with Ronald Henderson. (Joan and I were married a fortnight before we left and we have, truly, lived happily ever after.) I intended to work on the implications for the theory of the firm and the trade cycle of the assumption that secure profits were as important as maximum ones; by the time I submitted in August 1958, it had become a study of the economic implications of using historical cost accounting procedures to measure income for dividend and tax purposes and to set prices in a period of inflation (with hindsight, not *that* unconnected).

While I was in Cambridge, Joan Robinson published *The Accumulation of Capital* (1956). I locked myself up with the book for a term, then emerged to read a paper on it to a research students seminar, with Robin Marris in the chair and the author herself attending the second session. This paper marks the beginning of my friendship with Joan Robinson, though I had met her at a previous research students seminar (these were usually chaired by Piero Sraffa). Incidentally, 'the class of 1955–58' included Tom Asimakopulos, Charles Feinstein, Pierangelo Garegnani, Luigi Pasinetti, Amartya Sen and John Whitaker, as well as a host of bright Australians (such as Keith Frearson, Hugh Hudson and Duncan Ironmonger) who were later to make their mark on Australian academic and public life.

The Accumulation of Capital had a profound effect on me. It presented a 'vision' of how capitalism works over time and, more tentatively, a conceptual framework with which to think about the processes involved and make sense of what I saw happening around me. It formed the core from which my own work and teaching were subsequently always to start. I realize now that, apart from her own very considerable contributions, not least the marvellous introduction (to which Lawrence Klein paid tribute in 1988), Joan Robinson had also synthesized strands of thought from other economists who had influenced me – Smith, Ricardo, Marx, Marshall, Keynes, Kahn, Kalecki and, increasingly in the years to follow, Sraffa.

I returned to Australia in March 1958 to take up a lecturing post in the Economics department of the University of Adelaide with which I was to be associated for 27 very happy years. There my mentors were, first and foremost, the late Eric Russell, who was ten years older than myself, and Bob Wallace, who was one year older and with whom I had overlapped at Melbourne. I wrote my first book, *Economic Activity*, with Bob Wallace and Peter Karmel, our dynamic youthful professor.

At Adelaide I developed my interest in the links between accounting practices and economic performances, at firm and economy levels. This culminated in 1962–63 in 'The Accountant in a Golden Age', a project first suggested to me by Harold Lydall. I was introduced to Wilfred Salter's seminal work on vintage models when Peter Karmel asked me to write a review article of Salter's 1960 classic, *Productivity and Technical Change*, for the *Economic Record*. I lectured to the interim honours class on Kaldor's economics and wrote a critique of his (then) theories of distribution and growth (1963), concentrating on his strange assumption of full employment. Though naturally I welcomed the macrotheories of distribution as an alternative to marginal productivity, I was puzzled by the peculiar pricing behaviour inflicted on the consumption and investment goods sectors in Kaldor's version, principally because of the full employment constraint. I was also politically active in a conventional sense, becoming president of our local branch of the ALP and secretary of the South Australian branch of the Howard League for Penal Reform.

In 1963 I returned to Cambridge, I thought for a year's study leave. Richard Kahn and Joan Robinson made me extremely welcome. (I had been corresponding with Joan Robinson about my 1963 paper criticizing Kaldor's models. She also wanted me to be a witness to fair play in her debates with Solow and Arrow who were also in Cambridge on study leave.) I made a nostalgic return to the research students seminar to read a paper on the determination of the level of employment and the distribution of income in the short period in a two-sector model. The paper was inspired by hearing Bob Solow's 1963 Marshall lectures on two mythical creatures, Joan and Nicky. Its themes jelled with my continuing interest in the process of price formation in oligopolistic industries, with the work I had done on Kaldor and Salter in Adelaide, and with the beginnings of the hardest intellectual task of my life – to try to master the argument of Sraffa's 1960 classic, *Production of Commodities*. (I was then reading the book with Vincent Massaro; we agreed not to go on to the next sentence until we had understood the one before.)

I read the paper to an audience which included Arrow, Meade, Sraffa, Kahn and Joan Robinson. Evidently it went well for Joan Robinson and Meade both complimented me on it; Kahn asked me to dinner and to join the 'secret seminar'. Then, to my amazement, I was offered in effect a lecturing post in the Faculty. As I was on leave from Adelaide, I felt I could only accept this for a limited period, so I obtained three years leave without pay to do so. Trinity Hall elected me as their first teaching fellow in economics. (The Vice Master clinched my election by saying that even if it were a disaster, it would only be a short-run one.)

I am personally very fond of the two-sector model paper, which was published in the *Economic Record* (1965b), after which it vanished, virtually without trace. So I was delighted when Robert Dixon wrote in 1988: 'This much under-rated paper is one of the major building blocks of post-Keynesian economics' (p.247).

Then commenced what were probably the most productive years of my life. Drawing on my Adelaide experiences and working in one of the best faculties in the world, I wrote a number of papers which I can now see were in the post-Keynesian tradition. There was a unity to them, as reviewers of the volumes of my selected essays have pointed out. In addition to finishing 'The Accountant in a Golden Age' (can we use accountants' methods to find out what economic profits are?) and the two-sector model, I wrote a satirical critique of the CES production function (1966a) in which I incorporated the implications of Salterian vintages into the Robinsonian critique of the aggregate production function as it applied to econometric exercises. I also began to work on investment decision rules, investment incentive schemes and the choice of technique, including in this an analysis of the implications of the results of 'The Accountant in a Golden Age' for a bonus scheme for managers in the Soviet Union (1966b). The papers under this rubric illustrated how models which were based on what business people or managers actually do result in significantly different predictions from those which may be obtained from models which incorporate standard profit-maximizing assumptions. In these papers, unwittingly at the time and as very small fry, I was allying myself with heretics such as Kaldor and P. W. S. Andrews. I also began the work on pricing and the investment decision which was to reach fruition ten years later in a *Kyklos* paper (1976b) with Peter Kenyon, who was then a graduate student at Adelaide. This was an attempt to explain the sizes of the mark-ups set by firms in oligopolistic industries by relating them to the financial requirements of the firms' investment programmes. Finally, with Vincent Massaro I wrote two papers on Sraffa's 1960 book, one of which was a review article for the *Economic Record*. It had Sraffa's blessing in the sense that we had discussed virtually every word of it with him!

Joan, the children (then three) and I left Cambridge for Adelaide at the end of 1966, loathe to leave yet excited to be going home (and to be able to play Australian Rules Football again). As it turned out, I was about to embark on actions which fundamentally changed my life. In 1965 I began to get agitated about the Vietnam war especially, of course, Australia's involvement in it, with the accompanying conscription of 18-year-olds. I went back to Australia armed with well-prepared information from some of my Cambridge colleagues, who were already attacking Harold Wilson's and Michael Stewart's appalling acquiescence in the role of the US. When the Campaign for Peace in Vietnam (CPV) was set up in Adelaide in mid-1967, I became a Foundation Committee Member and later the Chairperson. Thus began five-and-a-half years of intense direct political action, during which I averaged about two-and-a-half days a week on anti-war activities, as well as having a full teaching load, jointly editing *Australian Economic Papers* (which at that time was one of the few outlets for maverick opinion), and helping to bring up four young children (I reneged a *lot* on this count – the great support and love of my wife seems more extraordinary to me now than it did even at the time). I must confess, too, that I played cricket in the summer and Aussie Rules in the winter.

Because of my Jewish origins, I was doubly a target for the right. I received more death threats than most people have had hot dinners, as well as one actual attempt when someone tried to blow up our car. I have never regretted the involvement in direct-action protests, moratoria and so on. In the actual debates I tried not to forget the role for dispassionate argument, and that the people I disagreed with were nevertheless people. The works of two scholars had a great influence on me at the time – Hugh Stretton's *The Political Sciences* (1969) and Noam Chomsky's 'The Responsibility of Intellectuals' (1967). They made me realize that ideology and analysis are indissolubly mixed and that we must always tell our students and our contemporaries where we stand, both in the classroom and in society at large. Since then I have never given a course of lectures without an opening burst on values, ideology and analysis, and what my own political, religious and economic views are, so that the students may be on their guard from the beginning.

The other significant event was the request in August 1968, by the editor Mark Perlman, (at the suggestion of my former professor at Melbourne, Wilfred Prest), that I write the survey article on capital theory for the second issue of the newly-formed *Journal of Economic Literature*. The rest, as they say, is history!

I shut myself away for four months behind a usually open door and, between protest marches and meetings, wrote 'Some Cambridge Controversies in the Theory of Capital' (1969). In order to make the task manageable, I split the topic into a number of self-contained working papers which I sent to about 30 people in Australia, UK and US. The then economics editor of CUP saw them and asked me to make a book of the survey. A Leverhulme Exchange Fellowship, which took us all to Keio University in Tokyo for three months over the long vacation period, December 1969 to March 1970, allowed me to escape from ceaseless political activities, live the selfish life of a scholar and write the book, the first draft in two months. I have never, before or since, worked so intensively. I wanted to get on paper what I saw in my mind as a unity.

Although many saw the reswitching episode as the centrepiece of both the survey article and the book, I thought the methodological critique by Joan Robinson concerning changes *versus* differences at least equally as important. Certainly Joan Robinson had already decided on the primacy of this aspect of the critique. When I sent her the first draft of the book in May 1970, her major criticism (apart from her reaction to some of the jokes) was that I had not emphasized it enough.

Cambridge Controversies was published in early 1972. I went back to Cambridge for a year at Clare Hall in 1972–73, venturing forth to give upwards of 50 seminars on the book's themes. I also wrote a sequel paper, which was published in *Oxford Economic Papers* (1976a).

To be known for these papers and the book became something of a bind, for I spent the next ten years or so writing commissioned articles on these themes. The only paper that had to meet the refereeing test, as it were, was the one written with Kenyon; it fell at the *Economic Journal* hurdle (courtesy of my old chums, David Champernowne and Brian Reddaway) but cleared the *Kyklos* one in style (1976b). Personally, I think it a good example of post-Keynesian analysis of a problem set in historical time and starting from 'real world' observations. I also chaired, at John Hicks's suggestion, the 1975 IEA Conference at S'Agaro on 'The Microeconomic Foundations of Macroeconomics' and edited the volume of the conference (1977a). Writing the 'Introduction' was one of the hardest tasks I have ever undertaken, so I was chuffed when Hicks said how much he liked it, adding that he thought it could not be done. The issues of the conference were, of course, those I had been grappling with, ever since my undergraduate dissertation.

In the 1970s, partly from the impetus of giving the Edward Shann Memorial Lecture on the social significance of the Cambridge controversies (1975), but mainly because of the emergence of the great inflation and the attempts to tackle it by monetarist policies, I became increasingly involved in policy debates and policy-making in Australia. With Eric Russell and other colleagues, I attempted to apply post-Keynesian analysis – containing strong Kaleckian-Robinsonian inputs and using the Meade-Russell model of the Australian economy (1957) – to the problem of inflation within the context of the Australian institutions of centralized wage-setting through the Arbitration Commission. As the economist on the ALP's 1978 National Committee of Enquiry, I drew together the party's progressive strands of thought on economic policy in a discussion paper which emerged from the enquiry. My own ideas may be found in a paper written with Prue Kerr (1980) and in the 1982 John Curtin Memorial Lecture, 'Making Socialism in Your Own Country' (1982b). When Hans Jensen (1988–89) wrote about my 'civilized economics', he discerned a structure running through the two volumes of my selected essays (1982a, 1986) from which emerged a coherent set of policy proposals. This involved a package deal of redistribution through the public sector as the *quid pro quo* to wage-earning groups for accepting incomes policies directed at the rate of increase of *money* incomes, using the traditional Australian institutions of indexation and the Arbitration Commission. Fiscal and monetary measures were to be directed towards the level of activity and the rate of growth. I put nationalization of certain key industries, including financial intermediaries, back on the agenda for discussion but sat on the fence concerning the tariff (leave it as it is and concentrate on export promotion). I opted for a fixed exchange rate, with the proviso that in an economy like Australia's, a change may have to be contemplated from time to time. I like to think that Bob Hawke toyed with the idea of implementing such a package deal for a good half hour after the election of the ALP government in 1983.

The bottom dropped out of my personal and intellectual world in February 1977 when Eric Russell died, completely unexpectedly, after playing squash. This happened while I was on six months unpaid leave from Adelaide, teaching at the Scarborough Campus of the University of Toronto with the wonderful group that Lorie Tarshis had gathered there. To help to cope with the (shared) grief of Eric's death, I wrote the first of what was to become a regular series of intellectual biographies. My memoir of Eric was published in the *Economic Record* (1977b); I then wrote a fuller study for the Newcastle Lecture in Political Economy (1977c). One of my more encouraging colleagues at Cambridge calls my essays on Tarshis, Shackle, Boulding and Goodwin, for example, 'mere chit chat'. I think they serve a more serious purpose of attempting to show how people's background and personalities influence their approaches to economics, and how ideas arise in the form that they do.

I was in Canada again in 1980, working especially with Jon Cohen. I wrote an exploratory and speculative paper on 'Marshall, Sraffa and Keynes: Incompatible Bedfellows'? (1981), in which I tried to think through the issues associated with the concept of centres of gravitation both in their work and in the make-up of modern economies. I remain ambivalent about its value but several of my research students have taken the paper as the starting point for their own work, and a number of papers have also appeared in the literature on convergence to natural prices in classical models.

I returned to Cambridge in 1982 to try to carry out one last research project – to document the intellectual history of those we may loosely think of as Keynes's pupils. I call it 'Joan Robinson and her Circle' for I want to use her contributions as the focal point around which to put the writings of Kahn, Kalecki, Kaldor, Sraffa, Pasinetti and the other gifted people, most of whom worked at Cambridge in the Cambridge tradition before and after Keynes's death. I believe it to be a worthwhile object to explore what is coherent and lasting in the contributions of these scholars. Most of the papers that I have written in the 1980s may therefore be seen as prefatory to this task. I am also an editor of the *Cambridge Journal of Economics* and am associated with other journals with furnish outlets for non-mainstream publications.

Omar Hamouda (who edited the second volume of my essays) asked me to record what I thought the purpose of economics is. Evidently, I said that the purpose is:

> to make the world a better place for ordinary men and women, to produce a more just and equitable society. In order to do that, you have to understand how particular societies work and where the pockets of power are, and how you can either alter those or work within them and produce desirable results for ordinary people, not just for the people who have the power. I see economics as very much a moral as well as a social science and very much a handmaiden to progressive thought. It is really the study of the processes whereby surpluses are created in economies, how they are extracted, who gets them and what they do with them. All economies have created surpluses in one way or another. Capitalism does it in a particular way and that is the process in which I am most interested because I live in capitalist economies. At the same time, I would like

to help to create a society where the surplus is extracted and used in a way quite different from that of a capitalist society.

Sheila Dow kindly suggested that this could stand as a succinct statement of the post-Keynesian credo.

Harcourt's Major Writings

* reprinted in (1982a)   + reprinted in (1986)

*(1962), 'Review Article of W.E.G. Salter, *Productivity and Technical Change* (1960)', *Economic Record*, **38**.

*(1963), 'A Critique of Mr Kaldor's Model of Income Distribution and Economic Growth', *Australian Economic Papers*, **2**.

*(1965a), 'The Accountant in a Golden Age', *Oxford Economic Papers*, **17**.

*(1965b), 'A Two-Sector Model of the Distribution of Income and the level of Employment in the Short Run', *Economic Record*, **41**.

*(1966a), 'Biases in Empirical Estimates of the Elasticities of Substitution CES Production Functions', *Review of Economic Studies*, **33**.

*(1966b), 'The Measurement of the Rate of Profit and the Bonus Scheme for Managers in the Soviet Union', *Oxford Economic Papers*, **18**.

(1967), *Economic Activity* (with P.H. Karmel and R.H. Wallace), Cambridge: Cambridge University Press.

+(1969), 'Some Cambridge Controversies in the Theory of Capital', *Journal of Economic Literature*, **7**.

(1972), Some Cambridge Controversies in the Theory of Capital, Cambridge: Cambridge University Press.

(1975), *Theoretical Controversy and Social Significance: An Evaluation of the Cambridge Controversies* (The Fifteenth Edward Shann Memorial Lecture in Economics), University of Western Australia Press.

*(1976a), 'The Cambridge Controversies: Old Ways and New Horizons – Or Dead End?' *Oxford Economic Papers*, **28**.

*(1976b), 'Pricing and the Investment Decision' (with P. Kenyon), *Kylos*, **29**.

(1977a), *The Microeconomic Foundations of Macroeconomics* (editor), London: Macmillan.

(1977b), 'Eric Russell 1921–77: A Memoir', *Economic Record*, **53**.

*(1977c), 'Eric Russell 1921–77: A Great Australian Political Economist' (The 1977 Newcastle Lecture in Political Economy).

(1980), 'The Mixed Economy' (with P. Kerr), in J. North and P. Weller (eds), *Labor: Directions for the Eighties*, Sydney: Ian Novak.

(1981), 'Marshall, Sraffa and Keynes: Incompatible Bedfellows?', *Eastern Economic Journal*, **7**.

(1982a), *The Social Science Imperialists; Selected Essays* (edited by Prue Kerr), London: Routledge and Kegan Paul.

+(1982b), 'Making Socialism in Your Own Country' (The twelfth annual John Curtin Memorial Lecture).

(1986), *Controversies in Political Economy; Selected Essays of G.C. Harcourt* (edited by O.F. Hamouda), New York University Press and Wheatsheaf Books Ltd.

Other References

Chomsky, N. (1967), 'The Responsibility of Intellectuals', in I. Roszak (ed), *The Dissenting Academy*, New York: Pantheon Books.

Dixon, R. (1988), 'Geoff Harcourt's Selected Essays: A Review Article', *Economic Analysis and Policy*, **18**.

Jensen, H.E. (1988–89), 'The Civilized Economies of Geoffrey C. Harcourt – A Review Article', *Journal of Post Keynesian Economics*, **11**.

Klein, R.L. (1989), 'The Economic Principles of Joan Robinson', in George R. Feiwel (ed), *Joan Robinson and Modern Economic Theory*, London: Macmillan.

Meade, J.E. and Russel, E.A. (1957), 'Wage Rates, the Cost of Living and the Balance of Payments', *The Economic Record*, **33**.

Robinson, J. (1956), *The Accumulation of Capital*, London: Macmillan.

Rothschild, K.W. (1946), 'Price Theory and Oligopoly', *Economic Journal*, **57**.

Sraffa, P. (1960), *Production of Commodities by Means of Commodities*, Cambridge: Cambridge University Press.

Stretton, H. (1969), *The Political Sciences: General Principles of Selection in Social Science and History*, London: Routledge and Kegan Paul.

Robert L. HEILBRONER (born 1919)

I was born on 24 March 1919 and began my intellectual life as an economist at a propitious moment, in the autumn of 1936, when I matriculated at Harvard, quite caught up in the full flush of Rooseveltian political ideals and ignorant of the name, much less the pronunciation, of John Maynard Keynes. It is difficult today to convey the sense of discovery that permeated economics in the late 1930s, when neither growth nor general equilibrium, rational or any other kind of expectations, choice theoretics or, for that matter, micro nor macro had yet entered the economic vocabulary. One of my most vivid academic recollections was a debate mounted by the economics faculty in a crowded hall, where distinguished professors argued with trembling voices and empurpled faces as to whether savings did or did not equal investment. It speaks to the innocence of the age that six years later I was able to publish a small article in the *American Economic Review* (1942) on the perplexing question of why a changing level of income was required to bring about equality between these two variables when they were defined to be equal at all levels of income.

Thus, I was certainly not distanced from the emerging consensus of the times. When Alvin Hansen, already Keynes's foremost American disciple, spoke to us about prospects for stagnation and possibilities for deficit finance, 'Keynesian' economics seemed capable of offering self-evidently clear solutions. I also recall very well the sense of disbelief when Schumpeter lectured in Hansen's course to tell us, in his inimitable Viennese accent and manner, that 'a depression is for capitalism a good cold douche', a statement rendered all the more shocking in that not many of us knew that a douche was a shower.

I begin with this nostalgic sketch to establish the point of my subsequent departure from conventional pieties towards both radical and conservative scepticism, and from analytic simplicities into interpretational complexities. The change began in 1946 when, after returning from the war, I decided to continue my economic education and had the immense good fortune to fall into the class, and under the spell, of Adolph Lowe at the Graduate Faculty of the New School for Social Research. There I extended my knowledge of Keynes to include growth theory (I recall that Hansen had noted with interest that the trough of every other Kitchens cycle was typically higher than that of two cycles before); learned a little calculus (there had been no mathematics required in the Harvard economics curriculum); heard for the first time of a field called 'underdevelopment', a subject unmentioned in the Harvard catalogue; and – much more important – discovered the existence of a wholly new perspective on economics in Lowe's seminars on the history of thought. Reading Smith and Ricardo under Lowe's guidance, I discovered classical political economy as an approach to economics compared with which Keynesianism appeared less revolutionary than parochial. Behind this growing enthusiasm for the work of the classics was the dawning comprehension that the ideas from which Keynes sought to extricate himself – what he misnamed 'classical' economic theory – were less constraining than others that Keynes accepted without much difficulty, namely the framework of what we have come to call neoclassical economics.

What Lowe conveyed was the idea of the economic process as a force imposing a powerful order-bestowing shape and impetus to the material activities of society. Classical political economy could thus be seen as a succession of attempts to explicate this process from (roughly) the mideighteenth to the mid-nineteenth centuries. Of special interest to myself, as a burgeoning student of the history of economic thought, was the way in which the investigators of different periods fastened on, or interpreted, different aspects of society as strategic for its evolution. To take only the most elementary example, the successive views of 'rent' from the Physiocrats through to Ricardo could thus be seen not merely as a refinement of analytic capabilities, but as a gradual redefinition of the very idea of 'land' as an economic, not as a natural, category. With this redefinition, rent is no longer perceived as a gift of nature but as an absorptive wedge inserting itself between wages and profits. In this way, I began to see economics as something other than the analysis of a wholly unambiguous object of investigation called 'economic reality'. In its place emerged the problem of identifying an 'economy' within the totality of perceived social relations – an act that determined both the boundaries of the object to be studied and the constitutive elements and properties of the discipline that studied it. Although I do not think I yet knew the word, I was thus orientated towards what has come to be known as a hermeneutic, as opposed to a positive, approach to economic inquiry.

In the course of these studies I began writing *The Worldly Philosophers* (1953), at first somewhat to the consternation of Lowe, but soon thereafter under his invaluable guidance. The book took everyone by surprise, its publisher and author not least, by finding a place for itself on enough syllabi to multiply its initial printing a thousand-fold. Over successive revisions, the cast of characters has remained essentially unchanged, minor entrances and exits excepted, but one substantial alteration marks the last edition. Earlier texts have always concluded in efforts to take the measure of the current socio-economic state of affairs, but these have invariably proved to be dated almost as soon as they appeared. The last version, in 1986, ends on a different note. It asks whether Schumpeter, who occupies the penultimate chapter, will be followed by other scenarists of his imagination and scope; and it answers the question in the negative. The reason is that, following Lowe's diagnosis (*On Economic Knowledge*, 1965), I have come to doubt that the historic course of contemporary capitalism can be depicted in terms of a self-regulating socio-economic drama. For reasons of institutional size and complexity, changes in social attitudes and ever-more-urgent political imperatives, all capitalist economies are today subject to political direction of one sort or another, including the very important political decision as to the areas in which, and the extent to which, market processes will be allowed to work their way unhindered. This is a setting so different from that of the past as to make the purely economic scenarios of the classical thinkers largely irrelevant. Schumpeter is himself the paradigmatic example of this change in that his optimistic projection of a 'plausible capitalism' is, in the end, undone by socio-political changes that undermine and annul its economic vitality.

This changing relationship of economics and history applies in particular to the most ambitious of all economic prognoses, that of Marx. I had not yet studied Marx at any length when I first wrote *The Worldly Philosophers*. At Harvard I read the *Manifesto* and some historical essays; later, with Lowe, Volume I and *Theories of Surplus Value*; but I only studied Volumes II and III still later, after I became Chair of the Economics Department at the New School in 1968. The Department had already begun to take on a radical orientation with the accession of E.J. Nell, and this drift was accelerated through the hiring of Stephen Hymer, Anwar Shaikh, David Gordon and still others. These new colleagues, and the climate of student radicalism during the 1960s, contributed to the next clear phase in my own distancing from conventional economics, culminating in *Marxism: For and Against* (1980a). This book was an effort on my part to assess the body of Marxian work in which I had become increasingly interested and immersed. As I have had occasion to remark many times, the contentious word in the book's title was its innocuous 'and' which drew fire from both those who wanted me to embrace and those who wanted me to reject Marxian ideas without reservation.

In fact, the conjunction 'and' describes very precisely my intellectual stance. In the book I define Marxism as consisting of four interrelated but distinct parts: (i) a dialectical approach to knowledge, construed as a relational rather than positivist epistemology; (ii) a materialist conception of history, centring on the importance of production activities, and class struggle over distribution; (iii) a general view of capitalism that emphasized the ideological aspects of Marxian economics – above all, its demystification of 'labour' and 'capital' as comprised of social relations, not individuals or things; and (iv) a commitment to socialism, defined as the 'practice' of Marxian social theory. This four-way definition allowed me to see Marxism 'as embodying the promise of a grand synthesis of human understanding – a synthesis that begins with a basic philosophic perspective, goes on to apply this perspective to the interpretation of history, moves thereafter to an analysis of the present as the working-out of historical forces in the existing social order, and culminates in an orientation to the future that continues the line of analysis in an unbroken trajectory of action' (pp.22-23). At the same time, the categorization of Marxism also allowed me to define my stance as *for* the first three elements mentioned above, and *against* the last – namely, a commitment to socialism as an historical destination that can be attained by 'scientifically' guided analysis.

This general endorsement of Marxian historical analysis, coupled with grave misgivings with respect to its usefulness as an historical *vade mecum*, allows me to introduce another theme in my general dissent from established economic doctrines. This is an interest in the ill-defined but inescapable concept of human nature as the bedrock of drives and needs that underlies all institutions, whether socialist or capitalist. This theme first surfaces in *The Future as History*, a book written in reaction against the facile optimism of the late 1950s. A central tenet of the book – that economic development was unavoidably a revolutionary, and not an evolutionary process, more likely to occur under the guidance of 'strong-man' regimes or 'military socialism' than as a consequence of free market practices – sharply indicates its distance from the conventional wisdom of the time. But this 'radical' view was entwined with another, whose much more conservative character was suggested by the subtitles of the concluding chapter: 'The Limits of the Possible', 'The Inertia of History' and 'The Ambiguity of Events'. These subtitles indicate a facet of my inquiries that has distanced me from conventional views of the left as well as of the right. The distancing arises from a recognition of the power of social resistance to change. In *Marxism: For and Against* this idea takes the form of doubts as to the degree of malleability of the human species – doubts which, once expressed, impose constraints on the socialist project; or which, if not admitted, force us to consider that under the appropriate conditions any human behaviour would be compatible with 'socialism'. These considerations can be easily pressed into service as arguments against the feasibility – or even the morality – of all movements of socialist reform, but I raise them not for that reason, but rather to protect the socialist movement from unnecessary disappointments and unwanted abuse.

The limits of social change come to the fore again in *An Inquiry Into the Human Prospect* (1974a) which was in part concerned with the then just emerging problems of massive ecological disturbance. Its main object of inquiry, however, was less on the size and complexity of the ecological challenge than on the degree of socio-economic disruption required to bring that challenge under control. Here the crucial matter for consideration was the degree of adaptability of capitalism and socialism as social orders and, anterior to that, some assessment of the fundamental psycho-social basis on which these orders were raised and on whose support they depended.

In retrospect, my treatment of the adaptive capabilities of the two orders seems flawed, according too little adaptability to capitalism and too much to socialism, but the direction of inquiry leads nonetheless towards my most recent work, above all *The Nature and Logic of Capitalism* (1980b) and my article 'Capitalism' in *The New Palgrave* (1987). There the central question becomes, more explicitly than ever before, the manner in which all socio-economic formations rest on patterns of indoctrinated belief and behaviour that endow them with a specific 'nature' and an ensuing 'logic'. Thus primitive, imperial and of course capitalist social orders are characterized by general behaviour-shaping institutions that not only set each order apart from others, but that bestow on each a characteristic historic dynamic. More specifically, despite many variants within each formation, we have no difficulty in recognizing a 'business world' that shapes the activities and mentalities of all members of the capitalist order, just as we can recognize the reciprocities and tradition-based orientations of primitive peoples, and the institutions and beliefs of kingship in imperial orders. From these differently constituted settings, we can also trace the historic movements associated with each – homeostatic adaptation in the case of primitive society, dynastic strategies in imperialist systems, and the complex dynamics of economic expansion in capitalism.

With respect to capitalism, the analysis singles out the accumulation of capital as the key element in its 'nature'. What separates this analysis from conventional Marxism is its consideration of the drive for accumulation not only as the means by which economic viability is achieved, but as the means by which the capitalist class continuously reestablishes and justifies its socio-political legitimacy. Therefore the approach searches for the roots of the drive for power and domination itself, rather than taking this drive for granted as do most socio-political analyses. I trace this drive to the universal experience of prolonged infantile helplessness, whence springs a central shaping aspect of human nature – its infantile frustrations and rages that find adult expression as the desire for power and/or acquiescence in existing structures of power. Under capitalism these universal social dynamics must be worked out in a setting in which the seamless cloak of rulership has been rent in two, according to government the traditional powers of war, law and order, and ceremony but denying it the rights of property invasion, while in turn according to the class of capitalists the rights to dominate the economic process but denying it the prerogatives of war, coercion, law-giving and the like.

In this fashion capitalism appears not as an 'economic system' but as a 'regime' – a social order with a central pillar of beliefs (and activities motivated by those beliefs) that endows it with the supra-rational drive enjoyed by social orders whose regimatic character is more readily recognized, such as monarchy, feudalism and the like. The differences between this view and that of conventional economics are too obvious to require comment, but it may be useful to add that without such a psychoanalytic approach, no explanation can be given for the drive to accumulate wealth, given the conventional belief in the diminishing marginal utility of wealth.

Behind the Veil of Economics (1988) pursues this general line of inquiry by searching for the degree of difference in the mechanisms of social control that distinguish the market 'mechanism' from that of tradition and command. The conventional wisdom sets the two apart, suggesting that the control mechanism of the market has no need for – indeed, has no lingering traces of – these earlier means of social coordination. My argument is that behind the veil of conventional economic rhetoric we can easily discern an understructure of traditional behaviour – trust, faith, honesty etc – as a necessary moral foundation for a market system to operate, as well as a concealed superstructure of power in the characteristic allocation by the market of a disproportionately large share of the social product to owners of the means of production. From various perspectives, the book examines these and other ambiguous boundaries of the economy, and of economics itself.

It only remains to add that I have pursued a few other lines of endeavour that should be noted in this brief intellectual self-profile. One of them is a lifelong interest in Adam Smith's large-scale endeavour, of which I might mention a general article on Smith in the *Encyclopedia Britannica* (15th ed, 1974) and 'The Socialization of the Individual in Adam Smith' (1982). Other long-pursued interests include problems and possibilities of socialism; technological determinism; the problem of value; and yet others, the more important of which have been gathered together in *Between Capitalism and Socialism* as well as in *Behind the Veil*. I have in addition written widely for non-academic audiences, in journals ranging from *Dissent* to *The New York Review of Books* and *The New Yorker*, as well as for professional journals, in particular *The Journal of Economic Issues* and *Challenge*.

It remains to say a word about the social philosophy that has made me a 'dissenting' economist. From what I have written, it is evident that liberal, radical and conservative promptings have successively coloured my social philosophy; but I could not describe those successive colourations as a movement from one end of the political spectrum towards the other. Rather, each orientation has imparted its distinctive dye to those previously there, a multi-colouring rather than a blending that I hope is as visible to the reader's eye as it is to my own. In all of this, one clear line of change is evident. This is an increasing impatience with, and finally a near total rejection of, neo-classical economics as an interpretation of social reality. I cannot resist illustrating this rejection by considering the fundamental building block of neoclassical economics itself. This is the concept of the rationally maximizing individual as the irreducible building block of economic analysis. What interests me in this conception is not the idea of 'rational' or 'maximizing', both of which are easily enough subjected to criticism but which remain useful as heuristics. Rather, the key self-destructive term is 'the individual'.

For what is the first act that this individual performs as the expression of its paradigmatic behaviour? A thousand textbooks tell us that it is to allocate his or her income in such fashion as to equalize the marginal utilities yielded by the commodities over which income is distributed. And what is the self-destructive element in this innocuous description? It is our individual's 'income'. *For how does an 'individual' acquire an income, if not from another individual?* Does not the 'fundamental building block' thereupon become a dyad – a metaphor for society? Does this not remove all possibility of creating a study of economics from an individual, rather than from a social, starting point?

On that matter alone, I find the space between myself and conventional economics too wide to allow of comfortable mutual adjustments to secure an amicable unity. Economics, in my view, can only be approached as a form of systematized power and of the socialized beliefs by which that power is depicted as a natural and necessary form of social life. We may – indeed, we have no option but to – utilize the remarkable analytical capabilities of the discipline that calls itself economics to understand the logic of our market system but, even at its best, analytical economics will tell us nothing about the nature of our social order. For that we require a standpoint outside the uncritical construals of reality that constitute the vocabulary of neoclassical economics.

Such a critical perspective allows us to see that 'economics' is by its nature always inextricably enmeshed in 'society', and that the 'problems' identified by economics are therefore always in some fashion entangled in the requirements of the larger order of which the economy is a part. Economics, in a word, is a construct, not a thing. Its analytic concerns are those of a particular social order, not of an immutable human condition. Its first and most difficult problem is therefore to make its practitioners aware of the responsibility they bear for the economic reality they place before us. Economics, thus self-consciously interpreted, is a valuable servant; but without those cautionary recognitions it is a dangerous master.

Heilbroner's Major Writings

(1942), 'Saving and Investment: Dynamic Aspects', *American Economic Review*, **32**(4).
(1953), *The Worldly Philosophers*, New York: Simon and Schuster. Sixth ed, 1986.
(1959), *The Future As History*, New York: Harper & Bros.
(1970), *Between Capitalism and Socialism*, New York: Random House.
(1974a), *An Inquiry Into the Human Prospect*, New York: W.W. Norton. Revised ed, 1980.
(1974b), 'Adam Smith', *Encyclopaedia Britannica*, Vol 16, 904–7.
(1980a), *Marxism: For and Against*, New York: W.W. Norton.
(1980b), *The Nature and Logic of Capitalism*, New York: W.W. Norton.
(1982), 'The Socialization of the Individual in Adam Smith', *History of Political Economy*, **14**(2), 427–39.
(1987), 'Capitalism', *The New Palgrave*, Vol I, London: Macmillan.
(1988), *Behind the Veil of Economics*, New York: W.W. Norton.

Other References

Lowe, A. (1965), *On Economic Knowledge*, M.E. Sharpe. Reprinted 1973.

Rudolf HILFERDING (1877–1941)   *Jerry Coakley*

Rudolf Hilferding was born into a prosperous Jewish family in Vienna (Austria) on 10 August 1877. He joined the student socialist movement at 15 while at the *Staatgymnasium* (secondary school) – hence his early and life-long interest in socialism. At the University of Vienna he studied medicine, obtaining his doctorate in 1901. By that time he had developed an interest in the social sciences and particularly economics. Thereafter he enjoyed a chequered career in a series of posts as editor, economist, doctor, lecturer, politician and Cabinet minister.

Hilferding practised as a doctor until 1906 and later during the First World War when he was stationed with the Austrian army on the Italian front. In 1902 Kautsky invited him to become a regular contributor on economic issues to *Die Neue Zeit*, the theoretical journal of the German Social Democratic Party (SDP). Five years later he was chosen to be the foreign editor of *Vorwärts*, the leading SPD newspaper. At the outbreak of the First World War Hilferding, along with a minority of the SDP, opposed the voting of war credits.

After the war he was invited to edit *Freheit*, the journal of the newly formed Independent Social Democratic Party (USPD) of Germany. As well as Bernstein and Kautsky, the latter included Rosa Luxemburg amongst its leading members. Hilferding opposed the affiliation of the USPD to the

(Communist) Third International and, in 1922, he rejoined the reunited German SPD, playing a prominent role in its activities during the following decade.

In 1920 he was appointed to the Reich Economic Council and briefly served as Minister of Finance from August to October 1923. He was elected to the *Reichstag* (parliament) in 1924 and remained a member until 1933. He again served as Minister of Finance in 1928–29. Along with other members of the German left he was perhaps slow to realize the menace of the rise of Hitler in the late 1920s and early 1930s. After Hitler's accession to power he was forced to flee the country and eventually settled in France. In 1941 the Pétain government handed him over to the Gestapo which tortured and probably executed him; the details of his death remain unknown.

One of the impressive features about Hilferding was his productivity in his adopted subject – economics. From the outset Hilferding was a dissenting economist whose main output was an elaboration and extension of Marxist economics. At the age of 27 he intervened in the debate between the Austrian neoclassical, subjectivist school and the Austro-Marxist school by publishing a riposte to Böhm-Bawerk's critique of Marx's value theory (1904). This formed part of the first volume of a *Marx-Studien* series which he had helped to establish with his friend, Max Adler.

One year later his magnum opus – *Das Finanzkapital* (hereafter *Finance Capital* or *FC* for short) – was substantially complete, as Hilferding tells us in a preface dated Christmas 1909. *FC*, published as part of the *Marx-Studien* series in 1910, was a monumental achievement by any standards. Unfortunately it proved to be the apogee of Hilferding's writings in economics, for his subsequent output pales into repetition and insignificance by comparison.

Despite its early impact and undoubted originality, *FC* has been allowed to gather dust on the shelves of Marxists. Why should this be so? One explanation is Hilferding's subsequent political career in which he allied himself with the centrist faction of the German SDP. This is borne out by Lenin's characterization of him as an 'ex-"Marxist", and now a comrade-in-arms of Kautsky and one of the chief exponents of bourgeois, reformist policy in the Independent Social Democratic Party of Germany' (Lenin, p.13).

The other explanation concerns Bukharin (1918) and Lenin (1920) who freely borrowed Hilferding's economic ideas for their theories of imperialism. Indeed it was Lenin who popularized many of Hilferding's economic theories and concepts in his classic pamphlet, *Imperialism, The Highest Stage of Capitalism*. But whereas *FC* makes for demanding and challenging reading, *Imperialism* is presented in Lenin's characteristically accessible and popular style. The upshot is that many of the central concepts of *Imperialism* are attributed to Lenin although their provenance can be traced directly to Hilferding.

Since Hilferding's enduring contribution as a dissenting economist was *FC*, this piece will focus on that work (see also other References, below).

When *FC* first appeared in print in 1910 it was hailed as a major achievement especially by his political allies, Bauer and Kautsky, who claimed it as the fourth volume of Marx's *Capital*. Certainly Hilferding was not lacking in ambition; he describes the object of his project as an attempt '...to arrive at a scientific understanding of the *economic characteristics* [my emphasis] of the latest phase of capitalist development. In other words, the object is to bring these characteristics within the theoretical system of classical political economy which begins with William Petty and finds its supreme expression in Marx' (p.21; hereafter all references are to the Bottomore's 1981 edition of *FC*).

The economic characteristics which Hilferding had in mind were those processes of concentration which: (i) lead to the formation of cartels and trusts and thus to the elimination of free competition; (ii) bring bank and industrial capital into an ever-closer relationship which he characterized as finance capital. These two aspects of concentration and their interplay form recurring themes throughout the book. On one hand they are related to the growing power of bank capital, and on the other to an analysis of finance capital as a stage of capitalism.

FC combines elements of theoretical and conjunctural analysis. The former draws heavily on Marx's *Capital*. It distinguishes three main fractions of capital: industrial, commercial and bank capital. At times the first two fractions are collectively described as 'productive capital', an apparent shorthand notation which also recognizes the fact that both fractions earn the average rate of profit; it does not appear to relate to the 'productive' and 'unproductive' labour debate.

Hilferding takes disaggregation of capital still further, identifying different sectors of industrial capital such as consumer goods industries and even individual enterprises. His conjunctural analysis is less systematic. Its focus clearly is Germany, but this does not blind Hilferding to the institutional differences of other countries as has been alleged at times. Nonetheless his discussion of other countries' peculiarities within the confines of one volume tends to be cursory and selective.

The juxtaposition of theoretical and conjunctural analysis is a feature of the whole of *FC*. Hilferding himself makes a distinction between the theoretical and policy components of his book. The former (Parts I–IV) deal respectively with money and credit, fictitious capital, the restriction of free competition, and crises and the trade cycle. The latter (Part V) traces the influence of developments in the theoretical component on economic and commercial policy.

Paul Sweezy, a leading Marxist, was confidently able to assert in 1942 that Hilferding had mistaken a transitional phase of capitalism for a lasting one. At issue was the permanence or otherwise of the power enjoyed by bank capital at the turn of the century. To get to the root of this issue, one needs to understand that Hilferding was employing the concept of 'bank capital' in its broadest sense of the German model of universal banks.

As the term itself suggests, these banks supply a wide or universal range of bank services including those associated with the institutionally separate categories of commercial and investment banks. Countries such as the US, Canada and Japan have segmented financial systems where commercial and investment banking are legally separate. In recent years the barriers within such systems have been subject to deregulatory pressures and are being eroded. Interestingly, the concept of universal banking underpins the European Commission's Second Banking Directive for the creation of a unified banking market within the European Financial Area by 1992. Moreover the principal rationale behind the whole 1992 project is to enable EC-based blocs of capital to compete with their US and Japanese rivals. In that context Hilferding's discussion must be seen as highly relevant today.

In Parts I and II Hilferding outlines the three major functions of bank capital which form the basis of the power and influence which he claims bank capital exerts over industrial capital under modern capitalism. These three functions of bank capital relate to money, credit and fictitious capital (this is capital represented by securities such as equities and bonds). I now examine these three functions as they relate to industrial capital.

Hilferding's analysis of the functions of money does not in itself add much to Marx's discussion in *Capital I*. However he highlights the major developments in the form money has taken under modern capitalism. In particular he argues that trade between capitalists is transacted not in terms of cash payments but rather through the use of credit money such as bills of exchange or cheques. A cheque or banker's draft is simply a bill of exchange payable on demand and drawn on a banker. Since credit money arises in circulation, Hilferding calls it 'circulation credit'. In the orthodox literature this is equivalent to trade credit or debtors' and creditors' items on a company's balance sheet.

Since the bulk of payments between capitalists takes the form of credit money, a system for netting out or clearing payments and receipts is necessary. Bank capital operates such payments and clearing systems as one of its major functions. Hilferding underlines the role of payments systems in facilitating trade on an ever-wider geographical basis. Initially credit money took the form of commercial credit (or bills), but Hilferding noted a tendency for bank credit, such as bankers' acceptances, to replace commercial credit as the major form of credit money.

One may wonder how the control of the payments mechanism and of the supply of bank credit would enable bank capital to exert influence over industrial capital. Indeed Hilferding believed that this function conferred no power on bank capital. Lenin, on the other hand, stressed how the operation of the payments mechanism enabled banks to ascertain the exact financial position of other capitalists. This would have been true in Lenin's day when most companies relied on just one bank for banking services. Today the monitoring of a company's financial position is complicated by multi-bank relationships.

Bank capital's second main function is the supply of capital credit or, in modern parlance, loan finance facilities. In this function bank capital collects the idle money of both the capitalist and non-capitalist classes as deposits and lends it as 'capital' credit, so-called since it involves a transfer of capital between capitalists. By contrast, credit money or 'circulation' credit is merely a payment in the exchange of equivalents. Hilferding notes that, historically, capital credit has tended to replace circulation credit, thus reinforcing the near monopoly of bank capital in the spheres of money and credit.

Hilferding contrasts the longer-term relationship between banks and enterprises implied by capital credit with the essentially short-term nature of circulation credit. However both his and Lenin's conceptions of the power conferred on bank capital by the supply of capital credit are couched in terms of competition for *access* implied by a developed credit system. They both overlooked the *conditionality* of such credit facilities which, to be fair to them, has only developed in recent decades. In other words capital credit today is advanced subject to detailed conditions inscribed as restrictive covenants in loan agreements which may limit and circumscribe the activities of the enterprises concerned.

One of the insights of *FC* is the distinction which Hilferding develops between money and credit on one hand, and fictitious capital on the other. In Part II he focuses on the mobilization of capital or the raising of equity on the stock exchange by the modern joint stock company or corporation. He contrasts the individually-owned enterprise with the modern corporation. In the former the industrial capitalist or entrepreneur owns and controls the means of production. In the corporation the raising of equity becomes the domain of money capitalists, including bankers, who become the owners of the corporation's equity stock. This implies that these money capitalists are the owners, not of the corporation's means of production (except, *in extremis*, on liquidation or receivership), but of claims to potential dividends. Hilferding describes shareholders as money capitalists rather than industrialists since, in principle, they can convert their shares into money capital at any time on the stock exchange.

What is the role of banks in this process? Unlike Lenin, Hilferding emphasizes the role of banks in the raising of new or additional equity capital. In this investment banking function Hilferding envisages banks earning a new source of revenue which he calls 'promoter's profit'. In the modern corporation the profits of enterprise are no longer appropriated by the industrialist but rather divided into dividends paid to shareholders and promoter's profit paid to banks. In this context Hilferding does not explicitly mention the role of retained profits in the corporation, though he does hint at it by referring to the competitive struggle between banks and corporations over the appropriation of promoter's profits. He also argues that the role of banks is further enhanced in modern capitalism by the demise of the stock exchange and the appropriation of its functions by banks.

A number of caveats must be added at this stage. First, the subordinate role of the stock exchange *vis-à-vis* bank capital is specific to Germany. In most other advanced economies the stock exchange plays an important role, although the role of banks has increased in the wake of various deregulatory measures known as 'Big Bangs'. Second, Hilferding seems to have overlooked the role of other financial institutions in relation to fictitious capital. In countries such as the UK and US the latter, in the guise of pension funds and insurance companies, dominate the ownership of equity claims on the stock exchange.

To sum up, the major functions of bank capital place it in a relatively powerful position *vis-à-vis* industrial capital. Both Hilferding and Lenin stress that this can lead to interlocking directorships and cross shareholdings between banks and industry. An important point stressed only by Lenin is that the power of bank capital is predicated on the combination of all its functions. Thus in both the US and Japan, for example, investment and commercial banking functions are segmented which limits the relative power of both type of banks as compared with their European competitors. Finally it seems curious that both Hilferding and Lenin saw power relations between banks and industry as uni-directional; they both overlooked Marx's view that bank capital ultimately depends on productive capital for its profits.

One of the merits of *FC* is that Hilferding does not present a static picture of the relationship between industrial and bank capital, but distinguishes between its secular and cyclical aspects. In addition he examines the change in the relationship of the capitalist class to the state which finance capital implies.

As already mentioned, Hilferding's focus in *FC* is on processes of concentration. One of the major secular tendencies of modern capitalism is that of concentration through the formation of cartels and trusts. However these processes are selective rather than general. For example, in Part III, Hilferding's elaboration of cartels and trusts appears confined to industry, contrasting sharply with Lenin's (1920) account of concentration within banking and industry. A curious aspect of Hilferding's discussion is the catch-all nature of the concept of concentration and the absence of any engagement with the concept of centralization. Instead he distinguishes between concentration of ownership of property and of production. Both processes need not be, and frequently are not, coterminous.

One of the recurring themes within *FC* is that developments within banking and industry are mutually reinforcing. It is by this circuitous route that Hilferding sees concentration as affecting the banking sector. One important consequence of concentration tendencies within the two sectors is that, by implication, other sectors get squeezed. Thus Hilferding charts the demise of commodity exchanges (Chapter 9) and of commerce and trade (Chapter 13) and the appropriation of their roles mainly by bank capital.

He sketches a musical-chairs picture of the role of fractions of capital since the beginnings of capitalist production. In the early era pre-capitalist fractions (like usurer's and merchant's capital) played an important role in accumulation. The next stage, heralded in by the industrial revolution, was one in which industrial capital subordinated bank and money-dealing capital to its needs. The latest or modern stage is finance capital in which bank capital is the hegemonic fraction and dominates industrial and other fractions of capital. Unfortunately such a schematic depiction of modern capitalism does not appear convincing towards the end of the twentieth century.

One problem with Hilferding's concept of concentration is that he appears to countenance no effective limits to the process. Indeed he explicitly mentions 'tendencies towards the establishment of a general cartel and ... a central bank' (p.234). This seems unsatisfactory for the following reason, which Lenin was later to formulate in terms of inter-imperialist rivalries. Even in a world dominated by the export of capital, it fails to take account of ongoing competition between corporations based in different national economies or groups of economies, as in the case of the European Community's plans for a single market by 1992 (see Coakley, 1991).

In Part IV Hilferding looks at the relationship between industrial and bank capital during the course of the business cycle and its fluctuations. His somewhat controversial view was that crises stem from disproportionalities in the course of the cycle. They arise from disturbances in the price structure when market prices deviate excessively from prices of production. If the rate of profit begins to fall, the exacerbation of these disproportionalities can lead to crisis. The development of cartels intensifies disproportionalities, although cartels can divert the burden of a crisis to non-cartelized sectors or enterprises.

Hilferding views developments in the credit system as obscuring dispro-portionalities during the business cycle. The upside of these developments is the elimination of the monetary crisis characteristic of the nineteenth century. By contrast the modern concentration of bank capital implies a redistribution of power in its favour at the expense of industrial and commercial capital. This development, combined with the absence of monetary crisis, safeguards against banking and stock exchange crashes. With the benefit of hindsight one can see that Hilferding was overly optimistic *vis-à-vis* the possibility of financial collapse, Third World debt crisis and the October 1987 crash being vivid reminders of the latter.

Despite the centrality of fractions of capital in Parts I–IV of *FC*, it is somewhat ironic that Hilferding concludes in Part V that the phase of finance capital unifies all fractions of capital as well as the opponents of finance capital. This unity means that capital is able to exert coordinated political pressure on the state to support its policies. These include measures relating to domestic protective tariffs for cartels and others designed to promote the export of capital. This is a relatively disappointing conclusion but, in Hilferding's defence, it must be said that the theory of the capitalist state was underdeveloped at the time of writing.

It is now some 70 years since Hilferding first published *Finance Capital*. In the interim capitalism has developed still further, especially in its international dimensions, and debate on its essential characteristics has continued to flourish. Nonetheless *FC* was and remains an impressive study of modern capitalism. One of its merits is Hilferding's lucid combination of elements of real and financial analysis. Even if Hilferding's most enduring concept – finance capital – has been found wanting in the light of developments this century, *FC* remains a landmark in Marxist scholarship which still repays close study for its many insights. For this reason alone Hilferding will be remembered as one of the leading dissenting economists of the twentieth century.

Hilferding's Major Writings

(1904), 'Böhm-Bawerk's Marx-Kritik', English translation by Eden and Cedar Paul in P. Sweezy (ed), *Karl Marx and the Close of his System: Böhm-Bawerk*, London: Merlin, 1975. First edition 1949, A.M. Kelley.

(1910), *Das Finanzkapital*, Vienna. Edited from translations by M. Watnick and S. Gordon with an introduction by T. Bottomore (ed), *Finance Capital: A Study of the Latest Phase of Capitalist Development*, London: Routledge and Kegan Paul, 1981.

(1954), *Das Historische Problem* (unfinished work, edited and with an introduction by B. Kautsky), *Zeitschrift für Politik*, **1**, New Series.

Other References

Bukharin, N. (1918), *Imperialism and World Economy*, London: Merlin.

Coakley, J. (1982), 'Hilferding's Finance Capital', *Capital and Class*, **17**.

Coakley, J. (1991), 'London as an International Financial Centre' in S. Whimster and L. Budd (eds), *Global Finance and Urban Living*, London: Routledge.

Harris, L. (1983), 'Finance Capital', in T. Bottomore (ed), *Dictionary of Marxist Thought*, Oxford: Blackwell.

Harvey, D. (1983), *The Limits to Capital*, Oxford: Blackwell.

Lenin, V.I. (1920), *Imperialism the Highest Stage of Capitalism*, Progress Press.

Sweezy, P.M. (1942), *The Theory of Capitalist Development*, New York: Monthly Review Press.

Tomlinson, J. (1987), 'Finance Capital' in J. Eatwell et al (eds), *The New Palgrave: A Dictionary of Economics*, Vol 2, Macmillan.

Albert O. HIRSCHMAN (born 1915)   *Michael S. McPherson*

Albert Hirschman was born on 7 April 1915 in Berlin. After attending the Sorbonne and the London School of Economics, he obtained a doctorate in economic science from the University of Trieste in 1938. His early career was dominated by the struggle against fascism in Europe. He left Germany for France in 1933 and, while in Italy with the French army until its defeat in June 1940, he actively supported the underground opposition to Mussolini. He stayed on in Marseilles six months more, engaging in clandestine operations to rescue political and intellectual refugees from Nazi-occupied Europe. He avoided arrest by leaving France for the United States in January 1941. There he produced his first book, *National Power and the Structure of Foreign Trade* (1945), which introduced some of the main themes of dependency theory.

After the war, Hirschman served as an economist in the Federal Reserve Board until 1952, when he left for Colombia where he stayed four years. Beginning in 1956 he held professorships successively at Yale, Columbia and Harvard, and in 1974 was appointed professor at the Institute for Advanced Study in Princeton.

The closest thing Albert Hirschman has written to a description of his own approach to social science is the essay, 'Political Economics and Possibilism' which introduces his collection, *A Bias for Hope* (1971). 'Possibilism' is tied up on the normative side with a hopeful attitude towards the prospects for constructive social change, but intellectually it is also closely connected to the proposition that available social science explanations of events rarely, if ever, exhaust the interesting features of those events. There is generally something further to be discovered. Possibilism thus seeks 'to widen the limits of what is or is perceived to be possible, be it at the cost of lowering our ability, real or imaginary, to discern the probable'. 'Quite possibly,' Hirschman observes, 'all the successive theories and models in the social sciences, and the immense efforts that go into them, are motivated by the noble, if unconscious, desire to demonstrate the irreducibility of the social world to general laws!' Hirschman characterizes his own work as a search for 'novelty, creativity, and uniqueness' (1971, p. 28).

Hirschman never sets this search of his for 'the unexplained phenomenon … the odd fact' (1971, p. 27) in opposition to the social scientific search for general laws. One could imagine such a nihilistic posture: a claim that since all putative general laws in social science are bound to fail, the search for them – the standard kind of social scientific activity – ought to stop. This would be quite foreign to Hirschman's purpose, which is to obtain 'equal rights of citizenship in social science to the search for general laws and to the search for uniqueness' (1971, p. 28). This is not mere tactical politeness; indeed, Hirschman himself has more than once propounded social scientific 'laws' of his own. Besides being useful in themselves, such general laws provide the necessary background against which the unique and the unexpected can stand out.

The feature of Hirschman's work that I shall focus on can be described metaphorically as one of peering around the edges and through the cracks in social scientific laws, to see what is being overlooked. This feature is pervasive in Hirschman's writings, from his early work on the virtues of unbalanced growth (1958), through his discovery of the 'tunnel effect' by which under certain circumstances the familiar emotion of envy is transmuted into pleasure at others' good fortune (1971), and on into more recent work like his uncovering of unexpected arguments for capitalism as a device for 'gentling' people's unruly passions (1977).

Even when Hirschman does express his findings in the form of law-like generalizations, these are typically couched in language that quietly reminds us not to endow the 'law' with too much finality and completeness. Thus in his book on cooperatives in Latin American he formulates the 'Law of Conservation and Mutation of Social Energy' to describe the tendency for those once involved in political or social action to find a way to return to it, often in another form (1984). The reference here to Newton's Laws serves both to capture an important finding in a memorable phrase and, implicitly, to remind us how much more limited and context-dependent such a finding is compared to the laws of classical mechanics.

Hirschman's insistence on the complexities that embarrass economists' attempts at simple generalizations is often presented with humour and irony, as in his observation that Mancur Olson's celebrated book demonstrating the irrationality (and hence unlikelihood) of mass political action appeared on the eve of the era of Vietnam protest (1982). Hirschman's tone, here and elsewhere, is one of 'playful seriousness', a questioning and amused attitude based on an awareness of our profound ignorance about the truth concerning social life, and hence of the pretentiousness of most claims to settled knowledge. This lack of certainty about how things work carries worrisome risks – but also hopeful possibilities. This persistent search for the new angle of vision, for the overlooked phenomenon, illuminates some important aspects of Hirschman's unique place in contemporary social science.

One such aspect is the 'unity within diversity' of Hirschman's work. Readers of Hirschman's writings are aware of the exceptionally wide variety of topics, themes and even structures of argument they display. Compare, for example, the detailed historical narrative of *Journeys Toward Progress* with the essentially abstract argument of *Exit, Voice and Loyalty* or the textual exegesis of *The Passions and the Interests*. Yet, at the same time, almost all his writings share a highly distinctive, almost unmistakable, style. A key element in his intellectual style, I would suggest, is precisely this 'contrapuntal' quality of thought. What has been neglected or overlooked will vary according to subject matter or occasion: it may be an abstract logical symmetry or a recalcitrant historical fact. But the common thread is found in the desire to search it out and discover the hidden features of reality it reveals.

Second, this feature of Hirschman's thought helps us to understand why, despite his widespread influence, he has never been the founder of a school. A school which numbered among its prime doctrines that of searching out what other doctrines had overlooked would have something in common with an anarchists' convention. Of course, it is possible to imagine people doing work in the spirit I have identified as Hirschman's, and there are many such. But they would not, and do not, look much like disciples in the conventional sense.

In fact, this point can be pushed further. It would probably be impossible for Hirschman's work (or those aspects of it stressed here) to be the norm or standard or 'paradigm' of a discipline. For in an important sense, his work is *reactive* to the main themes being undertaken in the disciplines he takes up. The search for the overlooked must be guided by what is being focused on. The point is analogous to the observation that altruism cannot be everybody's prime motivation: there have to be some folks out there who care substantially for their own satisfactions so that the altruists have somebody to help. Just so (to put it too mechanistically), somebody has to be promulgating the laws Hirschman finds the exceptions to.

It should follow that, when one of Hirschman's formulations becomes part of the prevailing wisdom, it becomes his task to peer around the edges of *that*, to see what it omits. There are, in fact, some interesting cases of this in Hirschman's writings, several of which are elaborated in his retrospective essay, 'A Dissenter's Confession' (1984), and in a reflective essay, 'Beyond Asymmetry: Critical Notes on Myself and some Other Old Friends' (in 1981). (This essay, which considers his early book on *National Power*, is a useful reminder that Hirschman is as willing to dissent from 'left' orthodoxies as from other kinds.) But perhaps the most striking instance appears in Hirschman's less personal essay on the history of his specialty, 'The Rise and Decline of Development Economics' (1981).

In that remarkable piece, Hirschman examines the historically quite exceptional circumstances that gave birth to development economics, and shows how its optimistic assumptions about the benefits of economic development ran afoul of the unfolding political disasters in many developing countries. The analysis thus uncovers a hidden or overlooked aspect of the relation between development economics and political outcomes, and thereby sheds light on many complexities in the recent evolution of development thought. The essay is indeed self-critical, since Hirschman plainly numbers himself among the development pioneers whose understanding of the vital relation between political and economic development has proved too naive. Yet this criticism of himself and his peers is, again, of a constructive sort. Hirschman recognizes the value of what development economists tried to, and in part did, achieve, and he employs his uncovering of the political limitations of development economics to enrich, rather than disparage, the field.

The final aspect of Hirschman's own work that I shall touch on is his attention – unusual in contemporary social science – to history. In contemporary economics, history has come to be viewed largely as a laboratory for testing general economic laws. For Hirschman, however, a principal purpose of historical study is to uncover the role of the exceptional or unpredictable in human affairs. A striking illustration, pointing to the normative as well as the explanatory value of such historical insight, appears in his comment on a paper by S. N. Eisenstadt concerning theories of revolution (1986). Hirschman observes there that any attempt to identify probabilistic laws of revolution is bound to be pessimistic: few oppressed groups will be in a condition that makes a successful revolution likely. In fact, any path one can discern that leads from authoritarianism to pluralist democracy will appear both quite narrow and highly improbable. But, Hirschman continues,

> such unlikely sounding combinations are the kind of stuff history is made of! It is a considerable paradox, but I believe it is true that the spelling out of such a priori quite unlikely *combinations* of needed favorable factors is less discouraging than the laying down of just *one* overriding precondition for redemocratization. The reason why the *less* probable turns out here to be subjectively *more* hopeful is, precisely, that the bringing together of various conditions conjures up the image of a conjunction of circumstances such as we are familiar with from history. The mere act of describing such a conjunction gives confidence that, even if this particular one cannot be translated into reality a second time, there must be quite a few other similarly far-fetched ones that history might have up its sleeve. For history is nothing if not far-fetched.

In addition to investigating the history of phenomena, Hirschman is also interested, for rather different reasons, in the history of thought in his specialist disciplines. A lively awareness of both the current state of thinking about a subject and how it has evolved is essential to Hirschman's distinctive approach to social theory. For it is only *relative* to current understandings and their background that Hirschman can define neglected and overlooked aspects. A sensitive and broad-ranging awareness of the currents of thought in the social sciences is an essential characteristic of Hirschman's make-up; although plainly a natural part of his personality, it is also central to his distinctive way of working. Hirschman's introductory remarks about an essay of his entitled 'Morality and the Social Sciences: A Durable Tension' (1981) capture this outlook nicely:

> If there is to be a fruitful re-encounter of morality and social science, then the strength of the resistance against such an enterprise must be realistically appreciated. The essay thus explores the historical and epistemological reasons why the many well-meaning exhortations to build moral values into economic analysis have not been notably effective.

Albert Hirschman is, indeed, a dissenting economist, but not one who dissents in favour of some other orthodoxy. Although anxious to show up inadequacies in existing theories, he is not typically concerned either to overthrow those theories or to replace them with a new alternative. The aim is rather to say, 'Yes, there is something right about the existing theories, *and also* there is something over here, not noticed by those theories, which we should keep in mind as well'. This 'something else' will not typically be a full-blown new theory, with law-like generalizations and testable hypotheses. It is more likely to consist of a narrative account of some instances where the theory breaks down, illustrations of aspects of reality that the theory overlooks, or a collection of admittedly fragmentary theoretical insights.

Good illustrations are provided by Hirschman's arguments that what look like obstacles to development sometimes are not, or that reliance on comparative advantage sometimes is not a satisfactory strategy for growth. A fully-fledged replacement for the present theory of development obstacles would say when apparent obstacles are real and when they are not, and would stipulate criteria and tests for determining which they are. And similarly for a modified theory of comparative advantage. Hirschman's arguments are not generally ambitious in this way.

The underlying rationale for this modest approach, I would suggest, is Hirschman's perception that anything approaching the 'whole truth' about any interesting piece of social reality is bound to be much more complicated than our available means of apprehending it. The theories we possess are inevitably partial, constrained by our limited point of view, our imperfect knowledge, and our finite imagination. But we should not, on that account, be contemptuous of those attempts at systematic theory that are available – they give us whatever grasp we have. There is no point at our current (or foreseeable) level of understanding to demand or try to produce a completely adequate view. Rather we have to find positive ways of living with our ignorance.

It is not, from that perspective, particularly helpful simply to refute available theories – given their limits, that is liable to be both fairly easy and not very illuminating. It can, however, be useful to be *reminded* of our ignorance, if that can be done in ways that encourage us to widen our vision, and to see possibilities we had overlooked.

As Kuhn and others have argued, it may be necessary for members of a scientific community to suppress awareness of the dubieties and the limits of available theories – to proceed *as if* the dominant paradigm is true until such time as it is replaced by a new one. Researchers may need to hold firmly to certain basic propositions and theories as they try to advance knowledge; it is both understandable and useful that they should evolve ways of agreeing among themselves in order to get on with the work. But, however necessary for a certain kind of theoretical work to put on blinders, in social science we also have to *live* with those theories and their implications. Such theories are not confined to the textbook or the laboratory. They help guide our deliberations about social policy and our judgements about the limits of social possibility. Indeed, in an era as 'theory-soaked' as our own (to borrow a phrase from Charles Taylor), social scientific theories may importantly shape our own self-understanding as well.

We need, in conducting our lives, to draw on the best available social science theories, but we also need to learn to keep our distance from them, to retain a measure of perplexity and puzzlement about the character of our social lives. Although for the sake of advancing theory, it may be highly functional for a social scientist to 'put on blinders' – to focus as narrowly as possible on extending and refining a theory – those same blinders may be quite disabling when we seek to conduct ourselves intelligently in society, as well as disastrous if worn by policy-makers equipped with executive energy and the means of coercion. The disability is, of course, all the greater if we forget that we are wearing blinders.

This suggests that there is a role to be played by maverick social thinkers in probing beyond the limits of accepted views, trying in a constructive fashion to remind us that there is indeed more to the story. There is no 'method' to playing this role; what is needed is a broad knowledge of society, a good imagination, and something of an adventurous spirit. Thought in this vein should be tolerant, indeed supportive, of the more 'single-minded' theorists (although not above poking fun at their exaggerated claims). Nor would such thinkers aspire to the lofty heights of abstraction and universality, but instead would see their work as deeply enmeshed with the particular needs and limits of contemporary social thought.

Some such posture seems to me to characterize at least one important aspect of Hirschman's role in social science today. Perhaps this analysis can be seen as an application of some of Hirschman's own views about the development of societies to the development of social science. Hirschman helped pioneer the attitude that the policy process was best understood, not as a well-informed optimization process, but instead as a disjointed search for improvements and opportunities. In that context he argued (along with Charles Lindblom) that putting too much faith in a systematic plan or an allegedly comprehensive theory could impede the process of effective search.

Hirschman wrote in 1958 that 'development depends not so much on finding optimal combinations for given resources and factors of production as on calling forth and enlisting for development purposes resources and abilities that are hidden, scattered or badly utilized'. Perhaps improvements in social science sometimes depend not so much on advancing more encompassing theories as on uncovering ideas that are hidden, scattered, or badly understood. Such, I suggest, has been Albert Hirschman's role.

Hirschman's Major Writings

(1945), *National Power and the Structure of Foreign Trade*, Berkeley and Los Angeles: Bureau of Business and Economic Research, University of California.

(1958), *The Strategy of Economic Development*, New Haven: Yale University Press.

(1963), *Journeys Toward Progress: Studies of Economic Policy-Making in Latin America*, New York: Twentieth Century Fund.

(1970), *Exit, Voice and Loyalty: Responses to Decline in Firms, Organizations and States*, Cambridge: Harvard University Press.

(1971), 'Introduction: Political Economics and Possibilism', in A. O. Hirschman, *A Bias for Hope: Essays on Development and Latin America*, New Haven: Yale University Press,

(1977), *The Passions and the Interests: Political Arguments for Capitalism before its Triumph*, Princeton: Princeton University Press.

(1981), *Essays in Trespassing: Economics to Politics and Beyond*, New York: Cambridge University Press.

(1982), *Shifting Involvements: Private Interest and Public Action*, Princeton: Princeton University Press.

(1984), *Getting Ahead Collectively: Grass Roots Experiences in Latin America*, New York: Pergamon Press.

(1986), *Rival Views of Market Society and Other Essays*, New York: Viking-Penguin International.

Other References

McPherson, Michael S. (1986), 'The Social Scientist as Constructive Skeptic: On Hirschman's Role' in *Development, Democracy and the Art of Trespassing: Essays in Honor of Albert O. Hirschman*, Notre Dame: Notre Dame University Press, 305–15. The foregoing entry draws heavily on this article.

John Atkinson HOBSON (1858–1940)   *John E. King*

John Atkinson Hobson was born in Derby on 6 July 1858, into a prosperous middle-class family. After reading classics at Oxford he became a school-teacher and extension lecturer in English and, for a time, in Economics, in which he was entirely self-taught. Hobson's heretical views made it impossible for him to obtain a regular university teaching position, and he spent most of his life as a freelance writer, publishing over 50 books in addition to innumerable articles in the radical press.

A leading theorist of 'New Liberalism', which attempted to synthesize liberal and democratic socialist ideas, Hobson resigned from the Liberal party in 1916 in protest at its war policy. He subsequently joined the Independent Labour party and, through it, the Labour party itself, exercising a profound influence on its economic thinking throughout the interwar period. Hobson continued to publish prolifically until his eightieth year. He died on 1 April 1940.

Hobson's intellectual interests were unusually wide-ranging, encompassing sociology, ethics, the rationalist critique of religion, and political theory, in addition to economics. His sources were equally diverse, including Spencer, Ruskin, Veblen, John Stuart Mill and Henry George. As an economist he is best-known, first, for his underconsumptionist theory of crisis which to some degree anticipated – and was in some ways superior to – the demand-deficiency theory of John Maynard Keynes and, second, his economic interpretation of imperialism, which attracted the interest of Lenin. No less important, but often overlooked, were Hobson's analysis of income distribution (in which he generalized the concept of rent to derive an idiosyncratic, non-Marxist theory of exploitation and economic surplus) and his critique of orthodox welfare economics. Hobson's continuing interest in economic policy found expression in a tireless campaign for the redistribution of income, selective public ownership of industry and international economic cooperation.

The central themes of Hobson's underconsumptionism were set out in 1889 in his first book, written with the businessman and mountaineer A.F. Mummery. In *The Physiology of Industry*, Mummery and Hobson identify over-saving as the underlying cause of trade depression. Their analysis is non-Keynesian, in the sense that savings are always invested, adding to society's stock of capital. Excessive levels of saving push up the ratio of capital to consumption above that consistent with macroeconomic equilibrium and a crisis of over-production ensues, with heavy unemployment and falling wages. Although a private virtue, Mummery and Hobson argue, thrift had become a social vice. Fiscal policy should discourage saving, and the labour market should be regulated to protect the interests of the workers.

After Mummery's death in 1895 during an unsuccessful attempt on Nanga Parbat, Hobson developed and refined their analysis but never repudiated its fundamentals. For instance, *The Physiology of Industry* did not contain a convincing explanation of the forces giving rise to a tendency for excessive saving. This gap was filled in 1902 in Hobson's *Imperialism*, when he attributed over-saving to the maldistribution of income:

> If a tendency to distribute income or consuming power according to needs were operative, it is evident that consumption would rise with every rise of producing power, for human needs are illimitable, and there could be no excess of saving. But it is quite otherwise in a state of economic society where distribution has no fixed relation to needs, but is determined by other conditions which assign to some people a consuming power vastly in excess of needs or possible uses, while others are destitute of consuming power enough to satisfy even the full demands of physical efficiency (*Imperialism*, p.83).

For the rest of his life Hobson would advocate egalitarianism and increased expenditure on social welfare, not merely on humanitarian grounds but also as an essential weapon against over-saving.

Orthodox economists were strongly opposed to Hobson's crisis theory, though it took the Great Depression to provoke explicit and detailed criticisms of his ideas. Their objections were two-fold. First, investment led to reduced costs and lower prices, which would stimulate consumption. Second, any tendency to over-saving would be rapidly reversed by a decline in the rate of interest. Both claims had been rejected, somewhat unsatisfactorily, in *The Physiology of Industry*. In his *Economics of Unemployment* (1922) and, more especially, in *Rationalisation and Unemployment* (1930), Hobson launched a more considered counter-attack. On the one hand, the price level was unlikely to fall, he maintained, since monopoly power involved rigid prices and widening profit margins. On the other hand, lower prices would lead to lower money incomes and reduced demand. Nor was saving at all sensitive to changes in the rate of interest; it was rather a function of the level and distribution of income.

In these later writings Hobson anticipated both the model of monopoly capitalism associated with the work of Paul Baran and Paul Sweezy, and some important aspects of the economics of Keynes, who praised Hobson in the *General Theory* and with whom he corresponded in 1931 and again in 1936. Towards the end of his life Hobson made significant concessions to Keynes's theory of under-investment (see for example 1938, pp.192–3), without abandoning his own contention that crises could also result from over-investment. In this he has been vindicated by the Harrod-Domar growth theory, which stresses the capacity-increasing effect of investment and the potential problems of effective demand which this creates.

Hobson's theory of imperialism represented less a direct challenge to contemporary orthodoxy than the application of economic ideas to issues which were generally regarded as essentially non-economic in nature. Drawing on his experiences in South Africa, where he was sent as correspondent of the *Manchester Guardian* during the Boer War, Hobson pointed to the intimate connection between economic interests and political decisions. Over-production had led to the dumping of surplus output in export markets, and over-saving had induced desperate attempts to find overseas outlets for surplus capital. Powerful financial lobbies had seized control of Britain's foreign policy to assist them in this, and were promoting militaristic and chauvinistic attitudes among the population at large. Over-saving, then, was 'the economic tap-root of imperialism', which could be combated only through social reforms to redistribute income and expand the home market.

This analysis, if not the associated policy conclusions, was taken up by Marxian theorists of imperialism, most notably by Rudolf Hilferding in his discussion of 'finance capital' and – very much less systematically – by Lenin. Hobson himself was not entirely consistent on the question, sometimes largely ignoring it and on occasion evidencing a much more sanguine view of the prospects for international capitalist cooperation along the lines of Karl Kautsky's notion of 'ultra-imperialism'. At other points, especially in the 1930s, Hobson brings to mind Rosa Luxemburg in arguing that imperialist expansion was inherently contradictory. Once absorbed by the metropolitan powers, peripheral areas no longer offered 'external' outlets for surplus capital, making the crisis of over-saving a truly global one (1932, p.26).

The third central feature of Hobson's economics, closely related to his views on underconsumption and on imperialism, was his distribution theory. First proposed in *The Physiology of Industry*, the analysis was fully developed in his *Economics of Distribution* in 1900. Hobson followed his friend Sidney Webb in generalizing the concept of economic rent from land to labour, capital and entrepreneurship. All payments to owners of productive inputs in excess of their minimum supply prices constituted 'forced gains' or 'surplus' income. Imperfections in competition were pervasive, Hobson argued, and the resulting surpluses were correspondingly large. Factor prices depended on the respective bargaining strengths of their suppliers. Labour in particular was at a permanent disadvantage relative to the owners of capital; this was reflected in the very large share of the total product which accrued as profits.

In principle none of this was inconsistent with the marginal productivity theory of relative income shares which John Bates Clark was advocating at the end of the last century. Then, as now, neoclassical writers tended to assert that competition was powerful enough largely to eliminate monopoly and monopsony power, which Hobson denied. This is an empirical question, on which Hobson's position is arguably the more plausible; no really important theoretical issue is at stake. Indeed, in two articles in the *Quarterly Journal of Economics* in 1891, Hobson had formulated his own analysis in marginal productivity terms. But in *The Economics of Distribution* he repudiated the whole Clarkian approach on the grounds that the marginal products of individual units can never be identified.

This was sufficient – it may not have been necessary – for his theory to be ignored by orthodox economists, or treated with disdain. It was, however, of great importance for the Hobsonian system. Surplus incomes were the source of the vast inequalities which he despised; they were the basic cause of over-saving, trade depression and imperialism. For Hobson 'the problem of absorbing the "surplus" for social uses' (*Poverty in Plenty*, 1931, p.35) was the most fundamental of all macroeconomic issues.

Hobson was also extremely hostile towards neoclassical welfare economics. Here he drew heavily on the passionate if rather diffuse humanism of John Ruskin and on the more biting criticism of Thorstein Veblen, in addition to his own ideas on ethics and social philosophy. In *The Industrial System*, Hobson argued for a 'human interpretation of industry' in which the quality of working life was given equal weight with the satisfactions afforded to the consumers. Twenty years later, in his *Wealth and Life*, he returned to this theme, attacking orthodox thinkers like Mill, Marshall and Pigou for failing to transform economic into human values. True wealth involved more than material goods, Hobson maintained. Under capitalism, individuals were alienated both at work and in consumption. Human personality, social relationships and individual creativity were all conditioned by productive activity and in consuming. None of these dimensions, according to Hobson, was adequately dealt with by orthodox economic analysis. A 'new utilitarianism' must be derived, which would take into account physical, intellectual and moral satisfactions and replace the neoclassical view of economic welfare with a more rounded conception of 'organic' well-being.

The breadth of Hobson's theoretical perspective was reflected in his writings on economic policy. Always a social reformer, he was by 1920 a socialist. But his was a socialism of an idiosyncratic kind, neither Fabian nor Marxist. In *The Physiology of Industry,* Mummery and Hobson had urged the redistribution of income through progressive taxation, both to promote social justice and to counteract the tendency to over-saving. They endorsed trade unionism for similar reasons, and throughout his life Hobson opposed wage reductions as a cure for trade depression. *Imperialism* added an extra dimension to his argument. Social reform was now seen as an essential means of avoiding war: 'Trade Unionism and Socialism are thus the natural enemies of Imperialism, for they take away from the "imperialist" classes the surplus incomes which form the economic stimulus of Imperialism' (*Imperialism*, p.90).

At this stage 'socialism' still meant little more to Hobson than redistribution and social welfare expenditures; in short, a welfare state. He later came to see state ownership of industry as the only way in which the abuses associated with monopoly power could be contained. But Hobson advocated a mixed economy rather than comprehensive nationalization. Public ownership should be confined to industries where mass-production techniques were indispensable, and large-scale operation could not be avoided. In other branches of industry, state control would stifle craftsmanship and individual initiative, and 'as much as possible of production and consumption [should] participate of the nature of the fine arts' (*Wealth and Life*, p.327).

All this was set against the background of an internationalism which owed more to Cobdenite liberalism than to Marxian revolutionary proletarian solidarity. Hobson was a tireless advocate of international economic cooperation, both to protect the interests of workers in the high-wage countries and to promote the development of the more backward regions. Always suspicious of the relevance of orthodox trade theory to a world of unemployment and crisis, Hobson was nevertheless no protectionist. He mourned the passing of free trade in 1931, but called, as so often in the past, for the international coordination of economic policy to stimulate consumption demand, adding a case for the establishment of a world bank. An internationally planned recovery, Hobson argued, offered the only realistic prospect of a return to free trade.

Orthodox economists were generally dismissive of Hobson's economic heresies. As far as his underconsumptionism was concerned, the tone was set by Edgeworth's hostile review of *The Physiology of Industry*, which in the longer term effectively excluded Hobson from British academia. Not until the 1930s had the climate changed sufficiently for him to receive some of the credit which he was due, and even then it was very much a case of reflected glory from Keynes. Hobson's theory of imperialism was neglected or opposed by neoclassical writers: sympathetically by Pigou, less so by Robbins; only the Marxists took it at all seriously. His views on income distribution and economic welfare made even less of a mark on professional economists, at least in Britain. (In the US, where the institutionalist tradition was much stronger, he found a somewhat friendlier reaction.) Hobson's greatest influence was at the political level. In 1928 he was described as 'economist "by special appointment" to the British Labour Party' and, to the extent that the programme of the 1945–50 Attlee government had any coherent intellectual basis, Hobson supplied it.

Of his theoretical contributions, only Hobson's theory of income distribution has sunk without trace. Something close to his theory of over-saving continues to thrive on the margins of Marxian and post-Keynesian political economy, along with his analysis of imperialism. And Hobson's quest for a humanist economics of welfare, however unsuccessful it might have been, finds an echo among many modern socialists and in the green movement inspired by E.F. Schumacher.

Hobson's Major Writings

(1889), *The Physiology of Industry*, (with A.F. Mummery). Reprinted by Kelley, New York, 1971.
(1891), 'The Law of Three Rents', *Quarterly Journal of Economics*, 5.

(1900), *The Economics of Distribution*. Reprinted by Kelley, Clifton, N.J., 1972.

(1902), *Imperialism: a Study*. Reprinted by Allen and Unwin, London, 1961.

(1909), *The Industrial System: an Inquiry into Earned and Unearned Income*, London: Longman, Green.

(1922), *The Economics of Unemployment*, London: Allen and Unwin.

(1929), *Wealth and Life: a Study in Values*, London: Macmillan.

(1930), *Rationalisation and Unemployment: an Economic Dilemma*, London: Allen and Unwin.

(1931), *Poverty in Plenty*, London: Allen and Unwin.

(1932), *From Capitalism to Socialism*, London: Hogarth Press.

(1938), *Confessions of an Economic Heretic*, London: Allen and Unwin.

Other References

Allett, J. (1981), *New Liberalism: the Political Economy of J.A. Hobson*, University of Toronto Press.

Freeden, M. (1978), *The New Liberalism: an Ideology of Social Reform*, Oxford: Clarendon Press.

King, J.E. (1988), *Economic Exiles*, London: Macmillan.

Nemmers, E.E. (1956), *Hobson and Underconsumptionism*, Amsterdam: North-Holland.

Stephen Herbert HYMER (1934–1974)   *Christos N. Pitelis*

Stephen Hymer is the undisputed leading figure in the theory of the multinational or transnational firm (TNC hereafter), his Ph.D. thesis being probably the most extensively cited ever. However, Hymer's contribution to economic theory extends well beyond the analysis of the TNC; he also wrote a most insightful and original account of the political economy of multinational corporate capital.

Stephen Hymer was born in Montreal (Canada) on 15 November 1934 and died tragically in 1974. His father, a Jewish immigrant from Eastern Europe, ran a small clothing store in which his mother worked as a bookkeeper.

His undergraduate studies were at McGill from where he graduated with first class honours in politics and economics. He then moved to MIT with his wife Gilda and their two sons. At the suggestion of Charles Kindleberger, he decided to combine his interests in industrial and international economics, by working on the area of the TNC. His now famous Ph.D. thesis on *The International Operations of National Firms: A Study of Foreign Direct Investment*, though completed in 1960, did not appear until 1976 due to MIT's original refusal to sponsor its publication.

Following the completion of his thesis, Hymer spent a year in Ghana, returned to MIT and Yale where he taught for two years and then went back to Ghana in 1963. Back at Yale in 1964, he worked at the Economic Growth Center until 1969. During this time he was also appointed to the Canadian Task Force in 1967 to examine the structure of Canadian industry and visited Cambridge (UK) where he worked with Bob Rowthorn in 1968. The following year he received a research fellowship at the University of West Indies (Trinidad), worked at the summer Institute for International Studies of the

University of Chile, made a 'public commitment to Marxism', and was refused tenure and promotion at Yale. From autumn 1970 until his death he worked as a Professor of Economics at the New School for Social Research in New York. In 1973 he separated and divorced; he also spent several months in the Max Planck Institute in Starnberg (West Germany). During his last years he acquired substantial acclaim, testifying before the UN study group on TNCs and appearing on the CBC several times. His death left an unfinished book where his various contributions to economics were to be brought together. A collection of 11 of his best papers was published in 1979 by a number of his friends and colleagues, entitled *The Multinational Corporation: A Radical Approach.*

By his own admission, Hymer's work and more general perceptions of capitalism were shaped by his family background during the early depression years. During his childhood he recalls how they felt 'aliens' in a land controlled by big business and government, coming to understand the importance of 'money as social power'. At McGill he and his fellow Canadians were also beginning to realize the special status of Canada as 'more than a colony but ... less than a nation'. In Ghana he experienced problems relating to the British colonial legacy; in particular he entertained the possibility that Britain discouraged Ghana's development. His experience in Chile reinforced a feeling that least developed countries (LDCs) needed more than the regulation of TNCs for survival.

Hymer's ideological attitudes developed in parallel with his experiences. From an orthodox but liberal criticism of the TNC in his thesis, through his nationalist radical proposals to curb US TNCs in Canada in his Task Force study developed his 'cathartic' commitment to Marxism and an associated focus on overthrowing rather than regulating the multinational corporate capital system.

In the following pages I begin with Hymer's theory of the TNC, describing its main strands and how it relates with current debate in the field. My belief that he virtually 'said it all' has not been accepted because of a tendency in the profession to focus on his thesis and ignore his later 'Marxist' (thus irrelevant?) papers. Particular emphasis is given below to his views on TNCs and labour, the TNC and the nation-state, uneven development and the industrialization of the LDCs. Discussion then follows of his more general assessment of the internationalization of capital and the transnational corporate capital system, as well as the implications of his views for policy towards TNCs and the system as a whole.

Hymer's starting point was that, for the coordination or the *division of labour*, the firm is a substitute for the market. Built around a special discovery or advantage, the strength of firms lies in their ability to reap the benefits of cooperation and the division of labour. Firms then obey a 'law of increasing size'. Historically they have developed from their early Marshallian years (an owner-controller), to becoming national corporations (public limited companies), then multi-divisional firms (separation of strategic decisions from operational ones) and finally transnationals. The distinctive characteristic of the last stage is that they control production activities outside their country of origin. Such control – the undertaking of foreign direct investment (FDI) – distinguishes transnationals from alternative forms of international operations, such as exporting or licencing. In the light of this, two obvious questions emerge: first, why are national corporations *willing and able* to undertake FDI; and, second, why do they prefer FDI to existing (market) alternatives. In other words, why do they choose to internalize the market on a global scale?

Concerning the first question, Hymer's theory had two strands, the first being the concept of an 'ownership advantage' ('specific advantage' or 'monopolistic advantage'); this would include such aspects as organization, technology, access to capital and product differentiation. According to this, firms are *able* to undertake FDI because they possess an advantage over indigenous firms abroad. Without FDI they would suffer a competitive disadvantage *vis à vis* indigenous firms, which have a better knowledge of the local market conditions, customs, language etc.

The second strand of Hymer's theory, explaining why firms are *willing* to undertake FDI, relies on the concept of firms operating in a framework of oligopolistic rivalry and collusion. The threat of (potential) rivalry leads firms to try to reduce competition and eliminate conflict (collude). TNCs increase their control over international product markets; bigness is paid by fewness and competition decreases.

Concerning the historical phenomenon of US firms investing overseas, particularly in Europe in the 1950s, Hymer observes that this was due to the threat of potential competition by expanding Japanese and European firms. US firms were obliged to undertake FDI overseas as a defensive measure against the threat of potential competition. FDI is therefore a device for restraining competition.

This still does not fully explain the choice of FDI over market alternatives such as exports or licencing. Already in his Ph.D. thesis, Hymer suggested that this choice was due to the inherent problems that firms have fully to appropriate their ownership advantages if they use the market, such as with licencing arrangements. Such problems could relate to contracting arrangements, 'externalities', 'opportunistic' behaviour (self-interest with guile), the desire to control raw materials and the need to 'defend the quasi-monopoly of knowledge'!

Other motives for FDI discussed by Hymer include market growth for firms' products overseas, the existence of cheaper labour, and macroeconomic factors such as higher growth rates abroad. Benefits of transnationalization include dividing the power of labour while uniting it in production. Also, because of the greater flexibility of their operations and their better organization compared with national firms, TNCs enjoy an enhanced bargaining position *vis-à-vis* nation-states. Hymer also viewed size and internationality as advantageous in themselves, in part due to the broadening of the TNCs' horizons.

In summary, Hymer's views on the TNC can be interpreted as follows. Oligopolistic rivalry, collusion and the law of increasing firm size provide the underlying framework. Within it 'ownership advantages' explain why firms can become TNCs (the necessary condition). International collusion explains why they wish to undertake FDI (the sufficient condition). Problems associated with the appropriation of quasi-rents explain why firms internalize the use of such advantages, that is supersede the market (the choice of institutional form). A number of locational factors provide additional motives for firms to undertake FDI. Others are their ability to increase their bargaining position *vis-à-vis* labour by dividing it spatially and *vis-à-vis* the nation-state. For all the above, size and internationality are advantages in themselves and thus additional motives.

Whether one follows the current TNC debate or just glances at the collection of papers in Pitelis and Sugden (1990), it becomes plain that virtually everything has been said by Hymer. In particular, 'ownership advantage' theories, 'global reach' theories, 'internalization' theories, the 'eclectic' theory (which combines ownership advantages with locational factors and internalization, OLI), 'oligopolistic interaction' theories, 'divide and rule' theories, as well as some macroeconomic considerations, are all there. This would seem to leave little basis for decrying Hymer's alleged focus on 'ownership advantages' alone, his alleged failures to account for locational factors and/or to distinguish between 'natural or cognitive' market failures from those that are 'structural'. Subsequent theories have obviously expanded, often substantially, on Hymer's groundwork but they have not extended the argument.

An important aspect of Hymer's work was the relationship between TNCs and labour. Generally he was in agreement with both Marx and Marshall in claiming that the division of labour was the key to solving the economic problem. He viewed the factory (firm) as a better means of coordinating the division of labour than market forces. He observed that the division of labour stemmed from the principle of 'divide and rule' and was based on the division between mental and manual labour. Control over labour was through spatial, horizontal, vertical and temporal divisions. Sexism, racism and hierarchical divisions among occupations extended this control. He regarded the TNC as a means of achieving a more productive division of labour, thus unleashing great sources of latent energy, by eliminating anarchy in international markets. Simultaneously TNCs further reduced the power of labour through extending its spatial division.

Hymer claimed that 'market economic power grows out of the subjugation barrel of a gun'. In his mind, the subjugation of labour to capital was originally achieved through an alliance between the merchants (the emerging capitalist class) and the feudal monarchs, based on mutual benefit. Ever since then, the capitalist class and the state have grown hand in hand. The emergence of the 'new industrial state' helped to complete the process of 'primitive accumulation', and led to the strengthening of the 'nation-state'. This gave rise to national rivalries externally and the use of the visible hand of the state, along with the invisible hand of the market internally.

However, the transnational corporation put an end to the symbiotic relationship between capital and the ability of nation-states to pursue autonomous policies. This erosion of power applies to all states, but asymmetrically. Strong states, such as the US, are in a better position in relation both to their own transnationals and to foreign TNCs. For example, Hymer observes, the US can stop her TNCs from 'trading with the enemy' whereas a less developed country cannot hold a US firm hostage for actions of its parent company. Concerning the bargaining power of TNCs *vis-à-vis* small, weaker, nation-states (DCs or LDCs), the TNC is always dominant both because of its locational flexibility of operations and its superior organization. More generally, TNCs no longer operate *under* the state, but alongside it or even above it.

The erosion of the power of nation-states generates a need for transnationals to mobilize new power bases to fill the vacuum (after all markets grow out of the barrel of a gun). This implies a need for international institutions such as the UN, the IMF etc. Still, it is not a foregone conclusion that TNCs will supersede the state. Hymer (with Rowthorn) asks the question whether France or IBM will have survived in a hundred years. Although the answer may not appear so obvious now as in 1970, Hymer observes that TNCs and/or international organizations still need to find an effective substitute to good old 'nationalism'. The 'struggle' between nation-states and TNCs is thus an ongoing one.

One of the most important aspects of Hymer's work was his views on uneven development and industrialization of the Less Developed Countries (LDCs). He observed that, unlike the earlier years of capitalist development when LDCs were banana republics, TNCs now needed industrialized LDCs in order to create new markets and extend their productive base globally. New markets are very important for TNCs for three reasons. First, the existence of fixed costs in the production of new products implies high marginal profits when these are sold in new markets. Second, in contrast to what income statistics suggest, a relatively wealthy middle class exists in

LDCs with similar aspirations and tastes to its counterpart in the developed countries, thus providing a ready clientele. Third, oligopolistic preemption: TNC operations in LDCs can be seen as a device to preempt potential rivals from entering these markets.

The importance of LDCs for TNCs need not imply development and/or equality: rather it implies uneven development and inequality. Hymer was careful to point out that TNCs' operations in LDCs did provide these countries with benefits – technology, skills etc. The vital issue for him, however, was who controls this process of development. To the extent that TNCs do, LDCs lose their economic independence and enter a condition of self-perpetuating dependency. The benefits moreover are spread unequally. TNCs tend to shape the world to their image (the 'correspondence principle'); they create superior and inferior states by using a 'pyramid of power' – a centre and a periphery (the hinterland) which involves decentralized decision-making but centralized control. A few metropoles in the centre concentrate all strategic decision-making. New products are first introduced there and then diffused to the periphery through international 'trickle down' and 'demonstration' effects.

Although the periphery might have been better off choosing an independent path to development, the chances of this happening through a national capitalist class are grim. According to Hymer, middle classes in the LDCs prefer to seek promotion within the transnational corporate capital system, and for good reason! Local capitalists are better off becoming shareowners of a TNC (possibly even running the local branch) than trying to compete. An obvious reason is that they are no longer locked in their firms and can thus join the international wealthy in diversifying their portfolios so as to share in the 'general social surplus'. This results in a branch-plant outlook in LDCs. In contrast to orthodox economists, Hymer claimed that it is *not* technology that leads to uneven development. On the contrary, technological developments in communications could make it easier for LDCs to develop independently. Rather, it is the centralization of control by TNCs that leads to dependency. The latter in turn increases TNCs' control over the 'labour aristocracy' at home, since they can always threaten to draw on the 'reserve army of labour' in the LDCs.

From his early inclination (expressed in his thesis) to regard TNCs as an institution of capitalism, Hymer gradually moved towards the view that the TNC was simply an institutional form of the tendency towards the *internationalization of capital*, a tendency arising from the interest/needs of capital to expand its productive base, the source of potential profit (labour power). Internationalization, Hymer observed, introduced profound changes in the world capitalist order. First, it reduced national capitalist competition, through *interpenetration* of investments. He specifically stressed the concept of interpenetration (rather than US imperialism) due to the growing power of European and Japanese capital. The former, he suggested, had had the opportunity to choose self-sufficiency but chose interpenetration; Japan was facing a similar situation, with all the pressures being for her to choose the same road. One such pressure was her stake in trade with the US. This interpenetration did not serve the national interest of any country; rather it served the interest of the 1 per cent of the world's wealthy who invest their money in the international social surplus. Unlike earlier periods, the wealthy had realized that their interest lay not in war, but rather in international market sharing and collusion, in particular the maintenance of the capitalist order through the TNC. Concerning the LDCs in particular, Hymer observed that the developed countries competed in providing loans but presented a united front in collecting debt repayments.

The new emerging world system, Hymer suggested, tended to create an international capital market, international production and international government. Competition and credit were the two levers of concentration of capital. Credit in particular was the prerequisite for expansion on a world scale. He regarded the joint stock company as a means of enhancing the ability of capital to obtain access to social saving without on the whole sacrificing control. By exchanging shares, he observed, the wealthy form a common front, thus 'generalizing their interests'. Similar to the national corporation abolishing 'private property', the TNC was now abolishing national capital. Although rivalry among capitals to obtain above average rates of return still existed, a dominant common interest for the *general* profit rate had emerged. While European and (probably) Japanese capital, together with the middle classes of the LDCs, became 'partners' in this new world system, trade unions promised little challenge due to their exclusive interest with their members. An important implication of this new world system was a tendency towards the globalization of the concentration and centralization of capital.

With remarkable foresight, Hymer identified a shift of emphasis in the new world order, away from production as such and towards marketing and new product development. This would allow TNCs to move away from production (thus allowing small firms to own the plants and take the risks) but still to control the 'intangibles' (such as software). This independence of small firms, would increase both the tactical flexibility of the TNCs and their planning capacity, thus extending their control of the market (through externalization rather than internalization!). The relevance of this for current debates on the TNC and the recent observed increase of subcontracting should be obvious here. A further means of enhancing control over the market, Hymer suggested, was an attempt by TNCs to extend the duration of their 'product cycles' by having projects in all stages moving to cheap places, controlling marketing etc.

It will come as no surprise that Hymer's feelings for capitalism were not sympathetic. He quoted approvingly Keynes's views on capitalism (that it is not beautiful, not just, not virtuous and that it does not deliver the goods) and of self-sufficiency. His proposed alternative to transnational corporate capital's strategy to integrate one industry over many nations was the integration of many industries over one nation and the use of socialist planning. Regarding in particular the issues of efficiency, he asked the question efficiency for whom? He claimed that the efficiency issue hinged not on the rate of change but rather on the direction of change, pointing to 'too much' (rather than too little) innovation under the system; the absence of consumer sovereignty, dependency and the international 'trickle down'; and the social, political and environmental costs of TNCs' control of the system. A way out for the LDC, he suggested, was to try and change the flow of information and to pursue a strategy of producing sufficient basic goods (self-sufficiency).

Hymer's predictions for the future of the TNC and the transnational corporate capital system were gloomy. He foresaw a tendency for wage rates in the LDCs not to grow in the future, partly due to the increasing costs of administering the empire. This would lead to workers' disillusionment with the system, as well as to a realization on their part of the need to control the investment process, thus provoking a politicalization of the class struggle. Although the possibility of international trade unionism was there, the fact that most of labour's historical gains were country specific implied a tendency for labour to become more nationalist and possibly socialist. Further, difficulties arose from the increased emancipation of LDCs' capital and thus their increased claims to a share of the social surplus, an example of which was OPEC. In this sense Hymer anticipated that the TNC might well be the swan song of capitalism.

The final outcome (capitalism versus socialism), however, was by no means a foregone conclusion. Labour in particular could well choose to shift to the right, joining with capital to create a 'new imperialist alliance' in order to get higher benefits in return for suppressing labour in LDCs and the various minorities in the centre. Accordingly, Hymer claimed, the question for scientists (equal radicals) was not to predict what will happen, but rather to choose sides.

To conclude, Hymer comprehensively grasped and stylishly expounded virtually all the existing 'theories' of the TNC, analysing in depth the transnational corporate system. His views on 'ownership advantages', 'internalization' and the 'correspondence principle' have generated (often independently) whole new schools of thought. Remarkably he did all this in a very short time. His early death was a tragic blow to the development of economic theory in general and to radical economic theory in particular. In his mind the two were one and the same thing in any case.

Hymer's Major Writings

(1970), 'Multinational Corporations and International Oligopoly: the Non-American Challenge', in C.P. Kindelberger (ed), *The International Corporation: a Symposium*, Cambridge, Mass: MIT Press.

(1976), *The International Operations of National Firms: A Study of Director Foreign Investment*, Cambridge, Mass: MIT Press.

(1979), *The Multinational Corporation: A Radical Approach, Papers by Stephen Herbert Hymer*, edited by R.B. Cohen, N. Felton, M. Nkosi and J. Van Liere, with the assistance of N. Dennis, Cambridge: Cambridge University Press. (This collection of 11 papers is undoubtedly the best source of information on Hymer's work, containing rich bibliographical material. The book has three parts: the nature and contradictions of the multinational corporation; accumulation, trade and exploitation; and the future of the world economy.)

Other References

'In Honour of Stephen H. Hymer', a collection of papers published in the *American Economic Review*, 75(2), 1985.

Pitelis, C. and Sugden, R. (eds)(1990), *The Nature of the Transnational Firm*, London: Routledge.

Nicholas August Ludwig Jacob JOHANNSEN

(1844–1928)

Christof Rühl

Knowledge of Nicholas Johannsen's life is still very limited. He was born in Berlin in 1844 and later moved to the US where after the turn of the century we find him in New York City, being employed in the import-export business. The exact date of this transition is not known, nor do we have any firm evidence on the extent to which he later became the independent businessman he sometimes claimed to be. It is obvious, however, that Johannsen did visit the US several times before his move and also that he must have been able to return to Germany on a regular basis after having settled down in New York. Throughout his life he was keenly interested in Germany's political and economic affairs, claiming that the 'crucial point of criticism' would be there (1913, p.220). Accordingly he published in both languages; he was engaged in the major political debates of his time and, besides economic theory, wrote on astrophysics.

Research has been hampered by the fact that Johannsen initially used two pen-names, apparently to avoid irritating an employer who did not quite approve of the idea of a clerk spending his nights at the writing desk. The names were A. Merwin (under which the first article appeared of which we have knowledge) and J.J.O. Lahn (for the publication of his first two books). Johannsen, who described himself as a 'self-taught' businessman entirely without academic blessings, died in Richmond (Staten Island) in 1928.

The fate of his contributions to economic theory – a story of contemporary neglect and gradual rediscovery – marks one of the strangest incidents of which we have record in the history of our 'dismal science'. Despite his constant efforts to receive criticism, recognition or at least a fair discussion, he was more or less persistently ignored by the academic profession which he so desperately tried to address. It was only in the aftermath of the Keynesian 'revolution', when the hunt for potential precursors finally became a legitimate and respectable enterprise, that Johannsen's writings were gradually removed from obscurity where they had lain for decades. Today, this 'amateur economist' (crank, some might say), as Keynes chose to label him in the *Treatise*, is rather unanimously honoured as one of the most important precursors of the *General Theory*.

This holds true with respect to three topics in particular: the anticipation of the Keynesian theory of effective demand entailed in Johannsen's treatment of the saving-investment nexus; the independent discovery of the principle of the multiplier; and, although less univocally accepted, his contributions to monetary and to business cycle theory.

From the record of Johannsen's own writings it becomes evident how continuously and desperately he sought to establish contact with economists blessed with an academic reputation. He was aware that his ideas challenged traditional viewpoints and correctly perceived that the theoretical framework and policy conclusions he drew from them ran counter to the conventional wisdom of his time. He was not, however, a revolutionary; with respect to the social function of economics (in an attitude similar to Keynes's), his work aimed at modifying the economic system in such a way as to increase its performance while leaving the premises of a private ownership economy untouched. Again similar to Keynes, he was deeply convinced that his analysis was not only fundamentally different from, but at the same time logically superior to, the prevailing neoclassical orthodoxy. Consequently, he tried to gain publicity by forcing his academic counterparts either publicly to accept his ideas or to prove where he was wrong.

He pursued his attempts to be recognized and to find partners in scientific discourse throughout his professional life: from his first confrontation with the German profession in 1898, to his most active period in the US when he tried to join the debate on currency reform (1907) and to address his academic counterparts by publishing open letters (1909), to the very end, when the 'aged outsider' (as the increasingly bitter octogenarian had come to call himself) warned against the onset of a prolonged period of stagnation (1928). There were a few notable exceptions such as a friendly review of one of his books by J.B. Clark in 1909; notes and passing remarks, for instance by the British underconsumptionist Hobson and the young Wesley Mitchell; and a somewhat more extensive consideration by German-language academics (by Gerwig, 1922, and later *in extenso* by Schnack, 1951). Johannsen largely remained the impertinent outcast, although the picture changed after the publication of the *General Theory*. The 'pseudonymous and itinerant writer' (Dorfman, 1949, p.413) became the 'sadly neglected crank' (Klein, 1947, p.143), and ever since Klein's appraisal, Johannsen's precursorial role has become more and more explicit (cf Hutchison, 1953; Shackle, 1967; Hagemann and Rühl, 1987, 1990).

This neglect by his contemporaries is reflected in Johannsen's publication record. Although he wrote four books and numerous articles, he never managed to be accepted in any of the leading professional journals. Most of the articles were printed and circulated privately but, due to the relentless efforts of their author, became widely distributed nevertheless. With regard to his treatment of effective demand failures and the multiplier, Johannsen's books represent an elaboration of his pamphlet material (1909 and 1925 contain useful summaries). However, with respect to monetary and business cycle theory and his policy conclusions, some of the papers are useful in evaluating the total scope of his contributions (see 1878, 1906a, 1906b and 1926).

The essentials of Johannsen's later reasoning were encapsulated in three papers he submitted to the German professor, Adolph Wagner, as early as 1898. Two of them were published shortly thereafter. The first contained a detailed and amazingly elaborate analysis of the circular flow of income, graphically depicted in the form of a complicated 'wheel of wealth' diagram (Patinkin, 1973). With Wagner's approval, it was subsequently published in Germany (1903a). The second paper drew on the consequences of this framework. Here Johannsen's revolutionary analysis of the investment-saving process and the multiplier were developed further, but Wagner's reaction was negative. Johannsen thereupon introduced it to the public in New York, even though it was written in German (1903b). *A Neglected Point in Connection with Crises* (1908a), the most often quoted of his works (and the only book written in English), together with his 1913 article represent attempts to make his theory more accessible to an international audience – either by combining the first two books (as in 1908) or by adding policy proposals such as the *Schwundgeld* scheme (which was included among the papers presented in 1898, but then disappeared from Johannsen's agenda until 1913).

Johannsen's analytical framework was based on a strong adherence to the 'income approach' in determining macroeconomic activity, much in the tradition of Tooke's famous thirteenth thesis on the quantity of money; it also depicted central economic relations in terms of a circular flow of money. Aggregate production, in this picture, was limited by effective demand. Perhaps for the first time in the history of economic analysis, here was the fundamental insight that decisions to save and decision to invest were not only made by different people but also had to be treated separately for all relevant analytical purposes. From the emphasis on aggregate income as the 'genuine source of all demand' it was just a short step to the question of how this aggregate is held or spent. The question of 'moneyed demand' thus became decisive and Say's law lost its appeal as a generally valid proposition. The income approach enabled Johannsen to discover the equilibrating role of output with respect to the potential discrepancies between the aggregates of saving and investment.

Aggregate demand, in this scheme, consists of consumption and investment, while aggregate income is either spent on consumption goods or saved. With no guarantee for a smooth translation of the 'saving funds' into productive investment, the act of saving *per se* could be perceived as anything but beneficial for the community as a whole – 'tend[ing] to impoverish others to the amount of the money saved' (1925, p.3). Consumption and saving are both a function of current income. In a striking parallel to Keynes's consumption function, Johannsen explicitly states that the marginal propensity to consume should be less than unity: with any increment in income the 'power to save' would increase, and this 'not only in proportion ... but at a faster rate' (1903b, p.90). A marginal propensity to consume of less than unity is one of the essential preconditions for assigning income the role of equilibrating saving and investment; today we know how hard Keynes (via the example of the banana plantation in the Treatise) had to struggle before he gained this insight. For Johannsen it was an offspring of his circular flow analysis, supported by what his observation of the real world seemed to suggest.

An initial position of full employment could be maintained only as long as all the forthcoming savings would find productive investment in real capital formation. Any 'failure' of the savings to do so (no matter whether due to a decrease in the rate of investment or an increment in the rate of saving) would cause aggregate real income to fall and the rate of saving to decline accordingly. Johannsen did not use Keynes's terms though. The decisive problem for him became the question how exactly this deterioration of income was brought about; what exactly happened to the 'unused' excess of savings in the first place?

Disregarding hoarding, he termed any surplus of planned saving over planned investment *impair savings*. They were matched by *impair investment*, such as the purchase of existing assets, mortgages or the act of lending money to others in the economy. 'Impair savings' differed from 'productive savings' insofar as they 'come to those who use them over the bridge of their own impoverishment' (1925, p.4): any decline in activity thus necessarily involved the redistribution of wealth in the economy. Obviously, 'impair savings' are not included in the Keynesian definition of net savings and net investment; the term simply represents an excess of *ex-ante* saving over *ex-ante* investment. Therefore the assertion that if Johannsen had 'reckoned dis-savings as negative savings, he would have ended up with the algebraic result that aggregate net savings equal aggregate net investment' (Klein, 1947, p.145) is perfectly valid. In Johannsen's scheme, any excess of planned saving over planned investment causes real income to shrink and the rate of savings to decline until a new level of aggregate income is restored. Moreover, any such discrepancy is subject to the 'multiplying principle', aggravating the baneful effects on income and employment.

Johannsen not only coined the expression 'multiplying principle' but also tried to calculate numerically the secondary effects of an initial reduction in total expenditure. In most of his writings he analysed the multiplier as a downward process in accordance with the problems posed by his depression theory. However, he also realized the potential for economic policy exhibited by such a relationship (1908b). Although the numerical examples were merely used to 'bring out the general principle' and not to 'establish exact proportions' (1908a, p.46), after long and heavy struggles in search for the correct *formula* he at least succeeded in obtaining the correct *result*. Given a marginal propensity to consume of two-thirds, a decline in investment would be tripled (1913, pp.280–81). However, his calculations were not free from errors, nor were they unanimously derived from his recognition of the principle of a geometrical progression. While in 1913 he came very close to the correct values entailed by computing such a series, the results were marred by the fact that he carried over an invalid example from his article of 1908a. Ultimately, and most likely due to his lack of mathematical sophistication, he was prevented from explicitly stating Kahn's formula – but on the other hand, who else had come so close at such an early date?

The denial of interest as a coordinating macroeconomic activity is yet another decisive prerequisite for assigning income the role it now plays in macroeconomic analysis. Johannsen did not develop a theory of the rate of interest; he merely contended that various and irregular forces in the money market have an influence on its determination. Certainly the notion of liquidity preference escaped him, and we do not find anything comparable to Keynes's MEC schedule in his discussions of investment behaviour. On the other hand, that Johannsen had no elaborate theory regarding the rate of interest did not prevent him from reaching conclusions remarkably similar to those of Keynes. In his picture of the economy, there was clearly no need for the interest rate to coordinate saving and investment, a fact he was very conscious about: 'This argument is one of those which is not based on practical experience ... in fact the activity of savings is very little affected by the level of the rate of interest' (Johannsen, 1903b, p.29). To understand why Johannsen did not feel obliged to deliver an explanation of the rate of interest, it may suffice to remember Keynes's claim that the theory of liquidity preference had occurred to him only *after* income had been put in place to guarantee the necessary equality between saving and investment. Keynes knew that to have an audience among professional economists one had to tackle the problem of how interest should be determined if not by productivity and thrift, and thus why it should not ultimately serve to coordinate saving and investment, whereas Johannsen – true amateur! – did not realize that his 'circular flow' analysis had to face the issue and therefore did not tackle it at all. Against this background, Keynes's sole comment on Johannsen where, at the time of the *Treatise*, he brushed off the latter's analysis as overlooking that a fall in the rate of interest would be the cure for the malady of an unemployment equilibrium (cf. Keynes, 1930, p.90) hardly did justice to the 'amateur'.

In general, Johannsen's contributions to monetary and trade cycle theory have been treated as distinct from his theory of effective demand failures, which is the better known part of his work (see Marget, 1938, and, more recently, Allsbrook, 1986). This dichotomy has produced unsatisfactory results, all the more surprising since no obvious reasons exist to justify the separation. On the contrary, Johannsen's writings on money and the trade cycle fit well into his overall framework. The confusion apparently has two sources: on the one hand and as pointed out above, Johannsen's 'Keynesian' results were derived despite his very 'unprofessional' treatment of the rate of interest. However, this limitation may have actually helped him to arrive at conclusions which even Wicksell (who was troubled by a very similar problem concerning the identity of saving and investment towards the end of Volume I of his *Lectures*) was unable to reach – ultimately due to his adherence to a natural rate concept. On the other hand, it has not often been noted that Johannsen's discussion of monetary and trade cycle theory closely resembles (as it was partially motivated by) the set of questions Keynes had to face after the publication of the *General Theory*.

The debate in question arose when Keynes had to respond to criticism directed against his 'causal nexus', with investment being treated as the independent variable. According to the loanable funds arguments of his critics, any increase in investment financed by bank loans should (through shifts in the structure of relative prices) 'force' into existence savings exactly equal to the amount of this particular investment. In this picture the interest rate would remain determined by the 'real' forces of productivity and thrift and would continue to perform the coordination function it had been assigned by neoclassical theory. In order to counter this criticism and to defend his position according to which an increase in investment had 'nothing to do with saving', Keynes introduced the conceptual device of the 'Finance Motive'. He argued that ultimately 'increased investment will always be accompanied by increased saving, but it can never be preceded by it. Dishoarding and credit expansion provide not an alternative to increased saving but a necessary preparation for it. It is the parent, not the twin of increased saving' (Keynes, 1973, p.281). Johannsen's contributions to monetary and trade cycle theory can be evaluated most sensibly in the context of this debate.

As early as 1878 Johannsen had included bank deposits in his definition of money; he had distinguished between 'saving funds' and 'credit money' (the equivalents of what Keynes later termed saving and finance). He shared the view that current production would have to be financed by the creation of credit, whether in a growing or a stationary economy. There was, for this reason, no need to consider prior savings as a prerequisite to an increase in the rate of investment since the argument (so popular in business cycle theories of the inter-war period) that an increase in thriftiness could promote social welfare by fostering accumulation was no longer valid. 'In accordance with this view economists very often argue that there exists an inherent need for the onset of a depression, namely to gain the financial strength for the later recovery – in order to prepare for future undertakings by thriftiness and abstinence. This is an assumption which may sound plausible but which lacks all factual reasoning. In reality the financial means [for an upswing] will be raised during the upswing and not before' (1913, pp. 250–51). The money supply in this situation was viewed as being at least partly determined endogenously. The impact of an increase in investment spending on the rate of interest depended on the extent to which the overdraft facilities of the banking system were employed; the repercussions on investment in turn depended on the investment schedule.

Although Johannsen did not fully realize the causal independence of investment from past savings, he clearly distinguished the need to finance production as well as any increase in activity by the creation of credit from the flow of savings. The need to take into account a developed banking system may then arise either by admitting the possibility of an (inherently stable) sub-optimal equilibrium with underutilized primary resources (as labour was in the case of Johannsen and Keynes) or by acknowledging the dynamics connected with the introduction of technological change (as in the writings of the young Schumpeter, historically, between Johannsen and Keynes). In all of these approaches, however, there was no need to consider prior savings as representing a meaningful concept, nor to accept the alleged virtue of thriftiness in order to increase the rate of accumulation. Investment, as in post-*General Theory* Keynes, could become congested by a shortage of cash, but never by a lack of saving.

Besides a shortfall of effective demand, a second reason for the onset of a sudden crisis may emerge. Due to an increased demand for cash the money market may become so tight as to suffer 'stringency' followed by a general loss of trust and a credit crunch. In Johannsen's view this scenario could be avoided by allowing for an accommodating money supply. However, he strongly advocated monetary control to guard against the inflationary dangers involved, advancing different proposals in this respect such as (interest-bearing) 'emergency money' or a tax on seignorage. At the other end of the scale he proposed a Gesellian type *Schwundgeld* to be issued in times of slackening demand. However unrealistic such proposals might be judged from our perspective, they were undoubtedly developed against the background of a very sophisticated theoretical framework. Not surprisingly, Johannsen's discussion of the upper turning point of the business cycle resembles Keynes's writings after the *General Theory* much more than those of his contemporaries.

How then are we to explain Johannsen's comparative neglect by most of his contemporaries? The comment that 'contempt for the "autodidact" is universal among continental academics' (Shackle, 1967, p.196) would have to apply to the continents on both sides of the Atlantic. Perhaps more important is that Johannsen's ideas were simply hard to grasp by contemporary economists working in the mainstream tradition; the fact that in his expositions he failed to comply with the formal standards imposed on the profession may have added to the difficulty. No doubt a far more important reason is that Johannsen's observations run counter to neoclassical opinion: it may indeed require a place inside the main castle to knock down the 'citadelle' Keynes talked about. Or so it seemed to Johannsen: 'To prove that I was wrong they could not do; to admit that I was right they did not want to do ... the only alternative left was to ignore the new theory' (1913, p. 219). For an evaluation of his achievements it seems only appropriate to quote again the economist who for so many reasons was better equipped to launch an attack on the 'citadelle' successfully. Surely Johannsen 'preferred to see the truth obscurely and imperfectly rather than to maintain error, reached indeed with clearness and consistency and by easy logic' (Keynes, 1936, p.371).

Johannsen's Major Writings

(1878), *New Capital, New Light on an Old Subject*, Edward Cuttle (published under the name A. Merwin).

(1903a), *Der Kreislauf des Geldes und der Mechanismus des Soziallebens*, Puttkammer und Mühlbrecht (published under the name J.J.O. Lahn).

(1903b), *Depressionsperioden und ihre einheitliche Ursache* (published under the name J.J.O. Lahn).

(1906a), 'The Coming Crisis and How to Meet It; A Plea for Currency Reform', privately printed and circulated.

(1906b), 'A Guide for Determining the Proper Rate of Taxation', privately printed and circulated.

(1907–9), 'Eight Open Letters on Currency Reform', privately printed and circulated.

(1908a), *A Neglected Point in Connection with Crises*, The Banker's Publishing Company.

(1908b), 'To Relieve the Depression: A Suggestion to Railroad Men and Bankers', *Journal of Commerce and Commercial Bulletin*, 18 April.

(1909), 'To the Economists of America; The New Depression Theory', privately printed and circulated.

(1913), *Die Steuer der Zukunft und ihre Auswirkungen auf geschäftliche Depressionen und volkswirtschaftliche Verhältnisse*, Puttkammer und Mühlbrecht.

(1925), 'Business Depressions; Their Cause. A Discovery in Economics', privately printed and circulated.

(1926), 'Two Depression Factors: The Minor One Known, Not the Other', private printed and circulated.

(1928), 'A Depression Manifest; A Lesson in Neglected Fundamental Economics', private printed and circulated.

Other References

Allsbrook, O.O. (1986), 'N.A.L.J. Johannsen: An Early Monetarist', *Journal of Institutional and Theoretical Economics*, **142**.

Clark, J.B. (1909), A New Depression Theory', *The Bankers Magazine*, February.

Dorfman, J. (1931), 'Some Documentary Notes on the Relations among J.M. Clark, N.A.L.J. Johannsen and J.M. Keynes', in J.M. Clark, *The Cost of the World War to the Amerikan People*, Reprint, August M. Kelley, 1970b.

Dorfman, J. (1949), *The Economic Mind in American Civilization*, Vol III, 1865–1918, Viking Press.

Gerwig, E. (1922), *Die nationaloekonomischen Theorien und wirtschaftspolitischen Vorschlaege N. Johannsen*, Ph.D. Thesis (University of Zürich), Moritz Schauenburg.

Hagemann, H. and Rühl, C. (1987), 'Nicholas Johannsen's Early Analysis of the Saving Investment Process and the Multiplier', *Studi Economici*, **42**(3).

Hagemann, H. and Rühl, C. (1990), 'Nicholas Johannsen and Keynes' "Finance Motive"', *Journal of Institutional and Theoretical Economics*, **146**(3).

Hegeland, H. (1961), *The Multiplier Theory*, Gleerup.

Hutchison, T.W. (1953), *A Review of Economic Doctrines 1870–1929*, Oxford: Clarendon Press.

Keynes, J.M. (1936), *The General Theory of Employment, Interest, and Money*, London: Macmillan.

Keynes, J.M. (1939), 'The Process of Capital Formation', *The Economic Journal*, September. Reprinted in *The Collected Writings of John Maynard Keynes*, XIV, Macmillan, 1973.

Klein, L. (1947), *The Keynesian Revolution*, London: Macmillan.

Marget, A.W. (1938), *The Theory of Prices, A Re-Examination of the Central Problems of Economic Theory*, Vol. I. Reprinted by Augustus M. Kelley, New York, 1966.

Patinkin, D. (1973), 'In Search of the "Wheel of Wealth": On the Origins of Frank Knight's Circular Flow Diagram', *American Economic Review*, **62**.

Schnack, H.-W. (1951), *Der Wirtschaftskreislauf bei N.A.L.J. Johannsen und J.M. Keynes*, Ph.D. Thesis, University of Kiel.

Shackle, G.L.S. (1967), *The Years of High Theory, Invention and Tradition in Economic Thought 1926–1939*, Cambridge: Cambridge University Press.

Richard KAHN (1905–1989) *John Eatwell*

Richard Ferdinand Kahn (Baron Kahn of Hampstead) was one of the most distinguished and influential economists of the twentieth century. His distinction rests on an article written at the age of 25 in which he invented the most powerful practical tool ever devised in 200 years of economics – the 'multiplier'. His influence derives from his close professional association first with John Maynard Keynes and later with Joan Robinson. Kahn himself wrote comparatively little, his ideas appearing most often in the writings of others.

Richard Kahn was born in London on 10 August 1905. He died in Cambridge on 6 June 1989 at the age of 83. He was educated at St Paul's School and at King's College (Cambridge) where he earned an upper second in physics in 1927. He then switched to economics and, with Keynes as one of his supervisors (the other being Gerald Shove), obtained a first in economics in one year, completed a Fellowship dissertation in a further year, and was elected to a Research Fellowship at King's in the spring of 1930.

The dissertation, 'The Economics of the Short Period', was a sustained critique of the orthodox theory of the firm. Its intellectual origins lay in Piero Sraffa's critique of Marshallian theory, which was elaborated both in his articles in *Annali di Economia* (1925) and the *Economic Journal* (1926), and in his more wide-ranging Cambridge lecture course on the theory of value which Kahn had attended. Sraffa had demonstrated in his *Economic Journal* article that neither decreasing costs *nor* increasing costs were compatible with the construction of the Marshallian industry supply curve (other than when economies or diseconomies are external to the firm and internal to the industry). Hence 'in normal circumstances the cost of production of commodities produced competitively ... must be regarded as constant in respect of small variations in the quantity produced'. But if this is the case then, except in quite peculiar circumstances, the Marshallian supply curve for a competitive industry is horizontal around the point of equilibrium, with no apparent role for demand in the determination of price. Sraffa concluded that the theory of value must therefore be developed *either* within a framework of general equilibrium *or* by means of an analysis in which individual firms face a downward-sloping demand curve for their products and falling marginal costs. It was this latter suggestion that Kahn developed into an economics of the short-period – an economy of what he called 'imperfect markets'. One of Kahn's most important conclusions was that, in an economy in which firms face negatively-sloped demand curves, a decline in industrial demand will result in *all* firms suffering under-utilization of capacity, not just the least efficient firms. Recession is therefore not an effective device for making the economy 'leaner and fitter'; it is just a means of wasting productive potential.

'The Problem of Duopoly' (1937) was the published version of a section of Kahn's dissertation. An Italian edition of the entire work appeared in 1983; 60 years after it was written, the dissertation was published in English in 1989. However, many of Kahn's results were incorporated into Joan Robinson's *Economics of Imperfect Competition*, the first fruit of the remarkably productive partnership between the two close friends which was to last until Joan Robinson's death in 1983.

Kahn wrote several papers during the 1930s couched within an essentially Marshallian (or Pigouvian) framework. 'Some Notes on Ideal Output' (1935) advanced the proposition that uniform imperfections of competition might be associated with a welfare optimum, since what matters is the relationship between relative prices and the *ratios* of marginal costs. This point is, in fact, not correct, since varying degrees of industrial integration will have a differential 'compounding' effect on the deviations of prices from their competitive levels. Kahn's interest in welfare economics (see also his 'Tariffs and the Terms of Trade', 1947; an analysis of the determination of the 'optimum tariff') was manifest later when he worked with J. de V. Graaff on Graaff's *Theoretical Welfare Economics* (1957).

In the summer of 1930, Richard Kahn wrote a paper in a quite different style from anything he had previously done. This paper would alter completely both the foundations of the theory of employment and the analytical framework of economic policy formation. The high levels of unemployment then prevailing had led a number of economists and politicians to advocate public works as a means of alleviating distress. The government had firmly resisted their pleas, arguing that public works were 'inefficient' and detracted from private sector investment.

In an article entitled 'The Relation of Home Investment to Unemployment' (1931), Kahn provided a precise measure of the ratio between the increase in employment associated with initial investment (road-building in Kahn's example) and the 'secondary employment' generated by the impact of successive rounds of consumption expenditure. The size of this multiplier (a term that Kahn did not then use) depended fundamentally, he argued, not on technical coefficients but on the proportions of wages and profits spent on domestic consumption (wages being expressed net of 'savings on the dole').

Kahn's analysis was devoted almost entirely to considering the 'employment multiplier'. But, on what he tells us was the prompting of James Meade, he also demonstrated the link between the employment multiplier and 'Mr Meade's relation', namely:

Cost of investment = saving on dole + increase in excess of imports over exports + increase in unspent profits − diminution in rate of saving due to rise in prices.

In other words, the increase in investment is matched by an equal increase in saving. (As Kahn later pointed out, he made the mistake of omitting increased tax revenues from the right-hand side of the equation.) In a prophetic passage Kahn commented: 'This relation should bring immediate relief and consolation to those who are worried about the monetary resources that are available to meet the cost of the roads. ...If one is looking for sources *outside* the banking system, they are available to precisely the right extent.'

All the material was available here to refute the government's so-called 'Treasury view' – that public investment would crowd out private investment. But Kahn did not draw such radical conclusions from his own analysis. Instead he concentrated on the problem of the measurement of 'secondary employment', as indeed, at this time, did Keynes. Kahn was later to claim that:

> Although it was, and still is, my estimate of the multiplier with which my article is mainly associated, it was far more important for a quite different contribution. My main concern – *from the start* – was to prove that the various offsets – the increase in the yield of taxation, savings of various kinds to the Exchequer, or rather (as we should put it now) to the Public Sector, the increase in imports over exports, the increase in private savings (mainly out of profits), and the change in the rate of saving due to the rise in prices – added up to the cost of the investment (1984, emphasis added).

But Kahn did not take the crucial step of extending his invention into a new theory of savings and investment, and hence creating an entirely new theory of output and employment.

It was in the *General Theory* that Keynes seized on Kahn's idea and used it to demonstrate both that investment *determines* savings and that equality between savings and investment is maintained by variations in the level of output and employment. There is no fixed amount of savings in the economy which can be used either for private or public investment. On the contrary, Keynes's use of the multiplier demonstrated that the increased income generated by more investment would in turn result in increased savings exactly equal to the extra expenditure on investment (though in an open economy those extra savings may take place overseas).

In an article published in the *Journal of the American Statistical Association* in 1933, Kahn had lamented the fact that whilst increased public spending was necessary to stimulate the economy, 'the advocacy of budget deficits must be regarded as a hopeless cause'. The *General Theory* was to provide the intellectual case for public spending in a depression. Keynes used his version of Kahn's multiplier precisely to demonstrate that public and private expenditure are not competitive but complementary. Hence economic efficiency requires that the budget should be in surplus or deficit, according to the overall balance of supply and demand in the economy as a whole. The idea that the government should balance its own budget without reference to the overall level of activity was now seen to be both inefficient and without intellectual foundation.

Kahn had played a major role in the genesis of the *General Theory*. As the intermediary between the famous 'circus' of young economists and Keynes himself, he conveyed back and forth the analytical problems thrown up by the new theory of money and employment – interpreting the ideas of the circus to Keynes, and interpreting Keynes to the young. As a meticulous critic he also sorted through successive proofs time after time (Keynes would write his articles in pencil and then have them set immediately into proofs). In the Preface to the *General Theory* Keynes acknowledged the importance of Kahn's advice: 'There is a great deal in this book which would not have taken the shape it has except at his suggestion'.

Over the same period (1931–35), Kahn prepared a translation of Wicksell's *Geldzins und Güterpreise*, a work with some similarities to the method of Keynes' *Treatise*, but none to the *General Theory*.

Kahn was to prove to be the most zealous defender of the Keynesian faith. In the bitter arguments on the theory of interest which erupted in the 1950s, he refused to acknowledge any ambiguity in Keynes's theory of liquidity preference – other than a little in the definition of the precautionary demand for money (see 1954). Non-Keynesian views were characterized as 'examples of heresy'. In Kahn's version of liquidity preference, as in Keynes's, expectations as to the future path of the rate of interest are simply taken as given; as Keynes put it in the *General Theory*: '*Any* level of interest which is accepted with sufficient conviction as *likely* to be durable *will* be durable'. The relationship between the rate of return on short and long bonds is therefore determined by the expectation of future interest rates held by those trading in the markets of today (the rate of return on long bonds is in no way an average of short-term rates). And the demand for money is determined by the relationship between the current rate of interest and the expected rate. This characterization of liquidity preference contrasts with the neoclassical synthesis view which transforms liquidity preference into a stable function of a single rate of interest.

In his 'Notes', Kahn did not address the fundamental problem of what determines the expected rate – the original lacuna which exposed Keynes's analysis to the neoclassical synthesis proposition that this expected rate was determined by the 'real rate of return', by 'the real forces of productivity and thrift'. In a rather odd passage, Kahn seemed to accept such a determination, referring to the impact of real output on the transactions demand for cash:

> It is not intended in these 'Notes' to discuss the various ways in which 'the real forces of productivity and thrift' exercise an influence on the rate of interest, but an

important point about Keynes' theory is that these forces exercise their influence through their effect on liquidity preference and on the quantity of money. ... In the limiting case in which [the elasticity of substitution between money and securities] is zero, the liquidity preference theory is compatible with any level of the rate of interest, which is therefore indeterminate except in so far as the real forces operate.

Defence of Keynesian orthodoxy was to produce a brilliant paper later in Kahn's career ('Malinvaud on Keynes', 1977). In a review of Edmond Malinvaud's *Theory of Unemployment Reconsidered* he attacked the 'neo-Keynesian' models which associated unemployment with 'sticky prices'.

Malinvaud had created a typology of unemployment in which 'Keynesian unemployment' could be alleviated by a rise in the real wage (an increase in effective demand), while 'classical unemployment' could be alleviated by a fall in the real wage (offsetting diminishing returns to increased output). Kahn pointed out that Malinvaud's 'classical unemployment' derived from the assumed coexistence of increasing costs (diminishing returns) with sticky mark-up pricing behaviour through the trade cycle. But, Kahn argued, sticky mark-ups are typical of industries which operate under increasing returns through the cycle (Okun's Law), whereas the industries which encounter decreasing returns (notably producers of primary products) are typically those whose prices are flexible. In either case, Malinvaud's classical unemployment disappears, the only remaining determinant of activity and employment being the level of effective demand.

Concern with problems of inflation – the problem of Keynesian success – dominated many of Kahn's later writings. Monetarism was dismissed as being without intellectual or empirical foundation, and he abhorred the idea that unemployment might be created deliberately as a means of controlling inflation:

economic waste ... is particularly great if demand is regulated by restricting productive investment, as will be the main result of relying on monetary policy. Not only is there the loss of potential investment. But the growth of productivity is thereby curtailed, thus narrowing the limit on the permissible rate of rise in wages and increasing the amount of unemployment required to secure observance of the limit. (Evidence to the Radcliffe Committee, 1959, para 38).

Inflation, he argued, was essentially a problem of money wage bargaining, and one of the major sources of inflationary pressures was the structure of relative wages and the 'leap-frogging' associated with the maintenance of differentials: 'If the *relative* wage problem could be solved ... it should not be too difficult to secure that the *absolute* wage level followed an acceptable course' (Evidence to the Radcliffe Committee, 1959, para 54).

A glance through the prefaces of her books reveals the importance which Richard Kahn played in the development of Joan Robinson's theoretical work. Kahn was an ever-present source of critical advice. For instance, from the *Economics of Imperfect Competition* in 1933:

> Of not all the new ideas, however, can I definitely say that 'this is my own invention'. In particular I have had the constant assistance of Mr. R. F. Kahn. The whole technical apparatus was built up with his aid, and many of the major problems ... were solved as much by him as by me.

And in her *Accumulation of Capital* in 1956, she wrote: 'As so often it was R. F. Kahn who saw the point that we were groping for and enabled us to get it into a comprehensible form'. Occasionally he would write an article clarifying the use of concepts they had developed together (see, for example, 'Exercises in the Analysis of Growth', 1959). But more typically, he remained in the background.

He also played a role in the development of Robin Marris's theory of the growth of the firm. In a paper written in 1964 but not published until 1972 ('Notes on the rate of interest and the growth of firms', in Kahn, 1972), he introduced a neat analysis of the determination of a company's 'valuation ratio' – the ratio of stock market valuation to the replacement cost of productive assets, a statistic later labelled 'q' by James Tobin. Kahn demonstrated that in a steadily growing economy in which shareholders are indifferent between dividend yields and capital gains, the valuation ratio 'v' equals $(r - g)/(i - g)$, where r is the rate of profit on real investment, i the overall return (dividends and capital gain) on share capital, and g the rate of growth. If v is less than one, the growth of firms will be biased towards growth by takeover. If v is greater that one, growth will be biased towards the expansion of real investment.

Richard Kahn was not just an academic theorist. The new Keynesian ideas which he helped to create are essentially practical. He was one of the brilliant young Keynesians who put the new ideas into practice in running Britain's economic policy during the war. Keynes had created the economics of excess demand in *How to Pay for the War*. In the wartime environment the problem was to manage both the scale and composition of effective demand to make as many resources as possible available for the war effort. At the Board of Trade, which he joined in December 1939, Kahn's task was, as he put it, 'concerned largely with helping to ensure that the supply of goods to civilians was restricted to an essential level ... and at the same time to ensure efficiency in the limited production of civilian goods, and equity in their distribution'. From 1941 to 1943 he pursued this task in the Middle East where 'the main objective was to restrict the use of ocean shipping space for non-military purposes to the maximum extent consistent with the avoidance of famine and serious unrest'. Later at the Ministry of Production and then, again, at the Board of Trade he worked on post-war supply problems, both in Europe and at home.

Kahn returned to King's in September 1946, and was Professor in the Faculty of Economics from 1951 until his retirement in 1972.

He continued to play an important role in public life, notably in his influential memorandum of evidence to the Radcliffe Committee on the working of the monetary system in 1958, and as (informal) Chairman of the OEEC Group of Experts studying the problem of rising prices (1959). As was to be expected from Kahn, the OEEC Report argued that 'leap-frogging', the 'wage-wage spiral', was one of the main causes of inflation.

From 1965 to 1969 Richard Kahn acted as an adviser to UNCTAD. In the 1965 UNCTAD report on *International Monetary Issues and the Developing Countries* he first advocated what was a typically Keynesian solution to some problems of developing countries. The 'link', as it was called, was typically Keynesian in that it rested on an analysis of the relationship between finance and demand and neatly solved two problems at the same time – the lack of finance in developing countries and the (then) lack of liquidity in the developed countries. The idea was that the direct grant (via the World Bank) of international liquidity to developing countries by the IMF would both facilitate their development and (as the developing countries spent their grants) provide liquidity and stimulate demand in the developed world. He later elaborated this idea by suggesting that the newly created SDRs should be issued to developing countries (see UNCTAD, 1969, and Kahn's article, 'SDRs and Aid', 1973).

Richard Kahn was a very practical economist, devoted, like Keynes, to the skilful use of the economist's 'toolbox'. But he also had a remarkable command of economic theory. His main characteristic as a theoretical economist was not the invention of new ideas. It was rather his ability to tease out the logic of ideas, to clarify, and thus to produce new insights.

Like Keynes, Kahn believed that rational solutions to economic problems may be found in a judicious balance of state and market. In the summer of 1930, in a flash of genius such as few ever enjoy, he created one of the means of attaining that balance.

Kahn's Major Writings

(An extensive list of Kahn's published work is to be found in *L'economia del breve periodo*, 1983, pp. 27–30. Items marked * are reprinted in Kahn, 1972.)

(1929), *The Economics of the Short Period*, unpublished Fellowship dissertation, King's College, Cambridge. Italian translation, *L'economia del breve periodo*, Milan: Boringhieri, 1983; published in English by Macmillan, London, 1989.

*(1931), 'The Relation of Home Investment to Unemployment', *Economic Journal*, **41**.

(1933), 'The Elasticity of Substitution and the Relative Share of a Factor', *Review of Economic Studies*, **1**.

(1933), 'Public Policy and Inflation', *Journal of the American Statistical Association*, **28**.

(1935), 'Some Notes on Ideal Output', *Economic Journal*, **45**.

(1937), 'The Problem of Duopoly', *Economic Journal*, **47**.

(1947), 'Tariffs and the Terms of Trade', *Review of Economic Studies*, **15**.

*(1954), 'Some Notes on Liquidity Preference', *Manchester School*, **22**.
(1956), *Economic Survey of Europe, 1955* (with others), Geneva: United Nations.
*(1958), 'The Pace of Development', in *The Challenge of Development*, Jerusalem: The Eliezer Kaplan School of Economics and Social Sciences, The Hebrew University.
*(1958), 'Memorandum of Evidence' submitted to the Radcliffe Committee (27 May 1958). Committee on the Working of the Monetary System.
(1959), 'Exercises in the Analysis of Growth', *Oxford Economic Papers*, **11**.
(1959), *The Problem of Rising Prices* (with others), Paris: OEEC.
(1960), *Principal Memoranda of Evidence*, Vol 3, London: HMSO.
(1972), *Selected Essays on Employment and Growth*, Cambridge: Cambridge University Press.
(1973), 'SDRs and Aid', *Lloyds Bank Review*, no 110.
(1977), 'Malinvaud on Keynes', *Cambridge Journal of Economics*, **1**.
(1984), *The Making of Keynes' General Theory*, Cambridge: Cambridge University Press.

Other References

Graff, J. de V. (1957), *Theoretical Welfare Economics*, Cambridge: Cambridge University Press.
Keynes, J.M. (1936), *The General Theory of Employment, Interest and Money*, London: Macmillan.
Robinson, J. (1933), *The Economics of Imperfect Competition*, London: Macmillan.
Sraffa, P. (1925), 'Sulle Relazioni fra Costo e Quantita Prodotta, *Annali di Economia*, **2**.
Sraffa, P. (1926), 'The Laws of Return under Competitive Conditions', *Economic Journal*, **36**.

Nicholas KALDOR (1908–1986)   *Ferdinando Targetti*

Nicholas Kaldor was born in Budapest on 12 May 1908. He became a student at the London School of Economics in 1927 and graduated with first-class honours in 1930 – in the meantime also graduating from Berlin University in 1929. He joined the LSE teaching staff in 1932 and remained there until 1947.

Although Kaldor's academic writings date back to 1932, his first important article was published two years later. In 'The Determinateness of Static Equilibrium' he described the conditions of existence, uniqueness and stability in Walrasian equilibrium. Although this was the theme on which his ideas would change most radically, the article is worthy of note as it introduces the 'cobweb theorem' which became a standard item in economics textbooks. In these early years, under the influence of Lionel Robbins and Friedrich von Hayek, he was a convinced adherent of the 'Austrian school' in the fields of capital theory and economic policy.

During this time Kaldor joined the debate on the theory of the firm initiated by Sraffa nine years previously, contributing two articles. The first (1934b) demonstrated the incompatibility between perfect competition and the long-term static equilibrium of the firm if a tendency exists for the size of the firm to grow relative to that of the industry. He returned to the theory of imperfect competition (1935) to show that free entry to an industry leads to perfect competition only under constant returns to scale. In the case of increasing returns, free entry increases both the number of producers and their costs per unit until such time as the entry of new firms ceases. In equilibrium each firm produces and sells less than its optimal output but, more importantly, earns a long-run positive profit. Kaldor's conclusion was somewhat unorthodox: competition increases costs and prices; it does not reduce profit to zero.

In 1934 Kaldor obtained British citizenship and in the same year married Clarissa Goldsmith. A Rockefeller Scholarship in the following year allowed him to visit the universities of Harvard (where he met Schumpeter, Chamberlin, Samuelson, Solow and Sweezy), Columbia, California and Chicago (where he met Jacob Viner and Milton Friedman). He went to several conferences, giving a paper on 'Wages Subsidies as a Remedy for Unemployment' at the meeting of the Econometric Society, while his contacts with Henry Simons and Irving Fisher gave him ideas on personal income that he would later develop in his work on taxation in the 1950s.

In 1937 he was still orthodox on the theory of capital (see 1937). In other areas, however, he was a swift convert to Keynes's ideas: the great economic crisis of those years placed economists under considerable pressure to reconcile fact with theory. An important factor in Kaldor's conversion were his readings in the monetary theory of the Swedish school (of Myrdal in particular) which his colleague, John Hicks, had recommended. Equally important were his discussions with his two closest friends at the LSE, Hicks and Allen, and with Abba Lerner, the leading Keynesian at the school. Finally, as Kaldor himself admits, while he was translating Hayek's article 'The Paradox of Savings' he was shocked by the gaps and flaws in Hayek's argument; this caused his enthusiasm for Austrian doctrine to begin to wane.

On the relation between money wages and employment, Kaldor was rigorously Keynesian from the very beginning of the debate that the *General Theory* provoked. He argued that the fundamental cause of increased employment was not a cut in wages as such, but the increase in the quantity of 'inactive balances' (1938). Increased employment is achieved by cutting wages *only if* this induces a fall in the rate of interest, which can be accomplished in other ways – for instance by increasing the money supply. Because this argument appears in the Appendix to Chapter 19 of the *General Theory*, it is known today as the 'Keynes effect'. But Kaldor had developed it independently of Keynes and was able to convince Pigou of its validity.

The relation between speculation and the underemployment equilibrium of the income level, and the related issue of the monetary nature of the interest rate, was the second Keynesian area in which Kaldor made an outstanding contribution. He sought to expand the *General Theory* and the multiplier principle by generalizing the theory of speculation to it (1939a). Kaldor's refutation of the (neo)classical thesis that saving determines investments was based on the stabilizing influence of speculators who dampen the fluctuations in interest rates. On the question of the determination of interest rates, Kaldor's 'Keynesian' treatment was again important for its rebuttal of the neoclassical criticisms advanced by Robertson, who accused Keynes of having left his theory of long-term rates of interest unsubstantiated ('hanging in the air by its own bootstraps'). Kaldor's article countered Robertson's objection by setting out a theory of the interest rate in which the short rate was determined by the monetary policy of the Central Bank. This constituted the foundation of the edifice: the structure of interest rates was determined by the 'risk premium' on securities of varying durations. Kaldor used this concept, which was analogous to the 'liquidity preference', to explain the *structure* of interest rates and not, as Keynes had done, their *level*. In 1986 Hicks wrote to his old friend saying that his 1939 article was 'the culmination of the Keynesian revolution in theory; you ought to have more honour for it'.

Kaldor made an equally important contribution on money and monetary policy, an area in which his work divides into two periods. Representative of the first is his memorandum to the Radcliffe Commission on British monetary policy of the 1950s and then his comments on the Commission's Report ('Monetary Policy, Economic Stability and Growth' and 'The Radcliffe Report', both in Volume 3 of the *Collected Papers*). The second period, from 1970 until his death, comprises several works launching a radical critique against the Neo-Monetarist School of Chicago.

The final Keynesian topic to be given seminal treatment by Kaldor was the theory of the trade cycle. His innovative approach (1940) expressed the saving and investment functions relative to income in *non-linear* form; it also gave a plausible explanation as to why the parameter values of these two functions changed through time. This gave rise to an entirely endogenous theory of the cycle. His model shows that the cycle is not engendered by random monetary shocks, but by the instability of the system, an instability which has been more or less severe in different periods of the history of capitalism.

Kaldor sought to provide a way out of the impasse in which economic theory became trapped after Robbins' hyper free-trade criticism of Pigou's utilitarianism (see 1939b). Taken to its logical extreme, such criticism would impede the economist, *qua* scientist, from making any judgement as to the consequence of any measure of political economy should there be the slightest detriment to any economic subject from a proposed change. Without resorting to the measurement of interpersonal utility, Kaldor propounded a criterion which took the name of 'Kaldor's compensation test'. This assessed the effects of a measure which, at the same time as increasing economic efficiency, entailed somebody's loss. The test was positive if the economic action still brought an increase in well-being even after the loss-maker had been compensated for her/his loss. Rarely has a short article generated such a wealth of literature as followed Kaldor's – a literature which took the name of 'New Welfare Economics'.

During the war the LSE had transferred to Cambridge; this strengthened the links between the young Hungarian economist and Cambridge University, where he was highly regarded by Keynes not only for his theoretical achievements but also for his work on war finance. Then in 1944 – in Appendix B to the Beveridge Report, which was to be highly influential with regard to post-war economic policy in both Britain and Europe – he quantified the fiscal policies necessary to achieve full employment.

On Keynes's suggestion the Cambridge Economics faculty invited Kaldor to teach a course on 'Value and Distribution', lectures which he gave from 1941 to 1943. These were years in which Kaldor and Keynes formed a close relationship; the Kaldors were often guests of Maynard and his wife Lydia at the Cambridge Arts Theatre. Keynes frequently used Kaldor as a referee for the *Economic Journal*, and in 1943 he wrote to Jesus College proposing Kaldor as a possible economics fellow of the college, declaring that he was of the calibre to become head of the Faculty.

After the war, Kaldor served abroad on an important mission in Hungary, France and Germany as head of the Planning Division for John Kenneth Galbraith's US Strategic Bombing Survey, which analysed the military and economic effects of the allied bombing campaign.

In 1947 the LSE refused to give Kaldor leave of absence to go to Geneva to work for the UNO, on an appointment offered to him by Gunnar Myrdal. In reaction to the LSE's unjustified obstructionism, Kaldor resigned his teaching post and went to Geneva in any case. Here he recruited a first-rate team of economists (R. Nield, W. Rostow, T. Barna and P. J. Verdoorn) which produced a series of annual reports on the economic conditions and prosperity of Europe. Three years later Kaldor was offered a fellowship at King's College, Cambridge, and in 1950 returned to academic life.

His move to Cambridge strengthened the close relationship that he had been developing since the war with Joan Robinson, Richard Khan and, especially, Piero Sraffa. The friendship among the four economists flourished not only personally but also intellectually. It was this small group of Keynes's ex-pupils (also heavily influenced by Kalecki) that founded what came to be known as the post-Keynesian Cambridge School. Unlike the orthodox 'synthesis' of neoclassical and Keynesian thought, this group applied the Keynesian principle of effective demand not only to the determination of income in the short period, but also to the determination of rate of growth of income and of income distribution in the long term. In 1948 Kaldor gave a first outline of these developing ideas in his entry on 'Distribution' in *Chambers Encyclopedia*. Over the period 1956 to 1962 he published four articles (1956, 1957, 1961 and, with J. Mirrlees, 1962) which constituted the cornerstones of what came to be called the post-Keynesian (or Cambridge) theory of distribution and growth.

The theory's basic idea was that under conditions of full employment (hypothesized as holding in the long period), the multiplier determines not the *level* (as in Keynes) but the *distribution* of income. This principle offered a way out of Harrod's dilemma: the rate of effective growth (equal to natural growth) is made equal to the warranted rate of growth by variation in the share of profits. If, therefore, the propensity to save of profit-earners (s_p) is given and greater than that of wage-earners (s_w), which is also given and is greater or equal to zero (as in Kalecki's theory of profit); if money wages are given and exogenous; and if the excess (shortfall) of ex-ante investment (I) over ex-ante saving (S) leads to a rise (fall) in the level of prices (as in Keynes's Treatise on Money) – then the share of profits (P/Y) will vary in such a way that, under full employment, it equalizes the income share of saving S/Y to that of ex-ante investment I/Y.

Given the natural rate of growth G_n, in the case where workers do not save ($s_w = 0$) the rate of profit r is yielded by the so-called Cambridge Equation: $r = s_p G_n$. If, further, one assumes that profit-earners save all their income ($s_p = 1$), one obtains the equation of von Neumann's model: $r = G_n$. (Kaldor and von Neumann were close friends in the early 1930s and often used to discuss economics together on long walks in the Buda Hills.)

At this level of analysis the natural rate of growth is still an exogenous datum: the model is more a theory of income distribution in a context of growth than a theory of growth in the strict sense. Nevertheless, it was precisely in the area of distribution that the Cambridge Equation took on its revolutionary character, because it enabled determination of the rate of profit without having to resort to a theory of value and, above all, omitting the marginal productivity of capital. Since publication of Sraffa's *Production of Commodities by Means of Commodities* (1960), the neoclassical theory of capital had been subjected to massive criticism. The Cambridge Equation now provided a new and more robust theory of the profit rate.

Kaldor's most thorough formulations of his models comprised a theory of growth in the strict sense – that is, they explained the determinants of what Kaldor considered to be the natural rate of growth. He thus gave explicit form to the investment function and invented what he called the 'technical progress function'. In contrast to the neoclassical tradition, this expressed the idea that the dynamism of an economic system is not the outcome of *exogenous* growth – for example, an exogenous increase in the population (Solow) or in per capita output (Harrod) – but of the desire to accumulate among entrepreneurs. For Kaldor it was impossible to distinguish between 'choice of techniques' and 'technical progress'. Technical progress is only partially independent capital accumulation; it is in fact mostly 'endogenous' because new ideas are introduced into the economic system by means of investment itself. Kaldor formalized this insight into a 'technical progress function' which tied the rate of growth of output per person to the rate of growth of capital per person. Beginning with a positive value on the axis of the ordinate, this constant measured autonomous technical progress.

It is the investment function, however specified, that explains the tendency of the system to move along the technical progress function until it reaches point G_n (Kaldor's long-period rate of growth) where the function cuts the bisector of the quadrant. G_n therefore represents both the rate of growth of output per person and the rate of growth of capital per person. Here the ratio between the two rates is unity which, in a growing economy, signifies constancy in the capital/output ratio.

Kaldor claimed that he had shown why post-war economies displayed (i) a tendency towards growth of output without cumulative discrepancies between *ex ante* saving and investment; (ii) a tendency towards stable growth of capital per person and output per person; and (iii) a constancy in the capital/output ratio and in distributive shares. These were the 'stylized facts' that capitalist economies displayed in their long-term growth and which neoclassical theory could not adequately explain.

The most important contribution in defence of Kaldor's theory was Pasinetti's 1962 article. Pasinetti was the first to show that if the propensity to save of wage-earners is higher than zero, they must receive interest on the savings lent to capitalists. Thus if wage-earners save, not all profit goes to capitalists. Nevertheless, Pasinetti demonstrated that the Cambridge Equation, under the valid hypothesis that $s_w < I/Y$, still held if the propensity to save out of profits was replaced by the propensity to save by capitalists s_c (that is, of the social class whose only income is profit).

Kaldor opened up new areas for investigation in his last article (1966a) on the subject. Here he clarified the hypothesis that the propensity to save of capitalists is higher than that of workers; this propensity is not to be attributed to families of capitalists, but to managerial firms which hold back part of their profits in order to finance their investment plans.

In 1951 Kaldor became a member of the Royal Commission on the Taxation of Profits and Income. Kaldor expressed his disagreement with the Commission's conclusions by writing his own minority report, the *Memorandum of Dissent*. This set out more radical ideas for the reform of the British tax system, which he accused of being 'absurd and unjust'. Kaldor's principal recommendation, an 'expenditure tax', became the title of a book (1955) which swiftly established his reputation as an international tax adviser and has become a classic of public finance. He was invited to every corner of the globe to give expert advice to governments, ministries and central banks. In 1964 he began a long period of serving as 'Special Adviser' to three Chancellors of the Exchequer (Callaghan 1964–67, Jenkins 1967–70 and Healey 1974–76). These were also years in which Kaldor's interest in economic dynamics shifted from the growth and distribution of a single country to the causes of different rates of growth among countries. The issue that now became central to his research was evidenced by *Causes of the Slow Rate of Growth in the United Kingdom* (1966).

The keystone of Kaldor's theory of the growth process was his first law of the 'manufacturing sector as the engine of growth'. This stated that a country's growth of income depends on the growth of productivity of its sectors, which in turn depends on the growth of output from the manufacturing sector. This is partly because the manufacturing sector alone is able to spread new techniques to the other sectors. But two other processes, represented by Kaldor's second and third laws, are also involved. The second law – the 'Kaldor-Verdoorn' law – stated (in Kaldor's version) that the rate of growth of productivity of the manufacturing sector depends on its rate of growth of output due to the operation, within this sector, of static and, above all, dynamic returns to scale. (Thus the mature Kaldor revived an idea he had first learnt from Allyn Young, his teacher at the LSE: that increasing returns are a macroeconomic and cumulative phenomenon.) Even mature economies, contrary to the neoclassical tenet, are 'dual' in character: they have an advanced sector with a faster growth of productivity and higher wages, and a backward sector with disguised unemployment. This gave rise to Kaldor's third law, of 'migration', which stated that the growth of output and employment in the manufacturing sector increases the productivity of the system as a whole because it withdraws workers from the agricultural sector where they have a zero or negative marginal product.

An economy reaches its 'maturity' when wages are equal in the two sectors and the dual economy has disappeared. Prior to this stage, other factors operating on the demand side – like the country's poor performance abroad – may be responsible for a slowdown in economic growth (1971).

For Kaldor, in an industrialized economy not only consumption but also manufacturing investment in the medium-long period are endogenous and induced by income (according to the principle of the super-multiplier).

Thus, if the 'inducement to growth' is to stem from an endogenous component of demand (the feature of Kaldor's theory that distinguishes it from the neoclassical theory of growth), it has to come from outside the manufacturing sector. Such 'external demand' takes three forms: demand from agriculture, whether one considers the growth of LDCs or the world economy as a whole (see 1986); demand from the public sector in a closed economy undergoing rearmament; and export demand under normal conditions in industrialized countries. Kaldor now formulated his fourth law, the 'Kaldor-Thirlwall' law, deduced from Harrod's foreign trade multiplier. It stated that a country's long-period rate of growth is approximated by the ratio between the rate of growth of exports and the income elasticity of demand for imports.

In contrast with the neoclassical theory of international trade, free trade between two countries does not necessarily increase their incomes or equalize their factor prices. The operation of the first, second and fourth of Kaldor's laws instead generates vicious circles for some countries and virtuous circles for others. This is why countries and regions grow at different rates and why the gap between rich and poor regions widens (see 1970b).

These cumulative processes led Kaldor insistently to urge the adoption of an export-led model of growth. His recommendations to successive British governments of frequent external adjustments to the exchange rate during the 1960s, of devaluation and budget restriction in the early 1970s, of 'import controls' in the late 1970s, and of opposition to Britain's joining the Common Market all followed from these premises. Most of them, especially his call for import controls, were highly unorthodox. Kaldor was also in favour of the free entry of manufacturing goods from LDCs in order to encourage their industrialization and economic progress.

In the last 15 years of his life, Kaldor was severely critical of two leading currents in the mainstream of economic thought: the static theory of equilibrium (see 1972 and 1984) and the monetarism of the Chicago School (see 1970a and 1982). As regards the former, he attacked the prevailing theory of value for being too static and grounded on false premises, offering an alternative model which interpreted world economic problems like stagflation in terms of two sectors – agriculture and industry. This provided the theoretical framework for his proposed reform of the international monetary system based on a buffer stock system of raw materials operating internationally (1976).

Kaldor's assault on Britain's new laissez-faire monetarist policy was conducted on two fronts. Theoretically, he criticized the government's monetarist policies for being based on an analytical model inappropriate to capitalist credit-money economies. In particular, he attacked the idea of a money supply wholly in the hands of the Central Bank and proposed instead that money supply be endogenously determined by demand (an idea which he had harboured ever since his 1939 article on speculation). Kaldor waged the second front to his critique before a wider public in the correspondence columns of *The Times* (he wrote more than 260 letters to the paper in his lifetime) and in numerous speeches from the benches of the House of Lords (where he sat from 1974 until his death in September 1986).

That Kaldor was a thinker in the great tradition of British political economy is demonstrated by the evident influence exerted on him by the classical economists. From Adam Smith he inherited his preoccupation with the link between the dynamics of the economic system and technical progress; from David Ricardo his interest in the distribution of income among classes and in the constraints on growth induced by diminishing returns to land. There are also numerous similarities between his thought and Marx's. Suffice it to mention his view of technical progress as a necessary condition for the survival of the individual capitalist in competition, his identification of market failures in economic dynamics, and his singling out of the cumulative processes that lead to unequal development. He also made a major contribution to continuing the typically Cambridge tradition, from Sidgwick to Keynes, of public intervention in the economic sphere.

Both Keynes and Kaldor were convinced of the effectiveness of market mechanisms. They were equally convinced that the market was unjust in its distribution of income and that society must have institutions able to guarantee a stability of production and employment that the market, if left to itself, cannot provide. But the most important feature shared by the two economists was the faith that inspired their economic policy beliefs – a faith summed up by Max Weber when he wrote: 'The possible would never be achieved if there was nobody in the world who attempted the impossible'.

Kaldor's Major Writings

The great majority of Kaldor's articles are collected in nine volumes published by Duckworth. A shorter selection of his most important articles can be found in *The Essential Kaldor*, edited by F. Targetti and A.P. Thirlwall, Duckworth, 1989.

(1934a), 'The Determinateness of Static Equilibrium', *Review of Economic Studies*, 1.

(1934b), 'Equilibrium of the Firm', *Economic Journal*, 44.

(1935), 'Market Imperfection and Excess Capacity', *Economica*, 1.

(1937), 'The Recent Controversy on the Theory of Capital', *Econometrica*, 5.

(1938), 'Professor Pigou on Money Wages in relation to Unemployment', *Economic Journal*, 48.

(1939a), 'Speculation and Economic Stability', *Review of Economic Studies*, 6.

(1939b), 'Welfare Propositions of Economics and Interpersonal Comparisons', *Economic Journal*, 49.

(1940), 'A Model of the Trade Cycle', *Economic Journal*, 50.

(1955), *An Expenditure Tax*, London: Allen and Unwin.

(1956), 'Alternative Theories of Distribution', *Review of Economic Studies*, 23.

(1957), 'A Model of Economic Growth', *Economic Journal*, 67.

(1961), 'Capital Accumulation and Economic Growth', in V. Lutz (ed), *The Theory of Capital*, London: Macmillan.

(1962), 'A New Model of Economic Growth' (with J. Mirrlees), *Review of Economic Studies*, 29.

(1966a), 'Marginal Productivity and the Macro-economic Theories of Distribution', *Review of Economic Studies*, 33.

(1966b), *Causes of the Slow Rate of Growth in the United Kingdom*, Cambridge University Press.

(1970a), 'The New Monetarism', *Lloyds Bank Review*, no. 97.

(1970b), 'The Case for Regional Policies', *Scottish Journal of Political Economy*, 17.

(1971), 'Conflicts in National Economic Objectives', *Economic Journal*, 81.

(1972), 'The Irrelevance of Equilibrium Economics', *Economic Journal*, 82.

(1976), 'Inflation and Recession in the World Economy', *Economic Journal*, 86.

(1982), *The Scourge of Monetarism*, Oxford University Press.

(1984), *Economics without Equilibrium*, New York: M.E. Sharpe.
(1986), 'Limits on Growth', *Oxford Economic Papers*, **38**.
(1991), *Causes of Growth and Stagnation in the World Economy*, Mattioli Lectures, Cambridge University Press.

Other References
Cambridge Journal of Economics, Special Issue on Kaldor, **13**, March 1989.
Pasinetti, L. (1962), 'The Rate of Profit and Income Distribution in Relation to the Rate of Economic Growth', *Review of Economic Studies*, **29**.
Targetti, F. (1988), *Nicholas Kaldor: Economia e politica di un capitilismo in mutamento*, il Mulino. English translation, Oxford University Press, 1991.
Thirlwall, A.P. (1987), *Nicholas Kaldor*, Brighton, Wheatsheaf Books.

Michal KALECKI (1899–1970)   *Malcolm C. Sawyer*

Michal Kalecki was born in 1899 into a Polish–Jewish family in Lodz (Poland), then occupied by Russia. His academic training was in the field of engineering; however, after an interruption for military service, his formal education was brought to an end by his father's unemployment. While his background in engineering gave him a good grounding in mathematics, he was self-taught in economics, studying first such writers as Rosa Luxemburg, Turan-Baranovski and Marx. Only at a relatively late stage was he exposed to neoclassical (Walrasian general equilibrium) ideas then dominant in Polish academic circles. His attitudes were also strongly influenced by the prevailing levels of unemployment in Poland.

Kalecki's employment during the 1920s varied widely, from making credit ratings of firms applying for loans to undertaking market research and economics journalism. He was also involved in political journalism and maintained close connections with left socialist movements. In late 1929, he obtained his first quasi-academic employment at the Research Institute of Business Cycles and Prices in Warsaw. His early work at this institute involved the study of business cycles and the preparation of reports on specific industries, often monopolies or cartels.

In 1933 he published a paper in Polish under the title, 'Outline of a Theory of the Business Cycle' (reprinted as Chapter 1 of *Selected Essays*, 1971) in which he presented the basic idea of the importance of fluctuations in investment expenditure as a generator of business cycles. This and some related papers form the basis of the claim that Kalecki published some of the key ideas of Keynes before Keynes himself (1933 versus 1936). The basic ideas which they share are the relevance of the level of aggregate demand, investment demand as the key element in aggregate demand and the fact of real wages not being determined in the labour market.

At the time of publication of the *General Theory* (February 1936), Kalecki was in Sweden on a Rockefeller Foundation Fellowship. When he realized the significance of Keynes's findings for his own research, he delayed developing his own ideas into a book. He travelled to England in April 1936 and made contact with Keynes, Joan Robinson and others. During the war Kalecki was employed at the Oxford University Institute of Statistics, undertaking some important independent work, as well as contributing to the current debate on economic policy. These commentaries reveal some general features of Kalecki's approach to economics, namely the interplay between theorizing and the observation of reality, concern for the 'underdog' and the pursuit of social justice. Kalecki's work at Oxford of lasting significance concerned prospects for the post-war economy including the socio-political difficulties of maintaining full employment and the limits on the use of investment stimulation as a means of achieving this end.

At the end of 1946, Kalecki was appointed deputy director of a section of the economics department of the United Nations secretariat. He resigned from the UN in 1954 in response to the restrictions placed on himself and others by the effects of McCarthyism then sweeping the US. From the beginning of 1955 until his death in 1970, Kalecki's home was in Poland. The first two years of his return to Poland coincided with the growth of overt political opposition to the Polish government; the Poznan workers' uprising in June 1956 and the spread of strikes across Poland; and the spontaneous creation of workers' councils in October 1956 (the 'Polish October'). In an environment of discontent with centralized planning and the emphasis on rapid industrialization, Kalecki was heavily involved in the debates over the roles of decentralization, workers' councils, the speed of industrialization and the relative size of consumption and investment. He did not have great enthusiasm either for decentralization or the use of market mechanisms which were advocated by many economists in Poland, in part as a reaction to the problems posed by centralized planning. In the second half of the 1950s, Kalecki was Chairman of the Commission of Perspective Planning, but his official role effectively ended in 1960. In the last decade of his life, Kalecki was heavily involved with problems of economic development, including seminars organized at the Academy of Sciences, Warsaw University and the Central School for Planning and Statistics. By 1968, the political climate in Poland had changed considerably for the worse and Kalecki's outspokenness, disagreement with the heavy industry investment programme (and an element of anti-Semitism) brought him into disfavour.

Kalecki made substantial contributions to the analysis of developed capitalist, socialist and developing economies, and these are now discussed in turn. Of the numerous differences between these three types of economies, Kalecki emphasized that capitalist economies are usually demand-constrained whilst socialist ones tend to be resource-constrained. In a similar vein, a major cause of unemployment in underdeveloped economies is the shortage of capital equipment, whereas in developed capitalist economies unemployment arises from an inadequacy of aggregate demand.

Throughout his writings on capitalist economies, Kalecki saw investment expenditure as having crucial importance as a component of aggregate demand and as generating business cycles. Investment expenditure is the active component of aggregate demand and thus seen as determining the level of income (rather than being determined by it), whereas consumer expenditure is largely constrained by the level of consumers' income. Investment expenditure and savings are (in a simple closed private economy) equal *ex post*, but Kalecki saw investment expenditure as causing (forcing) savings. Firms make investment plans for some future time period which are largely carried out and to which savings have to adjust in order that the national income accounts identities can hold.

Profits are the main source of savings. In the case of a classical savings function (where all profits are saved and all wages spent), the equality of savings and investment implies the equality also of profits and investment. At the aggregate level, the direction of causation was seen by Kalecki as running from investment expenditure to profits. At the level of the firm, there is also a relationship running from expected profits to the level of investment.

Firms have a preference for internal funds, which are less costly than external funds. The use of external funds involves various transactions costs of raising the loan or making new share issues. The volume of internal funds available to a firm will be largely determined by the volume of profits, so that current profits (or perhaps more accurately cash flow) are an important determinant of investment through considerations on the availability of finance. The use of external funds is limited eventually by the increasing costs of such funds through the 'principle of increasing risk'. In effect, the argument is that the greater the volume of borrowing which a firm wishes to undertake (relative to its profits and assets), the greater is the risk that it will be unable to repay the interest charges and the capital sum itself. Financial institutions take this increasing risk into account and charge higher rates of interest for larger volumes of borrowing.

Kalecki saw that a condition for expansion of aggregate demand is the granting of loans to finance the increase in demand. Investment expenditure above the prevailing level of savings can only occur if banks are willing to finance the increased investment expenditure. He generally assumed as a first approximation that loans to finance investment would be granted by the banks so that the investment could proceed. The extent of those loans would be limited by the desire of firms to borrow to finance investment rather than by the desire of banks to extend loans. Kalecki recognized that there could be times when banks would respond to an increased demand for loans by raising the rate of interest, thereby choking off the demand for loans and thus the planned increase in investment expenditure.

One rather general way of looking at Kalecki's approach is to ask why a firm would wish to increase its capital stock by net investment. In each time period, finance becomes available as profits are made and savings undertaken. Thus some potential investment delayed in the past because of a lack of finance can now proceed as finance becomes available. The incentive for a firm to own and operate capital equipment can be expected to depend on the prospective rate of profit on that capital equipment relative to the rate of interest at which the firm can borrow. A change in the relationship between the average rate of profit and the average rate of interest on borrowing would generate a change in the desired stock of capital equipment owned by firms, and thus stimulate investment. With the level of long-term interest rates (which are significant for investment decisions) rather stable, changes in the rate of profit are the predominant influence on investment. The rate of profit changes either because profits change or because the capital stock changes, which occurs automatically when there is non-zero net investment. The former would arise from, *inter alia*, fluctuations in the level of output (and thereby profits) or in the degree of monopoly (influencing the profits-to-sales ratio).

Kalecki dismissed the notion of perfect competition as being of any practical relevance for the analysis of capitalism, which he viewed as largely oligopolistic. He considered the concept of perfect competition 'as a most unrealistic assumption' which 'when its actual status of a handy model is forgotten becomes a dangerous myth' (*Essays*, 1971). The rejection of the concept of perfect competition applies to the product market for industrial goods and services, the labour market (where collective bargaining and trade unions are important features) and the financial markets. In particular, any theory of pricing has to recognize capitalism's oligopolistic nature. Although Kalecki's precise formulation of the analysis of pricing changed over time, two features can be highlighted. The first is that the mark-up of price over average direct costs which a firm incurs depends on the market power of the firm. The market power ('degree of monopoly') depends in turn on a range of factors such as the number of rivals, the conditions of entry into the industry concerned, level of advertising etc. The second feature is the link between pricing and the distribution of income (between wages and profits).

The degree of monopoly in an industry depends on factors such as the degree of concentration and the extent of effective collusion amongst firms, the conditions of entry into the industry, and the level of product differentiation. Each of these factors helps to secure the position of existing firms and to permit prices to be raised relative to costs. The extent of collusion is not mechanically determined by the level of concentration or by barriers to entry but also depends on the previous history of the industry concerned. The degree of monopoly in an industry will be reflected in the extent to which prices are above marginal costs.

Kalecki's 'degree of monopoly' approach is a theory in the sense that it produces potentially refutable predictions. The charge that it was a tautology rather than a theory was based on aspects of its presentation. The term degree of monopoly was sometimes used so as to be coincident with the mark-up of price over marginal costs, whereas the mark-up should be seen as a consequence of the degree of monopoly. The refutable proposition is that the mark-up of price over costs depends on factors such as the level of concentration, barriers to entry etc.

Following Kalecki's working assumption of the equality between marginal costs and average variable costs, the mark-up of price over average cost also depends on the degree of monopoly. The excess of price over average variable cost has to cover (the average) profit and fixed costs, from which it follows that the share of profits plus fixed costs in sales depend on the degree of monopoly. At the aggregate level, sales (gross output) by domestic firms are equal to domestic net output (value added) plus imported inputs. For each industry, the material inputs are separated into domestic and imported inputs, and the domestic inputs split down into their labour and material components. The share of profits in national income can then be shown to depend on the degree of monopoly and the terms of trade between the domestic economy and other economies.

Real wages depend on the balance between money wages and prices. On the whole Kalecki sees prices as set (based on the degree of monopoly) by reference to average labour costs and average material costs, which in turn depend on productivity, money wages and material costs. Turning this around suggests that real wages depend on the degree of monopoly, productivity and imported prices (relative to wages). This would also imply that conditions in the labour market are not seen as relevant to the determination of real wages.

A major constraint on the achievement of full employment in capitalism arises from limits on the manipulation of aggregate demand. Consumer expenditure could only be raised through a change in the distribution of income towards wage earners and the poor. This was a course of action generally favoured by Kalecki as much for its social benefits as its economic ones. He tended to see virtually all wages being spent so that it would be difficult to raise the propensity to save out of wages, but perhaps possible to distribute more income in the direction of wages. But here, as with a number of redistributive policies, whilst they could be viewed as beneficial from an economic or social welfare perspective, nevertheless there would be strong political constraints on governments undertaking such redistribution.

Investment expenditure could be encouraged by government subsidy, lower interest rates etc, but after a while would run into the difficulty that more investment leads to a greater capital stock and, *ceteris paribus*, a lower rate of profit. The limits on the net effect of government expenditure arise simply from the constraints of a rising national debt-to-income ratio and the consequent rising interest charges. Kalecki was critical of the 1944 White Paper on Full Employment as not grasping the nettle that full employment may require a permanent budget deficit.

Whilst Kalecki believed that the use of appropriate demand-management policies could remove unemployment, he argued that 'the assumption that a Government will maintain full employment in a capitalist economy if it knows how to do it is fallacious' (1943). He started from the view that capitalist economies would not generally maintain full employment since this would require substantial government intervention. A prolonged period of full employment underpinned by government intervention would generate significant social and political changes. Resistance to the maintenance of full employment would arise from dislike by some groups of those social and political changes and from dislike of government intervention in general and of whatever particular form it took.

Resistance to government intervention amongst business was seen to arise from a fear that the extension of government activity could be seen as foreshadowing the replacement of capitalism by state activity and socialism. Further, under laissez-faire capitalism the level of employment rests on the level of investment, which in turn depends on profitability and the 'state of confidence', whereas the use of government expenditure to underpin full employment would reduce the role of business.

Kalecki's writings on the economics of socialism were undertaken only after his return to Poland in December 1954. He was directly involved in many of the debates of the mid-1950s on the development and organization of the Polish economy. His general approach could be summarized by saying that he sought a departure from the system of bureaucratic centralism; the main lines of development in the economy would be centrally planned, with the market mechanism used in a subordinate role. Further, he advocated a substantial increase in self-management by workers (under a system of Workers' Councils), though acknowledging that there would be tension between central planning and workers' councils.

Soviet and later Eastern European economic planning policies placed great weight on rapid industrialization and a heavy investment programme. The tendency towards over-ambitious plans often led to the sacrifice of consumption in favour of investment when the overall plan could not be implemented. For long-term planning, 'Kalecki's fundamental principles …[were] that the plan should be realistic, internally balanced, and it should protect the current interests of the consumer' (Osiatynski, 1982). This approach brought Kalecki into conflict with the prevailing orthodoxy at both the theoretical and practical levels (over the construction of five-year and perspective 15-year plans).

Kalecki's approach to growth under socialism can be discovered by reference to a basic relationship in which the growth of output is equal to the impact on productive potential of new investment minus the loss of the (proportionate) amount of production due to depreciation plus the change in utilization of productive capacity. Some differences between socialism and capitalism can be illustrated by reference to this equation. Decisions on savings and investment are in the hands of the private sector (mainly capitalists) under capitalism, but lie with the planning authority under most forms of socialism. Viewed as demand-constrained, a major cause of year-to-year fluctuations of capacity utilization under capitalism is demand fluctuations. Under socialism 'the coefficient [of capacity utilization] begins to reflect solely the effect of organizational and technical improvements which do not require significant capital outlays' (1972a).

Much of Kalecki's theoretical work on economic growth under socialism stemmed from this equation for growth of output, with modifications for foreign trade, limited labour supply and technical progress. The emphasis was on the identification, and then the pushing back, of the effective constraints on economic growth.

Kalecki paid relatively little attention to the problems of achieving technical efficiency at the enterprise level or the role of incentives. He regarded the determination of patterns of consumption and investment as important political decisions, though he did seek to devise rules for investment decisions for central planners. This began with a 'generalized formula of the efficiency of investment' within the context of a recoupment period fixed by the planning commission in instructions issued to enterprises (1959). This was the number of years over which additional investment expenditure should be recouped by lower annual operating costs.

Kalecki was heavily involved with teaching and research in the area of development planning from the late 1950s to the late 1960s, organizing courses and seminars on underdeveloped economies.

In his writings on development it is useful to identify four themes. The first is that unemployment is seen to arise from a shortage of capital equipment (rather than from a deficiency of effective demand), so that constraints on employment and the pace of development arise more from the supply side than from the demand side. This led on to the identification of the binding constraints in any concrete situation: difficulties of expanding agricultural production, problems in achieving the desired rate of investment, and shortages of foreign exchange. These economic constraints were often compounded by the political resistance of powerful groups whose interests would be harmed by economic development.

A second theme is the need for the expansion of agricultural production as part of the development process, since development leads to an increased demand for food. If that increased demand is not satisfied, the price of food is likely to rise, with real wages being depressed as a consequence. The agricultural sector is likely to suffer from low productivity and backward techniques. Since there are often powerful obstacles to the development of agriculture, such as feudal or semi-feudal relations in land tenure and the domination of the peasants by merchants and moneylenders, substantial institutional changes would be required.

The third theme is that market mechanisms left to themselves are unlikely to produce outcomes which Kalecki would regard as acceptable or desirable. This can be reflected in inadequate or misdirected investment, in insufficient food production etc. Thus Kalecki saw a strong need for planning and direct government intervention, particularly in investment and foreign trade, though he was well aware that such intervention would be resisted by those with economic and political power.

The fourth theme is the distributional aspects of growth and development. Kalecki has always stressed the income distribution aspects of his analysis and of economic policies. In his writings on development, there is a concern that the process of development should benefit the poor. But there is also an awareness that prospective distributional consequences may block development.

In discussing the range of underdeveloped countries, Kalecki introduced the concept of an 'intermediate regime'. Countries in this category had generally achieved independence after the Second World War and, whilst seeking economic development with government involvement, could be considered neither socialist nor laissez-faire capitalist. The governments of these intermediate regimes represented the interests of the lower middle class, rich peasants and managers in the state sector. The poorest strata of society were still unorganized and lacked any political power. Kalecki argued that, following the political freedom from imperial occupation, 'representatives of the lower middle class rise in a way naturally to power. To keep power they must: (i) achieve not only political but also economic emancipation; ... (ii) carry out land reform; and (iii) assure continuous economic growth' (1976). State capitalism develops at the expense of socialism in the economies of intermediate regimes because it helps the middle class retain power, for example by aiding faster growth and economic emancipation.

Kalecki's Major Writings

The collected works of Michal Kalecki (edited by J. Osiatynski) have been published in Polish and are in the process of being published in English in seven volumes by Clarendon Press.

(1943), 'Political Aspects of Full Employment', *Political Quarterly*, **14**.

(1959), 'Generalized Formula of the Efficiency of Investment' (with M. Rakowski), *Gospodarka Planowa*, **11**.

(1966), *Studies in the Theory of the Business Cycle: 1933–39* (translated by Ada Kalecki), Oxford: Blackwell.

(1971), *Selected Essays on the Dynamics of the Capitalist Economy*, Cambridge: Cambridge University Press.

(1972a), *Selected Essays on the Economic Growth of the Socialist and the Mixed Economy*, Cambridge: Cambridge University Press.

(1972b), *The Last Phase in the Transformation of Capitalism*, New York: Monthly Review Press.

(1976), *Essays on Developing Economies*, Brighton: Harvester.

Other References

Kriesler, K. (1987), *Kalecki's Microanalysis*, Cambridge: Cambridge University Press.

Osiatynski, J. (1982), 'Michal Kalecki's Perspective Development Plan for Poland, 1960–1975', *Oeconomica Polona*.

Osiatynski, J. (1988), *Michal Kalecki on a Socialist Economy* (translated by Jan Toporowski), London: Macmillan.

Sawyer, M.C. (1985), *The Economics of Michal Kalecki*, London: Macmillan.

John Maynard (1st Baron) KEYNES
(1883–1946)   *Victoria Chick*

The legacy of Keynes's writing is so vast, and the external events of his life and his ideas both encompassed so much change, that the role Keynes plays in economics is very much in the eye of the beholder. While writing *The General Theory* (*Collected Writings of John Maynard Keynes*, hereafter *CW*, Vol VII), he declared himself to be working on a theory which would 'revolutionise the way the world thinks about economic problems' (letter to G.B. Shaw, *CW* XIII, p. 492). While some embrace the Keynesian Revolution, others see Keynes as the bourgeois reactionary, devising ways to shore up the capitalist system by a series of expedients. I shall argue that he was both profoundly revolutionary and profoundly conservative: in his life as in his writing there is both tradition and dissent, continuity and revolution, at almost every stage.

John Maynard Keynes was born in Cambridge, the eldest of three children of John Neville and Florence Ada Keynes. His father was a Cambridge don, a lecturer in Logic and Political Economy and, later, Registrar of the University. J. N. Keynes's *The Scope and Method of Political Economy* (1890) remains a classic. Maynard's instruction in economics thus began at home, and it was there, too, that he first met Alfred Marshall. Florence Keynes (née Brown), educated at Newnham in its early days, engaged in many progressive social projects and became Cambridge's first woman mayor.

This was a solid, cultured, late-Victorian background in an important and influential place. But its traditional appearance was tempered by important differences from the prevailing norm. First, there was the presence of an educated and independently-active mother. Second, the family was Congregationalist; Mrs Keynes 'was descended from a bewildering succession of Puritan divines' (R. Skidelsky, in *The End of the Keynesian Era,* p. 2). On that count, Keynes was a born Dissenter.

For a boy early perceived as intelligent – though the scope of his powers was not fully evident – the transition from his background into a career like his father's would have been quite expected and should have been comparatively easy. But although he became a Fellow of King's College, Cambridge, his path was not all that straightforward, nor did Keynes's ambitions end there. He became not only the greatest (and still the most controversial) economist this century, but also a civil servant, a financier and speculator, Bursar of his college, editor of *The Economic Journal*, patron of the arts, bibliophile and collector, and negotiator for Britain at the Paris Peace Conference and at Bretton Woods. He was a prolific writer: his *Collected Writings* run to 30 volumes, and much was excluded. His subjects were not only economics but also philosophy, history, politics and biography. And he wrote at many levels, as academic, journalist, pamphleteer and man of letters.

He won a scholarship to Eton and went on to King's, where philosophy and ethics claims his attention far more than the subject he was reading – not economics, but mathematics. His philosophical explorations (note the forthcoming *Collected Philosophical Writings of JMK*) formed the basis of his economic theory and policy.

Keynes was part of the generation destined to challenge Victorian values. In working out where they stood, Keynes and his circle were greatly influenced by G. E. Moore, whose philosophy elevated the enjoyment of beauty and the pleasure of human relationships and undermined the foundations of Victorian morality. Keynes was also keenly interested in Burke. In Keynes's life the enjoyment of beauty and the cultivation of friendships were balanced by a sense of duty and obligation in public life, which may reflect these two opposing influences or may stem from temperament and background. These matters are, at present, the active subject of scholarly investigation.

Keynes got his first class degree in Mathematics in 1905, coming a respectable but not-very-glorious 12th. He then debated whether to take the Economics degree examinations the following year. He studied for these with Marshall's encouragement and supervision, but decided to enter for the Civil Service examinations instead. He came second and joined the India Office. While he was there he not only took an interest, outside his duties, in the problems of India's monetary system, but also began to transform an early critique of Moore into a pioneering work on the philosophy of probability – what would become the *Treatise on Probability* (*CW* VIII). He submitted the work as a Fellowship dissertation to King's in 1908. Although not elected, he resigned from the India Office and returned to Cambridge to lecture in Economics, paid out of Pigou's own pocket. He revised the dissertation and gained his Fellowship the following year.

The *Treatise*, Keynes's main preoccupation between 1906 and 1912, was not published until 1921. By this time Keynes had published, in 1913, his first major work as an economist, *Indian Currency and Finance* (*CW* I); he had also caused a sensation by resigning from the Versailles Treaty negotiations in protest against the harsh reparations settlement. (He had entered the Treasury during the war and was its principal representative at the Paris Peace Conference.) He published his dissent in a brilliant and, in official circles, thoroughly offensive book, *The Economic Consequences of the Peace* (*CW* II), in 1919. He was now famous – not as an academic, but in the world of affairs.

After Versailles, Keynes resigned from the Treasury. In order to leave more time for writing, he also resigned his university Lectureship, though he retained his Fellowship (without pay) and continued to give some lectures and run the seminar he organized as the Political Economy Club. His financial activities now provided his main source of income. In the first six years after the war he revised and published the *Treatise on Probability*, opposed Britain's return to gold, wrote the *Tract on Monetary Reform* (*CW* IV) and, in 1925, married Lydia Lopokova, of Diaghilev's Ballet Russe.

Indian Currency and Finance (*ICF*) serves as a bridge to the first of these activities. *ICF* does not count as the work of a dissenting economist, yet one can discern two indications of dissent to come. First, *ICF* was traditional theory based on a thorough knowledge of institutions and supported policy proposals to improve those institutions. (Twenty-three years later Keynes expressed his irritation with his contemporaries whose policy prescription for the slump was correct but *did not follow from their theory*. Correcting this incoherence was given as a main motivation for writing *The General Theory*.) Second, in *ICF* he expresses strong support for discretion over rules in monetary arrangements – a position which echoes his early critique of Moore on rule-following – and a sceptical view of the gold standard. In an era when the gold standard was seen, unquestioningly, as the source of all monetary order, Keynes understood that its success was not a property of the standard itself, but was contingent on the existence of a single, strong financial centre – at the time, London.

The end of the war put this view to the test. Keynes and Reginald McKenna were virtually the only dissenters against Britain's return to the gold standard at pre-war parity. Today we are so used to thinking of the exchange rate as a policy variable that it is difficult to appreciate the moral overtones of the debate: the pro-gold faction, that is nearly everyone, felt that anything less than a return to gold at the old parity was tantamount to default, and default was unthinkable. Keynes and McKenna lost to the 'moral majority': Winston Churchill, as Chancellor the Exchequer, returned Britain to gold in 1925.

To Keynes the worst phase of the relatively long campaign to return to gold was the last year, 1924. American prices had failed to rise as far as had been expected; in an effort to reduce prices, policy turned to a concerted attack on the level of wages. In a term Keynes later developed in the *Treatise on Money* (TM), this was income deflation. He foresaw trouble since, to maintain parity, the policy would have to be continued after the return to gold. He wrote three newspaper articles to this effect; they were published (1925) as a pamphlet with a title he must have known was unfair, but who could resist?: *The Economic Consequences of Mr Churchill* (CW IX). True to Keynes's predictions, the workers resisted the attack on wages: the spring of 1926 saw the Coal Strike and the General Strike.

In the first two years after the war, Britain experienced one of the sharpest price fluctuations in her modern peacetime history. The retail price index rose 16 per cent in 1920, then fell 9 per cent and 19 per cent in the two succeeding years. During the inflation Keynes advocated the use of high interest rates to engineer (in *TM* terms) a profit deflation. He was optimistic that this policy would not cause much unemployment. His views were elaborated in *A Tract on Monetary Reform* (1923; *CW* IV). The *Tract* follows the Cambridge tradition of monetary analysis, based on the cash balance equation. The dissent is methodological: Keynes's impatience with the long-run orientation of monetary theory – not surprising after such wide and rapid fluctuations – is vented in a famous, if often misused, passage:

> But the *long run* is a misleading guide to current affairs. *In the long run* we are all dead. Economists set themselves too easy, too useless a task if in tempestuous seasons they can only tell us that when the storm is long past the ocean is flat again (*CW* IV, p. 65).

This attack on orthodox theory, which only discloses the properties of equilibrium, foreshadows the transition from the *Treatise on Money* to *The General Theory*.

In 1920, Keynes returned to the *Treatise on Probability* (TP), to revise it for publication (1921). Although virtually ignored by economists until very recently, *TP* is now the subject of enormous interest, as it is seen as the prime expression of the philosophy which led eventually to Keynes's crowning achievement, *The General Theory*. Keynes developed a theory of probability to establish principles of rational judgement and rational action in an uncertain world, where 'knowledge of the permanent facts of existence', including reliable conventions and scientific laws, provide little guidance. Keynes's *logical theory of probability* deals with events or propositions to which no numerical probability can be attached; indeed the probabilities may not even be comparable in terms of more or less. The classical, relative-frequency theory of probability is seen as a special case, applicable to a restricted class of events.

The logical theory of probability has direct relevance to decision-making under uncertainty – the hallmark of *The General Theory*. Entrepreneurs in the *GT* make their investment decisions by a combination of rational calculation (the marginal efficiency of capital) and the mixture of non-quanitifiable hunches and sheer urge to action which Keynes called 'animal spirits'.

Post-war events had brought to the fore the influence of banking and monetary policy on the economy. With *TP* and the *Tract* out of the way, Keynes determined to write – in between his journalistic excursions – *A Treatise on Money*, bringing together his accumulated knowledge. *A Treatise* is a solid, scholarly work, 'built to last'. Its appeal to scholarly tradition is evident in its structure. There are two volumes, mirroring the dichotomy of Marshall: *The Pure Theory of Money* (*CW* V) and *The Applied Theory of Money* (*CW* VI). But as Harrod pointed out, it was really impossible for someone like Keynes, whose thinking was undergoing continuous evolution (spurred on by his contemporaneous service on the Macmillan Committee) to write a definitive treatise. Indeed, not only does *TM* contain internal evidence of this evolution, but it is also well documented that Keynes was dissatisfied with it as soon as it was finished (*CW* XIII).

TM (1930) takes up the challenge of the *Tract*: its theoretical analysis is concerned with the processes of adjustment necessitated by variations in demand, or (equivalently) disparities of saving and investment, which result in windfall profits or losses. Windfalls are defined as unexpected deviations – the 'tempestuous seasons' – from the flat sea of a long-period equilibrium. The equilibrium is Wicksellian: just-normal profits, normal real wages, full employment of the factors of production, equality of saving and investment and of the market and natural rates of interest. The quantity of money determines the equilibrium price level. Departures from long-period (full) employment are explained by fluctuations in demand which are presumed temporary.

The framework of TM is firmly traditional, not only in the characterization of equilibrium as long-period but also in casting unemployment as a disequilibrium phenomenon and attributing it to entrepreneurial error: a proposition fully acceptable to classical and neoclassical economists to this day. The natural rate of interest is determined by saving and investment, as of old, but the money rate of interest is determined by banking policy and a new element – what we would now call liquidity preference – involving the deployment of the whole of financial wealth rather than, as in loanable funds theory, only the flow of saving. Here is another step towards *The General Theory*.

Disequilibrium provokes adjustment, which takes place in two time frames: within a single production period and in the moment at the beginning of the next period. Within the period, plainly the level of output has already been decided and cannot be altered, even if demand is greater or less that expected. Prices, however, may respond, either to changes in the costs of production (mainly changes in money wages) or to excess demand. The first Keynes called 'income inflation', the second, 'profit inflation'. Between periods, output and employment decisions may be altered in the light of realized profits. Thus profits are the spur to change. But given the way equilibrium is defined, *wages must fall to cure unemployment* – a very 'classical' conclusion!

When Keynes published *TM* in 1930, production in Britain had been depressed since 1921 and unemployment had never fallen below 10 per cent of the insured labour force. Was all this really only due to 'transitory monetary factors'? Money wages had fallen sharply in the early 1920s but, contrary to the *TM*, unemployment had persisted. Added to these facts of experience was theoretical criticism: a group of brilliant young economists at Cambridge, their own names now legendary in their subject, had persuaded Keynes that *TM* did not really admit of changes in output. In mid-1931, with work for the Macmillan Committee finished, Keynes resolved to spend more time in Cambridge, to revise *TM*. The stage was set for the Keynesian Revolution: what emerged, in 1936, was *The General Theory of Employment, Interest and Money* (*CW* VII).

The Keynesian Revolution is usually understood to be the policy conclusion associated with Keynes: government spending to counteract a slump. But others had advocated this policy long before Keynes. There are two, interdependent revolutions, neither to do with policy: one is a revolution in theory, the other in economic method. By means of these changes, the policy became, for the first time, consistent with economic theory.

Looking at *TM* from the point of view of Marshallian method, it is a classic example of the excluded middle: of Marshall's three 'periods' – market, short and long – only the two extremes are represented. The production period corresponds to the market period, in which output is perforce fixed at the beginning, while Keynes's point of reference is the long period. It is true that output decisions can be revised at the start of the next period, but this was not captured in the formal analysis of the Fundamental Equations. A sequence of production periods constitutes the short period, in which capital is fixed but output and employment, as well as prices, are variable. This construct, missing from *TM*, is the framework of most of the *GT*.

The move to the short period constituted a sharp break with the traditions of monetary theory. The 'classical dichotomy' between the real and monetary sectors states that 'real' factors, including saving and investment viewed as real resources, determine 'real' variables – output, the rate of interest and relative prices between goods. Money determines the 'absolute level' of prices. The real factors were seen as 'fundamentals', which determine the long-period equilibrium position to which the economic system would eventually return. 'Competition' – the expansion, entry and exit of firms – would ensure the bidding down of supernormal profits and of real wages to the point at which factors of production were fully employed. Economic fluctuations, including unemployment and price fluctuations, were caused by monetary factors and were by nature transitory.

In the short period the capital stock is taken as given; hence long-run competition cannot do its work, as entry and exit imply changes in the capital stock. All production decisions, and hence employment decisions, by definition take place in the short period – that is, with the capital stock on hand. A given capital stock implies the possibility of quasi-rents or supernormal profits which vary with the level of demand. When demand is correctly anticipated, there is short-period equilibrium, *which need not be a position of full employment.* In the *GT*, Keynes analyses the properties of this equilibrium and adjustment to it, relinquishing the sheet-anchor of the long run. Indeed, the classical frame of reference is turned upside down: instead of a theory of fluctuations being used to determine employment, Keynes uses his theory of employment to explain the trade cycle.

The definitive break with neoclassical economics is the Principle of Effective Demand. This Principle states that employment is determined by the expected demand for output, and that the demand for output along with supply conditions settles the price level. The quantity theory of money and a labour-market theory of employment are both abandoned. The real wage is determined as a macroeconomic outcome rather than being a determinant of employment and output; in place of a theory in which supply and demand for labour have equal weight, the Principle implies that labour has little control over either the volume of employment or the real wage. If effective demand is insufficient, there is *involuntary unemployment* – unemployment due to the operation of the system as a whole rather than labour's actions.

If producers' demand expectations are met at a level of production which does not absorb all labour willing to work at the going wage, unemployment can continue indefinitely; there is *unemployment equilibrium.* At this point many would equate the short period to a short run of time, as if to say 'this too shall pass'. But there is no guarantee of convergence to full employment. Nor would a fall in wages help, for it would reduce demand as well as cost. Therefore an 'exogenous shock' – such as government spending – is the best remedy.

The Principle of Effective Demand is, like so much in Keynes's life and thought, both radical and traditional. It denies the importance of supply and demand analysis in 'the labour market', yet it generalizes to the macroeconomic level Marshall's theorem that the demand for labour is a derived demand – derived from the demand for output.

In the *GT* the theory of the rate of interest is also radically revised. The determination of the rate of interest was taken away from the saving-investment nexus. Saving now adjusted to investment through the multiplier– an invention of Richard Kahn's – by a combination of price and output changes. That left the rate of interest 'in the air' until Keynes developed his *TM* idea of bearishness into the theory of liquidity preference, severing any direct connection with saving. The old identity of the rate of interest and the rate of profit was broken. Interest depended mainly on convention and speculators' expectations. The rate of interest, along with producers' highly uncertain expectations of future profit and their animal spirits, determined autonomous expenditure on investment, on which the level of economic activity utterly depended as long as the consumption function was stable. And worse! Preference for liquidity could keep the rate of interest above the level which would give full employment, even in the long period. The neoclassical long run was completely destroyed.

The General Theory, published in 1936, was too late. On top of the contractionary policies undertaken in pursuit of pre-war exchange rate parity in the 1920s there had been the Wall Street crash of 1929 and the American depression, which had spread worldwide. Britain had gone off gold in 1931 and interest rates had fallen, but the scale of the collapse of the world economy was far too great for national, monetary remedies. Much of the world seemed polarized between communism and fascism. Before anything 'Keynesian' could be done, employment in Britain improved – in anticipation of another war.

Keynes had his first heart attack in 1937. While this severely limited his activities, during the war he still managed a prodigious workload. *How to Pay for the War* (*CW* IX), which applies the *GT* analysis to inflation, was published early in 1940. Then he joined the Chancellor of the Exchequer's Consultative Council. Soon after, a room was found for him at the Treasury. He drew no salary and had no official status; he was just 'Keynes'. From this position he concerned himself not only with the internal and external financing of the war, but also with the shape of post-war trade and, especially, payments.

Keynes had ended the *Treatise on Money* with a plan for a supranational bank, an idea which had its roots even in *Indian Currency and Finance*. His proposal for an International Clearing Union – essentially a supranational central bank and thus a complete break with automatic monetary mechanisms – was the British starting point in negotiations which culminated at Bretton Woods. Keynes's concern, characteristically, was the prospect of creditor countries building up idle balances, thus exerting a deflationary influence. For the Americans the plan was far too radical: they feared an outpouring of (probably unproductive) dollar loans. Keynes could not protest too much: he knew he would soon have to negotiate an American loan to Britain. He did not dare walk out, as he had in Paris.

At every stage of these preparations for peacetime, Keynes argued for his proposals by all available means, including the House of Lords after his elevation to the peerage (for which he was much teased by his friends) in 1942.

The Loan Agreement was signed just in time for Parliament, which had been waiting for its outcome, to ratify the Bretton Woods Articles of Agreement. Three months later Keynes went to the first meeting of the Bretton Woods institutions at Savannah (Georgia) in March 1946. He had expected 'a pleasant party', but it all went horribly wrong. The agenda concerned only final details, but in them, all the old conflicts over the basic character of the institutions surfaced afresh. And the Americans had their way. A disappointed Keynes died at his home, Tilton, in Sussex on Easter Sunday 1946.

Keynes's Major Writings

All of Keynes's works cited in this biography are to be found in *The Collected Writings of John Maynard Keynes*, 30 volumes, D.E. Moggridge and E.A.G. Robinson (eds), Macmillan, 1971–1989. Volume numbers have been given to works cited in the text.

The Collected Philosophical Writings of John Maynard Keynes, R.M. O'Donnell (ed), five volumes, are forthcoming.

Biographies

Harrod, R.F. (1951), *The Life of John Maynard Keynes*, Macmillan.

Moggridge, D.E. (1976), *Keynes*, Macmillan. Second edition, 1980.

Skidelsky, R. (1983), *John Maynard Keynes*, Volume I, *1883-1920; Hopes Betrayed*, Macmillan. Other volumes forthcoming.

Moggridge, D.E. *Maynard Keynes: An Economist's Biography*, Routledge, forthcoming.

David P. LEVINE (born 1948)

David Levine was born in 1948 in Chicago. He was educated at the University of Wisconsin and Yale where he received the Ph.D. degree in 1973. He joined the faculty of the Yale Economics department in that year and remained there until denied tenure in 1980. In 1981 he accepted the position of Chair of the Economics department at the University of Denver, a position he occupied until 1987 when he accepted his current appointment as Professor of Economics in the university's Graduate School of International Studies.

Levine's main contributions to economics fall into three broad areas: methodology, the theory of need, and the theory of capital accumulation and capitalist development. His contributions in these areas are closely linked and together explore a conceptual framework for understanding the capitalist economy; he has been strongly influenced by the classical economists, by Hegel, Marx and by contemporary theorists including Joan Robinson, Josef Steindl, Michal Kalecki and Paul Sweezy.

Levine's distinctive approach to economic theory developed under the influence of Hegel and Marx. His first book, *Economic Studies* (1977), explores the conceptual structure of classical and modern analytical arguments in economic theory. Following the method sometimes employed by Marx in *Theories of Surplus Value*, Levine develops an internal critique of the theory of value and capital, defining the conceptual issues underlying and accounting for analytical arguments. The main theme of the book can be briefly summarized in the following way.

The important analytical errors in economic theory are made for reasons. Uncovering these reasons is more important than correcting the mistakes. The reasons have to do with implicit and explicit conceptual arguments. Errors arise because theorists attempt to hold inconsistent arguments simultaneously within a single analytical-conceptual construct. Theorists attempt to say two or more different things at once – in one theory, in one sentence, even in one word. Important examples include Ricardo's invariable measure of value; the so-called transformation of values into prices in Marxian theory; and the effort to measure capital as a scarce factor of production in the neoclassical theory. Levine's strategy in the critique of theory is to make *explicit* the tensions *implicit* in the theories and thus make the analytic errors intelligible, even inevitable given the contradictions of the intellectual project that spawned them. This should illuminate the basic structure of thought employed by the theorist, a structure of which the theorist may be unaware. For Levine, theory is about making known the often hidden structure of thought that underlies the explicit arguments presented.

A specific theme emerges out of Levine's critique of economic theory. The root of the contradictions and analytical confusions in economics is the conflict within the theories between two themes: the construction of economic relations as naturally, materially or subjectively determined, and the construction of economic relations as socially determined. Levine develops this theme in the Prologue to Volume I of *Economic Theory* (1978). There he investigates the materialist arguments of the classical economists, Marx and modern classical thinkers (such as Piero Sraffa), and proposes a methodological revision of their theory based on certain of their own arguments. In this respect, Levine's work is both critique and extension of the classical-Marxian traditions. This relationship becomes clear in the remainder of *Economic Theory* Volume I, where Levine explores the core of economic theory through a reconstruction of Marx's fundamental conceptual argument regarding value, money, capital, labour, production and circulation.

Levine's notion of social determination follows the Hegelian idea of reciprocal recognition and constitution of personhood. The idea of recognition as the constitution of social being seems far removed from economic analysis. Yet it relates intimately to the way we think of the core economic concepts, especially value and exchange. The Hegelian reference point led Levine to think of the market system as a constitutive rather than instrumental institution. In other words, the market is not essentially a means (as it is for Adam Smith to some extent and more exclusively for the neoclassicals); it is a world of relations that define (constitute) who we are, how we see ourselves, and how we relate to others.

In Levine's view, our social determination is not something that happens to us, it is what constitutes our self-hood. In this framework, our self-hood and individuality are not subject to social determinants: they *are* our social determination. They are created through, and only have meaning in, our relations with others and with the structure of social relations considered as a whole. This insight formed the basis for a continuing revision of the classical framework to take social determination into account. The implications of this idea, including its opposition to the neoclassical (utilitarian) theory, are developed in a series of works, most notably Chapter 1 of *Economic Studies*, Chapter 1 of Volume I of *Economic Theory* (1978), Chapter 7 of Volume II of *Economic Theory* (1981), and *Needs, Rights, and the Market* (1988).

In all of this work, Levine attempts to explore and resolve a difficulty in the theory of need as it comes down to us from the classical economists, Marx and the neoclassicals. These theories offer us, roughly speaking, two ways of conceptualizing needs and wants: as subsistence needs and as preferences. The virtue of the classical deployment of the notion of subsistence (and of modern variants of the classical strategy) lies in its determinacy: what we consume is not a matter of whim, caprice or arbitrary choice. The weakness of this approach is that it does not consider the individual agent, and thus the market system, in any meaningful way. The neoclassical approach reverses the strengths and weaknesses of the classical, giving up the sense of determinacy of individual wants in order to make subjective choice the main theme of economic affairs. We thus face a dilemma: determinacy of want without the individual agent or individual agency without determinacy.

Levine rejects the strategy of synthesizing what are, in important respects, incompatible frameworks. To attempt such a synthesis must lead to analytical-conceptual incoherence similar to that investigated in *Economic Studies*. Instead, he proposes a reconstruction of the theory of want aimed at making individual self-determination of wants central to economics without defining those wants in the problematic and conceptually incoherent language of preference and choice.

In *Economic Theory* Volume II (see also 'The Determinants of Capitalist Expansion') Levine presents a theory of capital accumulation based on the methodological considerations briefly outlined above. He argues that central to the process of capitalist expansion is the interaction and sometimes opposition between private accumulation and the growth of social wealth (between the firm and the market). This is a classically inspired theory within which the market (both aggregate and particular demand) plays a decisive role.

Levine modifies the classical-Marxian framework to highlight the constitutive role of the market. In doing so he integrates the demand side (both aggregate and product demand), employing insights of Michal Kalecki and Josef Steindl. Levine's critique of the classical theory of markets (1980) focuses on the weaknesses of the vision of the market as a passive mechanism for allocation or reproduction. In Steindl's work, competition of capitals and the struggle over market shares are central to capitalist dynamics. Levine develops this theory in a particular direction to take into account consumer demand. Levine's theory of consumer demand embodies his broader notion of the social determination of the individual, suggesting how that broader theory has concrete implications for analytical arguments concerning capital accumulation and economic development.

Levine's non-neoclassical account of consumer decision-making attempts to gain important ground for the classical approach without giving way to the subjective method and the problematic notions of utility and rational choice. If successful, this would enable the theory of accumulation to consider a set of vital concerns excluded by the subsistence notions traditionally employed in classically inspired theories.

Analytically, Levine's theory incorporates a version of the Keynesian-Kaleckian argument (particularly as formulated by Steindl and Baran and Sweezy). The expansion of the particular unit of capital, or firm, encounters limits in the growth of its market, which depends on the growth of the system as a whole. The latter, of course, is the result of particular investment strategies of firms, so a circular causation is established at the core of the capitalist process. Levine refers to this circle as self-replicating growth, a restatement of Joan Robinson's notion of 'desired growth'. But while Robinson is mainly concerned with the stability of growth, Levine is concerned with the implications of circularity for the relation of firm to market. When circular causation constrains the growth of the individual firm (as Levine argues it must inevitably do), the growth of the firm demands that it alter its relation to the market as a whole (concretely its market share). The inevitable translation of extensive growth into structural change involves various forms of competition and innovation.

Levine emphasizes three dimensions of structural change: price competition and the concentration of capital and markets; new product development and the transformation of modes of consumption; and the exploitation of external markets (potentially including government spending). Levine's aim is to root these dynamic features of capitalist economy in the logic of its fundamental structure by setting them in the dynamic relation (and opposition) between private accumulation and the growth of social wealth.

Beginning with his earliest publications, Levine emphasized the link between quantitative growth and economic development (see 1975). Levine's theory attempts to explain the development, and particularly the uneven development, of capitalist economy. It emphasizes the role of the particularization (differentiation) of firms and the development of their cost structures (especially wages) in the process of uneven growth and development. Uneven development is rooted in the connection between quantitative growth and competition. Since, as Levine argues, competition is the mode of growth, so also is unevenness born of winning and losing in the competitive struggle (and of building upon gains and losses in the circular and cumulative process). In Levine's theory uneven development is built into the logic of capitalist economic organization.

On a broader level, the theory culminates in a vision of the social purpose of the market or, as Marx would say, the historical mission of capitalism (see the last chapter of *Economic Theory* Volume II; also 1985 and 1988). Levine's exploration of the social purpose of the market centres on the meaning and role of private property and private ownership of capital.

In his more recent work, Levine moves towards a rights-based critique of private enterprise. Here, Levine brings his analysis of the social determination of wants and of the market system to bear on the question of rights to income and to ownership of capital. The revision of the theory of consumption is critical to this part of Levine's project since it is in the conception of the relation of individual to property that grounds can be found to argue for and against limits on property ownership.

In his work, Levine emphasizes the importance of thinking abstractly (see particularly 1989). He seeks to retrieve something of the spirit of theorizing that has lately come on hard times. In mainstream economics, theory means model. This equation effectively excludes the serious exploration of conceptual issues and of the links between conceptual framework and analytical argument. It prevents us from learning what we might from the work of reflecting on the structure of our thinking. The equation of theory with model has also taken its toll on those economists seeking to develop alternatives to the neoclassical approach. Among the latter, further barriers have been thrown in the way of theoretical thinking by a proclivity for politically and historically inspired modes of argument.

Under the early influence of Joan Robinson's work (especially her critique of the neoclassical theory of capital), Levine was impressed by the necessity of conceptual clarification as the essence of good analytical work. Levine continues to be an advocate of theory, not as a way of modelling the world but as a way of making sense of it.

Levine's Major Writings

(1975), 'The Theory of the Growth of the Capitalist Economy', *Economic Development and Cultural Change*, **24**(1), October.

(1977), *Economic Studies*, London: Routledge and Kegan Paul.

(1978), *Economic Theory*, Volume I, London: Routledge and Kegan Paul. Volume II, 1981.

(1980), 'Aspects of the Classical Theory of Markets', *Australian Economic Papers*, **19**, June.

(1982), 'The Determinants of Capitalist Expansion', *Economic Development and Cultural Change*, **30**(2), January.

(1985), 'Political Economy and the Argument for Inequality', *Social Concept*, **2**(3), September.

(1988), *Needs, Rights, and the Market*, Boulder: Lynne Rienner Publishers.

(1989), 'The Sense of Theory in Political Economy', *Rethinking Marxism*, **2**(1), Spring.

Adolph LOWE (born 1893)

I was born on 4 March 1893 in Stuttgart. From 1911 to 1918 I studied law, economics and philosophy at the universities of Munich, Berlin and Tubingen, the last granting me the Dr Juris in 1918. From 1919 to 1924 I served as section head in the Ministries of Labour and Economics, and in the period 1924 to 1926 I was head of the International Division of the Federal Statistical Bureau in the Weimar Republic. In 1926 I joined the University of Kiel as Professor of Economic Theory and Sociology; I also became Director of Research at the Institute of World Economics at the same university. It was at the latter that I established the centre for research into business cycles and their control and regulation through planning. In 1931 I was appointed Professor of Political Economy at the University of Frankfurt at Main where many leaders of socialist thinking had gathered. In March 1933 I became the first professor in the social sciences to be fired by Hitler.

I had to move, and was appointed Special Honorary Lecturer in economics and political philosophy at the University of Manchester. From there I joined the New School of Social Research in 1941 as Professor of Economics and Director of Research in the Institute of World Affairs where I stayed until my retirement in 1963. As Professor Emeritus I remained active in the department at the New School until my return to Germany in March 1983. In 1984 I was awarded the Dr Honoris Causa by the University of Bremen. I also hold the Veblen-Commons Award and the Grand Cross of the German Order of Merit.

My major publications include 'Wie ist Konjunkturtheorie ueberhaupt moeglich' (1926); 'The Classical Theory of Economic Growth' (1954); *On Economic Knowledge* (1965, 1977); *The Path of Economic Growth* (1976) and *Economic Means and Social Ends* (1969) which was edited by Robert L. Heilbroner and published on my 75th birthday.

My 'dissent' emanates from my concern with the central question of economics as being the determination of the path of economic growth in relation to technical progress and social change. The issues which I believe are in dispute can be summarized in the following manner.

There is dissent about the diagnosis of the contemporary socio-economic process – about the explanation of certain shortcomings of this process – and about the policies appropriate to overcome these shortcomings. There is, however, no dissent about the ultimate goal towards which the socio-economic process should tend; namely, a level of provision acceptable to all members of society combined with the maximum degree of personal freedom that is compatible with the viability of the system. Such a level of provision is to be obtained from the full utilization of resources, operating under conditions of balanced growth.

The political economist agrees with the neoclassical economist that the present state of the Western economies, in particular of the larger ones, can by no means pass as a realization of this goal. But when it comes to establishing the causes of what I define as 'systemic instability', opinions again diverge. To the neoclassicist such instability is ultimately the result of public controls that limit individual freedom. Contrariwise, in the view of the political economist, the prevailing controls, though largely imperfect expedients, are the very instruments that have so far kept destabilization within tolerable limits.

Still, in order to uphold this view, the political economist must refute an argument, with the help of which the neoclassicist tries to demonstrate that an uncontrolled system of laissez-faire *can* be both stable and capable of satisfactory provision. He refers as evidence to the liberal era of the nineteenth century.

Now it is true that, when compared with the centuries of feudalism and absolutism, revolutions as well as peaceful reforms which started in the latter part of the eighteenth century have gradually abolished most of the *personal constraints* formerly imposed by monarchs, priests, bureaucrats and guild masters. It must also be admitted that during this period, Western capitalism achieved a fair degree of resource utilization and a steady rise of provision for most strata of society. But was it unlimited personal freedom which provided the marketers with these benefits? Were they not subjected to impersonal constraints, stringent enough to narrow down the range of personal freedom in the economic realm almost to the limits of the pre-liberal era?

Among those impersonal constraints was the pressure of poverty upon the broad masses during the first half of the liberal century. No less effective was the pressure of unlimited competition upon the middle and upper strata of society, intensified by the repercussions of technological progress. More subtle was the constraining influence of Victorian culture, some variety of which dominated at least the overt behaviour of the relevant layers of all Western societies.

In the economic realm, the combined impact of these forces imposed on the partners in market transactions the uniform action directives of maximizing receipts and minimizing expenditures, formalized in the so-called law of supply and demand. It was those impersonal constraints which achieved that uniformity and thus compatibility of the behaviour of the market participants, which created what stability and balance the liberal system displayed.

However, it is a major characteristic of contemporary capitalism that those impersonal forces are steadily wearing away – through the democratization of political institutions with the indirect effect of raising the provision of the masses; through the limitation of competition on both sides of the social fence; through a new revolutionary technology; and through a general 'loosening' of the standards of behaviour.

By expanding the range of individual choice and also the range of persons and groups who can benefit from such expansion, the discarding of those impersonal constraints has indeed enhanced individual freedom. But at the same time the political economist must remind his opponent that ultimately not only the freedom but even the physical survival of the individual depends on the viability of the socio-political system of which he is a member. This viability cannot be maintained after the earlier constraints are discarded, unless it is strengthened by public controls of the action directives of those members. Therefore in his view it is the very approximation to the laissez-faire ideal of the neoclassicist that has become the main cause of the present instability.

This difference concerning the goal-adequate organization of contemporary markets extends to the nature and function of the *theories* from which the respective views are derived. To the neoclassicist the function of theory is entirely *explanatory*. It is to state the reasons for the by no means obvious fact that in a market in which the behaviour of members is totally unconstrained, the goal as defined above can be attained; also why, on the other hand, the goal will be missed if there is any interference with the unlimited freedom of the marketers.

In contrast, the function of theory in political economy is ultimately *practical*. It also starts with an explanatory argument, expounded above, which refutes the neoclassical idea that a socio-political process, operating through the unlimited autonomy of its members, can ever attain its goals. But from this analysis the conclusion is drawn that only a subsequent practical step, namely the *application* of public controls in the realm of practice, can transform an initially goal-inadequate state or process into a goal-adequate one. To do so, however, the political economist must know which public controls are goal-directed – again a task for theory. To answer this question, I make use of the *heuristic method*, a research technique which today leads a subterranean existence alongside the conventional hypothetico-deductive method for the history of the heuristic method and its potentiality (see Polya, 1957).

In order to facilitate understanding I will spell out the differences in the two methods between what is treated as known and as unknown. The conventional method treats as known the initial state of the system and a universal, changeless law of motion. The unknown is the future state of the system, whenever one or more of the data which make up the initial state change. In contrast, the heuristic method treats as known, besides the initial state, also the future state of the system – of course not as an accomplished reality, but as *stipulated by political decision*. The unknowns are the factors that can transform an undesired (unstable) initial state into a desired future state. Among those factors are: a suitable path of adjustment, behaviour patterns suitable to pursuing that path, individual motivations suitable to inducing the suitable behaviour patterns, and finally public controls suitable to inducing the motivations.

This procedure also indicates why I contrast neoclassicism with *political* economics. Political decisions enter in the course of this chain of analysis twice: when the goal of the adjustment process is stipulated (in a modern state in accord with the ruling constitutional principles), and when the heuristically-discovered public controls are applied by political administrators (see 1983).

But the achievements of political economy are not confined to the practice of goal attainment. They include the *restoration of deductive theory*. A new 'law of motion' is established through the uniformity of responses which the public controls prescribe. To the extent to which these controls succeed in transforming the initial behaviour patterns into goal-adequate ones, a 'quasi-law of motion' is created – 'quasi' because it is not a 'given' property of the system (in the way the law of motion is treated in conventional analysis), but the product of extra-systemic public controls. Still, such quasi-laws of motion can serve as the minor premise in a deductive procedure, the conclusion of which can be tested in the traditional manner by observing the movements which these controls induce in the transformed system. However, this favourable outcome depends on a very important, but by no means assured condition, namely that the public controls are *successful*. In other words, there may be a divergence between what appear as suitable controls at the level of analysis and what they achieve in practice. In order to explain this possible clash, I must be more explicit about the logical nature of the heuristic method.

Heuristics is a search procedure that does not 'derive' its conclusions in the usual sense of the term. There are no strict rules, the observance of which could safely guide us from one step of analysis to the next. It is a *regressive procedure*, leading from the consequent to the antecedent and thus resulting in a chain of 'discoveries'. The successive steps are, in Michael Polanyi's words, 'logical leaps'. But they are not leaps in the dark. They start from a detailed description of the initial state – the place from which we leap – and an equally detailed description of the place upon which we want to land. The more detailed and precise those descriptions are, the narrower are the boundaries within which the solution lies. Furthermore, within those boundaries our search is guided by past experience, analogies and other clues. Yet it remains true that our ultimate insight springs from a non-rational act of 'imagination' as Charles Pierce, the modern rediscoverer of heuristics, formulated.

To reassure the reader that no mystical powers are involved in this account, I refer to *induction* – the preliminary of deductive reasoning because it establishes the major premise of any syllogism. There are also no binding rules, according to which a researcher could decide in favour of one among many possible hypotheses. Which one he chooses in the end, adopting what is called 'induction by enumeration' or Einstein's 'free creation of the mind', is neither a strictly determinable nor an arbitrary decision. The researcher 'senses' a structural relationship between the hypothesis he chooses and the problem he wants to solve.

Still, as in the case of induction, the findings of heuristic analysis can be accepted only provisionally. At best they are plausible, but always remain in need of empirical confirmation. The locus for such a test is the structure of the new system as it evolves under the impact of the applied controls.

There we touch the weak spot of every attempt at theorizing about social processes. Their 'particles' do not respond blindly to external stimuli, as do molecules or cells. The effect of any external control depends on the subjective response of the controlled. This in turn depends on whether or not they understand its purpose and agree with it, but also on the type of control, ranging from mere suggestion to outright coercion. This 'looseness' of the interrelation between controls and behaviour is inherent in the very nature of social systems. It is due, not to the logic of heuristics, but to the *Erkenntnisobjekt* to which it is applied – man in society.

Therefore prediction in this realm is reduced to pragmatic experimentation, and we must accept that our 'quasi-law of motion' can never be as strict as the laws that govern nature. Speaking as scientists, we certainly deplore this outcome. As members of a modern society we feel comforted that our controllers can never destroy our basic freedoms.

Lowe's Major Writings

(1926), 'Wie ist Konjunkturtheorie ueberhaupt maglich?' *Weltwirtschaftliches Archiv*, **24**.
(1935), *Economics of Sociology*, Allen and Unwin.
(1937), *The Prices of Liberty*, Hogarth Press.
(1940), *The Universities in Transformation*, Macmillan.
(1954), 'The Classical Theory of Economic Growth', *Social Research*, **21**.
(1965), *On Economic Knowledge*, Evenston.
(1976), *The Path of Economic Growth*, Cambridge University Press.
(1983), *On Economic Knowledge*, Armonk, New York: M.E. Sharpe, second edition, Chapters 10–12 and Postscript.

Other References

Heilbroner, R.L. (ed) (1969), *Economic Means and Social Ends: Essays in Political Economics*, Englewood Cliffs: Prentice Hall.
Oakley, A. (1987), *Essays in Political Economics: Public Control in a Democratic Society*, Brighton: Wheatsheaf Books.
Polya, G. (1957), *How to Solve It*, New York: Doubleday Anchor Books, Second edition.

Rosa LUXEMBURG (1871–1919) *Meghnad Desai*

Rosa Luxemburg was born in Zamosc, in the Russian part of Poland, on 5 March 1871. She was a pioneer in the Polish Social Democratic party and a leading member of the German SPD. She made a marriage of convenience with Gustav Lubeck to obtain German citizenship, but was associated with Leo Jogiches and Karl Liebknecht as comrades-in-arms. She took a doctorate in economics at the University of Zurich in 1898, her thesis topic being the industrial development of Poland.

The main claim of Rosa Luxemburg as a dissenting economist rests on her book *The Accumulation of Capital*. Written in 1913, this generated a lot of debate at the Second International in which Bukharin, Hilferding and Lenin participated. Her reply to her critics was published posthumously in 1921 as *Anti-Critique* though it was written earlier in 1915. Rosa Luxemburg can also be seen as a major influence on Kalecki who used the Marxian reproduction schemes as a starting point for macroeconomics.

Soon after Marx's death in 1883, the two remaining volumes of *Capital* were published from his notes by Engels. Each volume sparked off a controversy among Marxists most of whom were active in the SPD (the German Socialist party) or in fraternal socialist parties in Europe. The controversy centred on the contradiction between the model of capitalist crisis in Volume I, Part VII – the classic Marxian model of business cycles – and Volume II, Chapter 21 entitled 'Accumulation and Reproduction on an Extended Scale'. The latter presented the possibility of a crisis- and cycle-free growth of capitalism in a two-department Scheme of Expanded Reproduction (SER). Thus at the level of abstract theory, there seemed to be two different possible scenarios for capitalism.

At that time, Eduard Bernstein had mounted a revisionist attack on Marxism, arguing that business cycles had become less violent and more controllable in the late nineteenth century. He thus argued that Marx's theory should be abandoned in favour of a reformist programme. On the publication of Volume III of *Capital* in 1894, Bohm-Bawerk wrote a polemical attack arguing that Marx contradicted himself as between Volumes I and III and that his central contention – that profits arose from surplus value – was logically false.

Logical contradiction or error and empirical misfit were the twin attacks with which the Marxists of late nineteenth century had to contend. The period 1883–1913 was characterized by debate on these two controversies. Hilferding participated in both, arguing for a qualitative rather than a quantitative interpretation of the value-price transformation, conceding in effect the logical error alleged by Bohm-Bawerk. As for the cycle problem, he accepted the Bernstein critique in its empirical aspects and proposed a revision of Marx's theory of (competitive) capitalism, replacing it with a model of monopoly capitalism in which finance capital played a dominating role over industrial capital. He did not offer a new value theory, but grafted empirical details on to the classical Marxist doctrine.

Rosa Luxemburg has the unique distinction of mounting an *immanent* rather than an empiricist critique of Marx's theory of accumulation. The problem as she saw it was not so much the mismatch between theory and facts, but that the theory was left at too high a level of abstraction to be useful for examining facts. Marx's theory was incomplete; it needed repair and completion rather than revision. She was unwilling to repeat the litany of the faithful about Marx. She examined him critically and in so doing enriched classical Marxism. She did not find the competitive assumptions of Marx problematical, since she did not conceptualize competition or monopoly in terms of the number of competing firms or their size etc. Instead she saw the problem in the internal logic of the Scheme of Expanded Reproduction.

It may be briefly recalled that in these Schemes Marx puts forward a two-department model in which the output of the machine sector (Dept I) exceeds the input demand at current levels of activity: $Y1 > C1 + C2$ and that of wage goods (Dept II) falls short: $Y2 < [V1+V2+S1+S2]$ (using standard notation for constant and variable capital and surplus value; all in value units). Faced with this imbalance, Marx proposed that a decision by Dept I capitalists to invest a constant one-half proportion of surplus value (keeping the organic composition of capital unchanged and with Dept II capitalists absorbing the remaining output of Dept I) will ensure, year after year, sustained growth of the economy with no falling profit rate, no cycles and no breakdown.

The conflict of the Scheme with the rest of Marx's work is obvious. Was Marx trying to point out the difficulty of achieving equilibrium reproduction without overall planning (i.e. who would order the capitalists of Dept I to invest one-half of surplus value) or was this another of those gross contradictions between Volume I and subsequent volumes?

Rosa Luxemburg subjects Marx's Scheme to a thorough logical analysis. Unlike any other Marxist writer of her time (or even the anti Marxists for that matter) she reveals an immanent logical flaw in Marx's analysis. It is logically impossible, she says, for capitalists to invest surplus value *before* it is realized; there just is not the money. Since credit supply is not part of Marx's original Scheme, she is correct in saying that investment *plans* are not sufficient to ensure reproduction in a capitalist system. *Actual* expenditure has to be incurred, value produced has to be converted into money before it can be spent on expansion. If, however, the realization of surplus value is contingent upon the investment plans being actualized, we are in a logically circular situation. This is not the type of circularity that Dimitriev defended Ricardo against; nor is this the sort of vulgar attack that Bohm-Bawerk launched against Marx about the price value problem. Her objection to the Scheme does not hinge on the issue of their being no aggregate Departments, only individual capitalists in the 'real' world. Marx's scheme is logically inconsistent, although it may well be a super convergent two-sector growth model as Morishima (1973) has argued.

The vital point, though not made in this way by her, is that Marx had no business to consider *the circuit of commodity capital* in isolation from *the circuit of money capital*: the first third of Volume II contradicts the last third. Commodity fetishism being what it is, no one at the aggregate level, much less at the individual capital level, can operate in terms of labour values of constant capital etc. Where, she asked, did these Dept I capitalists get the money to buy these goods?

Accumulation and reproduction in capitalism cannot logically be conceptualized in terms of commodity capital circuits; money has to be at the beginning and the end of the process, as the first part of Volume II of *Capital* convincingly demonstrates. Thus the transitions from money to productive capital and from output produced back to money are essential links in the chains of converting (transforming) surplus value into profits. Money is thus not superficial or nonessential to capitalism. In playing with the SER, Marx overlooked this fundamental requirement. The incomplete and unpublished state in which he left his manuscript was probably partly to account for this.

But if Marx were to be treated critically rather than in an unquestioning way, it was vital that the incompleteness be repaired. Rosa Luxemburg saw clearly that the missing monetary links of the SER relate to the unsolved question of realization: who buys the ever-expanding output produced by the two Departments and, more important, why do they buy it? Thus effective demand is explicitly posed as a problem.

Given the two-Department/two-class framework, she argues that no purely internal/endogenous resolution is possible. Capitalists of the two Departments cannot be expected to go on accumulating and expanding the scale of their operations merely because that makes the numbers add up. Although she does not put it in these terms, Marx's scheme lacks an investment behaviour relationship: is it profitability that drives accumulation; is it the fear of competition or of erosion of profitability? The cycle of profit rate and accumulation working – the pressure in rate of surplus value that is in Part VII of Volume I of *Capital* – needs to be integrated with the two-Department scheme of Volume II. In particular, why does the profit rate not fall in SER as it does in the Volume I theory? Why is there no pressure via exhaustion of the reserve army on the rate of surplus value?

Rosa Luxemburg tackles these questions in the last section of the book which occupies eight chapters. Having rejected a purely internal logical solution (for instance by positing an *ex ante* equilibrium of plans and expectation as in Desai, 1979, Chapter 18), she looks for an extension of the model beyond the two Departments and two classes. She introduces in turn the pre-capitalist peasant economy within a country, the pre-capitalist periphery abroad, the developed capitalist economy in the international arena and finally government and militarism. Each extension puts Marx's model in a richer historical, as well as analytical, context: historically this is how capitalism *did* expand; logically these are the only ways it *can* expand. Of course once the various external spheres are conquered, internalized, the question to come up is, historically and logically, where can capitalism expand next?

One particular solution that she proposed to the realization problem was military spending, the very last chapter of *The Accumulation of Capital* being entitled 'Militarism as a Province of Accumulation'. It is here that Rosa Luxemburg suggested that military spending, being prototypically wasteful, could form a structural part of the reproduction strategy of capitalism. This was by treating military spending as Dept III. As was her method in the rest of the book, she set up a numerical example. She did not however treat the military sector as a 'Third' Department explicitly, but tacked it on separately. Armaments expenditure was seen as an indirect tax on wages, a diversion of variable capital to maintain an army. Excluding the armament output from the social product, it can be shown that the diversion of variable capital by a tax on wages causes a decline in total social product – a multiplier working negatively (see Rowthorn, 1980, for a corrected version of Rosa Luxemburg's example). However the armaments industry represents a market for Dept I; in an extreme case a suitably high taxation of wages can, via a balanced budget, leave the output for Dept I and total surplus value unchanged (see Desai, 1979, for details). Subsequent debates on militarism and Dept III have taken this idea further, but Rosa Luxemburg herself did not attach too much weight to this argument. Thus in her *Anti-Critique* she does not refer to militarism, although ironically her life ended in a struggle against militarism.

Critics have not always understood the power of her logical arguments. Thus the problem is not solved by saying that capitalists buy from each other for ever and ever; *effective demand* has to be backed by purchasing power, which presumes the sale of existing production. It is possible to envisage a bootstrapping mechanism of capitalists' expectations such that the plans of the two departments are consistent; but the logical structure for such investment behaviour is not in line with profit-orientated motives. If capitalists lived to clear each others' markets and not for their own profit, one might accept bootstrapping. Steady-state theories require that capitalists have always lived in the steady state and hence behave as if they always will and thereby bring about this happy outcome. (As the late Prof. Joan Robinson once said to me during a seminar I gave on this problem: capitalists of Dept I invest one-half of their surplus value because they have always done so. Where is the problem?) Such growth scenarios require rational expectations based on output growth as an objective of capitalists, together with steady-state growth in the past, to meet Rosa Luxemburg's cogent objection.

The point is that even *ex ante* equilibrium is difficult enough to envisage without begging the question. Actual capitalist behaviour at any except a single-good/single-capitalist level cannot be modelled as equilibrium without removing money, uncertainty and past history from the discussion. The problem of modelling capitalist dynamics as a monetary, disequilibrium phenomenon arising out of plausible behavioural rules for investing capitalists in a competitive framework still remains unsolved. Rosa Luxemburg's challenge has yet to be answered.

On the broader political economy front, she extended Marx's theory of capitalism to include the pre-capitalist formations at home and abroad, as well as integrating the State via militarism into the accumulation process.

The long years of Stalinist orthodoxy reduced the impact she should have had on the development of political economy. There is now, again, much to be gained from returning to Rosa Luxemburg.

Luxemburg's Major Writings

(1913), *The Accumulation of Capital* (translated by Agnes Schwarzchild), London: Routledge and Kegan Paul, 1951.
(1921), *The Accumulation of Capital – An Anti-Critique,* in N. Bukharin (ed), *Imperialism and the Accumulation of Capital* (translated by K. Tarbuck), London: Allen Lane, 1972.

Other References

Desai, M. (1979), *Marxian Economics*, Oxford: Basil Blackwell.
Morishima, M. (1973), *Marx's Economics*, Cambridge: Cambridge University Press.
Rowthorn, R. (1980), 'Rosa Luxemburg and the Political Economy of Militarism', in R. Rowthorn, *Capitalism, Conflict and Inflation*, London: Lawrence and Wishart.

Bruce McFARLANE (born 1936)

Bruce McFarlane was born in Mudgee (New South Wales). At school he read Joseph Dietzgen's *Excursions...* and Engels' *Ludwig Feuerbach*, both classic statements of the distinction between mechanical and dialectical materialism. At school and university he studied economic theory and the history of economic thought in order to understand the anatomy of civil society.

In the 1950s, the Faculty of Economics at the University of Sydney offered courses, taught by J.R. Wilson and E.L. Wheelwright, which included the study of Marx, Sraffa, Kaldor, Kalecki and Lange. Attracted to the deep analysis of these writers, McFarlane attempted in later years, not only to expound them to new generations of students (1982b, Parts I and II, and 1985), but also to apply the major insights to Australian conditions (1968a, Chapters 4-8, and 1982a). In company with Professor P.D. Groenewegen of the University of Sydney, he has also written the first comprehensive history of Australian economic thought since the offering of Crauford Goodwin, a visiting Canadian, almost 25 years ago (1990).

Graduating with first-class Honours in Economics, he failed to win the support of the Dean of the Faculty of Economics, Professor S.J. Butlin, in obtaining the normal scholarship to pursue the further study of economics in Cambridge. Instead he got the support of the Yugoslav Department of Cultural Relations with Foreign Countries, being appointed by its chief, Madame Regner, as 'Oceanic Scholar' for 1958.

As a result, McFarlane was able to study techniques and analysis of economic planning under conditions of market socialism. His mentor at this time was Dr Jakov Sirotkovic, a young and brilliant economic planner not long returned from post-graduate work in Manchester (later Premier of Yugoslavia). Following the completion of one-year's intensive instruction in the theory and practice of economic planning and the mysteries of the Yugoslav economy (1966, 1988), McFarlane joined the Perspective Planning Division of the Indian Planning Commission. He was for a time member of a small team headed by Michal Kalecki, who was visiting adviser to the Nehru administration on the Third Five-Year Plan (other members of the group included Vinod Prakhash, Jagdish Bhagwati, A.K. Sen and Ms I. Grace). Inevitably he came under the influence of the powerful personality of Michal Kalecki with whom he travelled to parts of India. Personal contact with Michal and Ada Kalecki left a deep impression that the study of political fetters on economic growth and of the institutional settings in particular countries must form an integral part of what later came to be called 'development economics'.

Consequently, after completing a five-year stint as a Research Fellow in Economics at the Australian National University under the good care of

Professor Heinz Arndt, McFarlane devoted a number of years to the study of political institutions, to the ideas of Mao Tse Tung insofar as they related to development strategy (1968b), to the Soviet industrialization debates of the 1920s and to Maurice Dobb's corpus of writings on these and related subjects. In 1976 he was appointed to the Chair in Politics at the University of Adelaide, where he continued to specialize in political economy. There he collaborated with the Professor of economics. G.C. Harcourt, in exposing students to the ideas of the 'Anglo-Italian school' which included Piero Sraffa, Joan Robinson, N. Kaldor, L.L. Pasinetti and D.M. Nuti.

In 1971 McFarlane became associated with the *Journal of Contemporary Asia,* which had been established in Stockholm to counter CIA investigations on Vietnam and the South East Asian national liberation movements. In 1980 he succeeded Hamza Alavi as co-editor with Peter Limqueco. Since then, and with the stationing of the *Journal* in Manila, he has been involved in fieldwork concerning the issues of labour and industry in countries of South East Asia conducting, with P. Limqueco and J. Odhnoff, a survey of some thousands of workers on 16 industrial sites in Manila, Bangkok, Penang and Kuala Lumpur (1989).

McFarlane has also increasingly been concerned with encouraging Asian scholars to analyse the development situation in their own countries and has offered them publishing outlets. What has been sought is a body of economic analysis which throws light on such topics as social relations in agriculture, problems of economic planning and economic democracy (1983), the emergence and consciousness of the Asian working class and the enrichment of the Marxian analysis of development. For McFarlane has from the beginning accepted the view that ruling classes live off the labour of others, and as both Dietzgen and Engels had demonstrated, this is an historical datum, not something that has to be proved by a logical syllogism.

McFarlane's Major Writings

(1966), 'Yugoslavia's Crossroads', in J. Saville and R. Miliband (eds), *The Socialist Register,* London: Merlin.

(1968a), *Economic Policy in Australia,* Melbourne: Cheshire.

(1968b), *The Chinese Road to Socialism: Economics of the Cultural Revolution* (with E. Wheelwright), Harmondsworth: Penguin. Also Amsterdam: Van Gennep, 1975; Torino: Einaudi, 1973; Tokyo: Simul, 1973; Oslo: Gylenal Norsk Forlag, 1974.

(1982a), 'A Kaleckian Analysis of the Australian Economic Crisis' (with D. Beresford), in P. Boreham and G. Dow (eds), *Work and Inequality,* Melbourne: Macmillan.

(1982b), *Radical Economics,* London: Croom Helm; Peking: China Resource Holdings.

(1983), *Neo-Marxian Theories of Development* (with P. Limqueco), London: Croom Helm; Tokyo: Tsuge Shobo, 1988.

(1985), *A Manual of Political Economy* (with D. Beresford), Manila: Karrel Inc.

(1988), *Yugoslavia: Politics, Economics and Society,* London: Frances Pinter.

(1989), *Labour and Industry in ASEAN* (with P. Limqueco and J. Odhnoff), Manila: JCA Publishers.

(1990), *A History of Australian Economics* (with P. Groenewegen), London: Routledge.

Ernest MANDEL (born 1923)

Ernest Mandel was born in 1923 into a Flemish-Jewish family. He was educated at the Université Libre de Bruxelles, the Ecole Pratique des Hautes Etudes (Sorbonne), where he got his certificate, and the Free University of Berlin, where he received his Ph.D. After working as a journalist and a member of the Economic Studies Commission of the Belgian Trade Union Federation, he became professor at the Vrije Universiteit (Brussels) in 1972, teaching Marxist economic theory and political science. Until retiring, he was also Director of the Institute of Political Studies at Vrije. He has been politically active all his life in the Fourth International.

His first book appeared in 1962, translated into English under the title *Marxist Economic Theory*. Many other books have followed. Mandel would consider the contributions discussed below as his main ones, in which he generally dissents from the mainstream of economic thought in the West as well as in the East. Some of the publications have been quite seminal; others are still largely ignored by 'official' science.

With his article 'The Heyday of Neo-Capitalism and its Aftermath' (1964), Mandel revived the long-wave theory of economic development under capitalism, generally known as the Kondratief-Schumpeter theory. But he counterposed the idea of 'long waves' to the concept of 'long cycles'. This meant rejecting any great regularity in the duration of long waves; it especially meant establishing the asymmetry between the turning of a 'long expansive wave' into a depression, and a 'long depressive wave' into a long-term expansion. While the first turn is inevitable, according to Mandel, the second one is not endogenous in the economic process properly speaking. It requires 'system shocks', to use a term introduced by Prof. Forrester. Only such external shocks can explain what might appear as a paradox from a Marxist point of view: a sudden and lasting upturn of the average rate of profit, without which no long-term increase in the rate of capital accumulation and of economic growth is possible. Such sudden upturns have occurred thrice in the history of capitalism: in 1848–49, in 1893 and in 1948 (in the Anglo-Saxon countries in 1940). It remains controversial whether a first reversal of this kind can also be dated to the beginning of the Napoleonic Wars.

According to Mandel, such system shocks are essentially the results of radical changes in the relationship of forces between the classes, which induce a radical increase in the rate of surplus-value (rate of exploitation of wage labour), and radical declines in the value of the money-commodity gold (as distinct from paper money or bank money). Revolutions, counter-revolutions, sudden radical expansions of the world market, wars, the appearance of a hegemonic capitalist power on the world market – all play an important role in these processes. In the light of this theory, the 'soft landing' of the long depression which started in the late 1960s and early 1970s is neither automatic nor certain. Once an upsurge of the rate of profit begins, however, a technological revolution tends to make the higher rate of growth cumulative for several decades.

These ideas were further developed in Chapter IV of the book *Late Capitalism* (which appeared in German in 1972) and especially in the book *Long Waves of Capitalist Development* (an extension of the Alfred Marshall Lectures which Mandel delivered at the University of Cambridge in 1978).

In his book *Late Capitalism*, Mandel tries to explain that, with World War II, there came about a new sub-phase in the history of capitalism which, while maintaining the main characteristics of monopoly capitalism (imperialism according to Lenin's vocabulary), adds significant new features. Mandel does not deny the important role of state intervention in the contemporary capitalist economy. But contrary to prevailing economic doctrine in the West (Samuelson, Galbraith, neo-Keynesians in general) and in the East (theory of 'state monopoly capitalism'), he considers the growing internationalization of the productive forces and of capital, triggered off by the third technological revolution, as the main trend of international capitalism in the last 50 years. The emergence of the multinational (transnational) corporation as the main form of business organization synthetically expresses this tendency. Mandel was thereby able to predict both the decline of American hegemony on the world market and the decline of the power (efficiency) of nation-states to intervene in the economic process before either actually occurred. He considers the relative decline of neo-Keynesianism in favour of neo-liberalism as the prevailing doctrine of economic policy not as the cause, but as the consequence, of that reversal.

In his 1984 article Mandel analysed the emergence of semi-industrialized capitalist countries (Brazil, South Korea, Taiwan, Mexico etc) as a result of transformations in the metropolitan countries and in these countries themselves. Since the latter remain dependent in the fields of finance and technology, Mandel rejects both the 'dependency' theory (which denies the possibility of semi-industrialization under capitalism) and the theory of 'sub-imperialism'. He sees the vulnerability of these economies especially enhanced by successive international recessions (generalized crises of over-production) in the metropolitan countries.

Mandel tries to restate and refine classical business cycle (crises) theory, out of grace in academic and even Marxist (neo-Marxist) circles during the long post-war boom. He rejects any mono-causal explanation of crises of overproduction and, following Marx, stresses that all the inner contradictions of the capitalist mode of production and of bourgeois society are involved in the process leading up to such crises. In particular, he rejects any attempt to explain crises of overproduction simply in terms of what occurs in the sphere of production. Instead he insists that the problems of realizing surplus-value, of markets, of precise division of 'purchasing power' (national income) into effective demand for each basic category of commodity (with its peculiar use-value) play a key role in bringing about such crises. These problems cannot be automatically 'solved' by the structure of output, the rate and amount of surplus-value etc.

This analysis, which implies a fundamental 'rehabilitation' of Volume II of Marx's *Capital* in the general corpus of economic theory, is further developed in the following: Chapters 10 and 11 of *Marxist Economic Theory*; Chapter IV of *Late Capitalism*; in Mandel's 'Introductions' to the first paperback edition of the three volumes of *Capital* in the Pelican Marx library, and in his books *The Second Slump* and *Cash, Crash and Crises*. The roles of inflation, of credit explosion ('the debt economy') and the subsequent emergence of a large sector of speculative capital inside the capitalist economy (both as a means of temporarily delaying the crisis and of making it more explosive in the long run) are extensively analysed in these successive books.

Mandel has devoted a systematic effort at determining the nature of the post-capitalist economies (Eastern Europe, China and especially the USSR) and at trying to lay out their long-term laws of motion. This was done especially in Chapters 15 and 16 of *Marxist Economic Theory*, in his article 'The Laws of Motion of the Soviet Economy' and in his book *Beyond Perestroika*. It is systematized most recently in *The Marxist Theory of Bureaucracy* (1990).

Mandel rejects any definition of these economies as 'socialist', as 'capitalist' (state capitalist), or as dominated by a new ruling class (bureaucratic collectivism). He sees them essentially as economies in transition between capitalism and socialism, frozen at that phase by the stranglehold of a privileged parasitic bureaucracy and by the stalemate of the worldwide struggle between capital and labour. In these economies, the law of value does not apply anymore (which proves that they are not capitalist), but it does still influence the economy (which confirms that they are not socialist or collectivist).

Contrary to a view long prevailing in left- as well as right-wing circles critical of these economies, Mandel sees their main feature not in a hypertrophy of Dept I (of productive accumulation, of heavy industry), but in a hypertrophy of Dept III (unproductive state expenditure, not only and not even essentially of a military nature). This enabled him to predict a trend in the rate of growth of these economies. The principal cause of this decline is not the intrinsic nature of central planning. It is due to the nature of bureaucratic management (mismanagement, including built-in disproportions), flowing from the very nature of bureaucracy itself.

The bureaucratic 'caste' is basically motivated by the appropriation, extension and consolidation of privileges in the sphere of consumption. It wants to maintain its control over the social surplus product only in order to keep its monopoly of political power, which is the basis of these material privileges. It does not share with the capitalist class any bias towards maximizing profit, output or economic efficiency at firm (plant) level. It is not interested in systematically insuring a greater efficiency of the system as such. Mandel affirms that the basic ills of the Soviet economy do not result from too much but rather from too little planning, while he accepts that the artificial reduction of market relations in the fields of distribution and of light industry, as well as agriculture, also contribute to the growing disfunctioning of the system.

This basic critique of bureaucratic (as opposed to socialist) planning and the analysis of the social nature of bureaucratic power (bureaucratic dictatorship) linked to it are related to what Mandel considers one of his main contributions to economic analysis: the nature of goods and services consumed by producers as 'indirect producer goods'.

According to Mandel, there is no direct mechanical relation between investment (productive accumulation) and the rate of economic growth. Any extension of accumulation which results in a reduction of the level of consumption desired by producers will lead to a rate of economic growth lower than expected (to a rise of the 'capital coefficient'). Realized (as opposed to expected) productivity of labour is not only a function of the level of technology, of labour organization etc. It is also a function of labour's willingness to work, of labour's motivation to contribute to the process of production, which is undermined by consumption levels below expectations (not to say by consumption levels which decline absolutely) and by the degree of producers' control over their work conditions. This fact in turn pushes the administrators (planners, managers, political bureaucrats) to increase the expanded dimensions of the apparatuses of control over producers, production and distribution, which in turn inflates tremendously unproductive expenditure (Dept III).

This is not only true for post-capitalist societies, but also increasingly for 'late capitalism'. This emerged embryonically during the final stages of World War II in Japan, where productivity of labour declined severely. Since the late 1960s, this has appeared on a broader and broader scale in many capitalist countries where, contrary to the prevailing (according to Mandel, largely mystifying) thesis, the 'work ethos' of the direct producers is in constant decline, resulting in a huge part of the productive potential of society being underutilized. In fact, the overall, total rationality of the system (as distinct from its partial rationality at the level of the firm) is in growing disarray which expresses itself in a general crisis of bourgeois social relations and values. Without a workforce which feels itself responsible for production because it is the master of the economy, the full potential of the third technological revolution cannot be realized. The search for increased 'quality of life', for a radical reduction of the work week, the irruption of ecological consciousness both into general social behaviour and into economic science, are but different expressions of this basic thrust.

According to Mandel, it follows that democratic socialist planning, planned workers' (producers') self-management and socialist democracy (political pluralism, the possibility for all citizens to decide consciously about key priorities in the allocation of scarce resources) represent a fundamental 'third model' of economic and social order, distinct from bureaucratic central (state) planning and from the generalized (prevailing) market economy. Mandel considers both these models as despotic, the despotism of the market (of the pocketbook) being no less detrimental to human self-determination and freedom than the despotism of the state (of the bureaucracy). Real human freedom and self-determination are linked to the capacity of men and women consciously to determine their fate (their priorities) in the field of economic life as well as in the realm of politics. 'Economic democracy' cannot be restricted to having the state reduce the worst evils of capitalism (*soziale Marktwirtschaft*). Economic democracy is just that: the power of the mass of the people to decide where priorities should lie in the field of investment and consumption. These ideas were developed in Mandel's polemic with Alex Nove in his articles 'In Defence of Socialist Planning' and 'The Myth of Market Socialism'.

Thus Mandel tries to develop a unified theory of economic and social/political science, based upon a dialectical (parametrical) concept of determinism as opposed to a mechanistic one. Such a concept of determinism integrates into the economic and social processes the possibility, nay the inevitability, of choice – but choice within certain given constraints and choice, in the last analysis, determined by social interests which will remain conflicting ones unless a classless society can one day be established.

Mandel's Major Writings

(1962), *Marxist Economic Theory*, London: Merlin Press.
(1964), 'The Heyday of Neo-Capitalism and its Aftermath', *Temps Modernes*, no. 219–20.
(1972), *Late Capitalism*, London: New Left Books/Verso Press.
(1976, 1978, 1981), 'Introductions' to Volumes I, II and III of *Capital*, The Penguin Marx Library.
(1979), *Long Waves Capitalist Development*, Cambridge University Press.
(1980), 'The Laws of Motion of the Soviet Economy', *Critique*.
(1983), *The Second Slump*, London: Verso Press.
(1984), 'Pays semi-coloniaux et pays dependants semi-industrialisés', *Quatrième International*, **13**, April.
(1986), 'In Defence of Socialist Planning', *New Left Review*, no. 159.
(1988), *Beyond Perestroika*, London: Verso Press.
(1988), 'The Myth of Market Socialism', *New Left Review*, no. 169.

(1989), *Cash, Crash and Crises* (in German).
(1990), *The Marxist Theory of Bureaucracy*, London: Verso Press.

Gardiner C. MEANS (1896–1988)   *Frederic S. Lee*

Gardiner Coit Means was born on 8 June 1896 in Windham (Connecticut) and grew up in Massachusetts and Maine. He entered Harvard at the age of 18, majoring in chemistry. With the outbreak of war in 1917, Means left Harvard to enlist in the Army and was sent to an officers' training camp in Plattsburgh (New York). After receiving his commission, he transferred to the Aviation Section of the Signal Corps in January 1918 and spent the rest of the war learning how to fly planes. Upon his discharge in January 1919, Means joined the Near East Relief, an organization dealing with Armenian refugees, and went off to Turkey. He was sent to Harput (now Elizaer) where he provided technical training and industrial expertise for the industrial activities set up by Near East Relief to finance the Armenian (and Greek) orphans under its care. As part of his job, Means had to engage in price and quantity bargaining with local merchants to get the industrial supplies he needed. Thus he experienced at first hand a market situation in which prices were determined in the course of carrying out the transaction itself.

Returning to the US in 1920, Means entered Lowell Textile School in September, a decision prompted by his exposure to handweaving in Turkey. After two years of studying wool manufacturing, he left in March 1922 to set up Means Weave Shop to make a high-quality (and high-priced) handwoven blanket of his own design that was very different from others then available. Through the running of his firm, Means became well acquainted with the Boston wool market and the textile machinery market, quickly coming to the conclusion that American industrial life was very different from what he had experienced in Turkey. In particular, Means found himself setting his price prior to any transaction in the market and then engaging in many sequential transactions at this price. For one five-year period in the 1920s, he maintained the same price, even though his costs and sales varied, and sold many thousands of blankets.

While still maintaining his textile firm, Means became interested in learning more about business methods and about the operation of the economy, such as the causes of business depressions and unemployment. Therefore he enrolled in Harvard's Department of Economics in February 1924. The course he took from W.Z. Ripley on the corporation and industry undoubtedly met his goal of learning how the American economy operated. He also listened to the James Bonbright lecture on public utility regulation. As for economic theory, Means took F.W. Taussig's well-known course and A. Young's 'Money and Banking'. In spite of this excellent introduction to neoclassical theory, Means found it hard to take it seriously as a means of explaining the operations of the American economy of the twentieth century, since to him it appeared relevant only to the kind of pre-industrial economy he had dealt with in Turkey. So by the time he received his M.A. in 1927, Means had become quite disenchanted with orthodox theory.

In 1927 A.A. Berle asked Means to help him with a research project on the modern corporation, the outcome of this collaboration being *The Modern Corporation and Private Property* (1932). Means's contribution to the book included the tripartite distinction between ownership, control and management; the economic arguments that the separation of ownership from control implied for the traditional theoretical roles of private property, wealth and the profit motive in directing economic activity and increasing social welfare; and the economic arguments regarding both the implications of firm size for costs and the coordination of economic activities by the forces of supply and demand in the marketplace. However, the main theoretical focus of *The Modern Corporation* was on the implications of the separation of ownership from control; Means did not pursue these implications until he began writing his Ph.D. dissertation.

After finishing his work for Berle and the subsequent publication of some articles in the *American Economic Review* and the *Quarterly Journal of Economics*, the Harvard Department of Economics suggested that Means could combine these articles with an additional interpretive section for his doctoral dissertation. This Means did and in January 1933 submitted 'The Corporate Revolution: The Modern Corporation and Its Effect on Certain Fundamental Economic Postulates'. However, his committee, which included E.S. Mason and E.H. Chamberlain, did not accept the dissertation because they felt that the theoretical section was not 'well developed'. Perhaps the real truth behind the rejection was their dislike of the theoretical interpretations which Means drew from the factual evidence – which boldly attacked neoclassical theory. Nevertheless, possibly with some prodding from Berle, the committee later accepted the first part of the dissertation which contained the factual material, awarding Means his Ph.D. in 1933.

In the summer of that year, Means went to Washington to take a position as Economic Adviser on Finance to Henry Wallace, the Secretary of Agriculture under Roosevelt. In taking the job, Means took it for granted that he would be trying to develop policies and instruments that would make the economy work more effectively. However he found that his suggestions were not taken seriously by the policy-makers. Believing that his ideas might gain more attention if accompanied by dramatic empirical evidence, Means undertook, in the late spring of 1934, a statistical analysis of wholesale prices to bring out the basic difference in behaviour between farm commodity prices and the administered prices of industry. He found the results much more startling than he had expected as well as in conflict with neoclassical price theory. Consequently, drawing upon his previous analysis of administered prices, Means used the statistical evidence as a lead to writing a paper delineating the reasons for the failure of the National Recovery Administration (NRA) and the Agricultural Adjustment Administration (AAA) to formulate industrial policy and suggested possible techniques to improve the situation. He titled the paper 'NRA and AAA and the Reorganization of Industrial Policy Making' and had it widely distributed. The paper generated a great deal of response with regard to Means's statistical and economic analysis of administered prices and his discussion of industrial policy-making. It was eventually published in January 1935 as a government document under the title 'Industrial Prices and their Relative Inflexibility' (reprinted as Chapter 3 in 1991).

In 1935, Means became the Director of the Industrial Section of the Industrial Committee of the National Resources Committee (NRC). There he initiated a research project to develop a model of the American economy that could then be used for indicative national economic planning. In November 1936, Means wrote a memorandum (reprinted as Chapter 5 in 1991) on this subject to the NRC in which he argued that one of the concerns of a federal planning organization should be to bring about and maintain an effective overall balance of the use of the nation's resources. This implied an expansion of his research project to include an investigation into the forces which affect the coordination and organization of economic activity and hence the overall balance of the economy. The NRC accepted Means's suggestion, thus permitting him to develop a truly comprehensive multi-industry model of the American economy. The fruits of this research were published in *Patterns of Resource Use* and in *The Structure of the American Economy Part I: Basic Characteristics*. Although each of these develops various features of Means's multi-industry model of the American economy, no single publication presented the model in its entirety. This was due to the rise of American Keynesianism and its approach to national economic planning.

Aside from his work with Wallace and the NRC, Means also found time to write a short note (reprinted as Chapter 6 in 1991) in which he argued that corporate enterprise expenditure was a function of the current and the preceding year's level of production. This is quite possibly the first description of the sales-accelerator investment function popularized by Robert Eisner in the 1960s.

In 1943 Means became associate director of research for the Committee for Economic Development (CED), a business-sponsored, private research group originally concerned with government policies to ensure a full-employment transition to a peacetime economy. While at the CED he instigated the collection of statistical series on money flows, now regularly published by the Federal Reserve Board in its flow of funds accounts. He retired from the Committee in 1958 and spent his remaining years writing, lecturing, appearing before Congressional Committees and working as an economic consultant for several companies involved in antitrust suits.

In the theoretical section of his dissertation, which was titled 'Certain Theoretical Implications of the Modern Corporation', Means presented a detailed explanation of how the existence of the large corporation and the separation of ownership from control called into question the 'scientific' validity of neoclassical economic theory. Restricting himself to what he considered the most fundamental postulates of the theory – the principle of supply and demand in determining prices, the determinacy of costs, the saving and investment process, and the role of the profit motive in directing economic activity – Means argued that these could not be sustained in their traditional form once the large corporation and the separation of ownership from control became the dominant features of the economy. In particular, he argued that the demise of the principle of supply and demand in determining prices rested primarily upon the sheer size of the corporation enterprise, as opposed to the separation of ownership from control. Consequently, Means devoted a chapter of the theoretical section, which he titled 'The Modern Corporation and Basic Economic Thought', to the concept of administered prices and its destructive implications for supply and demand determination of prices.

Throughout the 1930s, Means maintained his interest in administered prices and their implications for the coordination of economic activity. Conceiving the economy as a continuous monetary flow of economic activity coordinated by market and administered prices, he sought to dispel the notion that the American economy operated as a cybernetic mechanism which automatically tended to eliminate underutilization of all economic resources. Given the existence of administered prices, Means argued that a serious deficiency of buying is unlikely to be corrected by any of the economic forces inherent in a modern economy in such a way as to bring about the full use of resources. Thus he concluded that the underutilization of economic resources was a problem of social organization which could only be corrected through social or government industrial policy-making.

During the 1940s and 1950s Means directed his energies towards developing his concept of administered prices into a doctrine. In 1943 he extended the concept to international trade (see Chapter 9 in 1991). He also devoted much effort to developing a macroeconomic equilibrium model which included both flexible and administered prices, such as found in the later Hickian flex-fix price models (see Chapter 10 in 1991). However he spent the majority of his time developing the foundation for his doctrine of administered prices based on the behaviour of firms and their approach to pricing. Stung by comments that he failed to utilize Chamberlin's description and analysis of monopolistic competition, Means first attempted to fashion an explanation of administered prices based on traditional monopoly analysis, but without utilizing the marginalist apparatus associated with the Chamberlin-Robinson theories. However, when the Brookings report on pricing in big business appeared in 1958, Means quickly refashioned his explanation of administered prices, basing it on target rate of return pricing procedures. Second, in the 1940s Means had begun to dismiss the notion that management tried to maximize current profits. He subsequently reached the more revolutionary position that management seeks neither short- nor long-period maximum profits nor frames its business strategies in terms of long or short periods. Rather management seeks profits over time which would not induce entry or otherwise inhibit the growth of corporate profits or the corporation itself. Third, Means integrated the concept of the pricing period and the flow principle of production into his definition of administered prices. Fourth, Means began to take seriously the importance of perverse prices which John M. Blair had brought to his attention. Lastly, Means worked on his concept of administrative inflation.

These developments during the 1940s and 1950s permitted Means to develop his doctrine of administered prices; this delineated the forces that affected the coordination of economic activity and determined the actual manner in which the modern corporate economy operated. With the doctrine in hand, Means could not only account for the persistent inflation that characterized the American economy since World War II, but also propose economic policies to deal with it (see 1962a, 1962b and Chapters 15, 16, 17 and 19 of 1991). More generally, given the economic relationships embodied in the doctrine – such as target rate of return pricing, administered prices, administrative inflation, market power and non-market control of economic activity – Means could emphasize their human and institutional nature and hence their amenability by social action. Thus, since the modern economy did not automatically tend to full employment, the implication of the doctrine of administered prices was that non-market government involvement in guiding economic activity was both necessary and desirable if the quality of human life was to be enhanced. Since the visible hand of coordination is both a necessary component as well as a necessary outcome of the doctrine, Means clearly developed a non-neoclassical analysis of the modern economy.

Means saw his doctrine of administered prices as a direct challenge to neoclassical economics whose adherents responded in a variety of ways, most commonly by denying the empirical existence of administered prices. The most noted attack in this regard came from George Stigler in his book with James Kindahl called *The Behavior of Industrial Prices* (1970). Upon examining the transaction price data which was collected especially for his study, Stigler claimed that it did not support the existence of administered prices. Means analysed the same price data and came to the opposite conclusion – that it did confirm them. His findings were published in the *American Economic Review* in 1972 and Stigler responded with a piece in the same journal in 1973. Means in turn submitted a rejoinder, alleging no less than 17 errors of fact in the interpretation of his position made by Stigler (reprinted as Chapter 12 in 1991). The editor of the *AER* refused to publish the paper. However subsequent research by D. Carlton on the Stigler-Kindahl price data (1986) clearly show that Means was correct in his allegations and that Stigler came very close to perpetrating a fraud when he claimed otherwise.

Means died on 15 February 1988, his obituary appearing in many newspapers in the US and elsewhere. However economists generally ignored his death. Perhaps this was fitting for an economist who had served his country and fellow citizens so well but at the same time – by trying to forge new non-neoclassical concepts and pictures of economic relationships appropriate for a modern economy – had incurred the displeasure of mainstream neoclassicists.

Means's Major Writings

(1932), *The Modern Corporation and Private Property* (with A.A. Berle), New York: Macmillan. Revised edition, Harcourt, Brace & Woruld, 1967.

(1938), *Patterns of Resource Use*, Washington, D.C.: Government Printing Office.

(1939), *The Structure of the American Economy.* Part I: *Basic Characteristics*, Washington, D.C.: Government Printing Office.

(1962a), *Pricing Power and The Public Interest*, New York: Harper and Brothers.

(1962b), *The Corporate Revolution In America*, New York: Crowell-Collier Press.

(1991), *The Heterodox Economics of Gardiner C. Means: A Collection*, edited by F.S. Lee and W.J. Samuels, Armonk: M.E. Sharpe.

Other References

Carlton, D. (1986), 'The Rigidity of Prices', *American Economic Review*, 637–58.

Eichner, A.S. (1980), 'Gardiner C. Means', *Challenge*, **22** (January–February), 56–9.

Lee, F.S. (1988), 'A New Dealer in Agriculture: G.C. Means and the Writing of *Industrial Prices*', *Review of Social Economy*, **46**.

Lee, F.S. (1990), 'From Multi-Industry Planning to Keynesian Planning: Gardiner Means, the American Keynesians, and National Economic Planning at the National Resources Committee', *Journal of Policy History*, 1990.

Lee, F.S. (1990), '*The Modern Corporation* and Gardiner Means's Critique of Neoclassical Economics', *The Journal of Economic Issues*, **24**.

Lee, F.S. (1990), 'G.C. Means's Doctrine of Administered Prices', in P. Arestis and Y. Kitromilides (eds), *Theory and Policy in Political Economy: Essays in Pricing, Distribution and Growth*, Aldershot: Edward Elgar.

Nossiter, B. (1962), 'The World of Gardiner Means', *The New Republic*, **146**, 7 May, 17–20.

Samuels, W.J. and Medema, S.G. (1990), *Gardiner C. Means's Institutional and Post-Keynesian Economics: An Interpretation and Assessment*, Armonk: M.E. Sharpe.

Ronald L. MEEK (1917–1978)   *Michael C. Howard*

Ronald Meek was born in Wellington (New Zealand) in July 1917. Here, at university in the 1930s, he read law and economics. Beginning in 1946 he studied under Piero Sraffa for a Ph.D. at Cambridge. His thesis, completed in 1949, was titled 'The Development of the Concept of Surplus in Economic Thought from Mun to Mill'. The idea of a 'surplus tradition in economics' developing parallel with, and in antagonistic relation to, the dominant tradition of supply and demand theory was to be the focus of much of his subsequent work. In 1948, Meek moved to the University of Glasgow to take up a teaching post in the department of political economy. He remained there until his appointment to the Tyler Chair of Economics at the University of Leicester in 1963, which he held until his death in 1978.

Meek's scholarship was exceedingly wide-ranging. His first publication was *Maori Problems Today* (1943), while at the time of his death he was working on a book dealing with the use of linear algebra in social theory (1986). During the 1950s he wrote a series of articles on Soviet economic thought, and in the 1960s published numerous papers on electricity pricing as part of his successful attempt to establish a specialism in public sector economics at the University of Leicester. He also found the time to write *Hill Walking in Arran* (1963) and *Figuring Out Society* (1971) which dealt with quantitative techniques in social and economic theory. One notable aspect of this latter work was the explanation of the concept of an 'optimum' in the context of the development of the science of hanging in nineteenth-century Britain – a mode of illustration designed to ensure that, once read, it would never be forgotten. This is but one example of Meek's very great abilities as a teacher. He put immense effort into his lectures and tutorials, and his writings are a model of structure and clarity.

Nevertheless, it will be as an historian of economic thought that Ronald Meek will be best remembered. Although he dealt extensively with the whole period between Physiocracy and neoclassicism, there were four areas of special concern to him: the labour theory of value, the surplus tradition in economic analysis, the ideas of Adam Smith and those of Karl Marx.

Meek's *Studies in the Labour Theory of Value* (1956) analysed the development of the theory from its medieval origins to its refinement in modern Marxism. The motivation for writing the *Studies* arose from Meek's correspondence in the early 1950s with Joan Robinson, and in particular from his inability to persuade her that she had failed to appreciate the structure and significance of the labour theory of value. He sought to show, therefore, that 'the labour theory was good science in Marx's time' and also 'that it was good science today' (p.7). The work not only stands as a piece of scholarship in its own right, but is also notable for the importance that Meek gave to the qualitative purposes which the theory served. He emphasized that it was through the medium of labour value categories that the social relations of commodity-producing economic systems were conceptualized. Marx, of course, was seen as doing so most explicitly and self-consciously, but Meek was able to trace the embryonic forms of the idea in earlier work on which Marx built. This explains why Meek viewed the 'historical transformation problem' as so important to Marxism. The transformation of values into prices of production, and surplus values into profits, was not simply a logical exercise; it was also, according to Meek's interpretation of Marx, a process in history as changing forms of commodity production made their impact upon quantitative economic variables and patterns of economic development. The capitalist mode of production emerged gradually, as the capital-labour relation dominated that of simple commodity production; capitalist competition intensified and created powerful tendencies towards the equalization of the rate of profit throughout the economy; and landed property, merchant and money capital were subordinated to the new mode of production. Meek argued that the labour theory of value, properly understood, was designed to treat these processes, and was misrepresented if considered only as a theory of equilibrium price in the conventional sense.

It was from this perspective, Meek also claimed, that the overall structure of Marx's *Capital* was best appreciated. It reflected the historical development of commodity-producing economies, albeit in a theoretically purified form. Meek christened this procedure 'the logical-historical method' and his description of it is of great relevance for assessing the most recent vintages of Marxian political economy. Both the 'Sraffian Marxists' and the otherwise very different 'Rational Choice Marxists' employ comparative static methodology extensively. In Meek's interpretation of Marx, this is not wholly out of accord with Marx's own manner of developing scientific propositions. However, it simultaneously indicates important limitations in the work of modern Marxists. Their use of the comparative static method follows that of neoclassical theorists and thereby requires that the exogenous elements are assumed to be independent of each other. Only then can singular *ceteris paribus* changes be made and their causal effect on endogenous variables be assessed. Marx, by contrast, considers only the 'special' cases which he believed were evident in history. Causal relations are understood by comparing historical configurations which are different in a number of respects, so that singular *ceteris paribus* variations cannot be legitimately attempted because changes in (what neoclassical economists would consider to be) parameters are joined together historically. Marx's method is thus expressly intended to capture actual interdependencies and to assess the significance of real changes in history; modern Marxists eschew this by requiring their methodology to handle hypothetical cases in the manner of neoclassical theorists.

Meek's research into the labour theory of value and Marx's method was part of a broader concern to establish the credentials of the 'surplus tradition' in economic thought against the views of orthodox intellectual historians. Undoubtedly, he derived much support from Sraffa's *Production of Commodities by Means of Commodities* (1960). Meek wrote one of the two most insightful reviews of this book, claiming that it provided a basis for a 'magnificent rehabilitation' of classical and Marxian political economy (1961). Subsequently, he elaborated on how Sraffa's framework could be used to treat Marx's problems in a Marxist fashion (see 'Introduction' to the second edition of *Studies in the Labour Theory of Value* and 1977). Meek wrote before the results of the Sraffa-based criticism of Marx, pioneered by Ian Steedman, were firmly established and consequently tended to minimize the tensions which actually exist between the two paradigms. Nevertheless, it remains broadly true that the points which he emphasized as crucial in connecting Sraffa to Marx were not affected by this critique; indeed, they are accepted by most Sraffians.

Meek was much more critical of Marx's 'laws of motion'. His analysis of the 'immiseration thesis' (1962b) remains one of the best treatments of Marxian distribution theory. His evaluation of the falling rate of profit (1960) has been overshadowed by Okishio's proof that cost-reducing innovations can never result in a lower profit rate in the way in which Marx believed they could. Nevertheless, Meek's examination of the various economic forces affecting profits is still useful for understanding why Marx thought as he did, and why he was wrong to do so. Meek also showed that while the account of the 'reserve army of the unemployed' was more soundly based, Marx had been unduly influenced by the transitory effects which capitalist production had had upon the pre-capitalist economy (1968).

Much of Meek's analysis of the 'surplus tradition' from Physiocracy, through Marx, to Sraffa was parallel to that of Maurice Dobb's *Theories of Value and Distribution Since Adam Smith* (1973). But there were also important differences. Meek never accepted that neoclassical theory had been completely undermined in the 'Capital Controversies' of the 1960s. He did not dispute that the Clarkian and Austrian forms of neoclassicism had been shown to be seriously defective, but he recognized that the other formulations of supply and demand theory were built on more secure foundations. In this Meek was undoubtedly correct, as theoretical developments after his death have shown. The Walrasian counter-attack on the conceptual structure of *The Production of Commodities* has exposed extremely serious limitations in the Sraffian framework and has clarified how General Equilibrium theory avoids them. Game theory, which was initially formulated by Edgeworth and has been formalized rather erratically over the last 50 years, is completely immune from the critical force of Sraffian economics. Meek criticized neoclassical theory, but it was the ideological vision and its origin in apologetic defences of capitalism which he emphasized (see 1950, 1957 and 1972b). Furthermore, Meek regarded Adam Smith much more favourably, relative to Ricardo, than did either Dobb or Sraffa. Two reasons lay behind this judgement, each buttressed by extensive research.

First, Smith was recognized as the leading member of the 'Scottish Historical School' which anticipated much of Marx's materialist conception of history. Meek summarized this as follows:

> [The] theory was that society 'naturally' or 'normally' progressed over time through four more or less distinct and consecutive stages each corresponding to a different mode of subsistence, these stages being defined as hunting, pasturage, agriculture and commerce. To each of these modes of subsistence... there corresponded different sets of ideas and institutions relating to law, property, and government and also different sets of customs, manners, and morals. [This] four-stages theory... was destined not only to dominate socio-economic thought in Europe in the latter half of the eighteenth century, but also to become of crucial significance in the subsequent development of economics, sociology, anthropology and historiography, right down to our own time (1976, p.2).

Meek also sought to understand how this view of history had arisen, and why the Scottish Historical School was so advanced relative to other thinkers of the time.

Second, Meek argued, Smith reformulated the class typology which he inherited from the Physiocrats, and in doing so provided the basic conceptual framework of the modern surplus tradition.

> One of the crucial features of a change from one paradigm to another... according to Professor Kuhn, is a 'shift in scientific perception', of such a character that 'objects that were grouped in the same set before are grouped in different ones afterward and vice versa'. It was precisely a 'basic shift of perception' of this type which was the main achievement of the *Wealth of Nations*. As I see it, the really central element of that work was Smith's new division of society into landlords, wage earners and capitalists. ... Before Smith, the socio-economic structure had almost always been defined in terms of a pattern which either virtually ignored the existence of the third of these 'orders', or implicitly denied its 'great, original and constituent' character by including it in some other 'order'. ... [T]his new way of looking at society made all the difference ... it paved the way for the idea that the drive by the third 'constituent order' to maximise its profits and to accumulate capital was the mainspring of the mechanism of the economic process – the principal medium ... through which the famous 'invisible hand' worked to improve human society. ... There was scarcely a single element in Smith's system which was new ... [but Smith made a paradigm shift] ... and when it ha[d] been made all the other elements fell into place – and very often into a new place. Thus it seems very unhelpful to regard Smith, as some historians have done, as a mere synthesizer (see 1973b, pp. viii–vii).

Meek's immense respect for the intellectual stature of Smith was evident in his dedication to the editing of *Adam Smith: Lectures on Jurisprudence* (1978). George Houston describes this work in the following way:

> The bicentenary of Adam Smith was to be marked by several publications, one of which was going to be onerous, indeed tedious, to prepare. A set of student notes for Smith's lectures on Jurisprudence had become available, the text had to be deciphered, annotated, edited and matched against Cannan's version. Although joint author with David Raphael and Peter Stein, Ronald accepted the main responsibility for the volume, especially the text, and he spent hours and hours on that text in the most meticulous checking and counter-checking. What he called his monocular vision must have made the task even more daunting for him (Bradley and Howard, 1982, p. vi).

Ronald Meek was thus a 'dissenter' not only within economics generally, but within the 'surplus tradition' as well. It is a mark of his success, however, that this judgement is truer for the beginning of his career in 1948, than it was at the end, 30 years later. Together with Maurice Dobb and Piero Sraffa, he did much to keep classical and Marxian ideas alive after the Second World War, and in the process contributed substantially to their elevation from the outer periphery to a more secure position in the intellectual development of economics. At the same time, however, Meek proved able to keep this in perspective. He recognized that the 'surplus tradition' had a vibrant and increasingly refined competitor in the evolution of supply and demand theory. Thus he did not exaggerate the intellectual stature of either Smith or Ricardo, nor that of Marx and Sraffa. Great economists they each were, but Meek realized that they did not monopolize all that was worthwhile in the history of economic thought, and that the surplus paradigm had to prove its worth by interpreting modern problems in an analytically satisfactory manner.

Meek's Major Writings

(1943), *Maori Problems Today*, Wellington: Progressive Publishing House.

(1950), 'The Decline of Ricardian Economics in England', *Economica*, **17**, 43–62.

(1956), *Studies in the Labour Theory of Value*, London: Lawrence and Wishart. Second edition, 1973.

(1957), 'Is Economics Biased? A Heretical View of a Leading Thesis in Schumpeter's History', *Scottish Journal of Political Economy*, **4**, 1–17.

(1960), 'The Falling Rate of Profit', *Science and Society*, **24**, 36–52.

(1961), 'Mr Sraffa's Rehabilitation of Classical Economics', *Scottish Journal of Political Economy*, **8**, 119–36.

(1962a), *The Economics of Physiocracy : Essays and Translations*, London: Allen and Unwin.

(1962), 'Marx's "Doctrine of Increasing Misery"', *Science and Society*, **26**, 422–41.

(1963), *Hill Walking in Arran*, Arran Tourist Association. Second edition 1972.

(1967), *Economics and Ideology and Other Essays: Studies in the Development of Economic Thought*, London: Chapman and Hall.

(1968), 'Karl Marx and the Industrial Revolution', in R.V. Eagly (ed), *Events, Ideology and Economic Theory*, Detroit: Wayne State University Press, 120–23.

(1971), *Figuring Out Society*, London: Collins.

(1972a), *Quesnay's 'Tableau Economique'* (with M. Kuczynski), London: Macmillan for the Royal Economic Society and the American Economic Association.

(1972b), 'Marginalism and Marxism', *History of Political Economy*, 4, 498–511.

(1973a), *Turgot on Progress, Sociology and Economics*, Cambridge University Press.

(1973b), *Precursors of Adam Smith*, London: Dent.

(1976), *Social Science and the Ignoble Savage*, Cambridge University Press.

(1977), *Smith, Marx and After: Ten Essays in the Development of Economic Thought*, London: Chapman and Hall.

(1978), *Adam Smith: Lectures on Jurisprudence* (with D.D. Raphael and P.G. Stein), Oxford: Clarendon Press.

(1986), *Matrices and Society* (with I. Bradley), Harmondsworth: Penguin.

Other References

Blaug, M. (1987), 'Classical Economics', in J. Eatwell, M. Milgate and P. Newman (eds), *The New Palgrave: A Dictionary of Economics*, Macmillan, Volume I, 434–45.

Bradley, I. and Howard, M. (eds) (1982), *Classical and Marxian Political Economy: Essays in Honour of Ronald L. Meek*, Macmillan.

Dobb, M. (1973), *Theories of Value and Distribution Since Adam Smith*, Cambridge University Press.

Garegnani, P. (1987), 'Surplus Approach to Value and Distribution', in *The New Palgrave*, Volume IV, 560–74.

Howard, M.C. and King, J.E. (1989), *A History of Marxian Economics, Volume I, 1883–1929*, Macmillan and Princeton University Press.

Howard, M.C. and King, J.E. (1991), *A History of Marxian Economics, Volume II, 1929–1990*, Macmillan and Princeton University Press.

Hyman P. MINSKY (born 1919)

Hyman P. Minsky was born in Chicago (Illinois) on 23 September 1919. His mother, Dora Zakon, had been active in the nascent Trade Union movement; his father, Sam Minsky, was active in the Jewish section of the Socialist party in Chicago, having left Russia in the aftermath of the unsuccessful revolution of 1905. According to family legend, the courtship of Dora Zakon by Sam Minsky began at a gala that the Jewish section of the Socialist party of Chicago held to celebrate the 100th anniversary of the birth of Karl Marx.

Minsky received his elementary and secondary education in Chicago, Lima (Ohio) and New York City. He attended the University of Chicago beginning in 1937 and graduated four years later with a degree in Mathematics. In the same year he commenced his graduate work in Economics also at Chicago. In the summer of 1942 he worked on the input/output study of W.W. Leontief at Harvard University, and stayed on there as a graduate student.

In February 1943, he entered the US Army and served in the Transportation Corp in New York City, Great Britain, France and Germany until late 1945. He then stayed in Berlin as a civilian employee in the manpower division of the US Military Government for Germany until August 1946. In September 1946 he returned to Harvard to resume his graduate studies, finishing his M.P.A. in 1947 and his Ph.D. in 1954.

He began his teaching career at Carnegie Tech (now Carnegie Mellon) University in the summer of 1947. Minsky worked on the Raymond Goldsmith study of savings in the summer of 1948. He was Assistant to Associate Professor at Brown University from 1949–1957, then visiting Associate Professor and Associate Professor at the University of California Berkeley from 1957–1965. In 1955 he married Esther De Pardo; they had two children: Diana, born in 1964 and Alan, born in 1965. From 1965 until his retirement he was Professor of Economics at Washington University (St Louis) and Professor Emeritus since 1 July 1990. Since his retirement from Washington University he has also been a Distinguished Scholar at the Jerome Levy Economics Institute (Bard College).

Hyman Minsky's professional interest in Economics was an outgrowth of a political and social commitment, as well as a reaction to the economic and social climate of his youth. He was a member of the youth division of the American Socialist party while in secondary school in Chicago.

As an undergraduate he had a strong interest in formal logic, the philosophy and methodology of science and the theory of probability. He intended to specialize in Mathematics and Physics despite his strong interest in social sciences.

The first work of Keynes that Minsky read was the *Treatise on Probability*. An emphasis upon the need to act in the face of uncertainty characterizes Minsky's view of both Keynes's *General Theory* and the capitalist economy. Minsky holds that present views about the uncertain future are determinants of the relative money prices of capital and financial assets, where the money price of money is always one.

Minsky treats the effect of uncertainty upon economic decisions by claiming that businessmen, portfolio managers and bankers are in a position logically analogous to that of a scientist when newly-available evidence tends to falsify accepted theory; a vacuum exists until a new theory can be formulated and accepted which resolves the doubts engendered by the new evidence. For a scientist, uncertainty prompts the development of research programmes in order to reach a clear perception of what constitutes 'normal' science. To businessmen, portfolio managers and bankers, uncertainty means that decisions are made in the absence of firm knowledge. For both the doubting scientist and the sceptical businessman, 'I don't know' is often the most appropriate answer to questions relevant to decision-making.

In the winter of Minsky's second year at the University of Chicago, Oscar Lange gave a short course for the Socialist party of Chicago on 'The Economic Theory of Socialism'. Minsky attended the lectures and became interested in economics as a discipline. Under the influence of Professor Lange he decided to shift his major interest from mathematics and physics to economics, although he remained a mathematics major, pioneering a mathematics-major/economics-minor degree.

Throughout the time they overlapped at the University of Chicago, Lange was a major influence upon Minsky's development, teaching the first course in which the then new economics of Keynes was the principal subject. Lange gave a precise, though somewhat mechanical, interpretation of Keynes.

Professor Henry Simons taught one of the first courses Minsky took in Economics after his decision to specialize. Although a strong advocate of the capitalist way of organizing production, Simons was at that time sympathetic to the ideals and objectives of Democratic Socialism, as evidenced in his writings. However, he doubted that the socialist mechanism would lead to the achievement of socialist goals. He was also aware of the shortcomings of capitalism, in particular the fact that a capitalist market economy led to an income distribution that was incompatible with democracy. He also deplored the debt deflations and therefore deep depressions which were characteristics of any capitalist economy with the financial structure necessary for capitalism to be dynamic. Simons encouraged dialogue with his students. Minsky's location of the principle flaw of laissez-faire capitalism in its financial structure (necessary if the capitalist way of managing the investment process is to be compatible with a dynamic economy) is a debt that the financial instability hypothesis owes to the influence of Henry Simons.

Other influences upon Minsky while he was at Chicago were Professors Jacob Viner, Paul Douglas, who became a liberal US Senator, and Gerhard Meyer, who taught an entire generation of University of Chicago undergraduates.

In the spring of 1942 Lange arranged for Minsky to spend the summer at Harvard University helping on a post-war planning research project of Professor Wasilly Leontief. This led to Minsky doing his doctoral degree at Harvard after World War II, although if Lange had remained an academic in America he quite likely would have taken his doctoral degree with Lange.

At Harvard the major influences upon Minsky were Alvin Hansen, John Williams (then a teaching assistant in their joint course on Money and Banking) and Joseph Schumpeter. After World War II Minsky became closely associated with Jerome Lettvin, Walter Pitts and Oliver Selfridge who were working with Professor Norbert Weiner at MIT.

Minsky began his doctoral dissertation research under Schumpeter; his untimely death in early 1950 meant that the dissertation was finished under the supervision of Leontief. Schumpeter's vision of the capitalist process required an integration of financial markets and investment behaviour which matched the approach that Minsky had acquired at Chicago. One facet of

Minsky's vision is that Keynesian theory does deal explicitly with an economy that is dynamic in the sense that Schumpeter described: Keynes's monetary theory was what Schumpeter needed to complete his own theory of the developing capitalist economy.

During Minsky's time at Harvard, Alvin Hansen was the leading apostle of Keynesian economics. From the perspective of the interpretations of Keynes which are associated with Minsky, Hansen's reading was strangely mechanical as it largely neglected the significance of money and finance. Uncertainty, which was so critical to Keynes's explanation of the dynamics of capitalist economies, was virtually ignored by Hansen.

Hansen's vision was dominated by the tragedy of the Great Depression. In his view the mission of economics was to help end the depression and to set in place a structure that would make a repetition of such a tragedy most unlikely. This meant that the rationalization of fiscal policy as an economic 'steering wheel' (to use a phrase we owe to Abba Lerner) was of primary importance.

The positive contribution of Hyman Minsky may be viewed as a struggle through the years to reconcile Lange and Simons and to integrate this reconciliation with the deep insights of Schumpeter and the pragmatism of Hansen.

Through the years at Berkeley, Brown and Washington Universities, Minsky had some occasions to interact with both the research departments of financial institutions and with operators at banks. Concern with the question, 'Can "it" happen again?' ('it' being a great depression) was an outgrowth of research he undertook at the instigation of the Commission on Money and Credit. He also conducted research sponsored by the Federal Reserve System and the Federal Deposit Insurance Corporation. One of his most influential studies, 'The Economics of Disaster', was prepared as a research paper for the Federal Reserve Board of Governors. For almost 20 years Minsky was also associated with the Mark Twain banks in St Louis; he often asserted that these banks were his laboratory.

The doctrines most associated with Hyman Minsky can be summarized as follows:

1. The interpretation of Keynes as an investment theory of the business cycle and a financial theory of investment. This interpretation emphasizes the 'two-price level' aspect of capitalism; that is, the prices of assets, capital and finance are based upon different proximate variables than the price level of current output.

2. The 'financial instability hypothesis' which holds that over a period of good times the financial structures of a dynamic capitalist economy endogenously evolve from being robust to being fragile, and that once there is a sufficient mix of financially fragile institutions, the economy becomes susceptible to debt deflations.

3. The significance and necessity of Central Banks to be lenders of last resort in order to help abort and contain debt deflations and therefore the thrust towards deep depressions.
4. The cash-flow analysis of financial relations, which emphasizes the flows of incomes (wages, gross capital income, taxes and foreign exchange earnings) from the productive part of the economy that can validate financial obligations. In particular, the significance of profits as the income flow that validates or fails to validate the business debt structure in capitalist economies (leading to an emphasis upon Kalecki's way of looking at National Income).
5. The necessity and significance of big government; that is, one whose budget is a 'large' percentage of national income so that government deficits are sufficient to act as a stabilizer to aggregate profits.
6. The significance of financial innovations as reactions to perceived profit opportunities, and
7. The tiers approach to the balance of payments, which emphasizes the significance of international payments as shifts of profits and other incomes among national economies, and how balance of payments cash flows are necessary to validate the payment commitments on international indebtedness.

By combining these doctrines, Minsky reached the position that a relevant research programme for understanding a capitalist economy cannot abstract from monetary and financial relations. In Minsky's view the orthodox theory reflects a 'village market' paradigm, where the basic transaction is the bartering of one good for another. He holds that the apt theory for a capitalist economy has to reflect a 'Wall Street' situation where the paradigmatic events are negotiations in board rooms among bankers and businessmen that deal with financing investment and positions in capital assets. Whereas in orthodox theory, money is neutral, in the Wall Street paradigm theory, money is not neutral. In Minsky's view the abstract problem set by Keynes is the development of an economic theory in which the non-neutrality of money is an essential theorem that follows from the basic premises rather than a special case that reflects some informational asymmetry or market imperfection.

The interpretation of Keynes that Minsky developed – his special version of post-Keynesian economics – holds that Keynes solved the problem of the non-neutrality of money by recognizing that there are two key price levels in a capitalist economy: the price level of current output and the price level of financial and real assets, and that these two price levels are based upon two quite different relations.

The prices of current output are the means by which the producing and distribution apparatus recovers its costs. Output is produced because the producer, and the banker who finances production, believe that the sales revenue will enable costs to be recovered and a profit to be earned. But the costs of production are mainly labour costs. In a capitalist economy bankers are repaid and businesses make a profit only if sales revenue exceed labour costs by a large enough margin: the price level of current output can be interpreted as a mark-up on unit labour costs. Labour costs per unit of output, even in a world without trade unions, react with a lag to the ratio of employed labour to available labour. The price level of current output will lag behind what happens to overall employment.

Current output in a no-government, no-foreign trade skeletal model of a capitalist economy consists of consumption goods and investment goods production. The price level of investment output can be considered to move along with the price level of consumption output. Producers of investment outputs set their prices to recover their labour costs: the price level of investment output equals unit labour costs plus a mark-up.

Liquidity preference is in Minsky's view a theory of the price level in money and of relative prices of capital and financial assets in conditions of uncertainty. Capital assets and financial instruments are valuable only as they yield incomes. But such yields occur through time: the present prices of capital assets and financial instruments reflect the present valuations of incomes that will be realized as the economy functions through time. Because investment production occurs through time and because today is the future for the past, a capitalist economy (especially if it has a complex financial structure) is one in which the past, the present and the future affect the output of the economy at every date.

But the future exists today only in the minds of the actors in the economy. In Minsky's view, one essential aspect in understanding a capitalist economy are the rules of behaviour formulated by actors in that economy in the light of the uncertainty that they must acknowledge.

Minsky's work has significant policy implications. Capitalism is a flawed system in that, if its development is not constrained, it will lead to periodic deep depressions and the perpetuation of poverty. Appropriate government interventions and an apt structure of central bank controls can lead to an adequate performance: the period 1946–1980 or so is interpreted as a practical 'best' for the real-world economy. However even when the economy functions well, agents feel constrained by interventions that make for its aggregate success. This sets in motion institutional changes which lead to evasions and avoidance of the constraints. In this manner what is an apt structure of intervention in initial circumstances becomes inept as time goes by. Capitalism can be made to function in an adequate manner, but it is a constant struggle to determine the interventions that are necessary and to put these into place.

Minsky's Major Writings
(1975), *John Maynard Keynes*, Columbia University Press.
(1982), *Can 'It' Happen Again?* M.E. Sharpe.
(1986), *Stabilising an Unstable Economy*, Yale University Press.

Wesley Clair MITCHELL (1874–1948)   *Philip A. Klein*

Wesley Clair Mitchell was born in Rushville (Illinois) in 1874, the son of Dr John Wesley Mitchell, a physician who served in the Union Army during the Civil War, and Lucy Medora McClellan, born on a farm in Yorkville (Illinois) but raised by her aunt in Chicago.

Raised and educated in Illinois, Mitchell entered the University of Chicago in the autumn of 1896. Here he was diverted from the field of classics by two of his professors, John Dewey and Thorstein Veblen, both of whom had enormous influence on young Clair. It was undoubtedly from them that Mitchell developed the institutionalist perspective which he retained throughout his professional life and in turn influenced so significantly.

Like Schumpeter and Veblen, Mitchell insisted that the economy as an allocating mechanism could be properly understood and appreciated only if it were examined and evaluated as part of the larger societal and cultural structure within which it is embedded.

Mitchell devoted his professional life in large part to studying business cycles; he ultimately came to feel that economic instability is an integral aspect of the evolving economy and is best approached in terms which include the institutionalist perspective. Mitchell himself came to this view only gradually. From his early efforts to understand business cycles he came to feel that cycles grow out of, and reflect back on, the whole economy of which instability is but one aspect. Ultimately understanding instability came to mean understanding how economies grow and change. Thus his early reflections on business cycles led him to consider the nature of the evolving economy and, subsequently, to contemplate writing a volume on economic theory which unfortunately he never managed to complete.

Of the three American economists customarily regarded as the fathers of American Institutionalism, Mitchell would appear to have the most secure current reputation. Veblen has perhaps been relegated by mainstream economists to the position of a turn-of-the-century gadfly, interesting and provocative perhaps, but disorganized and ultimately not particularly relevant to the discipline of economics as it is perceived today. Commons worked more closely to the currently agreed parameters of the discipline, but his contributions are often overlooked. Mitchell is acknowledged by all to have had a profound influence on quantitative research. The fact that today the United States has what is probably the best set of detailed historical statistics on the basis of which the past can be studied is in no small part due to the influence of Mitchell and his National Bureau. Ultimately, under Mitchell's stimulus, improved statistics for studying instability grew in coverage and sophistication to encompass national income accounting, the flow of funds, international trade, and virtually every applied field of modern economics. Mitchell's institutionalism may be overlooked or ignored, but his quantitative emphasis continues to influence modern economic research.

In addition to Veblen and Dewey, Mitchell studied monetary economics with J. Lawrence Laughlin at the University of Chicago. Under Laughlin's influence, his doctoral dissertation dealt with the monetary crises of the Civil War period (published as *A History of the Greenbacks,* 1903). Mitchell moved from Chicago to the University of California at Berkeley in 1903 where he spent a highly productive decade. Early in his career Mitchell was already focusing on careful empirical investigations. This became even more evident in his second book (1908) in which he expanded and enriched his doctoral study, covering the period 1862 to 1878.

Attention to statistical procedures and methodology, along with efforts to improve the quality and coverage of data, were hallmarks of Mitchell's output virtually from the outset of his career. In coverage, his work moved from a monetary focus to a broader examination of forces making for instability and, ultimately, to an examination of the evolving economy as a whole. Methodologically his work moved from an initial recognition of the need for statistical data to support any interpretation, to increasingly complex and sophisticated techniques for organizing, summarizing and averaging that data. In this connection his 1913 *Business Cycles* revealed Mitchell's lifelong preoccupation with acquiring detailed and accurate statistical records to analyse. Moreover, this went far beyond the earlier monetary studies. Joseph Dorfman summarized Mitchell's viewpoint well by noting that his aim was 'to work out the logic and technique of the money economy, to show how it affected men's actions and habits of thought ...' (Burns, p.130). Mitchell's early views on instability already emphasized the stresses and strains which evolve in market-orientated economies, which is to say in economies motivated by the quest for profits:

> Now the recurrent phases presented by economic activity, wherever it is dominated by the quest for profits, grow out of and grow into each other. An incipient revival of activity, for example, develops into full prosperity, prosperity gradually breeds a crisis, the crisis merges into depression, depression becomes deeper for a while, but ultimately engenders a fresh revival of activity, which is the beginning of another cycle. A theory of business cycles must therefore be a descriptive analysis of the cumulative changes by which one set of business conditions transforms itself into another set (1913, reprinted 1941, p. ix).

These cumulative changes involve alterations (and ultimately stresses and strains) in the shifting psychological, financial or monetary, and real interrelationships which emerge from the recurring widening and narrowing of cost/price (profit) margins, along with the resulting fluctuation over the cycle in entrepreneurial perceptions of profitable investment opportunities.

Because he stressed these many divergent factors, his theory of instability is often called a 'business-economy' or 'eclectic' theory of the cycle. Indeed, when he began investigating the nature and causes of instability he did not so much ignore previous cycle theory (as has sometimes been charged) as argue that there might well be correct elements in many theories. Indeed the immediate or proximate cause of downturns and upturns need not invariably be the same among the many possible interrelationships which shift over the cycle. That business cycles were part of the process which ineluctably emerges in economies organized around making money was clear to him very early. That business instability was itself part of a larger evolutionary pattern which institutionalists stressed became clear to him as his work progressed. While much of his theoretical viewpoint was an outgrowth of the 1913 volume, his methodological perspective was rendered more concrete by his 1915 seminal publication, *The Making and Using of Index Numbers*. This pioneering monograph, reprinted as late as 1938, illustrated his lifelong concern with finding better methods of presenting statistical data.

In 1913 Mitchell moved to Columbia University where, except for the period 1919-22 when he and Alvin Johnson established the New School for Social Research in New York City, he remained until he retired in 1944. Mitchell was, as noted, significantly responsible for launching the National Bureau of Economic Research in 1920 to further his insistence that economic research in any field, including business cycles, could only proceed if first 'the facts' were known. Good economic theory, Mitchell insisted, must be empirically grounded. Thus from its inception the essential function of the Bureau was to fill out, and in as great detail as possible, the empirical record so that theorists could proceed from reality to significant generalizations for testing.

Virtually from the start, Bureau publications included a statement which proclaimed: 'The object of the National Bureau of Economic Research is to ascertain and to present to the public important economic facts and their interpretation in a scientific and impartial manner'. While the Bureau earned much of its early reputation through its painstaking work in developing and analysing times series in an effort to isolate and understand business cycles (W.I. King, Willard Thorp, and ultimately Burns along with Mitchell), it always worked in other areas as well. Under Mitchell's direction in its first two decades, Bureau studies tackled trade union developments (Leo Wolman), income distribution (King, Macaulay, Oswald Knauth) and price behaviour

(Frederic Mills). Still later the Bureau was intimately involved in setting up the system of national income accounting (Simon Kuznets), studying American transportation (Thor Hultgren), inventory behaviour (Moses Abramowitz, Thomas Stanback), international trade (Ilse Mintz, Oskar Morgenstern), business cycle indicators (Geoffrey H. Moore, Julius Shiskin), monetary behaviour (Milton Friedman and Anna J. Schwartz), productivity trends (Solomon Fabricant), consumption (Ruth P. Mack) and trends in philanthropy (W.I King). This by no means exhausts the range of areas studied by Bureau economists. The special genius of Mitchell's direction was that the Bureau earned an enormous reputation for precision, accuracy and objectivity which made its work both useful and appealing to economists of all persuasions. If Mitchell, as is argued below, is best regarded as a dissenting economist, the Bureau under his leadership attracted both dissenting and mainstream economists and produced empirical research that could be and was utilized by all.

The field of business cycle research, of course, continued to be the principal focus of Mitchell's own work, as well as the field in which the reputation of the Bureau was established. Mitchell began by collecting an enormous number of time series dealing with the past behaviour of the economy. At the Bureau he was able to apply vastly greater resources in the service of his belief – that efforts to understand the cycle could best be enhanced by organizing systematically a great deal of data pertaining to the real world and searching therein for patterns of interrelationships. Therefore his approach continued to be vigorously and emphatically empirical. Because, as in his early work, there were no obvious or simple hypotheses set out in advance, his approach to cycles was not only labelled 'eclectic' (as we have seen) but also 'measurement without theory'.

It may be argued that Mitchell's reputation with mainstream economists lies with his influence in persuading them that quantitative economics – empirically grounded economic research – was the most appropriate (Mitchell might have argued the only) way to make progress in understanding the economy. The traditional tendency of mainstream economists to reject empirical research in favour of logically consistent models has burgeoned anew in recent years and in new forms, even more relentlessly sympathetic to 'rigour' at the expense of 'relevance' (unless the relevance is measured against 'stylized facts' rather than mere 'real facts'). Mitchell himself regarded economics as a social science 'to aid in social amelioration'. If, moreover, he had a 'blind faith' that 'the evolutionary process of cumulative causation is amenable to intelligent social control' (in the words of Paul T. Homan in Burns, 1952), all economists at the Bureau in those days did not agree with him nor did Mitchell ask them to. Others at the Bureau found it congenial to join Mitchell in collecting facts, but only to understand how market forces operate, rather than to control them in any way. Thus Milton Friedman, a quintessential mainstream economist, was comfortable at the Bureau virtually from the outset of his career. If Mitchell was personally an interventionist, he regarded the Bureau as a source of empirical information neither in the service of interventionism nor of non-interventionism. His personal objective may have been to improve social control, as Homan suggests. The Bureau's role, however, was only to enrich the empirical record available to all economists.

The Bureau of today continues but with no particular emphasis on business cycles; its empiricism is closely tied to the model-building approach of mainstream economics (stylized facts); and it is under the direction of economists customarily associated with devotion to market solutions. It was charged – and arguably to be sure – that the Bureau under Mitchell was 'measurement without theory'. Today the Bureau may perhaps be appropriately characterized as 'measurement comfortable with mainstream theory'. One wonders what Mitchell would think.

In terms of publications, the major works Mitchell produced at the National Bureau undoubtedly were *Business Cycles: The Problem and Its Setting* and *Measuring Business Cycles*, co-authored with Arthur F. Burns. The former book was an extension and revision of part of the 1913 volume. We may note that Part I of the 1913 study of business cycles presented and summarized leading extant theories of the cycle; it then included Mitchell's efforts at presenting year-to-year statistical records for the US, France, England, and Germany during the period 1890–1911. In 1927 Mitchell was able to include a good many monthly or quarterly series covering the period 1850–1925, particularly for the US and England.. This more extensive study did not cause him to alter his basic views of what happened during business cycles.

Over the years Mitchell and his colleagues were involved in the detailed analysis of statistical series designed to update and improve Part II of the 1913 volume. Part II of that study was eventually reprinted in the early 1940s on grounds that 'a contribution to economic theory does not pass out of date so automatically as do business annals and business statistics' (1941, p. vi). This body of work from 1913 through 1927 is, in terms of its perspective and approach, consistent (as is all his subsequent work with Burns). Throughout his career Mitchell did not so much change his view of the causes of instability as corroborate, extend, refine, enrich and empirically verify his 1913 views.

The 1946 book with Burns summarized the methodology developed by Mitchell and his associates over many years at the NBER and was designed to bring out the critical business cycle relationship patterns Mitchell had been in the process of refining since his early California days. It was this work which led ultimately to the creation of the first of a number of 'short lists' of 'most reliable business cycle indicators' of the sort eventually embraced by the US Department of Commerce and now monitored monthly in their publication, *Business Conditions Digest.* It has been correctly observed that this publication serves as proof that monitoring instability with business cycle indicators is the only method of forecasting business cycles which has the imprimatur of the US government.

Mitchell's lifelong preoccupation with improving statistics so as to ascertain 'the main facts of economic history' pertaining to the 'congeries of interrelated phenomena' (which he always perceived as constituting business cycles) was a major impetus to careful quantitative empirical research in economics in general. When it is recalled that mainstream economics of this period customarily assumed not only Say's Law of markets and full employment, but also flexible wages and prices leading to 'cleared markets' and equilibrium, it was also one of the major examples in the history of economic thought of the profound impact which responsible dissent can have on the techniques, if not the perspective, of mainstream analysis and thought.

Mitchell would never have acknowledged any dichotomy between one aspect of himself as the analyst of business cycles and another as the institutional economist. It is not clear that he ever applied the term 'institutionalist' or 'evolutionary economist' or even 'dissenting economist' to himself, but he was clearly sympathetic to the work of both Veblen and Commons, as a reading of his notes on these economists in *Types of Economic Theory* will corroborate. Moreover, the closeness between Mitchell's two kinds of work is underscored by Joseph Dorfman's comment in his Professional Sketch in Burns's volume dedicated to Mitchell: 'His theory was that business cycles were not "natural" nor were they the outcome strictly of industrial forces; rather they were a product of the peculiar institutions and habits associated with the money economy' (1951, p.131).

Today, however, the disjunction between 'the two Mitchells' is almost complete. Those who work in the tradition of the original NBER and do quantitative research dedicated to understanding business cycles rarely if ever think of Mitchell as an institutionalist, or indeed as a dissenting economist. On the other hand, those who regard Mitchell as a leading dissenter and/or a founder of American institutionalism rarely if ever focus in any detail on the enormous contribution to the technical manipulation of statistical data, which formed the central core of Mitchell's business cycle research.

It seems clear, however, that these 'two Mitchells' were a unity, as shown conspicuously in his conception of the task of economics. In the last of his famous *Lectures in Types of Economic Theory*, Mitchell expresses his own views and suggests that economics is fundamentally a 'science which deals with economic behavior' (p.296). Moreover, he was at pains to define 'behavior' in broad – which is to say – institutionalist terms.

As Frederick Mills has noted, Mitchell never wrote the capstone volume on economic theory which he planned. Nevertheless he developed a consistent system of 'concepts and beliefs' which Mills summarized as follows:

1. The emphasis on objective behaviour as an object of study, as against the 'intellectualist' fallacy of the nineteenth century.
2. The conception of economics as one of the sciences of human behaviour.
3. A concern with reality and a conviction that the objective of economics is the understanding of the institutions and processes by which men make their living. All available instruments to this understanding should be utilized by the economist, but it is the understanding of reality and not the formulation of a body of concepts to be judged in terms of their own internal consistency which is the end-purpose of economics.
4. The belief that pecuniary institutions, and the money economy generally, provide keys of central importance to an understanding of contemporary economic processes.
5. The notion of sequence, the concept of cumulative, consecutive growth, as opposed to the Newtonian concept of equilibrium.
6. The notion that inquiries should be framed from the start in such a way as to permit testing of the hypothetical conclusions; profound belief in the interplay of reason and observation as the way to achieve warranted conclusions.
7. The confidence in statistical measurement as a means of ensuring the cumulative growth of a body of factual knowledge; such quantitative, substantive knowledge would not only provide tests of hypotheses, but would constitute a seed-bed for the germination of new hypotheses (Mills, in Burns, 1952, pp.119–20.)

Consideration of this list of beliefs reveals the profound influence of Veblen as well as Mitchell's sympathy for the approach taken by Commons. Mitchell's approach was unequivocally evolutionary. In his introduction to *What Veblen Taught*, Mitchell asserts: 'The biological view of man's evolution suggests that habits of thought are formed by the activities in which individuals engage. ... Hence economic factors have had and still have a major share in shaping mass habits of thought. ... The theory of evolution begun by biologists must be continued by students of culture, and primarily by economists' (1936, p. xxi–xxiii). Modern institutionalists can relate to this approach of 'evolutionary economics', even as they may note the influence on more recent institutionalist work of the more explicit juxtaposition of

Dewey with the Veblenian tradition. Nonetheless Dewey's instrumentalism is surely to be perceived in the Mitchellian perspective.

Mills noted further that 'no man did more to turn economists toward the study of the actual functioning of our economic system' (p.120). If another name might be added in the twentieth century it would surely be Keynes, thereby suggesting that a 'reality-based' approach to economic analysis was common to both. (This no doubt accounts for Mitchell's willingness, like Keynes's, always to serve on commissions and as a consultant to government.) However, even Mitchell's close friend and colleague Arthur F. Burns thought that the 'disaggregative approach of Mitchell and the aggregative approach' of Keynes were antithetical (cf Burns, *Economic Research and the Keynesian Thinking of Our Times*, 1946). It is ironic that modern institutionalists still debate the compatibility of Keynes and Mitchell. In any case, much of the recent 'new classical' economic theory is not only a rejection of Keynes, it is also a rejection of the Mitchellian perspective – so critical in the evolution of modern institutionalist thought.

Mitchell's Major Writings

(1903), *A History of the Greenbacks, With Special Reference to the Consequences of Their Issue, 1862–1865*, Chicago: University of Chicago Press.

(1908), *Gold, Prices, and Wages Under the Greenback Standard*, University of California Press.

(1913), *Business Cycles*, University of California Press. (Part III was reprinted under the title, *Business Cycles and Their Causes*, University of California Press, 1941; Third printing, 1959.)

(1915), *The Making and Using of Index Numbers*, US Bureau of Labor Statistics, Bulletin no 656. (Reprinted 1938).

(1927), *Business Cycles: The Problem and Its Setting*, New York: National Bureau of Economic Research.

(1936), *What Veblen Taught* (edited and with an Introduction by Wesley C. Mitchell), New York: The Viking Press.

(1937), *The Backward Art of Spending Money, and Other Essays* (written 1912–36), New York: McGraw-Hill.

(1946), *Measuring Business Cycles* (with Arthur F. Burns), New York: National Bureau of Economic Research, Studies in Business Cycles.

(1949), *Lecture Notes on Types of Economic Theory*, New York: Augustus M. Kelley. (Stenographic Record of Class Notes from 1934–35. Unauthorized, published posthumously.)

(1951), *What Happens During Business Cycles: A Progress Report*, National Bureau of Economic Research, Studies in Business Cycles, No 5. (Published posthumously.)

Other References

Burns, A.F. (1946), 'Economic Research and the Keynesian Thinking of our Time', in Twenty-sixth Annual Report of the National Bureau of Economic Research, June 1946, reprinted in A.F. Burns, (1954), *The Frontiers of Economic Knowledge*, National Bureau of Economic Research, Publication No. 56, Princeton: Princeton University Press.

Burns, A.F. (ed) (1952), *Wesley Clair Mitchell: The Economic Scientist*, New York: National Bureau of Economic Research, Publication No 53.

Klein, P. (1983), 'The Neglected Institutionalism of Wesley Clair Mitchell: The Theoretical Basis for Business Cycle Indicators', *Journal of Economic Issues*, **17** (4), December.

Mitchell, L.S. (1953), *Two Lives*, New York: Simon and Schuster.

Moore, G.H. (1978), 'Wesley Mitchell in Retrospect', *Journal of Economic Issues*, **12** (2), June.

Gunnar MYRDAL (1898–1987)   *Malcolm C. Sawyer*

Gunnar Myrdal was born in the province of Dalarna in Sweden in 1898 and grew up in a farming environment. His early interests were in the natural sciences, but he initially read law at the University of Stockholm. He soon switched to economics and in 1927 completed his doctoral thesis on the problem of price formation under conditions of economic change, with an emphasis on the role of anticipations. Many of the ideas and concepts in his doctoral thesis appeared again in Myrdal's writings on macroeconomic analysis published in the 1930s (in English as *Monetary Equilibrium*). Myrdal was initially a 'pure' economic theorist, but became deeply involved in economic policy debates. He moved towards a multi-disciplinary perspective (as reflected in his writings from the early 1940s onwards) describing himself as an institutionalist. Throughout his career, Myrdal worked on the 'big issues', conscious of the multi-faceted nature of economic and social problems and of the need for careful research.

After spending a year in the United States as a Rockefeller Fellow in 1929, Myrdal wrote a survey of Sweden's monetary and exchange problems. He became an adviser to the new Social Democratic government from 1932, and a Member of Parliament in 1935. Myrdal was strongly involved in showing the possible benefits of an expansionary fiscal policy, playing a pioneering role in the development of a theoretical framework for the analysis of fiscal policy (1934). As a member of the 'Stockholm School', he was closely involved in the development of many notions which were later regarded as Keynesian, particularly the role of demand and fiscal policy. From 1933 to 1939, he was Professor of Political Economy at Stockholm University. He was actively involved in Swedish political life in the 1940s, returning to Parliament and appointed Director of the Central Bank, Chair of the Planning Commission and Minister for Trade and Commerce (1945–47). He became Executive Secretary of the United Nations Economic Commission for Europe in 1947, a post he held for ten years. On return to Sweden, he established the Institute of International Economic Research in Stockholm to undertake work on trade and development. A ten-year study of Asia culminated in his three-volume *Asian Drama*. He shared the Nobel prize for economics in 1973.

His first book, *Monetary Equilibrium* (1939), focused on the Wicksellian notion of cumulative causation applied to credit creation, a general idea that recurs in different forms in much of Myrdal's work. Viewing this book as an 'immanent criticism' of Wicksell, he pointed to the links between the real and the monetary sides of the economy, in particular to the influence of the money rate of interest on relative prices. He also focused on the Wicksellian cumulative process, arising from any difference between the 'natural' rate and the money rate of interest. For example, a fall in the money rate of interest means that future profits are discounted at a lower rate, leading to a rise in capital values (based on discounted future profits). There is a consequent shift to investment goods and away from consumer goods; the prices of consumer goods rise which further stimulates investment. This cumulative process only comes to an end when the banking system changes the conditions under which credit is granted. Whilst general (non-monetary) equilibrium is viewed as stable, monetary equilibrium is seen as 'labile' (prone to change). The main purpose of the analysis was apparently to include anticipations in the monetary system. Myrdal saw the chief contribution of this book as derived from the concepts *ex post* and *ex ante*, which were applied in particular to saving and investment. The major problem in monetary theory was 'how does this tendency to disparity in the saving-investment equation develop into an *ex post* balance'? (p.46). The answer was seen to lie with unexpected gains and losses and fluctuations in prices.

An early book, *The Political Element in the Development of Economic Theory* (originally published in Swedish in 1930 but not appearing in English until 1953), combined a study of economic ideas with the intention of identifying the value premises underlying economic theories. In it he advocated a clear statement both of these value premises and of the institutional assumptions underpinning the economic theories. Myrdal appeared to accept the division between positive and normative in economic analysis, arguing that such analysis can contribute to political debate by scrutinizing the facts and analysing causal relations between them. However, there are discrepancies between the principles of economic analysis and practice. For example,

> the theory of 'free competition' is not intended to be merely a scientific explanation of what course economic relations would take under certain specified assumptions. It simultaneously constitutes a kind of proof that these hypothetical conditions would result in maximum 'total income' or the greatest possible 'satisfaction of needs' in society as a whole (p.4).

Further, most general terms used in economic analysis have two meanings, one positive and the other normative (consider equilibrium, balance or productivity). Myrdal was particularly critical of notions of 'natural laws' which often make their appearance in economic analysis. Much of the book was an analysis of a range of economic theories (such as classical and neoclassical value theory, free trade), with the aim of bringing to the fore their normative elements.

In 1938 the Carnegie Corporation commissioned Myrdal to investigate the position of blacks in the US; this resulted in *The American Dilemma*, completed by the end of 1942. The 'dilemma' of the title is the conflict between the ideals of the American constitution, the values of the American people and the actual situation of American Negroes (amongst others). The book was seen as the first full-scale scientific analysis of the status of America's black population. It ranged over the economic, social and political position of the American Negro, and drew on anthropology, social and intellectual history, law and sociology. 'Our task in this inquiry is to ascertain social reality as it is. We shall seek to depict the actual life conditions of the American Negro people and their manifold relations to the larger American society' (p.lxxiii). An outstanding feature of the book is its scholarly approach to a highly emotive issue but where the author is fully aware of the moral aspects, particularly as seen by those involved.

The idea of cumulative causation was seen as a main explanatory scheme in this inquiry. This general idea, as seen above, can be traced back to Wicksell and was later extended in *Economic Theory and Underdeveloped Regions*. The discussion on 'the principle of cumulation' has elements of the ideas of instability of equilibrium and of multiplier effects; thus the final effects of a change of much greater magnitude than the size of the change itself. The multiplier effects arise from the interaction between interdependent economic, social and political factors, which involves the rejection of any notion of a single basic factor (which is anyway seen as a narrow approach). The 'principle of causation ... has a much wider application in social relations. It is, or should be, developed into a main theoretical tool in studying social change' (p.75). Two sets of forces may balance out in a static 'accommodation' but that would be accidental. A change in one force leads to mutually reinforcing changes in the other.

Myrdal drew a parallel between the position of Negroes and that of women and children (especially in Appendix 5), showing many similarities between the status of the two groups. One of Myrdal's main conclusions was relatively optimistic when he said that '*not since Reconstruction has there been more reason to anticipate fundamental changes in American race relations, changes which will involve a development toward the American ideals*' (p. lxi, italics in original). In his preface to the 20th anniversary edition of The American Dilemma, Myrdal pointed to the dramatic changes which had taken place in inter-racial relations and which bore out his optimism.

Economic Theory and Underdeveloped Regions, based on lectures given in Cairo in 1955, continued the themes of cumulative causation and the role of ideology in economics (but placed in the context of economic and social development), discussing also the appropriate roles of market forces and planning. Market forces are viewed as tending to increase (rather than decrease) inequalities between regions. Internal and external economies, widely interpreted, fortify the growth of successful regions while others stagnate (at least in relative terms). The movement of labour and capital tends to exacerbate these tendencies. Migration of labour generally involves the more productive and more enterprising, with savings siphoned off from poorer regions to the richer ones where profitability is high. In fact these 'backwash effects' are modified by 'spread effects' of the momentum towards expansion which come from the centres of economic expansion into other regions. However, the existence of these 'spread effects' does not re-establish the usefulness of equilibrium analysis, for even if by chance the 'backwash' and 'spread' effects are in balance, this does not represent a stable equilibrium because any change in the balance of forces will trigger off a cumulative movement.

Myrdal clearly welcomed the wide acceptance (in the 1950s) of the idea that underdeveloped countries should have an integrated national plan. However, this was not detailed centralized planning; rather it was closer to what would now be called 'strategic' planning. The national plan was seen as a programme for the strategy of the government in interventions with the operation of market forces so that those forces could be conditioned to aid social progress. State policies, as built into the national plan, should be used to increase the strength of the spread effects, and in that way to use the forces of cumulative causation to lead to virtuous rather than vicious circles. The modernization of most underdeveloped countries was heavily constrained by the existence of outmoded institutions and of social and economic inequality which often could not easily be changed. The national plan should not be restricted to economic planning but also encompass social planning.

Myrdal stressed that a national economic plan could not be rationally constructed by using the criteria of the price system based on private profitability; instead it had to consist of a blueprint 'in real terms of a cumulative process of circular causation, in the final analysis directed by political decisions, I am not preaching a gospel of licence but quite the contrary'. It is necessary to investigate below the surface of market phenomena, and to provide an analysis of the causal inter-relationships involved, which is 'an analytical task of supreme difficulty' (p.91).

Myrdal criticized the standard theory of international trade for being unable to explain the existence and persistence of international economic inequalities, seeing part of its shortcomings as arising from the use of a stable equilibrium framework. For reasons such as the infant industry case and externalities arising from industrialization and employment creation, Myrdal argued in favour of some trade protection in underdeveloped economies. He stressed, though, that this was not an 'invitation to licence' but rather an appeal for the application of a set of criteria different from those derived from the doctrine of free trade.

In *Beyond the Welfare State*, published in 1960 and based on lectures delivered at Yale University in 1958, Myrdal identified a general trend towards planning. A range of forces – such as the impact of economic crises and pressures for equality and democracy – lay behind this trend. He argued that the discussion of a 'free market' versus a 'planned economy' was divorced from reality and an obstacle to the development of economic policy (for example the stereotype of 'socialized medicine' blocked clear thinking on health care in the US). Myrdal pointed to the distinction between government intervention and planning, with the former coming historically before the latter. The first stages of the development of the 'welfare state' had involved government intervention, often uncoordinated. But Myrdal looked ahead to further developments of the welfare state, when planning could help to simplify and coordinate interventions. There could be a decrease of state intervention with a strengthening of local self-government and the growth of an infrastructure of organized interest groups with increased participation of individuals in decision-making. He looked forward to the replacement of an 'etatist' approach to the welfare state by a participatory democratic one.

A central concern of Myrdal in the post-war period was the economic structure and development of the less developed countries, culminating in *Asian Drama* published in 1968 in three volumes and nearly 2,300 pages. In *Asian Drama*, Myrdal considered the history and prospects of eight South Asian countries (India, Pakistan, Malaya, Burma, Thailand, Indonesia, Philippines, Ceylon: the name of countries at the time of the study are used here), with the inclusion of South Vietnam, Cambodia and Laos on occasions. The scope of this study was enormous, ranging over, for example, the value premises of the study, inadequacy of statistics, and the causes and effects of corruption. Throughout considerable attention was paid to the historical and institutional backgrounds in the different countries.

The prologue (entitled 'The beam in our eyes') and Part One reiterated Myrdal's concern with bias and value judgements in economic analysis (and the social sciences more generally). He argued for less naiviety about ourselves and our motivations, and for a degree of sophistication on the ways in which research activity is subject to personal and social conditioning. In the context of the study of Third World countries, there were biases arising from treating their internal problems from the point of view of Western political and military interests and the transfer of concepts valid for industrialized economies over to non-industrialized ones. Since objectivity in analysis is aided by making value assumptions explicit, one chapter is entirely devoted to discussing the value premises chosen for the study. Myrdal considered that his task was to look at problems in South Asia from the viewpoint of the interests and ideals, norms and goals, which were relevant in those countries. The value premises chosen were described as 'the modernization ideals', which have several, sometimes conflicting, dimensions including rationality, development and planning for development, rise of levels of living, social and economic equalization etc.

Although described as 'institutional', such an approach involved much more than merely qualifying conventional Western economic analysis to allow for so-called non-economic factors. Instead the analysis had to be based from the beginning on theories and concepts relevant to the societies being studied. Moreover, the institutional approach imposes severe demands such as logical consistency and relevance to reality.

The unreliability of available statistical material was a considerable handicap to research and to the analysis of the development problems of the countries concerned. But the statistics also had to be measured in a way appropriate to the South Asian situation.

Myrdal argued that there were particularly significant differences in the prevailing conditions in South Asia as compared with those existing in Western countries prior to industrialization (and of course even more so compared with current conditions in the West). These differences worked to the disadvantage of the underdeveloped countries in South Asia, preventing growth such as had occurred in developed Western countries.

Myrdal saw the ideology of economic planning as rationalist in approach, with the state taking an active role to steer economic development. Further, planning in the South Asian countries was closely linked with the drive for modernization. However, factors such as the pool of competent administrators inherited from colonial times and tendencies towards paternalism and authoritarianism encouraged the use of state planning. Whilst economic planning (of the developed 'welfare state' variety) had arisen as a consequence of industrialization, in South Asia the role of planning was to foster industrialization. Of course Myrdal recognized that the rhetoric of planning was often used to justify any form of state intervention.

A range of preconditions is required for successful economic planning which involve the conditioning and direction of economic life. Myrdal saw these as including a stable and effective government, conditions of law and order, 'social discipline and, more generally, national consolidation'. In general, the South Asian countries do not satisfy these preconditions. Although the ideology of planning was widely accepted, few South Asian countries had made serious attempts to 'bring their economic life under the discipline of economic planning' (p.714). Further, the ideology of planning could serve to justify a wide range of government interventions undertaken for spurious reasons (rewarding supporters etc) which have nothing to do with economic planning.

Myrdal viewed all the countries studied as being 'soft states', which he defined as arising when policies decided upon 'are often not enforced, even if they are enacted at all, in that the authorities ... are reluctant to place obligations on people' (p.66). A low level of social discipline was seen as a fundamental difference between South Asian countries in the 1960s and Western countries at the beginning of their industrialization process. Yet, 'rapid development will be exceedingly difficult to engender without an increase in social discipline in all strata and even in the villages' (p.899).

Myrdal argued that the concepts of underemployment and unemployment derived for Western economies were inappropriate in South Asia and elsewhere. In Western economies it can reasonably be assumed that those able to work but not employed are involuntarily idle. But in South Asia, there was a blurring between voluntary and involuntary unemployment. Low levels of labour participation in South Asia were the result of a range of cultural and institutional factors which would not be overcome merely by raising aggregate demand. The size of the labour reserve was seen as dependent on policy measures applied; it could not be measured independently of policy assumptions.

Industrialization was seen as part of the drive for modernization. Given the low levels of industrialization and the rapid growth of population, modern industry would not be able to provide employment for much of the growth of the labour force. But industrialization needed to be pursued since it would have important employment-creation effects in the longer term. Myrdal argued that 'South Asian countries now run the risk of creating petty islands of highly organized Western-type industries that will remain surrounded by a sea of stagnation', which could be avoided by policies to stimulate development of other sectors (p.1203). Industrial development should be directed towards either the production of exports or import substitutes; Myrdal argued that the latter was a more promising prospect. A strong case could be made for the protection and promotion of craft industries in the villages of South Asia, in particular because of the lack of alternative employment for most craftspeople. Promotion of small-scale industrial enterprises in urban areas and the preservation of cottage industries in the villages were seen as advantageous in the provision of employment and in spreading modernization outside of the large-scale enterprises.

Volume 3 of *The Asian Drama* was largely devoted to problems of 'population quality', dealing with investment in people, health and education. This reviewed past policies in these areas and culminated in a range of policy recommendations.

In this entry, we have focused on a relatively small number of Myrdal's writings, albeit those which were major contributions by any standard, involving many years of toil and ranging over many disciplines. We have also sought to illustrate a number of themes which run through Myrdal's work including, first, the notion of cumulative causation and the associated dismissal of equilibrium analysis and, second, his concern with the detailed and rigorous analysis of important economic and social issues using a range of social sciences and with a full awareness of the value judgements made by those being investigated as well as by the investigator. It is significant that he chose 'the equality issue in world development' as the theme for his Nobel Memorial lecture (1975). The final sentences of that lecture provide a good summary of Myrdal's approach to economics:

I am hopeful about the development of our science. We can by immanent criticism in logical terms challenge our own thinking and cleanse it from opportunistic conformism. And we can widen our perspective. Everything can be studied. We are free to expand and perfect our knowledge about the world, only restricted by the number of scientists working and, of course, the degree of their diligence, brightness and their openness to fresh approaches.

Myrdal's Major Writings

A full bibliography is given in Harald Bohrn, *Gunnar Myrdal: A Bibliography 1919–1976*, Acta Bibliothecae Reglae, Stockholmiensis. Also up to 1970 in Reynolds (1974).

(1934), 'Finanspolitikens ekonomiska verkningar' ('The Economic Effects of Fiscal Policy') SOU. A Report to the Unemployment Committee, Stockholm, 1934.

(1939), *Monetary Equilibrium*, London: Hodge.

(1944), *The American Dilemma*, New York: Harper & Row. Twentieth anniversary edition, 1962.

(1953), *The Political Element in the Development of Economic Theory*, Routledge & Kegan Paul. Translated from German by Paul Streeten. Originally published in Swedish in 1930.

(1957), *Economic Theory and Underdeveloped Regions*, London: Duckworth. American title *Rich Lands and Poor*, New York: Harper.

(1958), *Value in Social Theory: A Selection of Essays on Methodology* (edited by Paul Streeten), London: Routledge & Kegan Paul.

(1960), *Beyond the Welfare State*, New Haven: Yale University Press.

(1968), *Asian Drama: An Inquiry into the Poverty of Nations*, New York: Twentieth Century Fund.

(1972), *Against the Stream: Critical Essays on Economics*, New York: Pantheon.

(1975), The Equality Issue in World Development, *Swedish Journal of Economics*, **77**.

Other References

Lundberg, E. (1974), 'Gunnar Myrdal's Contributions to Economic Theory', *Swedish Journal of Economics*, **76**.

Reynolds, L.G. (1974), 'Gunnar Myrdal's Contributions to Economic Theory, 1940–1970', *Swedish Journal of Economics*, **76**.

Claudio NAPOLEONI (1924–1988)   *Marina Colonna*

Claudio Napoleoni was born in L'Aquila on 5 March 1924, and died in Andorno Micca on 31 July 1988. For the generation of Italian economists who were trained in the 1960s, Napoleoni was a leading thinker, active in both economic theory and policy and in the political debate. From 1968 until the early 1970s, he was regarded by university students as a cultural and political point of reference, as the philosopher-economist who had been able to promote a revival of Marx and a critique of political economy, and who had helped to renew the study of economics in Italy. For the entire Italian left-wing movement, Napoleoni has frequently played the role of provocative critic, commanding attention even from those scholars and politicians who did not share his views and beliefs.

Napoleoni's political and cultural training started soon after the war, when he became a member of the Constituent Ministry, worked with the Communist Finance Minister M. Scoccimarro (1945–46), joined the Economic Committee of the Italian Communist party, and participated with M. Rossi Doria in the study for agrarian reform in Calabria. In 1948–50 he was editor of *La realtà economica,* a fortnightly magazine of the Consigli di Gestione, which influenced the left-wing movement and the development of its economic policy. The aim of the magazine was to make the 'production process and the public institutions increasingly democratic' through widespread information about important events of Italian economic life. Consequently, the magazine paid great attention to the Marshall Plan, and in 1948 published the first Italian translation of the ECA Country Study on Italy. The publication included an unsigned introduction, probably written by Napoleoni, in which a careful explanation was given of the terms of the bill through which the US government intended to control Italian productive development. It was also pointed out that the material and financial help which was agreed upon would not solve the problem of unemployment. In order to face the Italian economic crisis of those years, the magazine strongly supported the CGIL economic plan against the government and Confindustria, recommending that the workers' movement support that plan through the organization of 'Conferenze di produzione' and by their participation in the 'Piani di produzione' of the enterprises.

At the beginning of the 1950s Napoleoni, together with the philosopher Felice Balbo, contributed to the journal *Cultura e realtà* and joined the cultural and political group of Catholic-communists, whose influence was perhaps responsible for his conversion to Catholicism. From 1953 to 1968, he was appointed researcher and afterwards lecturer at the Svimez (Associazione per lo sviluppo dell'industria nel Mezzogiorno). This Association, born in 1946 because of interest by the Socialist Industry Minister, R. Morandi, had the purpose of analysing the industrial situation in the south of Italy and of identifying its possible development. This activity was conceived as an experimental joint effort between private and public institutions. Important outcomes of this cooperation were the numerous writings on economic dualism and national economic planning which contributed to the drafts of the 'Rapporto Vanoni' (1955–1964) of the 'Nota aggiuntiva la Malfa' (1962), two of the first attempts at economic planning in Italy. Napoleoni also had a hand in gathering together a group of very good scholars for the Association, who greatly contributed both at home and abroad to the debate on the economic problems of Southern Italy, and to the spread of knowledge in Italy of foreign scholars and theories.

In 1962 Napoleoni founded, together with Franco Rodano, *La Rivista Trimestrale,* of which he was joint editor until 1970. In that journal Napoleoni published many important articles on two main issues: the redirection of post-war economic development in Italy, and the critique and revision of Marx's theories of exploitation and alienation. Even if Napoleoni's views on both issues underwent some changes in the 1970s, those articles remain an important point of reference in the development of his theoretical and political approach. They greatly help us to understand Napoleoni's writings of the 1980s and, together with the contributions of his co-editor F. Rodano, they express the most significant political and cultural ideas of the Italian Catholic-communists in those years.

From 1968 to 1974 Napoleoni was head of the Sispe (Scuola Italiana di Scienze Politiche ed Economiche), a school open to anyone whose purpose was to study the more relevant theoretical problems seen mainly in the light of their historical evolution. In 1977 Napoleoni was elected a Member of Parliament in the list of the Sinistra Indipendente, and from 1979 he was elected a Member of the Upper House.

At university, Napoleoni's education and career had been irregular. Before the war he attended courses on natural science; in 1947, after having been enrolled for some time in philosophy, he left the university. Between 1962 and 1966 he taught the history of economic doctrines, econometrics, and financial mathematics in Ancona (University of Urbino). In 1965 he received a university teaching qualification, thus becoming, in 1966, one of the few professors in Italian universities without a degree. In 1966–68 he taught in Ancona; and in 1968–70 he moved to a Full Professorship at the University of Naples where his very successful lectures on *Das Capital* were attended by an extremely varied audience of students and others interested in Marx. During the 1960s he held several Visiting Professorships at the Centro di Specializzazione e Ricerche Economico-Agrarie per il Mezzogiorno in Portici and, in 1968-69, at the University of Rome. From 1970 to 1977 he taught economic and financial policy at the University of Turin. In 1978, owing to his political commitments, he left the university, going back only occasionally for some conferences and short courses.

A complete list and review of Napoleoni's writings would be very long. He covered the three main topics in economics: economic policy, history of economic thought, and theory. His analysis of Italian economic problems and his comments on trade union and government policies followed the changing sceneries in Italy from the 1950s till the early 1980s, and were published both in scientific journals and in newspapers such as *Settegiorni, Rinascita, il manifesto, Mondo economico, la Repubblica* and *Paese Sera*. In the 1960s, his view on Italian dualism informed the debate on the problems of Southern Italy. Napoleoni's most important contribution to the history of economic thought was *Il pensiero economico del 900* (1961). For the first time in that book the substantial difference between classical and neoclassical theories was pointed out and made intelligible for a large audience. Other important writings on history are entries in the *Dizionario di economia politica* (1956) and articles published in *La Rivista Trimestrale* (1962–70), *Smith, Ricardo, Marx* (1970, 1973), *Lezioni sul Capitolo sesto inedito di Marx* (1972) and *Valore* (1976).

Napoleoni's contributions to political economy are closely intertwined with the history of economic thought, and are contained within his critiques of those great theoreticians whose works have laid the very foundations of economic theory: Smith, Ricardo, Malthus, Marx, Walras, Robbins, Keynes, Schumpeter and Sraffa. For this reason it has been said that Napoleoni regarded political economy as an open framework which could embrace its history, its critique, and the new frontiers of knowledge; also that the history of economic thought was a fruitful field which he researched in order to solve theoretical questions. This method of research, which has sometimes caused Napoleoni to interpret well-known authors and established concepts rather freely, has been criticized by some scholars (see, for example, Ginzburg, 1971). On the other hand, Napoleoni's procedure may also be regarded as a useful interpretive key. It implies that what is really fruitful and interesting is Napoleoni's various attempts positively to reconstruct political economy through his personal reading of the economic literature. That revision or reconstruction was finally transformed by him into the uneasy and still debated theoretical proposal expounded in *Discorso sull'economia politica* (1985).

An overall view of Napoleoni's reflections on political economy shows his constant effort to find a satisfactory solution to the problems of the theory of value. In 1956 Napoleoni himself stated the centrality of this topic: 'The theory of value is like the heart of economic science; ... the nodal points of the history of political economy are reflected in the fortune of the theory of value' (*Dizionario*, p.1675). Attention will be concentrated below on Napoleoni's critique of Marx's theory of value and on the relation he established between Marx, Sraffa and neoclassical theory. This choice will leave out some interesting suggestions which Napoleoni has put forward on Smith's and Schumpeter's theories of growth, as well as his writings about more philosophical issues. On the other hand, Napoleoni's reflections on the theory of value constitute the most original part of his work. Moreover, their partial translation into English makes it possible for non-Italian readers to appreciate them.

Marx's theory of value – its revival, critique and the way to go beyond it – can be regarded as the linchpin of Napoleoni's thought. In 1956 he regarded Marx as the author who gave the 'most finished and rigorous formulation' to classical political economy (that is, to a surplus value theory where 'capital and land have no independent influence on the exchange value of commodities'). The notion of the 'value of labour-power', the surplus value theory, and the connected theories of exploitation and alienation, were the further steps which, according to Napoleoni, enabled Marx to overcome Ricardo's contradictory notion of the 'value of labour' and to bring to light the *nature* of the capitalist system of production. At the same time, Marx's inability to find a correspondence between values and prices (the transformation problem) and, once again, the failure of the labour theory of value to explain price formation, made Napoleoni wonder whether the classical approach should be abandoned. Alternatively, Marx's theory of value could be regarded as the starting point for research whose aim was not the explanation of prices, but 'the understanding of the nature of the capitalist system and the rules which guide its working' (*Dizionario*, pp.1697–8).

In order to follow this second line of research, Napoleoni introduced into the critical re-examination of Marx's thought the assumption that any judgement on the validity of a theory cannot be only scientific, but must go back to the philosophical foundations of the theory. The idea was that within an enlarged analytical context, Marx's explanation of the origin of profit could still be regarded as an open problem (*Dizionario*, p.1699). Nevertheless, within a few years it became clear to Napoleoni himself that the introduction of philosophical reasoning into the economic sphere as an integral part of the latter could not replace the 'scientific verification' of the origin of profit. Napoleoni's attempts to solve this problem underwent substantial changes during his life. Here the survey will be confined to the views worked out by him in *Valore*.

Starting from the premise that in Marx's thought the notion of value differs from the notion of price, the main thesis advanced by Napoleoni in *Valore* was that Marx's difficulty in solving the transformation problem originates from his attempt to establish a *mathematical* relation between values and prices. The difficulty was seen in the fact that Marx's notion of value had to interpret the contradictory relation between labour and capital in the capitalist system, thus reflecting his idea of capitalism as a 'reversed' reality. Consequently, that notion was not shaped within the logic of non-contradiction, and could not be related to the (scientific) notion of price (*Valore,* pp.98–9). On the other hand, Napoleoni was also ready to recognize that, in order to preserve Marx's exploitation theory, the problem of the relation between value and price could not be avoided: even if it is true that in Marx's theory values are determined *before* prices, 'without exchange value as the "necessary phenomenal form" of value, Marx's notion of value would not exist at all' (*Valore,* p.174). This contradiction about a relation which is both unattainable and necessary, was the basis for Napoleoni's final conclusion that, even within an enlarged context including philosophical and methodological considerations, 'the hope of preserving [Marx's] theory of exploitation ... appears groundless' (*Valore,* p.175).

Napoleoni's relinquishment of Marx's theories of value, which in 1963 he had defined as 'logically untenable, but historically significant', was based on his negative view of economists, such as Bortkiewicz (1907), Seton (1956–57) and Sraffa (1960), who 'completed' Marx's transformation, as well as of those who saw in Sraffa's model the possibility of preserving Marx's theory of exploitation (Dobb, 1964; Meek, 1967; Vianello, 1970).

Napoleoni was one of the very few scholars who read the manuscript of Sraffa's book. His review of that book appeared in Italy only a few months after its publication (in *Il Giornale degli Economisti e Annali di Economia,* **20** (1), 1960). From the beginning he regarded Sraffa's model as the final critique of both the classical labour theory of value and the neoclassical theory of distribution (see also 1961, Chapter 12), but his views on the relation between Marx and Sraffa underwent substantial changes. His views followed the same path as Napoleoni's attempts to preserve Marx's notions of exploitation; in the 1970s he finally rejected Sraffa's model as a continuation of Marx's more significant themes. The reasons given by Napoleoni in support of this interpretation are numerous, and have been put forward on several occasions. Here a brief account will be given only of those arguments most closely linked with the relation between values and prices.

One of the outcomes of Sraffa's solution of Marx's transformation problem is that its logical sequence – value, rate of profit, price – could not be preserved: the rate of profit could not be determined before prices were set and, at the same time, prices could not be set before the determination of the rate of profit. According to Napoleoni, Sraffa's solution – the simultaneous determination of the rate of profit and prices (given the rate of wage) – entailed the final suppression of two related features of Marx's theory: (i) the idea that the notion of value *differs* from the notion of price, so that prices are *derived* from values; and (ii) his attempt to find an 'economic' explanation of the origin of profit. In Sraffa's model the amount of commodities is measured by the amount of labour, while the latter can be replaced by the physical quantities of the former. According to Napoleoni, this means that 'labour' is no longer essential in the determination of values, and that values themselves have disappeared from the scene. In Napoleoni's words, Sraffa's price theory is 'the first theory expounded outside [classical and neoclassical] theory of value' (*Valore*, pp.96, 177). Napoleoni also pointed out that, once the labour theory of value is rejected, it becomes impossible to compare Marx's and Sraffa's theories of distribution. Even if both Marx and Sraffa assume a given rate of wage, Marx's distribution finds its 'economic' explanation in the analytical notion of surplus value, while in the case of Sraffa the distribution of the surplus between profit and wage can only be determined outside the model, by social class relations. Consequently, the notion of surplus itself necessarily loses its original meaning and becomes 'an occurrence' which will always be 'empirically ascertained', but which, from a theoretical point of view, is a 'neutral' or 'dumb' concept *'consistent with any theory'* (see 1985, pp.15–19; also *Valore*, p.177).

Napoleoni's further comments on Sraffa's use of 'labour', can be regarded as an introduction to his attempt to go beyond Marx. In Sraffa's 'reduction [of prices] to quantities of timed labour', the price of each commodity depends not only on the quantity of labour which directly or indirectly has been used for its production, but also on the distribution of that labour over time. This means that the quantities of labour alone are not sufficient to determine prices, and that another factor, 'time', must be taken into account. According to Napoleoni, this result 'opens the way to the theory of the "factors" of production (the modern and "bourgeois" one): labour has become one factor of production among others' (*Valore*, p.98). This brings us directly to Napoleoni's reflections on neoclassical theory.

Napoleoni's critique of neoclassical theory of prices and distribution started as early as 1957. After 1960 it incorporated arguments derived from Sraffa's *Production of Commodities by means of Commodities*, and was then extended to the inconsistency of the methodological approach of that theory. Garegnani's *Il capitale nelle teorie della distribuzione*, was regarded as the final critique of that part of the neoclassical theory of distribution which is based on the notion of the productivity of capital. Nevertheless, from the very beginning Napoleoni seems to have appreciated some related elements in neoclassical analysis, namely Robbins's definition of economics as the science of scarcity, and Senior's notion of abstinence.

Napoleoni regarded Senior as an author who tried to reconcile Ricardo's and Say's explanations of the origin of profit, when, in the supply analysis, 'he considered elements [labour, nature and abstinence] which are "real" just as Ricardo's labour is "real"' (*Dizionario*, p.1701). In 1976, even if Napoleoni recognized that Senior's intuition entailed the abandonment of the classical notion of surplus and the related distribution theory based on class struggle, he pointed out that Senior's substitution of abstinence for capital made it possible for him to avoid Ricardo's error and 'to achieve the necessary symmetry in the theory of distribution: abstinence is to profit as labour is to wage' (*Valore*, p.102). Finally, in 1985, Senior's idea of 'indirect consumption' (abstinence), and Böhm-Bawerk's idea of the 'indirect application of labour to nature' (the roundabout processes of production) were seen as the starting point of a representation of the productive process where the postponement of consumption leads to the creation of new capital which, in turn, determines an increase in the productivity of labour. The result of this increased productivity Napoleoni called 'surplus', and that representation he regarded as the neoclassical explanation of the origin of surplus. This explanation did not have any necessary connection with the neoclassical theory of distribution which, in turn, had to be replaced (1985, pp.21, 28).

Napoleoni's first attempt at a preliminary formulation of an alternative theory of distribution was put forward in 1963 ('Sfruttamento, alienazione e capitalismo', reprinted in *Smith, Ricardo and Marx*, 1970, but not reprinted in 1973), and was restated in 1985 (pp. 29–33) and in 1987 ('La teoria del valore dopo Sraffa', reprinted in L. Pasinetti (ed), *Aspetti controversi della teoria del valore*, 1989, p.42). The solution was seen in the introduction of Schumpeter's theory of innovation in order to explain how the surplus produced by labour and abstinence distributes itself between wages and profits over time. The Schumpeterian theory was also used by Napoleoni in order to 'close' Sraffa's model by substituting a dynamic and 'immanent market rule' (in harmony with the neoclassical 'centrality of the market'), for Sraffa's static and 'sociological' theory of distribution. The new theoretical core, according to Napoleoni, would retain Marx's idea of 'the indirect and mediate nature of the relationship between human being and reality', and would thus provide a new basis for Marx's notion of 'abstract labour'. Napoleoni then assumed that core to be the basis of his concept of 'general alienation' (an alienation which involves either workers or capitalists), and of the related thesis according to which the main characteristic of the capitalist system is 'the sway of "things" upon man'. (With different arguments, the notion of general alienation and the centrality of the reification process were expounded by Napoleoni as early as 1963, in 'Sfruttamento, alienazione e capitalismo'.) One of the outcomes of this interpretation of the capitalist system is that a general struggle against an abstract entity – 'the sway of things' – was finally substituted for the Marxian notion of class struggle.

While in 1985 (and in some subsequent articles) Napoleoni enriched his theoretical proposal with several philosophical, methodological and even theological arguments which gained the attention of philosophers, he did not take further the theory of distribution which would result from the synthesis of Schumpeter's and Sraffa's theories. The proposal was explicitly left by

Napoleoni to be examined by younger economists (in 1985 he was already very ill). It was regarded by himself as an attempt at drawing a broad framework within which, once again, he tried to connect different spheres of knowledge in order to point out and question not only the inhuman (alienated) character of present society, but also the too-narrow limits of the theoretical debate in economics.

Napoleoni's Major Writings

(1956), *Dizionario di economia politica* (edited by C. Napoleoni), Milano: Comunita.

(1960), 'Sulla teoria del produzione come processo circolare', *Il Giornale degli Economisti e Annali di Economia*, **20** (1). Reprinted in F. Botta (ed), *Il Dibattio su Sraffa*, De Donato, 1974.

(1961), *Il pensero economico del 900*, Roma: ERI; Torino: Einaudi, 1963. English translation, *Economic Thought of the Twentieth Century*, by M. Robertson, 1972. C. Napoleoni and F. Ranchetti, *Il pensiero economico del Novecento*, Torino: Einaudi, 1990. This new edition includes five new chapters (13–18) covering the history of economic thought of the last 30 years.

(1970), *Smith, Ricardo, Marx*, Boringhieri. Second edition partially rewritten, 1973. English translation, Basil Blackwell, 1975.

(1972), *Lezioni sul capitolo sesto inedito di Marx*, Boringhieri.

(1976), *Valore*, ISEDI.

(1978), 'Ci obliga a ricominciare tutto da capo', *Rinascita*, 4 August. English translation, 'Sraffa's "Tabula Rasa"', *New Left Review*, no 112.

(1985), *Discorso sull' economia politica*, Boringhieri.

(1986), 'Il Discorso sull'economia politica: Critica ai crittici', *La Rivista Trimestrale*, terza serie, 2.

(1991), 'Value and Exploitation: Marx's Economic Theory and Beyond', in G. Caravale (ed), *Marx and Modern Economic Analysis*, Vol 1, Aldershot: E. Elgar.

Other References

Becattini, G. (1988), 'Per Napoleoni oltre Napoleoni', *Il Ponte*, **44** (4–5).

Bellofiore, R. (1989), 'In ricordo di un economista critico: Il percorso intellectuale di Claudio Napoleoni', *Rivista di Storia Economica* n.s. **4** (1).

Cafaro, G. and Messori, M. (1980), *La teoria del valore e l' altro*, Feltrinelli.

Cavalieri, D. (1988), 'L'utopia della ragione in Claudio Napoleoni (1924–1988)', *Quaderni di storia del' economia politica*, **6** (2).

Ginxburg, A. (1971), 'Dal capitalismo borghese al capitalismo, proletario. Ovvero: da Adamo (Smith) and Eva all'economia "volgare"', *Quaderni piacentini*, **10** (44–45).

Graziani, A. (1962), 'Il pensiero economico del Novecento' (review), *Nord e Sud*, April.

Graziani, A. (1962), 'Sulla storia del pensiero economico del 900 – Postilla', *La Rivisita Trimestrale*, **1**.

Il discorso sull' economia politica, di Claudio Napoleoni: un dibattio con l'autore', *Quaderni di storia dell' economia politica*, **4** (1–2), 1986.

Edward J. NELL (born 1935)

Edward Nell was born in Chicago in 1935, the only son of professional parents. His father was a journalist, editor and educator; his mother first a teacher, then an administrator and finally, in a second career, a professor of education. He grew up in a small, select suburb, where his was the only liberal and socialist family in a Republican, conservative town. He attended Princeton, then Oxford as a Rhodes Scholar, finding there, for the first time, an intellectual home where rigorous, careful thought combined with liberal sympathies to produce an outlook that sought to direct the economy (and so the material basis of history) for the benefit of humanity.

After leaving Oxford, Nell taught at Wesleyan University and later at the University of East Anglia. In 1969 he became Professor at the Graduate Faculty of the New School for Social Research in New York City, where he served for many years as Chair of the Department, linking it with the leading research in Europe and the Third World, and making it a world centre for alternative, critical and progressive visions of the economy.

At Oxford he began his work in philosophy, publishing his first six papers in logic and philosophical analysis. These questioned the adequacy of the analytic-synthetic distinction, later a major issue in Hollis and Nell (1975), but preliminary to his main concern at the time which was understanding the processes of social change. This required a grasp of the way economic forces developed historically – the theory of growth. Growth economics, however, appeared to him to take too narrow a perspective; in particular, the analysis of technical change confined itself to the study of the quantitative enhancement of productivity. But qualitative changes were obviously more significant. These early considerations prepared the way for his major contribution – the theory of transformational growth.

But before the theory of growth could be rebuilt, the foundations of the theory of value had to be re-examined. For if scarcity and substitution were the foundations of value, then they could also be expected to govern the processes of growth. Understanding growth would be a question of finding the optimal path of expansion over time, given the various factor constraints and the time preferences of the agents. But there were reasons to believe that this way of thinking was flawed.

The neoclassical approach derived value – by which it means the set of equilibrium prices – from a consideration of choices based on preferences in circumstances in which there are given amounts of factors of production. But value is a stable, relatively permanent construct; values are used as the basis for the formation of plans and expectations in the economy. Yet the wants and preferences people actually have are transient and changeable. People grow and change, age and die. How can their actual wants form an adequate basis for value? But the wants they *ought* to have cannot be the foundation of value either, for notoriously, people do not behave as they ought, nor do they agree as to what ought to be. Hence there would be neither consensus nor predictability (1975, Chapter 5).

The device of a 'representative individual' only makes the problems worse, for it raises the additional issue of how to decide what is truly representative.

It seemed, in short, that value could not be based on behaviour; that is, on choices in the context of given endowments. However, the scarcity approach should not be dismissed altogether. Rather than being a descriptive theory of value or normal prices, it has a legitimate role as a prescriptive approach. In given circumstances it tells us how to find the best position, although the usual mainstream models are less useful than the more concrete ones favoured by operations research (Lowe, 1964; Hollis and Nell, 1975, Chapter 7).

Conventional theory starts on the wrong foot; neither preferences nor endowments can be fundamental, for both are social products. People are the products of their experience, and the world we live in is man-made. Even 'nature' itself is the product of our impact on the planet. Value, then, must arise from the system of production, from relatively permanent features of that system – its structure. The structure of a socio-economic system endures through change. As agents carry out their duties they use up material products. To be able to continue, to act in a regular repetitive manner, these material products must be replaced. The conditions for such replacement provide the foundations for a set of valuations.

Foundations, yes, but not a determination. For the basic production system will not only reproduce the materials used up in the course of normal activities, it may also produce a surplus; in that case the disposition of that surplus must be known to determine normal prices (Sraffa, 1960, Chapters 1–5). And the causes of the surplus must be explained.

Drawing on Marx's distinction between 'constant' and 'variable' capital, Nell argued that the origin of the surplus was to be found in the fact that consumption goods supported workers for a given period of time, regardless of how much they accomplished during that time. The output of any viable system must at least support the necessary workers for the time required to produce that minimal output. Taking a viable system, so defined as a base: if workers can be cajoled or coerced into speeding up the process, producing the same amounts but in less time, a surplus will be created. This introduces technical progress at the most fundamental level, relates it to incentives and coercion, and bases it on the different temporal characteristics of consumer goods (which support workers for a period of time) and means of production (which are required in certain amounts, per unit output, independently of time). This approach also provides a solution to the problem of heterogeneous labour and sheds a favourable light on certain claims of the labour theory of value. By contrast, in neoclassical theory technical progress is an afterthought, the initial level of productivity an unexplained given (see 1990b and 1980).

In neoclassical theory distribution is considered a form of exchange, and this has a curious significance for the theory of money. Every market transaction is considered an exchange and thus, in the absence of money, barter.

Hence money simply breaks the unity of barter into two parts, in each of which money exchanges against goods. But when value is based on production and the system generates a surplus, distribution is not an exchange, but a transfer. So some money exchanges against goods, and some money is transferred to the appropriate recipients of distribution payments. Money must play two different roles, which must be coordinated. How does the given stock of money exchange, first, for the aggregate inputs as producers buy what they need and, second, for the larger volume of output when producers sell? At first glance the same amount of money appears to swap for two different amounts of goods. A theory of circulation is required, as both Marx and Wicksell realized (see 1967b). Nell's solution to the problem builds on the above differences in the temporal relationships of different kinds of outputs, and so ties the concept of velocity to the time rate of production and, therefore, to productivity (see 1986).

The Capital Controversy intruded at this point; distribution is not an exchange; the rate of profit is not a price. The neoclassical story of the demand and supply of capital is flawed – there is no regular inverse relationship between the quantity of capital and the rate of return. Nell's contribution was, first, to provide an interpretation of Sraffa showing that prices in his equations, and the rate of profit (and therefore capital), were not determined by a maximizing procedure. The formal process was different; also, mathematically, prices were a vector, but the rate of profit was derived from the root of the equation system. Understanding the rate of profit correctly made it possible (i) to dispose of Solow's claims that it necessarily equalled the 'social rate of return'; (ii) to expose the mistake in Gallaway and Shukla's proposed construction of a neoclassical production function, and (iii) to show that both Marx and J.B. Clark had a more sophisticated understanding of capital value in relation to capital goods than that found in modern neoclassical thinking (see 1974, 1977 and 1967a).

The rejection of the neoclassical perspective left the way open for a reconstruction of economic theory which would make room for an adequate treatment of growth and technical change, something Joan Robinson always urged (see 1989a). The 'choice of technique' framework set forth in neoclassical theory has effectively stood in the way of a theoretically satisfying approach to the emergence of new products and new processes. According to this perspective, firms choose techniques of production from among a set of pre-existing blueprints, rather than developing new methods in response to incentives and pressure thrown up by the market. It is this latter which is the central idea of transformational growth: the transformation comes about as the result of responses to pressures generated by market processes.

In the redevelopment of economic theory, a central task had to be the redefinition of the place of money and of effective demand. Remarkably, Nell showed that the temporal relationships underlying technical progress and the generation of the surplus also govern the circulation of money and determine its velocity (see 1986). Velocity turns out to be a reflection of productivity, and when the money supply is endogenous it will exactly mirror the aggregate mark-up, the ratio of profits to wages (see 1990f). The development of endogenous money in turn parallels the rise of mass production.

Following the Kaleckian tradition, Nell distinguishes investment as the expansion of productive capacity from investment spending, the demand for capital goods. The latter but not the former is sensitive to financial variables, not only the rate of interest but also the appreciation of stock prices, which in turn reflect (among other things) the financial community's judgement of the effectiveness of real investment. There will therefore be a three-way arbitrage between investment spending, bonds and stocks as alternatives to holding money (see 1989b). But the long-term expansion of productive capacity must be coordinated with long-term pricing policies.

The results on monetary circulation and investment spending are reached on the assumption that prices reflect a stable distribution – or rate of profit – and established conditions of production. While short-term or market prices may reflect 'supply and demand', long-term or normal prices do not. This, in turn, requires a new understanding of the relation between supply and demand and the determination of market prices, and prices of production. And this leads to a central methodological point in Nell's perspective: apparently competing theories of the market actually apply to different historical stages of market development. Marshallian 'supply and demand' curves may be a good rough approximation of adjustment patterns for an earlier stage of capitalism, in which employment and output were comparatively fixed.

Demand fluctuations may be considered, in a closed economy, to result from the volatility of the expectations governing investment, as Keynes argued. Supply conditions, on the other hand, will necessarily be stable, in the sense that fixed capital, once in place, cannot be changed rapidly – perhaps not at all in the short run. But there are two quite different cases to consider. In the first, corresponding to a 'craft economy' (1988, Chapter 4), employment as well as fixed capital cannot easily be changed. Output can therefore only vary as a result of changes in productivity. If demand collapses because of unfavourable expectations concerning the future, then output can only be adjusted downwards by allowing productivity to fall. In these circumstances firms will try to produce close to their normal output and sell for whatever they can get. Prices will be driven down.

In the second case, that of 'mass production' (1988, Chapter 5), the methods and conditions of production have been reconstructed so that employment and output can be varied *pari passu* with demand. When demand falls or rises, employment – and thus variable costs – and output can be adjusted appropriately. When demand unexpectedly drops there will be no excessive production forcing prices down. Nor will productivity have to change. Recovery from a slump need not lead to price rises (1990c, especially 'Transformational Growth: Mass Production and the Multiplier'). With prices stable, the adjustment will bring output into line with demand in each industry or sector. However, the effects of adjusting costs and employment in any one sector will be felt as changes in demand in other sectors – those that supply the first, or in which the wages of the first are spent. Hence such a pattern of adjustment sets up a matrix multiplier.

Broadly speaking, then, flexible prices are associated with fixed employment and fixed output; that is, when demand fluctuates, prices are the first to respond. Employment and output may also vary eventually, but only after the variations in prices have failed to bring about a successful adaptation. On the other hand, flexible employment and output will be associated with relatively fixed prices.

When employment and output can vary, there will be no pressure for prices to change when demand changes, but producers could still adjust prices if they found it optimal to do so. That will not be the case, however. Nell shows that under conditions of mass production, the best strategy for producers will normally be to keep prices steady when demand fluctuates. A crucial reason for this concerns investment: a central feature of mass production is that economies of scale are available, particularly as learning-by-doing enhances the productivity of the technologies in use. Hence the existing firms in a market will undertake regular investment to maintain their market share and prevent newcomers from entering. They will set their prices with an eye to generating the profits, at normal output, that will financially underwrite this investment. The prices that firms set are thus associated with the growth of output, not, as in the conventional view, with the level (1990b, IV).

These will be normal prices and will be set in association with normal growth. But short-term fluctuations may lead to deviations from the pattern of normal growth. In general, Nell shows that prices will not be affected much by small deviations. For a representative firm, to cut prices when demand falls will not be a worthwhile strategy unless it expects a proportional increase in sales greater than the proportional cut in prices. This will be unlikely in the case of manufacturers, which tend to be price-inelastic overall, and to involve differentiated products, so that customers will be hard to attract from competitors. Prices of primary products, however, may be sensitive to demand, as may some services.

By contrast, in the craft or fixed-employment economy the flexibility of prices will lead to changes in the real wage. Precisely because employment is relatively fixed, price changes will tend to be of greater amplitude than money wage changes. But the changes in the real wage will affect consumption. A fall in spending on investment will thus lead to a greater fall in prices than in money wages, so too a rise in the real wage results, therefore, in a rise in consumption demand in real terms, as the same money income now commands more goods. In other words, variations in effective demand tend to set up offsetting patterns of movement. Expressing this in a compact formula, Nell shows that under certain conditions the elasticity of consumption spending with respect to investment will be -1. By contrast, in a mass production system, the elasticity will be $+1$. In the former, the adjustment process is such that the product I x C remains constant; in the latter, the ratio I/C is kept constant. (This, of course, provides an explanation of the relative constancy of the share of investment in output in conditions of mass production, and can be considered a generalization – and correction – of the so-called Cambridge Theory of Distribution.)

A mass production system, however, unlike a fixed-employment economy, can operate in two distinct modes. In one, represented by modern mixed economies, aggregate demand chronically falls short of productive capacity; both grow at approximately the same rate, and the gap between them, though it may fluctuate, on average also grows at the same rate. In the other, represented by the post-war centrally planned economies, aggregate demand chronically tends to exceed productive capacity, creating shortages and imbalances, because of which growth will be slowed. Again both demand and capacity will tend to grow together, and the gap will be stable (see 1988, especially 'Demand Scarcity and Supply Shortage'). The striking point in Nell's analysis is that he shows that these two modes of operation are institutionally distinct and unconnected. An economy cannot, for example, begin with excess capacity and then move to full utilization, finally spilling over into a state of excess demand. Once a system is operating, there are forces that tend to keep it either in a state of excess capacity or in a state of excess demand. It cannot move from one condition to the other, although the levels of either excess demand or excess capacity may fluctuate.

An excess capacity economy ('capitalism') is demand-constrained; because of this, businesses must compete to sell. Hence they must please their customers, and competition will lead to product improvement and cost-cutting. A shortage economy ('socialism') is a seller's market; whatever is produced, within reason, will find a buyer. Cost overruns are acceptable and quality is no object; the incentive is to meet the guidelines of the Plan. In an excess-capacity economy inflation will arise from the cost rather than the demand side; in an excess-demand economy, inflation will reflect demand pressures. Expansionist policies will promote the welfare of the common people in excess-capacity economies, although they will be unpopular with capitalists since they strengthen the bargaining power of workers (see 1988, Chapter 10).

Transformational growth is the process of change that arises out of the incentives thrown up by the normal working of the system. Because of these incentives, innovations are developed. As these are put into practice, the linkages between the parts of the system are changed, and the system comes to work differently. It is necessary to see what the problems are in the way the system is working at a given time, and what rewards there are for solving such problems. Nell wrote a striking series of articles on early agriculture, Feudalism, Mercantilism and the Industrial Revolution, illustrating in each case the development of pressures that led to specific forms of innovation which, when widely adopted, led to changes in the way the markets worked (see 1990c, Part 3).

The change from a fixed-employment to a flexible-employment system resulted from the fact that those firms able to reduce their employment and costs, and adjust their output, when demand fell, improved their chances to survive. The incentive was to reduce losses; the reward was survival. But by making employment, costs and output flexible, the innovating firms reduced and eventually removed the pressure on prices, in the process creating a chain-linkage of new effects, with the result that the system came to work differently.

But the move from fixed to variable employment is not a simple change; it requires altering not just the technology, but also the institutions of control. The firm must be reorganized, and this will create both opportunities and pressures for changes both in the methods of finance and in the organization of capital. A fixed-employment firm tends to reach an optimal size and remain there (Robinson, 1932); it will be a family business in a traditional mode. But variable employment technology will require a corporate structure, and the firm will try to achieve, not an optimal size, but the most appropriate growth pattern. It will regularly invest and, drawing on technical progress, will from time to time undertake reorganization (see 1988, Chapter 6).

The change from family firms to modern corporations alters the nature of capital. Once held by families and passed from generation to generation through inheritance, it takes on an increasingly institutionalized character. Capital is invested in funds, managed by professionals and often regulated by the state; those who would formerly have held ownership increasingly have the status of beneficiaries. What were once the prerogatives of owner-ship are now divided between the managers of the corporations and those of the funds. Not only has the firm become a corporate institution, so have its owners. And the institution in which ownership of capital was once vested, the family, has fragmented and is being reshaped by social and economic pressures. Most of its traditional functions have been shifted to the state or have become marketable commodities in the private sector. This accounts in part, for the growth of the state as a proportion of GNP and for the shrinking of the extended family to the nuclear which, like the atom, is splitting under the impact of modern technology.

'The owl of Minerva takes wing only at dusk'. Just as we are beginning to understand the deeper nature of Western capitalism, it has entered another period of wrenching change. Even as the pundits celebrate what they see as its triumph over centrally planned socialism, new stresses are forming. Information systems now permit worldwide coordination of production, more flexible designs and more varied production runs, bringing massive unemployment to the traditional 'rust belts' of the West. New materials and new processes create new products and new jobs. A more complex mix of services and goods in output is changing the definition of the marketable commodity from an 'item' to a 'system'. Complementarities and 'public goods effects' can be expected to increase; a widening gap between social and private returns is already evident and the impact on the environment is near catastrophic. Will markets and prices continue to function in the same way? Should there be further changes in the relationships between governments and markets? This is the field for the theory of transformational growth.

Nell's Major Writings

(1967a), 'Theories of Growth and Theories of Value', *Economic Development and Cultural Change*, 16(1), December. Reprinted in G.C. Harcourt (ed), *Capital and Growth*, Penguin, 1974.

(1967b), 'Wicksell's Theory of Circulation', *Journal of Political Economy*, August.

(1974), 'The Black Box Rate of Return', *Kyklos*, 28, fasc 4.

(1975), *Rational Economic Man* (with Martin Hollis), Cambridge University Press.

(1977), 'Reswitching, Wicksell Effects and the Neo-Classical Production Function' (with D. Laibman), *American Economic Review*, December.

(1980), *Growth, Profits and Property*, Cambridge University Press.

(1984), *Historia y Teoria Economica* (translated by A. Barcelo y Lluis Argemi), Grijalbo: Editorial Critica.

(1986), 'On Monetary Circulation and the Rate of Exploitation', *Thames Papers in Political Economy*, Summer. Reprinted in P. Arestis (ed), *Post-Keynesian Monetary Economics*, Edward Elgar, 1988.

(1988), *Prosperity and Public Spending*, Unwin Hyman.

(1989a), 'Accumulation and Capital Theory', in G. Feiwel (ed), *Joan Robinson and Modern Economics*, New York University Press.

(1989b), 'Notes on Finance, Risk and Investment Spending', in B. Barrere (ed), *Money, Credit and Prices in Keynesian Perspective*, Macmillan.

(1990a), *Economics at the Princeton Club*, Macmillan.

(1990b), *Keynes after Sraffa*, Unwin Hyman.

(1990c), *Transformational Growth and Effective Demand*, Macmillan.

(1990d), 'Demand Scarcity and Supply Shortage in Capitalism and Socialism', in E.J. Nell and W. Semmler (eds), *Nicholas Kaldor and Mainstream Economics*, Macmillan.

(1990e), 'Pricing, Profits and Corporate Investment', in D. Papadimitriou (ed), *Profits, Deficits and Instability*, Macmillan.

(1990f), 'Velocity of Circulation and the Mark-up', *Economie Appliquée*, Summer.

Other References

Harcourt, G.C. (1972), *Cambridge Controversies in Capital Theory*, Cambridge University Press.

Lowe, A. (1964), *The Path of Economic Growth*, Harper and Row.
Robinson, E.A.G. (1932), *The Structure of Competitive Industry*, Cambridge University Press.
Sraffa, P. (1960), *Production of Commodities by Means of Commodities*, Cambridge University Press.

Alec NOVE (born 1915)

I was born in 1915 in what was then Petrograd, into a Russian Jewish family. We moved to Moscow in 1918. My father had been an active Menshevik, which landed him in gaol both under the Tsars and under the Bolsheviks. From exile in Siberia he was allowed to leave the country, and my mother and I followed, in 1923. Fortunately he, and we, settled in Britain. I attended King Alfred School in North London, and the London School of Economics, graduating in 1936 with an upper second. After some research jobs, the last of them for a trade union, came a long period of army service, from 1939 to 1946, holding various ranks from Signalman to Major. After demobilization I found a job in the Board of Trade, as it was then called, and remained in the Civil Service until 1958. In my spare time I had written a review article on Soviet constitutional law, published in the *Modern Law Review* (in 1948), and a critique of what had seemed to me an over-favourable view of Soviet collective farms for *Soviet Studies*. There was at that time very little hope of any academic appointment. However, I then had a stroke of luck. With the progressive abandonment of wartime controls the Board of Trade was over-staffed and the then permanent secretary, Sir Frank Lee, was persuaded by Alec Cairncross (who had been economic adviser to that ministry) to give me two years' paid leave to study the Soviet economy in Glasgow. Sir Alec Cairncross is now Chancellor of Glasgow University; I owe much to him.

So I was in Glasgow when Stalin died. I tried to reconstruct the Soviet national income – a frustrating task when so many figures were unpublished, but most educational! I returned to the Civil Service in 1954. In 1955 I went to the USSR for the first time since childhood as a member of the British agricultural delegation. In 1956 I was borrowed by the Foreign Office and sent for five months to serve in the British Embassy in Moscow. Around this time I wrote a article on 'The Problem of Success Indicators in Soviet Industry', published in *Economica* in 1959. Finally, in 1958, I was appointed to a Readership at the University of London, spending most of my time at the LSE.

I was glad to switch, rather late in life, to a university career. Already then I felt two kinds of dissent: from the theory and practice of Soviet planning, but also from neoclassical orthodoxy. It seemed to me that much had changed since I was a student (I had been out of touch with academic economics for 20 years). Not only was there a substantial increase in the amount of mathematical formalism, but the emphasis was much more on equilibrium than on process. Questions of organization, real decision-making under uncertainty, the historical context, seemed to be ignored or downgraded. Astonishingly few of my colleagues took an interest in the real problems of any particular country, area or system. There was a long struggle before development economics could be taught at all.

In 1963 I was offered a Chair in Glasgow, where I was to set up an Institute of Soviet and East European Studies (on the basis, laid over several years, by Jack Miller and Rudolf Schlesinger), and also to organize courses on development economics. As far as the latter were concerned I took a special interest in Latin America and made many visits, especially to Mexico and Chile (my sad account of the economics of the Allende administration appeared in 1976 in a volume on Chile edited by P. O'Brien). Meanwhile, while still in London I had written the textbook *The Soviet Economy* and also *An Economic History of the USSR*, which were translated into many languages. A collection of my papers appeared under the challenging title *Was Stalin Really Necessary?* There also appeared a short historical introduction, *Stalinism and After*, which went (as did the textbooks) through several editions. A rewrite of *The Soviet Economy* was given the title *The Soviet Economic System*. Two more collections of papers were published, and one more is in the press. I will come in a moment to the two books which most clearly reflect dissent from orthodoxies.

A close study of the Soviet economic record convinced me of the inherent inefficiency of the system of centralized planning. Oskar Lange had been right to describe it as a 'war economy *sui generis*'. In wartime in all countries, the market is subordinated to the overwhelming and incommensurate priorities of war. In more normal times the needs of citizens, and of the production process itself, are so complex as inevitably to overwhelm the informational and decision-making capacity of the planners. Many if not most of the known and familiar deficiencies of the centralized model follow from 'the curse of scale'. Faced with a vastly excessive number of decisions and with informational overload, the centre becomes split into departments which compete for resources and are exceedingly hard to coordinate. The precise requirements of the customer get lost owing to the necessity of aggregating plan targets. The attempt to fulfil targets expressed in roubles, tons or thousands of units leads to familiar distortions: management produces not for the customer but for plan-fulfilment statistics. A theory of value based on human effort, a price system based on cost-plus, fail to reflect use-value and have the perverse effect of rewarding wasteful use of inputs. And so on.

Thus far my critique of Soviet practice did not diverge significantly from that of Barone or even Mises. The difference lay in the fact that I was, on the whole, favourably inclined to the socialist idea. I could see that the Stalinist model, which survived his death, represented some sort of monstrous perversion, was closely linked with despotism and terror. It is far easier to control people if nearly everyone works for the state and nearly everything is supplied by the state. Indeed, it is possible that the centralized system requires a despot at the top to set and impose priorities, that the dilution of priorities and the abandonment of terror after Stalin's death made inevitable the decay of the system. But what was, what could be, a socialist alternative?

This led me into conflict with the then quite numerous neo-Marxists and some other left-wing intellectuals, whose criticism of the Soviet Union seemed to me to be based on unreal and Utopian assumptions about what socialist planning *could* be. They saw, indeed they stressed, the inefficiencies of the Soviet economic system. They also saw the link between the centralized control over the means of production and the despotic and hierarchical nature of the society. But they counterposed to it some sort of democratic planning by 'the associated producers', in which what needed to be done would be decided by comradely discussion. The market mechanism could be tolerated (indeed at times *had* to be tolerated) during a transition period, but for them socialism and the market were inherently incompatible. And indeed they could claim to be following in the tradition of Marx, Engels, Bebel and Kautsky. In this respect they were right: Marx and his followers had assumed that socialist planning would be simple and transparent, once the market and 'commodity fetishism' were eliminated along with the capitalist class. The kind of planning that the founding fathers had in mind was quite different from what had existed in the Soviet Union – that at least was clear. But such men as Sweezy, Bettelheim, Ernest Mandel and Ticktin drew from this the conclusion that Stalin and his successors were guilty of distortion and betrayal, since they had failed to introduce the socialist planning system envisaged by Marx, Engels and Lenin.

This seemed to me to miss the essential point. They failed to look critically at the concepts of the founding fathers. A non-market economy spawned bureaucratic centralism not because of somebody's betrayal, but through functional necessity. If, for example, materials and components are not *sold*, they have to be allocated. All have numerous alternative uses. Most are scarce relatively to what demand would be at zero price. This requires the creation of a large number of allocating offices, related to each other within a hierarchy and staffed by professional bureaucrats. The vast scale of interconnected planning decisions, called upon to replace the market, is not due to the deficiencies of the Soviet economic and political system; they are among the principal causes of these deficiencies.

I went back to Marx and to those who followed him, including Lenin, who had said (1917): 'to run the entire economy on the lines of the post office, under the control of the armed workers, this is our immediate task'.

The experience of war-communism taught Lenin and his comrades a hard lesson, but even for Bukharin the market in the mixed economy of NEP represented a stage in the transition to a real socialism in which the market would wither away. Out of all this emerged several critical articles (for instance, 'Market Socialism and its Critics', directed particularly at Bettelheim) and a book, *Economics of Feasible Socialism* (1983). Along with a critique of the Utopian aspects of Marx's view of socialism, plus the lessons to be drawn from Soviet experience, and of reform attempts in other countries such as Hungary, I tried to sketch out a possible model of social-ism which included the market and a variety of forms of property. The book was translated into several languages, including Chinese and Hungarian. It may appear in Russian too, since many of its ideas are shared by Soviet reformers who are close to Gorbachev. In fact by now the dogmatists who had been my target when I was writing that book are on the retreat (though Mandel and Ticktin still hold to their anti-market ideology, still imagine that one can have no market *and* no bureaucracy outside of Cloud Cuckoo Land). So perhaps even in the context of socialist ideas I have ceased to be a dissenter, having possibly made a marginal contribution to a change in the ideological climate on the left.

However, my critique both of Soviet practice and of neo-Marxist ('new left') dogmatism was not undertaken in an anti-socialist spirit. For reasons to be expounded in a moment, I was far from happy with the dogmas of neoclassical economics and strongly opposed to the laissez-faire extremists who surrounded Mrs Thatcher. Consequently some recent articles written in Russian and published in the Soviet Union (thanks to Gorbachev's *glasnost*) have been around the theme of 'Yes, the market is necessary, but ...'. There is an alarming tendency, in reaction to the pseudo-socialist dogmatism im-posed on them in the past, for economists in the USSR and Eastern Europe to regard the market as a panacea, to see only the virtues and not the limitations. My paper, about to be published in Hungary, on 'Soviet Economic Reform and Neoclassical Economics', develops the theme that, while the dogmas of the 'political economy of socialism' are indeed useless and mis-leading, the neoclassical axioms are (almost as) irrelevant to their real prob-lems. In fact they are largely irrelevant to ours.

Which brings me to my dissent with much of conventional Western academic economics. It found its most systematic expression in a book entitled *Efficiency Criteria for Nationalised Industries*, published in 1973, with its ideas expanded and (I hope) deepened following encounters with Thatcherite economics. As I said frequently in articles and lectures, neoclas-sical economics as such bears little or no blame for the errors and excesses I was criticizing, save in one important respect: its emphases, plus the things it chooses (with some honourable exceptions) not to mention or not to stress.

Thus externalities, the 'free rider' problem, do get a mention, but almost literally as footnotes within a paradigm where laissez-faire permits, or almost guarantees, equilibrium at a Pareto optimum. So when the British government cuts grants to scientific research, arguing that private firms would undertake it if it were profitable, the average graduate in economics might well not see why this is myopic, or indeed why no other industrial country is as foolish as this.

For me all this began long before Mrs Thatcher, when perusing the advice being given by academic economists on how to make nationalized industries efficient. Most such industries in Britain were monopolies, in many instances *natural* monopolies. One reason for their being in the public sector was surely that efficiency could not be detached from purpose, that private profitability would be an inadequate guide. This was particularly obvious in the case of urban transportation. Efficient rapid-transit reduces congestion, benefiting even those that do not use it in a variety of ways (through the effect on property values, or not having to fetch friends to visit them, or enabling them to get to work when their car is off the road etc etc). Profits can be enhanced by reducing the quality and frequency of service or by squeezing in more standing passengers. It was equally obvious that the post office could increase its profits by having more customers waiting longer to be served by fewer staff, and closing offices in rural areas. All this highlighted a gap in conventional monopoly theory: it was, with few exceptions, concerned with just two variables – quantity and price. What about quality? I tried an experiment: in six well-known textbooks I looked for the word in the index; in five it was not there, in the sixth it appeared under the heading of product differentiation. A given product or service was of a given quality. Yet a given product has many characteristics, and quality *can* deteriorate, a monopolist (public or private) would find that such deterioration pays, since to maintain quality (sharpness, after-sales service, punctual deliveries, durability, availability of spares etc) incurs a cost.

It struck me, as I read papers in which nationalized industries were supposed to act 'commercially', that the authors of these papers had a somewhat odd view of how real private firms functioned in the real world. Clearly, the textbooks had not taught them the meaning of such words as function, duty, purpose or responsibility. Suppose one considers the transport department of any largish private corporation. It would be crazy, would it not, to consider its efficiency in terms purely of its own profit-and-loss account, without taking into consideration the punctuality with which it delivered whatever loads it was supposed to carry, that is the very purpose of its existence. Yet just this myopia could be seen in the evaluation of public transport, and indeed of other forms of infrastructure, which almost by definition have important external effects. These external effects become internal within a firm. Indeed one function of a firm, private or public, is the internalization of what otherwise would be externalities. It is intuitively obvious that what it appears rational to do, or not to do, depends in some degree on the area of responsibility of the decision-maker, since this determines what factors he or she takes into account. Yet in not a single textbook known to me is this rather important point ever mentioned.

This led me to question the meaning of the term 'margin'. By this I do not mean that I suffered from an ideological hostility to marginalism as such. But the textbooks never explain the term, leave it to be supposed that it is clear and unambiguous, such as the marginal batch of shoes, the marginal labourer, or whatever. Yet this is to abstract from some very important distinctions. Production of almost any good or service takes place in stages, interconnected instalments, through time. Within this process marginal decisions interrelate and affect each other in varying degrees. Thus, to take one of many examples, the location and equipment of a pumping station on an oil pipeline call for decisions which could be characterized as marginal, but which make sense only within its context. The marginal productivity of the pump, or of whoever operates it, makes very little sense, if the absence of the pump brings the entire operation to a halt. Decisions are taken in relation to contexts, purpose, strategy. If they cannot be adequately considered at lower levels, where their wider effects cannot be perceived, they have to be referred upwards. Hence hierarchies, public or private. To a hierarchy of decision-makers there corresponds a hierarchy of margins.

Furthermore, the interrelationships could be of many kinds: technological (such as successive stages and processes) but also via goodwill. But the word 'goodwill', of vital importance in the real world of competition, is as rare in a textbook as is the word 'quality', despite (or because of) the fact that the two are closely linked: one maintains quality for fear of losing customer goodwill. Why, I asked myself, do textbooks ignore so obvious a fact? The answer, in my view, brings one back to the over-emphasis on equilibrium and perfect competition. As should be clear, under 'perfect competition' there is not and cannot be any competition: there is full employment of all resources (so there is nothing left to compete *with*), and by definition oil agents can sell all of their (homogeneous) product at *the* price. Goodwill, like quality, are irrelevant in such a model. And under monopoly the customer cannot go elsewhere, so once again goodwill matters not. Finally, our textbooks tend silently to assume that all transactions are directly market-related, and it would seem theoretically untidy to remind students that different transactions undertaken by the same firm react upon one another. Even though this is a major reason for the existence of firms!

In fact orthodox theory has a struggle to find reasons why firms exist at all, and then its explanations are plainly incomplete. As H. Demsetz pointed

out, the so-called perfect competitive model is in fact one of perfect decentralization, with no role for a coordinating function. Nor, let it be added, for
an entrepreneur (hence in equilibrium profits tend to zero, or to whatever is
the current rate of interest; there is no reward for a non-existent function). O.
Williamson tried to find a *raison d'être* for firms through the concept of
transaction costs (Coase had explored this avenue decades earlier). Yes, in
respect of a *given* transaction it is relevant and interesting to ask the question: should the firm undertake it itself (hierarchy) or use a sub-contractor
(market)? But this approach misses out not only on the coordinating function, it also fails to ask the question: where does that particular transaction fit
into a firm's purposes, role, strategy or responsibility, these being terms that
have meaning when applied to firms, and none if applied to transactions
viewed in isolation from the firm and from other transactions. My attempt to
point this out, in a note I sent to *Economica*, was not understood; it was not
printed. Maybe I drafted it badly. Or maybe the orthodox economist just is
not trained to see the point I was making. I will quote in a moment other
examples of mutual incomprehension.

This brings me to what I like to call 'myopic marginalism', by which I
mean an attitude which sees every marginal decision as, firstly, market-
related and, secondly, as profitable in itself. (Were it not so, it would not be
undertaken.) To cover loss-making activities out of profits is 'cross-
subsidization' and, it seems, economically irrational. In fact (to my mind
incredibly) cross-subsidization has been made *illegal* in urban transport in
Britain. Needless to say, such insanity is unknown elsewhere, so one cannot
blame economic theory – except for sins of omission: it has had far too little
to say about systems and sub-systems, about indivisibilities and
complementarities. Myopic marginalists *fragment*. For them there is no wood,
there are only trees.

Examples that can be quoted are legion, and I will omit the supermarket
'loss leader', and take instead the (real) example of a major food shop in the
centre of a provincial town. It was famous for its vast range of choice. It was
taken over, and the new owners put in myopic accountants. They recommended the removal from the shelves of products that turned over slowly.
Soon the shop lost its *raison d'être*. It closed. Passing to the more important
case of public transport, no *network* has ever existed in which there is not an
element of cross-subsidization. Costs and revenues vary widely. Services
interconnect. For purposes of marginal cost pricing, where is the margin? If
there is a standard charge of any sort (zonal, per-mile, or any season ticket,
capital card, *carte orange* or whatever), some bits of the network, if separately evaluated, are loss-making, others profitable. This is even true of the
same service at different times of the day. Every scheduled bus, train or
plane that leaves half empty may be said to be cross-subsidized. Standby or

reserve capacity does not pay as such, and is maintained in the real world either from consideration of goodwill (without it customers would be upset and go elsewhere) or because of a sense of duty or of imposed obligation (such as having enough back-up generating capacity in the event of a very cold day). Supermarkets 'cross-subsidize' car parks. Arsenal Football Club, plc, cross-subsidizes its reserve team. If *The Times* costs the same in Wick as it does in Wapping then this is *prima-facie* evidence of cross-subsidization. And so on.

The point about systems has been well made by Brian Loasby: 'Highly complex sub-systems such as firms, or even whole sectors of the economy, containing within themselves many layers of great complexity, are regularly treated as simple elements, while components of a complex system are analysed as isolated units' (1975, p.30).

The neoclassical textbooks tend, with few exceptions, to be based on the assumptions of methodological individualism. The whole is *only* the sum of its parts. 'There is no such thing as society' (Mrs Thatcher). And individuals 'maximize' their personal utility, save at occasional moments of 'altruism'. From this gross oversimplification of human motivation one can derive a theory according to which public servants think only of themselves. Also the ludicrous belief that involuntary unemployment is impossible, and so in 1933 some 17 million Americans 'preferred leisure'. There is no room in such theories for loyalty, commitment or pride in work well done – of vital importance in public *and* private sectors. All this invites the sort of critique made by Tibor Scitovsky in *The Joyless Economy*, but (like the present author) he did not find it easy to be understood. I have recently heard of a case where a labour economist was not considered for a post in a reputable American university since, in the formal mathematical equilibrium world – where human beings might as well be robots – there ain't no such thing as labour economics.

But above all the excesses of methodological individualism lead, at least in Britain, to fragmentation. If the whole is but the sum of (profitable) parts, eliminate the whole, divide up, opt out. This has been done in recent years for London, the post office, urban transportation, health, education and electricity generation. Of course there is nothing in the formal doctrines of neoclassical economics which compel its practitioners to recommend, for example, the break-up of London or Glasgow Transport. No such absurdities are to be seen in New York, Toronto, Washington, Zurich, Paris, Dusseldorf, Munich. ... But our students are not trained to see the inherent fallacy involved in fragmenting a system such as Paris transport, and they will be predisposed also against subsidy, because externalities are downgraded. Many years ago, the late Denys Munby told a committee that if the head of London Transport thought he had some sort of social contract with Londoners he could not run an efficient service. In other words, efficiency in his view must be detached from purpose! The same Munby believed in the separate evaluation, as far as practically possible, of every portion of line, station, train and marshalling yard, of a railway. A classic instance of the militant-ideological externalization of internalities!

A simple example of what we do not teach. Virtually every airport in the United States is in the public sector. Why? Our students would usually be unaware of the fact, and would not know how to approach the question. Yet this is another example of the relationship between efficiency and purpose, which in this instance is to provide good service to the businesses and citizens of (say) Pittsburgh, which is not identical with profit maximization of the airport seen in isolation from these external effects. Or to take a Scottish example: if a consortium of Scottish businessmen operated Prestwick airport, they would surely charge much lower landing fees (the ones currently operative are actually higher than at Gatwick). For that matter, if they or their interests were represented on the Board of British Airways, we would not be facing a fares structure apparently designed to penalize anyone booking direct flights to Scotland from the continent of Europe. These are all variations on the theme of the consequences of myopic fragmentation, a result of what neoclassical orthodoxy chooses not to emphasize – interconnections between the parts, or between the parts and the whole.

My final example of the mental distortions engendered by the standard neoclassical textbook relates to investment. Frank Hahn has remarked that under perfect competition the investment process is 'profoundly mysterious'. Thirty years ago, G.B. Richardson demonstrated most rigorously that the orthodox model fails to generate the information on the basis of which investment decisions can be taken. Nor is this only a matter of prices (and interest and exchange and wage rates) in future years not being known. Let us suppose that they are known; that it is quite clear that there will be additional demand at a price which will definitely make this investment profitable. A moment's thought should show that the preceding sentence is contradictory. If, as Richardson, Loasby and a very few others realize, this information is available to all the competitors, none will know what to do, since the model does not generate information about the investment choices made by others. If they all respond, then the future price will be lower and the profit will vanish. If many people know that a horse will win a race at odds of 10 to 1, the odds will not be 10 to 1. In fact investment occurs because of so-called imperfections: actual or anticipated market domination, information which others do not have, collusion, long-term links with customers, or governmental coordination which has played so large a role in Japan and South Korea.

I once put forward this sort of objection to an investment model presented by a well-known neoclassical economist. He looked at me with total puzzlement and replied: 'But I am assuming profit maximization!' I think that he meant that such an assumption was sufficient to make his model in a formal sense determinate. So my (Richardson's) objection literally had no meaning for him. A more recent example: the *Economic Journal* published an interesting note contrasting investment decisions taken by a public monopoly, in this case electricity generation, with those that would be taken by several private firms. I wrote a note, drawing attention to two points. One was that the monopolist does have the responsibility to estimate future requirements and to take investment decisions accordingly, whereas none of the separate generating firms supplying the national grid would have any basis for investing unless they had some notion of what the others were doing; also that, demand being ever uneven, the required *reserve* capacity, not profitable as such, may simply not be provided. Once again the point was not understood; my note was not published. Please, I am not paranoid about non-publication, since my publication list is a very long one. It is simply that I am surprised that these seemingly legitimate and relevant points are as water off a duck's back, and I am not sure why.

Let me make it clear that I am not against mathematics. I do, however, feel at one with that minority of 'institutionalists' who criticize those for whom mathematical models are the be-all and end-all of economic science. This does lead to inattention to those problems and statements which cannot be given mathematical expression. To give just one more example, no one can possibly deny that economic performance is affected by the attitude of the worker to his or her work, by management-labour relations and by changes of organizational structures. But because such matters cannot be given meaningful expression in formal models, they tend to be omitted from microeconomics, as if they do not matter or do not belong to our subject. I once attended a seminar in California which related to indeterminacy. We had an hour of mathematical exposition in which the speaker showed that his model was, unlike its rivals, determinate. Yet throughout he uttered not one word, nor cited a single statistic, relating to any aspect of the economic situation in the real world. He was concerned only with mathematical consistency.

The concept of equilibrium, and Walrasian general equilibrium, must of course be taught. What worries me is what is not taught. It is as if a course on bridge-building, quite sound as far as it goes, omits mention of the fact that water-levels and currents vary at different times of the year, that on tidal rivers they could flow in both directions, that there could be ice in winter. Of course I agree that economic theory must and should abstract from much of everyday reality, must rise above mere institutional description and what the Russians call 'naked empiricism'. What it must not do is to divert attention away from frequently-encountered problem areas. If technical progress and entrepreneurship are virtually always concerned with actual and/or anticipated *DIS*equilibrium, and if investments are almost always made in conditions of uncertainty, then to treat such matters within a general equilibrium framework is, shall we say, not very helpful. In my (rejected) note for the *Economic Journal*, I wrote that it seemed to me that investment decisions are inappropriately considered in an equilibrium framework, since it is disequilibrium that provides motive and the anticipated profit-making opportunity. The referee found this (elementary) point unacceptable!

Not very helpful either is 'mainstream' neoclassical economics to those in the Soviet Union who, understandably exasperated by the irrelevance of received Marxist doctrine, seek theoretical help from the West. Indeed some Western econometricians, applying their concepts to the very different situation of Eastern non-market economies, can and do reach misleading conclusions. Thus several scholars have denied the existence of aggregate excess demand in the USSR, Poland etc or the prevalence of frustrated purchasing power, dismissing evidence to the contrary as 'anecdotal'. A paper presented at an American Association for the Advancement of Slavic Studies conference asked us to believe that the USSR would get nearer to the efficiency frontier (wherever that is; who has ever seen one?) by transferring resources *from* services *to* heavy industry!! The error here lies in assuming that Soviet prices and relative incomes are an appropriate unit of measure. Still another sought to show that incentives in collective farms are particularly effective because, in the model, they equal average and not (the lower) marginal productivity! Apart from the fact that no one, in any economy, knows what his or her marginal productivity *is* (a not unimportant point if one is discussing human response to incentives), such a conclusion flies in the face of all that is known about the Soviet collective farms as an institution (my note was rejected by the *Journal of Comparative Economics*).

What could Soviet economists learn from a typical neoclassical course in micro and macro economics, which would help them replace their useless theoretical ballast? Clearly, there are some elementary principles of the most vital importance: on the relationship of supply to demand, the role of prices (so long as one also says, with Kornai, that major decisions are not taken in the real world on the basis of price information alone); the consequences of price and exchange controls; and the dangers of a lax monetary and credit policy. One needs to tell them about real markets and real competition (in other words to treat perfect markets and perfect competition as an unreal but theoretically interesting extreme). It should also be said that competition and choice logically require that supply exceeds demand, that there be some unused resources (otherwise what is there to compete WITH?). Marginal analysis must be used, but qualified in the manner discussed above, seen (as it so often is, in real life) in the context of complementarities, indivisibilities, networks and sub-systems – in a word, real firms. One must introduce the notion of maximizing behaviour, but qualify it, since it is by no means clear what institutions and human beings in fact maximize. (I do not know what I maximize; do you? Unless one tautologically and axiomatically assumes that whatever I or you do is maximizing behaviour, which helps us not at all to understand anything.)

They should be made aware of the yawning gap between macro and micro analysis, which helps to explain why the British government fails to see the connection between industrial decline and the balance of payments crisis (even denying the seriousness of the latter). They must be told about 'rational expectations', though one must hope that this fashion will pass. I for one continue to be incredulous: how could such a doctrine gain such widespread acceptance, other than as a theoretically convenient but totally unreal surrogate for certainty – and as a crudely ideological tool for those who wish to 'prove' that governments cannot affect the 'real economy'. (Tell that to the Japanese and South Koreans!)

We all need a new and relevant economics!

Nove's Major Writings
(1959), 'The Problem of Success Indicators in Soviet Industry', *Economica*, **26**.
(1962), *The Soviet Economy: An Introduction*, Allen and Unwin. New editions 1965, 1968.
(1964), *Was Stalin Really Necessary?* Allen and Unwin.
(1969), *An Economic History of the USSR*, Allen Lane. Penguin 1970; new edition 1988.
(1972), 'Market Socialism and its Critics', *Soviet Studies*, July.
(1973), *Political Economy as Soviet Socialism*, Allen and Unwin.
(1975), *Stalinism and After*, Allen and Unwin. New edition 1988
(1976), 'The Political Economy of the Allende Regime', in P. O'Brien (ed), *Allende's Chile*, London and New York: Praeger.
(1977), *The Soviet Economic System*, Allen and Unwin. New edition 1986
(1980), *Studies in Economics and Russia*, Macmillan.
(1983), *Economics of Feasible Socialism*, Allen and Unwin. Revised edition under name of *Economics of Feasible Socialism Revisited* scheduled for 1991.
(1986), *Socialism, Economics and Development*, Allen and Unwin.

Other References
Loasby, B. (1975), *Choice, Complexity and Ignorance*, Cambridge University Press.
Scitovsky, T. (1976), *The Joyless Economy*, Oxford: Oxford University Press.

Domenico Mario NUTI (born 1937)
I was born in the Tuscan town of Arezzo and grew up in a small village, a poor agricultural centre of fewer than 1,000 souls. With 50-50 sharecropping the only form of land tenure, it had two latifundia, a usurer and two shopkeepers, and only one car even in the 1950s. It is now a polluted, overgrown industrial centre. I had a classical education. My interest in economics was generated by both personal and social circumstances. My father – a teacher and journalist – was a small landowner financially ruined by post-war Italian

hyperinflation and by the pig cycle. I still remember his astonishment when, many years later, I explained to him the cobweb theorem.

A self-supporting student of law at Rome University in the mid-1950s, I got in touch with Danilo Dolci, a practitioner of self-help and non-violent action for civil rights, working in Sicilian mafialand. A stay in Palermo and Trappeto in 1958, and the sight of road-building by volunteers asserting their right to work (guaranteed on paper by Article 4 of the Italian Constitution) made a great impression on me. Helping to organize and attending a conference on 'Planning from Below' arranged by Dolci in Palermo did the rest. They gave me the motivation and contacts to do my degree dissertation in development economics and to get a research post with the Inter-Ministerial Committee for the Development of Southern Italy. The job took me to field visits throughout the Mezzogiorno, with a team whose task it was to identify suitable locations for concentrating industrial infrastructures, in line with the 'growth poles' approach of Albert Hirschmann, Gunnar Myrdal and François Perroux. This early personal and social background vaccinated me for good against economic theories relying on malleable capital, voluntary unemployment and rational expectations.

Graduating 'cum laude', I was placed in a queue for a Bank of Italy scholarship to study abroad. While waiting to go to Cambridge (England), I obtained a fellowship from the Polish Academy of Sciences; I wanted to see socialism and central planning in action, and I knew that in Warsaw I would find outstanding economists. I joined a course for planners from developing countries at the Warsaw School of Planning and Statistics, where I was fortunate to be taught by Oskar Lange, Michal Kalecki, Wlodek Brus, Kazimierz Laski and others. I learned Polish and attended Lange's lectures at the University. Poland at that time was the most liberal Eastern European country; there were no food shortages and the arts were thriving. There were obvious inefficiencies and in many ways the place was uninspiring, but there were also expectations of early improvements and of further progress towards a better, market-orientated model of socialism. In addition to my modest grant, I turned a few hundred dollars into a very large sum at a vast multiple of the official exchange rate – openly and legally – by importing from Switzerland a small amount of a crucial scarce input used to make scent and sold it to a cooperative producing for the Soviet market. I lived comfortably, demonstrated the twist to Polish teenagers and learned a great deal.

From Warsaw I went to King's College, Cambridge, as a research student where I was to remain, in various capacities, for the next 17 years. I was taught first by Nicky Kaldor, a most inspiring lecturer, 'maestro' and challenger of orthodoxies. I shone in the Cambridge Tripos and began work on a Ph.D. thesis on 'Problems of Investment Planning in the Socialist Economies'. By virtue of being a leading specialist in my chosen field, Maurice Dobb soon replaced Kaldor as my supervisor. My first research output on socialist economies – three essays on enterprise incentives, investment criteria and inflation – gained me the Stevenson Prize (1965) and a Research Fellowship at King's, followed by a tutorship, teaching lectureship and directorship of studies accompanied, from 1970, by a parallel appointment at the Faculty of Economics.

At Cambridge in the 1960s a lively debate was taking place between the followers of the neoclassical approach and those seeking alternatives in the Marxian and Ricardian tradition. A major issue was the measurability of capital, capital malleability and substitutability, the shape and very existence of aggregate production functions. The questions may seem highly esoteric but have devastating policy implications: an innocent-looking assumption of a Cobb-Douglas aggregate production function implicitly leads to assertions that income distribution is given by 'God and the engineers' (Joan Robinson) and cannot and should not be altered; that unemployment is not due to Keynesian deficit demand but to excessive high real wages; that investment mistakes can be costlessly rectified. Like me, many knew that this was not and could not be the case and clung to the promises of any seemingly plausible alternative approach, like Piero Sraffa's cryptic *Production of Commodities by Means of Commodities*, neo-Marxian and neo-Ricardian cost-based prices, or neo-Keynesian propositions about income distribution and their possible microeconomic extension.

As it turned out, these were dead ends, not viable alternatives. Production prices (that is, cost-based prices embodying a uniform rate of profit) are relevant under special conditions: constant returns to scale, only one primary factor (labour) and no joint production. In this situation, demand – if correctly anticipated by producers – will have no influence on relative prices. In such conditions production prices are part of every economist's education and are not controversial as they correspond to the prices of Paul Samuelson's dynamic non-substitution theorem. Sraffa never conceded the necessity of constant returns, and fudged the questions of land and joint production by referring to marginal land and equi-profitable joint production techniques. To establish which land is marginal and which equi-profitable techniques to use, one needs to know precisely those demand conditions that Sraffa claimed to dismiss. Wage bargaining has no connection whatever with his 'standard commodity', nor can it or should it because, for a start, in a world of technical alternatives, such a composite commodity must differ for different real rates of wage or profit. Production prices could be expressed as 'transformed' values but these is no general way of preserving the total surplus value/total profit equality postulated by Marx. Outside distribution theory, capital aggregates are inaccurate but harmless. Neo-Keynesians express the extreme implications of constant behavioural parameters (such as propensities to save or to import, technical coefficients) whose invariance cannot be justified and is at odds with their findings; they have no alternative microeconomics.

These exercises had great pedagogical value, but ultimately could not provide new and unorthodox answers. Neoclassical theorists moved on to discuss important questions such as temporary equilibria, transaction costs, the nature of money, exhaustible resources, uncertainty, information, principal-agent relations, games. They replaced malleable capital with equally implausible constructs such as rational expectations, but also gained new insights and, whether right or wrong, had something to say. Most practitioners of the alternative approaches – with notable exceptions such as my good friend Bob Rowthorn – remained silent on crucial old and new questions, stuck as they were in their grooves. I do not mind that this kind of dissent had made me somewhat unpopular.

A by-product of my research on socialist investment planning was an analysis of intertemporal allocation in a steady growth, flow-input flow-output model in the 'putty-clay' tradition (that is, with *ex ante* but not *ex post* substitutability). The model produced the desired reswitching techniques and capital-reversal, as well as a crop of other results (consumption-growth wage-profit duality, golden rules of accumulation etc). They were interesting negative results since, even in a steady state, the time dimension of production ruled out the conventional treatment of capital. But I over-claimed, asserting that capital measurements were redundant and that socialism would yield a better consumption performance than capitalism (which it would in such a model, but in the real world this claim was soon to be contradicted by events). The paper, inspired by Kalecki's project selection rules, developed what John Hicks labelled a 'neo-Austrian' approach (not to be confused with later neo-Austrian ultra-laissez-faire theories) and was published in 1970. I beat Hicks to print, which is to his credit because he later told me he had actually refereed that paper (lesser men might have been less generous).

I subsequently played with Marx's transformation problem in an essay published in 1977 (though written much earlier), reacting to Marx's gross neglect of the importance of entrepreneurship and of price adjustment. I developed the 'neo-Austrian' approach further to handle the truncation of production flows and unsteady states (still fully anticipated) in a 1973 article, but I soon realized – alerted by Jack Hirshleifer's book on *Investment, Interest and Capital* – the limits of both the so-called Cambridge School and of neoclassical theory. My change of mind was already clear from my article (1974b) and my edition of the *Economic Essays* by V.K. Dmitiev (1974a), an anti-Ricardian pioneer. Of course I would not renege a single word of what I have ever written: *habent sua fata libelli* – writings have a life of their own, and are there to be judged within their context and on their own terms. I have never believed that one had to be consistent over time. But my views on alternative approaches and on economic systems naturally have changed.

Ultimately, I believe the neoclassical picture of the capitalist economy is fantasy because markets are both incomplete (where are the future markets for manufactured goods, or the contingent commodity markets?) and, most importantly, sequential. Hence resource allocation is ruled by price (and quantity) expectations as much as by actual spot prices, and therefore from Arrow-Debreu we instantly fall into a Keynesian world of expectations – whether self-fulfilling or false – of underemployment equilibria and economic fluctuations. It is precisely the essence of Keynes that savings decisions do not signal demand for future goods, and that money balances can be a bottomless pit draining purchasing power no matter how low the money interest rate.

If neoclassical theory cannot support the claim that private ownership and a market economy are the best of all possible worlds, this does not mean that markets can be dispensed with, that individual agents (both households and firms) do not respond to relative prices as neoclassical microeconomics predicts, or that central planning is necessarily superior. Markets are automatic self-regulating mechanisms (as Dick Goodwin taught me); they produce some of the economic anarchy stressed by Marx but also some order, in due course – too fast or too slowly, imperfectly, mercilessly for the poor, the unemployed and the bankrupt – but surely. Lack of such an automatic response is one of the reasons why the Soviet-type socialist model failed: through the inertia of central planners in the face of a changing world, including changing technology, domestic demand and world trade opportunities.

The other main economic drawback of the centrally planned socialist system of the Soviet-type is over-ambition, aiming at an impossible set of targets. This has been the spirit of Soviet planning from the First Five-Year Plan onwards, the pretence that 2+2=5: that there is no fortress that the Soviets cannot storm; that planning is like an act of war and tight plans mobilize resources; that socialism marks the end of economics. Thus the passive adjustment of monetary flows to impossible targets and the parallel commitment to price stability – to avoid one of the evils of capitalism – set up a lethal time bomb, as inflationary gaps piled up over time to construct an inordinate monetary overhang (see 1986c). Socialist planners would have fared much better by following Friedmanite policies of a steady and slow growth of the money supply (profligacy is also, I believe, the main cause of decline of the Scandinavian alternative). Instead, the misguided commitment to price stability in the face of persistent monetary indiscipline and planners' inertia – rather than the informational and coordination problems usually investigated by economists working on planning – aggravated by communist political monopoly have made Soviet-type production relations and infrastructure (in Marxian parlance) inadequate to the level of development of productive forces. As a result, economic and political fluctuations have been generated since the mid-1950s, which I have tried to analyse using Marx's own approach to the dynamics of 'modes of production' (see 1979; EUI Working Papers nos 26 and 85/156; and my *New Palgrave* entry on 'Cycles in the Socialist Economy', 1987).

From Cambridge I moved to Birmingham to direct the Centre for Russian and East European Studies (1980–83), where I was in a much better position to monitor East European developments and learned much from my colleagues, especially Bob Davies, Phil Hanson, Ron Amann and Julian Cooper. I was much encouraged by the rise of Solidarity and Polish 'party renewal' (see 1981), but I correctly predicted Polish military rule (in the *New Left Review*, November 1981). With British university cuts, I sold my chair back to Thatcher and retired to the ivory tower of the European University Institute at Florence, where I was able to pursue my research on the dynamics of socialism from 1983 to 1990 (see, for instance, 1986c, 1988 and 1989). I set up a working group on comparative economic systems, to whose members and visitors (including many East Europeans now holding ministerial posts) I am much indebted, and watched in disbelief the collapse of the Soviet-type system.

Protracted and obtuse procrastination by communist leaders – including also, indeed especially, Mikhail Gorbachev – brought about the Soviet economic catastrophe of 1990, disintegrated the Union and CMEA, freed Eastern Europe, justified the restoration of private property and the reswitching to capitalism (see my contribution to the OECD volume, 1990). The tasks of stabilization, restructuring and systemic transition are massive and provide an exciting field of research. I have been particularly interested by the questions of appropriate sequencing, speed and credibility of economic reform, the role of foreign trade liberalization and the routes to convertibility. I believe in the primacy of stabilization, preferably fast; the need to demonopolize and restructure before large-scale privatization, avoiding undue appropriation or dilapidation of state property; the need for commercial banking and financial markets immediately afterwards; the possibility of instant improvements but of slow completion of trade liberalization and convertibility (see 1990b, 1990c and other forthcoming papers on these subjects).

Yet market socialism has not failed: it was never fully designed or even imagined, let alone implemented (see 1991b). Today it is still literally a Utopia, but well worth exploring. I have always liked investigating Utopias (and cacotopias, see my paper on Orwell in *Coexistence*, July 1985). As the Eastern European economic crisis unfolded, I turned my interest to economic institutions that might make up such a market socialist model. These included cooperatives and similar Yugoslav-type self-managed firms; profit-sharing; wage-earners' investment funds; workers' participation à la Mitbestimmung; basic income schemes; labour-capital partnerships and neo-corporatist institutions. I found (i) that cooperatives were microsocialist, almost monastic, institutions with defective incentives (1990a); (ii) that profit-sharing does not have the employment enhancement properties believed by Martin Weitzman (*Industrial Relations*, 1987). Moreover, for proper incentives, profit must be defined to include such capital gains as dividends plus all increments in an enterprise's capital value (see the 'Profit-Sharing' entry in 1991a); (iii) that workers' investment funds cannot be the painless nationalization machines hoped for by Rudolf Meidner, except for the brief period while they are being set up, before they pay out dividends and redemptions; (iv) that democracy in the workplace is an essential concomitant of profit-sharing; and (v) that the guarantee of a basic income is a luxury that few economies can afford. None of these steps on its own would make much difference, but all of them together could add up to a coherent alternative model, where dependent workers would genuinely transform themselves, to the extent that they wished, into entrepreneurs (1991a). This model is very close to James Meade's *Agathotopia* (Aberdeen UP, 1989) – a better Utopia than most (see 1990a).

I also explored Kalecki's version of vertically-integrated, self-managed and planned socialism (1986b) and possible new instruments and institutions, such as the replication of financial markets without private ownership (1989), contingent policy commitments, possible state agencies undertaking the role of employer (or investor or international trader) of last resort (in 1986a). The need for a better system will be intensified once lessons are drawn from the collapse of both the Soviet-type and the Scandinavian models; after the unavoidable disappointment with the restoration of crude capitalism in Eastern Europe, as excessive doses of IMF medicine are taken, as in Poland in 1990 (see 1990b); and as incomplete and out of sequence reforms fail to yield the expected results. Capitalism will bring improvements but will not solve the problems of Central Eastern Europe; it will transform them into other problems – unemployment, open inflation, market turbulence and social conflicts – with which we are only too familiar.

I am glad I never joined any political party. For all my penchant for Utopias, I have never been an armchair economist. Besides my spell in the Mezzogiorno, I worked in Egypt for FAO, helped to set up the Italian Trade Union CGTL research department and worked in Zambia on a large-scale irrigation and resettlement scheme at Mpongwe. I helped the Zambian Ministry of Power to regain control over its share of Kariba electricity, leading to much higher prices for electricity exports to Rhodesia. I was nearly napalmed in a Rhodesian raid on Lusaka and was held at gunpoint in the bush, but I cost Ian Smith the equivalent of a few dozen helicopters. I was then involved in undoing what I had contributed, and helped to restore cooperation between Zambia and Zimbabwe. I joined three World Bank and one UNDP missions to Poland, as well as one to Algeria (a disconcerting Mediterranean cross between Poland and Hungary) in the late 1980s. I also joined a 'task force' of Western and Soviet economists under Wassily Leontief and Ivan Ivanov (of the Soviet State Committee for Foreign Economic Relations), sponsored by George Soros, on the opening up of the Soviet economy. I am now – while on leave from the University of Siena – an economic adviser on Central Eastern Europe at the EC Commission in Brussels, where I am pleased to work with some former students of mine (needless to say, my views should not necessarily be associated with those of the Commission). I know no better way of doing economics.

I have been very fortunate in having good teachers, many good colleagues, good secretaries, students, friends and opportunities. I used to reproach myself for not doing enough work, for I only regarded research as true work, but I now regret not having spent more of my time on a beach.

Nuti's Major Writings

(1970), 'Capitalism, Socialism and Steady Growth', *Economic Journal*, **80**.

(1973), 'On the Truncation of Production Flows', *Kyklos*, **26**.

(1974a), Introductory essay and notes, *Economic Essays on Value, Competition and Utility* by U.K. Dmitriev, Cambridge University Press.

(1974b), 'On the Rates of Return of Investment', *Kyklos*, **27**.

(1977), 'The Transformation of Labour Values into Production Prices in the Marxian Theory of Exploitation', in J. Schwartz (ed), *The Subtle Anatomy of Capitalism*, Santa Monica, Calif.: Goodyear Publishers.

(1979), 'The Contradictions of Socialist Economies – a Marxian Interpretation', in R. Miliband and J. Saville (eds), *Socialist Register 1979*, London: Merlin Press.

(1981), 'Socialism on Earth' (Inaugural lecture), *Cambridge Journal of Economics*, **5**.

(1986a), 'Economic Planning in Market Economies: Scope, Instruments, Institutions', in P. Nolan and S. Paine (eds), *Rethinking Socialist Economics*, Oxford: Polity Press.

(1986b), 'Michal Kalecki's Contributions to the Theory and Practice of Socialist Planning', *Cambridge Journal of Economics*, **10**.

(1986c), 'Hidden and Repressed Inflation in Soviet-Type Economies: Definitions, Measurement and Stabilisation', *Contributions to Political Economy*, **5**. Reprinted in C. Davis and W. Charemza (eds), *Models of Disequilibrium and Shortage in Centrally Planned Economies*, London: Chapman and Hall, 1989.

(1987), 'Profit-Sharing and Employment: Claims and Overclaims', *Industrial Relations*, **26**.

(1988), 'Perestroika: Transition between Central Planning and Market Socialism', *Economic Policy*, no 7.

(1989), 'Feasible Financial Innovation under Market Socialism', in C. Kessides, T. King, M. Nuti and K. Sokil (eds), *Financial Reform in Centrally Planned Economies*, Washington: EDI-World Bank.

(1990a), 'Traditional Co-operatives and James Meade's Labour-Capital Discriminating Partnerships', in D. Jones and J. Svejnar (eds), *Advances in the Economic Analysis of Participatory and Labor-Managed Firms*, 4, JAI Press.

(1990b), 'Privatisation of Socialist Economies: General Issues and the Polish Case', in H. Bloomenstein and M. Marrese (eds), *The Transformation of Planned Economies*, Paris: OECD.

(1990c), 'Stabilisation and Reform Sequencing in the Soviet Union', *Recherches Economiques de Louvain*, **56**.

(1991a), 'Profit Sharing', in G. Szell (ed), *Concise Encyclopedia of Participation and Co-Management*, Berlin and New York: de Gruyter.

(1991b), 'Market Socialism: The Model that Might Have Been but Never Was', in A. Aslund (ed), *Market Socialism or Restoration of Capitalism?*, Cambridge University Press.

Other References

Hirshleifer, J. (1970), *Investment, Interest and Capital*, Englewood Cliffs, New Jersey: Prentice Hall.

Nobuo OKISHIO (born 1926)

I was born on 11 December 1926. However, my official birth date is 2 January 1927. Before the Second World War, Japanese people counted age by calendar year. My parents were anxious about my becoming two years old after only one month; they feared that people might underestimate me when compared with other babies of the same age. So they registered my birth date as 2 January illegally.

My father had a small store in which he sold women's trinkets. He expected me to succeed him in his business. He sent me to Kobe Commercial School, hoping it would produce a reliable assistant for him after my graduation. His pretty dream did not come true as I entered Kobe Higher Commercial School instead. The Japanese ruling class, headed by Emperor Hirohito, had tried to solve the economic difficulties of the 1930s by a military invasion of China. As their criminal activities became wider, they began to mobilize all economic capacity for war. The government ordered my father's business to shut down, shouting 'Luxury is Our Enemy'. My father was compelled to obey and he was drafted into a munitions factory, working there until Japan was defeated in 1945. At that time, the Communist party had collapsed and was banned; reading Marxian books was forbidden.

The US army occupied Japan and Emperor Hirohito declared 'I am not a God but a mere human'. After graduation from Kobe Higher Commercial School, I entered the faculty of Economics at Kobe University. My teacher in Higher School had recommended Keynes's *General Theory*, a 'safe book'. Then, at university, I concentrated on Hicks's *Value and Capital*. Though Keynes's brilliant attack against 'classical' economics and Hicks's beautiful technique for analysing interdependent economic relationships satisfied my intellectual hunger, I felt somewhat uneasy. Just after the war we looked at the drastic changes in social and political structures in Japan. We also experienced enhanced movements of people. I felt that the economics of Keynes and Hicks did not reflect these occurrences. Marx's work, when I began to read him, struck me as deeper and more relevant.

Many economists dissenting from the neoclassical school have attacked its adherence to marginalist and equilibrium theories. For example, Mr Kaldor in his 'A Model of Economic Growth' rejected the marginalist theory of the firm. In its place he built a model assuming full employment of labour – labelling it Keynesian. However, as I wrote in 'On Mr Kaldor's Growth Model' (*Kobe University Economic Review* [*KER*], 1967), his model is not Keynesian, but neoclassical. In my opinion, Keynes did not deny the marginalist theory of the firm; on the contrary, in *The General Theory* he admitted its first postulate, mainly taking exception to its assumption of full employment. But Kaldor did deny the marginalist theory of the firm and admitted the assumption of full employment of labour. This is quite anti-Keynesian.

As to the marginalist theory of the firm, it reflects, I think, the most important aspect of capitalism: production decisions are made by capitalists with wage-labourers excluded. Capitalists make decisions on the criterion of profit maximization. The marginalist approach theorizes on these capitalist decisions. If we want to have an economic analysis of capitalism, we cannot dispense with a theory of capitalist decision-making. In certain cases, the marginalist theory of the firm is of use. Though not quite satisfactory, it is wrong to abandon it as a means of explaining capitalist decisions on production, employment, investment and choice of technique. If we are not satisfied by such a theory, we must improve it so as to make clearer the characteristics of capitalist decision-making. It is a pity that people interpret such efforts as 'neoclassical'.

As to the concept of 'equilibrium', recent young dissenting economists regard this assumption as the most serious crime of the neoclassicals. Among them it is very popular to make disequilibrium models. I can understand their feeling. The neoclassicals usually assume full employment of labour, normal utilization of productive capacity and even rational expectations. This ignores almost all the important facets of capitalism. No unemployment, no over-production and no economic anarchy. It is just a daydream.

However I think that it is not reasonable to refute the concept of equilibrium completely. Since capitalism has maintained itself for more than one hundred years, there must exist a mechanism for its reproduction. In order to analyse this mechanism, the concept of equilibrium is indispensable. Marx gave us a reproduction scheme in *Das Capital*. He had three aims in this analysis, as I wrote in 'On Marx's Reproduction Scheme' (*KER*, 1988): (i) to show the possibility of equilibrium reproduction and its conditions, (ii) to show inner contradictions which exist even in equilibrium reproduction, and (iii) to show how a capitalist economy moves when these conditions are disturbed by its anarchic character. In this analysis the concept of equilibrium played an important role.

Neoclassical growth theory usually calculates the path of movement of an economy satisfying full employment of labour and normal utilization of productive capacity. Such a model is vain as a description of an actual capitalist economy; from the viewpoint of realism, it is quite irrelevant. However we can get some important information from such a model if we look at it from a different angle. For example, in neoclassical growth theory, Harrodian neutral technical progress is a necessary condition for the sustainability of the equilibrium growth path. This means that if the type of technical progress is something other than Harrodian neutral, sooner or later the equilibrium path must face difficulties which cannot be removed by Keynesian devices. This is very close to Marx's argument of the adverse effects of increasing organic composition of capital on the rate of profit.

Keynes criticized heavily the neoclassical assertion that capital competition automatically leads to full employment. Essential in his theory is that a certain level of new investment demand is necessary for maintaining full employment when the propensity to consume is low. Therefore, the investment function is most important in his theory. Neoclassicals put great emphasis on the role of interest rates in investment decision-making, believing that interest rates can guide investment decisions successfully for maintaining full employment. Though Keynes did not deny the relationship between interest rates and investment, he paid more attention to capitalists' 'animal spirits' in investment decision-making.

His focus on capitalists' investment decision-making is his great contribution for understanding capitalism. But it is not so surprising that if investment demand is low, aggregate demand becomes insufficient for full employment. The problem is why investment demand can continue to remain at a low level. To answer this question we must have dynamic theory.

Roy Harrod initiated this. He asserted that once the economy diverges from equilibrium growth, in which an economy satisfies supply/demand equalities and keeps a normal utilization of productive capacity, disequilibrium becomes cumulative. As shown in my paper 'Instability of Harrod-Domar Equilibrium Growth' (*KER,* 1966), his conclusion is derived from his investment function, though he did not clearly formulate and recognize its importance. I think Harrod's Instability Thesis is the most important antineoclassical analysis after Keynes.

Keynes introduced monetary and fiscal policies from his theory as remedies for unemployment. These policies are all measures to increase effective demand. On this point I could not agree with him. In *The General Theory*, the amount of employment is determined at the intersection of the aggregate demand and supply functions. All his proposed policies are designed to shift the aggregate demand function. Nothing is mentioned about policies to change the aggregate supply function.

Keynes stated that the aggregate supply function is determined only by existing equipment and techniques. However, as shown in my book *Keynes' Economics*, the function describes capitalistic decision behaviour. Therefore even if existing equipment and techniques remain unchanged, the function can still be altered by changes in the behaviour of capitalists. Their decisions are different, for example, according to the degree of monopoly they enjoy. It is a great weakness that Keynes did not analyse the relationship between the aggregate supply function and monopoly. Consequently he did not propose policies to regulate capitalists' behaviour to increase employment. Such a bias in Keynes stemmed from his commitment to the bourgeois point of view.

The great merit of Marx over the neoclassicals and Keynes is his effort to explain economic phenomena from the basic social structure. During the early years after World War II, Japanese capitalism was thoroughly shaken. Without US troops it could not maintain itself. I felt great charm in Marx who offered a theory which treated basic social structures as variable.

However, analytically I could not accept *Das Capital* literally. A stumbling stone was his assumption that prices are proportional to values. Standing on this assumption, Marx demonstrated that the source of profit is the exploitation of wage-labour. I endeavoured to prove this proposition dispensing with the value/price assumption, succeeding in my paper 'Value and Price' (Kobel University Economics Studies, 1954, in Japanese). Soon after I wrote 'Monopoly and Rates of Profit' (1955) showing the proof of the proposition and its application to the problem of monopoly. Years later, Morishima christened this the 'Marxian Fundamental Theorem'.

Many Marxian economists thought and still think that the central assertion of labour-value theory is 'value determines price'. I cannot accept this; it is too narrow. Labour-value theory is the doctrine which requires us to analyse economic phenomena from the point of view of labour. Who works and who reaps? What kind of special phenomena occur when social relations of labour have certain characteristics? These are questions which the labour-value theory must answer.

When I had successfully demonstrated Marx's fundamental theorem, I recognized that his theory was tough enough to build mathematical arguments on. So I proceeded to examine Marx's law on the rate of profit. According to this law, the rate of profit has a tendency to fall. Many people have criticized this, their main point being that if the organic composition of capital increases, as Marx thought, the rate of exploitation must also increase owing to the rise of labour-productivity. Thus a falling rate of profit cannot be said to be inevitable. As I wrote in my paper 'Technical Change and the Rate of Profit', this critique is illogical. If we accept Marx's assumption that dead labour embodied in the means of production increases sufficiently relative to living labour, the rate of profit must tend to fall. This must occur because living labour is the sole source of profit.

Marx thought that capitalists are compelled to introduce new techniques to get extra profit and escape from bankruptcy. New techniques increase both the ratio of dead labour to living labour and labour productivity. If we accept this assumption about technical progress, the law is derived logically, as shown in my paper 'Formal Proof of Marx's Two Theorems' (*KER* 1972). But I suspected that capitalists introduce such a technique when the real wage remains constant. Examining capitalists' criterion for technical choice, I arrived at the conclusion (in my 'Technical Change' paper mentioned above) that if the real wage is unchanged, the rate of profit necessarily rises when capitalists introduce new techniques. This conclusion has provoked heated controversies, which continue.

The implication of this conclusion is that capitalism has more energy than Marx thought. Some Marxian economists predict the downfall of capitalism because of increases in the organic composition of capital. But the introduction of new production techniques has in fact helped capitalism to survive, the rate of profit having usually been maintained at acceptable levels.

The relationship between capitalism and technical progress has two opposite facets (see 1977a). Technical progress is necessary for capitalism to maintain itself, for without the former capitalism cannot surmount the limits set by the labour supply and natural resources. Technical progress is also the most important factor in switching from the downward to the upward phase in the trade cycle. On the other hand, technical progress produces situations in which it becomes difficult for capitalism to operate. The minimum fund required to introduce new techniques becomes too great for private sources of finance to bear alone. Public funds must be mobilized for capitalists. This is fertile ground for bribery and corruption. New techniques also influence the natural environment, seriously and globally. It becomes very dangerous to leave investment and production decisions in the hands of private capitalists. And new techniques necessarily foster a remarkable increase in the average person's information-processing capacities. The exclusion of informed working people from making fundamental production decisions, which is the indispensable characteristic of capitalism, becomes difficult to maintain.

What are the tasks of economics? This is the question which I have cherished from the beginning of my studies. In my opinion, as explored in my paper 'Problems of Political Economy' (*KER*, 1989), the basic problems of economics are as follows. When we study economic phenomena in any society – say capitalism or socialism – we must ask what are the characteristic human relations of that society? Who grasps the fundamental production decisions? What kinds of economic phenomena occur as a result of these decisions? How do various economic phenomena mutually interrelate? How do these economic phenomena function to maintain the society under study? And, finally, how do these economic phenomena function to compel the society to transform in order to assure human survival?

Looked at in relation to this list of problems, neoclassical and Keynesian economics ignore many important concepts. Especially, they regard capitalism as a given, constant, untouchable set of sacred precepts. They do not see the feedback, positive and negative, between economic phenomena and social structures. Their proposed policies are therefore kept within bounds which generally leave deep social structures undisturbed. Though this is their fundamental fault, I cannot agree with the opinion that schools other than Marxian are completely unscientific. Their results about interrelationships

among economic phenomena and their study of the so-called micro-foundations of economic phenomena are indispensable components of our science.

However, I believe that Marx's *Das Capital* proposed all of the above tasks.
Marx urged us to analyse capitalism dialectically. This means that we must
understand the reproduction mechanism and also reveal the growth of factors which change and revolutionize the social structure. Analytically, this is
the same as the above list. In order to perform these tasks we must utilize the
scientific results of both non-Marxian and Marxian economics.

In order to analyse socialist economies specifically, we must address the
same list of problems introduced above. As written in my book *Problems of
Contemporary Capitalism*, the characteristic human relations in a socialist
society must be a sharing by all members in fundamental production decisions. Violation of this principle was the serious fault of the Stalinistic
system. The reasons such a system cannot survive are obvious.

How is it possible for all members to participate in fundamental production decisions? The prerequisite is that all members of society have enough
capacity and will for making decisions. Both the size of a society and the
issues requiring decision-making are problems. As these sizes are usually
tremendous, it is not feasible to have direct conferences. Therefore, socialist
societies must have the following channels for its members to participate,
directly or indirectly, in production decisions: (a) all members participate
directly in deciding fundamental rules; for example, the basic economic
structures and the minimum standard of living; (b) all members participate
directly in the election and recall of persons who are entrusted to decide
macroeconomic plans and common consumption priorities; for example,
education and medical care; (c) as members of a firm, people participate
directly in production decisions including election of the head of a firm (of
course, firms are free to make production decisions, while obeying basic
rules); (d) as residents in the area where firms locate, people have procedures for participation in the decisions which influence their living environments; (e) as consumers of goods, including services, people have procedures
for participating in firms' decisions which influence their lives and amenities.
Finally, (f) all members choose goods through effective demand by money
in markets.

The channels (a)–(e) cannot become effective without political democracy and subsidized information. In order to maintain democratic procedures,
over-concentration of decisions must be avoided, and separation of power is
essential. Channel (f) cannot work without (i) strict discipline of money
supply, (ii) non-monopolistic behaviour of firms, and (iii) fair distribution of
money which functions as votes. The working of the socialist economy thus
offers many theoretical topics to us economists to pursue further.

Okishio's Major Writings

1. Main Books in Japanese

(1957a), *Keynes' Economics*, San-ichi Shobou.

(1957b), *Theory of Reproduction*, So-bun Sha.

(1965), *Fundamental Theory of Capitalist Economy*, So-bun Sha.

(1967), *Theory of Accumulation*, Shikuma Shobou.

(1980), *Problems of Contemporary Capitalism*, Iwanami Shoten.

2. Collected Papers in Japanese

(1977), *Marxian Economics: Value and Price*, Shikuma Shobou.

(1987), *Marxian Economics: Accumulation*, Shikuma Shobou.

3. Main Papers in English

(1955), 'Monopoly and the Rates of Profits', *Kobe University Economic Review* (KER), **1**.

(1961), 'Technical Change and the Rate of Profit', *KER*, **7**.

(1963), 'Mathematical Note on Marxian Theorems', *Weltwirtschaftliches Archiv*, **99**.

(1966), 'Instability of Harrod-Domar Equilibrium Growth', *KER*, **12**.

(1972), 'Formal Proof of Marx's Two Theorems', *KER*, **18**.

(1977a), 'Note on Technical Progress and Capitalistic Society', *Cambridge Journal of Economics*, **1**.

(1977b), 'Inflation as an Expression of Class Antagonism', *KER*, **23**.

(1985), 'Measurement of the Rate of Surplus Value', *KER*, **31**.

(1988), 'On Marx's Reproduction Scheme', *KER*, **34**.

(1989), 'Problems of Political Economy', *KER*, **35**.

Other References

Kaldor, N. (1957), 'A Model of Economic Growth', *Economic Journal*, December.

Luigi Lodovico PASINETTI (born 1930)   *Mauro Baranzini*

Luigi Lodovico Pasinetti was born on 12 September 1930 at Zanica, near Bergamo (Northern Italy). He received his first degree (laurea) from the Catholic University of Milan in 1954; after graduate work at Cambridge (UK) and at Harvard he got a Ph.D. in economics at the University of Cambridge in 1962 with a now well-known dissertation on 'A Multi-Sector Model of Economic Growth'. As he was later to write, he came into close contact 'with that remarkable group of thinkers – Richard Kahn, Nicholas Kaldor, Joan Robinson and Piero Sraffa – whom I had the rare fortune of meeting, discussing with so often, and then being associated with, in Cambridge, which has been to me the most stimulating place I could possibly imagine for progressive thought in economic theory'. His first official appointment (to a research fellowship) was at Nuffield College, Oxford (1959–61), but in 1961 he was called by Lord Richard Kahn back to Cambridge where he became Fellow of King's College, remaining there until 1976 (in 1973, at a time when this was reputed to be of great distinction, he was appointed economics Reader at the University of Cambridge). In 1976 he returned to Italy to his economics chair at his old *alma mater*, the Catholic University of Milan, where in quick succession he was chairman of the Faculty of Economics (1980–83), director of the Department of Economics (1983–86) and director of the doctorate programme (1986–). He has held a number of visiting appointments (in the US several times, Canada, Japan, India and Cambridge, UK), has been a member of the Executive Committee of the International Economic Association (1980–89), fellow of the Econometric Society, president of the Società Italiana degli Economisti (1986–89), and has received a large number of academic distinctions (including membership of the Accademia Nazionale dei Lincei, Rome, and a Doctor Honoris Causa from the Swiss University of Fribourg).

In the address given in honour of Lord Richard Kahn, held in King's College Chapel in Cambridge on 21 October 1989, Luigi Pasinetti made reference to the previous commemorations of Joan Robinson and Nicholas Kaldor:

> This is the third time, over a short span of years, that the Congregation assembles in this Chapel to commemorate, and reflect upon the life of, a major contributor to that intellectual breakthrough that has become known in the world of economics and politics as 'the Keynesian Revolution'. ... If one adds that another memorial service, shortly after that of Joan Robinson, was held in Cambridge, though in another Chapel, for yet another close associate of Keynes, Piero Sraffa, one cannot resist the impression that today's ceremony concludes a whole historical phase, almost an era, in the recent history of economic thought. This group of Cambridge economists had been protagonist of one of those extraordinary and unique events in the history of ideas that decisively pushed knowledge ahead and created a break with the past.

Pasinetti himself is one of the most representative, if not *the* most representative, heir of the 'post-Keynesian' school, since he was first a student and then a colleague and friend of all the above-mentioned scholars. He was also a major animator of the controversies on capital theory, income distribution and theory of value that were fought out between Cambridge (England) and Cambridge (Mass) during the 'raging' 1950s, 1960s and 1970s. The battle was, as we shall see, won by Cambridge (England) but paradoxically the losing side was awarded a number of Nobel prizes over the years (while significantly none of the above-quoted UK economists ever got one). Notwithstanding the strength and the high analytical rigour of such a group of thinkers, as time passed the 'Keynesians' and later the 'neo-Keynesians' have progressively become a 'minority' school of thinking, while the marginalists have taken over and, numerically at least, become the dominant school in most of the Western world. In a sense the first 'Keynesian Revolution', led by Keynes himself, Kahn and Joan Robinson, had been able to 'create a break with the past' and to take with them most of the leading economists and fellow politicians from the 1930s to the 1950s. However, when the time was ripe for a further refinement, development and establishment of a 'Keynesian Programme', its leading members found themselves besieged and forced to fight off the neoclassical counter-attack. Eventually, over the last two decades as the founding fathers have passed away, the Keynesian School has dispersed and continued elsewhere. (This is not new in the history of science, as the setting up of medieval learning centres like Oxford and Padua has shown.)

Pasinetti's 30-year-old 'research programme' has followed a coherent thread, first outlining the weaknesses of the marginalist model, and then step-by-step laying the foundations of the reconstruction – on mixed classical/'pure' Keynesian bases – of a 'more general theory' in order to identify, explain and analytically recompose the mechanisms and dynamics of modern economic systems. This is carried out with powerful tools of analysis, in particular the method of vertical integration, allowing for the understanding of a number of very complicated economic phenomena. These include the unequal distribution and unequal pace of technical progress, the non-linear variations in the composition of demand, the presence of a large number of asymmetric behaviours and the complex role of institutions (although a characteristic of his research programme is that the core is institution free).

Pasinetti's scientific output consists to date of some 90 papers published in the most prestigious journals, and of seven books (three edited by himself) published with the best presses and usually translated into several languages. To give some order to these contributions, I shall link them with five different, yet strictly interconnected, partial research lines. They are (i) on Ricardo and classical political economy; (ii) on capital theory; (iii) on income distribution and growth theory; (iv) on structural dynamics and vertical integration, and (v) on the 'pure' labour theory of value. To these we should add a number of papers on models of unstable growth, economics of effective demand, development economics and monetary theory. Let me review the above-mentioned areas of research in some detail.

In one of his first major contributions, Pasinetti proved that the mathematical formulation of the classical model is possible (1960). He provides representation, in a rigorous and concise notation of the Ricardian dynamic process, in particular the process of economic growth and structural dynamics, stressing the multi-sectorality of the model with its specific structural dynamics. Additionally the solutions of Ricardo's 'natural system' are shown to exist and to be unique (but not always stable). Such solutions 'reach a perfect stability only in the equilibrium of the stationary state'. These important results led Pasinetti to conclude that 'Ricardian analysis, with all the naïveté and the limits of its particular theories, appears less primitive now-a-days than it appeared some decades ago' (1960, p.92).

As will become clear later, the Ricardian model represents a starting point for Pasinetti in at least two ways. First it provides a sort of 'foundation' for his 'pure' labour theory of value (see below): in fact, Pasinetti himself notes that for Ricardo 'the theory of value as stated in terms of quantities of labour, and independently of the distribution of income among the classes of the society, does hold, if not exactly at least as a very good approximation' (1960, p.80). (We may recall that a remarkable result obtained within the Ricardian model is that all macroeconomic variables and all prices are determined independently of demand conditions.) Secondly the Ricardian model allows for the exploration of the classical foundations of Keynesian and post-Keynesian economic theory. In fact, as Pasinetti himself notes, 'Keynes' theory of effective demand, which has remained so impervious to reconciliation with marginal economic theory, raises almost no problem when directly inserted into the earlier discussions of the classical economists' (1974, p. ix).

Pasinetti's fundamental contribution to the *capital theory controversy* has often erroneously been labelled a 'paradox' – as has the Kaldor/Pasinetti income distribution theorem expounded below. Yet the significance of paradox may be better understood in terms of the following passage.

Economists sometimes tend to examine a large domain of economic phenomena by adapting theoretical concepts that had originally been devised for a much narrower range of special issues. The discoveries of 'paradoxical' relations derive from the fact that their process of generalization often turns out to be ill-conceived and misleading, if not entirely unwarranted. (Pasinetti and Scazzieri, *New Palgrave Dictionary*, 1987, pp. 363–7).

It was in the 1960s that economists came to doubt whether it could still be taken for granted that there is a unique, unambiguous profitability ranking of production techniques in terms of physical capital intensity along the scale variation of the rate of profits. (On the historical development of this concept, see 1987.) It was originally Paul Samuelson who, with a number of other American economists, started looking for the conditions that would ensure a strictly monotonic relation between the rate of profit and capital intensity (capital/labour ratio) even in the presence of a non-linear relation between the wage rate and the rate of profits. This was claimed to be found by a pupil of Paul Samuelson's, David Levhari, in an article published in 1965 in the *Quarterly Journal of Economics*: in the case of 'indecomposability' of the whole technological matrix, the reswitching of techniques is impossible and hence one may extend the use of Samuelson's 'surrogate production function' to the non-linear relation between w and r. Seemingly encouraged by Sraffa himself, Pasinetti promptly refuted the neoclassical thesis in a paper presented at the Rome First World Congress of the Econometric Society in 1965. That paper gave rise to a host of others (and to a discussion on both sides of the Atlantic among economists who had participated at the World Congress) collected in the 'Symposium on Capital Theory' of the *Quarterly Journal of Economics*, November 1966. In this 'Symposium' a number of contributions, among which of course Pasinetti's, showed from different points of view that reswitching of techniques might occur both with 'decomposable' and 'indecomposable' technologies. Samuelson himself conceded defeat and concluded the 'Symposium' by stressing that the rule put forward by neoclassical theory, according to which a falling interest rate is unambiguously linked with higher capital intensive techniques, 'cannot be universally valid'.

Pasinetti's most widely known contribution (but not necessarily most original in our opinion) is surely in the field of *income distribution, profit determination and growth theory*: his works in this field have generated at least 200 papers in learned reviews, several books and a compulsory reference in a large number of textbooks on economic analysis (for an exhaustive list, see Baranzini, 1990). In his famous 1962 article, Pasinetti begins with a critique of Kaldor's growth model where two saving rates exist, one for workers and one for capitalists. He shows that the equilibrium rate of profits is totally independent of the behaviour of the working class, being determined only by the saving rate of pure capitalists (s_c) and by the rate of growth of the system. (The solution $P/K=n/s_c$ is known as *Pasinetti's Theorem* or the *New Cambridge Equation*.) Such a rate of profit is, however, independent of the production function and of the capital/output ratio. In this way the Cambridge (or post-Keynesian) School was in a position (i) to provide a solution to the Harrod-Domar dilemma by specifying an aggregate saving ratio determined by the exogenously given rate of growth of population, capital/output ratio and capitalists' propensity to save; (ii) to determine the long-run equilibrium value of the rate of profits, the distribution of income between profits and wages, and the distribution of disposable income between the classes; (iii) to allow for the existence of an income residual (very much in line with classical and neo-Ricardian models) namely wages, consistent with the assumption of a relationship between the savings of the class of individuals (the capitalists or entrepreneurs) who determine the process of production and the patterns of capital accumulation; and (iv) to give some insights into the process of accumulation of capital by specifying the equilibrium capital shares of the socio-economic classes. This range of results is obtained by Pasinetti (1974, Chapter 6) within a fairly simple framework and on the basis of relatively few assumptions, much less 'hybrid, opposite and extreme' than those of the neoclassical model.

Thanks to the contributions of Kaldor and Pasinetti, post-Keynesian distribution theory now occupies an undisputed place in most macroeconomic textbooks. Its fruitfulness is proved by the very high number of subsequent contributions which have branched out in various directions, covering many aspects of research relevant to the general topics of income distribution, profit determination and capital accumulation, both from a theoretical and an empirical point of view. Among these new research lines we find: (i) the introduction of a differentiated interest rate of return for different classes; (ii) the introduction of the monetary sector and of a portfolio choice; (iii) the analysis of the stability and of the long-term properties of the model; (iv) the introduction of the public sector with either a balanced or unbalanced budget (which both ensure the high robustness of the Pasinetti theorem in relation to the Meade-Samuelson and Modigliani dual); (v) the extension of the model to include other kinds of socio-economic classes; (vi) the introduction of the life-cycle theory into the model, thus providing a microeconomic base; (vii) the analysis of the long-term distribution of wealth and of the income share of various classes. The post-Keynesian distributive model thus now offers a completeness of analysis which may well challenge the neoclassical alternative, the latter requiring so many artificial assumptions in order to be reconciled with marginal productivity (as in the case of the Meade-Samuelson-Modigliani dual or anti-Pasinetti theorem).

The relevance of *structural dynamics and vertical integration* was stressed by Pasinetti as early as 1962 in his Ph.D. dissertation at Cambridge (England), partly published in 1965 and finally completed in 1981. Pasinetti studies the conditions under which an economic system may reach and maintain full employment and full capacity utilization over the long run when it is subject to major pressures leading to structural change. These are technical progress, non-uniform productivity increases and changes in the consumption structure (or consumers' preferences) according to Engel's law. This new approach, which entirely leaves aside the analytical tools of marginalist economics, faces technical change by giving up the input-output scheme and focusing instead on the 'vertically integrated sectors' approach (see Baranzini and Scazzieri, 1990). As Scazzieri has pointed out (1983, p.73):

> Within the classical tradition, Pasinetti's work reveals a strong intellectual sympathy with Adam Smith, as is shown by the representation of the productive system as a set of vertically integrated sectors, and by the associated idea (common to Pasinetti and Smith) that labour may be considered as the ultimate source of wealth. ... The study of natural dynamics is intended by Pasinetti as a benchmark for the explanation of the historical dynamics of the economic systems. From such a point of view, it turns out that an economic system where producers and consumers have only limited learning abilities is normally subject to perturbations deriving from the very nature of technical progress. Short-run difficulties (unemployment, spare productive capacity, the stagnation of once important industries) have to be considered as the necessary conditions for long-run expansion.

As already indicated, a specific feature of Pasinetti's contribution is to split the overall economic system into so many sub-systems as there are final uses of commodities. Each sub-system or 'vertically integrated sector' consists of the corresponding vertically integrated labour coefficient, which expresses 'in a consolidated way the quantity of labour directly or indirectly required in the whole economic system to obtain one physical unit of a particular commodity as a final good' (1973, p.6) and of a particular composite commodity called 'unit of vertically integrated productive capacity' relative to the same sub-system. Such a composite commodity (which collapses all the inter-industry relations so that one sees only the final measure) 'expresses in a consolidated way the series of heterogeneous physical quantities of [all] commodities ... which are directly or indirectly required as stocks, in the whole economic system, in order to obtain one physical unit of [a specific commodity] as a final good' (1973, p.6). Note that the use of vertically integrated sectors permits the author to overlook the network of inter-industry transactions which may blur the picture when we use the input-output approach. Additionally such an analytical formulation provides a logical framework in which both technological and demand conditions may be integrated in order to give a comprehensive interpretation of the dynamics of the 'wealth of nations', both concerning its absolute level and possible changes in its composition. Finally it must be mentioned that Pasinetti has chosen an analytical device that focuses on the 'natural' properties of the economic system, leaving aside the institutional mechanisms (such as the tendency towards the equalization of the rate of profits in a competitive market economy).

Starting from this analytical scheme Pasinetti has more recently put forward the 'pure' labour theory of value and distribution, around which his more recent work is centred. He first defines (1986, 1988) a 'newly defined sub-system', more comprehensive than those considered earlier (1973, 1981), which 'include not only the labour and the means of production for the reproduction of each sub-system, but *also* the labour and the means of production necessary to its *expansion* and its particular rate of growth $(g+r_i)$' (1988, pp.126–7). By additionally assuming that the rates of growth of these 'newly defined sub-systems' are different (due to a different rate of growth of technical progress and changes in the level and/or composition of demand) and defining by $1^{(i)}$ the vector (equal for all sectors) of the vertically hyper-integrated labour physical coefficient i, Pasinetti obtains the specific set of natural prices $p^{(i)}=1^{(i)}.w$, where w is the wage rate (1988, p.29). This result is remarkable since, as Pasinetti himself points out, it is a complete generalization of the pure labour theory of value; in fact each physical quantity of consumption good comes to be 'unambiguously related' to each physical quantity of labour.

Linked with this issue we find another work of Pasinetti (1980–81) in which he shows that, at a stage which precedes the introduction of capital accumulation and thus the emergence of any rate of profit, the theoretical scheme of a pure dynamic labour economy already contains a complete theory of the rate of interest and hence a theory of income distribution. More specifically, in a pure labour economic system characterized by structural dynamics of technology and of prices, there exists a rate of interest on interpersonal loans – that is, a rate of interest equal to the growth rate of the wage rate, which Pasinetti calls the 'natural' rate of interest – that keeps 'labour commanded' equal to 'labour embodied' through time. Hence there exists a level of interest on interpersonal loans (a 'natural' interest) which 'if paid annually by debtors to creditors, keeps income flowing to each single individual, through time as well as at any given point of time, in proportion to labour contributed to the production process' (1980–81, p.181).

Pasinetti's results are far-reaching and prove, among other things, that there is no need for Keynesian dynamic analysis to be carried out exclusively in macroeconomic terms. Besides the consideration of socio-economic classes of savers, the vertically integrated approach actually provides a sort of micro foundations of the model where the dynamics are much more easily described and understood. Secondly, as Scazzieri has pointed out (1983, p.87), the interpretation of the overall historical dynamics of an economic system requires that Pasinetti, or somebody else, attempt a full-scale analysis of the patterns of expansion that can be expected as a result of the interaction between the fundamental factors of change and the special features of each particular institutional or technological set-up.

At this point we may reassess the significance of Pasinetti's truly and overall 'dissenting' vast research programme, which provides a comprehensive alternative to neoclassical economics based on alternative foundations of how the industrialized system works. More specifically, Pasinetti has provided a new theoretical framework capable of synthesizing the works of Smith, Ricardo, Keynes and Kaldor in a single and coherent whole, by appropriately modifying parts of their foundations and completing still other parts. As may be inferred from the previous pages, we expect further contributions from Pasinetti himself, especially for the refinement of the theory of value and capital and of the link between institutions and economic dynamics. Taking into account the size, complexity and comprehensiveness of the task, however, it is unrealistic to expect a completion of the whole research programme by Pasinetti himself. For the final fruition to be reached, contributions by his pupils and other scholars will be necessary.

Pasinetti's Major Writings

(1960), 'A Mathematical Formulation of the Ricardian System', *The Review of Economic Studies*, **27**, February, 78–98.

(1962), 'Rate of Profit and Income Distribution in Relation to the Rate of Economic Growth', *The Review of Economic Studies*, **29**, 267–79.

(1965), 'A New Theoretical Approach to the Problems of Economic Growth', *Pontificiae Academiae Scientiarum Scripta Varia*, n. 28. Reprinted in *Econometric Approach to Development Planning*, Amsterdam: North Holland, 1965, 571–696.

(1966), 'Changes in the Rate of Profit and Switches of Techniques', *Quarterly Journal of Economics*, **80**, 503–17. Completed by 'Switches of Techniques and the "Rate of Return"' in *The Economic Journal*, **79**, 1969, 508–31.

(1973), 'The Notion of Vertical Integration in Economic Analysis', *Metroeconomica*, **25**, 1–29. Reprinted in L.L. Pasinetti (ed), *Essays on the Theory of Joint Production*, London: Macmillan and Columbia University Press, 1980.

(1974), *Growth and Income Distribution: Essays in Economic Theory*, Cambridge University Press.

(1977), *Lectures on the Theory of Production*, London: Macmillan and Columbia University Press.

(1980), 'The Rate of Interest and the Distribution of Income in a Pure Labour Economy', *Journal of Post Keynesian Economics*, **3**(2), 1980–81, 170–82.

(1981), *Structural Change and Economic Growth: A Theoretical Essay on the Dynamics of the Wealth of Nations*, Cambridge University Press.

(1986), 'Theory of Value – A Source of Alternative Paradigms in Economic Analysis', in M. Baranzini and R. Scazzieri (eds), *Foundations of Economics: Structures of Inquiry and Economic Theory*, Oxford: Basil Blackwell, 409–31.

(1987), 'Capital Theory: Paradoxes, (with R. Scazzieri), *The New Palgrave*, 1987, Volume I, London: Macmillan.

(1988), 'Growing Subsystems, Vertically Hyper-Integrated Sectors and the Labour Theory of Value', *Cambridge Journal of Economics*, **12**, 125–34.

Other References

Baranzini, M. (1990), *A Theory of Wealth Distribution and Accumulation*, Oxford University Press, Chapters 2 and 3.

Baranzini, M. and Scazzieri, R. (eds), (1990), *The Economic Theory of Structure and Change*, Cambridge University Press, Chapters 3–6 and 9.

Blaug, M. (1985), *Great Economists since Keynes: An Introduction to the Lives and Works of One Hundred Modern Economists*, Brighton: Wheatsheaf.

Scazzieri, R. (1983), 'Economic Dynamics and Structural Change: A Comment on Pasinetti', *Rivista Internazionale di Scienze Economiche e Commerciali*, **30**.

Scazzieri, R. (1990), 'Vertical Integration in Economic Theory', *Journal of Post-Keynesian Economics*, **13**, 1–15.

François PERROUX (1903–1987)   BY *G. Destanne de Bernis*

Born in Lyon in 1903, François Perroux often spoke of the debt he owed to his family and to the 'Monts du Lyonnais', to which he would ultimately return in 1987 to be with his wife, also from Lyon in the little cemetery of Saint Romain de Popey. Such fidelity to his origins did not limit his outlook; quite the contrary. He was very much a citizen of the world and this nourished his non-conformity.

To begin with, his family influenced him profoundly. Most significant was the fact that his father, a craftsman maker of shoes, had been, like so many others, eliminated by competition (neither pure nor perfect). 'Progress' for him was always an equivocal concept: what was progress for some generated costs for others, the social accounts only being in balance if they allowed for this.

When he recalled in his personal notes, or with friends, what he owed to his parents, three powerful ideas emerged. The *Christian faith* had been his personal way towards a 'humanisme scientifique'. This faith in mankind set at the foundation of his philosophy a refusal to kill and, even more basically, the solidarity of all men in the search for peace, the primary requirement for the satisfaction of every need: 'nourrir les hommes, soigner les hommes, libérer les esclaves' (*La coexistence pacifique*, PUF, 1958, 3 vols). *Respect for work*, particularly manual work, was for him a permanent stance. On the night of his election to the Collège de France, the centre of educational excellence in France, recalling to mind his father, he wrote: 'My studies must be as fine as a pair of shoes'. Moreover, this respect for work placed him in the great philosophical tradition of Thomas Aquinas, Spinoza, Marx, Sartre and Lacroix, for whom work, over and above the output of goods, is the product of man himself. He made full-time employment the condition for the 'liberation' of man. His *mistrust of money* ('money must be de-glorified', he wrote in *Le pain et la parole*, ed. du Cerf, 1969) sprang from the same source, a combination of Christianity and family. A rule for living, proven by his innate generosity, this principle quickened his conception of a world yet to be built. He praised the effectiveness of capitalism (and of profits, which he analyses carefully in his doctoral thesis, *Le problème du profit*, Giard, 1926), but purposely challenges it, as the glorification of money cannot be the foundation on which humanity is built.

Lyon was then an ancient city of learning and culture with a wonderful past, one of the high places of nineteenth-century industrialism, where could be found the ten biggest industrial and financial groups of France. But Lyon suffered the full force of the depression and eventually fell victim to a centralization based on Paris. It was in his time, however, a favoured place to grasp the capitalist dynamic, its power, its contradictions and the part played by its active agents and social groups.

Perroux was a student of R. Gonnard and E. Antonelli. One taught him the history of economic ideas which constantly nourished his subsequent thinking; the other, concerned to put back into its sociological framework the mathematical economics of L. Walras, prepared him for the encounter between pure economics and socio-economics, the fruitfulness of which he was to realize in full. A. Aftalion, the important critic of the quantitative theory of money, which Perroux was to espouse, also initiated him into the dynamics of fluctuations. It was at Lyon that Perroux started to teach in 1928. His thesis had brought him into contact with Schumpeter, who gave him his friendship, and it was to Schumpeter that his first significant work, published in 1935, was dedicated.

He himself considered 1934 to be the year of his 'birth certificate' in economics. That year a Rockefeller scholarship made possible a stay in Vienna. There he received 'lessons from a high, refined and omnipresent culture', the most important, certainly, being the privileged opportunity to study the 'second marginalism' at its very source. The clear perception of its true foundations illuminated his critical analysis: he rejected any theory which demolished the active agent, reduced it, made it passive, a mere point of intersection on a pair of curves or a substitute among a great multitude of substitutes. He understood very early that one must choose to 'either change reality (to conform with the textbooks) or change the textbooks'. He undertook to change the textbooks.

This stay in Vienna provided the opportunity to form firm friendships with O. Morgenstern, already 'showing reservations with respect to marginal utility and to the general construction one can place upon it': with O. Spann, sociologist, philosopher and analyst of the relationship between social structures and economics; and with H. Gaitskell, for whom Mises already foresaw, mockingly, a 'socialist career'.

From Vienna he went to visit W. Sombart in Berlin, where his friendship with F. Neumark was born. There he became interested in the philosophical basis of politics. In Rome he deepened his study of Paretian thought with the experts Pantaleoni and Dalonne. 'It produces', he wrote, 'analytical frameworks and a methodological approach which mark whoever has benefited from it, above all, perhaps, he who refuses to stick to it with too much docility.' From this visit date his close links with Ugo Papi, G. Demaria and G. Palomba, who are also well removed from orthodoxy.

One can understand his interest in the developments underway in that part of Europe both because he felt that the future of society was at risk there and because he deeply admired its culture but saw it as going astray. An economist cannot remain indifferent to national structures. He had already published several studies on the fascism of Salazar. It was German fascism and the dangers it presented for the whole of Europe that he attacked in his two books, *Les mythes hitlériens* (PUF, 1936) and *Les mythes hitlériens et l'Europe allemande* (PUF, 1940).

The war prevented him from making a trip he had planned to the United States. As a professor in Paris since 1937, he had devoted himself to a profound study of various equilibria, that of Walras certainly, but just as much those of assorted marginalisms, that of Myrdal and of Wicksell (*La valeur*, PUF, 1943 and *Cours d'économie politique*, CDU, 1947).

In October 1944, a few weeks after the liberation of Paris, Perroux set up the Institut de Sciences Economiques Appliquées (ISEA – Institute of Applied Economic Sciences). One of its first patrons was Keynes. The ISEA, his veritable instrument of work, very soon became a place for encounters, exchange of ideas and discussions where liberty with respect to all views was assured and where no one was excluded, provided the rules of freedom of thought and of research were accepted. The friends which Perroux had made before the war were joined by the American Dr Sanders, the biologist from the Soviet Union S. Tchakotine, as well as R. Harrod, N. Kaldor, J. Robinson, T. Balogh, P. Streeten, J. Schumpeter, R. Triffin, E. Chamberlin and M. Kalecki, who was permanently associated with ISEA. There were also J.R. Hicks, P. Samuelson and many more. They came to ISEA to present their research studies and discuss them with P. Uri, M. Bartoli, M. Bye, Y. Mainguy, M. Allais, G. Th. Guilbaud, J. Dessau and many others. Some of them wrote in the journal *Economie Appliquée*, which, from 1945, welcomed all who could contribute to the development of a 'scientifically verified knowledge'. It was not enough, indeed, to comment on prevailing ideas; it was necessary to produce an alternative theory.

Perroux consciously dedicated himself to this task. His first presentations at Harvard dealt with economic spaces: space as a homogeneous structure, polarized space, space as defined by a plan and macro unities and macro decisions. His taking into account asymmetrical relationships (the three parameters of which are size, nature of the activities and the negotiating power of the active agent) force one to go beyond the static equilibrium of perfect concurrence and prepare for a radical change of outlook in order to understand general interdependence.

The central assumption of asymmetrical relationships illuminates his research into the workings of the capitalism of his time. Although not alone, Perroux contributed decisively to the development of the theory of dominance largely accepted today. To avoid the interpretation of 'dominance' as the substitution of one unit's decision for that of another, he defined influence, dominance and partial dominance, which he expressed by topological displays and graphic methods. He showed that transnational corporations assert themselves as the dominant form of capitalist production and transform the nature of international commerce. The depression between the two World Wars can be understood primarily as rivalry between England, the former dominant international economy unwilling to relinquish this role, and the United States, which felt itself ready to take over the part. Because the latter did not conduct itself like the former, this substitution of one dominant international economy for another resulted, over the long term, in a global recombination of all the links between national economic spaces.

In his analysis of the new, global links between these spaces, he laid stress upon the following:

1. the dominant role of the dollar: money is power;
2. the integration of the 'little European cape' into one Community, including all the ambiguities of the word 'integration': 'who integrates and for the benefit of whom? he asked;
3. the conditions for 'peaceful coexistence' between East and West; and, above all,
4. underdevelopment, for him the central issue of this period, which he defined by three characteristics: external dominance, disjointed internal economic structures and failure to cover 'les couts de l'homme' (the costs of a truly human life for all).

To explain these analyses he produced concepts which allowed asymmetrical relationships to be examined in greater depth. He studied conflict/ cooperation, struggle/ assistance, propulsion effects (poles of development are a key element in his ideas on long-term dynamics and industrialization), and actual tendencies (of work, change and innovation). The method can be generalized: income distribution cannot be understood other than by reference to successively dominant social roles etc.

It is not sufficient to see these as partial analyses only, no matter how interesting they may be as such. These ideas enabled him to renovate the theory of *general interdependence* and to make of it something quite other than a new kind of equilibrium. Every agent, private or public, is active, charged with the transformation energy of its surroundings, has a strategy, is unequally endowed with power – power, this 'recalcitrant exile', finds once again a place at the heart of economic theory – makes decisions about the agents which it has at its disposal, and makes plans for its spaces of operations. Every economic action combines free choices and relationships between forces. An economy is a whole, made up of structured, hierarchical elements linked together. The 'great' impose constraints on the 'small'; the cost of the struggle between the great can lead them to call a halt, their mutual satisfaction being compatible with the strong discontent of the small. What is true at the national level is also often true on a global scale; direct overseas investment brings large corporations and small states face to face.

An equilibrium conceived in terms of stopping all movement thus stands in contrast to encounters between dissimilar, unequal agents, loaded with strategies not necessarily compatible nor susceptible to becoming so, inserted into structures which themselves have the same characteristics. Uncertainty, risk, conflict and inequality of information are not only the properties of things, but are inherent in man and his activities. The equilibration of activities in historical time endowed with content is foreign to the equilibration of objects in logical time.

This 'equilibrage' allows one to construct the *dynamization* of the system, all dynamism deriving from money and unfolding in irreversible time. Perroux rediscovered in this way the broad, significant and prolific dynamics of the original 'classicists', who had already interpreted long-term developments in terms of human activity and struggle/assistance relationships between social groups. The study of these relationships must be placed, as they had done, within the *contextual motive forces* where economics finds its coordinates within a social system. Population, techniques and the institutions or rules of the game can be treated endogenously and inserted into the economic working equations of the whole. Cycle and trend replace one another in periods of development; cyclic contraction and structural crisis are no longer confused. In a word, economic motive force is linked to the dynamism of social groups.

In contemporary capitalism, the state cannot in fact stand aside from the workings of the economy. It does not intervene through objects, public goods or meritorious goods, but through activities – the finality, the time horizon and the means of which are specific. These present fresh opportunities for cooperation/conflict or organizational activity by social groups. Here originates the collective reckoning which, if it is genuine (which implies that it be the subject of debate), obeys other rules than does private economic reckoning. Perroux is thus situated well away from welfare analysis, from consumer surplus or the terms of political economy set down by Pigou. He challenges all ideas of collective advantage; it is rather the very shape of society which counts, and every capitalist society is essentially marked by conflict.

Thus Perroux breaks openly with all orthodoxy, that is to say, with all predominant thinking, be it neoclassical, Keynesian or other. R. Di Ruzza notes five points of rupture: (i) his taking into consideration social relationships; (ii) his rejection of the market as a balancing principle; (iii) his conception of money as a constraint, force or standard; (iv) his need to analyse capitalism directly in its spatio-temporal dynamic; and (v) his rejection of the distinction between micro and macro.

These breaks also show up if one examines the way in which Perroux reads the important writers and, as it were, argues with them. Perroux had carried out many field studies; he was a prolific author but, even more, he was well read. He had drawn many of his observations from literature – Balzac, Hugo, Zola – but not that alone. The history of economic thought had constantly enriched his thinking and from it he nourished his own theories. He learned all he knew, he said, from Schumpeter. Even so, he departed from him on four major points:

1.   The stationary circuit is an advance compared with the Walrasian equilibrium, but it remains indeterminate and can represent no more than historical curiosities, for even if objects can repeat a circuit, this is not the case with money.
2.   To the monistic dynamic of innovation he contrasts that of dominances, of inequalities and of creativity: innovation which, ceasing to be that of individuals, has become a phenomenon of collective creativity, usually public or semi-public, diffusing not through Schumpeterian channels but across perfectly structured social environments, often with the help of macro decisions.
3.   He similarly enriched the relationship between profit and innovation by three determinants: tendency to create (one of the mainsprings of progress, along with the will to work), risk-taking on new structures, and social struggles.
4.   Finally, he never experienced the aversion which Schumpeter felt for socialism.

His relationship with Keynes was more complicated. He argued, step by step, the whole Keynesian edifice – the *General Theory* as well as the *Treatise* – and that without any reduction in the manner of Hicks-Hansen, but built up at least part of his own structure of ideas in counterpoint to his analysis of Keynes. Many examples of this can be found. If interest is indeed the price of liquidity, then this conclusion on its own remains too abstract. Full employment is a fundamental concept but it must be stated each time which of four possible definitions applies. As to the difference between 'autonomous' and 'induced' investments, he prefers to use 'propelling' and 'propelled', the latter not blending into the former. He agreed to argue in terms of global quantities – he had participated sufficiently in the development of the French national accounting system for that to be clear – but this kind of reasoning demands the possession of a concept of macro decision, which was not present in Keynes. Moreover, the level which he called archi-global must not exclude meso-analysis (by sector or by branch), including all that concerns the role of money, for no money could be introduced into an economy if not by decisions, be they private, public or mixed, at the sector or branch level. In other words, in the monetary economy of production, Keynes had focused more on the analysis of money than on that of production.

It is even more difficult to speak of the relationship between Perroux and Marx, which went beyond the strictly scientific. Concerning Marx, Perroux always felt a current of attraction and repulsion, perhaps due in large measure to the dogmatism which had long characterized Marxists. Perroux held a conception of the world closer to that of Marx than to that of Schumpeter or Keynes; he saw men as active in society in order to satisfy their needs. In this sense many of Perroux's questions are also those of Marx, even if Perroux gave them different answers. He did not hold the same theory of value but nevertheless acknowledged the need for such a theory; he asserted that man is primarily concerned with his needs (indeed, certain writers consider that one cannot understand *Das Kapital* without reference to an implicit idea of need); he does not make use of Marx's two sectors, but his sector of machines producing machines is indeed fully in the Marxist line of thinking and in that of intermediaries such as Tugan-Baranowski and others.

The profound difference between Perroux and Marx lies in the central question of the class struggle. The definition which each gives to the social classes was not the same (for Perroux, the definitions given by Marx for the different classes are too narrow), but both acknowledge their existence; the argument about their composition depends, at least in part, upon the difference in time between the works of these two writers. Marx would probably have accepted Perroux's observation that to tie together the working class and proletarianism prevents an understanding of today's Third World. Similarly, the capitalist class of Marx is not homogeneous, and he would have admitted the existence of competition between entrepreneurs as well as between them and the suppliers of capital. The central contrasting point lies in the fact that, for Perroux, competition within a class is not of a different kind from that between classes. He does not deny the conflict between capital and labour: he had analysed unionism, the right to work, alienation, the formation of the mass of workers, the phenomena of poverty and working conditions, particularly in his works on 'human resources'. He points out that 'since the beginnings of modern industry, Western societies have been societies based on domination. When the right to speak was granted, it was to discuss everything except what was essential. It would be naive to confuse social dialogue with those unequal conflicts where one uses words.' But he adds immediately that there is no pure conflict, only conflict/cooperation and struggle/assistance. And he concludes that the antagonistic struggle between capital and labour, defined as the struggle which entails destruction of an enemy, will never suffice to ensure the conditions for a reconciled society. Here he is in radical disagreement with Marx.

Perroux's Major Writings
(1948), *Le Plan Marshall ou l'Europe Nécessaire au Monde*, Paris: Libr. de Médecis.
(1954), *L'Europe sans fivages*, Paris: PUF.
(1956), *Théorie Générale du Progrès Economique*, Cahiers de l'ISMEA, Série I, 3 vol, 1956 et 1957.
(1960), *Economie et Société, Contrainte, Echange, Dons*, Paris: PUF.
(1964), *Industrie et Création Collective*, 2 vol, Paris: PUF, 1964 and 1970.
(1969), *L'Economie du XXème siècle*, Paris: PUF, 3ème éd.
(1970), *Aliénation et Société Industrielle*, préface à l'édition complète des oeuvres de Karl Marx par Maximilien Rubel, coll. La Pleiade, Paris: Gallimard.
(1973), *Pouvoir et Economie*, coll. Etudes, Paris: Bordas.
(1975), *Unités Actives et Mathématiques Nouvelles: Révision de la Théorie de l'Equilibre Economique Général*, Paris: Dunod.
(1983), *A New Concept of Development*, London: Croom/UNESCO.

Karl POLANYI (1886–1964)   *Geoffrey M. Hodgson*

Karl Polanyi was born in Vienna on 21 October 1886 of middle-class parents of Jewish descent. The intellectual vitality of the household is evidenced by the fact that Karl's brother also achieved world fame. After a career as a chemist, Michael Polanyi became influential for his contributions to philosophy.

Karl was raised in Budapest and he entered the university there to study law. Polanyi read widely in the social sciences and was influenced in particular by Aristotle and socialist writers such as Robert Owen and Karl Marx. One heady political debate developed into a fist fight, led to his expulsion from Budapest and forced him to finish his degree at the University of Kolozsvar.

His short career as a practising lawyer was interrupted by the First World War. As a cavalry officer in the Austro-Hungarian army he was badly wounded on the Galician front in 1917, and returned to Budapest. From 1924 to 1933 Polanyi worked as feature writer and associate editor for the influential periodical *Der Österreichische Volkswirt*. With the rise of Nazism, Polanyi fled to England and lectured for the Workers' Educational Association. After a lecture tour in the United States, he was enabled by a two-year Rockefeller Foundation fellowship at Bennington College, Vermont to write the bulk of his classic work *The Great Transformation* in 1941–43.

Subsequently, Polanyi and his wife returned to England to complete that book. In 1947 he crossed the Atlantic once more to take up a post as Professor of Economics at Columbia University (New York). However, they were obliged to live across the Canadian border, near Toronto, because of his wife's former membership of the Hungarian Communist Party. He formally retired in 1953, but continued his association with Columbia as an Adjunct Professor. Thereupon he co-directed the interdisciplinary project on the Institutional Aspects of Economic Growth, from which emerged his volume on *Trade and Market in Early Empires*. He died on 23 April 1964.

Although Polanyi's influence has been greatest amongst anthropologists and economic historians, he has also made an important contribution to economic theory. Indeed, his work addresses fundamental issues for economists, disputing both the basic concepts and the typical policy conclusions of neoclassical analysis.

Polanyi challenges both the subjectivist and the utilitarian foundations of economic orthodoxy, asserting a different type of value theory and welfare analysis. Like Smith, Ricardo and Marx, Polanyi took the distinction from Aristotle's *Politics* (Book I, Chapters 8–10) between value in exchange and value in use. However, his interpretation of these concepts was closer to Aristotle than some modern interpretations which have wrongly identified use-value with subjective utility. For Polanyi, as for Aristotle, use-value had an objective quality relating to the usefulness of an item for humankind. Its pursuit was more obvious in traditional institutions such as the household, and eclipsed by the quest for monetary gain in the market.

Partly influenced by his observations of the poverty and disharmony of industrial capitalism in Britain and elsewhere, Polanyi concluded that Adam Smith's dictum that people had a natural propensity 'to truck, barter and exchange' was the reverse of the truth. Rich support for this opinion was obtained from anthropology, particularly from Thurnwald's and Malinowski's studies of primitive communities. Therein the desire to make profits from production and exchange was absent. The usual gain from labour was not a contracted payment but social approbation, reciprocal gift-giving, and joy from work itself. In general, even hunger cannot be presumed to transform itself automatically into incentives to produce, to buy, or to sell. Instead it may lead to beggary or plunder, depending upon the prevailing social culture and institutions. Polanyi concluded that although there is such a thing as human nature, the Smithian propensities are not generally manifest.

Although they have a long history, exchange, markets and money have been peripheral to most economies prior to the modern era. Polanyi argued that economic relations were always embedded in complex social relations, without which the economy could not function. One cannot assert that 'in the beginning there were markets' – to use Oliver Williamson's recent phrase – as these are always dependent upon, and embedded within, the institutions, relations and culture of social life. It is only in modern capitalist society that market and exchange relations between rational, calculating agents have appeared autonomous or disembedded. But by undermining this institutional and cultural support, 'free' markets have placed modern civilization in crisis.

Here Polanyi reaches conclusions similar to those proposed by Joseph Schumpeter in his *Capitalism, Socialism and Democracy*, where 'rational habits of mind' are seen to disable the structures of class and tradition upon which the system depends. Polanyi goes much further than Schumpeter, however, in examining the anthropological basis of social structures and the historical processes involved in the capitalist transformation.

Polanyi believed that although markets and exchange were not predominant in all human societies, certain fundamental types of integrative arrangement could be found in them all. He identified principles of behaviour which seem to have universality across all forms of economic and social organization. One is called *reciprocity*, defined as obligatory and reciprocal gift-giving between persons who stand in some specific social relationship with each other. Another, *redistribution*, involves obligatory transfers to some central and encompassing authority. Each of these basic integrative mechanisms can take different forms in different socio-economic systems.

For instance, reciprocity may take the form of regular and ritualized two-way transfers of gifts. To the modern mind, such behaviour may appear simply as underdeveloped barter or trade. However, even in a capitalist society reciprocity takes a variety of forms – such as within the household – which obtain their particular meaning precisely because they are not reducible to commodity exchange, and are disregarded by any overt calculus of gain or loss. There may be an expectation that the giving of a gift, for instance, will lead to the receipt of one in the future, but it is not definite or contractual, and is regulated by the nature of the social occasion and the social positions of the persons involved. To drive the point home, Polanyi quotes examples of ritualized gift-giving in primitive societies in which the very same object is transferred back and forth. The 'sole purpose of the exchange is to draw relationships closer by strengthening the ties of reciprocity'.

The concept of redistribution can be understood in its modern manifestation of taxation for the provision of defence and other state services. However, it has a much more general meaning and can take many forms such as tributes, tithes, or labour services. Redistribution serves not only to provision central services but to emphasize the boundaries and unity of the group and the authority and legitimacy of its leaders and central institutions.

Such anthropological ideas form the backdrop for Polanyi's studies of the rise of the capitalist economy. While markets in some form had existed since the Stone Age, only in modern society do they dominate and largely regulate the economy as a whole. Even before the development of markets there was barter and trade for tokens or money, sometimes on a long-distance basis. Under classical antiquity and feudalism markets existed in the sense of places or occasions, defined and set apart, where people met and exchanged goods. In contrast, in modern society the market is associated with a complex and widespread mechanism of supply and demand, leading to the formation and adjustment of prices, and assuming important self-regulating functions for the system as a whole. More particularly, the market is associated with a whole social culture and shared set of meanings, of higgling and haggling and the deliberate pursuit of gain.

Polanyi thus emphasizes that the market is not a natural phenomenon, reflecting some of the supposed fundamentals of human nature. It is also wrong to see the modern market as the inevitable result of growth from 'small beginnings', thus heralded by the trade and markets of the past. Against this, Polanyi argues that the modern market is the result of the contingent combination of varied and independent cultural and ideological elements, stemming from a diverse and changing institutional background.

Furthermore, the modern market system did not emerge spontaneously, but was in many respects the result of political action and even conscious design. Polanyi did not make the error of assuming that all social institutions are the manifestations of preconceived plans, and admitted, like Marx and others, that unintended consequences were important in social life. Concerning the market, however, his key point is that it required political intervention and legislation of a fairly specific kind. In particular, the 'fiction' had to be established that land, labour and money were commodities, along with other less problematic items. Thus in the case of land there was a succession of enclosure acts, while the creation of a labour market involved radical legislation, the removal of legal restrictions on physical liberty and parochial rights, and 'the wholesale destruction of the traditional fabric of society'. Consequently, as Polanyi put it in *The Great Transformation*:

> There was nothing natural about laissez-faire; free markets could never have come into being merely by allowing things to take their course; ... laissez-faire itself was enforced by the state. ... To the typical utilitarian ... laissez-faire was not a method to achieve a thing, it was the thing to be achieved (pp. 139–41).

This conception of the market, as something contingent rather than natural, as something intended rather than spontaneous, is fundamentally incompatible with the treatment of the market in orthodox economic theory. In the case of the latter a market is presumed to exist in the interstices of human existence, appearing whenever goods or services are transferred from one agent to another. In contrast, for Polanyi, the market is an *historically specific social institution*, created, like other institutions, in part through conscious design.

Not only was the state necessary to establish laissez-faire, but once a relatively 'free' market system had been established, as in Britain in the first half of the nineteenth century, the very operation of the supposedly 'self-regulating' system required continuous meddling and monitoring by the state:

> The road to the free market was opened and kept open by an enormous increase in continuous, centrally organized and controlled interventionism. To make Adam Smith's 'simple and natural liberty' compatible with the needs of a human society was a most complicated affair. Witness the complexity of the provisions in the innumerable enclosure laws; the amount of bureaucratic control involved in the administration of the New Poor Laws ... or the increase in governmental administration entailed in the meritorious task of municipal reform. And yet all these strongholds of governmental interference were erected with a view to the organizing of some simple freedom – such as that of land, labour or municipal administration. ... [T]he introduction of free markets, far from doing away with the need for control, regulation and intervention, enormously increased their range. Administrators had to be constantly on the watch to ensure the free workings of the system. Thus even those who wished most ardently to free the state from all unnecessary duties, and whose whole philosophy demanded the restriction of state activities, could not but entrust the self-same state with new powers, organs, and instruments required for the establishment of laissez-faire.

Polanyi describes this as a 'double movement':

> While on the one hand markets spread all over the face of the globe and the amount of goods involved grew to unbelievable proportions, on the other hand a network of measures and policies was integrated into powerful institutions designed to check the action of the market relative to labour, land and money. ... Society protected itself against the perils inherent in a self-regulating market system – this was the one comprehensive feature in the history of the age (p.76).

Polanyi thus rebuts libertarian protestations against state intervention in the market. For him, this is as 'natural', or otherwise, as the earlier creation of the comprehensive market. He even makes a case that such 'protective' measures emerged more spontaneously in the nineteenth century than the evolution of the market system itself.

What is Polanyi's relevance today? Obviously, Polanyi provides a thorough and forceful critique of neo-liberalism, his ideas providing an important counter to those of Friedrich Hayek, Milton Friedman and others of the New Right. But there are other reasons why he remains a relevant thinker, unjustifiably neglected by economists.

First, at the fundamental theoretical level, Polanyi's economic anthropology rehabilitates Aristotle's non-subjectivist concept of use-value that was taken up by Smith, Ricardo and Marx. Consequently, his work provides an alternative to the utilitarianism and subjectivism that has dominated economics for more than one hundred years. It points to the study and evaluation of real human needs as an alternative to the unquestioning acceptance of the sovereignty of individual wants.

Second, Polanyi showed that the creation of the 'free' market necessitated continuous and extensive state intervention to make the market 'work'. Although Polanyi did not envisage this, his argument has clear application to the case of an attempt to move from a social-democratic mixed economy to an economy where the market plays a greater role, through privatization and the intrusion of market accounting methods into the remaining government and public sectors. Such attempts have been made in Britain and the United States in the 1980s, under the leaderships of Margaret Thatcher and Ronald Reagan, and in the name of 'rolling back the state'. Polanyi's analysis shows that any such movement is not likely to lead to the announced diminution of state powers, but instead to increasing intrusion and regulation by the central state. This has been borne out acutely in Britain and to some extent in the US.

Third, in the case of the transformation of the European economy in the 1990s and beyond, and the creation there of a 'single market', Polanyi's argument counters the belief – held by Mrs Thatcher and other neo-liberals – that such an integrated market is possible without corresponding federation or integration at the political level, and the genesis of a European State. It is forcefully implied that extended and integrated markets require a corresponding extension of the supervisory and regulatory apparatus, at a minimum to establish standards, and to ensure contract compliance. For Polanyi, furthermore, extended markets depend upon the symbolic and practical support of a unified currency and integrated banking system. And finally, in a democratic system subject to sustained pressure from trade unions and enlightened employers, the extension of market is likely, in response, to stimulate general measures to protect working conditions and to safeguard employees.

In one sense Polanyi's work may appear less relevant today. He wrote at a time when central planning had a degree of popular and intellectual support in the West. With the dismantling of central planning throughout the Eastern bloc in the 1990s, support for some kind of market system extends well beyond the New Right; it is embraced by market socialists and social-democrats as well. In this context, and dressed up in a anti-market guise, Polanyi's views could appear old-fashioned, utopian and theoretically naive.

However, whilst in Polanyi's writing we can detect the influence of an intellectual environment which has passed, it is far too simplistic to interpret him as a straightforward anti-marketeer. Indeed, his sophisticated conception of markets can be given a modern relevance. As noted above, he stressed the unavoidable connections between markets and social relations and institutions, the manner in which markets can tend to generate social legislation to ameliorate their undesired effects, and the important proposition that to pursue a pure and free market system is itself to chase a hallucinatory and unobtainable dream.

Consequently, Polanyi's work has a direct relevance for the economies of the former Eastern bloc. Leaving on one side the question of whether the extension of the market there is desirable or necessary, Polanyi's work suggests that the market cannot be sustained without both state regulation and the type of developed and ingrained social culture that is necessary to sustain a market system. Without the full development of such a culture, the extension of the market in the East will bring severe problems and by no means act as the panacea anticipated by some economists.

In sum, Polanyi's theoretical work retains much of its force and relevance today, and its subtlety makes it viable for further extension and development. He deserves a following amongst economists to match his already-existing high reputation amongst historians and anthropologists. It is appropriate that the Karl Polanyi Institute for Political Economy was founded after the centenary of his birth in 1986. Located in Concordia University (Montreal, Canada), it publishes a regular bulletin, houses his archives and helps to propagate his ideas.

Polanyi's Major Writings

(1944), *The Great Transformation*, New York: Rinehart.
(1957), *Trade and Market in Early Empires* (with K. Conrad, M. Arensburg and H.W. Pearson), Chicago: Henry Regnery.
(1966), *Dahomey and the Slave Trade* (with Abraham Rotstein), Seattle: University of Washington Press.
(1968), *Primitive, Archaic, and Modern Economics: Essays of Karl Polanyi* (edited by G. Dalton), New York: Doubleday.
(1977), *The Livelihood of Man* (with Harry W. Pearson), New York: Academic Press.

Other References

Dalton, G. (ed), (1971), *Economic Development and Social Change*, New York: Natural History Press.
Granovetter, M. (1985), 'Economic Action and Social Structures: The Problem of Embeddedness', *American Journal of Sociology*, **91**(3).
Hechter, M. (1981), 'Karl Polanyi's Social Theory: A Critique', *Politics and Society*, **10**(4).
North, D.C. (1977), 'Markets and Other Allocation Systems in History: The Challenges of Karl Polanyi', *Journal of European Economic History*, **6**.
Sahlins, M. (1974), *Stone Age Economics*, Tavistock and Aldine.
Stanfield, J.R. (1986), *The Economic Thought of Karl Polanyi: Lives and Livelihood*, Macmillan.

Raül PREBISCH (1901–1985)   *J. Gabriel Palma*

Raül Prebisch was born on 17 April 1901 in Tucumàn, (Argentina) and died at the age of 84 in Santiago de Chile. He graduated in Economics at the University of Buenos Aires in 1923, having already published six articles;

his first paper – written at the age of 17 – was (not surprisingly) on the subject of industrialization.

He was Professor of Political Economy at the University of Buenos Aires from 1925 to 1948. In addition he held various other positions in Argentina, the two most important being Under-Secretary of Finance (at the age of 27) and first Director-General of Argentina's Central Bank (aged 32). In 1950 he moved to the UN as Executive Secretary of the Economic Commission for Latin America (ECLA), and in 1963 to the UN's Conference on Trade and Development (UNCTAD) as its first Secretary-General. When his term of office ended in 1969, he went back to Santiago de Chile as Director-General of the UN's Latin American Institute for Economic and Social Planning (ILPES).

Although his main intellectual and political concern was always the need for industrialization in peripheral countries, he acknowledged near the end of his life that he had first viewed the problem from the perspective of conventional economic thinking. It was not until he had witnessed the Great Depression and read *The General Theory* that he began to search for more 'heterodox' mechanisms to stimulate this process of peripheral industrialization.

Towards the end of the 1940s, having written several articles and an influential book on Keynes, he began to develop his well-known theses on the obstacles to economic development in the periphery. His ideas became known all over the world in the 1950s when he led his ECLA team to the formulation of what became known as the 'structuralist' approach to the analysis of these problems – the first major contribution to the social sciences coming from Latin America.

From an early stage, Prebisch and his ECLA team used the concept of 'structuralism' to describe their theoretical and methodological approach to the analysis of the process of economic development in Latin America. 'Structuralism' is usually understood to be a method of enquiry which challenges the assumptions of empiricism and positivism. This method is found in literary criticism, linguistics, aesthetics, and both Marxist and non-Marxist social sciences.

The principle characteristic of structuralism is that it takes as its object of investigation a 'system' – that is, the reciprocal relations between parts of a whole, rather than studying the different parts in isolation. In a more specific sense, this concept is used by those theories that claim the existence of a set of social and economic structures that are themselves unobservable but which generate observable social and economic phenomena. In anthropology, structuralism is particularly associated with Lèvi-Strauss and Godelier. The main structuralist current in Marxist thought originates from Althuser and opposes the version of Marxist theory developed by Lukacs, Gramsci and the Frankfurt School. Whilst the first group seeks to explain social phenomena by reference to the underlying structure of the mode of production, the second group of Marxist theorists stresses the role of human consciousness and action in social life.

The key to the internal unity of ECLA thought lay in the early postulation of the 'structuralist nature' of the original ideas and hypotheses around which its subsequent contributions were to be organized. Prebisch and his ECLA team were basically concerned with what they saw as the four 'stylized facts' of underdevelopment: (i) the growing gap in the level of income between centre and periphery; (ii) the persistent unemployment in the periphery; (iii) the persistent balance of payments disequilibrium in the periphery, which imposed an important external constraint to the process of economic growth; and (iv) the tendency to deterioration of the terms of trade of the periphery. Prebisch's main analytical concerns were to build a theoretical framework to explain these four phenomena – tracing their causes to the level of production (economic structure of the periphery) and of circulation (pattern of international trade) – and to develop a comprehensive set of economic policies to help developing countries overcome these 'stylized facts' of underdevelopment in practice.

At the core of Prebisch's analysis lies his differentiation of the *economic structures* of the centre and periphery. In the former, the economic structure is seen as *homogeneous* and *diversified*; in the latter as *heterogeneous* and *specialized*. He associated the problem of unemployment in the periphery with structural heterogeneity, and that of the balance of payments and terms of trade with the excessive degree of specialization. Together they were responsible for the increase in income differentials between the centre and the periphery.

For Prebisch the two poles of the world economy were closely bound together, conditioning each other mutually and reciprocally. Therefore, the structural differences between the centre and the periphery could not be defined or understood in static terms, as the transformation of either pole would be conditioned by the interaction between them. Thus centre and periphery formed a single, dynamic system. 'Structural' factors can be described more fully as follows:

1. *Structural heterogeneity and unemployment.* The economic structure of the periphery was understood as 'heterogeneous' by Prebisch because in it coexisted economic activities with significant productivity differences, the two extremes being the export sector with relatively high productivity of labour, and subsistence agriculture with particularly low productivity.

   In this context, the labour market in the periphery has two tasks: the absorption of additions to the active population, and the reabsorption of the labour force of the most backward areas into economic activities with higher productivity. As Prebisch's and ECLA's analyses assume that the demand for labour is proportionate to the level of investment, and as this takes place almost exclusively in the 'modern' sector, full employment of the labour force at adequate levels of productivity can only be achieved if the rate of capital accumulation in the modern sector (export and import-substituting manufacturing activities) is sufficient not only to absorb the growth in the whole of the active population, but also to reabsorb labour coming from the 'traditional' sector. It is from this heavy burden on the modern sector that the structural tendency towards unemployment can be deduced.

2. *Specialization in production and external disequilibrium.* The economic structure of the periphery was understood by Prebisch as 'specialized' in a double sense: the export sector typically represents a substantial proportion of the national product, and the economy in general is poorly integrated. As a rule, exports are concentrated upon a few primary products, with production characteristically confined to an 'enclave' within the peripheral economic structure (or, in other words, having very limited backward and forward linkage effects with the rest of the economy). One of the main economic consequences of this phenomenon is that a significant proportion of the demand for manufactured products has to be met by imports from the centre. Given that the income elasticity for these products is greater than unity, imports from the centre will tend to grow faster than the level of real income. The opposite is the case in the centre in relation to their primary commodities imports from the periphery since their income elasticities are usually less than unity; hence the centre's imports from the periphery grow less rapidly than the periphery's imports from the centre and, often, even less rapidly than real income in the centre.

Thus for a given rate of growth of real income in the centre, the disparity between the income elasticities of imports at each pole will impose a limit upon the rate of growth of real income in the periphery. This will not only tend to be less than that of the centre, but less in proportion to the degree of the disparity between the respective income elasticities of demand for imports. As the periphery has constantly attempted to surpass this limit, it has exposed itself to successive deficits in its balance of trade (resulting in continuous devaluations and/or foreign borrowing); the only long-term solution to relieve the periphery from this external constraint on its rate of growth would be an increased effort to satisfy the highly income-elastic demand for manufactured products with local production (so as to make imports less income-elastic), and/or to diversify its export trade towards more income-elastic products (so as to increase the centre's income elasticity for imports from the periphery). For Prebisch, only a process of industrialization could achieve these objectives and thus enable the periphery to enjoy a higher rate of growth of real income compatible with balance of payments equilibrium.

3. *Specialization, heterogeneity and the tendency to deterioration of the terms of trade.*   Prebisch's best-known thesis concerns the tendency to deterioration of the terms of trade of the periphery, developed at the same time as Hans Singer's theory on the subject (1950). (It is not clear whether Prebisch saw this as the most important part of his work, but this hypothesis was a seductive challenge to that part of the North American academic establishment which is ever anxious to extract from the structuralist approach unidimensional hypotheses referring to clearly established variables for its own consumption.) Prebisch was concerned with the effect of *economic growth on the terms of trade.* His hypothesis was that both from the point of view of the demand for imports and that of supply of exports there are reinforcing elements that, if left to an unregulated international market, would tend to work against the terms of trade of the periphery, creating a *tendency* for its secular deterioration. This 'tendency' and the disparity in the distribution of gains from trade which it brings with it are, according to Prebisch and ECLA, a logical analytical deduction from the phenomena of specialization and hetero-geneity.

There are demand and supply elements behind these phenomena. From a demand point of view – given the problem of specialization and the differ-ence in income elasticities for imports between the centre and the periphery with respect to each other – the 'consumption path' of the periphery (the changes in the composition of local consumption as incomes grow) is more biased towards trade than that of the centre with respect to the periphery. From the point of view of supply – given the effect of heterogeneity on technological change and the differences in price elasticities of supply of exports between the centre and the periphery – the 'production path' of the periphery (the changes in the composition of local production as incomes grow) is also more biased towards trade than that of the centre (the share of exports to the other pole in total output in the periphery grows faster). In this respect, Prebisch put great emphasis on the peculiarities of productivity change. For him there was one similarity and two differences in terms of the creation and diffusion of technological change in the centre and the periphery. The similarity is that technological change and increases in productivity are relatively high in both export sectors. The differences, on the one hand, are that those of the manufacturing sector tend to spread more to the rest of the economy (externalities are higher) than those of primary production (export-led growth based on primary commodities could in fact reinforce structural heterogeneity). On the other hand, the increases in productivity in the manu-facturing sector in the centre do not tend to be transferred into lower prices as do those of primary production (mainly due to market 'imperfections' in the centre both in product and labour markets).

The combined effects would be an excess demand for imports of manu-factured goods and an excess supply of exports of primary products from the periphery. If left to the 'invisible hand' of international markets, these phe-nomena would tend to push up prices of manufactured goods demanded by the periphery and push down prices of primary commodities exported by the periphery – thus the tendency towards the deterioration of the terms of trade of the periphery.

Within this context, if the periphery is to avoid a slower rate of growth than the centre (or avoid the need to increase its requirements of foreign borrowing), it must obviously have a consumption and production path less biased for trade. It must produce locally more of the highly income-elastic importables and diversify exports towards more price-elastic, productivity-spreading commodities – a process of industrialization.

In summary, the essence of Prebisch's thought is that if the periphery is to achieve accelerated and sustained economic growth, it has to avoid unem-ployment, external disequilibrium and the deterioration of the terms of trade. A necessary condition – and some ECLA writings seem to suggest a suffi-cient one – is the development of a process of import-substituting industri-alization. However this process cannot be expected to take place spontane-ously, for it would be inhibited by the international division of labour and by a series of structural obstacles internal to the peripheral economies. Conse-quently, a series of measures were proposed intended to promote a process of deliberate or 'forced' industrialization; these included state intervention in the economy, both in the formulation of economic policies orientated towards those ends and as a directly productive agent. Among the economic policies suggested were those of 'healthy' protectionism, exchange controls, the attraction of foreign capital into manufacturing industry, and the stimu-lation and orientation of domestic investment. The intervention of the state in directly productive activities was recommended in those areas where large amounts of slow-maturing investment were needed, and particularly where those needs coincided with the production of essential goods and services.

Of these policies the two most contentious turned out to be those of encouraging the role of the state as a direct producer, and the preference of tariffs to devaluation as a mechanism of adjustment of the balance of pay-ments of the periphery. The former was justified on the grounds of the weakness of the private sector in developing countries. The latter, and more controversially, on the set of assumptions and hypotheses concerning the nature of international trade between centre and periphery. Prebisch's and ECLA's scepticism regarding the effectiveness of devaluation was based both on the belief that the 'Marshall-Lerner' condition would not hold for the periphery, and due to its possible deflationary effects. It was thought that both the local demand for imports and the international demand for the periphery's exports were very inelastic, while the local supply for exports was 'excessively' elastic (at least to price increases); tariffs, on the other hand, work directly on imports and only indirectly on exports. The direct effect of a tariff is to restrict the volume of imports, increasing the price of the respective commodities; some of the indirect effects are to stimulate domestic production of these commodities, restrict their domestic consumption and increase public revenues. In this way, a tariff would tend to improve the balance of payments via import-substituting industrialization.

In one of his last articles, Prebisch summarizes his and ECLA's task as having been that of 'showing that industrialization was an unavoidable prerequisite for development' (1980, p. viii). Furthermore the article in question at times uses the concepts of 'industrialization' and 'development' synonymously.

It is important to stress that for Prebisch the argument for industrialization does not emerge only from a 'demand side' approach to the process of development – differences in income and price elasticities of demand for imports and exports between the centre and the periphery (arguments at the level of circulation of commodities). It is also due to a 'supply side' analysis, pointing *to the very nature of manufacturing production*, especially its externalities (an argument at the level of production similar to that of Verdoorn and Kaldor). For Prebisch *each* of these two sets of arguments is a *sufficient* condition for industrialization; together, they amount to an overwhelming case.

From this analysis it is clear that one of the nuclei of Prebisch's thought was his critique of the conventional theory of international trade (as expressed in the Heckscher-Ohlin-Samuelson version of Ricardo's theory of comparative advantage). This critique aimed to show that the international division of labour, which conventional theory claimed to be 'naturally' produced by world trade, was of much greater benefit to the centre. Prebisch's theory contradicts Ricardo's comparative advantage theory due to its static nature. For Prebisch, given his assumptions, the higher the rate of growth of productivity in the export sector of the periphery (primary commodities), the greater the need for import-substituting industrialization (see 1983, p.1082). His theory also contradicts the 'classical approach' to the terms of trade (shared by economists from Mill to Keynes) which argued that in the long term they should move in favour of primary production. On the other hand, Prebisch would certainly be in agreement with Joan Robinson's argument that in Ricardo's classical example of the mutual benefits from trade between Portugal and England, the former, having destroyed its promising textile industry, ended up with a low rate of accumulation, while the latter, having concentrated in manufacturing production, ended up with an industrial revolution (1979).

It is not particularly surprising that Prebisch and ECLA should have attracted their share of criticism, particularly as they went beyond theoretical pronouncements to offer packages of policy recommendations. They were condemned from sectors of the left for failing to denounce sufficiently the mechanism of exploitation within the capitalist system, and for criticizing the conventional theory of international trade only from 'within'. On the other hand, from the right the reaction was immediate and at times ferocious. Prebisch's and ECLA's policy recommendations were totally heretical from the point of view of conventional theory, threatening the political and economic interests of significant sectors. Leading critics in academic circles were R. E. Baldwin and G. Haberler.

On the political front, the right accused ECLA of being the 'Trojan horse of Marxism' on the strength of the degree of coincidence between both analyses. In both cases the principal obstacle was located overseas (the international division of labour imposed by the centre) and both shared the conviction that without extraneous effort to remove internal obstacles to development (the traditional sectors), the process of industrialization could be greatly impeded.

Furthermore, the coincidence between crucial elements of the analysis of the two respective lines of thought is made more evident by the fact that the processes of reformulation in each occurred simultaneously. Thus when it became evident that capitalist development in Latin America was taking a different path from that expected, a number of ECLA members began a process of reformulating the traditional thought of that Institution. At the same time an important sector of the Latin American left was breaking with the traditional Marxist view that capitalist development was both necessary and possible in Latin America, but hindered by the 'feudal-imperialist' alliance. Moreover, both reformulations had one extremely important element in common: *pessimism* regarding the possibility of capitalist development in the periphery (see Palma, 1978 and 1988).

As Rodriguez rightly points out (1980), it is also important to note that the structuralist nature of Prebisch's thought not only contributes to its internal unity, but is also responsible for some of its limitations. At Prebisch's level of analysis no consideration was given to the social relations of production which are at the base of the process of import-substituting industrialization, or to the related transformation in other structures of society that this induces in its wake.

Prebisch and ECLA propose an ideal model of sectoral growth designed in such a way that the three tendencies peculiar to economic development of the periphery are avoided; from this are derived the necessary conditions of accumulation which will allow the proportionality required for the transformation of different sectors of material production. Nevertheless, even when pushed to the limits of its potential internal coherence, the structural approach is insufficient for the analysis of the long-term evolution of the economic system as a whole which clearly involves more than just the transformation of the structure of production. Prebisch's and ECLA's theories describe and examine certain aspects of the development of the forces of production (to the extent that they deal with the productivity of labour and the degree of diversification and homogeneity of the structure of production), but do not touch upon the relations of production, nor, as a result, on the manner in which the two interact.

Furthermore, the analysis of the inequalities of development cannot be carried out solely in terms of the patterns of accumulation necessary to avoid the creation of certain disproportions between the different sectors of material production, since inequalities of development are clearly linked to the possibilities of savings and accumulation in each pole. The requirements as far as accumulation is concerned are derived from those disproportions, but their feasibility depends more on the general conditions in which accumulation occurs at world level. In other words, if the intention is to analyse the polarity of the centre-periphery system, it is not enough to postulate the inequality of development of the forces of production; it is necessary also to bear in mind that those forces of production develop in a framework of a process of generation, appropriation and utilization of the economic surplus. That process, and the relations of exploitation upon which it is based, are not produced purely within each pole, but also between the two poles of the world economy.

Some additional problems related to Prebisch's contribution to development economics are as follows:

1. Although it was not their intention, Prebisch's and ECLA's ideas have undoubtedly led to a clear bias in many countries of the periphery against the production of primary commodities *per se* (with very unpleasant consequences in many cases).

2. Recent studies have shown that far from being an 'enclave', the primary commodities export sector of many developed countries has had significant linkages (both backward and forward) with the rest of the economic structure (see, for example, Palma, 1979).

3. Prebisch's work does not sufficiently take into account the fact that some countries of the centre are major producers of primary commodities,

and some in the periphery of manufactured goods, and that there are important conflicts of interest within the periphery. For example, there could be significant gains in the short term for a peripheral country rapidly to expand its exports of a given primary commodity even when its competitors in the periphery were controlling their own output.

4. Prebisch did not sufficiently stress that in order to benefit significantly from industrialization, the periphery should not only produce the highly income elastic importables for the home market, but should also diversify its exports towards manufactured goods *as soon as possible*.

Some of Prebisch's and ECLA's analyses reemerged in the 1980s in some Latin and North American academic circles (the most important contributions coming from Taylor, see especially 1983). In some cases this was more as conventional economic analysis attempting to integrate some of the structuralist assumptions and hypotheses, or as an attempt to formalize classical ECLA thought (which has, nevertheless, proved to be an important contribution, and a much needed one, to mainstream economics) rather than an attempt to use structuralism as a different method of enquiry for economic analysis.

There can be little doubt that Prebisch is the best Latin American economist, and one of the very best development economists, ever. His 'trade mark' was always to be concerned with the real world. Most of his contributions originated in the examination of specific problems, around which a series of theoretical arguments were articulated in an attempt to isolate their causes and to justify those economic policy measures recommended to resolve them. Basically, he belonged to the 'markets are good servants, but bad masters' Keynesian school of economic thought. If individual and anonymous decisions in unregulated markets tend to produce disequilibria and slow rate of growth in the periphery, this can be avoided by the collected decisions of individuals through the state. In this way, Prebisch, in the Keynesian tradition, was opposed not only to the 'harmony of unregulated classical liberal capitalism', but also to the traditional Marxist view that the growing and cumulative contradictions of capitalism would necessarily become unmanageable in the end. Following this, he spent 60 years of a very productive professional life continuously trying, in theory and in practice, to develop the ideal framework in which markets could best serve the process of economic development in peripheral countries. His eclectic – and often heretical – views on the role of markets not only made him a notorious 'dissident' (which probably cost him the Nobel Prize), but also brought him continuously into conflict with the mainstream of our profession which prefers to look at the 'invisible hand' more as an object of idolatry than as a subject of scientific analysis.

Prebisch's Major Writings

(1949), 'The Economic Development of Latin America and its Principal Problems', *Economic Bulletin for Latin America*, 7, 1962. (First published in Santiago by UN ECLA in 1949.)

(1951a), 'The Spread of Technical Progress and the Terms of Trade', New York: UN Department of Economic Affairs.

(1951b), *Problemas Teòricos y Pràcticos del Crecimiento Econòmico*, ECLA.

(1959), 'Commercial Policy in the Underdeveloped Countries', *American Economic Review, Papers and Proceedings*, 49, May.

(1962), 'El falso dilema entre desarrollo econòmico y estabilidad monetaria', *Boletin Econòmico de America Latina*, 64(1).

(1963), *Towards a Dynamic Development Policy for Latin America*, UN.

(1964), *Towards a New Trade Policy for Development. Report of the Secretary-General of the United Nations Conference on Trade and Development*, UN.

(1968), 'A New Strategy for Development', *Journal of Economic Studies*, 3(1).

(1971a), *Latin America: A Problem in Development*, Institute of Latin American Studies, University of Texas at Austin.

(1971b), *Change and Development – Latin America's Great Task: Report submitted to the Inter-American Development Bank*. Praeger and Fondo de Cultura Econòmico (Mexico).

(1976), 'A Critique of Peripheral Capitalism', *Cepal Review*, 1.

(1981), *Capitalismo Perifèrico: Crisis y Transformaciones*, Mexico: Fondo de Cultura Econòmico.

(1983), 'Tres Etapas de mi Pensamiento Econòmico', *El Trimestre Econòmico*, 50(2).

Other References

Cardoso, F.H. (1977), 'The Originality of the Copy: CEPAL and the Idea of Development', *Cepal Review*, 4.

Di Marco, L.E. (ed), (1972), *International Economics and Development: Essays in Honour of Raül Prebisch*, London: Academic Press.

ECLA (1969), *El Pensamiento de la Cepal*, Santiago: UN (CEPAL).

Palma, J.G. (1978), 'Dependency: A Formal Theory of Underdevelopment, or a Methodology for the Analysis of Concrete Situations of Underdevelopment?', *World Development*, 6(7/8).

Palma, J.G. (1979), *Growth and Structure of Chilean Manufacturing Industry from 1830 to 1935: Origins and Development of a Process of Industrialization in an Export Economy*. D. Phil. Thesis, Oxford University. Oxford University Press, forthcoming.

Palma, J.G. (1988), *Development Dependency and Marxism: a Critical Reappraisal and Case Study of Chile*, D.Phil. Thesis, Sussex University. Academic Press, forthcoming.

Robinson, J.V. (1979), *Aspects of Development and Underdevelopment*, Cambridge University Press.

Rodriguez, O. (1980), *La Teoria del Subdesarrollo de la CEPAL*, Mexico, Siglo XXI Editores.

Singer, H. (1950), 'The Distribution of Gains Between Investing and Borrowing Countries', *American Economic Review*, 40.

Taylor, L. (1983), *Structuralist Macroeconomics*, New York: Basic Books.

Michael REICH (born 1945)

I was born at the end of the Second World War, on 18 October 1945, in Trzbina, Poland (near Cracow) to Polish-Jewish Holocaust-survivor parents. After moving temporarily to Stuttgart (Germany) in 1946, my family settled in the United States in 1949. I went to public schools in New York City and then enrolled at Swarthmore College (in Pennsylvania), graduating with a B.A. with Honours in 1966.

A child of the Sputnik age, I went to college initially intending to become a physicist and so concentrated my courses in science and mathematics. During two summers I supplemented my college instruction by working as a solid state physics trainee at the US Naval Research Laboratory in Washington D.C. This research led to my first scientific publication, 'The F-Band in Isotopically Enriched Lithium Fluoride' (with H. Rabin) in *The Physical Review* (1964).

During my college years I became drawn to the New Left, first by the involvement of my fellow students in the beginnings of the civil rights movement in the North, and then by the student movements for participatory democracy. My activism became most intense on behalf of poor urban community organizations and in community and student movements protesting against US military intervention in Vietnam. As with so many others of my generation, these experiences profoundly influenced my career decisions and intellectual outlook.

Believing that a better understanding of the economy was important for social change, I decided to pursue graduate training in Economics. Perhaps naively, I chose Harvard's Ph.D. programme because of its faculty's highly-publicized role in innovative social and economic policy under President Kennedy. In fact, the required courses were quite conventional. My first research experience in graduate school proved to be considerably more interesting, however, as it involved fieldwork in low-income labour markets in Boston and an evaluation of local training and employment programmes. This research, which I conducted with David M. Gordon (under the supervision of John T. Dunlop, Peter B. Doeringer and Michael J. Piore) provided some of the impetus both for Doeringer and Piore's institutionalist theory of dual labour markets and for the radical theory of labour market segmentation developed by myself, David Gordon and Richard Edwards (and published in the *American Economic Review*, 1973).

In contrast to competitive neoclassical models, both versions of segmentation theory emphasized the coexistence of distinct segments of the labour market – primary and secondary. The primary market is characterized by high wages, stable job ladders and mobility within the firm (internal labour markets) and therefore low turnover; the secondary market is characterized by low wages, unstable and dead-end jobs and high turnover. We suggested that poverty and low earnings are not just the result of unemployment or inadequate individual investments in 'human capital'. They also result from the structural barriers that separate the two segments and trap many workers in the secondary labour market.

The radical version of segmentation theory differed initially from the institutionalist account in emphasizing how primary employers benefit from a variety of specific strategies, including, but not limited to, job ladders and racial discrimination in access to primary jobs; such strategies fragment the overall workforce and reduce workers' bargaining power relative to capital. Primary employers and workers also benefit because primary firms can smoothe their cyclical variations by shifting a disproportionate share of business cycle adjustments to the secondary sector. Our fuller statement of segmentation theory (published as *Segmented Work, Divided Workers*, 1982) provides a more historically differentiated account of these relationships, emphasizing the compromises that capital was forced to make with the unionized section of the labour force in the 1930s and 1940s. More on this below.

While a graduate student at Harvard in 1968, I helped to found the Union for Radical Political Economics and to organize an influential circle of radical economists. This was indeed a time of exciting intellectual and political ferment. Our radical economic perspective was formed both by the crucible of the civil rights, antiwar, student power and feminist movements, and as a reaction to what seemed to us to be the ideologically apologetic role of most liberal economists and of what Samuelson then called the 'neoclassical economics synthesis'. (More recently, as liberal economists have lost influence relative to free-market conservatives, and as neoclassical economics has become more diverse than in the 1960s, I have become more impressed with the width of the ideological spectrum encompassed by the neoclassical label.) We tried out our ideas in a collectively taught course and then developed them into the most widely-read textbook of radical economics, *The Capitalist System* (1972).

The main thesis of the first edition of our book argued that whereas neoclassical economics presented capitalism as the best (most efficient) of all possible worlds, we regarded capitalism as deeply implicated in the multiple oppressions that we saw around us: inequality, alienation, racism, sexism, imperialism, waste and irrationality. Our vision of radical economics differed from traditional Marxism both in our fundamental dissatisfaction with the undemocratic character of Stalinist countries – we preferred a decentralized, democratic participatory socialism that did not and still does not exist – and in our lack of concern with such standard Marxian economic topics as the labour theory of value and the falling rate of profit. To be sure, we placed the concepts of class conflict and power at the centre of radical economic theory. But we were more influenced by the broader Marxian fare, notably the theories of alienation and of historical change, and by the new social movements (such as feminism and environmentalism) whose concerns were not narrowly economistic and whose political visions and strategies seemed more transformative than those of the established labour movement.

Besides working on the overall conceptualization and the substantial chapter introductions (and on the thoroughly revised second and third editions), my contributions to *The Capitalist System* include articles on the following: the evolution of the US labour force, which argues that both proletarianization (the expansion of wage and salary labour) and stratification among workers characterized the US class structure; the stimulus of military spending to the US economy in a period of demand-constrained growth; the relation of the US political party system to the evolution of its class structure; and an article on the economics of racism, which had become the focus of my dissertation research.

'The Economics of Racism' (originally published in 1970 and reprinted in *The Capitalist System*) summarized my surprising econometric finding that black-white racial income differences hurt most whites, while benefiting only the very top of the white income distribution. I suggested that this finding was consistent with a divide-and-conquer theory of racism, in which capitalists were the beneficiaries (even though they were not the sole agents) of racial discrimination against blacks. At the same time, these results were inconsistent with neoclassical theories of discrimination, such as that of Gary Becker, in which capitalists are hurt and white workers gain from discrimination.

I expanded this study into a doctoral dissertation, under the supervision of Kenneth Arrow, Samuel Bowles and Stephen Marglin, and then developed it further into book form. *Racial Inequality* (1981) also includes documentation and analysis of the persistence of black-white income differences in the post-Civil Rights Act era; a microeconomic model of the profitability of discrimination under competitive conditions; an historical study of the vicissitudes of black-white race relations relative to labour-capital struggles, and elaborated econometric analyses of the distributional impacts of racism upon whites.

After teaching for three years at Boston University, in 1974 I was appointed Assistant Professor of Economics at the University of California at Berkeley, with promotions to tenure in 1981 and to full Professor in 1989. At Berkeley I introduced a new graduate field in Political Economy, and have regularly taught courses on Marxist economics, political economy, and the history of economic thought. My teaching responsibilities have stimulated some of my writing, including an article on 'Empirical and Ideological Elements in the Decline of Ricardian Economics' (1980) and a work in progress provisionally entitled *The Political Economy of Capitalism*.

The bulk of my research has continued to focus on labour economics. This research has benefited from my association with Berkeley's Institute of Industrial Relations, and I have served as editor of its scholarly journal, *Industrial Relations*, since 1986. I had previously served terms on the editorial boards of the *Review of Radical Political Economics* and *Socialist Review*.

A central and continuing theme in my research concerns the persistence of inequality among workers in capitalist economies. In my work on racial inequality I argue, contrary to what was once received neoclassical wisdom, that competition among employers is not sufficient to eliminate labour market discrimination. Employers' profits are not maximized simply by equating wages with marginal productivity, but by organizing the best relation between the effort expended by labour and the associated wage and supervision costs. (These once-dissenting ideas have since gained some currency in liberal neoclassical circles, under the label of efficiency wage and rent-sharing theories of wage determination.) Since workers have both an interest in and some capacity to cooperate and act collectively, employers gain from structures that inhibit worker cooperation and enhance worker competition. Such structures include job ladders and competition for promotion, as well as discriminatory patterns and practices by white workers that reproduce race rather than class orientations.

Since racial differences in employment and wages hurt white workers, efforts to eliminate discrimination can be part of a non-zero sum game among all workers, provided that class and racial issues are addressed simultaneously. In the 1970s, however, conservatives argued vociferously that white workers were hurt by policies such as affirmative action, which had only a racial basis. I argue that this incorrect perception fuelled a white backlash and contributed to the conservative turn of the 1970s and 1980s (see 1988b).

The economic crisis that began in the mid-1970s heightened the interest of many radical economists in processes of macroeconomic transformation. Together with David Gordon and Richard Edwards, I developed a theory of Social Structures of Accumulation (SSA) to explain the relationship that we observed between long swings in economic activity and distinct stages of US capitalist development, particularly in the sectors involving labour (1982).

Segmented Work, Divided Workers argues that the US economy has undergone three significant transformations, or stages of development. A stage of competitive capitalism stretched from about the mid-1840s to the mid-1890s, with initial proletarianization as the dominant labour trend. A second stage, monopoly capitalism, lasted from about the mid-1890s to about the mid-1930s, with homogenization of the workforce as the dominant labour trend. A third stage of 'post-war' capitalism ranged from about the mid-1930s to the mid-1980s, with labour market segmentation as its dominant labour trend. The economic recovery of capitalism since the mid-1980s suggests that a fourth stage has begun.

SSA theory is concerned with providing an account of these historical transformations of US capitalism. An SSA consists of the 'institutional' environment that surrounds the process of capitalist accumulation. This includes economic institutions such as the structure of labour markets and industrial relations, the supply of raw materials, corporate governance structures, the degree of competition in product markets, the structure of banking, finance and credit, and the international environment. The SSA is also comprised of political and social institutions, such as the role of the state, the structure of political parties, the strength and composition of middle classes, the structure of the educational system, and the character of race and gender relations, for these can also significantly impinge upon the process of capital accumulation.

In each stage of US capitalism a distinctive SSA initially facilitated rapid growth for a time and then came apart in a long period of economic crisis. The development of each new SSA and the ushering in of a new stage of capitalism involved institutional and ideological experimentation, political conflict and the construction of a new political coalition, including a political party realignment. SSA theory suggests that socio-political factors – such as collective action and popular aspirations and struggles for democratic rights and social justice – are just as important as the drive for profits and efficiency in explaining how capitalist economies evolve. The elaboration of these themes, as well as investigations into the changing character of labour market segmentation in the 1980s, constitute the subject of four published articles (1984, 1988a, 1988b and 1990).

SSA theory provides a framework for analysing the institutional variations that characterize contemporary capitalist countries. The presence or absence of markets in labour and capital does not define a unique capitalist economy, for the social structure within which these markets are embedded and organized has decisive effects upon the nature of the economy. SSA theory helps organize, for example, our understanding of the differences among the US, Japanese and German variants of capitalism. I am currently preparing for publication a collection of research essays on SSA theory, together with David Kotz and Terry McDonough. These essays expand and develop SSA theory and will facilitate further discussion of this approach.

My current research focuses on ongoing developments in labour market institutions in the United States. To gain a first-hand account of these changes I have returned to the fieldwork methods of my graduate student days and have been conducting (together with my Berkeley colleagues Clair Brown and David Stern) on-site case studies of a number of US companies and unions. We are examining the impacts of the changed conditions of the

1980s and 1990s upon the organization of work, collective bargaining and governance structures in the US economy.

While it appears that US labour market institutions are changing rapidly, their new structure and their coherence with other elements of the new stage of capitalism that is emerging remain an important research question. The decline of the primary labour market and of traditional unionism and the record growth of inequality among workers are occurring simultaneously with an apparent managerial embrace of 'Japanese-style' systems of team-work and employee involvement in decision-making (see 1989).

My career in economics began with the study of conventional analytical methods, and then broadened to the non-neoclassical approaches of institutional labour economics and the conflict and power perspectives of radical economics. These approaches are well suited to advancing our understanding of the changing nature of capitalism, and they continue to inform my own research.

Reich's Major Writings

(1972), *The Capitalist System* (with R. Edwards and T. Weisskopf), Englewood Cliffs: Prentice Hall. Second edition 1978; third edition 1986.

(1973), 'A Theory of Labor Market Segmentation' (with R. Edwards and D. Gordon), *American Economic Review*, **63**, May.

(1980), 'Empirical and Ideological Elements in the Decline of Ricardian Economics', *Review of Radical Political Economics*, **12**, Fall.

(1981), *Racial Inequality: a Political-Economic Analysis*, Princeton University Press.

(1982), *Segmented Work, Divided Workers: The Historical Transformation of Labor in the United States* (with R. Edwards and D. Gordon), Cambridge University Press.

(1984), 'Segmented Labor: Time Series Hypotheses', *Cambridge Journal of Economics*, March.

(1988a), 'Income Distribution: an Inter-Industry Approach' (with C. Davidson), *Industrial Relations*, Fall.

(1988b), 'Postwar Racial Income Differentials: Trends and Theories', in G. Mangum and P. Philips (eds), *The Three Worlds of Labor Economics*, New York: M.E. Sharpe.

(1989), 'When Does Union-Management Cooperation Work?: A Look at NUMMI and GM-Van Nuys' (with C. Brown), *California Management Review*, Summer.

(1990), 'Capitalist Development, Class Relations and Labor History', in A. Kessler-Harris and C. Moody (eds), *Perspectives on Labor History*, Northern Illinois University Press.

Joan ROBINSON (1903–1983)   *G.C. Harcourt*

Joan Robinson was born in 1903 into an upper middle-class English family with a tradition of dissent. Her great-grandfather was F.D. Maurice, the Christian Socialist; her father was Major-General Sir Frederick Maurice, the victim of the infamous Maurice debate in 1918. Her mother, Helen Margaret Marsh, was the daughter of Frederick Howard Marsh, Professor of Surgery and Master of Downing at Cambridge. An uncle was Edward Marsh, civil servant, patron of the arts and scholar. Joan Robinson was one of five children, four daughters and one son. She went to St Paul's Girls School where she read history. She came up to Cambridge in 1922, to Girton, to read economics because she wanted to know why poverty in general, and unemployment in particular, occurred. She 'graduated' in 1925 with a second – 'a great disappointment'. In 1926 she married Austin Robinson, the economist, and they went to India for over two years. This was the start of Joan Robinson's love affair with the subcontinent and her interest in what we now call development economics.

In 1929 the Robinsons returned to Cambridge which was to be their base for the rest of their lives (Joan Robinson died in 1983). She was appointed to a university assistant lectureship in economics and politics in 1934, became a university lecturer in 1937, a reader in 1949 and a professor of economics in 1965. She was elected to an unofficial fellowship at Newnham in 1962 and to a professorial fellowship in 1965. She became an honorary fellow of Girton in 1965, of Newnham in 1971 when she retired from her chair, and of King's in 1979.

Joan Robinson was regarded as an outstanding teacher, especially in the 1930s and 1940s, and as an exemplary supervisor of research students, as demanding as she was supportive. She lectured all over the world to students, often at their request, never refusing their invitations if it were humanly possible to get there. In 1973 she published, with John Eatwell, a new type of text book, *An Introduction to Modern Economics*, which she hoped would herald a new dawn in the teaching of the subject. It was splendid in conception but rough in execution, too ambitious because it tried to distil into one work a lifetime's ponderings on economics.

Joan Robinson travelled extensively during her life, spending many (northern) summers in India, in later years (1972–82) with K.N. Raj at the Centre for Development Studies, Trivandrum in Kerala State. She made many trips to China after the revolution in 1949. She used to say that she came to learn, not to teach; in fact, among her papers are notes of the lectures which she gave on the economics of planning a newly-emerging nation. She both inspired the Western young and irritated the old (and not so old) with her lectures and articles on China, especially in the 1960s. She admitted that there was a leaven of advocacy in the presentation of her views to offset what she saw as basic hostility from most other quarters. Others went further, accusing her, unfairly in my view, of dishonesty.

Elsewhere (Harcourt 1982), I have described Joan Robinson as the rebel with a cause *par excellence*. Perhaps it should have been causes, though there was an underlying unity in all her endeavours. She passionately hated injustice, whether it be the byproduct of a class-ridden society such as the UK, or a caste-ridden one such as India, doubly disadvantaged in her view by the aftermath of the British Raj. (She did say that as imperialist powers went, the UK was not that bad.) All her life she searched for ways of creating a more just and equitable society, in the process analysing and trenchantly critizing the societies she knew and the theories of other people about them. She fervently hoped, for example, that China would create a society in which poverty would be vanquished and the potential of all its citizens would be realized in an environment of cooperation, hard work, mutual respect and affection – inevitably, as she was to admit, an impossible dream but no less noble for that.

Joan Robinson had a passion for truth and honest argument, no matter how unpleasant were the conclusions to which it led. She was as hard on herself as on others, changing her views over her life, yet at any moment of time fiercely defending them, often with what John Vaizey called 'bleak Cambridge rudeness'. This could be extraordinarily disconcerting for those who did not know of it or her. She could be harsh and unfair, but she was also warm-hearted, a loyal friend and quixotically courageous, an indomitable free spirit who never gave up nor ever accepted the limitations of age and ill-health.

As an undergraduate, Joan Robinson absorbed Marshall's *Principles* (when she came up to Cambridge in 1922, it was said that Marshall was economics), in her case, through the lectures and writings of Pigou and Gerald Shove. That she understood Marshall through and through may be seen from the delightful essay she wrote as an undergraduate (with Dorothea Morison), 'Beauty and the Beast' (*CEP* I). It concludes: 'With this happy union of producers' and consumers' surplus they then lived happily ever after, constantly keeping in mind their higher ideals and maximizing their satisfaction by equalizing the marginal utility of each object of expenditure'. That she was eager to criticize Marshall's views because of her increasing inability to square them with the unfolding experiences of UK industry in the 1920s is borne out by the publication in 1933, at the age of 29, of her first major book, *The Economics of Imperfect Competition*. It must be stressed, as she herself pointed out, that the writing of the book was a group effort, the bringing together of ideas circulating in Cambridge, Oxford and London at the time (and, of course, in the US, with the concurrent publication of Edward Chamberlin's *The Theory of Monopolistic Competition*).

The Marshallian/Pigovian theory of competitive behaviour predicted that the reaction to a sustained fall in demand would be the closing down of the least efficient firms, often permanently, with the rest operating at full capacity with price equal to marginal cost. In fact, most firms operated at less than capacity with prices greater than marginal costs. In 1926, Piero Sraffa reacted to this state of affairs with the 'pregnant suggestion' that firms should be analysed as mini-monopolies operating in a competitive environment, constrained by demand, not by rising marginal costs. This idea – together with the invention of the marginal revenue curve (by Charles Gifford),

Richard Kahn's 1929 fellowship dissertation, 'The Economics of the Short Period' (now, at last, published in English in 1989) and Shove's lectures – led to Joan Robinson's book.

She herself saw it at the time as a critique of the benefits of laissez-faire competitive capitalism, for it seemed to deny that the beneficial purging of the unfit in fact occurred in a slump. 'With the aid of Richard Kahn... [she] used the newly invented concept of "marginal revenue" to show how short-period profits are positive even at under-capacity working' (1978, p. xi). She was to say later, though, that her analysis undermined the simple statements and the normative implications of the marginal productivity theory of distribution. With their 'new apparatus' they 'produced a complete restatement of the Pigovian system with various amendments', in particular the demonstration that 'it is not true that wages are equal to the marginal product of labour [so refuting] the orthodox theory of wages, which had stuck in [her] gizzard as a student' (1978, p. x).

Though Joan Robinson continued to contribute to the literature on imperfect competition in the 1930s, she quickly turned away from it as her main interest. With Kahn, Austin Robinson, Sraffa, James Meade and the bright undergraduates of the 'Cambridge Circus', she became absorbed in arguing out the *Treatise on Money* and helping Keynes in the development of what was to become *The General Theory*, the theory of the level of output and employment as a whole in a monetary production economy. This analysis was to reveal another and much more damning indictment of the operation of laissez-faire – the failure to provide full employment of labour because of the possibility of under-employment equilibrium with which was associated the phenomenon of involuntary unemployment.

In this endeavour Joan Robinson played an important role. She criticized the various drafts of the book and the lectures by Keynes which led up to it; she wrote a number of 'progress reports' (1933a, 1933b). After its publication, she brought out her 'told to the children' version, *Introduction to the Theory of Employment* (1937a). She extended Keynes's analysis to the long period (in the Marshallian sense) to see whether sustained involuntary unemployment could be a characteristic of long-period equilibrium and whether there were long-period counterparts of some of the paradoxes of *The General Theory* such as that of thrift (1937b). Her approach was to take as given the rate of interest, allow the appropriate accumulation to occur on Keynesian principles, and then see if the resulting long-period level of output at which net savings and investment were zero implied permanent unemployment or not. In her *Essays in the Theory of Employment* (1937b), as well as in her introductory book, she explained systematically the extension of Keynes' system to an open economy. Her essay on 'The Foreign Exchanges' (1937b), which is Keynesian as well as Marshallian in inspiration, is a classic in the literature.

In the mid-1930s another major influence on Joan Robinson emerged – her interest in Marx, which was sparked off by her review in the *Economic Journal* of John Strachey's *The Nature of Capitalist Crisis* (1935) and then by the beginnings of her friendship with Michal Kalecki. He first came to Cambridge just after the publication of *The General Theory* and amazed Joan Robinson in particular by knowing all about its contents and more. 'I still remember my first meeting with Michal Kalecki – a strange visitor who was not only already familiar with our brand new theories, but had even invented some of our private jokes. It gave me a kind of Pirandello feeling – was it he who was speaking or I?' (*CEP* III, p. 95). He had come to his results mainly through Marx's framework of analysis and his own practical experience and research. He was to have a lasting effect on the direction of Joan Robinson's thought for the rest of her life.

It resulted, first, in her little book in 1942, *An Essay on Marxian Economics*, in which she tried to distil out for the orthodox the economic structure of Marx's thought. She compared his results with orthodox teaching on various issues (and, of course, showed that Marx operated on a larger scale and was interested in problems that had been expunged by the advent of neoclassical economics with its preoccupation with value, distribution and resource allocation theory within a static framework). Shove (1944) was to point out that while on the whole, her assessment of Marx was sympathetic, acute and accurate, give or take a few howlers, her presentation of orthodoxy on many counts left much to be desired, a charge that was often to be repeated for the rest of her life.

Be that as it may, the combination of the Keynesian revolution, her interest in Marx and Harrod's work on growth theory, just before and after the Second World War, focused her major efforts for the post-war period on two separate but related endeavours. The focus was reinforced and strongly influenced by the joint Sraffa-Dobb editions of Ricardo (1951–55) and then in 1960 by the publication of *Production of Commodities...* . The first was a critique of the orthodox theory of value and distribution itself, together, and increasingly, with a critique of what she took to be its basic method. Secondly, there was her attempt, together with Kahn and Kaldor and others, to bring about the generalization of *The General Theory* to the long period, but this time to go over the classical preoccupations with accumulation, distribution and growth in the light of the findings of, and the insights gained from, the Keynesian revolution. Joan Robinson was also to make, along with Kahn, extensive criticisms and developments of the theory of money and the rate of interest in the context of the debates over liquidity preference versus loanable funds in the post-war period. In these debates, she drew on her Keynesian heritage, pointing out that in an analysis of the economy as a whole, it was not always possible to use the device of the representative individual, for so often macroeconomic outcomes reflected the balancing of forces associated with the behaviour of different individuals or groups, often with different power and, most importantly, different expectations in uncertain situations.

Her work on growth theory led her to attempt to analyse the choice of technique in the economy as a whole as part of the process of accumulation. In her view it was a very secondary part. Thus, the principal results of *The Accumulation of Capital* (1956) are obtained from a model in which there is only one technique of production available at any moment of time. To examine the choice of technique she went back to Wicksell and Marshall, as well as to Hicks in *The Theory of Wages* (1932). The result was the article for which she is perhaps best known in the post-war period, 'The Production Function and the Theory of Capital' (1953–54). Alongside this particular analytical issue was her increasing preoccupation with how she thought traditional neoclassical economists handled time in their theories, usually by 'pretending' it could be treated as if it only had the characteristics of space.

Her basic criticism was that on a plane diagram there was no place for time as it ran, as she was often to say, at right angles from the blackboard. Moreover, often this was ignored in discussions of the existence, uniqueness and stability of equilibrium of a firm, an industry or an economy. One of the earliest and most readable statements of this point of view is in her 1953 'Lecture delivered at Oxford by a Cambridge Economist' (*CEP* IV, pp. 254– 63). The most comprehensive statement is 'History versus Equilibrium' (*CEP* V, pp. 48–58). In the 1953–54 article the criticism was reflected in the form of an attack on the procedure of using comparisons of equilibrium positions to analyse processes following a disturbance, the failure, as she was to say later, to distinguish between a difference and a change. This she referred to as 'a profound methodological error', adding: 'The neoclassical economist thinks of a position of equilibrium as a position towards which an economy is tending to move as time goes by. But it is impossible for a system to *get into* a position of equilibrium, for the very nature of equilib-rium is that the system is already in it, and has been in it for a certain length of past time' (*CEP* II, p. 120, emphasis in the original). Sir Dennis Robertson (I, 1951, p. 95) thought, 'with respect', that the last sentence was 'great nonsense'. Joan Robinson (*CEP* II, p. 130) agreed it was not 'well worded', adding that in the case of long-lived capital equipment, if each individual was 'satisfied today that he could not do better by changing his behaviour [the definition of a state of equilibrium] ...[then] the stock in existence today is in all respects what it would have been if those concerned had known, at the relevant dates in the past, what expectations about the future they would be holding today'.

Another favourite analogy was a pendulum. Its ultimate resting place is independent of whether it is given a slight nudge or arbitrarily lifted high and let go: not so for analogous disturbances in a market or an economy. Thus, with hindsight, we may see that she was putting back on the agenda an issue that was discussed very early on in the modern literature by Kaldor, the problem of path-determined equilibria (except that, ultimately, she went on to say that there may not ever be equilibria out there to be found). But this was *not* the issue that was latched onto in her 1953–54 article; rather it was the problem of the meaning and measurement of capital within the neoclassical framework. What meaning could be given to a quantity of 'capital' so that we could say that the rate of profits was high or low partly because we had a 'little' or a 'lot' of 'it'? Could we also mean something when we talked of 'its' marginal product? This conceptual issue continues to be debated up to the present day when its implications for the foundations of monetary theory are being assessed. Joan Robinson herself was quickly to back off from it and from the related reswitching and capital-reversing debates, and to stress, as we have seen, the methodological critique. She applied this both to her allies, the so-called neo-Ricardians (who defended the long-period method), and to her opponents, as she saw them, the neo-neoclassicals (who used the long-period method whether they knew it or not); on this, see Samuelson (1975, pp. 43–5) and Robinson (1980, pp. 135–8).

In the positive aspects of her work she tried to deal with real issues, using a model of an unregulated free enterprise economy in which firms 'within the limits set by their command of finance determine the rate of accumulation' while members of the public, constrained 'by their command of purchasing power, are free to make the rate of expenditure what they please'. The model was then used 'to analyse the chances and changes of development of an economy as time goes by', by considering 'four distinct groups of questions':

1. Comparing situations, each with its own past, developing into its own future, which are different in some respect (for instance the rate of accumulation going on in each) in order to see what the postulated difference entails.
2. Tracing the path which a single economy follows when the technical conditions (including their rate of change) and the propensities to consume and to invest are constant through time.
3. Tracing the consequences of a change in any of these conditions for the future development of the economy.
4. Examining the short period reaction of the economy to unexpected events.

Much of this analysis is comparative dynamics, the use of steady-state comparisons which were often interpreted by her readers as applying to real economies. They did not. Rather, they were statements of consistency conditions in order to reveal how rarely, in actual capitalist economies, they were likely to be brought about, the procedure which Marx had adopted with his schemes of reproduction and the mythical nature of which Joan Robinson indicated by her title, 'Golden Age'. These ideas were developed, first, in *CEP* II (pp. 74–87) and then in her 1956 book, *The Accumulation of Capital* (the above quotes come from an unpublished preface to later editions of this) and finally in articles and an explanatory book, *Essays in the Theory of Economic Growth* (1962). Her famous banana diagram illustrating the two-sided relationship between profitability and accumulation is in the second 1962 essay.

The central model incorporated Keynesian, Kaleckian, Marxian and classical ideas. Saving behaviour was class determined, so that the distribution of the product between classes determined the saving ratio, principally because wage-earners effectively do not save and profit-receivers do, especially through their companies. In turn, this affected the determination of the level and rate of profits by the level and rate of accumulation, reflecting Kalecki's maxim that capitalists' incomes depend on what they spend. Moreover, what they spend is not constrained by their incomes but by their overall access to finance, a point of view shared by Keynes, especially following the publication of *The General Theory*.

The other relationship is Keynesian in inspiration – the 'animal spirits' function expressing the dependence of planned accumulation on expected profitability (itself related in turn to current profitability). If the accumulation induced by a given expectation of profitability happens to create an income distribution which implies that this profitability is indeed achieved, a sort of economy equilibrium is obtained. The business people are happy (the growth rate is akin to Harrod's warranted rate of growth), but the wage-earners may not be; there may be considerable unemployment, for example. There is no suggestion that it is a stable, long-period or sustainable equilibrium because the mere passage of time, during which replacements associated with rates of accumulation of past periods become due and new methods of production emerge, can rupture the 'equilibrium' by changing the positions of the underlying functions.

In her 1977 *Journal of Economic Literature* essay, 'What are the Questions?' (*CEP* V, pp. 1–31), she argued that ideology and analysis are indissolubly mixed and that the dominant ideology exerts disproportionate power in the discipline at any moment of time. She deplored the major distinction made between macro and micro in modern mainstream economics, arguing that the one cannot exist without the other. Moreover, when the dominant models of each are put together, the background macro setting for micro theory is a kind of vague Say's Law world which, until recently anyway, is *not* the macro world that is analysed in its *own* separate compartment.

In her last years, Joan Robinson became more and more pessimistic and even nihilistic. In her last substantial paper, originally called 'Spring Cleaning' (1985), she urged us all to start again. She also set out what she still believed to be valuable from the Sraffian critique of neoclassical economics and the structure he put upon the surplus approach of the classical political economists and Marx, in his attempted revival of classical political economy. She herself despaired of ever obtaining a satisfactory long-period theory. She felt that Keynes's short-period analysis (in its Kaleckian form) was about as far as we could go, giving us the ingredients of a theory of cyclical growth in the form of linked short periods, the happenings of each helping to determine what happened next.

Clearly Joan Robinson *may* have been too pessimistic at the end. Perhaps a more balanced view of her final opinion is contained in the following statement: 'In reality, all the interesting and important questions lie in the gap between pure short-period and pure long-period analysis' (*CEP* V, p. 261). Certainly, her own example will continue to be an inspiring guide to those who are now trying to implement such an agenda.

Robinson's Major Writings

Basil Blackwell has published five volumes of Joan Robinson's *Collected Economic Papers* (*CEP*) (Vol I, 1951; II, 1960; III, 1965; IV, 1973; V, 1979) and two volumes of (mainly) selections from them (1978 and 1980 below).

(1933a), 'A Parable on Savings and Investment', *Economica*, **13**.

(1933b), 'A Theory of Money and the Analysis of Output', *Review of Economic Studies*, **1**. Reprinted in Vol I.

(1933c), *Economics of Imperfect Competition*, Macmillan.

(1937a), *Introduction to the Theory of Employment*, Macmillan.

(1937b), *Essays in the Theory of Employment*, Basil Blackwell. Second edition, 1947.

(1942), *An Essay on Marxian Economics*, Macmillan.

(1952), 'The Model of an Expanding Economy', *Economic Journal*, **62**. Reprinted in Vol II.

(1953), 'The Production Function and the Theory of Capital', *Review of Economic Studies*, **21**, 1953–54. Part reprinted in CEP.

(1956), *The Accumulation of Capital*, Macmillan.

(1962), *Essays in the Theory of Economic Growth*, Macmillan.

(1964), 'Kalecki and Keynes', in *Problems of Economic Dynamics and Planning: Essays in Honour of Michal Kalecki*, Warsaw: PWN-Polish Scientific Publishers. Reprinted in *CEP* III and in 1978.

(1973), *An Introduction to Modern Economics* (with J. Eatwell), McGraw-Hill.

(1978), *Contributions to Modern Economics*, Basil Blackwell.

(1980), *Further Contributions to Modern Economics*, Basil Blackwell.

(1985), 'Spring Cleaning', published as 'The Theory of Normal Prices and Reconstruction of Economic Theory', in G. Feiwel (ed), *Issues in Contemporary Macroeconomics and Distribution*, Macmillan.

Other References

Harcourt, G.C. (1982), 'Joan Robinson', in G.C. Harcourt, *Social Science Imperialists, Selected Essays*, Routledge and Kegan Paul.

Hicks, J.R. (1932), *The Theory of Wages*, Macmillan.

Kahn, R.F. (1989), *The Economics of the Short Period*, Macmillan.

Robertson, D. (1957), *Lectures on Economic Principles*, Vol I, Staples Printers.
Samuelson, P.A. (1975), 'Steady-State and Transient Relations: A Reply on Reswitching', *Quarterly Journal of Economics*, **89**.
Shove, G.F. (1944), 'Mrs. Robinson on Marxian Economics', *Economic Journal*, **54**.
Sraffa, P. (1960), *Production of Commodities by Means of Commodities*, Cambridge University Press.
Sraffa, P. and Dobb, M.H. (eds), *The Works and Correspondence of David Ricardo*, Cambridge University Press, 1951–55.
Stratchey, J. (1935), *The Nature of Capitalist Crisis*, Victor Gollanz.

John E. ROEMER (born 1945)

John E. Roemer was born in Washington D.C. in 1945, and graduated from Harvard College in 1966 with a degree in mathematics. During the last years of his undergraduate work, Roemer became a Marxist and began participating in political work against the US war in Vietnam. During 1967, while a graduate student in mathematics at the University of California at Berkeley, he switched his major to economics, taking courses until the autumn of 1968 at which time he was suspended from the university for a year on account of political activities relating to the Vietnam war. He taught mathematics in San Francisco secondary schools during the years 1969–74 and was involved in forming the Teachers' Action Caucus within the American Federation of Teachers, a group who organized parents and teachers around educational issues and working conditions. During 1973–74, he wrote a dissertation in economics (*US–Japanese Competition in International Markets: A Study of the Trade-Investment Cycle in Modern Capitalism*), was awarded the Ph.D. degree from Berkeley and began teaching at the University of California at Davis.

In 1975, Roemer encountered the work of Michio Morishima (1973) which deeply influenced him. There had been no courses in Marxian economics at Berkeley during the late 1960s; Morishima showed that Marx's economic ideas could be studied rigorously using techniques of modern economic theory. During the next four years, Roemer worked on classic Marxian questions, building on the model that had been pioneered by Okishio and Morishima. He formulated a general equilibrium model of a capitalist economy and derived a necessary and sufficient condition on its technology for the validity of what Morishima called the 'Fundamental Marxian Theorem': that the exploitation of workers is equivalent to a positive rate of profit at equilibrium. (The so-called Fundamental Marxian Theorem was true without caveats with the Leontief technology that Morishima employed, but with a general convex cone technology, this failed to be the case.) In Roemer's model, moreover, the equality of the rate of profit in different firms arose as an equilibrium condition: Morishima's model, not being an equilibrium model, had simply assumed this (see 1980).

During this period, Roemer wrote several papers on the doctrine of the falling rate of profit, in which he generalized Okishio's observation that, in an economy where capitalists introduce cost-saving innovations, the rate of profit would never fall so long as the real wage remained constant. Okishio had demonstrated this proposition with a Leontief model of production; Roemer generalized it to the von Neumann activity analysis model, capable of handling issues such as fixed capital, differential turnover times and the use of capital of different vintages. Okishio's result remained true; thus it was no longer possible to argue, as some had done, that the presence of fixed capital could validate Marx's claim that rational capitalist behaviour could bring about crisis due to a falling rate of profit. In Roemer's model, it is assumed that capitalists have rational expectations concerning the economic lifetime of a new technique. If, however, fixed capital becomes economically obsolete earlier than expected, due to a rapid rate of technical change, then the rate of profit can fall. The other avenue for a falling rate of profit is via a rising real wage. Thus the empirical question of whether capitalism tends to suffer from a falling rate of profit involves the association between the real wage and technical change, and whether capitalists are myopic. (These papers and others on the transformation problem are collected in 1981.)

Roemer's work in Marxian economics during this period was more technically sophisticated than what had come before, but was derivative in studying issues that had been raised by earlier writers: Okishio's formulation of the falling-rate-of-profit model and Morishima's presentation of the Fundamental Marxian Theorem. During 1979–80, while Roemer held a Guggenheim fellowship at Yale University, he completed a book which widened the repertoire of Marxian economics considerably, *A General Theory of Exploitation and Class* (hereafter *GTEC*). In the introduction, he stated that the book was motivated by an interest in understanding the development of class society in socialist countries. Marx had a theory of exploitation for feudalism and for capitalism, but none for socialism. Was it possible to propose a general theory of exploitation which would have, as special cases, feudal, capitalist and socialist exploitation?

In the first part of *GTEC*, a general equilibrium model of a private ownership economy was studied, in which agents are characterized as being endowed with labour and goods which could be used as inputs into production (that is, capital). Each agent has access to the technology; there are no firms that act as independent agents, as in the Arrow-Debreu model. Facing a vector of prices and wages, each agent seeks to maximize his utility subject to several constraints: a budget constraint stating that consumption is limited to total net income, which comes from wages, profits from hiring others, and profits from working in one's own shop: and a cash-in-advance constraint, stating that the inputs needed in the agent's chosen production plan must be financed from the value of his current endowment. A vector of prices and an allocation constitute a *reproducible solution* (a kind of steady state equilibrium) if, when all agents maximize utility subject to their constraints, all input markets and all output markets clear. Since the income in the budget constraint is income net of replacement of capital, each agent ends up with capital equal in value to what he began with; hence, the reproducibility.

An agent can, in this model, choose to hire labour that works in 'his shop' on his capital, to use his own labour in his shop on his capital, and/or to sell labour on the labour market (to work in someone else's shop.) At the optimum to an agent's utility maximization problem, he has a solution which is schematically of one of the five types in Table 1.

Table 1: Class Position of Agents

Own	Hire	Sell	
0	+	0	pure capitalist
+	+	0	semi-capitalist
+	0	0	independent artisan
+	0	+	semi-proletarian
0	+	0	proletarian

'Own,' 'Hire,' and 'Sell' mean 'working in one's own shop,' 'hiring labour,' and 'selling labour on the market,' and '+' means that the agent engages in that activity and '0' means that he does not. Each of these five possible combinations of activities defines a *class position*: a class is defined by the relationship of an agent to the labour process, not by his wealth. Thus at a reproducible solution in the model, each agent places himself in one of the above five classes. Class formation is endogenous: as agent's class emerges from economic activity; it is not part of his primitive characterization.

What is the relationship between an agent's class position and whether or not he is exploited? Roemer defined exploitation as a generalization of Marx's idea that exploitation was measured by the unequal exchange of labour. For Marx, the proletariat is exploited because the hours of labour socially embodied in the subsistence wage that proletarians receive (what Marx called 'necessary labour') are fewer than the hours of labour they provide to earn that subsistence wage: the difference Marx called surplus labour, and he measured the rate of exploitation as the ratio of surplus labour to necessary labour. The surplus labour which workers provide to capitalists can be viewed as a rent that they pay in order to use the capital stock that capitalists own, thereby enabling themselves to earn a living. In Roemer's general model there is no subsistence wage: rather, each agent chooses the vector of labour and goods which maximizes a utility function whose arguments are goods and leisure, subject to his budget and capital constraints (see 1986c). An agent is exploited at a reproducible solution if his earnings do not suffice to purchase a bundle of goods embodying as much labour as he expended, and he is an exploiter if, no matter how he spends his earnings, he must always purchase a bundle embodying more labour than he expended. Earnings consist of wages, profits and revenue from own-production.

Exploitation and class position are two independently-defined concepts in the model. The main theorem, the Class-Exploitation Correspondence Principle (CECP), states that *any agent who is a capital or semi-capitalist at equilibrium is an exploiter, and any agent who is a semi-proletarian or proletarian is exploited*. The exploitation status of independent artisans is indeterminate; depending on their wealth, they can be either exploiters, exploited or neither. (In a model with only one good, there is no ambiguity: independent artisans are exploitation-neutral.) Thus the model proves a relationship between classical Marxian categories which had been assumed in earlier Marxist work.

The first version of the CECP was proved for a model with a Leontief technology. The next step involved generalizing it to a model whose technology is a convex cone. In so doing, the concept of 'embodied labour time' becomes ambiguous: there are several possible definitions of embodied labour. Roemer showed that the CECP remains true in his model only if embodied labour time is defined to depend upon equilibrium prices in the following way: the labour embodied in a bundle of goods is the amount of labour needed to produce those goods as a net output when only techniques are used that maximize profits at equilibrium prices. For a general model of production, there may be many more 'processes' than goods, and thus a choice of technique. But those techniques cannot be known until equilibrium prices are known. Thus, *embodied labour times, or labour values, must depend upon equilibrium prices* for the CECP to remain true. This conclusion was heretical to some Marxists who, along with Marx, viewed labour values as more fundamental than prices in constructing a theory of value. Roemer's method – to accept the CECP as an important fact, and to adopt that definition of labour value which preserved the theorem in a general context – also aroused some objections.

In the latter part of the book, Roemer proposed a general theory of exploitation, using the concept of the core from cooperative game theory in which feudal, capitalist and socialist exploitation emerged as special cases. For example, a coalition of agents at an equilibrium in a private ownership economy is exploited if, by withdrawing with its per capita share of society's alienable assets, there exists an allocation for it which renders each of its members better off than at the original equilibrium, and there exists no allocation for its complement, rendering each of them as well off as they are at equilibrium. For simple models, this definition is equivalent to that of exploitation in terms of embodied labour times. In more complex models, the two definitions diverge. One virtue of the game-theoretic or 'property relations' definition of exploitation is that it makes no mention of embodied labour time, and therefore can be applied when there is no sensible notion of embodied labour (for example, when there are several non-produced resources in the model, or heterogeneous labour. There has been considerable debate about the salience of this definition, especially among philosophers (see, for example, Elster, 1982; Reiman, 1987 and Roemer, 1989b, which is a reply to Reiman).

The models of GTEC aroused debate, not only because of their use of neoclassical models of equilibrium and game theory, but because the cause of exploitation and class lay in the differential endowments of the agents (and their differential preferences). The theory of class and exploitation was thus liberated from the labour theory of value. Furthermore, the labour process was assumed not to be a locus of struggle: workers and capitalists signed wage contracts, and labour came forth without a contest. Roemer's defence of this (1988) was that his models show that exploitation and class can emerge in a private ownership economy *even if* the labour process is perfectly transparent and contracts signed on the labour market are costlessly enforceable. Of course Marxists associated with the 'labour process school' (deriving from the seminal 1974 book by Harry Braverman) viewed the essential locus of exploitation as being in the capitalists' control of the labour process. But Roemer propounded a theory of capitalism in which the emergence of exploitation and class are based primarily on property relations, not the relations of workers and capitalists at the point of production. In principle, one could conceive of a capitalism replete with exploitation and class, but in which the labour process was democratic.

During 1981, Roemer spent three months at University College London, where he talked with G.A. Cohen (1978) who influenced him to think more about the fundamental ethical roots of the concept of exploitation. Roemer concluded that exploitation, measured as the difference between labour expended by the agent and labour embodied in the goods which the agent could purchase with his earnings, was not of rock-bottom ethical importance. In 'Should Marxists be Interested in Exploitation?' (1985c), he argued that exploitation was a surrogate for an interest in equality; however, if one admitted the possibility of general preferences, it was an unreliable statistic of inequality. There could be cases where the poor exploit the rich, according to the surplus-labour definition of exploitation (though not according to the property-relations definition). While the CECP was true for an arbitrary profile of preferences, the natural relationship between class and wealth (and therefore exploitation and wealth) depends upon preferences. In the mono-graph *Value, Exploitation and Class* (1986c), Roemer provided a sufficient condition on preferences for the 'class-wealth correspondence' to be true.

As a result of this work, Roemer moved away from the unequal exchange of labour as a concept of fundamental interest, and began studying inequal-ity in the ownership of assets. What kind of equality should one advocate as an ideal? The aim of socialism was to eliminate the inequality in ownership of alienable means of production by eliminating private property in those means. But would inequalities remaining in skills, and hence income, be just? Roemer was much influenced by Ronald Dworkin's two papers on the equality of welfare and of resources (1981). In the first of these, Dworkin argued that equality of welfare was not a philosophically attractive option since it did not hold people responsible for their expensive tastes, and that any cogent egalitarianism must be one of resource equality. Dworkin's con-ception of such egalitarianism, presented in the second paper, is comprehen-sive in that it includes as resources not only as alienable resources, but also the native talents of people. Dworkin stood for a kind of radical equality of opportunity. In his paper he proposed a mechanism for allocating alienable resources among a population which, he claimed, implemented a defensible conception of comprehensive resource equality: that is, it provided the untalented and handicapped with just the amount of alienable resources needed to compensate them for their poor endowments of internal resources. The mechanism involved agents insuring themselves against the luck of the birth lottery behind a thin veil of ignorance, in which each knows his prefer-ences but not his resource endowment.

Finding this position quite compelling (for it went one step farther than equalizing alienable assets, as suggested by the theory of exploitation), Roemer modelled the Dworkin idea. In 'Equality of Talent' (1985a), he revealed some perverse aspects of the Dworkin insurance mechanism: in some cases it could render the poorly-endowed agents even worse off than they would have been without insurance. The next question thus arose: is there an allocation mechanism that could be interpreted as equalizing re-sources (comprehensively defined) but which is not subject to the problems of the Dworkin insurance scheme?

Roemer approached this question by changing the focus of analysis from the distribution of resources to the class of allocation mechanisms that distribute resources. One cannot straightaway define what a comprehensive resource-equalizing mechanism is: what, indeed, constitutes appropriate compensation for a handicap, lack of a talent or even an expensive taste that one acquired unconsciously? The procedure was to propose four desiderata, or axioms, for a resource-equalizing allocation mechanism, each of which seemed incontestable. One of these axioms eliminated the perverse behaviour of Dworkin's mechanism. Roemer proved that the only allocation mechanism (defined on a broad class of possible worlds or economic environments) that obeyed all four axioms was that which always distributed alienable goods so as to equalize the *welfare* of all agents ('Equality of Resources Implies Equality of Welfare', 1986a). He concluded this paper not by arguing that any comprehensive opportunity egalitarianism must be for equality of outcome; rather, that attention must be focused on what aspects of a person should be considered part of his resource endowment, and what aspects part of his preferences. The model in which the equivalence theorem was true allowed no such division. Without such a split, surprisingly simple axioms forced the equivalence of resource and welfare egalitarianism. Roemer's model of the Dworkin equality problem stimulated some discussion in the philosophical literature (see, for instance, Scanlon, 1986).

The issue of interpersonal comparability of welfare has been central to discussions of egalitarianism. The two central conceptions of justice among philosophers are utilitarianism and the difference principle, each of which assumes a degree of comparability of welfare across agents. Yet economists have been unwilling to assume the comparability of welfare across persons, in large part because Walrasian general equilibrium theory requires no such comparability. In 1987–88, Jon Elster and Roemer organized two conferences on the subject of interpersonal comparisons of well-being, which were attended by philosophers, economists and cognitive psychologists. The book resulting from these conferences (Ortuño-Ortin and Roemer, 1990) included a paper that demonstrates the possibility of deducing interpersonal comparisons of welfare, given a degree of 'local expertise'; namely, that each person is capable of making correct interpersonal comparisons between himself and others very similar to himself.

Since 1987, Roemer's work has concentrated on studying public ownership and market socialism. The Marxist prescription for resolving the inequities and inefficiencies of capitalism was to dissolve private property in the alienable means of production, and replace it with public ownership. There is, however, no accepted definition of public ownership among economists. For instance, consider the following question. Suppose an economy is specified, including the agents with their preferences and endowments – some of which they privately own, some of which they own publicly with all others – and the firms with their technologies (again, some firms are privately owned, some publicly). What is the natural allocation of resources associated with such an economy, akin to the Walrasian equilibrium of a private ownership economy? Roemer and Silvestre attempted to answer this question, taking a mechanism-design approach (see 1987). By examining the case of a simple economy, they proposed that an allocation mechanism that respects both the private and public ownership rights of agents has four desiderata: Pareto optimality along with three others, A, B and C. They showed that each of these determined a unique allocation mechanism on a broad class of economic environments. The most novel of these proposals they named the 'proportional solution'. Roughly speaking, the proportional solution for an economy is a Pareto optimal allocation of goods and labour in which the value of labour provided by agents (at efficiency prices) is proportional to the value of goods (also at efficiency prices) they receive. If public ownership is so interpreted, then it can be achieved by regulating access to the publicly-owned asset, so that the economy does not suffer the 'tragedy of the commons' which results when there is unlimited access to a publicly-owned resource. In 'A Public Ownership Resolution to the Tragedy of the Commons' (1989a), Roemer applied the results from the Roemer-Silvestre paper to criticize Robert Nozick's (1974) neo-Lockean view that appropriation of natural resources by individuals could lead to a just and efficient allocation of such resources.

In their mechanism-design approach to public ownership, Roemer and Silvestre assumed a classical economic environment in which all technologies were of constant or decreasing returns to scale. But public ownership of firms in actual capitalist economies is often an alternative to private ownership when the firm is a natural monopoly (that is, when there are indivisibilities in production or increasing returns to scale). It is well known that profit maximization does not lead to efficiency with such firms, leaving governments with two alternatives: to try to regulate a privately-operated natural monopoly, or to nationalize and then regulate it as a public firm. Conventional wisdom in the 1980s was that the first option is superior from an economic point of view. Roemer and Silvetre challenged this (1989c). In an environment of asymmetric information where the regulators do not know the exact cost function of the firm, they compared the welfare consequences of regulating a private monopoly and regulating or subsidizing a public firm. Neither regime uniformly dominates the other; which is welfare-superior depends on various parameters of the economy. In the model, it is not assumed that the public manager attempts to maximize profits; his objective function includes a concern with popularity among consumers (for they elect politicians who may have power over the manager) and a concern with workers' wages (for workers in public firms reputedly receive higher wages than in private firms). Nevertheless, the public firm may welfare-dominate the regulated private monopoly under reasonable conditions.

Along with many other Marxists, Roemer had for some time advocated a system of democratic market socialism as the only feasible form of socialism in modern times. With Ortuño and Silvestre, he began studying precisely how such a democratic market socialism could be organized. In 'Market Socialism' (1990b), these three authors defined democratic market socialism as an economy in which (i) all private goods, including labour, are distributed via markets; (ii) firms are profit maximizing and publicly owned – the latter means that profits are distributed to citizens in a manner that is democratically decided upon; (iii) the pattern and level of investment are decided upon democratically, perhaps through the competition of political parties; and (iv) the government uses price, quantity and tax instruments to implement the desired pattern of investment. Three models are constructed, each of which obeys these four requirements. The authors view their work in the tradition of Oskar Lange's pioneering paper of 1938.

Whether or not Roemer's work should be considered Marxist is a matter of interpretation, since it has shown that much of Marx's theoretical economics is wrong. On the other hand, using methods of contemporary economic theory, he has studied several of Marx's principal ideas about capitalism and has attempted to formulate rigorous definitions of public ownership and market socialism. His work in political philosophy has been heavily influenced by the Marxist G.A. Cohen, and the non-Marxist philosophers Ronald Dworkin and John Rawls.

Roemer's Major Writings

(1975), *US–Japanese Competition in International Markets: A Study of the Trade-Investment Cycle in Modern Capitalism*, University of California, Berkeley: Institute of International Studies.

(1977), 'Technical Change and the "Tendency of the Rate of Profit to Fall"', *Journal of Economic Theory*, **16**.

(1980), 'A General Equilibrium Approach to Marxian Economics', *Econometrica*, **48**, March.

(1981), *Analytical Foundations of Marxian Economic Theory*, Cambridge University Press.

(1982), *A General Theory of Exploitation and Class*, Harvard University Press.

(1985a), 'Equality of Talent', *Economics and Philosophy* **1**(2).

(1985b), 'Rationalizing Revolutionary Ideology', *Econometrica*, **53**.

(1985c), 'Should Marxists be Interested in Exploitation?' *Philosophy and Public Affairs*, **14**.

(1986a), 'Equality of Resources Implies Equality of Welfare', *Quarterly Journal of Economics*, November.

(1986b), 'The Mismarriage of Bargaining Theory and Distributive Justice', *Ethics*, **97**.

(1986c), *Value, Exploitation, and Class*, London and New York: Harwood Academic Publishers.

(1987), 'Public Ownership: Three Proposals for Resource Allocation' (with J. Silvestre), U.C. Davis Dept of Economics Working Paper 307.

(1988), *Free to Lose: An Introduction to Marxist Economic Philosophy*, Harvard University Press.

(1989a), 'A Public Ownership Resolution of the Tragedy of the Commons', *Social Philosophy and Policy*, **6**.

(1989b), 'What is Exploitation? Reply to Jeffrey Reiman', *Philosophy and Public Affairs*, **18**(1).

(1989c), 'A Welfare Comparison of Private and Public Monopoly' (with J. Silvestre), U.C. Davis Dept of Economics Working Paper 340.

(1990a), 'Deducing Interpersonal Comparisons from Local Expertise' (with I. Ortuño-Ortin), in J. Elster and J.E. Roemer (eds), *Interpersonal Comparisons of Well-Being*, Cambridge University Press.

(1990b), 'Market Socialism' (with I. Ortuño-Ortin and J. Silvestre), U.C. Davis Dept of Economics Working Paper 355.

Other References

Braverman, H. (1974), *Labor and Monopoly Capital*, New York: Monthly Review Press.
Cohen, G.A. (1978), *Karl Marx's Theory of History: A Defence*, Oxford University Press.
Dworkin, R. (1981), 'What is Equality? Part 1: Equality of Welfare' and 'Part 2: Equality of Resources', *Philosophy and Public Affairs*, **10**.
Elster, J. (1982), 'Roemer versus Roemer', *Politics & Society*, **11**(3).
Lange, O. (1938), *On the Economic Theory of Socialism*, University of Minnesota Press.
Morishima, M. (1973), *Marx's Economics*, Cambridge University Press.
Nozick, R. (1974), *Anarchy, State and Utopia*, New York: Basic Books.
Okishio, N. (1961), 'Technical Change and the Rate of Profit', *Kobe University Economic Review*, **7**.
Reiman, J. (1987), 'Exploitation, Force and the Moral Assessment of Capitalism: Thoughts on Roemer and Cohen', *Philosophy and Public Affairs*, **16**(1).
Scanlon, T.J. (1986), 'Equality of Resources and Equality of Welfare: A Forced Marriage?' *Ethics*, **97**.

Kurt W. ROTHSCHILD (born 1914)

Zwei Seelen wohnen, ach!
in meiner Brust

Goethe (*Faust*)

I was born in Vienna in 1914, the son of Ernst and Philippine Rothschild. My father was a salesman working for the National Cash Register Company most of the time. After finishing secondary school in 1933 I entered the University of Vienna. I should have liked to study physics; but the poor employment chances at that time, the length of a degree course, and the fact that I had to earn sufficient money (through tutoring) to finance my continued education enforced a different course of action. I turned towards the study of law both because of the shorter duration of legal studies and because of vague hopes that a job of some sort could be found on that basis.

At that time no Social Science faculties existed at the Austrian universities; the study of economics was an integral and important part of the legal studies curriculum. (All the well-known representatives of the 'Austrian School' – Menger, Böhm-Bawerk, Wieser, Schumpeter, Mises, Hayek, Haberler, Machlup – had been students of law at the University of Vienna.) When I came into touch with economics during my studies, my interests were quickly transferred from the (main) legal subjects to this subsidiary element of my course. While I did not dare even to think of a chance to make economics my profession (the chances in the academic sphere being extremely poor and for a Jew almost nil), I nevertheless spent more time than necessary for work and seminars in this field.

The motives driving me in this direction had different roots. In the university, where I came under the influence of Hans Mayer, a pupil of Friedrich Wieser and an enthusiastic proponent of a rigid marginal utility framework as the sole path to economic knowledge, I was attracted by the 'beauties' of analytical reasoning which contrasted so favourably (in my eyes) to the comparatively dull accumulation of legal facts and rules. A formal affinity to the natural sciences also played a certain role. At the same time an interest in economic matters from a quite different angle was kindled by my contact with the Socialist Youth Movement (before it was destroyed by the Austro-Fascist coup in 1934) where one was induced to get acquainted with Marx and the Austro-Marxist thinkers. Their views, though less 'exact' and structured than those expounded by the anti-Marxian teachers at the university, were far more relevant and stimulating when one looked at the rapid economic and political deterioration taking place in Austria in those days. And, last not least, it was this actual situation, in particular the mass unemployment of the 1930s – worse in Austria than in most other countries – which provided a strong impulse to turn to economics in order to find ways and means to overcome the economic and social miseries of the depression and of the 'lower classes'.

These three 'roots' – love and respect for economic theory as an impressive analytical instrument, dynamic perspectives as an important key to an understanding of socio-political developments, and a problem-orientated approach in view of the economic and social ills of society – have remained the 'prime movers' of my work in the field of economics, although it is not always easy or even possible to find a common denominator for these different approaches. Thus I had (and have) full understanding for Schumpeter's split personality when it came to an evaluation of the contributions of past economists: he was torn between an admiration for the precision of Walras' analysis on the one hand and the wide 'vision' of Marx on the other. And he himself tried to keep in touch with both elements, the detailed analysis and the extended research encompassing economic, sociological, and historical factors. I was (and I am) also impressed by economists like Oscar Lange and Paul Sweezy who were equally at home in classical and neoclassical, and in Marxian and non-orthodox fields. In naming these 'heroes' I do not want to suggest that I regard myself as belonging to this elite circle or even as one who tries to follow in their footsteps; I only mention them because I feel that they were faced by similar 'inner divisions' as those which I experienced.

When Hitler invaded Austria in 1938 it was clear to me that as a Jew I had to leave the country if I wanted to survive. I fled to Switzerland and in the autumn of 1938 I had the extreme luck to obtain one of two refugee scholarships at Glasgow University which enabled me to study economics in the two following years. These scholarships had been organized by the Glasgow branch of the International Student Service. The person in charge of the programme was a young economics lecturer, Alec Cairncross (now Sir Alec Cairncross). Before I came to Glasgow he wrote to me that it would be a good thing if I read a fairly new book by Keynes called *The General Theory of Employment, Interest and Money* since this played an important role in current university teaching and discussions. When I sat down in the university library of Basle trying to read Keynes, I could not make head or tail of his book. My narrow training in a 'pure' Austrian framework had not prepared me for such a strange menu. But then I came across Joan Robinson's slim *Introduction to the General Theory* and that proved an excellent brain- and eye-opener. So when I came to Glasgow in December of 1938 I already had a vaguely formed idea that here was a leading economist who was fully in command of traditional economics but was not prepared to stick to the niceties of a given analytical structure if it meant losing touch with the most pressing economic and social problems of the time.

When I studied Economics and Political Philosophy at Glasgow University, the 'high years of theory' (Shackle) were still in full swing and it was fascinating for me to see how, in the debate among Keynesians, theory became a pliable tool subordinated to a problem-solving approach rather than constituting an aim in itself. If an approach like this could be kept sufficiently open to permit the entry of non-economic factors and dynamic considerations, then – I felt – it should be possible to come nearer to a combination of the different aspects of economic theorizing.

In 1940 I finished my studies at Glasgow University, but continued there as Assistant Lecturer and later as Lecturer in Economics from 1940 to 1947. In 1947 I returned to Austria, joining the Austrian Institute of Economic Research in Vienna as Senior Research Worker with responsibility for the Labour Market and Foreign Trade sections. This helped me to get acquainted with the opportunities and pitfalls of empirical work. In 1966 I moved to a Chair in Economics in the newly-founded University of Linz (in the province of Upper Austria) which was created with a view of fostering social sciences and interdisciplinary relationships between the social sciences themselves and with technical studies. I retired in 1985 but have kept – through all the years – a link (as consultant) with the Austrian Institute of Economic Research.

The varying requirements on the path of my occupational career, the limited scope for specialization in a country with an (until quite recently) rather small academic establishment in economics, and last but not least a problem-orientated attitude, all contributed to the fact that my research has not been narrowly concentrated on a specific field. Its main directions cover wages and income distribution, employment and unemployment, price theory and market forms, some aspects of international trade, and occasional excursions into methodology and the history of economic thought. But I believe that behind all this diversity the different roots of my devotion to economics and their partly contradictory nature remain visible. This I shall try to indicate in the following short remarks.

Though Keynes's stress on macroeconomics impressed me as soon as I grasped the importance of his approach for the over-riding socio-economic problem of unemployment, I was still geared by my Viennese training to microeconomic problems and analysis in the early years. The main line in this early work was an attempt to transcend the predominant thinking in terms of full (or even perfect) competition which seemed to me to falsify many of the conclusions which were drawn from theory for practical policy. So I was naturally attracted by the 'monopolistic competition revolution' which had preceded that of Keynes but was (unfortunately?) not incorporated in his *General Theory* (in contrast to Kalecki who accounted for it in all his writings). In my article 'The Degree of Monopoly' I tried to develop – in the framework of Chamberlinian theory – a measure of the degree of monopoly power based on the hold which the individual producer can exert on the public's loyalty. While this paper stressed the importance of monopolistic elements, it remained in the sphere of atomistic (though heterogeneous) competition and transparent markets (at least on the side of the producers). Five years later in the paper 'Price Theory and Oligopoly', I turned to the market form, which seemed to me the most relevant one in modern capitalism – oligopoly; that asked for a definite farewell to traditional neoclassical price mechanics. Uncertainty, fewness, collusion all pointed to a different approach which was indicated (though not fully developed) by heuristic parallels to strategic behaviour in war-like situations.

In both these papers the 'power' of the enterprise in fixing prices – absent by definition in competitive markets – was an important factor. But while monopolistic power in the narrower sense, which was the essence of the first paper, had long ago obtained a firm (though often neglected) place in mainstream economics, the large oligopolistic firms of the second paper brought up a much wider power problem, extending to price wars, extra-market operations, political influence etc. This problem of power, elusive as the term may be, continued to hold my attention in much of my further work, because I feel that – in contrast to Marxian and other non-orthodox theories – neoclassical theory has neither the apparatus nor the inclination to give proper weight to power influences. The power problem came up once more in connection with prices in a paper (contributed to a conference on Böhm-Bawerk's essay 'Markt oder ökonomisches Gesetz?') entitled 'Macht: Die Lücke in der Preistheorie'; also, in a very general way, in an essay on the importance and different aspects of power in the Introduction to a volume of articles dealing with this subject (1971) for which I chose the following quotation from Bertrand Russell as a leading motive: 'Economics as a separate science is unrealistic, and misleading if taken as a guide to practice. It is one element – a very important element, it is true – in a wider study, the science of power'. Finally, the problem of power also came to the fore in some papers on international economic relations where (in the tradition of List, Balogh, Perroux and others) differences in the size and economic capacity of nations were given greater weight, leading to a more differentiated judgement regarding free trade than is typical for mainstream international trade theory (see, for example, 1963).

All through the years my interests were again and again drawn towards employment and unemployment and labour market problems in general. The stark reality of these problems and their social and political consequences, as well as the impact of Keynes, Kalecki and the early discussions surrounding their publications, were formative experiences. Both my first book (*The Theory of Wages*) and my most recent publication (*Theorien der Arbeitslosigkeit*) deal with this theme. In all these publications I have tried to give a balanced view of mainstream neoclassical thought and its possible contribution to the subject. At the same time I have pointed out that this approach can only be a partial theory which covers only certain aspects of the problem. It may be applicable in certain situations ('classical unemployment'), and it may be helpful as an additional factor in some others, but it would definitely be misleading if taken as the decisive approach to the entire problem. A much wider theoretical approach and the consideration of non-economic factors (institutions, psychological attitudes etc) were indicated as essential elements of an investigation in depth. To some extent I welcomed the rise of the disequilibrium theories of the 1970s as a possible bridge between the purely neoclassical theories and the Keynesian and other alternatives (see 1981), but even there the attempt to stick to an equilibrium framework and to the basic axioms of neoclassical theory proved to be a stumbling block for a fuller and more relevant investigation.

These special methodological problems which arose in the context of my employment research were also taken up in some more general papers on methodology where the possibilities and limits of the neoclassical orthodoxy were scrutinized. Thus in 'Political Economy or Economics?' I argued the necessity of making due allowance for political elements either in the economic theories themselves or at least 'at the back of one's head' (Keynes), while stressing at the same time that the economic theory of politics ('economic imperialism') *can not* be the solution to this problem because it tries to preserve the narrowness of the neoclassical paradigm rather than go beyond it. In 'Micro-Foundations, Ad Hocery and Keynesian Theory' I tried to show why Keynesian macroeconomics (and other varieties) can be viable without micro foundations (though they may be desirable), and why – if such foundations are sought – the neoclassical axioms would not be a suitable solution. All these methodological considerations were not concerned with a refutation of mainstream economic theory as such, but were directed against the arrogance and the hegemonial tendencies of neoclassical theory, against its explicit or implicit claim to be the only high road to a 'true' scientific theory of the economic universe.

Rothschild's Major Writings

(1942), 'The Degree of Monopoly', *Economica*, 9.

(1947), 'Price Theory and Oligopoly', *Economic Journal*, 57.

(1954), *The Theory of Wages*, Oxford: Blackwell.

(1963), 'Kleinstaat und Integration' ('Small Nations and Economic Integration'), *Weltwirtschaftliches Archiv*, 90.

(1971), Introduction to K.W. Rothschild (ed), *Power in Economics*, Harmondsworth: Penguin Books.

(1973), 'Macht: Die Lücke in der Preistheorie' ('Power: The Gap in Price Theory'), in H.K. Schneider and Chr. Watrin (eds), *Macht und ökonomisches Gesetz*, Berlin: Duncker & Humblot.

(1981), *Einführung in die Ungleichgewichtstheorie* (Introduction to Disequilibrium Theory), Berlin: Springer.

(1988a), 'Micro-Foundations, Ad Hocery and Keynesian Theory', *Atlantic Economic Journal*, 16.

(1988b), *Theorien der Arbeitslosigkeit* (Theories of Unemployment), München: Oldenbourg-Verlag.

(1989), 'Political Economy or Economics?' *European Journal of Political Economy*, 5.

Warren J. SAMUELS (born 1933)

I grew up, an only child, in the Bronx, New York City, and, after 12 years of age, in Miami Beach, Florida. My father and my mother's parents had been immigrants from Lithuania and Germany respectively. In high school I benefited from a strong academic programme, won essay contests and also engaged successfully in field events on the track team.

My undergraduate training was at the University of Miami (Florida) where I majored in economics, accounting and government, with a minor in philosophy. In addition to a course in the history of economic thought taught by a Marxist, the intermediate economic theory courses were taught from a history-of-thought perspective, and a course in institutional economics was taken jointly and effectively by an institutionalist and a neoclassicist. These courses created my interests in the history of economic thought and the professorial life. They also provided me with (i) an institutionalist orientation; (ii) a sense that the several schools of thought comprehend and interpret the economy from different perspectives, each imposing its own order on reality, each constituting its own mode of discourse or world view, which *inter alia* meant that my institutionalist orientation was kept in perspective; and (iii) an understanding that there were fundamental questions for human society, the solutions to which had to be worked out in the continuous reconstruction of economy, polity and society, and which could be studied abstractly though not conclusively from any particular point of view. My individualistic and eclectic predisposition, together with the absence of a compulsion to identify the absolutely correct solution, led me to believe that something was to be learned from employing the insights of all schools of thought – philosophical and economic. This predisposition, I might note, governed my 1971–81 editorship of the *Journal of Economic Issues* and was not universally acclaimed among institutionalists.

My other principal interest was in the economic role of government, attributable in part to the convergence of my undergraduate majors. I learned from a treatise written by Robert Dahl and Charles Lindblom that there were fundamental questions about and interrelationships between polity and economy with regard to human welfare, and that the economic role of government could be studied more or less objectively (non-ideologically) in an abstract but meaningful manner.

I also did work in US constitutional history and in the philosophy of science. The former helped establish my understanding of human affairs as much more conflict-ridden than generally appreciated in economic theory (with its harmonistic world view); and the latter, my understanding of the problematic metafoundations of epistemological and other philosophical positions. Both taught me that the meaning of any method or technique of analysis or philosophical perspective was comprised of both its strengths and weaknesses. I also came to understand that in the social sciences 'meaning' was both critical and largely a human projection or construction, and not a determination of some absolute transcendent reality; that is, an imposed not a discovered order. Also, that just as data were theory-laden, theory was the product, in part, of selective experience and interests.

I pursued graduate work at the University of Wisconsin because of its institutionalist orientation, which was then – both fortunately for me and regrettably for the discipline – in its final years there. I was able to pursue both of my fields of interest. In addition to a splendid year sequence in the history of economic thought, I had courses in institutional economics, distribution theory and the theory of noncompetitive markets taught from diverse history-of-thought and alternative methodological perspectives. My outside field was in sociology, where I both studied Max Weber and gained additional insight into the history of economic and sociological thought. Between my undergraduate and graduate programmes, I had the advantage of many history-of-thought courses, each taught from a more or less different point of view. My other principal field, in addition to economic theory *per se*, was the economic role of government to which work in institutional economics, labour policy, public finance, government and business, and macroeconomic policy also contributed. My dissertation on the economic policy ideas of major business and labour organizations contributed to my skills and insights in both of my principal fields. I greatly benefited from the Wisconsin department's encouragement, or at least tolerance, of independent thought.

My central interest has been to generate greater and, to the extent possible, non-ideological clarity in understanding the economic role of government in the history of economic thought, in economic theory and in the real world. I have been most interested in identifying fundamentals otherwise obscured by misleading or incomplete ideological and theoretical formulations. A crux has been an emphasis on the economy both as process and as artifact generated through deliberative and non-deliberative human choice, and therefore as a matter of the social (re)construction of reality to which both economic theory and economic policy contribute.

Apropos of the history of economics, this has meant showing, on the one hand, that economics is essentially a socio-logical and discursive (and not solely an epistemological) phenomenon; and, on the other, that economics relates as both cause and consequence to the economic system in which it originates. Apropos of the economic role of government, this has meant identifying, on the one hand, the nature and role of the rights (re)determination process and, on the other, how economic analysis, through selective normative (often implicit) premises itself contributes to the definition of economic reality and thereby to the social (re)construction of reality through the rights ((re)determination process).

My analyses are fundamentally dissident in that they do not take as given either the status quo structure of power or the existing modes of revising the structure of power. Power, income and wealth distributions are seen as driving forces not to be eclipsed by the static economics of efficient allocation. I seek explanations and analyses which do not, through limiting assumptions of various kinds, merely selectively ratify and privilege established institutions. My analyses stress the continuing creativity of human choice in (re)constructing the economy. The foregoing is quite independent of my personal subjective and normative affinities for pluralistic, liberal democratic and truly competitive market economies in which no class (including the capitalist) dominates, especially in the control and use of government. These affinities are hardly radical by some criteria but very much so by others. Moreover, they decidedly neither reduce to the view that power connotes only control over price, nor mean that I am hoping or expecting to scrap our intellectual heritage and start anew.

My work in the history of economic thought has centred, therefore, in part, on (i) understanding how economics serves three functions: knowledge, social control and psychic balm; (ii) how schools of economic thought can be differently understood both from within each school and on the basis of the perspectives of other schools (the matrix approach); (iii) economics as a system of belief and mode of discourse rather than a hard science immediately and conclusively dealing with reality and applicable to explanation and policy; (iv) the operation of power and ideology as filtration mechanisms; and, *inter alia*, (v) the role of such desiderata as scientific status, professional expertise made applicable to policy and ideological safety in the rise to predominance of neoclassical economics. I have rejected the Whig approach to the history of economics as representing history written from one point of view and have stressed the richness of economics, for example with regard to power and policy, that is so often obscured by traditional treatments.

My work in law and economics (the economic role of government) has centred on the fundamental importance of government in the social (re)construction of the economy; law as both dependent and independent variable; the critical role of the selective perception of rights, power, freedom, coercion and government itself; intervention as legal change of law; government as an instrument available to whomever can control it; and government as an arena of power and power-play as well as a process of collective bargaining, with politics as a mode of self-government. All this is in the institutionalist tradition.

I have found that neoclassical, especially Marshallian, microeconomics tells us a great deal about the working of pure, abstract markets. I have also found that this body of theory does not deal with markets in the real world, which are not pure disembodied price systems but the results of rights, rules and other institutional structures which both produce and operate through them. This body of theory is seriously marked by the way in which description, explanation and analysis are limited by assumptions deemed necessary to produce determinate, optimal, equilibrium results. Puzzle-solving exercises are typically substituted for the analysis of real-world processes and/or the actions of economic actors, and data and techniques are manipulated to comport with such goals. This body of theory is also capable of being combined with latent, ideologically-driven normative premises and/or professionally naive constructions so as to produce results both highly stylized and unable conclusively to dispose of the issues to which they are usually applied.

This body of theory tends to be combined with laissez-faire or non-interventionist conceptions of the economic role of government, conceptions which either ignore or take implicit normative positions on the inexorably ubiquitous and deep operation of government. For example, the juxtaposition of markets to government ignores the facts that markets are largely formed by and within legal definitions and assignments of rights, and that the key question is not whether government will be present but which interests government will be used to support – that is, legal change of legal rights. Despite pretensions to the contrary by some schools, all schools of economic thought represent fundamental participation by government in economic affairs. I also have come to recognize that both theory and ideology pertaining to the economic role of government are intentionally and inadvertently manipulated in the service of material interests and general ideological positions. The crux of my dissent from neoclassicism is its neglect of power, especially the role of power (both in the real world and in typically implicit assumptions in analysis) in driving economic performance. The harmonistic, optimality nuances of mainstream theory are fundamentally incongruous with my perception of the economy as a system of power and conflict in which government is willy nilly important.

My most recent critique of mainstream, and also some heterodox, practices of economics has been to insist that the quest for determinate, optimal, equilibrium solutions has meant that economists have foreclosed the operation of process in the economy and also, in part, substituted their own preferences and definitions of the world for those of actual economic actors (see 1989a). I also have argued that on methodological, as well as substantive grounds, economic policy recommendations do not conclusively deal with the issues to which they are addressed and that, accordingly, economists should be quite restrained in making such recommendations (see 1989b). My overall emphasis is on how much more subtle, and less presumptuous, arguments and analyses with regard to policy should be. One example of the above is my rejection of the policy conclusions drawn from mainstream economic theories of rent-seeking (though agreeing with much of the description). The limiting assumptions and selective perceptions with regard to output, waste, legal change and the state generate artificial distinctions which cannot sustain the policy conclusions put forth (see 1984).

The idea of economics as a system of belief, laden with ideology and deployed less on the basis of epistemological credentials and more on the basis of received modes of discourse and consonance with the accepted paradigm, was developed in a critique of the Chicago School and in a restatement of Vilfredo Pareto's general system of social science. A congruent analysis was made of three discursive systems in distribution theory: the productivity and exploitation paradigms were presented as highly subjective and normative; the Weberian appropriation paradigm as reasonably objective and non-normative (see 1982).

In my work on the Physiocrats (1961 and 1962), on the classical economists (1966) and in later work on other economists, I attempted to identify the ideas of those writers investigating at the deepest level the economic role of government. In doing so I believe that I contributed to a body of modern interpretation which is more accurate and meaningful, and less ideologically presumptuous, than that previously available as to what their ideas on the economic role of government actually involved. In each case, government was deeply involved in the fundamental economic and social organization of society and as an instrument in the larger processes of socio-economic change. For all their supposed laissez-faire and naturalism, which are now understood to be modes of discourse (providing more tone than substance), the Physiocrats envisioned several critical roles for government: social reconstruction, economic development, economic stabilization and remedial welfare relief, as well as presiding over the evolution of the institution of private property. Similarly with the classical economists. Building on the work of Lionel Robbins, I showed that the conventional non-interventionist interpretation seriously neglected the roles which their work evidenced of legal and non-legal social control. This government control was most notable in providing the basic institutions which form the economic system and in serving as a mode of change in the continuing resolution of the conflicts between freedom and control, hierarchy and equality, and continuity and change. Subsequent work on Adam Smith has demonstrated his understanding of the economy as a system of power and his much larger system of social science, all of which also demonstrated the simplistic nature of both the apologetic use and critique of Smith.

My work in law and economics has focused on power, on the inevitable and ubiquitous rights (re)determination process, on property as what is protected rather than as what is protected because it is property (that is, against reification), and on law and government as part of a large and complex system of mutual coercion (see 1971 and 1972, both reprinted in 1981).

In this context I have made many explorations: (i) the transformation of the individualist into a corporate economy, along with the subtle accompanying alterations in the mode of discourse; (ii) the false and/or tautological nature of the Coase Theorem (1974a); (iii) the nature of public utility regulation as both rights-dependent and rights-determining; (iv) externality and public goods theory as selectively restricting the consideration of interdependence in the economy, especially in light of the dual nature of rights and the reciprocal character of externalities; (v) regulation as the functional equivalent of deregulation in the protection of interests as rights; (vi) the role of selective, implicit, normative premises in regulatory theory; (vii) in light of the necessity of choice, the normative content of so-called *positive* theories of public choice; and (viii) a positive analysis of the compensation problem. This last stresses both the inevitability of non-compensated losses in the joint determination of rights and non-rights, and the selective role of the compensation principle as a check on government power, assuaging the anxieties of radical indeterminacy, and legitimizing rights' decisions which determine the distribution of gains and losses (see 1974b and 1979–80). That regulation is the logical and functional equivalent of deregulation implies the relevance of selective perception and what Pareto called rule by fraud, at least the susceptibility to manipulation. Anti-regulation and anti-statist positions are a matter of selective perception and operate in favour of otherwise privileged uses of government and hierarchic positions.

My most recent analysis rejects not only the possibility of governmental non-interventionism and the idea that polity and economy are separate and self-subsistent, but also the market-plus-framework model in which there is a set of interrelations between legal and economic (market) processes. Instead it favours an analysis of the 'legal-economic nexus' in which both economy and polity simultaneously and continuously originate. This view further emphasizes the role of government as both dependent and independent variable, but also stresses the jointness of the origin of economy and polity and the ontological-ideological primacy of neither (see 1989c).

I have tried to combine criticism and the construction of alternative, open, non-ideological analyses. Because economic theory and economic policy are so important in the inexorable and continuing social (re)construction of the economy, neither should be a monopoly of either the reactionaries or the radicals. Finally, I believe that there is much wisdom in recognizing the inexorable and potentially creative tension between a belief that one's own analysis is in some sense 'correct' and an understanding that that analysis is an exercise of a mode of discourse, telling one story among many and more or less inevitably laden with ideology.

Samuels's Major Writings

(1961), 'The Physiocratic Theory of Property and State', *Quarterly Journal of Economics*, **75**, February, 96–111.

(1962), 'The Physiocratic Theory of Economic Policy', *Quarterly Journal of Economics*, **76**, February, 145–62.

(1966), *The Classical Theory of Economic Policy*, Cleveland: World.

(1971), 'Interrelations between Legal and Economic Processes', *Journal of Law and Economics*, **14**, October, 435–50.

(1972), 'Welfare Economics, Power and Property', in G. Wunderlich and W.L. Gibson Jr (eds), *Perspectives of Property*, Pennsylvania State University: Institute for Research on Land and Water Resources, 61–146.

(1974a), 'The Coase Theorem and the Study of Law and Economics', *Natural Resources Journal*, **14**, January, 1–33.

(1974b), 'An Economic Perspective on the Compensation Problem', *Wayne Law Review*, **21**, November, 113–34.

(1979–80), 'The Role and Resolution of the Compensation Principle in Society' (with N. Mercuro), *Research in Law and Economics*, **1**, 1979, 157–94; **2**, 1980, 103–28.

(1981), *Law and Economics* (with A.A. Schmid), Boston: Martinus Nijhoff.

(1982), 'A Critique of the Discursive Systems and Foundation Concepts of Distribution Analysis', *Analyse & Kritik*, **4**, October, 4–12.

(1984), 'A Critique of Rent-Seeking Theory' (with N. Mercuro), in D.C. Colander (ed), *Neoclassical Political Economy*, Cambridge: Ballinger, 55–70.

(1989a), 'Determinate Solutions and Valuational Processes: Overcoming the Foreclosure of Process', *Journal of Post Keynesian Economics*, **11**, Summer, 531–46.

(1989b), 'The Methodology of Economics and the Case for Policy Diffidence and Restraint', *Review of Social Economy*, **47**, Summer, 113–33.

(1989c), 'The Legal-Economic Nexus', *George Washington Law Review*, **57**, August, 1556–78.

Bertram SCHEFOLD (born 1943)

My father, the archaeologist Karl Schefold, and my mother, Marianne Schefold, née von den Steinen, emigrated from Germany to Switzerland in the early 1930s. I was born on 28 December 1943 in Basel where I received a classical education at the Humanistisches Gymnasium which stimulated my private interests in literature, history and history of art. I took up my studies in mathematics in 1962 at the University of Munich, where a liberal curriculum allowed me to follow courses in other faculties (I spent one semester in Hamburg studying natural philosophy with Carl Friedrich von Weizsäcker). I graduated from Basel in 1967 in mathematics, theoretical physics and philosophy. At that time, I expected to become a philosopher, using mathematics to make a living, and for a while I felt drawn towards an academic career in mathematics. However, upon passing my examination, I found myself elected president of the Swiss National Union of Students. Such experiences as organizing the first national congress on university education and the challenge of the student movement changed my outlook: I took up the study of economics.

Having benefited particularly from Professor Bombach's courses on the theories of economic growth and distribution and from Professor Kapp's early introduction to environmental economics in Basel, I spent the years 1969 and 1970 in Cambridge, as a visitor to the Faculty of Economics and, afterwards, as an Advanced Student of King's College. However, I wrote my thesis *Mr Sraffa on Joint Production* for my home university (see 1971). I thus got no formal supervision in Cambridge, but I participated in the debates which then raged about Marx and Keynes. In my discussions with Joan Robinson, Kaldor, Sraffa and younger members of the faculty, I learned to respect the Cambridge style of arguing in which the recourse to formulae and invocation of authorities were regarded as improper.

After my Ph.D. examination in May 1971, I was nominated lecturer in mathematical economics in Basel and made an assistant to Edgar Salin, with the task of helping him to organize his last international conference, held at the time of the break-down of the Bretton Woods system; I also edited the proceedings, *Floating – Realignment – Integration* (1972). In 1972–73 I returned to Cambridge and acted as a supervisor for Trinity College. After spending 1973–74 at Harvard University as a research associate, having contact also with MIT, I was called to take a chair at the University of Frankfurt in 1974. At first I was mainly expected to raise the intellectual level of students in Marxian economics, but when offers came to move elsewhere, I was entrusted with the task of teaching general economic theory. Apart from a number of visiting appointments abroad, I have since remained in Frankfurt for various reasons, one being that the city and the university have an interesting past and a lively present; I even published a history of our Faculty.

When I came to Cambridge in 1969, there was a feeling of triumph because of the victory in the 'reswitching debate'. However, opinions about the usefulness of the classical theory of prices for a positive reconstruction of a non-neoclassical theory (beyond the framework of short-term Keynesian analysis) were divided. I decided to discuss the extension of Sraffa's theory of prices to joint production. I first proceeded by summarizing the results for single-product systems and tried to establish which of them held for joint-production systems as well. The generalization of some concepts allowed interesting differentiations, giving rise, for instance, to different notions of the basic system. In place of the maximum rate of profit, conditions were derived for the range in which prices remain positive. On the whole, Sraffa's assertions, based by him on stringent economic logic, could be confirmed through a mathematical reformulation (an important exception concerned the standard commodity). The treatment of fixed capital in terms of joint production proved most rewarding. The generality of the framework allowed an interesting reinterpretation of familiar concepts such as amortization and depreciation. Competition leads to the same outcome, whether prices of final goods are determined on the basis of 'correct' depreciation or whether there is, in addition, a market in which old machines are traded and their prices determined explicitly. In this theory, the equality between the cost of production of a machine and the value of its expected returns is not a long-period equilibrium condition to be posited as an *assumption*, as in Hicks and others, but a *result* of the uniformity of the rate of profit. It turned out that even land could be regarded as a special case of joint production. Sraffa's perspective thus shed a new light on the issue of specialization in the use of scarce resources which is also relevant for the theory of international trade. These were the main themes of my thesis, referred to above, and of some subsequent articles.

The classical theory aims at an explanation of growth and development in a process of accumulation in which technical progress, distributional shifts and institutional changes time and again threaten to upset the relative positions of investing entrepreneurs, workers and other groups. Full employment results only if the rate of growth of output, reduced by that of productivity, is large enough relative to the growth of the labour force. In an important application, the classical theory of prices allows a translation of the effects of different forms of technical progress and of the availability of natural resources at the microeconomic level into macroeconomic terms. Leontief's input-output analysis (which is classical in spirit) is often used to such purpose. A related theme of nineteenth-century economics can now be discussed in a Sraffian framework. Using the fixed capital model, it can be shown that mechanization as defined by Marx leads to a reduction of the maximum rate of profit since it consists in replacing manual production by machines without saving raw materials. It may thus tend to worsen the distributional conflict about the share of wages in much the same way as an extension of agricultural production without an increase of productivity or of the availability of productive land leads to a fall of the rate of profit, given the rate of real wages in Ricardo's corn model (see 1976).

However, the capital-output ratio moves less than our theories lead us to expect. A related puzzle is this: the comparison of different economic systems in terms of wage curves allows us to compare capital intensities for the theory of growth or to identify reswitching phenomena for the critique of capital theory. But if only two alternative methods for production in each of 1,000 sectors of an economy are known, the number of wage curves to be compared is so vast (2^{1000}) that any minute change of the rate of profit ought to trigger off an avalanche of switches which might raise or lower total output per head. Although there is less technological optimism today than three decades ago, this is not a result which one would expect, considering the steady accretion of innovations which appear to be of neutral effect on average (see 1979).

The most obvious theoretical problem in relation to joint production is this: whereas relative prices in a single product system are determined independently of demand (if there are constant returns and distribution is given), the composition of output matters in the case of joint production. I have analysed this problem in terms of models with balanced growth in a number of papers, with consumption needs taken as given, but one may also start from a prior determination of gross output (including investment). Square joint production systems then result from the choice of technique, in that at least as many processes are necessary to produce the commodities demanded (some of these may be domestic processes of production). There cannot be more processes than there are commodities with positive prices (that is, goods that are not overproduced) for there would otherwise be an overdetermination of prices incompatible with a uniform rate of profit. This principle of 'counting the equations' is reinforced if we think of a long-period equilibrium as one in which quantities and market prices fluctuate around normal values (these fluctuations are something different from the deviation of macroeconomic variables from a trend in business cycles). Demand for commodities may thus be subject to small changes in any direction, and this means that fewer than n processes to produce n commodities will not – even by accident – be sufficient to fulfil the demand conditions. Hence, joint production systems are square which implies that, given distribution, prices of joint products are determined in a classical framework – a problem never solved by the classical authors.

There are three difficulties with this result. The first is that, if the necessity of allowing for the small perturbations is not taken into account, fewer than n processes may suffice to produce n commodities in desired quantities just by a fluke. Another rather formal exception concerns so-called limiting means of production. The second, more interesting, difficulty is connected with different theories of demand. The system need not be square if other assumptions about demand are made, for instance because neoclassical preferences are introduced. Thirdly, it may be objected that square systems are not likely to be encountered in reality because non-square solutions have an important meaning as expressions of processes of transition. For instance, new domestic or industrial uses may be found for a good which until then had been a waste product (and therefore not a commodity to be counted). It will now not be disposed of at a zero price, but sold at a low market price; this market price will be an incentive to produce the commodity by other means, thereby introducing the new process. In the end, a system which had been square will thus be square again, but in the transition there is one commodity more than there are processes. An overdetermination of prices through the presence of too many processes, on the other hand, is familiar: it simply follows from the working of competition by which the least-cost-combination of methods is found. New methods may enjoy a cost-advantage, hence a more-than-normal rate of profit, for some time. I pursued these themes mainly in 1988 and in my contributions to 1989a.

To date the 'intertemporal theory' of general equilibrium seems to have been touched upon only marginally in the critique of neoclassical capital theory. The intertemporal theory, although referring to a long or even infinite horizon, does not describe a long-period equilibrium since there are different own rates of interest in terms of different commodities. They reflect the fact that initial endowments may be given in arbitrary proportions so that some are more scarce relative to demand (see 1985a). This kind of discrepancy can be shown to disappear if the time horizon is sufficiently far away. In this sense, the intertemporal equilibrium represents one particular form of a transition to a stationary state as the time horizon is pushed farther away. It is not surprising that the same effects which preclude the existence of a surrogate production function and, more generally, the existence of a demand function for aggregate capital, also preclude the convergence of an intertemporal equilibrium to a stationary state. Such a property – if it exists – has also been regarded as an extension of the turnpike theorems familiar from von Neumann models. This discovery ought to lead to a revival of interest in long-period equilibria by neoclassical economists themselves.

From the late 1970s onwards, I have been involved in research projects in the area of environmental economics. One was concerned with alpine regions in Switzerland; three with the future of the energy system in Germany. The best known of these, which I directed jointly with the physicist and philosopher K. M. Meyer-Abich of the University of Essen, was concerned with 'The Social Compatibility of Different Energy Systems in the Development of Industrial Societies' and employed about a dozen researchers from different disciplines in collaboration with a commission of the West German parliament. The task involved the implementation of energy scenarios in a large computer-based econometric model (run by the Institute for Economic Research of the Swiss Federal Polytechnic in Zurich) in order to investigate the economic consequences of choosing a particular energy path for the economy as a whole. Values for controversial data such as the future cost of reprocessing spent nuclear fuel were chosen in an exchange with the Kernforschungsanstalt Jülich, one of the two large nuclear research facilities in Germany. The final report, written by Meyer-Abich and myself, became a bestselling book, not least because it was published a few weeks before the accident of Chernobyl and was for some months very much discussed in the media (1986).

How shall we live in future decades? This question which motivated our research is political and its solution cannot be left entirely to autonomous forces. Technical progress has always to a large extent been directed by political decisions and by cultural forces which do not operate through the market alone. The popular attention paid to the energy debate does not arise simply from worries concerning the energy system taken in isolation. Rather, the energy system is correctly perceived as important in how it relates to economic, social and environmental developments. In fact, it also affects national and international relations and, through the consequent safeguards to maintain security, the national and international legal systems.

Clearly one cannot expect to obtain a vision of future developments by looking at individual technologies. Rather, it is necessary to see them as connected through international research priorities, technical linkages and institutional relations in the political sphere. The practice of isolating a small number of characteristic scenarios to compare their potential impact on society is thus theoretically justified. Interestingly, this methodological perspective has parallels in classical economic analysis as well as in the approach of the historical school, though it is less easy to integrate into neoclassical theory. For, whereas the latter is correct in postulating that external effects should be internalized whenever feasible, the idea of comparing different development paths with their associated social and cultural settings is alien to a theory which is accustomed to take preferences as given.

In this perspective, the research team published a series of books and articles, discussed beforehand at working conferences in order to assess the potential consequences of various scenarios on the legal system, the economy and society. We asked, conversely, which developments, in any of these areas might be favourable to the implementation of a given scenario, and we listed and explored political instruments. Historical parallels were also examined. This methodological approach to social choice, more than the details of our recommendations, may retain some interest.

Most environmental research projects require interdisciplinary collaboration and a readiness to transcend one's theoretical preconceptions. Thus, in contributions to books aimed at finding solutions for the double threat of pollution and unemployment, neoclassical concepts almost inevitably had to be used. I have so far, in English, made only one attempt explicitly to link applied work with my theoretical concepts (see 1985b).

Opposition to neoclassical models is often based on the allegation that neoclassicals fail to take social, historical and institutional factors into account. Certainly the classical model describes a highly idealized form of capitalism only. Interest in other historical periods has led me to reconsider the work of members of the historical school where one still finds challenging suggestions (beyond what has been preserved in Max Weber and apart from the particular historical scheme of economic evolution proposed by Marx). I have mainly studied Schmoller and Bücher and, to counterpoise, Schumpeter, but I have also tried, in a paper on 'Supply and Demand in

Classical Theory', to describe the historical element in the classical theory of consumption – as found mainly in Adam Smith. Here concepts such as necessary consumption, luxury consumption etc. refer to what is necessary or luxurious in specific social circumstances. Adam Smith's *Theory of Moral Sentiments* interprets the display of riches in order to please others as a cultural process and integrates it with a theory of luxury consumption and the diffusion of needs (see 1981).

One may seek precursors of modern ideas when working on the history of economic thought, but the 'Dogmenhistorischer Ausschuß' (section of the 'Verein für Socialpolitik') in which I have been active (now as President) has always been open to considerations of what was really characteristic of past authors. The Greek philosophers, for example, were not interested in economics as a causal science and made virtually no contribution to it. Like Plato in his 'Laws', their concern was to find those institutions in which the market might function without transforming or dissolving desirable social relationships; also to define, as in Aristotle, those concepts of justice and reciprocity which would allow the order of the polity to be maintained as the basis for striving for higher understanding. This presupposed a modest but comfortable supply of goods. The Greek philosophers were thus not opposed to the use of the market, but they thought that behavioural rules and political institutions were necessary to keep economic activity subordinated to higher goals. In analysing their position, they indirectly provided the first concepts for economics as a causal science (see 1989b).

At the time of writing of this entry, the idea to run economies by means of centralized planning seems almost globally discredited, but that does not mean that we are likely to return to a pure market system. In connection with a local emphasis on questions of comparative economic systems, I have repeatedly taught a course on 'Economic Systems in Historical Perspective', with a strong emphasis on the economies of pre-industrial societies but leading up to the social market economy. The unifying theme of my researches has thus been to try to understand the changing forms of interaction between the forces of the market, of centralized control and of social traditions which largely defy analysis in terms of neoclassical concepts of rationality.

Schefold's Major Writings

(1971), *Mr Sraffa on Joint Production*, Basel. (Enlarged in *Mr Sraffa on Joint Production and Other Essays*, 1989).

(1972), *Floating – Realignment – Integration*, Tübingen.

(1976), 'Different Forms of Technical Progress', *The Economic Journal*, **86**, 806–19.

(1979), 'Capital, Growth and Definitions of Technical Progress', *Kyklos*, **32**, 236–50.

(1981), 'Nachfrage and Zufuhr in der Klassischen Ökonomie'. Reprinted in B. Schefold (ed), *Ökonomische Klassik im Umbruch*, Frankfurt: 1986, 195–241.

(1985a), 'Cambridge Price Theory: Special Model or General Theory of Value?' *American Economic Review*, **75**, 140–45.

(1985b), 'Ecological Problems as a Challenge to Classical and Keynesian Economics', *Metroeconomica*, **37**, 21–61.

(1986), *Die Grenzen der Atomwirtschaft* (with K.M. Meyer-Abich), München.

(1988), 'The Dominant Technique in Joint Production Systems', *Cambridge Journal of Economics*, **12**, 97–123.

(1989a), *Essays in Honour of Piero Sraffa: Critical Perspectives on the Revival of Classical Theory* (edited with K. Bharadwaj), Cambridge: Cambridge University Press.

(1989b), 'Platon and Aristoteles', in J. Starbatty (ed), *Klassiker des Ökonomischen Denkens*, 19–55.

Dudley SEERS (1920–1983)   *Richard Jolly*

For three decades, Dudley Seers was one of the world's leading economists in the field of development studies. He wrote on a remarkably wide range of topics in development, working in some 35 countries and visiting many more. He was born in England and educated at Rugby School and Cambridge University. Initially undertaking statistical research in Oxford on income distribution in Britain, Seers rapidly developed viewpoints and approaches well outside the mainstream of neoclassical economics. It is oversimplistic to describe him as a dissident of development studies. Rather, he was something of a prophet: mainstream thinking on development often moved towards positions he had first put forward. It would be true to describe his influence as helping to make development studies a dissident wing of current economic orthodoxy. In his final book, the *Political Economy of Nationalism* , he provides a synthesis of his own contributions.

Seers espoused, taught, defended and worked largely within a structuralist paradigm. He focused on key structural relationships in the countries or situations under review (for example, the pattern of exports, the linkages between imports and production, the structure of ownership and of international and national political influence), relating these key relationships to the type of economy being analysed, the nature of its links with the international economy, and the phase or time-period in relation to broader world developments. This led Seers to a multi-disciplinary style of analysis that was, in many respects, situation-specific rather than universal. Seers's best and most quoted work focused on the study of individual national economies and their links with the 'world economy', rather than on isolated sectoral problems within them.

The foundations of Seers's way of viewing development problems grew out of his work in ECLA (Economic Commission for Latin America) from 1957–61, working under Raoul Prebisch and alongside Osvaldo Sunkel and other Latin American economists who were evolving the 'structuralist' and 'dependency' approaches. These experiences prompted one of Seers's most important articles, 'The Limitations of the Special Case' (1963), in which he analysed the dangers of naively transferring analytical models from the 'special case' of developed countries to the rest of the world. This article attracted more international attention than anything Seers had written until then.

This article (perhaps more accurately, this perspective) laid the basis for much country-specific work during the succeeding years, indeed throughout the rest of Seers's career until his final assignment in Fiji just before he died. Seers undertook further consultancy missions to Zambia (1964), Colombia (1970), Sri Lanka (1971), Nigeria (1979) and Uganda (1978); produced a major study on post-revolutionary Cuba (1962) and led or joined in many other country analyses. In the preface to his 1983 book, Seers lists some 35 countries where he had been involved in advisory work or research. These were mainly developing countries but included Canada, Ireland, New Zealand, Portugal, Japan and Spain of the so-called developed countries, as well as Czechoslovakia and Poland. The list explains his special interest in small, dependent economies; as he underlined, with characteristically self-awareness totally consistent with his structuralist position, the list reveals where he did *not* work.

> If I had undertaken research mainly in, say China, India, the United States and the Soviet Union, my approach would, without doubt, be very different. I would, for example, be less aware of the special problems of small countries (especially *vis-à-vis* the great powers) and more conscious of the importance of regional differences within countries – and of the economic, political and social costs of central bureaucracies (1983, x).

Seers added that the world was inconveniently large to cover all countries in one lifetime!

One of the self-imposed costs of structuralism and country-specific analysis is that they limit the field over which generalizations can be made. Seers, however, did develop more systematic models for certain classes of economy, which over the years became increasingly multi-disciplinary (see his papers published in 1959, 1962 and 1969 (which was reworked to become (1981a)). He also increasingly focused on a number of structural problems characteristic of different types of economies. From this emerged (1981b, 1982a) and the series of volumes on *Underdeveloped Europe* (1979) in which he analysed core-periphery relationships in Europe, using the dependency frame of analysis developed earlier for studying the relationships of developing with industrial countries.

The ILO employment missions of the 1970s provided Seers with the opportunity to apply structural analysis to internal problems and policy issues within particular countries. In Colombia the focus was on the problems of employment and income distribution; in Sri Lanka on unemployment and the mismatch between aspirations, skills and education; in Kenya (with

Hans Singer and Richard Jolly) on employment, incomes and equality, with special attention to the informal sector and, over time, to redistribution with growth. In 1979, Seers led a Commonwealth team on the Rehabilitation of Uganda after the destruction and wanton disregard of human life by Amin. In Nigeria, he led another ILO employment mission, which reviewed priorities for meeting basic human needs after the heady profligacy of the oil boom in the mid-1970s, producing a report entitled *First Things First* (ILO/JASPA, 1981).

In order to clarify further Seers's approach to structuralism and dependency, one can refer to his criticisms of what he saw as the major alternative approaches in the analysis of development – neoclassical economics and Marxism. In general attitude, Seers closely aligned himself with the position Joan Robinson set out in *Economic Philosophy,* in which economic philosophy in each period matches the interests of the ruling elites. Seers followed this approach in arguing that both neoclassical economics and Marxism have provided self-justifying rationales for those holding power in, respectively, capitalist and communist countries. But he achieved a shock effect – and strong reactions in response – by underlining the *common* features of both neoclassical economics and Marxism in their analysis of development. Both are in fact close relatives tracing their descent from the same European 19th century (classical economic) ancestors. And they share important common flaws:

1. the assumption of linear progress (towards some ill-defined Utopia) which encourages an optimism that continues to mislead, though it has frequently been dashed (1983);
2. they fail to take due account of non-material motives, especially nationalism;
3. both doctrines appeal to malcontents in the other system, more specifically on economic issues;
4. both treat the quantity of money as the determinant of inflation;
5. both emphasize capital investment as overwhelmingly the most important determinant of economic growth. Consequently the generation and allocation of savings are seen as the mainsprings of development.

Seers recognized some important differences between Marxists and neoclassical economists, however: the latter are characterized by a much greater belief in quantitative techniques and focus on variables which are quantifiable. They concentrate on equilibrium which for them is normative, whilst Marxists focus attention on social crises due to class relations, study the internal contradictions in capitalist (but not socialist) modes of production and stress how 'uneven development' is linked to 'imperialism'. Marxists therefore tend to emphasize the historic origins of problems and long-term dynamics (1983).

These critiques are important to an understanding of Seers's radicalism. They help to make clear where he stood – or, as he might have put it, where he did *not* stand. Seers took many positions critical of the status quo, whether of capitalism, of transational corporations, of communism, of the establishment in general, of administrators and of bureaucracy. He never tried to be even-handed in these criticisms because his values were egalitarian, anti-establishment, strongly for human rights. He had life-long friendships with and loyalties to key radicals of the Labour party in Britain (the pre-Bennite radical wing of the 1950s and 1960s). But notwithstanding his presidency of a Marxist Society in Cambridge as an undergraduate, his later views were anti-Marxist and anti-dogmatic.

In the area of national planning and statistics, Seers was masterly: creative and constructive, rigorous and professional, and at the same time deeply radical, perhaps more constructively radical than in any other area of his work. Seers was by training a statistician, and his early work in Oxford had been in statistical teaching and research. Two of his earliest papers are models of most careful statistical and analysis, directed to issues of major political concern (see 1949a and 1949b).

Over the years which followed, Seers never lost his statistical interests. He was always a trenchant critic of the unthinking use of statistics, taking delight in denouncing spurious precision in the presentation of data and in reminding both model builders and practical analysts of the arbitrary and often misleading conventions used for the calculation of statistical constructs such as GNP. But in statistical matters he was also a builder. In the late 1950s, he developed a modified (non-square) input-output table, adapted to the analytical needs and data availability of an export-orientated developing country. This was first applied to Jamaica, then used as the integrating frame for the UN/FAO/ECA mission report on the 'Economic Development of Zambia' and subsequently for Zambia's First National Development Plan 1966–70.

In 1969, as President of the Society of International Development, Seers launched a devastating attack on GNP in his address, subsequently revised and published in 1972 under the title 'What are We Trying to Measure?' He asked: if over the last decade in a country, GNP had grown, but unemployment had risen, income inequalities had widened and poverty had increased, is this development or not? This speech ended with an outspoken denunciation of 'the obscene inequalities that disfigure the world'. It became an early landmark in a succession of international initiatives and appeals over the decade to give more attention to inequality and poverty in development strategy.

Throughout his career Seers maintained a special interest in improving the quality and relevance of statistical indicators. In the late 1970s, he embarked on a major project to test the feasibility of using life expectancy as an integrating concept for social and demographic analysis and planning. The project involved trial applications in several countries. Although unfinished at the time of his death, Seers completed a comprehensive paper on his approach, entitled 'Active Life Profiles for Different Social Groups' (see 1982c).

As adviser and leader of international missions to many countries, Seers contributed creatively to the art of development planning. He believed that development planning should focus on strategy – in much the same way that good political or military strategy identifies a core of essential issues and concentrates on their rapid realization. This would mean moving 'to quite a different type of planning – longer term, less economistic, not entirely quantitative. And the object would not be necessarily – certainly not mainly – publication. Indeed the very fact that a plan is published raises doubts as to whether it deals with issues important to the government' (1983, p.95).

Seers indicated the types of issues that such planning would need to cover, the exact selection depending, of course, on the time and situation of the type of country concerned:

1. the basic political-economic and social pattern of the developments desired – and how they can be achieved (including the mobilization of 'an adequate coalition of diverse political forces in support');
2. a strategy to ensure sufficient control over the national economy and resources to achieve the objectives, including military strategy and attention to key economic issues such as oil imports, food production and technology;
3. distributional and social issues such as health policy, water, basic hygiene and information;
4. education for manpower development but with attention also to the role of education and religion in relation to the knowledge, attitudes and motivation needed for a self-reliant strategy. As Seers emphasized, patriotism, although unfashionable as a topic of concern for economic planners, is an obvious part of this. So also is the cultural heritage of a country, linguistic policy, especially in countries where there are large linguistic minorities etc.

In the final decade of his life, Seers turned his professional interests to Europe. First, he worked on 'underdeveloped Europe', analysing European problems and patterns of development with the same structural tools of analysis he had used earlier in developing countries, especially in Latin

America. Core-periphery models and tendencies became centre-pieces of this work, with the core identified as the industrial heart of central France and Germany, and the periphery as Greece and Southern Italy, Spain and Portugal, Ireland, Northern Ireland, much of Wales, Scotland and the North of England. (Scandinavia was clearly part of the geographical periphery – though not so obviously part of the underdeveloped and under-developing regions.) Seers contributed to three books on these themes (see 1979, 1980b and 1982b).

From this European perspective, Seers returned to the global view, emphasizing the forces at work within the international economy which made a tripartite division of the world – West, East and South – increasingly misleading. In the *Political Economy of Nationalism,* he argued the case for a more Euro-centred strategy in a world divided into a number of regional economic blocs.

Seers also at this time published a strong critique of the Brandt Commission's report, *North-South: a Programme for Survival.* In his review 'Muddling Morality and Mutuality' (1980a), he tore into the report for what he argued was a long list of confusions over 'mutual interests' which it had made a central point underlying its proposals. Seers challenged the implicit model of the Brandt Commission. He argued that there was no reality behind such phrases as 'international community', that the North-South division of the world was politically meaningless, and that experience had already demonstrated that OPEC solidarity with the non-oil exporting countries of the South was virtually without effect when it came to practical economic action. By 1980, countries were divided into other blocs too, which made the 'tripartite' view of the world dangerously misleading – as he himself had written several years earlier (see 1976). Fundamentally, Seers argued that a case based on mutuality of interests of countries was meaningless, because it failed to take account of the differing interests of key groups within each country. Moreover, the Brandt Commission ignored the *realpolitik* of industrial countries' policies at that time, in which monetarist ideas and priority for reducing inflation over reducing unemployment held sway.

In his final book, completed just before he died, Seers argued that to analyse regimes in terms of their orientation along some 'old left-right axis... is not much use'. Rather he put the case for a two axis analysis: nationalist-anti-nationalist and egalitarian-anti-egalitarian. This produced a four-fold classification, reproduced as Figure 1, which could be used to clarify not only the ideology and practice of regimes, but analytical approaches. Neoclassical economic analysis would tend to be in the anti-nationalist, anti-egalitarian segment; neo-Marxist in the egalitarian, nationalist segment.

Seers chose to stress in this book how he had moved to a nationalist – or rather European nationalist – position (somewhat playing down the contra-

ANTINATIONALIST (AN)

Marxists   Neoclassical
Liberals

EGALITARIAN (E) ——————————————— *ANTI-EGALITARIAN (AE)*

Dependency theorists   Traditional Conservatives
Populists, neo-Marxists   Fascists

NATIONALIST (N)

Figure 1

diction between being a nationalist and having *regional* affiliations, which seems to imply some residual internationalism). More importantly, Seers did not emphasize where he stood on the second main axis of analysis – egalitarianism. Nothing Seers wrote at this time suggests he had moved far from the concern with egalitarianism which had characterized so much of his professional work, from his statistical studies in Oxford in the 1940s to his call (with Gunnar Myrdal) in the 1980s for aid to be entirely devoted to poverty alleviation. On human rights, his concern, if anything, strengthened. The connecting thread of Seers's professional work over his lifetime is more clearly shown by this continuing focus on inequality and injustice than by moves over his last decade from internationalism to a European-centred nationalism.

Seers's Major Works

A full bibliography and other assessments of Dudley Seers appears in *IDS Bulletin, 20,* July 1989, which also contains an extended and earlier version of this entry.

(1949a), *Changes in the Cost of Living and the Distribution of Income since 1938,* Oxford: Blackwell.

(1949b), *The Levelling of Incomes since 1938,* Oxford: Blackwell.

(1959), 'An Approach to the Short-Period Analysis of Primary-Producing Economies', *Oxford Economic Papers,* 11.

(1962a), 'A Model of Comparative Rates of Growth in the World Economy', *Economic Journal,* 72.

(1962b), 'A General Theory of Inflation and Growth in Underdeveloped Countries based on the Experience of Latin America', *Oxford Economic Papers,* 14.

(1963), 'The Limitations of the Special Case', *Oxford University Institute of Economics and Statistics Bulletin,* 25.

(1964), *Cuba: The Economic and Social Revolution,* editor and part author, Chapel Hill: University of North Carolina Press.

(1969), 'A Step Towards a Political Economy of Development: Illustrated by the case of Trinidad/Tobago', *Social and Economic Studies,* 18.

(1970), *Towards Full Employment: A Programme for Colombia*, report by an inter-agency team led by Seers, Geneva: ILO.

(1971), *Development in a Divided World*, edited with L. Joy, Harmondsworth: Penguin.

(1972), 'What are We Trying to Measure?' *Journal of Development Studies*, **8**.

(1976), 'A New Look at the Three World Classification', *IDS Bulletin*, **7**.

(1979), 'The Periphery of Europe', in B. Schaffer, M. Kiljunen and D. Seers (eds), *Underdeveloped Europe: Studies in Core-Periphery Relations*, Brighton: Harvester Press.

(1980a), 'Muddling Morality and Mutality: a Review of the Brandt Report', *Third World Quarterly*, **2**.

(1980b), *Integration and Unequal Development: The Experience of the EEC*, edited with C. Vaitsos, London: Macmillan.

(1981a), 'The Life Cycle of a Petroleum Economy and its Implications for Development', *Research for Development*, **1**.

(1981b), 'The Tendency to Financial Irresponsibility of Socialist Governments and its Political Consequences', preface to S. Griffith-Jones, *The Role of Finance in the Transition to Socialism*, London: Frances Pinter.

(1982a), 'The New Role of Development Planning, with Special Reference to Small Countries', in B. Jamal (ed), *Problems and Policies in Small Economies*, Beckenham: Croom Helm.

(1982b), *The Second Enlargement of the EEC: The Integration of Unequal Partners*, edited with C. Vaistos, London: Macmillan.

(1982c), 'Active Life Profiles for Different Social Groups: A Contribution to Demographic Accounting, a Frame for Social Indicators and a Tool of Social and Economic Analysis', *Discussion Paper 178*, Sussex: IDS.

(1983), *The Political Economy of Nationalism*, Oxford University Press.

Amartya SEN (born 1933) *Louis Putterman*

Amartya Sen has been a leading figure in the fields of welfare economics, social choice theory, economic growth and economic development for over three decades. His published works include seven solely authored original books, two volumes of collected essays and a jointly authored development planning manual, as well as over 170 articles in books and periodicals. His topics range from the relationships between economics and ethics, economic methodology and the nature of well-being, to explorations of the Arrow impossibility theorem and a social impossibility theorem of his own (the impossibility of a Paretian liberal), to capital and growth theory, choice of technology, hunger and sex discrimination. Virtually unique among economists, he is highly regarded by the mainstream of the profession, which has awarded him prestigious chairs at Oxford, Harvard and other universities, published dozens of his contributions in its leading periodicals, and elected him to such positions as President of the Econometric Society. Yet he remains a vehement critic of core assumptions (such as the nature of welfare) and methodological propensities (including the separation of economics from ethics and other fields of inquiry) of neoclassical economics. Sen enjoys equally high stature among social philosophers and students of other social sciences. He is an accomplished economic theorist and proponent of rigorous statistical measures, but also a critic of the too exclusive focus of economists on mathematical refinements.

Born in 1933 in the village of Santiniketan in Bengal, Sen remains a citizen of India and an active contributor to debates on aspects of that country's development policies and experience. He earned his first bachelors degree in 1953 at Presidency College (Calcutta), then moved to Trinity College (Cambridge) where he earned B.A., M.A. and Ph.D. degrees. The last of these was awarded in 1959, by which time he had already published several articles on economic development and planning in leading journals. His doctoral thesis, supervised by Joan Robinson but also under the tutelage of Maurice Dobb, concerned the choice of techniques in economic development and led to his first book, published in 1960. The work focused on conditions under which more capital intensive techniques could be preferred in a capital-poor country.

After serving as a Fellow of Trinity College from 1957 to 1963, Sen became Professor at the Delhi School of Economics, University of Delhi, a position he held until 1971. He also held one-year visiting appointments as assistant professor at MIT in 1960–61 and as professor at Berkeley in 1964–65 and Harvard in 1968–69. During this period, he published work on the problem of labour surplus, mechanization and the farm size-productivity relationship in agricultural development; two important papers on the economic behaviour of peasant households (1966b and 1966c), and two equally important papers on externality and collective aspects of savings decisions (1961 and 1967). He also began publishing work in the fields of social choice theory and welfare economics (1963, 1964 and 1966a). This last line of investigation culminated in the book *Collective Choice and Social Welfare* (1970) which Mark Blaug, in his *Great Economists Since Keynes*, lists as one of the central pillars on which Sen's reputation rests. In addition, he published several papers on social and moral philosophy in journals such as *Philosophy* and *Philosophical Quarterly*.

Sen's work during this period contained a number of elements that he has emphasized and developed further in subsequent writing. Among these was a concern with different modes of organization, such as the peasant household and the cooperative, and an interest in investigating the implications of utility interdependencies, for example the concern of present individuals with members of a future generation. The latter interest also played a role in analyses of conflicts between individual and collective rationality, a theme that he explored in a number of papers making use of the game theoretic paradigm of the prisoners' dilemma, and of an important and original variant, the assurance game. Finally, Sen's concern with ethical and distributive issues fed into his evolving criticism of modern welfare economics and his analysis of the Arrow paradox, both of which emphasize the informational restrictions of ordinal utility-based social rankings.

For example, in 'Isolation, Assurance, and the Social Rate of Discount', Sen showed that if a is the value an individual places on a unit increment in income to his heirs, *b* the corresponding value for an increment to other members of the future generation, and *c* the value of an increment to a contemporary, then whenever $(b/a)>c$, the individual would be better off agreeing with others to save more than would be rational without such a collective decision. While the situation depicted has the character of a standard prisoners' dilemma, in which individuals most prefer that all others save according to the agreement while they themselves consume in contravention of it, and while a collective enforcement mechanism such as state taxation might therefore be desired, Sen also noted the existence of a game with slightly different payoffs. This he dubbed the assurance game, in which individuals are inclined not to cheat on the agreement to save provided they believe that all others are saving. Sen subsequently pointed out that prisoners' dilemmas could sometimes be transformed into assurance games, with likely benefits to the parties concerned, such changes would not necessarily be in objective options and outcomes, but possibly only in the subjective or moral valuation of those outcomes – that is, the individual would learn to prefer being a cooperator over being a cheater, although still wanting to avoid being 'suckered' by others. This point is of enormous importance to the study of such subjects as work incentives and cooperation in teams. The use of a highly abstract and somewhat methodologically focused argument to build a case for controversial policy intervention – here, state intervention to raise savings rates – is also typical of much of Sen's work.

In 1951, Kenneth Arrow had shown that it might be impossible to use individuals' rankings of alternative social states to construct a social choice function obeying such ostensibly reasonable and unrestrictive properties as acyclicity and absence of dictatorship by any single individual. In *Collective Choice and Social Welfare*, Sen sought to understand this result by examining which of Arrow's assumptions might be most responsible for it. While the work is extremely abstract and mathematically demanding, his conclusion may be summarized as follows: whereas the impossibility result continues to hold even after further weakening or dropping some of Arrow's requirements, that result should be viewed as a not surprising consequence due to the poverty of information permitted to enter the problem. That is, the utilized information about individuals' preferences is limited to orderings that give no inkling of the relative importance to any given individual of changes in welfare due to movements among different pairs of social states, or to the comparative significance of movement between a given pair of states for two different individuals. The argument is closely related to, and is in some respects a generalization of, the observation that without the possibility of making interpersonal comparisons of welfare or of welfare changes, the modern concept of 'social welfare' is unable to distinguish between even drastically different distributions of income.

Sen's critique of welfare economics went beyond pointing out the limitations of non-interpersonally comparable preferences, to criticism of what economists view as the relevant domain of preferences – individual welfare and social welfare – a domain usually restricted to the consumption and leisure of individuals. One of the most noticed salvos in this battle was an attempt to show that, far from being unobjectionable and virtually value neutral as many economists seemed to believe, the concept of Pareto optimality that lies at the heart of modern welfare economics is inconsistent with so widely accepted a philosophical value as liberalism (the idea that people should be permitted to do what they please provided that it does not prevent others from doing likewise). The argument appeared in 'The Impossibility of a Paretian Liberal' (1970b), and spawned a substantial further literature that, as with Arrow's impossibility theorem, focused on what elements (such as the utility interdependence used in Sen's example) were critical to the impossibility result.

In 1971, Sen return to England, where he was to teach for the next 17 years, the first six of these at the LSE and the remainder at Oxford. In 1972, *Guidelines for Project Evaluation* appeared, co-authored for UNIDO by Partha Dasgupta and Stephen Marglin. This book became a standard source on the methodology of development project evaluation. Other contributions at that time included work closely related with his interest in welfare economics, ethics and philosophy, and also contained some of Sen's major contributions to the statistical theory of the measurement of inequality and, later, of poverty. Also Sen considered new aspects of the issues explored in earlier work on technology choice and development, and gave special attention to differences between alternative modes of work organization, including wage employment and household production. Sen suggested that differences in the subjective valuation of labour under these alternative modes could help to account for the higher cost of wage than of family labour, thereby helping to explain the greater labour intensity exhibited by small family farms in developing countries. More generally, Sen argued that one cannot identify a most efficient technology by reference to input and output levels only, when factor proportions or scale differ among production arrangements and when the human agents concerned attach different levels of disutility to different work modes.

Despite Sen's continuing immersion in development issues, critical writing on welfare and social choice theory occupied much of his attention during the 1970s. During the same period, he published a number of additional papers on the measurement of inequality and poverty. He proposed a measure of poverty based upon the rank ordering of the poor and the distance of each below the poverty line; this measure bears a close relationship to the Gini coefficient of inequality and has stimulated a great deal of further, highly technical work in the area. The same period saw papers on capital theory and aggregation, and on ethical and moral philosophy, among other topics. In 1976, Sen was awarded the Mahalanobis Prize in India.

Sen's move to Nuffield College (Oxford) in 1977 coincided both with the publication of sharpened syntheses of his criticisms of welfare economics and neoclassical economics more generally, and with his development of a new and highly influential line of research on the subject of famines and hunger. Again, both the restrictive scope of concern of the 'utility' concept, and its informational impoverishment by restriction to intrapersonal ranking, featured prominently. Also emphasized was the equally fundamental criticism of the neoclassical model of man, which tends to ignore values, rights and motives other than material self-interest. The work on famine and hunger was presaged by articles appearing in the *Economic and Political Weekly* in 1976 and in the *Cambridge Journal of Economics* in 1977, then presented more fully in his book *Poverty and Famines* (1981) and in several more articles.

Prior to Sen, famine and hunger had generally been thought of as direct consequences of shortfalls in food production, with much of the fight against food deprivation in poor countries being focused upon the development of scientific methods for raising agricultural productivity. To be sure, it had been understood by many that the global food problem was not strictly one of production, since the US and other countries had the resources and the technology to meet existing shortfalls easily, if only those suffering deprivation had the purchasing power to elicit such production via the normal operation of the market mechanism. However, Sen took a step further the decoupling between the production and distribution of food (he conceptualized the latter as being based upon an institutionally specific system of 'entitlements'), arguing that famines could and did sometimes occur without any change in the availability of food to an economy. In particular, famine could result from a change in the distribution of entitlements caused by such seemingly remote factors as an increase in purchasing power in other regions or sectors of the economy. The argument was illustrated with historical evidence from the great Bengal famine of 1943, the Bangladesh famine of 1974, and famines in Ethiopia and the Sahel countries in the early 1970s.

The year before the publication of *Poverty and Famines*, Sen assumed the Drummond Professorship of Political Economy at All Souls College (Oxford), a position previously held by such illustrious figures as Sir John Hicks, Francis Edgeworth and Nassau Senior, and carrying with it a measure of leadership of Oxford's community of economic scholars. The eight years during which he held this position saw him working avidly on famine, hunger and other development interests, including questions of sexual division and inequality. Sen's writing in the areas of philosophy and ethics also continued apace, and he followed up on his earlier critiques of welfare economics by proposing a radical alternative that focused on human capabilities rather than consumption bundles. This was also a period in which Sen assumed numerous positions of leadership in the economics profession, including presidency of the Econometric Society in 1984 and of the International Economic Association in 1986–89, and in which his impact on research in the field of economic development was extended through a leading role at the World Institute of Development Economics Research in Helsinki.

Sen's further work on hunger and famine took a number of directions. Especially fruitful were comparisons of the experiences of various poor countries, including India, China and the nations of sub-Saharan Africa. For example, Sen pointed out that whereas Communist China had succeeded in reducing chronic hunger through policies that placed a floor beneath the food consumption levels of most of its people, contributing to an increase in life expectancy to roughly 69 years by the end of the 1970s, that country had not avoided a famine of unprecedented proportions in 1959–61; whereas India, with more chronic hunger and a life expectancy of only 56 years, had avoided famines through prompt governmental action. Exemplifying his attention to a broader range of phenomena, Sen argued that much of the difference could be attributed to the existence of a free press and electoral democracy in India but not China. However, he also argued that such instrumental advantages need not be the only, nor even the most important, reasons for valuing such institutions; these might be of intrinsic value to individuals and to the society as well – an example of Sen's position that social welfare needs to be defined over more than the set of commodity bundles consumed.

Sen's critique of what he came to call 'welfarism' – the identification of both individual and social well-being with the commodity bundles produced and consumed – added one more voice to a chorus of dissatisfaction expressed by many economists, including such senior figures as Tibor Scitovsky and Albert Hirschman. While the abstract and rigorous nature of much of Sen's critical work, and his well-earned position as an authority on welfare economics and social choice theory, distinguished his criticisms from some others, neoclassical defenders could brush off even the most refined of attacks by asserting that economists could not be expected to give up a workable and in many respects fruitful theoretical approach unless offered an operational alternative. This is precisely what Sen set out to do in *Commodities and Capabilities*, which was published in 1985, in his Tanner Lectures delivered in 1984 and published in *The Standard of Living* (1987a) and in other papers and lectures.

Like W.M. Gorman and Kelvin Lancaster before him, Sen noted that people value commodities not as goods in their own right but for their various properties and the needs that they can satisfy. Going beyond this, he pointed out that the satisfactions, achievements or other results of possessing or consuming commodities depend not only on the characteristics of the commodities, but also on the characteristics of the consumer and on his or her circumstances. For example, insulin and chocolate bars are of very different value depending upon whether one is a diabetic; and a particular income level may enable the person earning it to do very different things depending upon the average income in that person's society, and the amount necessary to achieve a life-style free from social humiliation. Moreover, Sen argued that well-being cannot be judged only by end states, and that options and the freedom to choose among them are also pertinent to well-being. This means that consuming bundle X when a large number of alternatives would have been possible, and when X is chosen freely by the consumer, is different from consuming X when no alternative is available, and when X is chosen by persons or institutions over whom the consumer has no influence. The standard of living or well-being should accordingly be judged by the person's 'capability' to lead the life that he or she has reason to value. Spelled in terms of elements, a person's living can be seen as a combination of 'functionings' – doing various things a person can value, varying from such elementary achievements as being well fed or clothed, being free from avoidable diseases and being able to live without fear of violent attack, to more complex accomplishments such as achieving self-respect, taking part in the life of the community, being able to feel that one lives in a just society, and so on.

Although it is too early to judge the impact of Sen's capabilities approach upon welfare economics, both his existing stature and the elegance of his arguments have assured it a respectful hearing among both economists and philosophers. Indeed, by the late 1970s and throughout the 1980s, Sen's views, although often far from what appeared to be orthodox in economics, were nonetheless frequently solicited and published in collections and handbooks presenting the state of the art in social choice, welfare, development, philosophy and other fields touched by his work. Two collections of his essays, the first on social choice and welfare (*Choice, Welfare, and Measurement*) the second on economic development (*Resources, Values, and Development*) were published in the early 1980s. Another book by Sen, *On Ethics and Economics*, appeared in 1987. Lectures he was invited to present in the late 1980s included the Yrjo Jahnsson Lectures in Helsinki in 1987, the Marshall Lectures at Cambridge University, the Simon Kuznets Memorial Lectures at Yale University and the Wicksell Lectures at the Stockholm School of Economics, all in 1988, followed by a Presidential Address to the International Economic Association in Athens in 1989. He also served on the editorial boards of a dozen journals.

Sen's Major Writings

(1961), 'On Optimizing the Rate of Saving', *Economic Journal*, **71**, September.

(1963), 'Distribution, Transivity and Little's Welfare Criterion', *Economic Journal*, **73**, December.

(1964), 'Preferences, Votes and the Transitivity of Majority Decisions', *Review of Economic Studies*, **31**, April.

(1966a), 'A Possibility Theorem on Majority Decisions', *Econometrica*, **34**, April.

(1966b), 'Labour Allocation in a Cooperative Enterprise', *Review of Economic Studies*, July.

(1966c), 'Peasants and Dualism with or without Surplus Labor', *Journal of Political Economy*, **74**, October.

(1967), 'Isolation, Assurance and the Social Rate of Discount', *Quarterly Journal of Economics*, **81**, February. Reprinted in R. Layard (ed), *Cost Benefit Analysis*, Penguin Modern Economics, 1972.

(1970a), *Collective Choice and Social Welfare*, Holden Day. Oliver and Boyd, 1971; North-Holland, 1979. Swedish translation: Bokforlaget Thales, 1988.

(1970b), 'The Impossibility of a Paretian Liberal', *Journal of Political Economy*, **78**, January/February. Reprinted in F. Hahn and M. Hollis (eds), *Philosophy and Economic Theory*, Oxford University Press, 1979.

(1972), *Guidelines for Project Evaluation* (with P. Dasgupta and S.A. Marglin), UNIDO, United Nations.

(1981), *Poverty and Famines: An Essay on Entitlement and Deprivation*, Oxford: Clarendon Press. Oxford University Press, 1981, 1982.

(1982), *Choice, Welfare and Measurement*, Basil Blackwell. MIT Press, 1982; Oxford University Press, 1983, Italian translation: 11 Mulino, 1986.

(1984), *Resources, Values and Development*, Basil Blackwell. Harvard University Press, 1984; Oxford University Press, 1985.

(1985), *Commodities and Capabilities*, North-Holland. Oxford University Press, 1988; Japanese translations by Iwanami, 1988.

(1987a), *The Standard of Living*, Tanner Lectures with discussion, edited by G. Hawthorne, Cambridge University Press.

(1987b), *On Ethics and Economics*, Oxford: Basil Blackwell. Italian translation: Editori Laterza, 1988.

George L.S. SHACKLE (born 1903)

I was born in Cambridge in 1903, the only child of elderly parents. The family moved to the nearby village of Great Shelford shortly after, and we lived there until 1930. Family finances prevented me from accepting a place at St Catherine's College. I worked first in a bank, then in London for a tobacco firm and finally spent nine years as a schoolteacher. During this time I took an external degree at the University of London, part of which included political economy.

The discipline of political economy is like a city built on a raft. Its internal design springs in every respect, organ and arrangement from a scheme of interdependent, partly rival and partly cooperative purposes. Everything that goes on in this city looks for its worthwhileness to a time-to-come, sometimes immediate and almost within touch, sometimes showing glimpses of impending creative change, sometimes the mere stuff of dreams. This complex organism bends, heaves and swings in a manner that disturbs, upsets, inspires and challenges its citizens.

This restlessness is engendered by the inhabitants themselves as they endeavour to strengthen the raft and to perceive its destiny in the current that carries it along. We may liken the cohesiveness and ultimate unity of its design to the logic of a scholarly discipline – a logic, however, which is meaningful only by virtue of the seeming practical basis of the elements it handles.

Political economy employs and studies a factor far more widely operative than logic: the factor of *suggestion*. If conditions A and B, when they occur together, make possible the emergence of C, may it not turn out to be the case that conditions D and E occurring together will make possible the emergence of F? Logic is strict and demanding to the last degree in its requirements. Suggestion, by contrast, is ready to catch the fragrance of the flower borne on the faintest breeze. The character of economics, its delight in the *suggestion of the possible* but unproven, its creation and promotion of a new method of structuring and combining ideas, the pursuit of the *imagined deemed possible*, puts it in direct sympathy with the methods, aims and satisfactions of the businessman of adventurous fertility of mind. He also is the hunter-down of the imagined deemed possible.

Something of this flavour in our discipline must, I think, have been present in the works of J.A. Hobson which had an unmistakable, though perhaps undefinable, relevance in the late 1920s and early 1930s when a world of supposed scarcity allowed millions of people to be unemployed. On the mind of a young man who at the age of 20 had already spent three years working in a bank, Hobson's works fastened themselves irresistably. Then came the assured triumphant exposition of the nature of money, with a glimpse of its power of destroying, as well as subserving, the enterprise that could bring an industrial society to life again. Keynes's *Treatise on Money* showed me a field whose crop I could understand, a field across which I might even one day drive the plough. It appeared with a book whose enigmatic fascination held me engrossed, then and later, for many a wrestling hour. Hayek's *Prices and Production* sought to draw from the Austrian theory of capital an explanation of the paradox of massive unemployment by regarding business depression as a phase of the trade cycle, the supposed necessary alternation of boom and slump. Two men more different in personality, two books more different in atmosphere, two theories more mutually alien in structure than Keynes and his *Treatise* on one hand and Hayek and *Prices and Production* on the other would be difficult to conceive of. Was it not a task worth attempting to show that one scholarly discipline could make use of both these themes? One more small surge of history's tide launched me upon it. I was already subscribing to the LSE journal *Economica*. Amongst the pages of an issue in the early 1930s a leaflet was inserted announcing the forthcoming launch of a new economics journal whose pages would be open to the untried writer with ideas of his own. The launch would of course cost money. The bold projectors, amongst them Ursula Webb and Ralph Arakie, invited subscriptions. I sent a minute sum, with a letter asking whether it would be permissible for me to submit an article. I wrote 'Some Notes on Monetary Theories of the Trade Cycle' and under this deliberately low-key title I tried to relate Keynes and Hayek to each other. My article was published in the very first issue of the *Review of Economic Studies*. A year or two later, at some meeting at the London School of Economics, I had the opportunity to speak to Keynes for a few minutes. I explained my novitiate status, mentioned my article and confessed my ambition to become an economist. 'Oh,' said Keynes, 'if you have been published you *are* an economist.'

I had been urged by the editors of the *Review of Economic Studies* to apply for a Leverhulme Research Scholarship at LSE, but through some strange scruple I delayed for a year. Even when granted it, I asked if I might delay my arrival at the school for a further term in order not to inconvenience the boys' school at which I was teaching. Thus at last I arrived at LSE on New Year's Day, 1935.

I am writing what Lord Robbins would have called an *Apologia pro Vita Mea*, but I shall round off this chronicle swiftly and turn to ideas. The examiners for my London thesis were to be Professor Hayek and Redvers Opie of Magdalen College, Oxford. A day or two before the date set for my viva, I received two letters from Oxford, one from Dr Marschak, the Director of the Oxford University Institute of Statistics, and the other from Mr (now Sir Henry) Phelps Brown, each inviting me to become his research assistant. I was conscious of gaps in my technical knowledge of statistics, and thought they would seem less atrocious to Mr Phelps Brown than to Dr Marschak. I went to Oxford at the end of March 1937 and began to exploit Phelps Brown's ideas of using the data of inter-bank transactions as a (very large) sample of the business of the big five British banks. With an incomparable generosity, Phelps Brown allowed our results to be published under both our names. Thus I added an Oxford D.Phil. to my London Ph.D.

In the early summer of 1939 I was appointed to a post of Assistant (the Scottish equivalent of Assistant Lecturer) at St Andrews University. The outbreak of war brought a summons to become a member of Mr Churchill's personal small team of statistical researchers – which he called S. Branch – to study the needs and available resources for the war. Mr Harrod (later Sir Roy), Mr McDougal (now Sir Donald) and Miss Helen Makower were at first the other members. I shall pass over the work of S. Branch, for its concerns were practical and V.E. Day brought it abruptly to an end. Lord Robbins, who at that time was head of the economic section of the Cabinet Office, handed over that post to James Meade and returned to his chair at the LSE. Mr Meade a few months earlier had arranged that I should join him as soon as the war ended. This I did, remaining in the Cabinet Office until 1950 when I was offered a Readership at Leeds University by Professor Arthur Brown. After four terms at Leeds I was invited to apply for the Brunner Chair of Economic Science at the University of Liverpool, a position I held until retiring in 1969.

The story that I have to tell, if it is worth anything, is about a life of ideas. It is not only the writer of fiction whose method and procedure is to make his reader wonder, at every step, how the story is going to unfold. It is to keep him in uncertainty. Is not this what life itself does to us? The problems of life are the problems of knowing what the sequel will be if we do this, or if we do that. Especially it is the businessman, the controller and administrator of real resources, labour, fuel and constructional material whose mind is thus at all times faced with *uncertainty*.

Uncertainty in any matter consists in the recognition of plurality and diversity of non-excludable hypotheses. When hypotheses are suggested answers are sought to the question: what would be the sequel of such-and-such a course of action? Well-grounded choice amongst rival practicable courses, each of which presents this picture, cannot be made by immediate comparison. The complexity of each picture has somehow to be reduced into understandable simplicity, but this simplicity must accept and preserve the uncertainty which is the essence of the epistemic situation. It must recognize and retain a minimal plurality, namely a duality. Each conceived course of action, for example each investment of money in construction of a durable instrument, must be represented by just two hypotheses of its outcome, highly contrasted in its implications of success or failure. Which pair of hypotheses concerning the revenues, net of operating expense, that would be got from a specific investment (housing estate, ship, communications system) in which an investor might embark his money, would best represent to him the *meaning* of his investment for the purpose of comparing its attraction with that of others? Surely the best outcome and the worst that in some sense he deems possible are the relevant ideas. To say that he deems a particular outcome *perfectly possible* is, I think, the same as to say that its realization would cause him *no surprise*. I define the *epistemic interval* as the range of feelings separating *no surprise* from an extreme intensity of surprise. On an axis orthogonal to that on which we measure, from some zero point or origin, gain in one direction and loss in the other, we can mark a point representing the utmost surprise the investor is capable of. Thus we have gain-loss on one axis, potential surprise on the other, within or on the bounds of which we can mark points representing some combination of potential surprise or disbelief, and hypothetical gain or loss. A curve or series of such points will represent for the investor what I shall call the meaning for him of the specified investment at the moment when he is about to make his choice between several conceived investments. Some particular combination of hypothetical gain and the potential surprise he associates with it will seem more attractive to him than any other; similarly a particular combination of hypothetical loss and the associated potential surprise will seem more deterrent than any other. I call these two points, lying within or on the bounds of the two-spaces defined above, 'the focus-points' of the investment. To compare with each other several conceived investments will be to compare, according to some formal procedure, their respective pairs of focus-points. One further frame of reference is needed, where focus gains are measured on one axis and focus losses on the other. A system of indifference-curves in this frame would enable the superior attraction of one investment to be made explicit.

The suggestion I have tried to make in writing on economics may perhaps be summarized thus. Economics has in the main pictured the individual as someone going into a shop to choose amongst ready-made goods whose character is plainly visible to him. In my view economics should think of the individual as an artist-craftsman going into his workshop to select materials in a primitive state and shape them into objects of his own imagining. These objects, his life's courses and his enterprises, will not conform to his first design; they will be carved and stamped by circumstances and the actions of others. Choice is in the first place origination, the creation of the choosables. The individual has tastes, but we may credit him also with the capacity of inspiration. It is surely his originative power that allows us to reject determinism.

In all such thinking the greatest difficulties, as Marshall said, arise from the idea of time. The word *time* might be said to encompass the whole of human experience. So universally is it present in the background of all thought that much discussion of the business of life proceeds without explicit utterance of the word, and without direct consideration of the complex subtleties that are its content of meaning. Yet any system of economic ideas must depend essentially and intimately on ideas about time. Everything that individuals do or suffer is done or suffered in some *present moment*, the merciless once-for-ever opportunity, replaced but not repeated. The non-determinist view rests ultimately on the supposition that the human mind is capable of *absolute origination*, of bringing into being on occasion something not wholly implicit in experience. If this view is justified, there can evidently be no sure prediction of the course of history. The non-determinist view depends not on freedom but on the supposition of the occurrence of an *uncaused cause*. Such an idea is abhorrent to some attitudes of science, but it amounts to nothing other than the hypothesis of continuing rather than once-for-all creation.

Some say that time itself is an illusion from which we suffer. This view plainly has devastating consequences for the explanations we, as scientists or historians, give ourselves of our experience. But it is no more than an admission that ultimate understanding is essentially beyond us.

A theme which has long been in my mind, but has lately begun to seem more pressing and more clearly definable, is that of the *wastefulness* of modern life. There are two kinds of wastefulness, that of purpose and that of means. Men may engage in activities that do not benefit body, mind or moral stance. Or they may seek good ends by extravagant means. Wastefulness of purpose is not the direct concern of the economist. Wastefulness of means is his proper target, but here there are great difficulties. Elaborate packaging may be the opposite of wasteful if it protects what it encloses. Packaging may itself give pleasure by its beauty or its mere colourfulness. Advertising may be a valuable or even vital source of information. But beyond questions of purpose or of means there is the question of how far one generation is justified in using up irreplaceable resources. It is in the field of public choice that economics (that we should do well to call political economy) has its great task of clarification.

Shackle's Major Writings

(1949), *Expectation in Economics*, Cambridge University Press, second edition 1952.
(1955), *Uncertainty in Economics and Other Reflections*, Cambridge University Press.
(1961), *Decision, Order and Time in Human Affairs*, Cambridge University Press.
(1966), *The Nature of Economic Thought*, Cambridge University Press.
(1967), *The Years of High Theory: Invention and Tradition in Economic Thought*, Cambridge University Press.
(1972), *Epistemics and Economics*, Cambridge University Press.
(1974), *Keynesian Kaleidics*, Edinburgh University Press.
(1983), 'A Student's Pilgrimage', *Banca Nazionale del Lavoro Quarterly Review*, No 145, June. Reprinted in Frowen (1988).

Other References

Frowen, S. (ed), (1988), *Business, Time and Thought: Selected Papers of G.L.S. Shackle*, Macmillan.
Frowen, S. (ed), (1990), *Unknowledge and Choice in Economics*, Macmillan. This contains a full bibliography of G.L.S. Shackle.
Harcourt, G.C. (1990), 'Introduction: Notes on an Economic Querist – G.L.S. Shackle', in S. Frowen (ed), *Unknowledge and Choice in Economics*, Macmillan. A shorter version was published in *Journal of Post Keynesian Economics*, 4, 1981, 136–44.

Anwar M. SHAIKH (born 1945)

I was born in 1945 in Karachi (Pakistan) two years before the partition of India. My early years were spent in Karachi, but after my father joined the Pakistani Foreign Service in 1950, I also lived in Ankara, Washington D.C., New York, Lagos, Kuala Lumpur and Kuwait. I received a B.S.E. from Princeton University in 1965, worked for two years in Kuwait (as an engineer and a teacher of social science and physics), and returned to the US to study at Columbia University, from which I received my Ph.D. in Economics in 1973. In 1972 I joined the Economics Department at the Graduate Faculty of the New School for Social Research, where I am presently employed.

Several factors have shaped my present political and economic orientation. My travels led me to the view that capitalism is a powerful social force which steadily transforms all cultures and institutions in its path, bending those which will bend and breaking those which will not. It develops the forces of production in an unparalleled manner, yet does not abolish poverty or social misery. Old bastions of privilege and power fall, but new ones inevitably emerge to take their place. It is this perspective that led me to the study of economics.

Like many others of my generation in the US, I was profoundly influenced by the civil rights and feminist movements of the 1960s. While in graduate school, I lived and worked (as a teacher of social science and mathematics) in Harlem, was active in the 1968 strike at Columbia University, in the Union for Radical Political Economy (from its founding in 1968) and in the anti-war movement.

The Graduate Faculty of the New School for Social Research, long tolerant of dissenting points of view, has generally provided a supportive climate for such efforts. The structure of the Economics Department has made it possible to pursue basic research, and its active student body (with at least half from the Third World) has consistently provided critical feedback.

The central concern of my work has been the attempt to understand the fundamental processes at work in capitalist economies. How do market economies work, and why do they generate certain intrinsic patterns which seem to cut across differences in origin, in culture, and even historical epochs? Why is capitalist growth characterized by order-within-disorder, periodically punctuated by episodes of general economic crisis? Why is capitalist development so typically uneven across nations, across regions and across individuals? In approaching such questions, it has always seemed crucial to me that one should start from a solid theoretical foundation grounded in the actual phenomena of the object of one's investigation. This probably reflects the influence of my prior training in science and engineering.

My exposure to conventional economics left me convinced that neither neoclassical nor Keynesian theory was adequate to these concerns, although the particular contributions of Leontief, Kalecki, Joan Robinson (whom I came to know and admire) and Sraffa furnished much inspiration and solace. It was Marx, with his trenchant analysis of the origins, structure and inner logic of capitalist economic processes, who seemed to provide the most comprehensive and well-grounded foundation for further work. I therefore set out to try and show that Marx had furnished the elements of a solid foundation for modern economic analysis, capable of being extended to address current theoretical and empirical concerns, and resulting in a distinctive body of economic propositions which could be formalized and tested. As is always the case, this was a project in which many others were also engaged.

My published work has been motivated by the above project. It falls into six main areas, the first of which deals with the theory of value. Here, at the methodological level, I have always opposed the use of equilibrium analysis and comparative statics, on the grounds that such tools as these are quite inadequate to describe the real regulation processes of capitalist markets. The unplanned individual activities which characterize capitalist production are made socially coherent only by being forcibly articulated into a viable social division of labour, through some real process of oscillations, discrepancies, and errors around ever moving centres of gravity. It is one thing to study the properties of these centres of gravity, as Marx does in his analysis of prices of production or of balanced reproduction. But it is quite another to assume these conditions ever exist as such, or that one may analyse the behaviour of individual units beginning from some assumed state of equilibrium (as neoclassical and neo-Ricardian economists so often do).

The above perspective leads to the notion that the immediate regulators of individual behaviour (prices, wages, profits etc) will have inner tendencies which are only expressed through some average movement. Since any immediate division of labour must be forcibly articulated into some viable social division of labour, the structural labour requirements must assert themselves over the immediate incentives of the market system. Following Ricardo and Marx, I therefore look to the ultimate regulation and domination of market prices by quantities of social labour time. At the same time, precisely because this regulation process is not immediate (as in 'general equilibrium'), one must identify the various mediating links between abstract socially necessary labour time and money price, between surplus value and money profit etc. For instance, in the latter case I emphasize that even though modern capitalist profit rests on the surplus value produced by industrial capital, profit can also arise from transfers of wealth or value in or out of the circuit of capital. These latter transfers give rise to what Marx calls profit-on-alienation. They explain not only the profits of merchant capital (which pre-dates industrial capital and surplus value), but also the famous difference between aggregate profit and aggregate surplus value which arises when we compare prices of production with prices proportional to labour values, holding the sum of prices constant (the transformation problem). It can be shown that this difference is strictly limited, and is inversely related to the rate of growth when the system is in balanced reproduction. Moreover, such a difference will arise when we compare the effects of *any* two distinct sets of prices. Thus even the deviations of market prices (or monopoly prices) from prices of production will give rise to differing measures of the rate and mass of profit. The phenomenon is perfectly general (see 1984, 1990a).

At a theoretical level, I have shown that the deviations between fully transformed (i.e. Bortkiewicz-Sraffa) prices of production and Marxian labour values depend essentially on *vertically integrated* capital-labour ratios (or equivalently, on vertically integrated organic compositions of capital), and that such deviations will tend to be relatively small in actual economies. At the empirical level, input-output estimates for the US indicate that labour values account for about 85% of the structure of prices of production (as measured by the percentage average absolute deviation); that Marx's own procedure for calculating prices of production (which can be viewed as a linear approximation technique) captures about 95% of the structure of fully transformed prices of production; that the overlap between aggregates such as the Marxian value rate of profit and the Bortkiewicz-Sraffa type uniform rate of profit is greater than 96%; and that all empirically estimated aggregate wage-profit curves are virtually linear even when wage shares are relatively low and actual output proportions in the economy are very different from those of Sraffa's Standard Commodity (Shaikh, 1988; Ochoa, 1989). Comparisons to *market* prices reveal that labour values account for 88%, Marx's prices of production for 87%, and fully transformed (Bortkiewicz-Sraffa) prices for 86%. Recent theoretical and empirical investigations provide further support for this Ricardian-Marxian structural approach to the determination of prices (Petrovic, 1987; Bienenfeld, 1988). Such results cast an entirely different light on the longstanding debate about the determinants of prices of production and of price-value deviations.

I use the preceding results, along with other arguments, to criticize certain key constructions in opposing schools of thought. For instance, neoclassical economics contemptuously rejects any form of the labour theory of value. Yet Garegnani (1970) has shown that the neoclassical aggregate production function, supposedly the very antithesis of the classical-Marxian approach, is theoretically valid only if Ricardo's labour theory of price is strictly true! In the face of this devastating result, neoclassicals have generally taken refuge in the fact that 'well-behaved' aggregate production functions and their associated marginal productivity explanations of 'factor prices' appear to have considerable empirical strength. In a series of essays on the 'Humbug Production Function', I show that this purported empirical strength is simply an algebraic artifact. For instance, in a (Robinsonian) economy with a single fixed proportions technique undergoing Harrod-neutral technical change, the marginal product of labour and capital cannot even be defined. Yet, even this completely anti-neoclassical case is perfectly consistent with an aggregate pseudo-production function with pseudo-marginal products equal to so-called factor prices. It follows that a fitted aggregate production function tells us very little about the underlying economic processes (1986).

At the other pole, the branch of neo-Ricardian economics exemplified by Steedman's work attempts to 'modernize' Ricardo and Marx by restating them in conventional terms. In spite of its Sraffian roots, this school also rejects any connection between labour time and prices. Here, I argue that even though this approach clarifies some important issues, its basic framework is far too dependent on neoclassical constructs such as perfect competition, long-run equilibrium prices, and associated notions of capitalist choice of technique (1981). These neoclassical roots are apparent in its static equilibrium approach to prices, and in its consequent inability to grasp the theoretical and empirical connection between prices and labour times. They also surface in its analysis of the process whereby new methods of production enter into competition with existing ones. Marx argues that individual capitalists with new lower-cost methods of production 'make room for themselves' by cutting selling prices. This is also how the business literature generally see competition. Yet the neoclassical-neo-Ricardian notion of perfect competition rules out such behaviour altogether, by simply assuming that individual capitals take existing prices as 'given' even in the face of technical change.

The difference in the two conceptions of competitive behaviour has profound implications for the movements of the general rate of profit. The problem can be thought of in the following way. Both sides agree that investments are evaluated on the basis of estimates of their future rates of return. This requires estimates of both probable costs and *also* probable selling prices, since it is the difference between the two which determines the probable streams of profit. The crucial difference arises in the treatment of selling prices. In keeping with their assumption of perfect competition, neoclassicals and neo-Ricardians assume that even new competitors take prices as given at pre-existing levels. Under this assumption profit-rate maximizing behaviour necessarily leads to a *rising* general rate of profit for any given wage. This is the Okishio Theorem. On the other hand, if it is assumed that firms can engage in price-cutting behaviour, then firms with new lower-cost methods of production can always force down selling prices to a point where their own expected rate of profit is higher than those of their higher cost competitors. Under these circumstances, profit-rate maximizing behaviour will favour techniques which have lower unit costs, and the Okishio theorem does not hold. Then the movements of the general rate of profit turn out to depend precisely on the factors analysed by Marx: organic composition of capital, rate of surplus value etc.

The second area of my work develops Marx's theory of the falling rate of profit and tests it against empirical evidence. I argue that the struggle of capital against labour manifests itself as the continual *mechanization* of production. But the benefits of this process can only be realized in the struggle of capital against capital if mechanization also lowers unit production costs. On average, such lower unit costs are achieved by tying up greater amounts of fixed capital per unit output (a process which I call the increased *capitalization* of production). To put it in the language of microeconomics, capitalist production displays an inherent tendency towards lower average variable and average total costs, at the expense of higher average fixed costs. I show that such tendencies are sufficient to account for a rising aggregate capital-output ratio and hence a rising materialized composition of capital c/(v+s), which in turn produces a downward drift in the general rate of profit even when the rate of surplus value s/v is rising *faster* than the materialized composition of capital. Finally, I establish that a secularly falling rate will necessarily produce a 'long wave' in the mass of profit, in which total profit first accelerates, then decelerates, stagnates and even falls. On the empirical side, I develop measures of profitability and its determinants for the US from 1899–1987, separate out the underlying trends from cyclical and conjunctural factors, and show that these trends mirror the patterns outlined above. I would argue that both the Great Depression of the 1930s and the long stagnation of the present period can be analysed from this perspective (1991).

A third area of my work centres around the theory of effective demand implicit in a Marxian approach to growth. Marx's schemes of expanding reproduction imply that supply and demand oscillate around a path of expanding output. But there is no explicit treatment of the mechanisms which might cause such an outcome. Indeed, ever since Luxemburg's critique of Marx's schema, and certainly since Keynes and Kalecki, it has become fashionable to argue that modern theories of effective demand have vitiated the classical/Marxian notion that accumulation is driven through the reinvestment of profits. In my own work, I try to show that Marx's approach to capitalist reproduction provide the foundation for an alternate, dynamic and non-equilibrium, approach to the theory of effective demand. Any given discrepancy between aggregate demand and supply is shown to react back upon both of them in such a way that they end up cycling erratically around each other. Thus aggregate demand equals aggregate supply only over the average cycle, so that no state of equilibrium ever exists. Moreover, the path defined by this average balance is a growth path, so that growth is intrinsic to the system even in the 'short run'. The economic structure of such a theory is quite simple and intuitive, but its formalization requires an excursion into the world of nonlinear dynamical analysis in order to prove the generality of its results. The picture of turbulent cyclical growth which emerges is very much in line with Marx's arguments, as well as with historical experience. By the same token, it is quite different from the essentially static (in the sense of growth) equilibrium frameworks developed by Keynes and Kalecki. As in Marx, growth is internally driven, and factors such as technical change or government spending *modify* this trend (in particular, the falling rate of profit eventually undermines the trend altogether). By contrast, in Kalecki, technical change and government spending are needed to *induce* a growth trend, because the system's intrinsic tendency is towards stagnation. Such theoretical differences have important implications for the analysis of capitalist accumulation (1989).

A fourth area concerns the theory of international trade. Classical economics emphasized that technical change lowered unit costs, and that lower cost producers generally beat out higher cost ones. Thus, within any one country, more developed (i.e. technologically advanced) producers of a given set of products would have an absolute advantage over their less developed competitors. This is precisely why capitalists are impelled to continually develop the forces of production. It seems plausible that the outcome would not be materially different if the more advanced producers happened to be in one country and the less advanced ones in another. Indeed, this is what Marx implicitly assumes. Yet from Ricardo onward, orthodox economics has always assumed just the opposite: namely, that when it comes to international trade, the laws of competition are overturned because the law of international comparative advantage replaces that of national absolute advantage. Then, even if all the industries in some poor country are technologically backward compared to some rich country, trade between the two is supposed to operate in such a way that only *some* industries in each will be eliminated (the most backward set in the poor, the least advanced set in the rich), leaving the others to expand to the point where trade is balanced so that both countries end up gaining from trade. Within this framework backwardness is no detriment because trade ensures that the backward country or region will share in the advantages of the advanced ones. Indeed, the greater the differences between countries or regions, the greater the potential benefits claimed for free trade.

Marxists and many others have generally reacted to the grave discrepancies between the above theory and the historical facts by turning to alternate explanations based on historically specific factors such as monopoly capital (Hilferding/Lenin) or on substantial international wage differentials (Emmanuel). Interestingly enough, they seldom question the peculiar manner in which orthodox economics extends its theory of competition to trade between nations. I show that the Marxian theory of competition implies very different outcomes. Underdeveloped nations will generally be at a disadvantage because their backward technologies would imply higher unit costs, all other things being equal. It is precisely for this reason that low wages and/or rich resource deposits become central factors in the internationally competitive exports of Third World countries. These same factors attract powerful foreign capitals, which not only displace local capitals but also help keep a tight lid on wages. Low wages in turn favour relatively more labour-intensive methods of production. Therefore, the normal result of capitalist free trade is to exacerbate uneven development on a world scale. It is only under extraordinary circumstances that a poor country is able to break out of the gravitational well created by modern free trade. These results provide a basis for a critique of both orthodox trade theory and its Marxian and neo-Marxian counterparts (1980). In my most recent work, I have been able to extend the argument to a theory of exchange rates which seems to work quite well at an empirical level.

A fifth area of my work has to do with the relation between Marxist theoretical categories and the macroeconomic 'facts'. Clearly, any attempt to test Marxist theory must be grounded in a body of data which reflects the appropriate categories. For instance, without a measure of the rate of surplus value we cannot say whether it rose or fell over some interval. But since all existing national economic accounts are based on neoclassical and Keynesian categories, this means that we have to derive a detailed mapping between conventional national accounts and their Marxian counterparts. The crucial difference in this regard arises from the different definitions of production and consumption activities in the two approaches. Orthodox economics restricts the definition of consumption to *personal* consumption, and defines all else (except for transfer payments) as production. In contrast to this, classical economists define consumption to include not only personal consumption but also various forms of *social* consumption such as government administration, legislative and judicial activities, the military etc. This implies a correspondingly reduced definition of production. In conventional accounts, an increase in the government bureaucracy or in the size of the military is treated as an addition to national wealth. In classical and Marxian accounts, it is treated as an increase in social consumption. This is based on an evaluation of the objective impact of different activities, not on any notion that one is more desirable than the other. At a concrete level, a difference such as this profoundly affects the measures of national production, surplus, productivity etc. It also changes the way in which we analyse any concrete outcome, since it changes our understanding of the underlying factors. My initial estimates of Marxian accounts appeared in 1978, and a greatly expanded version now exists in book draft (1990a).

The sixth area of research concerns the relation between state taxation of wage income and corresponding state expenditures on items which enter into the standard of living of wage earners. This question had surfaced in the guise of the argument that the social expenditures of the welfare state constitute a large and growing net 'social wage' which workers receive over and above their apparent wages. But an examination of this argument reveals that it either ignored the taxes paid by workers or else seriously underestimated them. My earliest estimates for select post-war years in the US showed an entirely different pattern; namely, that workers paid more in taxes than was spent by the state on items which entered into their standard of living (including transfer payments, health, education, welfare, housing, roads, recreation and postal services etc.). That is to say, there was a net tax (negative net 'social wage') imposed on US workers (see 1978). Subsequent studies confirmed this pattern for the US (Tonak, 1984; Shaikh and Tonak, 1990a). However, similar studies by others (in collaboration with myself) on Britain, Australia, Canada, Sweden, and Germany over the post-war period reveal that the US is exceptional, in the sense that all other welfare states end up transferring a positive (albeit modest) social wage to wage earners. But by far the most striking finding of these studies is that the international range of variation of the net social wage is relatively narrow (seldom exceeding 6% of wages and salaries), and that for the combined working population of the six countries studied so far, the average net social wage over the post-war period seldom ranged beyond 3%. It would seem that the principal contribution of the welfare state in this regard is to redistribute income *within* the working class (and to dampen the effects of recessions). It certainly does not induce any significant transfer of surplus value to workers (1990b).

A good portion of my completed research, comprising both theoretical and empirical work on competition, skills, technical change, exchange rates and government policy remains unpublished. Most of it is slated for publication in a forthcoming book (1992).

All in all, my central concern has been to show that the capitalist system is regulated by powerful built-in forces which account for a great number of its characteristic patterns. Conjunctural factors and historical events play an important role, but the very stage upon which they are played out is itself constantly in motion. It may be ideologically convenient to portray capitalism as manageable and static. *E pur si mouove!*

Shaikh's Major Writings

(1978), 'National Income Accounts and Marxian Categories', mimeo, New School for Social Research.

(1980), 'On the Laws of International Exchange', in E.J. Nell (ed), *Growth, Profits and Property: Essays in the Revival of Political Economy*, Cambridge University Press.

(1981), 'The Poverty of Algebra: Critical Notes on Neo-Ricardian Economics', in *The Value Controversy*, London: New Left Books.

(1984), 'The Transformation from Marx to Sraffa: Prelude to a Critique of the Neo-Ricardians', in E. Mandel (ed), *Marx, Ricardo, Sraffa*, London: Verso.

(1986), 'The Humbug Production Function', in J. Eatwell, M. Milgate and P. Newman (eds), *The New Palgrave: A Dictionary of Economic Theory and Doctrine*, London: Macmillan.

(1989), 'Accumulation, Finance and Effective Demand in Marx, Keynes and Kalecki', in W. Semmler (ed), *Financial Dynamics and Business Cycles: New Prospects*, New York: M.E. Sharpe.

(1990a), *National Income Accounts and Marxian Categories* (with E.A. Tonak), mimeo.

(1990b), *The Welfare State and the Social Wage: An International Study* (with I. Bakket), mimeo.

(1991), 'The Falling Rate of Profit and Long Waves in Accumulation: Theory and Evidence', forthcoming in A. Kleinknecht, E. Mandel and I. Wallerstein (eds), *New Findings in Long Wave Research*, London: Macmillan.

(1992), *Marxian Economic Analysis*, Oxford: Basil Blackwell, forthcoming.

Other References

Bienefeld, M. (1988), 'Regularities in Price Changes as an Effect of Changes in Distribution', *Cambridge Journal of Economics*, **12** (2) June, 247–55.

Garegnani, P. (1990), 'Heterogenous Capital, the Production Function and the Theory of Distribution', *Review of Economic Studies*, **37**, 407–36.

Ochoa, E. (1989), 'Values, Prices and Wage-Profit Curves in the U.S. Economy', *Cambridge Journal of Economics*, **13** (3), September, 413–30.

Petrovic, P. (1987), 'The Deviation of Production Prices from Labour Values: Some Methodology and Empirical Evidence', *Cambridge Journal of Economics*, **11** (3), September, 197–210.

Tonak, E.A. (1984), *A Conceptualization of State Revenues and Expenditures: The U.S. 1952–1980*, unpublished Ph.D. Dissertation, New School for Social Research.

Howard J. SHERMAN (born 1931)

I was born on 3 January 1931 in Chicago (Illinois) where I went to school. I thus grew up in the Great Depression and have some childhood memories of my father going bankrupt and various relatives being unemployed. So my primary field has always been the macroeconomics of recessions, depressions, and crises. I have dedicated my knowledge of economics to the cause of removal of all unemployment and its associated human misery. I am a dissenting, radical political economist from my nose to my toes!

My memories of the Second World War from a child's viewpoint focus on the holocaust and the effects of prejudice. Since my family was Jewish and we had many relatives in Poland, I remember vividly being told that all of them had been killed by the Fascists. I have, therefore, always been deeply opposed to anything resembling Fascism, racism, or sexism.

The victory of the Russians at Stalingrad made me sympathetic to the Soviet Union and I took a near Stalinist position. This led to my interest in comparative systems. I had always wished to understand and improve Soviet 'socialism'. In 1956, I was shocked by Khrushchev's exposure of Stalin's many crimes. I asked what was wrong with Marxist theories of the state, since these theories indicated that 'socialism' was always democratic. Ever since, my main obsession in comparative analysis has been to understand how we could reach and operate a feasible, democratic socialism. My view has been that democracy requires socialism in order to remove the unequal power of wealth from the political scene. On the other hand, socialism requires democracy because otherwise 'public' ownership is not public, but only control by an elite.

Finally, I found that the best tool to understand capitalism and socialism is the Marxist paradigm of the social sciences. My Marxism is far from orthodox or fundamentalist. Marx asked many of the right questions, but his analysis – like all analyses – was limited by the historical circumstances in which he wrote. One should take from Marx what is useful, but one should add whatever is necessary from other sources. Thorstein Veblen is one source that has had considerable impact on my views. So have many others, including John Maynard Keynes. My view is perhaps best described as radical or critical, combining Marxist, institutionalist, and post-Keynesian elements.

My education – aside from the experiences of life – was the usual US variety, with a B.A. in Economics from UCLA, an M.A. from the University of Southern California, and a Ph.D. from the University of California, Berkeley. What was a little unusual was that I stopped in the middle to get a law degree (Jur. D.) from the University of Chicago Law School. After passing the bar exam, I was denied entry to the bar on the basis of my political activities. This was 1953, the height of McCarthyism in the US. It was also during the Korean War, so I was promptly drafted into the US Army. I then refused to take the Army anti-communist ('loyalty') oath, believing that it was an infringement of free speech. After 21 months in the Army, I was given an undesirable discharge because of my politics. After a struggle of many years, the US Supreme Court reversed all such discharges. So I finally emerged with a discharge under Honorable Conditions with full rights and benefits.

After teaching at various universities, I landed at the University of California at Riverside, which gave me tenure before realizing that I was a dissenter. U.C. Riverside has been very tolerant and has even made me Chair of the department on two occasions – though I always feel uncomfortable as Chair, being a dissenter by nature. Our department now has non-traditional economists of various varieties and is completely tolerant of all unorthodox views, so I find it a very pleasant place to work.

What follows is a detailed exposition of my views in each of the following three areas: (i) crises and business cycles, (ii) comparative analysis of capitalism and socialism, and (iii) the Marxist or radical method.

Marx always spoke of economic crises rather than business cycles, though he did discern a ten-year business cycle. He considered several different theories, but never gave a systematic analysis of the cycle. One theory of Marx was the underconsumptionist approach. The argument is that capitalist expansion leads to increasing exploitation of workers; that is, a lower labour share of the national income. Since worker's income is the main component of consumer demand, a decline in relative workers' income will lower the average propensity to consume in the aggregate. Early underconsumptionists jumped from that statement to the proposition that limited consumption must mean a depression. But many economists – including Marx – have criticized naive underconsumptionists for that leap. It is theoretically possible for consumer demand to stagnate while aggregate demand grows, based on the demand for investment goods. In other words, it is technically possible to build factories to build more factories ad infinitum.

Therefore, the most perceptive of the dissenting economists – including Marx, Keynes, and Kalecki – have focused on investment as the key factor in the business cycle. To the extent that investment is a function of the change in consumer demand, one can elaborate a consistent underconsumptionist view. This was one task undertaken in my first book, *Macrodynamic Economics: Growth, Employment, and Prices* (1964). Marx also paid attention to cases of rising costs cutting into profits; he mentioned high wages in extraordinary conditions, but also pioneered the analysis of rising costs of raw materials interfering with profits. My book attempted to synthesize a theory in which profits are squeezed in every expansion, both by rising costs and by limited demand. In formal models, I found that this approach had been explored in a most interesting way by Michal Kalecki.

In the realm of empirical data, a concentration on all of the elements of profit rates marks the work of Wesley Mitchell whose institutionalist approach has guided all of my empirical work on the business cycle. Mitchell developed methods of measuring cyclical behaviour which are still the best approach today. He does not use correlation, but merely description; when one has worked through his descriptive analysis, however, one does know how the business cycle behaves. Much of my work has consisted in updating Mitchell's empirical analysis to the present day. Ironically, his own followers at the National Bureau of Economic Research have lost his particular vision, so they seldom use his methods anymore, except his insight into leading indicators of the cycle. Leading indicators are fine if one wants to make short run predictions, but his other measurements remain more important for an understanding of why there are cyclical downturns. To combine Marx's theoretical insights with Mitchell's empirical methods has long been a major goal of mine – a somewhat unique research project because most institutionalists pay little attention to Marx's theories and most Marxists pay no attention to Mitchell's empirical methods.

I have followed the lead of Paul Baran and Paul Sweezy in their remarkable explorations of the role of monopoly capital as a central phenomenon of capitalism. I examined the inimical effects of monopoly power on the macroeconomy in my 1968 book, *Profits in the United States*. In the 1970s, in contradiction to most existing theories, I was fascinated by the combination of inflation and unemployment. I wrote a book about this phenomenon, called *Stagflation* (1976) which focused on the role of monopoly power in raising prices during recessions.

My work on economic crises and the business cycle has continued over the years in a number of articles, culminating in my most recent book, *The Business Cycle: Crises and Growth Under Capitalism*. This attempts to show the utter worthlessness of most neoclassical work on the business cycle, because all of it relies on Say's Law and assumes that all recessions and depressions are due to external shocks. Instead, it presents a coherent endogenous theory of the cycle, showing how profit is squeezed at the peak by both rising costs and limited demand, and then allowed to expand at the trough by both rising demand and limited costs. The scenario includes – by successive approximations – the power of monopoly, credit and finance, government, and international processes.

Since the strongest point of Soviet planning has been the lack of general unemployment, it has always seemed quite natural to me to combine an interest in capitalist unemployment with Soviet planning. I have never been a Sovietologist in the sense that I seldom did any empirical research on the day-to-day happenings in the Soviet political economic system. On the other hand, I have reviewed all of the secondary sources from time to time in order to construct an overview of the Soviet forest, since many Sovietologists tend to get lost in the trees.

When I began my systematic work on the Soviet system in the 1960s, most of the available literature fell into one of two camps: either it was from Communists extolling the Soviet economy as perfect, or from anti-communist theorists and Russian emigrés explaining that the Soviet economy has been going downhill since 1917. I wrote a book in 1969 designed to give a more balanced view of the Soviet economy as one with a high growth rate (at that time), but having many problems of overcentralized and non-democratic planning that were tending to push the growth rate downward.

It is amusing that I was attacked by both sides: my book was called an anti-Soviet diatribe by the US Communist party and a defence of Stalinism by some reviewers further to the right. Perhaps one lasting contribution of the book, other than its attempt to provide an objective tone, was the fact that I carefully set the Soviet economy into an historical context. My historical framework for viewing the Soviet economy has to some extent influenced other writers in the field away from the previous current-events type of approach.

My own view of Soviet history was heavily influenced by the magnificent writing of Isaac Deutscher. I was particularly affected by his view of the historical evolution of Soviet dictatorship and democracy. Deutscher's hypothesis was that the Soviet Union suffered from the start from all of the problems of an underdeveloped country, combined with an all-out drive to develop the economy overnight. Rapid development means the sacrifice of immediate consumption. When people are at the margin of starvation (as in the Soviet Union in 1930), it is not a popular policy to demand sacrifices for many years. For that reason, it was impossible to have both rapid industrialization and a democratic regime. The whole countryside was being squeezed, yet peasants were a majority and workers only a small minority at the time. It is not surprising that a repressive dictatorship emerged under these conditions. On the other hand, Deutscher was optimistic that, after the Soviet Union had industrialized and made education universal, the conditions would exist for a political revolution to restore democracy and build a democratic socialism. By hindsight, I believe that recent events have proved Deutscher to be correct. We are marking the end of a dictatorial socialism (or statism); if we are lucky, we will witness the emergence of a democratic socialism in the Soviet Union.

My most recent book in this field, co-authored with A. Zimbalist and S. Brown, is called *Comparing Economic Systems: A Political Economic Approach*. In that book, we decided on pedagogical grounds that each country would be given a good solid section – with the largest part going to the Soviet Union. We disagreed with the thematic approach often used elsewhere where there is a chapter on each subject, such as labour, with a few paragraphs on each country to illustrate. Our approach to the Soviet Union covers several chapters in a coherent fashion. Unfortunately, like all work on this country, it is already largely outdated even though written so recently. Fortunately, we continued to use an historical approach, so that it is not totally obsolete. Since the Soviet Union has suddenly become fascinating – after many years of instilling boredom and disillusionment – I am doing some more work in this field, at least in terms of its historical evolution from dictatorial statism towards democratic socialism.

Georg Lukacs once said that the only thing constant or orthodox about Marxism is its methodology, not its particular conclusions. Marx never wrote a systematic treatise on methodology, but his shorter pieces and stray comments add up to a fascinating approach to the social sciences. Because of their unhappiness with the neoclassical paradigm, this is an area in which many Marxists, radicals and other dissenters have written up a storm. My attempt has been to synthesize this material in order to create a widely-accepted approach that would be a sharp weapon for dissenters.

My first book contrasting the neoclassical with the radical paradigm was called *Radical Political Economy: Capitalism and Socialism from a Marxist Humanist Perspective* (1972). This arose out of the ferment of the 1960s, when all kinds of establishment ideology, including neoclassical economics, were being criticized. A new economics association called the Union for Radical Political Economics was established, of which I was a founding member. My attempt in this book was to state a complete radical paradigm, beginning with some methodology and history, but concentrating on the main substantive points of its approach to capitalism and socialism. This book was widely reviewed, and – not to my surprise – attacked from both right and left perspectives. The right-wing all stressed that the radical criticisms of capitalism were pure drivel, although they agreed with my critique of the Soviet 'socialist' system. The far left attacked the book for its critical stance toward the existing so-called socialist societies, but did agree that my criticisms of capitalism were excellent!

After 17 years, I published a new book called *Foundations of Radical Political Economy* (1988). This attempted to go somewhat further into the questions of methodology and reviewed the new historical situation and the flood of radical literature that had appeared since my first book in the area. Since the left has now become far more tolerant, reviews have been more favourable. But as radical economics is no longer chic, the right has largely ignored my new book.

In several articles and in continuing research, I am attempting to systematize the present methodological conflict between neoclassical and dissenting economics. Some of the issues that I have discussed – and am now trying to explore in depth – include the following:

1. Neoclassical economics begins with assumptions about individual psychology; the radical paradigm attempts to explain individual psychology within a context of the socio-economic structure. The radical view puts the concept of class in the centre of its perspective; class is the entry point to the issues of political economy. Neoclassical economics pays no attention to class, partly because of the methodological critique of any concept beyond the individual, and partly because the concept of class needs to be seen in the light of all of the social sciences, not just economics.

2. Neoclassical economics believes that it is possible to consider a pure economics, separate from the other social sciences. Radical economists aspire to an integrated social science; they believe that it is impossible to get a good grasp of most subjects without involving an integrated approach. How can one look at race or gender or class from an isolated, pure economics view? When neoclassicals examine race and gender from the view of their pure economics, the result is remarkable for its lack of realism.

3. Neoclassical economics focuses on adjustments resulting in equilibrium and can handle only incremental changes. Radical political economy

deals with dynamics and change, including both incremental, evolutionary change and qualitative, revolutionary change. It asks always where a socio-economic process is going and from whence it came.

4. Finally, neoclassical welfare economics is built on a view of harmony, such that it is possible to make significant changes that harm no one. This ties into the neoclassical view that their economics is value-free, dealing only with 'facts'. The radical view is based on the reality of class conflict in society. One cannot significantly improve the conditions of slavery, for example, without abolishing the right of the slaveowners to hold humans as property. Moreover, there is no such thing as value-free social science. A description of slavery, for example, is never value-free; the researcher chooses such a topic for ethical or political reasons, examines the data in the light of some world view, and reaches conclusions heavily influenced by that world view. The question that social scientists must always answer is: which side are you on? the side of the oppressed or the side of the oppressor?

To get ahead in economics, one should write abstract, abstruse, profound-sounding articles. Thus, writers such as Robert Heilbroner or J.K. Galbraith are always sneered at by the establishment, but their writings reach millions of people. It is my view that dissenters cannot afford to leave the writing of popular books or textbooks to the orthodox. I am very pleased that my book, co-authored with E.K. Hunt, *Economics: An Introduction to Traditional and Radical Views* has been read by thousands of students. It examines neoclassical economics in a critical light, but also presents a dissenting view on every topic of economics. Unlike the ahistorical and parochial textbooks of neoclassical economics, we stressed both the history of economic thought and the comparative analysis of capitalist and 'socialist' systems. It is our hope that this book has contributed to a better world by changing those who read it.

Sherman's Major Writings

(1964), *Macrodynamic Economics: Growth, Employment and Prices*, New York: Appleton-Century-Crofts.

(1968), *Profits in the United States: An Introduction to the Study of Economic Concentration and Business Cycles*, Ithaca: Cornell University Press.

(1969), *The Soviet Economy.* Boston: Little Brown and Company.

(1972), *Radical Political Economy: Capitalism and Socialism from a Marxist Humanist Perspective*, New York: Basic Books.

(1976) *Stagflation: A Radical Theory of Unemployment and Inflation*, New York: Harper and Row.

(1988), *Foundations of Radical Political Economy*, New York: M.E. Sharpe.

(1989a), *Comparing Economic Systems: A Political Economy Approach* (with A. Zimbalist and S. Brown), San Diego: Harcourt Brace Jovanovich, 2nd edition.

(1989b), *Economics: An Introduction to Traditional and Radical Views* (with E.K. Hunt), New York: Harper and Row, 6th edition.

(1990), *The Business Cycle: Crises and Growth Under Capitalism*, Princeton: Princeton University Press.

Hans Wolfgang SINGER (born 1910)

I am encouraged to be autobiographical and to explain in what ways I could be considered a 'dissenting' economist. So I will start off by explaining how I came to specialize in problems of development and Third World countries. For an economist trained by Schumpeter and Keynes, born in an industrial country and who never set foot in a developing country until 1947, this specialization could in itself be called an act of dissent – a sort of divorce from the mainstream of economics. In fact when I visited my old teacher, Schumpeter, at Harvard in 1947 and told him that I had joined the UN and specialized there on problems of Third World countries, his reply was: 'But you are an economist – isn't this more a matter for anthropologists, sociologists, geographers etc?' And this from the author of the *Theory of Economic Development*!

How did I come to leave the mainstream and join the then tiny, virtually non-existent, band of 'development economists'? In explaining this, there are two scenarios, one creditable and the other not so. The creditable scenario presents this choice as a deliberate decision and in line with interests as they developed after I went down from Cambridge with my Ph.D. in 1936. The other was the result of sheer accident, in the form of a linguistic misunderstanding due to different meanings of the same word in American English and English English. I will now explain both scenarios, but the reader familiar with debates among historians will notice that they correspond to two different versions of history: one of the gradual unfolding of an influential, innate meaning and the other of history as 'just one damn thing after another'.

The meaningful scenario: in 1936, on the recommendation of Keynes, I was recruited as one of three young men to carry out a two-year survey of long-term unemployment in what were then called the 'depressed areas' of the UK, a survey financed by the Pilgrim Trust and guided by an influential committee under the chairmanship of William Temple (then Archbishop of York, later Archbishop of Canterbury – a great man who deeply influenced me). This study led to two books (1937 and 1940) and a series of articles on unemployment statistics (for which I was awarded the Francis Wood Memorial Prize of the Royal Statistical Society). The analogy of the 'depressed areas' of the 1930s (both in terms of absolute poverty and of relative poverty compared with more prosperous areas) with the 'underdeveloped countries', as they were then called, is obvious. This study, which involved living with unemployed families, can also be said to have impressed on me the importance of 'human capital' or the 'human face' of development which led to an early and continuing association with UNICEF and other social agencies. A direct involvement with the problems of employment and unemployment in the development process was to be sharply revived later when, in 1968–69, I got involved in building up the World Employment Programme of the ILO and when, in 1971–72, (jointly with Richard Jolly), I headed the ILO Employment Mission to Kenya. The report of this mission for increasing productive employment (1972) is generally considered as highly influential, leading directly to the adoption of the development strategy of 'redistribution with growth' (see Chenery, 1974). This association with Richard Jolly in an ILO employment mission was later repeated in Zambia (1981).

So much for the creditable scenario. The accidental scenario is one where I drifted into becoming a development economist through a linguistic misunderstanding. Shortly after the war, under the Attlee government, I had joined the Ministry of Town and Country Planning for work connected with the nationalization of the development rights in urban land and the calculation of proper compensation for present owners – following upon my Cambridge Ph.D. dissertation in the same area. This of course figured in my C.V. and when I arrived in New York after my recruitment to the UN, in early 1947, I was received by the American Deputy Director of the department, David Weintraub, a sturdy New Dealer. Noting my experience in the Ministry of Town and Country Planning, Weintraub had earmarked me for the 'planned development' section within the nascent Economics Department of the UN since, following US terminology, 'country planning' was a description of development planning. I did not want to disappoint him and by the time the Director of the department (David Owen, an old friend and associate in the Pilgrim Trust Unemployment Enquiry) came back from trade negotiations in Havana, I had become sufficiently interested in development economics to offer or ask to continue in that post. Thus one strand leads from unemployment and depressed areas to an interest in the Third World; the other leads from a Cambridge Ph.D. dissertation on urban land values and the US meaning of the term 'country planning'. Both versions are true and both versions are false, depending on whether you think the half-filled glass is half-full or half-empty!

Once installed in the Development Division of the UN, I had a fairly free hand in finding a first area of work – a free hand because in the early days of UN recruitment things were fairly chaotic, more a collection of individuals than an organization. I think my attention was drawn to problems relating to terms of trade largely by the accident that among my early friends in the UN was Folke Hilgerdt, the Swedish economist who had transferred from the League of Nations where he had studied and reported on international trade problems, including terms of trade. In looking at the data on terms of trade between primary commodities and manufactures (at that time still a satisfactory proxy for trade between rich and poor countries), I came quickly to dissent from the conventional or classical position that terms of trade would move in favour of primary products, as a result of scarcities and increasing marginal costs of production for primary products and of increasing returns and technical progress in manufactured goods. This conventional view was related to an optimistic assumption that international income inequalities would tend to diminish. In Keynes's thinking there would be diminishing marginal efficiency of capital accumulation in the industrial countries and high rates of return on capital in the developing countries – all this leading through trade and capital flows to gradual income equalization. The data seemed to me incompatible with that position (which initially I had shared without much doubt), and on reflection I found a number of what seemed to me good reasons why the empirical data should be so far from supporting the conventional view. I proclaimed this new discovery in a paper presented in December 1949 to the annual meeting of the American Economic Association (AEA) in New York (published in 1950). This article, with its implication of 'export pessimism' and derived policy recommendation of 'import-substituting industrialization' (ISI), became my trade-mark; in spite of many subsequent modulations and qualifications, it still seems to me essentially correct (as maintained in 1984). However, it drew immediate and predictable fire from such supporters of the classical view as Jacob Viner and Gottfried Haberler. With the former I had a fierce debate in Rio de Janeiro in a series of lectures organized in 1950 by the then Finance Minister and Brazilian elder statesman, Eugenio Gudin.

I believe it was between presenting my paper to the AEA in December 1949 and its publication in the *Proceedings* volume of the AER in the summer of 1950 that I discovered that Raul Prebisch, my colleague at the UN, had developed very similar opinions and had also put the problem of poor terms of trade for primary products into the centre of thinking of the Economic Commission for Latin America, of which he was the Director. We formed a close alliance of ideas and were twinned in the economic literature as representing the 'Prebisch-Singer thesis' or PS for short. Subsequently I discovered a similar sympathetic bond with Gunnar Myrdal who was Prebisch's counterpart in Geneva as Director of the UN Economic Commission for Europe. It was this triple alliance cemented by personal friendship which gave me the strength to survive the dreadful McCarthy years in the UN. At that time to be a dissenter was also to be subversive.

Apart from this triple alliance on terms of trade, my policy conclusion for import-substituting industrialization, combined with a belief in constructive government intervention and social welfare planning – derived from Keynesianism, war-time planning in the UK, and the Beveridge plan for a social welfare state (for an indication of my association with the Beveridge Report see 1943). Such aspects created a strong link with India. At that time P. C. Mahanalobis in Calcutta was the great guru of development planning; the first two Indian five-year plans which he created were holy writ. Once again, as in the case of Prebisch and Myrdal, this link was strengthened by personal friendship, in this case with V.K.R.V. Rao who had been my fellow student in Cambridge.

After the experience of the 1980s, the PS thesis has become more or less part of accepted or conventional wisdom, having received the accolade of even the IMF (studies by David Sapsford), of the World Bank (studies by Grilli and Yang) and of the Bank of England (evidence by Andrew Crockett to the House of Commons Treasury and Civil Service Committee). But the policy recommendation of ISI has become even more controversial, in view of the great expansion of manufactured exports by developing countries and the firm belief in many quarters that 'outward-orientated' countries have done better than the 'inward-orientated'.

The expansion of manufactured exports by developing countries was not foreseen by the original PS thesis in 1949–50; it could not have been foreseen then by us nor by anybody else. However by 1964, when Prebisch made his inaugural speech in Geneva as the first Secretary-General of the newly-established UNCTAD, he expressed the hope that the expansion of manufactured exports would dispose of the terms of trade problem. My recent research, however, throws considerable doubt on whether this has in fact been the case. In any event the PS thesis puts more emphasis on the need for industrialization (the final I in ISI) than on import substitution (the IS). It was substitution away from primary production that was required, and export substitution would be as acceptable in contributing to industrialization as import substitution.

As for the belief that outward-orientated tend to do better than inward-orientated countries, I have expressed doubts on this thesis and the way in which the World Bank and economists associated with it in particular have tried to demonstrate the alleged superiority of outward orientation (see 1988a, 1988b and 1988c). My objection is to the definition of 'outward orientation', the empirical facts about such allegedly market-orientated countries as South Korea and the manipulation of statistics. My general conclusion is that outward orientation is a good thing for a developing country if the international climate is favourable (as it tended to be in the 1960s) but ceases to be so when the international climate becomes unfavourable (as it was in the 1980s). Furthermore, outward orientation seems to work better for middle-income countries already half way up the development ladder than for low-income countries.

My involvement in food aid was linked with the vain attempt, as a member of the UN Secretariat, to give the UN a leading role in providing multilateral aid for developing countries. This attempt failed, as part of the general decline and marginalization of the UN during the McCarthy years. The soft-aid agency for developing countries went to the World Bank instead, in the form of its 'second window' – the IDA (International Development Association). However the UN obtained two important consolation prizes in the more liberal Kennedy era of the early 1960s, in the form of the 'Special Fund' for multilateral technical assistance (now called the UN Development Programme or UNDP), and a multilateral food aid programme (the UN World Food Programme or WFP in Rome). Having been responsible on the Secretariat side for the vain attempt to establish a multilateral aid fund in the UN (the still-born SUNFED or Special United Nations Fund for Economic Development), I then became directly involved with both the establishment of the Special Fund, forerunner of the UNDP, and of the World Food Programme. In the latter case I became the chairman of the expert committee which established the basic guidelines of the UNDP (see *Development Through Food: A Strategy of Surplus Utilization,* Food and Agriculture Organization, 1961).

Where was the element of dissent? Many economists as well as development practitioners were contemptuous of food aid as very inferior to financial aid – more or less a throwback to the Stone Age. Moreover, food aid seemed to be entirely a North American matter and linked with US interests in getting rid of burdensome surpluses, subsidizing US farmers and developing US export markets. The original US food aid programme, established in 1954 under Public Law No 480, was in fact disarmingly and honestly described as a Surplus Disposal Programme; later on it was to become 'Food for Peace'! The idea of food aid also met with much scepticism and resistance because of its alleged disincentive effects, by lowering domestic food prices in the recipient countries and thus discouraging local food production.

I dissented from this view for a number of reasons. First of all, there seemed no empirical evidence that the enormous volume of food aid which had gone into Western Europe under the Marshall Plan, and then into South Korea, Israel, Greece and Turkey, had prevented these countries from increasing their own domestic food production. The clinching case was India which received masses of US food aid in the late 1950s and early 1960s and yet managed to use the revenue obtained from the sale of food aid to finance the costly infrastructure investments in transport and irrigation which created the foundation of the Green Revolution in the Punjab and others parts of India. Secondly, I foresaw that the availability of food surpluses would not remain limited to the US and Canada, but would become widespread among the misnamed 'industrial' countries, thus making possible a coordinated and fully multilateral food aid system. Thirdly, it seemed to me that the debate about whether food aid was 'inferior' to financial aid was largely beside the point, since food aid was available where financial aid would not be politically acceptable; thus the question was not whether food aid was better or worse than financial aid, but whether food aid could achieve positive results in terms of economic growth, employment creation and relief of poverty. Fourthly, even though food aid had evil origins in the agricultural policies of the industrial countries which led to the accumulation of surpluses and which on balance were harmful to developing countries, I thought this did not need to prevent us from plucking the flower of development from the nettle of surpluses. Finally, it seemed to me that the disincentive effects were not inherent in food aid but the result of bad administration; on the contrary, properly administered, food aid could be used for the promotion of local agricultural production. For the case of India I pointed out that this is what actually happened (see 1975).

I have picked out a few areas of dissent. This is by no means a full list. If space had permitted I would have mentioned dissent on the present role of the IMF and World Bank and the structural adjustment policies by which they attempt to deal with the debt problem; perhaps more generally, dissent from the currently triumphant neo-liberal ideology according to which the market can do no wrong and the state can do no right. I would have added dissent from the present priorities of the industrial countries putting control of inflation above full employment, as well as their protectionist policies. May I conclude with words from John Stuart Mill (surely an acceptable source to the neo-liberals of today) which could serve as a sort of Dissenters' Charter: 'We can never be sure that the opinion we are stifling is a false opinion; and even if we were sure, stifling it would be an evil still'.

Singer's Major Writings

(1937), *Men Without Work*, Cambridge University Press.
(1940), *Unemployment and the Unemployed*, London: King and Son.
(1943), *Can We Afford Beveridge?*, Fabian Society Research Pamphlet.
(1950), 'Gains and Losses from Trade and Investment in Under-Developed Countries', *American Economic Review*, **40**.
(1972), *Employment, Incomes and Equality: A Strategy for Increasing Productive Employment in Kenya* (with R. Jolly), ILO, 1972.
(1975), 'Food Aid: Disincentive Effects and their Policy Implications' (with P.J. Isenman), *IDS Communication*, No 116, December.
(1981), *Zambia: Basic Needs in an Economy Under Pressure* (with R. Jolly), ILO.
(1984), 'The Terms of Trade Controversy and the Evolution of Soft Financing: Early Years at the UN', in G.M. Meier and D. Seers (eds), *Pioneers of Development*, Oxford University Press/World Bank.
(1988a), 'The World Development Report 1987 on the Blessings of "Outward Orientation": A Necessary Correction', *The Journal of Development Studies*, **24** (2), January.
(1988b), 'Trade Policy and Growth of Developing Countries: Some New Data' (with P. Gray), *World Development*, **16** (3).

(1988c), 'Import Substitution Revisited in a Darkening External Environment' (with P. Alizadeh), in S. Dell (ed), *Policies for Development: Essays in Honour of Germani Corea*, Macmillan. Also in *Asian Journal of Economics and Social Studies*, **5** (3), 1988.

Other References

Chenery, H. *et al.* (1974), *Redistribution with Growth*, A Joint Study by the World Bank's Development Research Center and the Institute of Development Studies at the University of Sussex, Oxford University Press.

Grilli, E.R. and Yang, M.C. (1988), 'Primary Commodity Prices, Manufactured Goods Prices and the Terms of Trade', *World Bank Economic Review*, **2** (1).

International Monetary Arrangements: International Debt Strategy, House of Commons Treasury and Civil Service Committee Session 1988–89, Minutes of Evidence 5 July 1989, p.34.

Sapsford, D. (1985), 'The Statistical Debate on the Net Barter Terms of Trade between Primary Commodities and Manufactures: A Comment and Some Additional Evidence', *Economic Journal*, **95** (397).

Ajit SINGH (born 1940)

It is not difficult to be a dissenting economist if you were born and brought up in India during the years spanning the country's independence in 1947. You grow up in an intellectual climate and a nationalist tradition where it is 'natural' to blame all the country's economic ills on imperialism and colonialism. As an undergraduate at Government College, Chandigarh, Punjab University, I read Sanskrit (for nationalist reasons) and Mathematics as main subjects. However, in order to understand how the material condition of the people could be improved, and I suppose more significantly how India could become a modern, prosperous country, I also studied Economics.

For young men from my social milieu and background, it was normal to go into the civil service, the army or technical professions like engineering or medicine. For those who sought higher education abroad, the usual destination, notwithstanding colonialism, was Britain. It was therefore a double act of defiance when in 1958 at the age of 18 I went to the US, moreover to study economics! Another motivation for going to America was that the educational system there permitted one to work one's way through university, whereas in the UK studying could only have been at my parents' expense.

I studied for a Masters degree in Economics at Howard University. Not only was Howard very cheap, even for foreign students in those days, but also the graduate school functioned in the evenings. This enabled me to work during the day at the Indian Supply Mission and thus to pay my way. Both Howard and living in Washington, D.C. were important formative experiences: direct contact with the black situation made me aware of internal colonialism. In Washington, I greatly enjoyed working at the Library of Congress on my Masters thesis on the Indian steel industry. For my particular subject, the Library's holdings were incredible: it possessed almost every single report of the Indian Tariff Commission going back to the turn of the century. The work on the thesis further reinforced my prejudices: like many before me, I reached the conclusion that to develop properly in the 19th century the Indian steel industry would have required protection, a policy which colonial administrations refused.

After completing my Masters degree at Howard, I went to Berkeley in September 1960 to do a Ph.D. In 1961–62, I was awarded the Alice J. Rosenberg Research Fellowship. While the Free Speech Movement was gathering momentum, Berkeley in the early 1960s provided fertile ground for developing consciousness and defiance against America's imperialist forays. The Bay of Pigs, increasing American involvement in Vietnam and the Civil Rights movement in the South were all significant events for many fellow students and myself. During this period, 'US imperialism' came to be widely discussed among the avant garde of Berkeley students, although the concept was not recognized in respectable academic discourse.

At that time, the Berkeley Economics faculty was, in conventional terms, among the best in the country; notwithstanding heterodox intellects like Gordon, Scitovsky, Minsky and Leibenstein, the department was by and large orthodox in its outlook. To survive the orthodoxy of economic teaching, I had learned a little trick. Faced with an examination question, I would first ask myself how Milton Friedman would answer it and then go on to point out the shortcomings of a Friedmanian answer. The teachers who for various reasons influenced me most at Berkeley were Leibenstein, Scitovsky and Jorgensen.

Robin Marris came to visit Berkeley in 1961–62 when he was working on the economic theory of managerial capitalism. I was his research assistant in the summer of 1961 and, at his invitation, I went to Cambridge (UK) for the calendar year 1963 to do further work on the book and on other aspects of corporate capitalism. This led to a post at the Department of Applied Economics and then afterwards to an Assistant Lectureship in the Faculty of Economics in 1965. As Robin had just left Cambridge to work in Whitehall for the new Labour administration, I took over his course of lectures on the 'Modern Corporation: Social Organization and Economic Performance'.

My first book (with Geoff Whittington), *Growth, Profitability and Valuation* (1968), was an attempt to provide empirical evidence on a range of hypotheses emanating from the debate on the theory of the growth of the firm. The sequel to this book, *Takeovers* (1971), was concerned with the market for corporate control and with the important question of the nature of the competitive selection processes in a modern capitalist economy. I concluded that, contrary to the folklore of capitalism and the maintained hypothesis of much of neoclassical theory, survival for large corporations depends only to a limited extent on profitability or stock market valuation, and is much more a function of corporate size. Thus, a large, relatively unprofitable corporation has a much higher chance of survival than a small profitable one. This result, which has profoundly uncomfortable implications for neoclassical theory, has been sustained in a large number of subsequent studies (see 1990a for a recent review article on the subject). More generally, my research on large corporations and the stock market convinced me early on that if one wished to understand the working of a modern capitalist economy composed of giant multinational corporations and big trade unions, the last place even to start from is the orthodox model of fully idealized neoclassical markets and a profit-maximizing entrepreneur.

The two economists who influenced me most in Cambridge were Kaldor and Reddaway. I later regarded the central ideas of the later Kaldor (increasing returns, dynamic economies of scale and cumulative causation as well as his approach to technical change and equilibrium economics) as being much more powerful than those of Joan Robinson in their undermining of orthodox theory. Also unlike Joan, who was much more of a pure theorist and deeply involved in economic theory for its own sake, Kaldor's chief interest was to use economic theory to understand, to interpret and to change the capitalist world around him. More importantly for me (as I noted in 1989), Kaldor was an apostle of the rapid industrialization of the Third World since, in his view, this was the only means by which the developing countries could improve the standard of living of their people. My research on Third World industrial development, as well as my policy work as a senior economic adviser to the governments of Mexico and Tanzania, where my colleagues and I put forward fully-worked-out 'alternative' economic policy programmes from a reformist left perspective, have been very much influenced by Kaldorian ideas. I also developed an analysis of alternative economic strategies for Mexico (1988) and for Tanzania (1986). (My general views on Third World industrialization are explored in 1979 and 1989.)

Although Reddaway's political perspective is rather different from mine, many of us on the left in Cambridge admired him because of his resolutely empirical approach to economics. In an era when 'a-priorism' dominates and leading economists feel under no obligation even to point to the empirical relevance of their theoretical speculations, let alone systematically to verify their ideas against the touchstone of contemporary economic reality, many of us shared his scepticism about high theory for its own sake, whether of the neoclassical or of the Cambridge variety. These perceptions have been important in the teaching of economics in Cambridge and particularly in the major reform of the Economics Tripos which took place in the mid-1970s. To a significant degree similar ideas inspired a number of us – after the *Economic Journal* (which Reddaway used to co-edit with Champernowne) left Cambridge – to establish the *Cambridge Journal of Economics* of which I was one of the founding editors.

For many years my work on corporate capitalism in advanced countries and on Third World industrialization and economic development ran on parallel lines without much interaction. I was eventually able to bring both strands together within a single intellectual framework with my research on the de-industrialization of the UK economy (see 1977 for my first paper on the subject and 1987 for a recent review). As I observed in 1977:

> It is somewhat ironic that an Indian economist like myself should be discussing the question of the de-industrialization of the UK economy. For one of the major issues in the economic history of India during the 19th century is the contention of a number of Indian historians that, unlike the West European countries, which during that century were undergoing the process of industrial revolution, for the Indian economy it was an age of de-industrialization or ruralization. It is contended that, as a result of free trade and competition with imported machine-made goods from the UK, as well as other policies of the colonial government, traditional Indian manufacturing industry declined during this period, without being replaced by modern industry on a sufficient scale, or by expansion in other sectors of the economy.

In this paper I provided a rigorous conceptualization of the notion of de-industrialization for a modern industrial economy as well as a theoretical framework (built around the concept of long-term structural disequilibrium of an open economy) for its empirical measurement and analysis. More recently I have taken research into questions of international competitiveness, of de-industrialization in advanced countries and of industrialization in the Third World further by considering them within the over-arching context of the 'rise and fall' of the Golden Age; that is, why industrial countries grew at twice their long-term historical trend rate between 1950 and 1973 (the Golden Age), and why they have been unable to sustain that performance since (see 1990b).

Moreover, as many developing countries – particularly the NICs – have achieved a significant degree of industrialization during the last 40 years, work on the corporation economy, takeovers and the stock market has acquired a far wider field of application. In 1990c I examined the question of the desirability of establishing a stock market in a centrally planned economy. Although this paper was written with special reference to China, its argument is more general and applicable to many Third World countries as well. In 1991, Hamid and I provided the first systematic study of corporate financial structures in the NICs. The purpose of this research programme is to analyse the relationship between corporate organization, corporate finance and economic and industrial development. More generally, it is to discover what kinds of financial systems and property rights are most conducive to industrialization in developing countries, as well as to promoting international competitiveness in advanced economies. With the recent change in the political balance of power between the North and the South, and the East and the West, and the onslaught of international financial institutions – with their recipes of liberalization, privatization and deregulation for rich and poor countries alike – this work also has significant and timely policy implications.

Singh's Major Works

(1968), *Growth, Profitability and Valuation* (with G. Whittington), Cambridge University Press.
(1971), *Takeovers: Their Relevance to the Stock Market and The Theory of The Firm*, Cambridge University Press.
(1977), 'U.K. Industry and the World Economy: A Case of De-industrialization?', *Cambridge Journal of Economics*, **1**(2), June.
(1979), 'The "Basic Needs" Approach to Development and the New International Economic Order: the Significance of Third World Industrialization', *World Development*, **7**, June.
(1984), 'The Interrupted Industrial Revolution of the Third World: Prospects and Policies for Resumption', *Industry and Development*, no 12.
(1986), 'Tanzania and the IMF: The Analysis of Alternative Adjustment Programmes', *Development and Change*, **17**.
(1987), 'Manufacturing and Deindustrialization', in the *New Palgrave*, London: Macmillan.
(1988), 'Alternative Policy Options in Mexico' in M.J. Hopkins (ed), *Employment Forecasting*, London: Pinter Publishers.
(1989), 'Third World Competition and De-Industrialization in Advanced Countries', *Cambridge Journal of Economics*, **13**.
(1990a), 'Takeovers in the Stock Market' (with A. Hughes) in J. Eatwell, M. Milgate and P. Newman, *Finance, The New Palgrave*, London: Macmillan.
(1990b), 'The Rise and Fall of the Golden Age' (with A. Glyn, A. Hughes and A. Lipietz) in S. Marglin and J. Schor (eds), *The Golden Age of Capitalism: Reinterpreting the Post War Experience*, Oxford: Clarendon Press.
(1990c), 'The Stock Market in a Socialist Economy', in P. Nolan and D. Furang (eds), *Economic Reform in Post-Mao China*, Cambridge: Polity Press.
(1991), 'Corporate Financial Structures in Developing Countries' (with J. Hamid) in the International Finance Corporation Discussion Paper Series, Washington, D.C.

Piero SRAFFA (1898–1983)   *Gary Mongiovi*

The life and work of Piero Sraffa comprise an important chapter in the intellectual history of the twentieth century. His principal contributions to economic science are well known. In the 1920s he exposed a serious defect in the Marshallian theory of supply under competitive conditions, and set the stage in England for the discovery of the theory of imperfect competition. As a participant – with Joan and Austin Robinson, Richard Kahn and Dennis Robertson – in the discussions on monetary theory and employment that took place in Cambridge during 1927–37, Sraffa contributed to the development of the ideas worked out by Keynes in the *Treatise on Money* (1930) and *The General Theory* (1936). Sraffa's ten-volume edition of the *Works and Correspondence of David Ricardo* (1951–73) is a peerless scholarly achievement. The interpretation of Ricardo's theory of value and distribution advanced by Sraffa in his Introduction to the *Works and Correspondence* can be recognized in retrospect as a crucial element of a larger project, the aim of which was to provide a foundation for the reconstruction of economic theory along the lines established by classical economists and Marx. The culmination of that project was achieved by Sraffa in 1960 with the publication of *Production of Commodities by Means of Commodities*, the work for which he is best remembered.

Sraffa's influence extended beyond economics. Before completing his studies at the University of Turin, he had met the Marxist philosopher and political activist Antonio Gramsci (1891–1937), with whom he became a close friend. From 1919 to 1925 Sraffa was active in the political and philosophical debates that were taking place within Gramsci's *Ordine Nuovo* circle in Turin and Milan; these discussions focused on the role of the intellectual and culture in the socialist movement, and on strategies for mobilizing the labouring classes and fostering among them an ideological commitment to socialism. When Gramsci was incarcerated by the Fascists in 1927, for allegedly subversive activities, Sraffa played a major part, at considerable risk to himself, in an unsuccessful campaign to secure his release. Throughout the period of Gramsci's imprisonment, Sraffa provided encouragement and practical support to Gramsci and his family; he arranged to have books and periodicals sent to Gramsci, and acted as his main link with contemporary intellectual and political developments. Upon Gramsci's death, Sraffa helped to ensure the safe transfer of his papers and notebooks to the Soviet Union.

Sraffa also influenced modern philosophy through his friendship with Ludwig Wittgenstein (1889–1951). Little is known about the exact nature of Sraffa's influence on Wittgenstein or vice versa. Their friendship probably began in 1929. There is anecdotal evidence that in the late 1920s and early 1930s Sraffa had raised doubts about the claim, made by Wittgenstein in the *Tractatus Logico-Philosophicus* (1922), that a proposition and the thing it describes must have the same 'logical form'. The insight, which runs through the philosopher's later work, that meaning depends upon context, was evidently an outcome of discussions with Sraffa. In the Foreword to his *Philosophical Investigations* (1945), Wittgenstein acknowledges the importance of the criticisms which Sraffa 'for many years unceasingly practised on my thoughts. I am indebted to *this* stimulus for the most consequential ideas of this book.'

Sraffa was born on 5 August 1898 in Turin (Italy) to an affluent and cultured Jewish family. His father, Angelo Sraffa (1865–1937), was a respected lawyer and university professor, a passionate opponent of fascism and (according to Salvemini) 'a man of great integrity'; this last trait was passed on to his son. Piero completed his secondary education in Turin, at the prestigious Liceo Massimo D'Azeglio, where he was taught and influenced by the socialist literary scholar Umberto Cosmo (1868–1944) who would later introduce him to Gramsci. In 1916 Sraffa began further studies in the Faculty of Law at the University of Turin. His studies were interrupted in 1917 when he was conscripted into the Italian army where he was made an officer the following year. His term of service ended shortly thereafter, whereupon he returned to Turin to complete his degree.

Sraffa's baccalaureate thesis (1920), written under the direction of the economist Luigi Einaudi (1874–1961), examined the Italian inflation of 1914–20. Sraffa masterfully outlines (with characteristic succinctness) the tangle of irresponsible, corrupt and collusive behaviour, on the part of the banks and the state, which led to the inflation. The theoretical framework implicit in the thesis represents an attempt to move beyond the simple quantity theory of money by looking at the differential impact of price level variations on different groups within the economy (an approach Keynes was to take three years later in his *Tract on Monetary Reform*). The chief policy issues addressed in the thesis involve two related questions: (i) the choice between price stabilization at the post-war parity with gold, or revaluation of the currency to its pre-war gold value; and (ii) the choice between domestic price stability or exchange rate stability. Sraffa came down on the side of stabilization rather than revaluation, and domestic price stability rather than exchange rate stability. His position rests on the recognition that inflation and deflation do not play themselves out in a symmetric fashion: during an inflation, workers must take the initiative in requesting wage increases; until such increases are put into effect, workers experience a gradual erosion of their standards of living, *but they will remain employed*. During a general fall of prices, however, the first step towards renegotiation of labour agreements is taken by entrepreneurs, who seek wage concessions from workers. If the required concessions are not forthcoming, enterprises will find it convenient to suspend their operations and throw workers out of employment. Thus a policy of monetary contraction 'would provoke a stagnation of trade and industry, many failures and high unemployment' (1920, p. 41; my translation).

After completing his degree Sraffa took employment at an Italian bank, with a view to obtaining practical knowledge of the internal operations of financial institutions. He left this employment in the spring of 1921 to spend three months in England, where he attended the lectures of T.E. Gregory and Edwin Cannan at the London School of Economics. During this period he worked at deepening his understanding of monetary problems and of English economic thought. It was on this trip that Sraffa met John Maynard Keynes. Keynes was impressed with the young Sraffa, whose ideas about monetary theory and policy were strikingly compatible with his own. (The arguments of Keynes's *Tract on Monetary Reform*, 1923, parallel those found in Sraffa's thesis; the policy conclusions of the two works are identical and are achieved by similar reasoning. Not surprisingly, Keynes later entrusted Sraffa to prepare an Italian translation of the *Tract*.)

Sraffa spent the academic year 1921–22 attending lectures at the LSE. In 1922, at the invitation of Keynes, he published two articles on the state of the Italian banking system (1922a and 1922b). These described in meticulous detail the incompetence and corruption with which the banks were managed by their directors and regulated by the state. The second article, which appeared in the *Manchester Guardian Supplement*, provoked an angry telegram from Mussolini to Angelo Sraffa demanding that the latter compel his son to publish a retraction. Angelo replied with a firm and dignified refusal, indicating that, since the facts which Piero had reported were a matter of public record and had never been called into question, there were no grounds for a modification of the claims of the original article.

Sraffa's interest in purely theoretical problems began in 1923 when he obtained an academic post at the University of Perugia and was required to deliver a course of lectures on economic theory. The issue to which he then directed his attention was the soundness of the Marshallian theory of supply under competitive conditions. In 1925 he published the outcome of these investigations – his brilliant paper 'Sulle Relazioni fra Costo e Quantità Prodotta'. The argument, simply put, was this: Marshallian partial competitive analysis of price determination requires that movements *along* the market supply and demand curves in a particular industry do not give rise to *shifts* in the positions of the curves. In other words, the prices of other commodities must be left unaffected by movements along the supply and demand curves under consideration. In the long period, rising industry costs can only be due to increases in a factor's price induced by an expansion of the output of a product which utilizes that factor; but if other industries use that factor, *their* prices will be affected by the same increase and the *ceteris paribus* condition is violated. If, on the other hand, the industry under consideration uses so little of the factor that the price of the latter remains unchanged when industry output increases, the cost of production of other goods remains unaffected; but then so will the cost of production of the good under consideration. *Ceteris paribus* is preserved and the partial equilibrium method can be applied, but the industry's unit cost curve will be horizontal. Thus a rising industry cost curve is possible in a competitive market only if the industry is the sole user of a scarce input.

A similar difficulty applies to the case of a falling long-run cost curve. In a competitive setting, the only way to confine the effects of increasing returns to the particular industry under investigation is to suppose that the increasing returns are external to the firm and internal to the industry.

Both of these conditions are rarely observed in reality. Sraffa therefore concluded that if competitive conditions are to be assumed, the most plausible supposition about unit costs is that they are constant. To sum up, the point of the critique is that unless extremely unrealistic assumptions are made about the environment within which firms operate, Marshall's theory cannot accommodate increasing or diminishing returns: the theory is inadequate because it cannot take account of important features of economic reality – in particular, increasing returns.

The following year, Keynes (at Edgeworth's suggestion) invited Sraffa to contribute an article on Marshall's treatment of costs to the *Economic Journal*. In 'The Laws of Returns under Competitive Conditions', Sraffa briefly summarizes the argument of his 1925 paper, and then attempts to show how value theory might proceed beyond the 'first approximation' of constant costs to take account of increasing, and to a lesser extent, diminishing returns. Rejecting the general equilibrium approach as unsuitable for the analysis of practical problems, Sraffa suggests that increasing returns can be accommodated by abandoning the competitive framework – that is, by recognizing that an industry's output is typically limited *not* by rising production costs, but by the difficulty of selling larger quantities of a good without lowering its price. Each firm, then, is to be viewed as having its own distinct market; its price is set so as to maximize profits on the supposition that the relevant demand curve is not infinitely elastic.

The solution suggested by Sraffa in 1926 provided the inspiration for Joan Robinson's work on *The Economics of Imperfect Competition* (1933). Ironically, Sraffa had already abandoned this solution by 1928, for reasons that are connected with his growing understanding of the classical approach to the theory of value and distribution.

The article of 1926 established Sraffa's reputation as an outstanding economic theorist. In 1927 Keynes was able to arrange to have Sraffa appointed as a lecturer at the University of Cambridge. During 1927 and 1928 Sraffa presented lectures on the theory of value. He did not enjoy lecturing, however, and in 1929 gave up his position to become Marshall Librarian and to supervise student research.

In 1931 F.A. von Hayek published a profoundly unfavourable review of Keynes's *Treatise on Money* (1930). Keynes responded with his own, equally unkind, assessment of Hayek's *Prices and Production* (1931), and he asked Sraffa to prepare a review of Hayek's book for the *Economic Journal*. Sraffa's review (1932) attacked the foundations of Hayek's Austrian trade cycle theory. Hayek had begun from the idea that there is a natural rate of interest that corresponds to the equality between saving and investment; trade cycles occur because banks have a tendency to hold their money rates below this natural rate, thereby creating distortions in the economy's capital structure. Sraffa considers an economy in which loans are made in physical units. The interest rate can be conceived in terms of differences between spot and forward prices (measured in units of any *numéraire*) for a particular commodity. Outside of long-period equilibrium, spot and forward prices do not coincide; they therefore define a set of sectoral rates of return, each of which is 'natural' in the sense that is represents the rate at which physically homogeneous goods available at different points in time exchange for one another. The convergence of all of these natural rates to a single equilibrium rate is a necessary outcome of the process by which market prices are brought into equality with long-period prices of production. But this process occurs in both monetary and non-monetary economies. Even if commodities exchange against one another in physical terms, there will be as many natural rates, when the economy is out of equilibrium, as there are commodities; and none of these rates could be considered an equilibrium rate.

The point is that cyclical fluctuations cannot be attributed to the divergence of the money rate of interest from *the* natural rate, since there are a multiplicity of natural rates, all of which will diverge from one another when the economy is not in equilibrium. On the basis of his own analysis, Hayek had advocated a policy of monetary 'neutrality', by which he meant that the effective money supply, MV, should be held constant. Such a policy would imply, for a growing economy, a secular decline of money prices. Sraffa's earlier work on monetary problems had convinced him of the potentially devastating impact of a deflation of prices. The immediate practical aim of his critique, therefore, was to undermine the theoretical rationale for a deflationary monetary policy – a fact which helps to explain the intensity of his, and Keynes's, opposition to Hayek's theory.

In the course of his polemic with Hayek, Sraffa notes that the significance of money lies mainly in the role it plays as a store of value. The deficiencies of Hayek's theory derive from his failure to take account of this aspect of money:

> Money is not only the medium of exchange, but also a store of value, and the standard in which debts, and other legal obligations, habits, opinions, conventions, in short all kinds of relations between men are more or less rigidly fixed. ...The money which [Dr Hayek] contemplates is in effect used purely and simply as a medium of exchange. There are no debts, no money-contracts, no wage-agreements, no sticky prices in his suppositions. Thus he is able to neglect altogether the most obvious effects of a general fall, or rise, of prices (1932, pp. 43–4).

Here Sraffa anticipates ideas that have come to be associated with the post-Keynesian tradition represented by Davidson, Kaldor and Minsky; yet this passage has received relatively little attention because discussions of the Hayek-Sraffa debate have been concerned almost exclusively with the concept of a commodity's own rate of return. Sraffa introduced the concept solely in order to expose the defects of Hayek's trade cycle theory, and he never contemplated the possibility of using it in a constructive, as opposed to a critical, context.

During the 1930s Sraffa continued to discuss monetary theory with Keynes and with other Cambridge colleagues. There is (so far) no clear indication of his attitude towards *The General Theory*. Joan Robinson has suggested that Sraffa harboured some misgivings about the book; it is unlikely, though, that he was antagonistic towards it. Sraffa may have been more sensitive than other members of Keynes's circle to the book's vulnerabilities; in particular, he may have recognized that Keynes's retention of several Marshallian constructs – an interest-elastic investment function, and the notion that the real wage must coincide with labour's marginal product – left the theory of effective demand open to logical attack and to assimilation into the neoclassical mainstream.

In the early 1930s, Sraffa began work on a definitive edition, sponsored by the Royal Economic Society, of the *Works and Correspondence of David Ricardo*, a project that would occupy him for over 20 years. Sraffa's 1925–26 investigations of the laws of return had led him to reflect upon how the classical economists of the nineteenth century had dealt with such phenomena. Probably by 1928, he had come to realize that the classical theory separates the analyses of value, distribution and outputs into distinct logical stages – an altogether different approach from what is found in marginalist (i.e. neoclassical) theory, where all relevant economic variables are determined simultaneously. Thus Ricardo did not suppose that the cost curve is horizontal with respect to output (as Sraffa, following Marshall, had previously believed); rather, he regarded outputs as parametric when determining relative prices, so that questions relating to non-constant returns did not arise. Such questions could be examined at subsequent analytical stages, when the effects of changes in distribution or outputs are investigated.

The essential features of the classical theory (and also of Marx) are outlined by Sraffa in his Introduction to Ricardo's *Works*. Value theoretic issues arose for Ricardo in connection with his attempt to refute Adam Smith's so-called 'adding-up' theory of price, which appears to suggest that the wage rate and the profit rate can vary independently of one another. Ricardo's attempt to demonstrate that this is not the case was complicated by the interdependence of prices and distribution. A change in the wage rate alters relative prices, causing some prices to rise and others to call according to their technical conditions of production; and since the profit rate is itself sensitive to changes in the prices at which inputs and outputs are evaluated, the relationship between the wage and the profit rates could not easily be isolated.

Ricardo's first solution to this difficulty, according to Sraffa, took the form of a 'corn-model' in which the rate of return in agriculture is asserted to regulate the rate of profit in all lines of production. In agriculture, Ricardo supposed, wages, output and inputs are all comprised of the same physical commodity – grain. Taking the output of corn, the technical conditions of its production and the corn-wage of agricultural workers as given, the profit rate could be determined without reference to prices; the necessary connection between wages and the profit rate could thus be clearly seen. Malthus pointed out to Ricardo that workers consume things other than corn and that the capital used in agriculture is not comprised entirely of that grain, so that the corn model does not really solve the problem of the interdependence between prices and distribution. Ricardo had to admit the validity of Malthus's point and in his *Principles of Political Economy and Taxation* (1821), he sought to avoid the interdependence problem by supposing that ratios of embodied labour-time are close approximations to relative prices. He realized, though, that the ratios at which commodities exchange do not in general coincide with their labour values; his ongoing search for an invariable standard of value reflects his awareness of the tentative nature of this approach. A correct solution was provided by Sraffa in his book of 1960.

The basic elements of the classical theory were identified by Sraffa in the late 1920s. Aside from the polemic with Hayek, virtually all of his subsequent scientific work was concerned with clarifying and refining that theoretical framework. The equations contained in Parts I and II of Sraffa's *Production of Commodities* summarize, in rigorously formal terms, the classical theory of value and distribution.

The fundamental data of Sraffa's model are: (i) the level and composition of the social product; (ii) the technical conditions of production; and (iii) the profit rate (or alternatively the real wage). When combined with the supposition that under competitive conditions market forces establish a tendency towards a uniform rate of return across sectors, these data determine relative prices and the remaining distribution variable. In effect, the model of *Production of Commodities* can be said to generalize Ricardo's corn model to the case of more than one basic commodity, where a 'basic commodity' is one that is used directly or indirectly in the production of all commodities.

Sraffa also provided a solution, in the form of the 'standard commodity', to the problem that had hindered Ricardo's attempts to expose the connection between the real wage rate and the profit rate. The standard commodity is a composite constructed in such a way that the proportions in which commodities appear as outputs are equal to the proportions in which they are used as inputs. When the real wage is measured in terms of such a commodity, the relationship between the wage and the profit rate will be linear: $r = R(1-w)$, where R is the maximum possible profit rate and w is the real wage measured in units of the standard commodity. The purpose of the device is simply to demonstrate the validity of Ricardo's insight that the real wage and the profit rate cannot vary independently of one another.

Production of Commodities was subtitled 'Prelude to a Critique of Economic Theory'. Sraffa himself did not carry out the critique, but he clearly identified the lines it would have to follow. The fact that commodities are produced by commodities implies that autonomous changes in the profit or wage rate can (and generally will) influence any single commodity's price in a complex and non-monotonic fashion. Thus, an increase in the wage rate might result in a *decrease* in the price of a commodity the production of which requires a relatively high proportion of labour to produced means of production.

> The reason for this seeming contradiction is that the means of production of an industry are themselves the product of one or more industries which may in their turn employ a still lower proportion of labour to means of production (and the same may be the case with these latter means of production; and so on); in that case, the price of the product ... might *fall* in terms of its means of production (1960, p.13).

Since underlying the production of any commodity are numerous layers of production located at successively earlier conceptual stages, there is no way to identify a production process as unambiguously 'labour intensive' or 'capital intensive'. Moreover, subsequent work by P. Garegnani, L. Pasinetti and others has demonstrated that, owing to this feature of capitalist production, the capital intensity of production need not be a monotonically decreasing function of the profit rate; that is to say, there is no logical basis for the construction of a demand curve for capital – or indeed for any factor of production. In as much as the conventional theory of distribution is firmly grounded in the substitution mechanism implicit in such factor demand curves, Sraffa's work has powerfully destructive implications for orthodox economics.

The brilliance of Sraffa's theoretical work is widely acknowledged. Its significance is less easy to assess, in part because the research programme to which it has given rise is still in the early stages of development.

It appears, first of all, that Sraffa's work opens the way to an analysis of distribution that can take account of the role that history and institutions play in determining the division of the social product. A similar approach can be taken to the analysis of consumption patterns, which appear in reality to have very little basis in the price-elastic demand functions of conventional analysis. By removing the logical basis for interest-elastic investment functions and wage-elastic labour demand curves, Sraffa has also cleared the way for a rehabilitation of the theory of effective demand – an area in which much fruitful work has been done since 1960.

Sraffa's Major Writings

(1920), *L'Inflazione Monetaria in Italia durante e dopo la Guerra* (privately printed baccalaureate thesis), Tipo-grafica Salesiana.
(1922a), 'The Bank Crisis in Italy', *Economic Journal*, **32**.
(1922b), 'The Current Situation of the Italian Banks', *Manchester Guardian Commercial – The Reconstruction of Europe*, No 11.
(1925), 'Sulle Relazioni fra Costo e Quantità Prodotta', *Annali di Economia*, **2**.
(1926), 'The Laws of Returns under Competitive Conditions', *Economic Journal*, **36**.
(1930), '"A Criticism" and "Rejoinder": Contributions to a Symposium on "Increasing Returns" and the Representative Firm', *Economic Journal*, **40**.
(1932), 'Dr Hayek on Money and Capital', *Economic Journal*, **42**.
(1951–73), *Works and Correspondence of David Ricardo* (Vols I–X), Cambridge University Press.
(1960), *Production of Commodities by Means of Commodities*, Cambridge University Press.
(1961), 'Production of Commodities: A Comment', *Economic Journal*, **71**.

Ian STEEDMAN (born 1941)

Born in London in 1941, I went to school in London and then studied at the Universities of Cambridge (1961–64) and Manchester (1964–67). Subsequently, a year's research work at the University of Florence, as a Nuffield Foundation Fellow (1970–71), was also influential in the formation of my style of work. My interest in the writing of Sraffa began earlier, however, when Maurice Dobb ended a Cambridge lecture in the history of economic thought with the almost throw-away remark that Mr Sraffa had recently published a small but very important book. I was never taught by Sraffa but his work has, without question, been by far the greatest single influence on my own. I refer here not only to Sraffa's influence on (some of) the questions in which I have been interested, but also to the example of his immense (and usually successful) effort to be precise. It has never seemed to me that vagueness is a virtue in the work of a 'dissenting' economist who should, on the contrary, match or surpass the degree of precision achieved by the 'orthodox' economist. 'It is better to be vaguely right than precisely wrong' is a self-indulgent slogan, giving too much encouragement to what is both vague and wrong.

One common misunderstanding of the so-called 'capital theory debates' of the 1960s was the idea that Cambridge theorists were obliged to ignore the heterogeneity of primary inputs: in fact, homogeneous labour had been assumed, and the role of land ignored, purely for simplicity. It was partly for this reason that J.S. Metcalfe and I wrote 'Reswitching and Primary Input Use' (1972a) which showed that, in the presence of a *positive* rate of return on the value of produced inputs, the competitively chosen land-labour ratio in production might be *positively* related to the rent-wage ratio. It followed from this that a number of standard theorems, in the two-commodity/two-primary input model, fail in the presence of a positive rate of return on capital. Thus the relative output of a commodity need not be increasing with respect to its relative price; a more intense demand for, say, the labour-intensive commodity might be associated with a lower price for that commodity and a lower wage rate; and a higher labour supply could be associated with a higher wage rate and a higher relative price of the labour-intensive commodity. As might be expected, this has a number of implications for familiar results concerning production possibility frontiers, tax incidence theory and Heckscher-Ohlin-Samuelson (H-O-S) trade theory (see below).

Also in 1972, I published a critique of Jevons's theory of capital, emphasizing that his rather 'Austrian' approach to capital and interest theory was just as vulnerable to internal criticism as was any $Q = F (K,L)$ version of marginal distribution theory. It was shown, for example, that his concepts of 'amount of investment' and the 'average period' of production failed in the presence either of compound interest or (independently) of fixed capital. Jevons was not in fact able to establish his claimed relationships between the interest rate, the 'average period' and the value of capital per man; and only by supposing simple rather than compound interest was he able to avoid the possibility of reswitching between techniques (see 1972b). I have maintained my interest in capital theory, applying it in more recent years, for example, to technical progress theory (see 1985). It was thus shown that, in an input-output economy, Hicks-neutral technical change is virtually impossible when there is a choice of technique – as is normally assumed, after all, in discussions of Hicksian neutrality and bias in technical change.

An interest in Sraffa-based capital theory led to a criticism of H-O-S trade theory, both when it starts from endowments of land and labour (see above) and when it postulates given endowments of 'capital' and labour. To dissent from H-O-S trade theory was not, however, to defend 'Ricardian' trade theory, for both Ricardo's own treatment, in the famous Chapter VII of his *Principles*, and the modern textbook travesty of that treatment are subject to capital theoretic criticism which, at root, is the same as that directed at H-O-S theory. Whether one is discussing H-O-S theory, textbook 'Ricardian' theory or Ricardo's own theory, one must recognize that, other than under fluke technical conditions, relative commodity prices depend on the rate of profit (interest), so that 'factor intensities' do not reflect technical conditions alone. This leads to difficulties for the internal logic of each of the kinds of trade theory referred to. In Ricardo's theory, for example, the pattern of trade cannot, in fact, be predicted from a knowledge of technical conditions alone, since autarky prices would also depend on distributional considerations. It then follows, in turn, that a trading country need not necessarily achieve a (comparative static) positive gain from trade. In H-O-S theory with land, labour and a common positive rate of interest in both countries, the pattern of trade theorem is not logically valid in its price form; trade need not harm a country's scarce factor, and uniqueness of international equilibrium is a special case. If the interest rate differs between the two countries, the position is far worse for H-O-S theory. And so it is when the endowments are taken to consist of labour and given 'values of capital'; in this case only the Rybczynski theorem survives. The reason for this is that commodity prices are fixed by assumption in the Rybczynski theorem and hence the dependence of prices on distribution (which undermines so much standard trade theory) can play no role here. It need hardly be added that the dependence of relative commodity prices on the rate of return to capital is the root of *all* the capital theory issues discussed in the 1960s. (For a range of relevant articles, see 1979a; for an attempt at an alternative approach to trade theory, see 1979b).

Any would-be 'dissenting' economist who dissents from one orthodoxy only to defend another is not a dissenter but a dissembler. Sraffa's work provided the basis not only for an acute criticism of certain marginalist theories but also for the critique of 'Anglo-Saxon' Marxian economic theory. (Some would argue that Sraffa's work also provides a superior framework for rebuilding classical/Marxian theory without some of its previous flaws, but that is another matter.) This line of thought led to *Marx after Sraffa* (1977) in which it is shown how Sraffa's method of analysis can be used to reject and replace Marx's theory of the profit rate and prices of production. It was internally inconsistent of Marx to attempt to define the rate of profit directly in terms of labour values when, by his own account, the very presence of a uniform rate of profit required that labour values not be proportional to prices of production (other than under fluke conditions). For the rate of profit is, by definition, calculated in terms of prices of production. Closely related to this point is the fact that Marx was quite wrong to reject Ricardo's idea that some commodities play no role in the determination of the profit rate. The fact is that, under reasonable assumptions, the rate of profit and prices of production are determined by real wages and their (direct and indirect) conditions of production; labour values play no role whatever in this determination. Moreover, this Sraffian approach can be used to analyse the labour process and can readily deal with heterogeneous labour *without* any need to 'reduce' all forms of labour to one 'simple' form. It was shown, too, how Marx's 'labour value' accounting for fixed capital is seriously misleading and how, in the presence of joint production (which is, empirically, the norm), positive profits can coexist with 'negative surplus value' calculated in Marx's additive value accounts. (Joint production is also, it may be noted, an issue over which the careful theorist has to dissent from certain statements made by Sraffa, for his usual precision failed him occasionally in this particular area, in relation to basic commodities, the maximum rate of profit and the choice of technique. Interestingly, joint production can also cause difficulties for certain propositions in marginalist theory: it seems to be a problem for many! See, for example, 1988 and 1990.)

Although there is a notably objective cast to Sraffa's economic writings, this obviously need not prevent someone greatly influenced by Sraffa from taking an interest in the source and nature of the purposes and preferences of economic agents. I have thus been led to argue that it is intrinsically impossible for agents' beliefs and preferences to be completely independent of what is and has been happening in the economy (with immediate implications for welfare 'assessments'), and that P.H. Wicksteed was correct to maintain that rationality and altruism are compatible with one another. Similarly, the familiar Fisherian theory of interest becomes suspect as soon as one recognizes that wealth ownership can be valued *per se*, so that saving is not merely a means of shifting consumption through time; Fisher himself occasionally recognized the phenomenon in question! (The three works referred to here may all be found in 1989.)

I do not distinguish sharply between my interest in economic theory and my interest in the history of economic thought. (But then I am not 'a historian's historian of thought'.) It is in this light that I have studied Ricardo, Marx, Jevons and Wicksteed – and, on occasion, the relations between them. Reference has already been made to some of my relevant work, so here I mention only a discussion of Marx's misuse of Ricardo in 'Marx on Ricardo', which analyses the role of heterogeneous labour in classical theory and in Marx, as well as a discussion of Wicksteed's 1884 critique of *Das Kapital, Volume I* (see 1981 and 1989 respectively).

The proper job of the dissenting economist is to search for the flaws in *all* economic theories; it is not to proclaim loudly the shortcomings of some particular kind(s) of theory and then to gloss over those of some other, favoured kind. And if the dominating presence of one particular, mainstream orthodoxy should lead 'dissenting' economists to forget this, they would cease to deserve the title of dissenter. Kalecki, Keynes and Sraffa, for example, were great economists but were naturally not infallible. Since one can never expect an economic theory to be better than partially true, and can always expect that there will be a ready supply of people to maintain that 'their' theory is an exception to this rule, the truly dissenting economist will always have plenty of useful work to do.

Steedman's Major Writings
(1972a), 'Reswitching and Primary Input Use' (with J.S. Metcalfe), *Economic Journal*, **82**, March.

(1972b), 'Jevons' Theory of Capital and Interest', *Manchester School*, March.

(1977), *Marx after Sraffa*, London: New Left Books.

(1979a), *Fundamental Issues in Trade Theory*, London: Macmillan.

(1979b), *Trade amongst Growing Economies*, Cambridge University Press.

(1981), 'Marx on Ricardo' in I. Bradley and M. Howard (eds), *Classical and Marxian Political Economy Essays in Honour of Ronald L. Meek*, London: Macmillan.

(1985), 'On the "Impossibility" of Hicks-Neutral Technical Change', *Economic Journal*, **95**, September.

(1988), *Sraffian Economics*, Two Volumes, Aldershot: Edward Elgar.

(1989), *From Exploitation to Altruism*, Cambridge: Polity Press.

(1990), *Joint Production of Commodities* (edited with N. Salvadori), Aldershot: Edward Elgar.

Josef STEINDL (born 1912) *Nina Shapiro*

Vienna was Steindl's birthplace (14 April 1912) and home for much of his life. There he received his academic training in economics (at what is now the Economic University) and his first position in the field, at the Austrian Institute for Economic Research. The position was obtained upon completion of his doctorate in 1935 and held until the German annexation of Austria, when he and other like-minded intellectuals lost their jobs due to their hostility to the Nazi regime. In 1938 he emigrated to England where he worked, first, as a lecturer at Balliol College, Oxford (1938–41), and then as a researcher at the Oxford University Institute of Statistics (1941–50). Upon his return to Vienna in 1950, he resumed his position at the Austrian Institute for Economic Research. Steindl worked there until his retirement in 1978 and, except for a year spent as a visiting professor at Stanford University (1974–75), he remained in Vienna. In 1970 the University of Vienna awarded him an honorary professorship, and in 1987 an International Conference on his work was held in Trieste, Italy.

Steindl's university days (the early 1930s) were a time of great economic hardship and political upheaval. The ideas dominant at the university were the anti-rationalist, nationalist ones connected with the developing Fascist movements. These ideas, and especially the militarism they supported, were repugnant to Steindl, and while his upbringing had been apolitical, he 'could not fail to be impressed' by the 'unemployment and misery' that surrounded him (see 1989); other personal reminiscences can be found in 'Reflections on the Present State of Economics' (1984).

The Austrian school of economics, which was then centred in Vienna, provided a counter to the reactionary intellectual currents of the day. Its liberal views were embraced by Steindl, who learned them from Richard Strigl, a professor at the university and pupil of one of the Austrian school's founders, Bohm-Bawerk. While Steindl's acceptance of the school's economic doctrines was short-lived, the school and its members played an important role in his life. The Austrian Institute for Economic Research, where he was employed upon his graduation and worked for many years, was a creation of the school (Ludwig von Mises was the institute's founder). A member of the school and associate of the institute, Gerhard Tintner, introduced Steindl to the work of Keynes; moreover, it was the support of von Mises, Haberler, Hayek and others of the school which secured Steindl his 1938 post at Balliol College. Without their help, his emigration to England would not have been possible.

The years spent in England were critical to Steindl's career. It was there that he developed his theoretical system, which is Keynesian in content but Marxian in outlook. The approach is historical and the analysis dynamic; while the historical perspective was the result of Marx's influence, the Keynesian framework was the result of Kalecki's, who was at the Oxford Institute of Statistics when Steindl joined it and worked there with him until 1944. Kalecki was the most important influence in Steindl's life; he 'inspired' his work and was its 'reference system' (1984).

During his first years at the institute in Oxford, Steindl worked on the issues of firm profitability, growth and competition. In *Small and Big Business* he investigated the problem of the large firm's dominance and the related question of the small firm's survival, both of which were concerns of the time. Industry was highly concentrated; there was little evidence of the economists' 'perfect competition' or of Marshall's 'upward movement' of small entrepreneurs into the ranks of the large ones. Clearly the large-sized firm had important competitive advantages, and Steindl wanted to know what the source of these advantages was and how, in the face of them, small firms could coexist with large ones (which they did, in fact, do).

The investigation began with the cost factors which favoured large enterprise, the plant- and firm-level economies of scale. While these economies were not ubiquitous, they were significant, for the technology was capital-using (mechanized) and its development required large investments in industrial research. Only the big concern could afford these investments, and since it could also afford any innovation open to the small firm – whereas the small one could not realize the innovations (and plant sizes) open to the large one – the latter was 'technically superior' and would, as a rule, have lower costs than the small concern.

Of course the cost advantages of large size would not necessarily bring higher ('abnormal') profits. Competition could keep down the profits of large firms, as traditionally assumed. But in the case of the large firm, there would not *be* much competition, for neither enterprise formation nor firm growth would produce many large-size concerns. Firm growth would not do so, because of the financial frailty of the small enterprise, whose contingency reserves were slim and capital too restricted to secure large funds or obtain them on favourable terms. And the capital restrictions on borrowing that impeded the growth of a small firm would also impede the founding of a large one. Only the wealthy could start up a large concern.

Large capitals were 'scarce'; it was because they were scarce that the lower costs of large-scale production brought extraordinary profits. The higher profit of the large firm was a 'differential rent', and its dominance was not the result of technology alone, but of technology in conjunction with the economic conditions under which it operated. For while it was economies of scale that made the large capitals more productive, it was the capital market's ('imperfect') operation and inequities of wealth distribution that made the capitals scarce (this implication of the analysis is developed further in 1945b).

Market 'imperfections' were also important in the case of the small firm's survival. Labour market segmentation gave the small firm the opportunity of drawing on a cheaper labour supply (the unorganized segment) than the one available to the large firm, while the imperfections of the product market protected the small firm's sales from the competition of lower-cost producers. Because the small firm had its loyal clientele ('goodwill'), its market could not be invaded without a special sales effort, and in many cases the revenue that could be gained through that effort would not justify the cost (the price reductions of advertizing expenses). The other important factor in the small firm's survival was the high social valuation of the entrepreneurial position, the importance given to being one's own boss, which kept up the supply of small entrepreneurs and led them to hold on to their business in spite of the often negligible profit and odds against success. (Steindl returns to this issue of the small firm's survival in 1965.)

While *Small and Big Business* dealt with the microeconomic effects of firm size, the work that followed showed the critical macroeconomic ones. This work, *Maturity and Stagnation in American Capitalism*, was also done at the institute in Oxford. It was the result of a research project on the Great Depression which had been undertaken at Kalecki's suggestion.

The economic crisis of the 1930s was difficult to explain in terms of the laissez-faire doctrines of orthodox economics. Unemployment was hardly an 'optimal' economic outcome, and the unemployment of the period was massive: a third of the labour force in the case of the American economy, and a greater proportion in that of the German (44% in 1932). It was inconceivable that so many could have been unemployed 'voluntarily', and because the unemployment was protracted as well as massive (in America it lasted over an entire decade), it could not have been 'frictional' either. But while the market's hand in the crisis was evident and the depression was certainly no 'accident' (which was the orthodox economists' explanation), it was not clear what 'exactly' had caused the stagnation. It was this that Steindl set out to discover in the work that culminated in *Maturity and Stag-*

nation (Steindl's account of the work's progression is in his contribution to 1989).

The roots of the crisis were found in a long-run development: oligopoly. When the output of an industry was concentrated in the hands of a few large firms, competition fell off, and when competition fell off, so did investment. It was the growth of oligopoly that had brought on the stagnation. Because the concentration of industry was a slow process, the stagnation had come on gradually through the exhaustion of the system's growth potentialities – its 'maturation'.

The importance of competition was due to the interconnections between investment, capacity utilization and profit margins. Because investment increased output capacity, and unused capacity depressed the firm's profits, investment would be cut if capacity utilization could not be kept up. The maintenance of normal capacity-utilization rates was essential: sustained investment was impossible without it, and what had kept utilization rates at their normal levels in the past was the competition that occurred when they fell below them. When investment in an industry overshot demand or depressed conditions brought sales down, a competitive war would break out. Firms would try to pass the excess capacity off onto their rivals, and the special sales efforts undertaken for this purpose would drive the higher-cost 'marginal' firms out. The excess capacity that depressed investment would be eliminated through the elimination of firms.

The elimination of excess capacity was the macroeconomic function of competition, and because it was achieved through price reductions and/or sales cost increases, competition not only kept utilization rates up, it also held profit margins down. It kept them at a level that was just sufficient for the financing of the industry's growth. This, also, had important macroeconomic consequences, for it meant that the profit share would fall when the growth rate did. The long-run effect of an investment decline would be a real wage rise, and instead of unemployment rising when investment fell, consumption would (workers' 'saving propensity' being less than capitalists').

The effects of an investment decline under oligopolistic conditions were quite different. In this case, the decline would increase unemployment in the long run as well as in the short run. There would be no real wage (consumption) increase to offset the negative effect of the decline in demand, nor would there be the 'other side' of the profit margin squeeze – restoration of normal utilization rates. Excess capacity cannot be knocked out of an oligopolistic industry through the elimination of firms: there are no small, financially weak firms to eliminate. All the oligopolist can do in the face of an unwanted increase in excess capacity is cut investment, and since the investment cuts of one firm depress the sales of others, the oligopolistic method of excess capacity elimination is self-defeating. Instead of reducing the excess capacity in industry, investment cuts enlarge it, and the increase in excess capacity reduces investment further. In an oligopolistic economy, investment declines are cumulative, and while the contractions of a competitive economy give way to expansion, those of the oligopolistic one result in stagnation.

The oligopolization of industry ends the cut-throat competition that revitalizes investment, and by the turn of the century the American economy (the one examined in the work) had been oligopolized. The industrial concentration of the nineteenth century thus set the stage for the stagnation of the twentieth. And while it was the oligopolistic structure of industry that pushed the downturn of the 1930s into the first decade-long slump, it was the structure's development that had brought it on. The 'primary' decline, firstly the fall in investment, was caused by the profit margin increase that came with industrial concentration. The enlargement of margins depressed demand (reduced real wages), which generated excess capacity and thus reduced investment. While the rise in security values that occurred in the early part of the century held off the cumulative decline, when the rise ended, in the crash of 1929, the full effects of the concentration were felt. The economy collapsed and remained depressed until an exogenous development, the war, pulled it up.

While the depression was an outgrowth of the oligopolization of industry, the oligopoly itself was a product of the competition that preceded it. Because the larger firms won out in the competitive warfare, competition and concentration were two sides of the same process. And what underlay them both was the 'aggressiveness' of business saving which seeks investment outlets and, under competitive conditions, finds them in the markets of small-sized firms. The oligopoly that impaired accumulation was thus created by the process itself; far from being a chance event, the depression was rooted in the logic of capitalist development.

Although there was not much interest in *Maturity and Stagnation* when the work first appeared – unemployment was low and the post-war growth boom had begun – it has since become a classic in the field. Its macroeconomic analysis has formed the basis of the Marxian theory of monopoly capitalism (Paul Sweezy was one of the few to recognize the work's significance), and when the economic climate changed in the 1970s (stagnation occurred again), the work became widely known, with a second edition printed in 1976. In the meantime Steindl had further developed his analysis (1966), and in the late 1970s and 1980s applied it to the problems of the post-war era.

The most important economic development of the post-war era was a political one: the increased economic role of government. This had a positive effect on employment in the first decades of the era; indeed, as detailed in 'Stagnation Theory and Policy', government expenditure and fiscal policies of the 1950s and 1960s were largely responsible for the high growth of the period. Although the expenditure was financed out of taxes rather than borrowings, because the taxes were levied on 'large savers' (firms), the overall effect was expansionary. Demand and capacity utilization increased, which stimulated investment, as did the business confidence that was created by the political acceptance and assurance of Keynesian (demand maintenance) policies.

The international political climate, and especially economic cooperation among Western nations, were also critical factors in the expansion. The liberalization of trade relations opened the European markets to America and transferred a 'backlog of innovations' to Europe, those that had been developed in America during the interwar period. Because these were embodied in new American products, trade expansion with America transferred the technology across national borders (1980), and this in turn greatly boosted growth in Europe through its effect on the investment incentive. Technical progress can generate an upward trend if the economic conditions are propitious (1982), and in the Europe of the time they were: the Marshall Plan provided the finance required to exploit the technology, while the buoyant demand provided the market (the importance of economic conditions in the productivity growth of the period is discussed further in 1985).

Trade liberalization not only brought new markets and investment opportunities, but also new competition. As trade barriers were lifted, foreign competition intensified which had a salutary effect. It held down profit margins, as did the increased bargaining strength of the workers, which had been enhanced by tight labour market conditions. Wage pressure along with foreign competition kept the wage share constant, and because real wages rose with productivity growth, the overcapacity that normally halts an expansion did not materialize (1989).

But the real wage growth that sustained the expansion had its long-run costs. As the incomes of workers grew, so did their expectations and demands. The increased demands of workers, especially for worker participation, provoked a political reaction against the unions and the welfare state that was associated with their strength, and it was this change in the political climate that brought the post-war growth boom to a halt. The stagnation of the 1970s was set off by a political development – the shift to the deflationary policies of the monetarists – though there were other, more purely economic, factors at work as well. The income growth of the 1950s and 1960s, along with the inequity of its distribution, had increased household saving which had a depressive effect on demand. Oligopoly also played a role in the crisis, though not the same one as in the 1930's stagnation. Large concerns had become increasingly preoccupied with the ends of market power and dominance, and since these were achieved through mergers and takeovers, financial considerations had come to dominate their investment decisions. Real estate and speculative investment had grown in importance at the expense of the more productive investment in equipment, technology and new products (1989).

Just as Marx 'lived very much in his times', Steindl has lived very much in his. From the early writings on industrial concentration to the most recent work on the saving rate (1990a), the economic problems of his era have been Steindl's main concern. Few of his contemporaries (or ours) have been as engrossed as he in these problems, and fewer still have provided as penetrating an analysis of their causes.

Steindl's Major Writings
(1945a), *Small and Big Business: Economic Problems of the Size of Firms*, Oxford: Basil Blackwell.

(1945b), 'Capitalist Enterprise and Risk', *Oxford Economic Papers*, no. 5.

(1952), *Maturity and Stagnation in American Capitalism*, Oxford: Basil Blackwell. Reprinted, with new introduction, by Monthly Review Press, 1976.

(1965), *Random Processes and the Growth of Firms*, London: Hafner Publishing Co.

(1966), 'On Maturity in Capitalist Economies', in *Problems of Economic Dynamics and Planning: Essays in Honour of Michal Kalecki*, Oxford: Pergamon Press.

(1979), 'Stagnation: Theory and Policy', *Cambridge Journal of Economics*, 3.

(1980), 'Technical Progress and Evolution', in D. Sahal (ed), *Research, Development and Technological Innovation*, Lexington: Lexington Books.

(1982a), 'Technology and the Economy: the Case of Falling Productivity Growth in the 1970s', in D. Sahal (ed), *Transfer and Utilization of Technical Knowledge*, Lexington: Lexington Books.

(1982b), 'The Role of Household Saving in the Modern Economy', *Banca Nazionale del Lavoro*, no. 140.

(1983), 'The Control of the Economy', *Banca Nazionale del Lavoro*, no. 146.

(1984), 'Reflections on the Present State of Economics', *Banca Nazionale del Lavoro*, no. 148.

(1985), 'Structural Problems of the Crisis', *Banca Nazionale del Lavoro*, no. 154.

(1989), 'From Stagnation in the 30s to Slow Growth in the 70s', in M. Berg (ed), *Political Economy in the Twentieth Century*, Deddington: Philip Alan.

(1990a), 'Capital Gains, Pension Funds, and the Low Savings Ratio in the United States', *Banca Nazionale del Lavoro*.

(1990b). *Economic Papers 1941–88*, London: Macmillan. This reprints most of Steindl's important papers.

Paul STREETEN (born 1917)

One of my childhood memories is that of the Viennese court singers or court musicians. These were not performers at the court of the Habsburgs, but musicians who sang and played in the courtyard of the blocks of flats in which we lived. The inhabitants of these flats would wrap a few coins into newspaper and throw the packet out of the window into the court. But since these musicians, particularly the organ grinders, frequently did not add to celestial harmonies but made disturbing noises, the money was often thrown to these court musicians to make them go away and permit peace and quiet to be restored.

These court singers became for me paradigmatic figures that later, when I learned economics, made me sceptical of the national income as a measure of economic welfare, and of the assumptions of neoclassical economics generally. Here was an instance of people who were able to extract money, not for a benefit bestowed, but for the removal of a self-created nuisance. They did not produce a good, but a 'bad', and received in payment an anti-bad. Was this a rare exception or was it typical of many other payments normally counted as net benefits? Nuisances or 'bads' can be generated by our enemies, by nature or by our productive activities themselves.

Those generated by our enemies call for an army and its weapons of defence. Many would not regard these as additions to our economic welfare, though they may be a necessary condition for carrying on production. The 'bads' generated by nature call for the anti-bads of protection against cold and extreme heat, against the vicissitudes of the weather, against starvation, everything that is needed to keep the body in productive shape. Should we then not deduct heating appliances, air conditioners, clothes, food etc also from our national accounts, not perhaps as regrettable necessities like defence, but as preconditions of net income?

Finally, what about the anti-bads that remove nuisances, such as the bads created by pollution? Scrubbers that reduce air pollution from chimneys would be an example. Going one small step further, how should we account for the means used to meet desires aroused by advertising and the social pressures of emulation? Everyone is reminded constantly from all directions that wives must continue to be charming and nice-smelling enough and husbands dandruff-free in order to be re-chosen every day at breakfast. If people buy deodorants because the fear has been evoked in them that they will be ostracized if they do not buy them, is this not exactly parallel to the court singers, or to the kidnapper asking for ransom or to the blackmailer asking for money (though he may not have created the occasion for the threat of blackmail)? Barbara Ward (Lady Jackson) once proposed to me that we should found a Society for the Propagation of Anti-Bads.

There is, of course, as Nordhaus and Tobin have pointed out, a danger that a consistent application of this line of reasoning would make the national income tautologically equal to zero. At best only frills and luxuries would be left over as adding to our net welfare. And even the desire for them might well be the result of an effective promotion campaign. Are then all created desires that require resources to fill a gaping void to be deducted from net welfare and to be categorized as anti-bads?

Surely not. Some of the finest as well as some of the basest desires are created by 'artificial' stimulation. The longing for truth, goodness and beauty, just like the desire to have the organ grinder leave, has been created, in the former case by educators, books, orchestras and role models, in the second case by the musician. The organ grinder may produce such appalling noises that we pay him to take away his organ, or he may produce such heavenly melodies that we are happy to give up a fortune for the pleasure of listening.

It follows that we cannot do without value judgements in deciding which are goods and which are anti-bads, which items add to our welfare and which bring us just back to square one. It was this discovery that made me look on economics as a moral study, or at least a study shot through with value judgements, as well as a study full of controversial, sometimes dubious, often implicit, assumptions.

At the same time, when Lionel Robbins wrote that the science of economics cannot make interpersonal comparisons of utility, I was startled. Surely, everyone of us makes them daily as matters of fact, not as matters of moral judgement. When parents decide on what their children need, or when we decide to which charities to subscribe, or when the Chancellor of the Exchequer decides on new taxes, a large part of these decisions has nothing to do with morality but with observations of comparative needs, abilities, talents, etc. Of course, questions of desert will also enter. But to say that such comparisons are 'impossible' or 'meaningless' or 'illegitimate' is silly in the technical sense (as defined by the philosopher C.D. Broad); that is, denying the possibility of legitimacy of something that happens constantly, rejecting an assumption that we all must make and do make every day.

So when I started to study economics in Aberdeen before the war, I found the need for value premises where the profession professed to be dealing in facts, and empirical facts where it presumed morality. This led me later to Gunnar Myrdal, the translation of his *The Political Element in the Development of Economic Theory* (1953) and the editing of *Value in Social Theory* (1958). My Introduction to this book, entitled 'Programmes and Prognoses', I regard as one of my best efforts. It contains a fundamental critique of welfare economics; it was enthusiastically reviewed; it had no impact at all. Perhaps David Colander's theory applies: I did not provide work for the drones.

There was another component that I found missing in the economics of the textbooks. That was the role of institutions in economic analysis and policy. Clearly, their existence cannot be denied, but their role and importance for study and policy are minimized by both neoclassical and Marxist economists. Neoclassical mainstream economists assume that institutions such as private property, joint stock companies, the monetary system and the state are given and fully adapted to the economic variables. They are therefore among the constants in an analysis. The Marxists, on the other hand, regard them not as *adapted* but as fully *adaptable*. They are part of the superstructure which follows from the modes of production. Hence again, a special study, let alone attention to policy-shaping, is unnecessary. Indeed, it was the preoccupation with institutional planning that Marx and Engels ridiculed in the 'Utopian' socialists Robert Owen, Saint Simon, Fourier and Proudhon, whose exercise of their institutional imagination seemed to me much less utopian and more realistic than the 'scientific' approach of Marx and Engels. In several contributions on the multinational corporation to volumes edited by John Dunning, I discussed the state as (partly) manipulated by particular interest groups and criticized the assumption, then quite common, that it looks after the public interest.

Having been born in Vienna in 1917, and having lived there in the inter-war period, it was not difficult to acquire a social conscience. When I was about eight years old, I had to write an essay on the topic 'If any would not work, neither should he eat' and made it an occasion for a harangue against the idle rich. My commitment has always been to the underdog, the poor and oppressed, although my views as to how they can be liberated have changed over the years. Like others, I had excessive confidence in the power of governments to do good, though I still do not believe that any form of government failure automatically constitutes a case for eliminating the intervention, just as any form of market failure does not by itself constitute a case for government intervention.

G.D.H. Cole, the Fabian professor of political theory at Oxford, used to draw a useful distinction between two types of socialist: the A- and the B-type. The As are the anarchists, the Bs the bureaucrats. Douglas Cole himself was a passionate syndicalist, had a healthy distrust of governments, and therefore was an A-type. Although I was always aware that it would be wrong to assume that government can be fully entrusted with the public interest, it took me some time to see the full range of its shortcomings. And I am still convinced that we can design hybrid institutions that draw on the best of free enterprise, individual initiative and the market, as well as of public responsibility and accountability.

I have dissented on many fronts: on the theory of the firm, on the compensation principle in the New Welfare Economics, on the economic case for the Common Market, on the doctrine of 'balanced growth', on the widespread use of the capital-output ratio in development planning, on the calculations of returns from education, on simple-minded models directly applied to policy-making, on the view popular in the 1950s and 1960s among economists that flexible exchange rates will cure our ills and that raising interest rates and tight money are remedies for inflation. I have had no reason to retract my words on these issues. Hardly any economist today is in favour of freely floating exchange rates. When Harry Johnson read my article on this subject he sent it to Milton Friedman, who wrote to me saying it reminded him of an abstract picture, beautiful and coherent in itself, but without any relationship to the real world. This is precisely the impression much current orthodox writing makes on me.

I have been better as a critic than as an apologist, propagator or advocate. My first two published articles contained a critique of the theory of the firm and the theory of profit. During a performance of *Aida*, Thomas Beecham, the famous conductor, introduced an elephant into the scene of the triumphal march. On one occasion, the elephant started to shit on the stage. Beecham, proudly pointing at him, exclaimed, 'Ah, I behold, not only an artist, but also a critic!' I had never felt comfortable when in charge of work on 'Basic Needs' at the World Bank in the late 1970s and, after having left the Bank, felt rather like that elephant.

I always wished I had learned more mathematics. Without this grounding, one feels nowadays like a handloom weaver after the introduction of the power loom. But the thought is made bearable by the fact that most of the power-loom weavers seem to be making the Emperor's clothes. The rigour achieved by mathematical modelling is all too often the *rigor mortis*. And the models, shapely and elegant though they may be, too often lack vital parts.

As one born into the expiring Austro-Hungarian empire, who spent most of his life in post-imperial Britain, and who came to the post-Watergate, post-Vietnam United States in 1976, I regard myself as something of an expert in imperial decay. It is a useful vantage point from which to criticize the nostalgic dreamers of imperial glory. It is from this position that I have been critical of the economic arguments for Britain's joining the Common Market in the late 1950s and 1960s (see 1961) and have analysed the need for global or transnational institutions that would replace the hegemonic power or dominant economies of the past. The public goods on which world peace and world order depend are no longer provided by the US and no other power has taken over.

Orthodoxy has a powerful grip on people's minds. Gunner Myrdal maintained that 'facts kick'. He meant that the crust of flawed orthodox thinking cannot withstand the empirical evidence and has, sooner or later, to yield to it. I, on the other hand, denied this in our lengthy conversations. I pointed to the existence of mass unemployment during the Great Depression, when orthodox economists clung to Say's Law and asserted the necessity of full employment equilibrium. I said that it requires an alternative model (or 'paradigm' as it has since come to be called) to kick out the orthodox one. Alfred North Whitehead had said this before, and Thomas Kuhn since.

Orthodox economics has been charged with being unrealistic, irrelevant, unproductive and amoral. When critics levy these charges, the defence normally is, 'can you produce a theory that is more realistic, relevant, productive and moral?' The critics are charged with having no constructive alternative. During the Lisbon earthquake on 1 November 1755 a hawker was selling anti-earthquake pills. When hauled before the judge for violating the rules of the then equivalent of the Food and Drug Administration, his defence was, 'What would you put in their place, your Honour'? If something is of no use, we should say so, even if we have no alternative and even if what we say has little impact.

It is true that scholars such as Thorstein Veblen (in spite of Wesley Clair Mitchell), Joseph Schumpeter, Kenneth Galbraith and Abba Lerner (in spite of David Colander) all had a good sense of reality, but formed no schools of disciples. They had no systematic nucleus round which ideas could be crystallized. And it is noteworthy that the formalized ideas round which schools have grouped themselves have often been rejected by their founders. Marx said that he was not a Marxist; Keynes that he was not a Keynesian (the originality of Keynes' contribution does not consist in the IS-LM diagram, as Hicks himself came to realize late in life); Kuznets rejected the Kuznets curve, and Pigou had to ask, 'What is the Pigou Effect'? This petrification of the original and revolutionary ideas of the founder is not peculiar to economics; it is shared by other intellectual, social and religious movements. Peter's petrification of the Church might have led Jesus to say, had he seen the result, 'I am not a Christian'. The point is made by Fyodor Dostoyevsky's Grand Inquisitor in *The Brothers Karamasov*.

The differences between dissenters such as Galbraith and Lerner on the one hand, and schoolmen such as Friedman and Samuelson on the other, are repeated within the messages of the school-makers. Two souls dwell in their breasts: one innovative but impossible to formalize; the other readily crystallized. These two souls are revealed in Keynes, in Marshall, in Samuelson. Marshall's insistence on the moral, social and human aspects of economics, Samuelson's emphasis in *The Foundations* on inequalities and discontinuities, got lost in the formulations of neoclassical economics.

Given the flow of publications by the mainstream, there are some minor reputations to be made by criticizing it. This is not a way of forming schools, but it can contribute to what Albert Hirschman, a great dissenter, has called 'obituary-enhancing' activities. David Colander has pointed out that for some scholars it is the process of confrontation, not the result, that matters and he tells of a Columbia University student who was turned on by confrontations with orthodox guys, 'and good sex is hard to come by'. To the extent that this is so, the dissenter needs the orthodox world in order to be able to live in his counter-world. I do not think this motivation is important in my case but, by definition, one cannot know one's unconscious.

My conclusion is that the contrast between orthodoxy and heterodoxy, between mainstream and side-stream, between consent and dissent can be overdrawn. There is heterodoxy in the founders of orthodoxy, and orthodoxy in the heterodox yappers.

The heterodox dissenters often think that it would be nice if they could band together and form an alternative paradigm. Yet it may be against the temperament of the dissenters to consent to this. Dissenters dissent, sometimes even or especially, from the dissent of others. My friend Mahbub ul Haq had a plaque on his office wall which read, 'It's too late to agree with me; I've changed my mind'. They cannot take 'yes' for an answer. On the other hand I remember a strip cartoon in which Penny says to her boyfriend, 'Why can't you be different – like all the others'?

All thought calls for structure. Models can serve as scaffolds or as crutches for better access to an incoherent, highly complex reality. But they can also become shutters or blinkers. A sharp focus illuminates a small area, but also excludes what is outside it. At any given time there is only one orthodoxy, but many heterodoxies. Some heterodoxies turn, in the course of time, into orthodoxies. The classical revolution in the 19th century can be regarded as a revolt against the pre-classical 'common sense' orthodoxies that read today very much like Keynesian writings. Keynes's previous underworld of economics became for a time the mainstream.

I regard the principal function of the dissenting, heterodox economist not to produce an alternative paradigm, but to serve as an intellectual muscle therapist, to cure us of intellectual cramps, to prevent the premature crystallization of flawed orthodoxies. We should be prepared to consider options. His function is more therapeutic than substantive. Like Oliver Cromwell in 1650, he says, 'I beseech you, in the bowels of Christ, think it possible you may be mistaken'.

The heterodox dissenter should stand for humility and tolerance, Keynes looked forward to the day when economists would be like dentists: humble and competent people. I am not sure that my dentist is either humble or competent, but I know that few economists of my acquaintance live up to Keynes's hope. Competence and humility should be cultivated, and with them the ability to talk across barriers. Our subject is in danger of being fragmented into non-communicating groups; the neoclassicals, the Chicago School, the new classicals, the radicals, women's studies, black studies, the greens and so on. It is of the utmost importance to keep the lines of communication open.

If I had to choose, I would rather be accused of fuzziness than of reductionism. For the orthodox consenters, the worst sin is fuzziness. Without agreeing with the late David McCord Wright, who once said, 'When people tell me I am fuzzy, I reply, "life is fuzzy"', the heterodox dissenters prefer, I think, to be accused of fuzziness. They prefer to be vaguely right to being precisely wrong. It is a matter of taste. The orthodox may say, 'reductionism is not the occupational disease of economists, it is their occupation'. But if in the process they throw out the baby *instead of* the bathwater, the reduction surely loses its point.

Streeten's Major Writings

(1949), 'The Theory of Profit', *The Manchester School*, **17**(3), September.

(1950a), 'Mängel des Preismechanismus', *Vollbeschäftigung*, Cologne: Bundverlag.

(1950b). 'The Inappropriateness of Simple "Elasticity" Concepts in the Analysis of International Trade' and 'Exchange Rates and National Income' (both with Thomas Balogh), *Banca Nazionale del Lavoro Quarterly Review*, **15**, October–December.

(1953), 'Appendix; Recent Controversies', in G. Myrdal, *The Political Element in the Development of Economic Theory*, London: Routledge and Kegan Paul.

(1954), 'Elasticity, Optimism and Pessimism in International Trade', *Economia Internazionale*, **7**(1).

(1957), 'A Reconsideration of Monetary Policy', *Bulletin of the Oxford University Institute of Statistics*, **19**(4), November.

(1958), 'Introduction' to *Value in Social Theory* by G. Myrdal, New York: Harper & Brothers.

(1961), *Economic Integration*, Leyden: Sythoff. Second edition 1964.

(1962), 'Wages, Prices and Productivity', *Kyklos*, **15**.

(1967), 'The Use and Abuse of Models in Development Planning', in K. Martin and J. Knapp (eds), *The Teaching of Development Economics*, London: Frank Cass.

(1972), *The Frontiers of Development Studies*, Basingstoke: Macmillan.

(1981), *Development Perspectives*, Basingstoke: Macmillan.

Paul Marlor SWEEZY (born 1910)   *John B. Foster*

Paul Sweezy, the world-renowned Marxist economist and social theorist, was born 10 April 1910 in New York. The son of a top officer of the First National Bank of New York, Sweezy was educated at Exeter and Harvard University, where he received his B.A. in 1931. He published his first academic article on 'The Thinness of the Stock Market' in the *American Economic Review* in December 1930, while still an undergraduate. In 1932 he left Cambridge (Massachusetts) for a year of graduate study at the London School of Economics. Already shaken by the onset of the Great Depression, Sweezy was further awakened during his year in Britain by the intellectual and political ferment associated with what was to be a turning point in world history, and soon gained sympathy for the Marxist perspective to which he was introduced for the first time. Returning to the US in 1933 to do graduate studies at Harvard, he found the intellectual climate much changed, with Marxism becoming a topic of discussion in some of the larger universities. As he recalled decades later:

> It was under these circumstances that I acquired a mission in life, not all at once and self-consciously, but gradually and through a practice that had a logic of its own. That mission was to do what I could to make Marxism an integral and respected part of the intellectual life of the country, or, put in other terms, to take part in establishing a serious and authentic North American brand of Marxism.

In pursuing these interests at Harvard, Sweezy received encouragement from the great conservative economist Joseph Schumpeter, whose analysis of the origins, development and impending decline of capitalism revealed a complex and critical appreciation of Marxist analysis.

Obtaining his Ph.D. in 1937, Sweezy took a job as an instructor at Harvard until 1939 when he rose to the rank of assistant professor. During these years he played a key role in two areas of debate then sweeping economics: the theory of imperfect competition and the issue of secular stagnation. Sweezy's interest in the monopoly question began early in his career, as shown by his 1937 article 'On the Definition of Monopoly' in the *Quarterly Journal of Economics*, and by his first book (winner of the David A. Wells prize), *Monopoly and Competition in the English Coal Trade 1550-1850* (1938b). His 1939a article, 'Demand under Conditions of Oligopoly', in which he presented the kinked demand curve analysis of oligopolistic pricing, remains one of the classic essays in modern price theory. While carrying out his teaching responsibilities at Harvard, Sweezy also worked for various New Deal agencies investigating the concentration of economic power (including the National Resources Committee and the Temporary National Economic Committee). His influential study, 'Interest Groups in the American Economy' was published as an appendix to the NRC's well-known report, *The Structure of the American Economy* (1939b).

During these years Sweezy was also deeply concerned about the economic stagnation of the depression decade, and its effects on disadvantaged sectors of the population. Along with a small group of Harvard and Tufts economists, he was one of the authors and signatories of the influential Keynesian tract, *An Economic Program for American Democracy* (1938a), which provided a convincing rationale for a sustained increase in public spending during the final years of the New Deal and soon became a Washington, D.C. bestseller. At Harvard Sweezy also took an active part in the great 'stagnation debate' involving such notable figures as Alvin Hansen and Joseph Schumpeter. The opposing (but in many ways complementary) historical answers provided by Hansen and Schumpeter to the question 'Why Stagnation?' were to influence Sweezy's economic analysis throughout his subsequent career.

Although deeply influenced by the Keynesian revolution, Sweezy was also an important contributor to Marxist economics by the late 1930s. From the lecture notes to his Harvard course on the economics of socialism, he soon produced his classic work, *The Theory of Capitalist Development: Principles of Marxian Political Economy* (1942). Especially notable for its review of the entire field of Marxian political economy; its emphasis, following Japanese economist Shigeto Tsuru, on the significance of the qualitative value problem for the labour theory of value; its elaboration of the Bortkiewitz solution to the transformation problem; and its discussions of crisis theory and monopoly capitalism, *The Theory of Capitalist Development* quickly established Sweezy's reputation as the foremost Marxian economist of his generation. In Schumpeter's monumental *History of Economic Analysis* (1954), which included more than a dozen entries on Sweezy's work, he referred to *The Theory of Capitalist Development* as 'the best introduction to Marxist literature I know'.

During the Second World War Sweezy served in the Office of Strategic Services (OSS) and was assigned to the monitoring of British plans for postwar economic development. With a number of years still remaining in his Harvard contract when the war ended, he opted to resign his position rather than resume teaching, recognizing that his political and intellectual stance would inhibit his receiving tenure. In this period, Sweezy wrote *Socialism* (1949), authored numerous articles on the history of political economy and Marxism, and edited a volume containing three classic works on the 'transformation problem': *Karl Marx and the Close of his System* by Eugene Bohm-Bawerk; *Bohm-Bawerk's Criticism of Marx* by Rudolf Hilferding; and 'On the Correction of Marx's Fundamental Theoretical Construction in the Third Volume of *Capital*' by Bortkiewitz (which Sweezy translated into English). His 1950 critique of Maurice Dobb's *Studies in the Development of Capitalism* (in which Sweezy, following Marx, emphasized the role of the world market in the decline of feudalism) launched the famous debate over the transition from feudalism to capitalism that has played a central role in Marxian historiography ever since.

With the financial backing of literary critic F.O. Matthieson, Sweezy and the historian Leo Huberman founded *Monthly Review* (subtitled 'An Independent Socialist Magazine') in 1949 as an intellectual forum for American socialists threatened by anti-Communist hysteria. Albert Einstein wrote his famous article 'Why Socialism?' for the first issue. Huberman and Sweezy began publishing books under the imprint of Monthly Review Press in 1951 when it came to their attention that, due to the repressive climate of the times, even such celebrated authors as I.F. Stone and Harvey O'Connor were unable to find publishers for their manuscripts.

In 1953, at the height of the McCarthyite period in the US, the state of New Hampshire conferred wide-ranging powers on its Attorney-General to investigate 'subversive activities'. On this dubious basis, Sweezy was summoned to appear before the state Attorney-General on two occasions in 1954. Adopting a principled opposition to the proceedings, he refused to answer questions regarding the membership and activities of former US Vice President Henry Wallace's Progressive Party; the contents of a guest lecture delivered at the University of New Hampshire; and whether or not he believed in Communism. As a result, Sweezy was declared in contempt of court and consigned to the county gaol (from which he was released on bail) until purged of contempt by the Superior Court of Merimack County, New Hampshire. On appeal, this decision was upheld by the New Hampshire Supreme Court. In response to a further appeal, the US Supreme Court overturned the verdict of the state court in 1957, on the grounds that there was no legal evidence that the New Hampshire legislators actually wanted the Attorney-General to obtain answers to these questions; and that the violation of Sweezy's constitutional liberties could not be justified on the basis of political activities only 'remotely connected to actual subversion' (US Supreme Court, *US Reports*, Vol. 354, October Term, 1956).

Despite the adverse political environment, Sweezy continued to author articles on all aspects of Marxian theory, adding up to hundreds of essays by the 1980s. MR Press's publication of Paul Baran's *The Political Economy of Growth* (1957) marked the beginning of Marxian dependency theory and helped to establish *Monthly Review's* primary identity as a backer of Third World liberation struggles. Visiting Cuba shortly after the revolutionary triumph of 1959, Huberman and Sweezy were among the first to recognize that Cuba would necessarily evolve in a socialist direction, and co-authored two influential tracts on the transformation of Cuban economic society: *Cuba: Anatomy of a Revolution* (1960) and *Socialism in Cuba* (1969).

Even before *The Political Economy of Growth* was finished, Baran and Sweezy began to co-author *Monopoly Capital*, which was eventually published in 1966, two years after Baran's death. Although described by the authors themselves as a mere 'essay-sketch', it rapidly gained widespread recognition as the most important attempt thus far to bring Marx's *Capital* up to date, as well as providing a formidable critique of the prevailing Keynesian orthodoxy.

In Sweezy's own case, *Monopoly Capital* partly reflected dissatisfaction with the analysis of accumulation advanced in *The Theory of Capitalist Development*. His earlier study had been written when orthodox economics was experiencing a sea-change due to the Keynesian 'revolution' and the rise of imperfect competition theory. Hence, he had provided a detailed elaboration of both Marx's theory of realization crisis (or demand-side constraints in the accumulation process), and of work by Marx and later Marxian theorists on the concentration and centralization of capital. As with mainstream theory, however, these two aspects of Sweezy's analysis remained separate; hence he failed to develop an adequate explanation of the concrete factors conditioning investment demand in an economic world dominated by the modern large enterprise. It was essentially this critique of *The Theory of Capitalist Development* that was provided by Josef Steindl in *Maturity and Stagnation in American Capitalism* (1952); Steindl went on to demonstrate how a more unified theory could 'be organically developed out of the underconsumptionist approach of Marx' based on Kalecki's model of capitalist dynamics, which had connected the phenomenon of realization crisis to the increasing 'degree of monopoly' in the economy as a whole.

Steindl's work thus exerted a direct influence on the model that Baran and Sweezy were to develop in *Monopoly Capital*. In this work they argue that

Marx's fundamental 'law of the tendency of the rate of profit to fall', associated with accumulation in the age of freely competitive capitalism, has been replaced, in the more restrictive competitive environment of capitalism's monopoly stage, by a law of the tendency of the surplus to rise (defining surplus as the gap, at any given level of production, between output and socially necessary costs of production). Under these circumstances, the critical economic problem is not so much one of surplus extraction as surplus absorption. Capitalist class consumption (which is unable to surmount its personal character) tends to absorb a decreasing share of surplus as the surplus share of GNP grows, while investment, which takes the form of new productive capacity, is itself impeded by investment that has taken place in the past, since plant and equipment cannot be expanded for long periods of time independently of final, wage-based demand. And although there is always the possibility of new 'epoch-making innovations' emerging that will help absorb the surplus, all such innovations – akin to the steam engine, the railroad and the automobile in their total economic repercussions – are extremely rare. To make matters worse, international economic transactions, which have sometimes been seen as a means of surplus absorption, are caught up in the imperialistic structure of world capitalism, and hence tend to generate a return flow of surplus to the core of the system that is greater than the outflow to the periphery, thus constituting little real help where problems of surplus absorption are concerned. Hence, Baran and Sweezy conclude that monopoly capitalism has a built-in tendency towards stagnation, largely staved off thus far through the promotion of economic waste by means of 'the sales effort' and military expenditures, and through the expansion of the financial sector. All such 'countervailing factors', however, are self-limiting by nature and can be expected either to wane of their own accord or to lead to a doubling-over of contradictions in the not too distant future.

For the authors themselves, the importance of *Monopoly Capital* lay not so much in its analysis of the underlying stagnation tendency – which had been thoroughly explored in the 1930s and in the work of Steindl – as in its account of those 'protective reactions' thrown up by the system that had allowed capitalism to prosper after the Second World War. To expand on the discussion above, these included such crucial historical elements as:

1. the epoch-making impetus provided by the second great wave of 'automobilization' in the US (encompassing the expansion of the glass, rubber, steel and petroleum industries, the building of the interstate highway system, and the rapid suburbanization of America);
2. the rise of 'Pentagon capitalism' in the Cold War period, including the economic boosts provided by the Korean and Vietnam wars;

3. the vast expansion of what Marx in his day had called 'expenses of circulation' in the form of the modern 'sales effort'; and

4. the historic augmentation of the role of finance (which they discussed briefly at the end of their chapter on the sales effort).

By analysing the way in which the surplus was absorbed through these and other channels, Baran and Sweezy enlarged the usual boundaries of economics to take into account its wider historical context. Of particular importance was their emphasis on the wasteful allocation of surplus under monopoly capital, which drew on the issue of use value that had been a central part of Sweezy's work ever since *The Theory of Capitalist Development*.

Any revolt against the increasingly contradictory conditions of monopoly capitalist society of a magnitude that would be likely to shake the US imperial power structure, Baran and Sweezy emphasized in their book, would probably emanate first and foremost (as the history of the post-Second World War period had already shown) from the neo-colonized peoples in the outlying regions of the capitalist world empire, and from their natural allies among African Americans and other racially oppressed populations systematically confined to the lowest rungs on the economic ladder within the US itself. Indeed, Baran and Sweezy devoted a whole chapter of their book to a systematic critique of the overly-optimistic liberal account of US race relations advanced by Gunnar Myrdal in *The American Dilemma* (1942), which they countered with an argument dialectically relating class and race, inspired largely by Oliver Cox, that was to reflect much more accurately the actual black experience in the US, not only in the 1960s but in subsequent decades as well. Hence, Baran and Sweezy's *Monopoly Capital* encompassed within a single framework of analysis the three major fields of crisis in the US social order of the 1960s: the underlying tendency towards economic stagnation, the growth of the civil rights and black power movements, and the imperial war in Indochina.

The re-emergence of conditions of relative economic stagnation in the 1970s, not long after *Monopoly Capital* was published, convinced at least some of the more free-thinking economists that the key to contemporary economic evolution was to be found neither in orthodox models nor in Keynesian fiscal and monetary 'fine-tuning', but rather in the impact of various world-historical factors (of the kind emphasized in *Monopoly Capital*) including the following: increasing aggregate concentration; the global ascendence of multinational corporations; an emerging world-glut of productive capacity; the clustering of technological innovations; the continuing existence of high levels of war and war-related spending; the spread of the world market hierarchy; the intensification of the sales effort, and the changing role of finance and speculation.

Yet, despite the fact that *Monopoly Capital* had both foreseen the advent of stagnation and had highlighted many of the key historical factors that increasingly drew attention as the 1970s and 1980s unfolded – and even though no work of equal synthetic unity in the field of Marxian economics came along to replace it – Baran and Sweezy's magnum opus had lost much of its influence and prestige even among left economists within 20 years of its publication. This is no doubt all the more surprising given the fact that *Monopoly Capital* constituted the initial theoretical common ground for the entire younger generation of radical economists in the US who emerged largely in response to the Vietnam war and who formed the Union for Radical Political Economics in 1968. In 1971, Sweezy delivered the Marshall Lecture at Cambridge University, and from 1974–76 served on the executive of the American Economic Association. In the early 1970s *Monthly Review* was perhaps the most influential publication among younger Marxist economists in the US. But by the 1980s most radical economists were drawn elsewhere – usually towards more fashionable supply-side theories of crisis that arose on the left as well as on the right during this period, and away from *Monopoly Capital* and *Monthly Review*.

Still, Sweezy, whose frame of reference was global and long-term, was not discouraged by these changing fashions and, together with Harry Magdoff (who replaced Huberman as co-editor of *Monthly Review* after the latter's death in 1968), he has continued to strengthen, extend and where necessary modify the analysis of *Monopoly Capital* in the decades following its publication. Utilizing the original framework to explain the re-emergence of stagnation, the rise of financial instability, and the further evolution of imperialism, he has published a series of works that represent a running commentary on capitalist development in the late twentieth century: *The Dynamics of US Capitalism* (1972), *The End of Prosperity* (1977), *The Deepening Crisis of US Capitalism* (1979), *Four Lectures on Marxism* (1981), *Stagnation and Financial Explosion* (1987) and *The Irreversible Crisis* (1989).

In addition to his central work on capitalist development, Sweezy has also made notable contributions to the analysis of the contradictory economic and social path of post-revolutionary societies in Eastern Europe. In *On the Transition to Socialism* (1971, with Charles Bettelheim), Sweezy boldly contended (against the theory and practice of market socialism rapidly gaining ground in Eastern Europe) that attempts to utilize the market mechanism as the key to building socialism were likely to lead to nothing less than the restoration of capitalism. It was the Stalinist political system rather than central planning as such, Sweezy argued, that constituted the real weakness of Soviet society (although the two obviously could not easily be separated and failure to grant more political power to the masses would eventually generate mounting economic problems as well). A decade later in

Post-Revolutionary Society (1980) he advanced the thesis that, although the original socialist character of the October Revolution was not open to question, a qualitative break had occurred during the early Stalin era, leading to the emergence of a class-exploitative system of a new kind. In the concluding paragraph of that book (which preceded by five years the rise of Gorbachev), Sweezy declared that the Soviet system had 'entered a period of stagnation, different from the stagflation of the advanced capitalist world but showing no more visible signs of a way out'. More recently, in a new preface to the 1990 Japanese edition of *Post-Revolutionary Society*, he has argued that as a result of *perestroika* and 'the revolution of 1989' in Eastern Europe, it has now become clear to the entire world that the new class system that arose in the Soviet Union and Eastern Europe in the Stalin period has come at last to 'a dead end'. 'The conclusion that emerges from this analysis,' Sweezy went on to observe, 'is that the crisis of the Soviet Union and the collapse of its East European allies was not due to the failure of socialism. The struggle for socialism in the Soviet Union as recounted above, was lost long before with the consolidation of a [new] class system, and it was this system which, despite its undoubted achievements, ultimately failed.'

Indeed, Sweezy had consistently argued at least since the early 1960s that those interested in the future of socialism should place their main hopes not at present with the working class in the advanced capitalist states, nor with the new class societies of the Soviet Union and Eastern Europe (now in the process of dissolution and reconstitution on capitalist terms), but rather with the insurgent populations of the periphery of the world capitalist system. It is here, if anywhere, that the modern proletariat in the fullest Marxist sense ('the focal point of all inhuman conditions') continues to struggle in the name of humanity itself.

In recognition of a lifetime of achievement, Sweezy was granted an honorary doctorate of literature from Jawaharlal Nehru University in India in 1983.

Sweezy's Major Writings

(1938a), *An Economic Program for American Democracy* (with others), Cambridge, Mass: Vanguard.

(1938b), *Monopoly and Competition in the English Coal Trade, 1550–1850*, Cambridge, Mass: Harvard University Press.

(1939a), 'Demand Under Conditions of Oligopoly', *Journal of Political Economy*, **47**, August, 568–73.

(1939b), 'Interest Groups in the American Economy', in US National Resources Committee, *The Structure of the American Economy*, Part 1, US Government Printing Office.

(1942), *The Theory of Capitalist Development*, New York: Monthly Review Press.

(1953), *The Present as History*, New York: Monthly Review Press.

(1960), *Cuba: Anatomy of a Revolution* (with Leo Huberman), New York: Monthly Review Press.

(1966), *Monopoly Capital* (with Paul Baran), New York: Monthly Review Press.

(1969), *Socialism in Cuba* (with Leo Huberman), New York: Monthly Review Press.

(1971), *On the Transition to Socialism* (with Charles Bettelheim), New York: Monthly Review Press.

(1972a), *The Dynamics of US Capitalism* (with Harry Magdoff), New York: Monthly Review Press.

(1972b), *Modern Capitalism and Other Essays*, New York: Monthly Review Press.

(1976), *The Transition from Feudalism to Capitalism* (with others), London: New Left Books.

(1977), *The End of Prosperity* (with Harry Magdoff), New York: Monthly Review Press.

(1979), *The Deepening Crisis of US Capitalism* (with Harry Magdoff), New York: Monthly Review Press.

(1981a), *Four Lectures on Marxism*, New York: Monthly Review Press.

(1981b), *Post-Revolutionary Society*, New York: Monthly Review Press.

(1987), *Stagnation and Financial Explosion* (with Harry Magdoff), New York: Monthly Review Press.

(1989), *The Irreversible Crisis* (with Harry Magdoff), New York: Monthly Review Press.

Other References

Foster, J.B. (1986), *The Theory of Monopoly Capitalism*, New York: Monthly Review Press.

Foster, J.B. and Szlajfer, H. (eds), (1984), *The Faltering Economy*, New York: Monthly Review Press.

Lebowitz, M.A. (1990), 'Paul M. Sweezy', in *Political Economy in the Twentieth Century*, New York: Barnes and Noble Imports.

Resnick, S. and Wolff, R. (eds), (1985), *Rethinking Marxism: Essays for Harry Magdoff and Paul Sweezy*, Autonomedia.

Sweezy, P.M. (ed) (1949), *Karl Marx and the Close of his System by Eugen Bohm-Bawerk and Bohm-Bawerk's Criticism of Marx by Rudolf Hilferding*, reprinted Merlin Press.

US Supreme Court, 'Sweezy v. New Hampshire', October Term 1956, *US Reports* 1957.

Lorie TARSHIS (born 1911)   *O.F. Hamouda and B.B. Price*

Lorie Tarshis was born into a middle-class family of Toronto on 22 March 1911. His father, Dr Singer, a medical doctor and Toronto City Coroner, died during the typhoid epidemic of 1915. In 1917 their mother married Tarshis whose name Lorie took. Tarshis started school at Huron Street Public Elementary School and found the competition very poor. Already by age ten and against his stepfather's wishes, he chose to leave the City of Toronto public school system. He was attracted to the highly competitive University of Toronto School run as a 'laboratory' school by the university for its education students.

Although he had intended to go into medicine, because of his enthusiasm and skill for mathematics he was counselled to go into economics. Undergraduate study of economics at the University of Toronto at that time meant entering a core programme called 'Commerce and Finance'. The first year was from the standpoint of economics modest, focusing on economic geography. In the second year economics was more seriously undertaken, with the main courses being Principles of Economics, Industry and Trade and Economic History. The students had to read Alfred Marshall's *Principles of Economics*. Thus Tarshis was immediately confronted with the challenge of reading the actual works of great economists, which he enjoyed.

Rather early in his second year of university, Tarshis's professor of Economic History, C.R. Fay, came to class one morning looking ashen and said, 'Gentlemen, I think you should know that you will remember yesterday for the rest of your lives'. Fay's pontifical tone and message did stay in Tarshis's mind: it was the day of the first big crash on Wall Street. The crash touched Tarshis and his fellow students in a very simple way. They were all involved in 'playing' the Stock Market, 'investing' in gold mines and the like, which until a few months before had been going up and up. The students played the game competitively, but Tarshis remained unconvinced that he learned any economics thereby.

Among Tarshis's third-year courses were Labour Economics, Money and Banking and Public Finance. He found the course in Labour Economics highly interesting because his instructor, H. Cassidy, introduced his class to the leaders of the local unions of the Ladies' Garment Workers and the Amalgamated Clothing Workers that were on strike in Toronto for most of 1931. In getting to know some of the strikers, Tarshis was persuaded that the strike was fair and sympathized with them.

The most memorable course of that year for Tarshis was Money and Banking, offered for the first time by A.F.W. Plumptre, a young Canadian instructor who had graduated from the University of Cambridge five years earlier. At the first meeting of the course Plumptre announced, 'Gentlemen, I have decided that I shall not use any of these American textbooks; I am going instead to use a very decent and reliable book by a magnificent Cambridge economist John Maynard Keynes'. This was the two-volume work, *Treatise on Money*. Tarshis thus had his first introduction to the work of the man who was to have the greatest influence on his intellectual life. Tarshis spent the greater part of his third year of university working through the book, finding it difficult.

Lorie Tarshis owed his dissent largely to force of circumstances. By 1931 he had begun to take economics quite seriously, aware that the visible economic situation in Toronto was getting drastic, with suicides over business failures, bread lines, riots or the remains of riots around the Parliament building and the main streets. Orthodox economists at the University of Toronto considered the depression a temporary phenomenon and spoke of a long-run return to normalcy. As the months passed and nothing seemed to be getting better but instead worse, he began to lose faith in their idea that market forces would eventually take care of the economy's woes. As his own understanding of economics and his observation of the growing wedge between what was happening in the real world and what the authoritative economists said would happen grew clearer and clearer, a dissenting opinion seemed the only sensible one for him.

Tarshis applied for a Rhodes Scholarship; his mentor, A.F.W. Plumptre, urged him to try for the Massey Scholarship which he subsequently won. In 1932, Tarshis set off for Cambridge where he was an undergraduate for two years preparing the second part of the Economics Tripos. He earned a first at the end of his second year and was subsequently awarded the Trinity Exhibitioner Fellowship at Trinity College. This enabled him to stay for two more years in Cambridge to begin his doctoral work.

Tarshis found the whole atmosphere at Cambridge favourable to dissent, and in economics Keynes was certainly the example. While a student he recognized the importance of Keynes's lectures and took detailed notes (recently published with others' lecture notes, in T. Rymes (ed) *Keynes's Lecture 1932–35: Notes of a Representative Student*, Ann Arbor: Macmillan, 1989).

On the morning of the very first lecture of his first term (October 1932) at Cambridge, Tarshis sensed the general atmosphere of excitement in the room. While waiting he wrote down in his notebook 'Theory of Money and Prices', which had been the title of the course Keynes was to offer. When Keynes came in, he announced, 'Gentlemen, I have decided to change the title of my course of lectures from "Theory of Money and Prices" to "Monetary Theory of Production"'. Tarshis crossed out the title on the front of his notebook and wrote down 'Monetary Theory of Production' and then began to puzzle over the title. He wrote a great big question mark, which was his shorthand for 'what is Keynes talking about?' None of the students had to wait too long for an answer, as Keynes very quickly revealed his new ideas.

In that first lecture Keynes raised a question which Tarshis has continued to think is still given insufficient attention. Keynes asked, 'What would you think if you were a businessman and you were advised to treat your workers in the same way as you treat your capital assets?' He continued,

> How would a society work if the employer treated his labour force in the way he treats his capital assets (protecting them with canvas tenting material or whatever can be got to keep the moisture off, greasing the wheels and so on), rather than as he does now, throwing them out on the street and saying waste away? If you are a worker, you're simply thrown out of work; you're simply told, 'come back in two months, we may have something for you then'. The employer is the boss; if he does not have work for his workers he says good-bye and good luck. But that's the limit of his concern.

Tarshis wrote the reflections down and thought about them extensively. Keynes asserted that the situation would be very different if the labour force were treated as a capital asset; then, for all practical purposes, unemployment would disappear.

Tarshis had quite a lot of contact with Keynes, since during his four-year stay in Cambridge he heard Keynes at the 'Political Economy Club' every two or three weeks on average. When Tarshis arrived in Cambridge in 1932, an invitation from Keynes to become a member of the Club awaited him. The Club met in Keynes's room four or five times a term on Monday nights from 7.30 to shortly before midnight. Tarshis found Keynes's Club very exciting, feeling that its discussions were on the cutting edge of economics.

Tarshis's first concern as a publishing scholar was money and real wages. He had started thinking about the issue in his third year at Cambridge, initially in a vague way for a thesis. In the next few years Tarshis developed his interest very concretely into his doctoral study, aimed at using the insights of microeconomics to tackle a macroeconomic problem – the distribution of wage income. Tarshis's analysis started with the firm and profit maximizing and then generalized to a collection of firms. Although he did not coin the graceful concepts of 'mark-up' and 'degree of monopoly' that Kalecki soon would, the results in Tarshis's thesis, 'The Determination of Labour Income' (1939), independently echoed those Kalecki had published, where labour share depends on the degree of monopoly and the elasticity of the typical marginal cost function.

Tarshis completed his dissertation under the remote supervision of M. Dobb and D. Robertson while coping with a heavy teaching load during his first years at Tufts College. Although not aware of it at the time, with his thesis Tarshis was assuming a role he would often play throughout his life – a dissenter from dissenters. Tarshis's dissertation was dissenting in that it rested for anything really novel on the *General Theory* and the not-yet-accepted ideas of J.M. Keynes; it dissented from that dissent in not accepting every conclusion of the *General Theory*. It accepted Keynes's major conclusions; Tarshis never saw any reason to reject them. He did, however, maintain that the *General Theory* oversimplified matters.

With government demands interrupting his teaching at the outbreak of war, Keynes did not read Tarshis's dissertation. He did, however, see some of the ideas which had crystallized from it into 'Changes in Money and Real Wages' which Tarshis sent to him as a note for publication in the *Economic Journal*. He had already formulated some of his ideas on the subject in 'Real Wages in the United States and Great Britain'. In the *General Theory* Keynes had written that he would not be surprised to find that in a period in which money wages are rising real wages are falling and vice-versa. The hypothesis was based, it seemed, on the notion that money wages will rise when employment is rising and vice-versa; real wages will fall when employment is rising because there are rising marginal costs. Prices go up even if money wages stay the same, therefore real wages drop. Tarshis found that Keynes's hypothesis was not right: if money wages were rising, real wages might be rising, but they might also be falling. He concluded that the picture was much more complicated than Keynes had depicted. Real wages depend on many factors, of which the level of output is only one.

Intrigued by Tarshis's findings, Keynes immediately accepted the note. He even asked Tarshis to add a paragraph or two based on his comparison of changes in the level of real wages and changes in output (or unemployment, where data were available). Both economists were certainly unaware that, ever since Marshall, no data would be found to confirm the thesis. Tarshis, like Keynes, felt that his conclusion had no effect on the validity of the *General Theory*'s assertion that aggregate supply and aggregate demand between them determine price and output.

In September 1936 Tarshis assumed a teaching job at Tufts College in Medford (Massachusetts) at the amazing salary of $2500. In the Boston area, he found himself among a small group of compatible colleagues from Harvard and Tufts. They began meeting regularly to discuss the economic situation in the US and by September 1937 decided to write a book together. The result, *An Economic Program for American Democracy* (1938b) signed by 'seven Harvard and Tufts economists', did not dissent from Keynesian conclusions; instead, it complained about the failure by US policy-makers of the late 1930s to use Keynesian analysis properly. It argued that things are more complicated than they appear; while a general statement or theory might justify assumptions in academic discussion, it may not be adequate when action is required to face a particular economic situation. The message was aimed at the inconsequent economic policies of the US government whose economists professed to have adopted the tenets of the *General Theory*. They were not aware, the book argued, of the implications of raising taxes for reasons other than fighting inflation as Keynes recommended. The current situation was that the US government was raising taxes to finance the introduction of the Social Security programme. Taxes were thus going up not in an effort to suppress inflation, but simply to balance the budget.

On the issue of the deficit, Tarshis found himself at odds with some of the authors of *An Economic Program*. The deficit was a great worry at the time. Having been brought up in Toronto and at Cambridge to believe that a deficit was next to the devil, Tarshis was extremely surprised by the impressive beauty of the *General Theory* in which Keynes had not concerned himself much with deficits. In fact, the atmosphere at Keynes's club was one of suspicion in anyone's excessive concern about the deficit. Thus, early on Tarshis had adopted an anti-anti-deficit posture. He felt that if an economy is allowed to grow, any deficit will take care of itself. Many of Tarshis's ideas on internal and external deficits were developed later in *The US Balance of Payments in 1968*, a study commissioned on the eve of an anticipated intractable US balance of payments deficit and in 'The Dollar Standard' (1974).

In 1946 Tarshis signed a contract to write a textbook of economics, which appeared the following year. The primary contributions of *The Elements of Economics: An Introduction to the Theory of Price and Employment* were conceived to be the introduction of Keynes into economic teaching and of macroeconomics into introductory courses. Whereas only fourth-year students studied macroeconomics at the time, *The Elements* set about introducing the beginning student to its intricacies. Although its third section was truly dissenting, Tarshis's textbook was a serious effort to explain all the 'elements' of modern economics. It began with an introductory section of three chapters describing the labour force in size, gender, wages etc. The second section was a study of microeconomics, based on Tarshis's paedagogical conviction that a student must first understand a good deal of microeconomics before he or she can really understand macroeconomics. Tarshis's treatment of microeconomics differed from the universally-espoused Marshallian approach which assumed free competition; he also introduced into his text diagrams of the firm which showed both the average and the marginal revenue curves as horizontal.

Tarshis was thus the first writer to include Joan Robinson's ideas in textbook form. To these ideas he added one important original element: his own 'mark-up theory'. He guided students not simply to recognize, as Joan Robinson had insisted, that firms very often do make marginal calculations (such as, marginal cost equals marginal revenue), but also to appreciate that firms will more likely use a formula approach. Tarshis offered both the evidence and a rationale for this observation: (i) in the real world, the estimate of marginal cost for a multi-product firm is based on so many assumptions, each of them of doubtful validity, that the effort of estimating hardly seems worth it; (ii) the elasticity of demand for the firm is virtually impossible to estimate when there is either monopolistic or imperfect competition.

Both political and economic attacks were laid against *The Elements of Economics*. It was condemned for being 'communist-inspired'. Malicious rumours began to circulate about Tarshis's disloyalty to capitalism which provoked a response among academics in defence of Tarshis and academic dignity. The economic arguments against the book were remarkably nonspecific, being put forward by those who felt that monetarism ought to be used for analysing macroeconomic problems. One could say the book was simply a casualty in the early war on Keynes. In the textbook itself, Tarshis revealed one staunch aspect of his dissent from general opinion: his reluctance to ignore either aggregate supply or aggregate demand. As a consequence of the attack on Tarshis's character, sales of his *Elements of Economics* immediately plunged. Later Tarshis substantially reworked the book for re-publication as *Modern Economics* (1967), although once again his ideas were a casualty of poor timing; the text appeared just as Keynes was being routed by prominent economists.

In 'Price Ratios and International Trade: an Empirical and Analytical Survey', Tarshis criticized the hypothesis of comparative costs. With data acquired on the relation of prices and costs for the production of steel plates of specific size, thickness and weight in various countries, he found that the exporting source of a product was often not its cheapest production source, and that a country such as the US was exporting things for which it had a comparative disadvantage. Tarshis concluded that the hypothesis that trade follows comparative advantage is an over-simplification; there are many other influencing factors such as trade ties.

Tarshis's article, 'The Elasticity of the Marginal Efficiency Function' was novel for its direction rather than for its conclusion. It maintained that the problem of assessing elasticity must be tackled, not by assuming *a priori* the marginal efficiency function as more or less elastic, but by asking 'why is it more or less elastic?' The elasticity of any function really depends on the diversity of opinions that lie behind it. A key element in discussing the marginal efficiency of such a function would be how diverse or close to uniform are the expectations. Great diversities in expected return yield a very low degree of elasticity.

In 'The Aggregate Supply Function in Keynes's *General Theory*' Tarshis maintained that an adverse shift in the aggregate supply function can help answer the question of the cause of inflation better than excess demand. Efforts to suppress inflation or to slow it down by raising interest rates or taxes are bound to make the situation worse. While the article recognized that orthodox economics has a role to play, Tarshis firmly maintained that Keynes's (or even Marshall's) notion of the aggregate supply function was far richer than that of many of Marshall's followers. The point of the article was that in the aggregate where the supply functions of all firms are combined, the supply curve is not vertical. Also, as things change, the movement is not only along the curve; the slope of the curve itself is altered. Any change in policy would not necessarily cause motion on the supply curve and thus inflation. It would be very likely to affect both the demand and the supply functions. Implicit in most policy decisions is that the supply functions stays the same and only demand is moved. The introduction of a new tax, especially one which heavily influences the supply of almost everything, will surely affect the position of the aggregate supply function drawn as a line that rises to the right and not straight; it may move it up or down, alter its elasticity etc.

Since the beginning of the 1980s Tarshis has developed a passionate interest in the state of international debt. His involvement in the issue sprang from his interest in the Euro-dollar currency markets. In his *World Economy in Crisis: Unemployment, Inflation and International Debt*, Tarshis introduced the notion of a banking system that is running wild and unrestrained. He maintained that if Euro-currency banking were to come into being, an individual central bank on its own could do nothing to control the negative effect of capital movement. As it is, the international lending-borrowing situation has become so uncontrolled that it has created an unprecedented strain on the less-developed countries in terms of their international debt. In *World Economy in Crisis* and numerous articles following, Tarshis has thus advanced a method of analysis and a scheme for bringing international debt under control, by the following steps:

1. The Federal Reserve System or the US government must take the initiative to approach the banks in the developed world which have lent to the developing world and offer to buy the bonds which those banks hold. This must be done internationally so that non-US banks are not faced with bankruptcy. The Federal Reserve System must run the plan, with international cooperation, since all the debt is in dollars and cannot be denominated from dollars and since the central banks of the other countries are in no condition to buy up the bonds and to pay for them in the dollars the banks need.

2. The banks sell to the Federal Reserve System or the US government which finances its buying by giving to the selling banks a credit which the selling banks can regard as reserve assets on the basis of which they can make further loans, which they are unable to do while they continue to hold the former bonds.

3. In order to avoid a dangerously rapid influx of new money and thus inflation, payment for the bonds must proceed slowly, in step with the growing economy's need for more reserve assets. Since banks will always need further reserve assets, they will eventually absorb all the credited reserves.

Lorie Tarshis can be recognized in all his writings as an independent thinker whose dissension has not been determined by any particular association, aside from his sympathy with Keynes. His friendships and intellectual acquaintances have crossed all political boundaries. Throughout his life Tarshis has principally shared the antipathies of other dissenters, although he has time and again found himself dissenting from them too. He felt that other dissenters – from the gold standard, from religion, from whatever – always focused frantically on one aspect of the picture, never seeing the whole, always leaving something out. While Keynes was right to dissent from the classical view, most Keynesians have also come to focus only on parts of his dissenting position. This has not been the case with Lorie Tarshis.

Tarshis's Major Writings

(1938a), 'Real Wages in the United States and Great Britain', *Canadian Journal of Economics and Political Science*, 4.

(1938b), *An Economic Program for American Democracy* (with nine others), Cambridge: Harvard, Vanguard Press. The economists were R. Bangs, R. Gilbert, W. Salant, A. Sweezy, P. Sweezy, J. Wilson and L. Tarshis (while L. Currie, E. Despres and W. Salant, though participants, remained unnamed as they were employed by the US government).

(1939), 'Changes in Money and Real Wages', *Economic Journal*, 49.

(1947), *The Elements of Economics: An Introduction to the Theory of Price and Employment*, Boston: Houghton Mifflin.

(1959), 'Price Ratios and International Trade: An Empirical and Analytical Survey', in M. Abramovitz et al (eds), *The Allocation of Economic Resources: Essays in Honour of B.F. Haley*, Stanford: Stanford University Press.

(1961), 'The Elasticity of the Marginal Efficiency Function', *American Economic Review*, 51.

(1962), 'Retained Earnings and Investment', in K. Kurihara (ed), *Post-Keynesian Economics*, London: Allen and Unwin.

(1963), *The U.S. Balance of Payments in 1968* (edited with W.S. Salant, E. Despres and A. Rivlin), Washington: Brooking Institution.

(1967), *Modern Economics*, Boston: Houghton Mifflin.

(1974), 'The Dollar Standard', in P.A. David and M.W. Reder (eds), *Nations and Households in Economic Growth*, New York: McGraw-Hill.

(1979), 'Aggregate Supply Function in Keynes' *General Theory*', in M. Boskin (ed), *Economics and Human Welfare: Essays in Honour of Tibor Scitovsky*, New York: Academic Press.

(1984), *World Economy in Crisis: Unemployment, Inflation and International Debt*, Toronto: James Lorimer for Canadian Institute for Economic Policy.

Lance TAYLOR (born 1940)

I spend much of my time teaching, doing applied research, and proffering policy advice in developing countries; the balance I devote to trying to understand how their economies work. Over the 20-odd years that I have been practising these vocations, I have convinced myself that economic change (or 'development') is highly constrained by conflicts over income distribution, and proceeds according to what Kaldor and Myrdal called 'cumulative processes' of distributional, institutional and technological change. The outcomes are strongly influenced by public interventions (for instance, to support import-substituting industrialization) and the political background. Putting all this complexity into policy suggestions or simple models that tell illuminating stories about how observable economies function is no easy task.

I got into economics by a back door, since after growing up in a small town in the rural American state of Idaho (where my family ran the local weekly newspaper), I went off to the California Institute of Technology to become a physicist. I did not succeed because I have minimal mechanical talent and thereby could not be an experimentalist, while I was not quick enough at mathematics to do theory. But I did learn two important things at Caltech. The first is that people who are mathematically able (like many neoclassical theorists in economics) are not always intellectually deep – there is no sense in being overwhelmed by algebraic fireworks. Second, I took a marvellous course in macroeconomics from Alan Sweezy who was devoted (like the wild duck) to diving into *The General Theory* in depth. Apparently, I did not drown in such excursions and, indeed, learned an enormous amount.

After a Fulbright scholarship year in Sweden, where I married and got my first look at a non-American culture at first hand, I ended up at Harvard to work towards a Ph.D. I did all right in the class examinations (manipulative mathematics is – or was – simpler in economics than in relativity or quantum electrodynamics), but was puzzled by the intellectual message most of the professors were trying to convey. 'Economics warps the mind' was my son's synopsis a generation later while describing the course material his college room mate was trying to figure out. He was right: individuals, enterprises, and the committees that make state policy never go through all the computational contortions that neoclassical theory says they undertake. They are much more cautious, flexible, and constrained by the 'dark forces of time and ignorance' as well as by socio-cultural and political pressures they do not fully comprehend. Asking how and to what end decisions about material life are made under such limitations is the natural subject-matter of economics, while my Harvard education (as well as most of the work of my MIT colleagues) boiled down to adorning 19th century Hamiltonian physics with dollar signs.

I wrote my Ph.D. thesis under Hollis Chenery. He passed along his practical view that economics should be applied to help poor people in poor countries, and also displayed a relatively open attitude towards dissent (many of the Harvard graduate students tending toward radicalism in the 1960s received a modicum of intellectual protection from him). The thesis was about how sectoral production structures change as development proceeds. It was an old theme, investigated by Kuznets and Chenery among others, but I added econometric twists which Chenery and collaborators such as Moshe Syrquin built into an impressive collection of papers and books.

After I finished my dissertation, I taught a year at Harvard (theory and econometrics). Then in 1968, through the old-boy network, I was shuttled to Chile as one of several new Ph.D.s helping with an 'advisory' mission to the Planning Office, set up by MIT's Paul Rosenstein-Rodan. The project served as stage scenery for Rodan's policy manoeuvring behind the government of Eduardo Frei; as one might have predicted, the impact of a collection of (mostly) *gringo* youngsters on state decisions was nil. However, I soaked up knowledge about how distributional conflict (implicit or explicit) determines economic change, as Chile's subsequent history amply attests. In his *History of Economic Analysis*, Schumpeter emphasizes how most economists spend their careers elaborating a 'vision' acquired around age 25. Certainly, I derived my basic economic views from my Chilean stay. They were heavily influenced by the structuralist ideas of the Economic Commission for Latin America that in the late 1960s were very much in the Santiago air. ECLA economists, in turn, owed intellectual debts to Kalecki and Kaldor.

The work we did in Santiago was quite standard: programming models, econometrics, commercial policy, and benefit-cost analysis. Edmar Bacha from Brazil (besides the occasionally visiting Carlos Diaz-Alejandro, the only non-*gringo* on the team) and I wrote papers on shadow pricing rules for foreign exchange which were cited for a few years before fancier neoclassical formulations made them obsolete.

More importantly than shadow exchange rates, Bacha and I read Cambridge economics and tried to fit the theory we had learned at Yale and Harvard into a Latin American context. We later took a stab at formalizing how regressive distributional change and more rapid growth may go hand-in-hand (1976). The paper is still discussed, even by mainstream theorists now beginning to put its notions together with Rodan's pet theme of economies of scale. The 1976 model, of course, drew on earlier institutional analysis by Latin Americans such as Celso Furtado and Maria da Conceição Tavares.

I taught at Harvard for three years after we got back from Chile, and then spent a year visiting at the University of Brasilia. The Brazil visit was financed by the World Bank (where Chenery had moved as chief economist and vice-president for research under Robert McNamara). Besides reading

Sraffa, Robinson, Kaldor, Kalecki and a lot of anthropology, I set up a computable general equilibrium (CGE) model which was supposed to describe Brazilian distributional change. The simulations were not informative, but along with Frank Lysy (a graduate student at Stanford who via the Bank had found his way to Brazil), I learned from contemplating the model that its results were highly sensitive to our assumptions regarding macroeconomic causality (such as saving responding to investment, or vice-versa) and also modes of macroeconomic adjustment (including output adjustment as in Keynes's *General Theory* or forced saving as in the *Treatise on Money* or Schumpeter's *Theory of Economic Development*, not to mention Kaldor). This recognition gave rise to a paper on model 'closure' (1979) which provokes neoclassical CGE model-builders to this day. More explicit theory along similar lines was worked out at about the same time by Amartya Sen and Stephen Marglin, following earlier hints by Joan Robinson and Kalecki.

After Brasilia, I moved from Harvard to MIT with a joint, tenured appointment in the Departments of Economics and Nutrition. Under the nutrition hat, I reinvented the two-sector model with a price-clearing 'agricultural' sector and quantity-clearing 'industry' which Kalecki, Kaldor, Hicks, Sylos-Labini and others had proposed. My original twist was to bring in Engel effects, to discuss how terms of trade increases may either stimulate or retard industrial growth, depending on the saving propensities of different classes and on income elasticities of demand. These distinctions are relevant in developing economies: the Indian industrial sector probably benefits from higher agricultural terms of trade while some of its Latin American counterparts may not.

The problems faced by a primary-exporting agricultural sector generalize fairly directly to those faced by poor countries as a group (the 'South') trading with an industrial 'North'. I wrote a paper on the theme 'South-North Trade and Southern Growth: Bleak Prospects from a Structuralist Point of View' (1981). Along with a more neoclassical formulation by Ronald Findlay (in turn preceded by a structuralist paper of Bacha's), this article started a cottage industry of North-South papers which flourished in the 1980s. The structuralist view on this question seems to be surviving rather well.

I also did applied work on food subsidy programmes, buffer stocks, and similar topics. On consulting missions for the World Bank and a joint Cairo University/MIT programme, I set up a CGE model about food subsidies in Egypt. The specification was broadly Kaleckian; the simulations showed that abolishing the subsidies would lead to output contraction and adverse nutritional change. These results did not strike me as surprising, but provoked debate with people opposed to subsidies because of their alleged micro-economic inefficiencies. My report (never published *per se*) became a mini-

cause célèbre when Cairo erupted in food riots after an attempt to end the subsidies in January 1977. Ill-planned distributional shifts can have substantial macroeconomic effects.

Richard Eckaus of the MIT economics department organized several advisory missions to Lisbon in the late 1970s in the wake of the Portuguese revolution. We mostly dealt with macroeconomic questions, although Eckaus and I also did a benefit-cost appraisal of a proposed superport at the fishing village of Sines. Swimming against the new government's optimistic stream, we argued that it would prove to be a white elephant; the port's subsequent unhappy history proved us right.

On the macro side, one of the hottest topics in Portugal was exchange devaluation. Along with Paul Krugman, then an MIT graduate student, I adapted the Egypt model to argue that depreciation can lead to both output contraction and price inflation in the short run (1978). This paper pulled together ideas about devaluation originally proposed by Albert Hirschman and Diaz-Alejandro. Hirschman said that more expensive foreign exchange benefits exporters with one hand but penalizes importers with the other. If imports initially exceed exports (the situation that usually provokes depreciation in the first place), then there is a real income loss. The consequent demand reduction is exacerbated along forced saving lines (Diaz Alejandro's observation) if money wages are fixed while devaluation drives up prices. Both effects are relevant in the context of semi-industrial economies. The likelihood that they will induce contraction was widely debated during the 1980s; consensus seems to be emerging that output losses following devaluation are more frequently observed than not.

During the 1980s I was mostly resident at MIT (except for a semester at the Delhi School of Economics in 1987), but continued to make frequent visits abroad, writing policy-orientated papers about Portugal, Pakistan, Mexico, Brazil, Egypt, Nigeria, Argentina, India, Kuwait and (recently) Nicaragua. In other policy-related areas, I worked with Emma Rothschild on the effects of military expenditure on growth and development (our contributions were partly merged in the report of the Olaf Palme commission on disarmament, published under the title *Common Security*) and, along with others from MIT, advocated subsidies directed towards the foods poor people preferentially consume. Both reducing military spending and providing these sorts of food subsidies are cropping up a decade later in recent policy recommendations of the IMF and World Bank. While serving as editor of the *Journal of Development Economics* for a dozen years, I tried to give space to good economists of both structuralist and neoclassical persuasions.

The main (only?) advantage of teaching at MIT or Harvard is access to graduate students. I have been fortunate in having a long string of brilliant ones, who have since gone on to their own academic successes and policy surprises (including the highly innovative but ultimately disastrous 'heterodox shock' inflation stabilizations in Argentina and Brazil in the mid-1980s; sad experience shows that the economy requires massive inflows of foreign exchange for such a package to work out).

Along with the students, I worked on a number of topics in macroeconomic theory for developing economies which are reviewed in a forthcoming book, *Income Distribution, Inflation and Growth.* These include the effects of redistribution on capacity utilization and growth (drawing on the ideas of Amitava Dutt); closure questions in past and present mainstream macroeconomic models (based on the work of Edward Amadeo); the etiology of financial crises in both industrial and semi-industrialized economies (with several models influenced by the work of Hyman Minsky); the respective roles of monetary forces and distributional conflict in causing inflation; more on the terms-of-trade, the agrarian question, and trade and debt problems faced by primary-exporting sectors and nations; and interactions of endogenous technical change and decreasing costs with income redistribution in affecting the course of economic growth.

The models we developed are very much in the Cambridge/Kalecki tradition, with an emphasis on internal consistency and closure questions. They are set up in simple algebra, not for the mathematics itself (although, admittedly, I enjoy working little puzzles out) but because formal reasoning helps sweep away cobwebs that verbal analysis cannot easily reach. For many questions of political economy, of course, comparative advantage favours verbal formulations.

Parallel to this theory, I collaborated with students and colleagues such as Bill Gibson, Nora Lustig, Jørn Rattsø, Jeffrey Rosensweig and Hiren Sarkar in putting together CGE models orientated towards practical development policy issues. A collection of these papers has recently been published (*Socially Relevant Policy Analysis*, 1990b); it is fair to say that at least the Indian and Mexican models we constructed have enriched the policy debate. Quantification of 'effects' and forcing one to think about the relative importance of different causal chains (for instance, will raising public enterprise prices increase inflation from the side of costs or ameliorate it by reducing the fiscal deficit?) are the major contributions that numerical contraptions can provide. In considering policy alternatives, this sort of information is often useful to have at hand.

Finally, both theory and the accounting built into CGE models lead naturally to empirical investigations with a Kuznets-Chenery twist. Agnes Quisumbing and I used a collection of social accounting matrixes to show that the agricultural trade surplus (or resource transfer to industry) is in fact small in countries apart from agro-exporters, contradicting a widely accepted dogma based on Taiwanese experience (see 1989). Using cross-country regressions, Desmond McCarthy, Cyrus Talati and I showed that export-led growth does not dominate in developing economies taken as a group (see 1987). Such investigations help provide useful background to industrial planning exercises of the type discussed below.

My interests began to take a more institutional turn in the mid-1980s. Along with Gerry Helleiner of the University of Toronto, I helped organize 18 comparative studies of recent economic stabilization experiences in developing countries, under the aegis of the newly-founded World Institute for Development Economics Research (or WIDER), a branch of the UN University set up in Helsinki. The results of the studies are reviewed in a recent book, *Varieties of Stabilization Experience* (1988). Along with other work supported by the UN, this publication helped generate healthy debate about the stabilization policies promoted by the IMF. The message may be penetrating – papers by Fund ideologues and even the contents of practitioners' policy packages have evolved over the past few years.

There is a parallel debate about the effects of orthodox, 'get the prices right', structural adjustment policies on prospects for progressive redistribution and growth. The World Bank emerged as the major advocate of liberalization in the 1980s, but the idea had surfaced in discussions about development 20 years before when neoclassical economics began to extend its intellectual hegemony toward the South (Bacha and I were hired to advocate price reform in Chile when we first got into the professional game).

Many of the same authors from the WIDER stabilization project are now working on medium-run issues in their own economies, drawing on successful planning experiences such as those in South Korea and Taiwan to suggest locally relevant policy initiatives that go beyond mindless liberalization. Their work relies not only on economic theory in the narrow sense, but also on the results of Kuznets-Chenery 'patterns of growth' studies and institutional and historical analysis more generally. Helen Shapiro and I drew the relevant questions together in a recent paper, along with tentative suggestions about how they might be answered in specific country contexts (see 1990a). In so doing, we followed Shapiro's lead in using common sense to criticize the reductionist theories of the state that neoclassical economists have recently dreamed up.

In summary, my main contributions have been to propose simple, direct approaches to practical issues in a number of fields, including macroeconomic theories of stabilization, adjustment, inflation and growth; studies of development patterns; computable general equilibrium modelling; and policy analysis and political economy more generally. In all these areas, people tell me that they found this paper or that book 'inspiring'. Compliments are nice to hear, but they refer less to the brilliance of my publications than to the intellectual poverty of economics as a whole. With most of the profession tied up with the latest theoretical fad or econometric wrinkle, senders of straightforward messages are rare. Being a dissident may amount to no more than studying an economy as it changes, advancing hypotheses about the forces that directed its evolution in the past, and drawing rudimentary inferences about what may be its next move. These activities are best undertaken without benefit of neoclassical blinders. But as Keynes observed, they are very difficult to shed.

Taylor's Major Writings

(1968), 'Development Patterns: Among Countries and over Time' (with H.B. Chenery), *Review of Economics and Statistics*, **50**, 391–416.

(1971), 'Foreign Exchange Shadow Prices: A Critical Evaluation of Current Theories' (with E.L. Bacha), *Quarterly Journal of Economics*, **85**, 197–224.

(1976), 'The Unequalizing Spiral: A First Growth Model for Belindia' (with E.L. Bacha), *Quarterly Journal of Economics*, **90**, 197–218.

(1978), 'Contractionary Effects of Devaluation' (with P. Krugman), *Journal of International Economics*, **8**, 445–56.

(1979), 'Vanishing Income Redistributions: Keynesian Clues about Model Surprises in the Short Run' (with F.J. Lysy), *Journal of Development Economics*, **6**, 11–29.

(1981), 'South-North Trade and Southern Growth: Bleak Prospects from a Structuralist Point of View', *Journal of International Economics*, **11**, 589–602.

(1982), 'Food Price Inflation, Terms of Trade and Growth', in M. Gersovitz, C.F. Diaz Alejandro, G. Ranis and M.R. Rosenzweig (eds), *The Theory and Experience of Economic Development: Essays in Honor of Sir W. Arthur Lewis*, London: George Allen and Unwin.

(1984), 'Defense Spending, Economic Structure and Growth' (with R. Faini and P. Annez), *Economic Development and Structural Change*, **32**, 487–98.

(1985), 'A Minsky Crisis' (with S.A. O'Connell), *Quarterly Journal of Economics*, **100**, 871–85.

(1986), 'Trade and Growth' (W. Arthur Lewis Lecture, National Economic Association), *Review of Black Political Economy*, **14**(4), 17–36.

(1987), 'Trade Patterns in Developing Countries, 1964–1982' (with F.D. McCarthy and C. Talati), *Journal of Development Economics*, **27**, 5–39.

(1988), *Varieties of Stabilization Experience*, Oxford: Clarendon Press.

(1989), 'Resource Transfers from Agriculture' (with M. Agnes Quisumbing), in S. Chakravarty (ed), *The Balance between Industry and Agriculture in Economic Development III: Manpower and Transfers*, London: Macmillan.

(1990a), 'The State and Industrial Strategy' (with H. Shapiro), *World Development*, **20**.

(1990b), *Socially Relevant Policy Analysis: Structuralist Computable General Equilibrium Models for the Developing World* (with others), Cambridge, Mass: MIT Press.

(1990c), 'Real and Money Wages, Output, and Inflation in the Semi-Industrialized World', *Economica*, **57**.

(1990d), *Common Security: A Blueprint for Survival* (The Independent Commission on Disarmament and Security Issues Staff), New York: Touchstone Books.

(1991), *Income Distribution, Inflation and Growth*, Cambridge, Mass: MIT Press.

Marc R. TOOL (born 1921)

My birthplace was a small rural town in eastern Nebraska; my birth year was 1921. My father, whose family traced its Scotch-Irish roots to the early 18th century in southeastern Pennsylvania, was a retail lumber dealer. My mother's parents left Alsace with five children after the Franco-Prussian War of the 1870s and settled in the midwest. I was the third son in a family of four children. When the Great Depression and drought savaged the agricultural sector and businesses dependent thereon, my father moved the family, in 1935, to Denver.

My first exposure to the character and merits of serious social thought occurred in a senior high school programme implementing a John Dewey-based 'progressive education' curriculum. Among the characteristics of this eight-year experiment were an inter-disciplinary approach to social analysis, the need to ground opinion or judgement in evidence, a pragmatic problem-solving orientation to public issues, and an apprentice-like exposure to career options. I now view that three-year experience as significantly stimulative and directive.

My undergraduate collegiate career began with a Business Administration programme at the University of Nebraska in 1939. I transferred to the University of Denver in 1941, and had the baccalaureate in Economics (all neoclassical) and Finance virtually in hand when I entered active military service in 1943 with the US 10th Mountain Division (infantry). Three years later (including seven months in northern Italy), I returned to the University of Denver to pursue a master's degree in Political Economy and Education, having by then decided to pursue a career as a professional scholar and teacher.

Shortly after my return, I was introduced to institutional economics as presented by John Fagg Foster, who was a student of Clarence E. Ayres. This was a watershed exposure for me. In some half dozen courses offered by Foster, I came to understand my consistent lack of enthusiasm for the main-stream neoclassical approach and found, in Foster's work and in the reference materials he recommended, an engrossing, exciting and heretical alternative mode of inquiry. Of greatest impact were his courses on the history of economic thought (how utility came to be the criterion of judgement in orthodoxy), modern economic thought (a profound critique of Hicks, Robinson, et al), comparative economic systems (why all economies are mixed systems), the American contribution to economic thought (the underpinnings and character of institutional thought) and value and its determinants (a comprehensive historical analysis of criteria of social value). Foster was a remarkably articulate, incisive and original contributor to the 'oral tradition' in the development of institutional thought. I began college level teaching with him and others in an introductory social inquiry source built around his heterodox approach. In the period from 1946 to 1951, I became an institutional economist.

Course work for a doctorate in economics at the University of Colorado in Boulder was begun in 1949 (commuting from Denver). After moving my family to Boulder in 1951, I completed the course work in another year. An interim faculty appointment provided an opportunity for me to teach several upper division courses, including doctrine and systems. My major fields of specialization were economic theory, history of thought, comparative economic systems and labour economics; corollary fields were political science and philosophy. My dissertation title was *The Philosophy of Neo-Institutionalism: Veblen, Dewey and Ayres*; the doctorate was awarded in 1953. Most memorable from the Boulder years were the running debates over the merits of neoclassicism, the vigorous pursuit of labour-orientated institutionalism, excursions into American philosophical traditions, and continuation of value inquiry. My dissertation topic, fortunately, required a comprehensive reading of much of the classical literature in institutional thought. The basic content of the dissertation – consideration of the contributions of Veblen, Dewey and Ayres to an institutionalist theory of knowledge, theory of human nature, theory of social change and theory of social value – has influenced much of my later scholarship.

In 1953, I accepted a position on the economics faculty at San Diego State College (later SDS University) where I had the opportunity, in addition to teaching the usual required mainstream courses, to develop institutional approaches to the economics of transportation and of social security. In the latter, for example, I found it impossible adequately to address questions of social justice and income transfers through recourse to presumptions of equational justice in neoclassical marginal productivity theory. For personal and professional reasons I transferred to Sacramento State College in 1955 (now California State University, Sacramento).

At the time of my arrival at Sacramento State, it was a very small and young institution. Instructional programmes and academic procedures were in large measure still being established. Accordingly, over my first decade there, in addition to developing my instructional specialities in economics, I was particularly concerned to help create non-dogmatic approaches to social inquiry generally, to help establish and maintain academic freedom, and to encourage the development of practices and instruments of collegial self-governance. In the mid-1960s I served as President of the statewide Association of California State College Professors in pursuit of these goals and others relating to economic welfare of instructional faculty. In that role, for example, I helped prepare, over just a few weeks, some dozen press releases vigorously challenging then newly-elected Governor Ronald Reagan's multifaceted assault on higher education. Shortly thereafter, at the request of the Statewide Academic Senate of the California State University System, I wrote a lengthy monograph analysing budgetary support levels and related matters for the State University system (see 1966).

My professional activities in these areas were largely concluded in the early 1970s with my two-year effort, assisted by a small *ad hoc* faculty committee, to formulate and secure state legislative sanction for a model of collegial governance for campuses of the California State University system. Although formal hearings were held, no implementing legislation was passed.

My post-Doctoral research and writing were reinvigorated in 1959 through participation in a Ford Foundation 'Summer Seminar for Faculty' on topics in economic development at an Oregon university (atypically, a third of the participants were institutionalists). In the course of assessing the explanatory capabilities of trade and development theories of neoclassical economics I saw even more clearly than before the disjunction between neoclassical theory and reality. Orthodox treatments simply could not address the range of variables and issues encountered in assessing development status, generating policy initiatives and appraising outcomes. Thus the conviction that orthodox doctrines were too ahistorical, too static, too acultural, too narrow and too archaic to guide those seeking to promote and accelerate economic development was dramatically reinforced.

While there I began drafting a manuscript, the working title of which was 'The Role of Ideology in Economic Development'. My original intent was to try to demonstrate the nature and significance of this gap between theoretical models and the reality of problem analysis and policy formation in development settings. It became increasingly obvious that efforts to employ any of the conventional isms – capitalism, socialism, communism, fascism – would lead to flawed policy and destructive consequences. The non-dogmatic, processual, pragmatic, instrumental approach of the institutionalists constituted a viable alternative approach. Indeed, as others have remarked, efforts seriously to address development problems compel abandonment of much received economic doctrine. I would later write about this phenomenon as a 'compulsive shift to institutional analysis' (*The Review of Institutional Thought*, 1 December 1981).

Starting with the common recognition that the ideology of capitalism is rooted in and validated by orthodox, neoclassical theory, that prominant versions of both socialism and communism in this century are grounded in Marxism, and that modern fascism purport to have theoretical and philosophical underpinnings, I refocused my research to comparative ideological assessments. The specific ties to development economics in the manuscript were dropped in favour of a more comprehensive structure. The title was changed to *Yesterday's Isms – and Beyond*. Work on this project extended over a decade and a half, culminating in a manuscript of nearly 1700 typescript pages. Some reference here to the contents of this manuscript is instructive in indicating how my subsequent research and writing evolved.

It opened with an introductory section on 'revolutions and ideologists' in which I contrasted contemporary pressures for change (economic, political, environmental, sexual and racial etc) with the claims of relevance of modern ideologists to direct that change. Then in each of five major sections – inquiry (theories of knowledge), people (theories of human nature), economy (institutional models of preferred or ideal systems), polity (loci of discretion and role of government), and value and goals (criteria of judgement) – I presented and evaluated the three main ideological belief systems: capitalism, Marxism and fascism. Each of the five main sections concluded with an '...and Beyond' chapter in which the institutionalist alternative perspective was introduced and defended. A brief substantive excursion into two of these five areas will suggest something of the character of the argument made by the book; sections on 'inquiry' and 'economy' will serve for present purposes. Characterizations that follow are indicative, not definitive.

In the introduction to the section on inquiry, I attempted to demonstrate that the selection of a mode of inquiry colours and shapes the choice of topics considered, the reasoning patterns pursued, the tests of significance imposed and the nature of outcomes realized. I then turned to the theories of knowledge reflected in the three major isms.

The mode of inquiry of orthodox theory undergirding capitalism is flawed by a rationalistic deference to deductivistic analysis, an insistence on a positivistic stance, presumptions of natural order, a preoccupation with equilibrium and a quest for *mere* predictive capabilities. The mode of inquiry of Marxism is flawed by universal claims of relevance, the rationalistic character of dialectics, exclusive insistence on scientific standing and the law-like progressivity of dialectical movement. The mode of inquiry of fascism is flawed by the dictum that thought is the pre-eminent reality, a reverence for a private world of intuitive knowledge, the claim that authority is the source of truth, and the corruption and manipulation of evidential grounding and logical reasoning.

Institutional inquiry, on the other hand, reflects the abandonment of Cartesian dualisms, the adoption of Dewey's theory of instrumental logic of inquiry, the employment of rationalist *and* empiricist modes in a processual quest for tentative truth, the continuing concern to explain complex causal determinants, the recognition that warranted knowledge emerges in an evolutionary and cumulative fashion, and the conviction that inquiry into the modes of inquiry must be a continuing responsibility of the scholar.

In an introductory chapter on economy I argued that, empirically viewed, all economies are in fact mixed and must be such. It appears that no people can indefinitely 'live an ism', as was recently demonstrated in Eastern Europe. The necessity of resolving an unending succession of problems requires that the structural fabric of any economy be subject to continuous revision. Problem-solving requires institutional *adjustment*.

In the capitalist model of an economy, the major structural elements – private property, profit motive, free markets, competition – are mistakenly characterized as natural (given) institutions; their autogenetic appearance will allegedly occur with the removal of 'artificial' restraints, mainly governmental 'interference'. Economic progress is naively perceived as a movement episodically from what is not capitalistic to what is capitalistic. Marxism offers an unacceptably deterministic succession of ism recipes, of which socialism (as transition) and communism (as culmination) are the preferred models. Economic change is primary and dialectic; class struggle is the omnipresent instrument of movement. Historical experience nowhere validates the succession and prime mover as detailed. Fascism proposes an hierarchically constituted political economy in which the *political* institutions are the givens, and the economic structure is subverted and adapted to political ends. The economy is corporatist in form and 'great men' are pretentious invokers of change.

In contrast, the institutional view is that *a priori* designs of institutional structure are nowhere relevant. One cannot know what new or revised structure to introduce until the 'imbecilic' flaws (Veblen) in existing structure have been determined. Democratically introduced changes are more likely to be efficient in the instrumental sense. All systems are in some measure evolutionary and developmental.

The *Yesterday's Isms and Beyond* volume was never published as such. Although one major publisher solicited 17 different reviewer evaluations, no supportive consensus emerged. The volume was thought to be too large, and its potential as a text too limited, to warrant publication. However, a different publisher finally did express an interest in a shorter version. As requested, I extracted and revised the institutionalist chapters; these were published as *The Discretionary Economy: A Normative Theory of Political Economy* (1979). The work offers a general introduction to an institutionalist perspective on political economy culminating in consideration of instrumental social value theory and social goals. The material on comparative ideology retained was minimal and largely incidental.

Through the early 1980s, I turned my research attention, in a series of essays, to a fuller and comparative consideration of theories of social value – criteria of judgement in economic analysis. These were published in 1986 under the title *Essays in Social Value Theory: A Neoinstitutionalist Contribution*. Two of the essays further developed the institutionalists' instrumental value principle. The first, reaching back to my dissertation, traced the contributions of institutionalists to social value theory beginning with a general consideration of Veblen's dichotomy of ceremonial versus technological judgements, and continuing through Dewey and Ayres to include Foster's principle of 'instrumental efficiency'. Another essay presented my version of the instrumental principle and its corollaries and applications. That principle is to act or judge in a manner 'to provide for the continuity of human life and the non-invidious recreation of community through the instrumental use of knowledge'. It is intended to provide criteria of judgement that will demonstrably permit the actual resolution of economic problems of impairment in the flow of real income. Four other essays address the differences between instrumental and non-instrumental value theory. Three of these present extensive critical assessments of the social value theory of neoclassical orthodoxy; a fourth provides a lengthy critique of Marxist normative analysis.

With regard to neoclassical orthodoxy, my argument is that all its utility-based criteria are inadmissible because they turn out to be tautological, relativistic and, in fact, inapplicable. Efforts to employ Paretian optimality, tenets of indifference demand, even theories of axiomatic choice, do not provide neoclassical orthodoxy with credible social value theory. By extension, conventional analyses of cost-benefit, delineations of externality conditions and formulations of market failure similarly offer no escape from the inherent, utilitarian 'methodological individualism' of orthodoxy and its persistent deference to given and unexamined preferences.

Heterodox institutional value theory, in contrast, is well-grounded in the inquiry logic of instrumentalism; it is processual and evidential analysis. It provides a cultural and judgemental context in which the institutional complexities can be assessed, employing the distinction between progressive (instrumental) and regressive (ceremonial or invidious) change. It disallows the normative use of any prefabricated institutional model as a criterion of policy judgement.

My critique of the normative dimensions of Marxism is pursued through an exegesis of selected works of both classical and especially contemporary Marxists. I applaud their normative concerns but find, through an exploration of both convergences and divergencies with institutionalism, that the latter overwhelm the former. I find them unconvincing in their view of dialectical inquiry as a finished mode, their implicit ethical relativism and their normative use of socialist and communist models. Also unacceptable are their lapses into ethical absolutism in the advocacy of communism as an ideal or a millennial stage, their insistence that only communism can provide for the full development of human potential and, finally, their invidious elevation of the interests of the proletariat to a predominate position. Only workers, so identified, have creative virtue. No instrumentalist can accept such claims.

The volume concludes with a reappearance of 'The Compulsive Shift to Institutional Analysis' essay in which I argue that Maynard Keynes in particular, as well as Arthur Okun, Gardner Ackley and other scholars not ordinarily identified with institutionalism have in fact moved theoretically in the direction of institutional analysis. Confronting real problems of instability, unemployment, maldistribution and the like *requires* serious researchers to develop analyses that substantively depart from the assumptions and tenets of orthodoxy. Those making such compulsive shifts, however, did not yet perceive the need for a comprehensive abandonment of the orthodox neoclassical paradigm.

In 1981, my professional responsibilities changed dramatically with my appointment as editor of *The Journal of Economic Issues*. The *JEI* is a major international quarterly that now focuses particularly on institutional economic theory and its applications to policy. In addition to the regular refereed issues of the journal, in 1984 (March) I solicited papers for, and edited, a special volume on 'Economic Policy for the Eighties and Beyond'. This work, republished under the title *An Institutionalist Guide to Economics and Public Policy* (1984), included policy recommendations on stabilization, unemployment, income maintenance, indicative planning, public utility regulation, environmental protection, agriculture and foreign economic relations.

After reading manuscripts submitted to the *JEI* for a couple of years, I came to see the need for more definitive referential volumes on the institutionalist perspective generally. With the guidance and encouragement, extending over three years, of an *ad hoc* committee of institutionalist colleagues, I solicited and edited manuscripts from 14 scholars to comprise a volume on the philosophical underpinnings and major concepts of institutional thought as our September 1987 issue of the *JEI*. Similarly, papers were requested from 16 scholars on institutional theory and its application to policy and were published as our December 1987 issue. These oversize issues were later republished under the titles *Evolutionary Economics, Volume I: Foundations of Institutional Thought* (1988a) and *Evolutionary Economics, Volume II: Institutional Theory and Policy* (1988b).

Over my terms as editor, and with the support of the sponsoring Association for Evolutionary Economics (AFEE), I have attempted through European travel (1981, 1984, 1987, 1988, 1989), lecturing (Sweden, Finland, Denmark, Switzerland, Austria, France) and personal contacts to help the *JEI* in particular, and institutionalism in general, acquire a more international focus and perspective.

Clearly, the highlight of my heterodox career was my receipt, in 1988, of the AFEE Veblen-Commons Award. When my editorship of the *JEI* concludes in 1991, I expect to continue my research and writing in the area of instrumental value theory and its operational applications.

Tool's Major Writings

(1966), *The California State Colleges Under the Master Plan*, Aztec Press, San Diego State College.
(1979), *The Discretionary Economy: A Normative Theory of Political Economy*, Santa Monica: Goodyear Publishing. Also Encore Edition, Boulder (Colorado): Westview Press, 1985.

(1984), *An Institutionalist Guide to Economics and Public Policy*, New York: M.E. Sharpe.

(1986), *Essays in Social Value Theory: A Neoinstitutionalist Contribution*, New York: M.E. Sharpe.

(1988a), *Evolutionary Economics, Volume I: Foundations of Institutional Thought*, New York: M.E. Sharpe.

(1988b), *Evolutionary Economics, Volume II: Institutional Theory and Policy*, New York: M.E. Sharpe.

Kozo UNO (1887–1977)   *Shohken Mawatari*

Kozo Uno was born in 1887 in Okayama prefecture 30 years after the Meiji Revolution, which is thought of as the beginning of modern Japan. He grew up the son of a merchant and studied at Tokyo University. His student life coincided with a time of stronger moves towards democracy, called the Taisho Democracy upsurge, which was reversed two decades later. Also at this time Hajime Kawakami, founder of Japanese Marxian economics and an orthodox Marxist, was publishing his personal journal, 'Social Problems Study', which included translations of Marx's books. Young intellectuals, such as Tamizo Kushida, Hyoe Ouchi, Itsuro Sakisaka and Kozo Uno, were attracted by Kawakami's introduction to Marxism. Some of them became major theoretical exponents of the Japan Communist party, while others followed the Japan Socialist (then called Rono) party, although Uno chose neither.

Uno first got a job at Ohara Social Problems Study Institute, a private institute founded by the philanthropic capitalist Ohara which hired some Marxian economists. The director at that time was Iwasaburo Takano. After marrying Maria, daughter of Takano and his German wife, Uno was allowed to go to Germany for two years from 1922–24. Besides observing the unprecedented German inflation and its aftermath, he mainly occupied himself there reading *Das Kapital*.

On returning to Japan, Uno was employed at Tohoku, one of seven 'Imperial' universities. He moved to Sendai and began to teach economic policy from a Marxist point of view. He continued to study *Das Kapital* and tried to formulate a Marxist theory of economic policy using Marx's ideas and the results of his own empirical study of history. He was able to concentrate on his research for about 14 years while an associate professor at Sendai.

Uno thought that the historical change of class interests largely influenced the type of economic policy pursued at any one time. Mercantilism, liberalism and imperialism were three of these types which reflected three stages of capitalist development. These three stages were in turn the main outcomes of the types of capital currently predominating: merchant, industrial and finance capital. His first book in 1936, *The Theory of Economic Policy*, included these ideas, though only its first volume ever appeared.

Also in 1936 he lectured on the principles of political economy on behalf of a colleague who was abroad for one year. A handwritten booklet remains showing that these lectures were organized extensively on the lines of Marx's *Das Kapital*. His lectures were extraordinary in two senses. Apart from Kawakami, who had been expelled from Kyoto University in 1927, no Japanese professor had given this type of lecture at an 'Imperial' university. Furthermore, Uno's lectures were different even from Kawakami's. The latter had just explained *Das Kapital*, while Uno analysed a capitalist economy using its terms. Kawakami only interpreted *Das Kapital*, but Uno tried to systematize his own theory about a capitalist economy using Marx's theories.

By 1936, Uno had formed his own ideas and established his fundamental points of view. He kept himself apart from communist and socialist party activities. He was greatly interested in the controversy concerning the Japanese economy about which Marxist economists disagreed violently in the mid-1930s. Uno avoided any involvement in these debates because he was not satisfied with either group's explanations. The pro-communist Koza-ha stressed the semi-feudal nature of the Japanese economy, echoing the Comintern thesis of 1932, whereas socialist Rono-ha stressed its advanced capitalist nature. Both views were linked with their respective political party programmes. Uno believed that Marxian economics should be independent from political party activities otherwise it would become subservient to Marxist political parties.

At this point Uno's academic career was suddenly interrupted: he was arrested by the special police of the Japanese militarist government, suspected of having worked as a member of the Rono (socialist) group. Although he had many close friends in this group, he himself was not a member. In explaining his viewpoint to the courts, he showed that his ideas were not compatible with those of Rono. Uno was finally proclaimed innocent even by the militarist government. But he did not return to the university when he was released after two years' detention in gaol. He took jobs with private research institutes during the Second World War. In 1947, two years after the war ended, he resumed his academic career, although this time as professor of the Tokyo University Research Institute of Social Science.

In contrast with the pre-war period, Uno's post-war years were not so dramatic. After 1945, in reaction to pre-war oppression, Marxism and Marxian economics were commonly accepted as progressive social ideas; they actually formed the mainstream in Japanese academic circles up to the 1960s. Uno's status as professor at Tokyo University was acceptable in Japanese society; he also became dean of the Tokyo University Research Institute of Social Science. His basic environment was encouraging except for attacks on his works by orthodox Marxists. In 1958 he retired from Tokyo University and moved to Hosei and later to Risho (private universities in Tokyo) where his disciples surrounded him.

Uno did not accept honourable status and he rejected awards. He liked to joke about a Nobel prize, saying that his theory of the measure of value would be worth a Nobel prize if one had existed for economics (and maybe if a scientific Marxist was the committee chairman). But, to his surprise, an economics prize was actually introduced after which he stopped making jokes on the subject.

What he wrote was important, but not easy to understand. However, his style of speaking was attractive. Many who felt his written work was difficult found his public lectures, discussions and interviews exciting. Uno attracted many talented disciples, mainly at Tokyo University. Some pre-war graduates of Tohoku University remained there to continue teaching his ideas. Other professors at Tokyo University, including the influential Koichiro Suzuki and Tsutomu Ouchi, converted to Unoism, while his younger graduate students became hard-core followers. Suzuki's and Ouchi's graduate students also became Unoists, some of them transferring to other universities. With such a following, Uno's methodology – the three-level approach – began to be termed the Uno School of economic thought. Its zenith was perhaps in the 1950s, 1960s and 1970s. But adherents are still influential: second- or third-generation Unoists continue to be leading professors at Tokyo, Tohoku, Tsukuba, Hosei and other universities.

In an academic sense, Uno has been a central figure in post-war Japanese Marxist economics. He published a series of major works at regular intervals, beginning with *An Introduction to Agricultural Problems* and *A Theory of Value* in 1947. Of his magnum opus, *The Principles of Political Economy*, Volume I appeared in 1950 and Volume II in 1952. *The Theory of Economic Crisis* was published in 1953 and followed by *The Theory of Economic Policy* in 1954, which was a fully condensed version of his pre-war work. *Das Kapital and Socialism*, appearing in 1958, dealt with philosophical matters. *The Methodology of Economics*, the first volume of the Unoist series covering all three levels of economics – the principles, the stage theory and the concrete analysis – was published in 1962 by Tokyo University Press. The condensed and revised version of *The Principles of Political Economy* was published in 1964. All of these works are in Japanese, but the last one was translated into English by Thomas Sekine and published by Harvester in 1980.

In 1970, Uno's biography was published in two volumes, using retrospective interviews. Almost all of his works were republished in *The Collected Works of Kozo Uno* in ten volumes, 1973–74. The first and second volumes of the *Collected Works* are devoted to the 'Principles of Political Economy', the third is to 'The Theory of Value', the fourth to 'Studies on Marxian Economics', the fifth to 'The Theory of Crisis' and the sixth to 'The Economics of Capital'. These six volumes cover economic theory. The remaining four volumes cover 'The Theory of Economic Policy', 'An Introduction to Agricultural Problems', '*Das Kapital* and Socialism' and 'The Methodology of Economics'. Uno saw all of his books published in his lifetime except for the English translation of the *Principles* which appeared three years after his death.

Uno's economics stemmed from Marx's *Das Kapital*. Uno read it for more than 50 years (*Reading Das Kapital For Fifty Years* was the title of his biographical volumes). But from reading it, he made it understandable by presenting his own system of political economy which is different from both orthodox Marxist and neoclassical economics. It is different from neoclassical economics, but it can be compared with this system.

The first problem he had to cope with was how the theory of *Das Kapital* related to the real process of capitalist development. Marx presented a theory of the capitalist economy which he called 'the capitalist mode of production'. However, the capitalist economy is not a static system, but a changing process. It has altered greatly since Marx's time. Is the theory of *Das Kapital* any longer valid?

In Uno's view, *Das Kapital* is fundamentally valid as a theory of 'pure capitalism'; that is, capitalism composed of three classes working under free competition. Such a theory is necessary to clarify what the capitalist system is and how it functions in principle. Marx's *Das Kapital* supplies the theoretical materials for this 'pure capitalism'.

Uno's model has some similarities with that of the neoclassicals but is very different in nature, being based on the historical tendency to 'pure capitalism'. In mid-19th century England, capitalism showed a tendency towards a three-class division and complete competition. 'Pure capitalism' is assumed as the utmost extent of this historical tendency (which in this case was reversed in later decades). Furthermore, this is a model of capitalist economic institutions, not a mere analytical tool. The theory of 'pure capitalism' supplies us with what Schumpeter calls a 'vision' of the capitalist economy, its structure and workings, as distinct from what he calls 'analytical engines'.

How is the theory of 'pure capitalism' organized? In Uno's view, according to the order and mutual relations of the institutional elements of a capitalist economy. Uno basically followed Marx, but stressed the initiative of economic agents; agents are not mere reflections of economic relations, but also creators of institutional systems. For example, a commodity-owner feels the contradiction between value and use-value: he wants to exchange his own commodity for whatever he particularly likes. He tries to solve this dilemma by obtaining a third commodity which is commonly needed. One of these commodities will develop into money through the behaviour of the commodity-owner as an economic agent. A money-owner has a dilemma: if he keeps a certain amount of money in hand, he cannot increase it. He has to release money to increase its amount. This behaviour creates capital. Money develops into capital through the behaviour of a money-owner.

Thus the logic of the theory of the institution of a capitalist economy is not mathematical, but dialectic, woven by economic agents (although Uno might have accepted a limited mathematical input). Uno stressed the importance of dialectics as the logic of the system of capitalist economies; on the other hand, he did not accept the dialectics of history and of nature.

Uno organized his theory of 'pure capitalism', the principles of political economy, in three parts: the theory of circulation, the theory of production and the theory of distribution. The theory of circulation deals with the basic forms of a capitalist market economy: commodity, money and capital. His theory of commodity does not involve the metaphysical extraction of the substance of value; it mainly demonstrates the necessity of money. The theory shows the functions of money such as measure of value, means of circulation and fund (object of savings, means of payment, object of increment). The theory of capital clarifies its main forms: merchant, money-lending and industrial. Uno intentionally separates these forms of market economy from production relations in order to specify what makes an economy capitalistic, concluding that it is the hiring relation or the 'commoditization' of labour power.

In the theory of production, Uno demonstrated why capitalism can exist as a self-sustained society. 'Capital' is in charge of production and circulation. He made use of the labour quantity theory of value to prove the capitalist manner of exploitation. By adopting the concept of abstract value and equal-value exchange, Uno showed that capitalists (in abstract, capital) exploit surplus labour through the market mechanism. Thus capital is a value-augmenting time-dependent circuit, which can be viewed both as stock and as flow. He analysed the periods of production and circulation, and various kinds of cost and capital which originated from these periods. Then he analysed the requirements of sectoral equilibrium, which he showed a capitalist society could fulfil completely through its market mechanism.

In the theory of distribution, Uno discussed the distribution of surplus-value under the market mechanism of complete competition. A capitalist maximizes his profit, not by adjusting his output given the capital invested, but by shifting his additional capital to more profitable sectors. This is a mid-term equilibrium mechanism following the classical-Marxist tradition. Equilibrium is attained when rates of profit in every sector are equalized. Further reallocation of capital is no longer needed and thus demand and supply of all commodities meet each other at that price. This equilibrium price is called 'production price' in which surplus-value is distributed among competitive capitalists.

Uno's theory of rent is not as original as his ideas on interest. Landowners attract portions of surplus-value as the differential rent or as the absolute rent through price mechanisms. He clarifies that the credit system is a capitalist device for utilizing temporarily idle funds among capitalists. The system is composed of commercial credit and banking credit. Commercial credit forms the basis of banking credit, which necessarily comprises commercial and central banking. Interest is paid and received among capitalists, which implies redistribution of surplus-value. Interest is determined by demand and supply of funds. Demand comes from various motives of capitalists; supply is affected by banking activity. Merchants receive a portion of surplus-value for acting as independent sales agents for industrial capitalists. Merchants utilize funds from credit systems.

Uno's theory of economic crisis clarifies the causal chains of business cycles in 'pure capitalism' under perfect competition. He reasons that capital accumulation necessarily increases to the point where a shortage of labour-power appears. This shortage of labour squeezes profits in real terms, though in monetary terms, prices and profits are kept high by credit expansion. The credit system first encounters difficulties by losing its gold reserves. Interest rates soar and firms become insolvent. Merchants begin to sell their stocks of commodities; prices fall dramatically; crisis begins and spreads. Depression starts when distrust among capitalists spreads, and continues until depreciation funds are accumulated to some extent in capitalists' hands. Using these funds, they replace old machinery with new and advanced models which reduce costs of production and increase the demand for means of production. Thus business recovers. This model of a business cycle approximately represents mid-19th century economic fluctuations.

Next to the theory of 'pure capitalism' comes the stage theory of capitalist development, as articulated in his *Theory of Economic Policy*. The stage theory describes the dominant forms of capital, their modes of accumulation and the characteristic features of the stages in the process of capitalist development. By this theory, he clearly demonstrated that capitalist society has had three stages of development; mercantilist, liberalist and imperialist. In the first stage the dominant capital was merchant capital which had productive bases by its putting-out systems; particularly representative are those of the British woollen industry of the 17th or 18th centuries. In the second stage, the dominant capital was industrial which was represented by machinery-based factories of the British cotton industry of the mid-19th century. German and American heavy industry represented the third stage, where imperialist conflicts among several powers led to 'the imperialist war'.

For Uno the decades after the First World War were not simply a capitalist era, rather one of coexistence of capitalist and socialist societies. Particularly after the Second World War, we have had the 'democratically organized societies' in advanced capitalist countries. Using these frameworks we must analyse the present state of capitalism.

Uno's methodology, the three-level approach, has some practical grounding by which he tried to connect theory to practice. For him theory is that of *Das Kapital*; practice is that of communist or socialist parties. The theory must be useful to these practices. Hence he stressed that the final goal of economics was the analysis of the present state of capitalism which can supply the scientific basis for judgements by these parties. For that analysis, the theory of *Das Kapital* must be utilized. But to be utilized, it must be logically purified and released from ideological prejudice. Furthermore it must be methodologically connected with capitalist development and with the present state of capitalism. To connect them, Uno separated theory from practice or ideology. Economics must supply practice with the result of a concrete analysis of the present state of a capitalist economy. Practice makes use of that analysis by connecting it with its ideal.

Uno was in a sense an old Marxist who did not lose his admiration for Marxist socialism. But he did not devote himself to transforming theory into practice. He was very critical of Soviet types of socialism and their ideological expression in Stalinism. Uno always said that the test of a socialist society was whether workers could decide their own wages, implying that a society where workers cannot take part in the economic planning process is not socialist. One wonders how Uno would have commented on the recent collapse of communist societies in Eastern Europe.

Uno's Major Writings

(1947a), *An Introduction to Agricultural Problems*, in Japanese.
(1947b), *A Theory of Value*, in Japanese.
(1950, 1952), *The Principles of Political Economy*, in Japanese. Volume I, 1950; Volume II, 1952. Condensed and revised version in 1964, the latter translated into English by T. Sekine, Harvester Press, 1980.
(1953), *The Theory of Economic Crisis*, in Japanese.
(1954), *The Theory of Economic Policy*, in Japanese.
(1958), *Das Kapital and Socialism*, in Japanese.
(1962), *The Methodology of Economics*, in Japanese.
(1970), *Reading* Das Capital *For Fifty Years*, 2 volumes, in Japanese.
(1973–74), *The Collected Works of Kozo Uno*, 10 volumes, Iwanami Publishers.

Other References

Albritton, R. (1986), *A Japanese Reconstruction of Marxist Theory*, London: Macmillan.
Itoh, M. (1980), *Value and Crisis*, New York: Monthly Review Press.
Itoh, M. (1988), *The Basic Theory of Capitalism*, London: Macmillan.
Mawatari, S. (1985), 'The Uno School: a Marxian Approach in Japan', *History of Political Economy*, **17**(3), Fall.
Sekine, T. (1975), 'Unoriron: a Japanese Contribution to Marxian Political Economy', *Journal of Economic Literature*, **13**(3), September.

Thorstein VEBLEN (1857–1929)   *Rick Tilman*

Thorstein Veblen was born in 1857 into a Norwegian-American family in Wisconsin. His academic training was in the field of philosophy but, after completion of his doctorate at Yale in 1884, a seven-year period of unemployment due to ill-health and inability to obtain an academic post followed before he turned to the study of economics. The seminal influences on Veblen's dissenting economics were Darwinism, particularly the work of Darwin himself, and American socialism, especially the ideas of the Utopian novelist Edward Bellamy.

During the next 30 years he held academic posts at Chicago, Stanford, Missouri and the New School for Social Research, during which time he became the most influential and best-known dissenting economist in the US. Veblen's heterodoxy was widely recognized by professional economists and sociologists after the publication in 1899 of his most famous book, *The Theory of the Leisure Class*, in which he developed his theory of status emulation. In this satirical study of the leisure class and the underlying social strata which emulate it, he argued that conspicuous consumption, conspicuous waste and ostentatious avoidance of useful work were practices by which social status was enhanced. In short, Veblen contended that individual utility functions could not be understood except in relation to the utility functions of others because individuals were emulating others in order to strengthen their own sense of self-worth by commanding more social esteem. The assumptions of atomistic individualism and consumer-sovereignty deemed valid by microeconomists were thus shown to be specious on social psychological grounds alone.

The Theory of the Leisure Class also contained many of Veblen's ideas regarding the nature of social value, ideas that were fundamentally different from those of the utilitarian tradition that formed the basis of the neoclassical approach to value. Veblen found unconvincing the conventional view of individuals as 'globules of desire' attempting to maximize pleasure and minimize pain. He was also caustic in his repudiation of the moral agnosticism he found pervasive in the neoclassical view of value as subjective preference measurable only by price. This had led to the claim that interpersonal comparisons of utility were impossible or irrelevant since consumer preferences were autonomously rooted in private, subjective states of mind.

Veblen's rejection of neoclassical value theory did not end in nihilism, however, for he outlined an alternative to both neoclassicism and classical Marxism. He wrote of the 'generic ends' of life 'impersonally considered' and of 'fullness of life'; in his evolutionary (that is Darwinian) mode of analysis, this implied the existence of some transcultural set of values. He found these values embedded in workmanship, parenthood and idle curiosity, all of which flourish in a properly-developing society. Veblen meant that proficiency of craftsmanship, altruism and critical intelligence were dominant values and processes in communities that were developing in a non-invidious manner. But in communities that were not so developing, these 'instincts' or propensities would be contaminated by their opposites, the pecuniary and sporting traits which were invidious.

Veblen's second book *The Theory of Business Enterprise* (1904) contains his explanation of business cycles and an extended treatment of the cultural and social psychological incidence of the machine process. Contrary to conventional analyses of business cycles, Veblen saw no natural equilibrating tendencies in the American economy. Instead, he argued that instability was endemic in the American business system because of excessive capitalization and credit inflation. His analysis focused on the tendency of firms to borrow too much by exaggerating their future earning power. At some point their creditors would recognize that loans made to these firms were unwarranted because their earning power was less than anticipated. The loans would then be called in with the inevitable consequences of liquidation and bankruptcy. A protracted period of depression would follow with large-scale unemployment and unused industrial capacity. Gradually, however, the earning power and credit rating of the firm would move towards convergence and recovery would occur. A period of prosperity would then ensue until over-capitalization and credit inflation recurred and the cycle began anew. Veblen anticipated that the growth of monopoly and wasteful government expenditures might check cyclical instability, but his disciples looked to the social control of industry and better economic planning to offset the deficiencies of the system.

Much of Veblen's reputation as a dissenting economist was based on his critique of classical and neoclassical economics. Included in his analysis of the received economic theory and doctrines was a rejection of the following: (i) hedonism and utilitarianism, (ii) the static bias of price theory, (iii) the taxonomic method, and (iv) the infection of economics with teleology. Veblen labelled these deficiencies 'pre-Darwinian'; that is, as rooted in a pre-evolutionary mindset which had not yet come to terms with the scientific revolution of which Darwin was the chief catalyst. Veblen criticized the hedonistic and utilitarian theory for portraying humankind as passive agents reacting to external forces only when impinged upon. His reading in cultural anthropology convinced him that humanity was active rather than quiescent and that, in any case, the Benthamite claim that pleasure and pain were the 'sovereign masters of us all' was merely tautological. When Veblen accused eminent neoclassicists such as his former teacher John Bates Clark and Irving Fisher of mere 'taxonomy' he was, of course, charging them with mistaking classification, inventorying and labelling for genuine scientific explanation, which in his view dealt primarily with the establishment of causal relationships.

Indeed, Veblen's essentially negative view of neoclassicism rested on his belief that it failed to move beyond the taxonomic stage of inquiry.

Veblen attacked the static bias of neoclassicism because it was unable to account for change; general and partial equilibrium theory failed to capture the flux of evolutionary processes, including both changes in the market mechanism and the underlying institutions which direct and channel exchange. Finally, Veblen criticized neoclassicism for its retention of the residues of teleology which so badly infected classical economics. His most often cited example was the neoclassical claim that equilibrium constitutes a 'normal' state of affairs towards which markets inevitably and invariably tend.

However, the central feature of Veblen's work as a dissenting economist was not his critique of neoclassicism, his contribution to business cycle theory, or even his theory of status emulation, as important as was the latter. Instead, what most set him off from the conventional paradigm was his development and use of the dichotomy between business and industry, what his disciples were later to call the 'ceremonial-technological dichotomy'. They and Veblen employed it as an analytical device, as an approach to the larger problem of value in economics and as part of a theory of social change. In his usage, the dichotomy was extended to include salesmanship as opposed to workmanship, free income versus tangible performance, individual gain as opposed to community serviceability, invidious emulation versus technological efficiency, and competitive advertizing versus the provision of valuable information and guidance. To Veblen much of the activity that the business community engaged in was wasteful and futile, for the profitability of market exchange did not necessarily measure its social value in achieving the generic ends of life. However, he was not adequately specific about which pursuits are industrial and which are businesslike or which have both traits. Nevertheless, it is clear in retrospect that such judgements depend on the meaning assigned by Veblen to 'fullness of life, impersonally considered' which was his way of indicating that the 'generic ends of life' are transcultural in nature and often not served by profit-making. The dichotomy between business and industry can be understood, as Veblen intended, if it is recognized that those values and processes most conducive to fullness of life – such as idle curiosity, the parental bent and proficiency of workmanship – cannot always be adequately measured by a price system or through market exchange. It follows that business enterprise will often dissipate resources rather than produce commodities that contribute to the generic ends of life. In the final analysis, what is business and what is industry in the Veblenian dichotomy can only be ascertained by reference to these ends.

Conventional income distribution theory, according to Veblen, is based on the untenable assumption that remuneration measures production. The modern captain of industry and the absentee owner are considered productive agents who receive in remuneration the equivalent of their productivity. Thus their pecuniary activities are not treated as the controlling factor about which the modern economic process turns, but are assumed to be productive operations effecting the distribution of goods from producer to consumer. At various times Veblen cast aspersions on all the prevailing theories and rationalizations of the existing distribution of income. He satirized, castigated or considered irrelevant the abstinence, risk and time rationales for the receipt of rent, interest and profit, and indicated that marginal utility theory was tautological and thus without explanatory power. He also criticized the Marxian theory because he thought it assigned to the individual worker the full value of his labour and ignored the fact that the forces of production were themselves a collective or social legacy and that, consequently, there was no objective way to ascertain the value of an individual's contribution. Although he never specifically articulated a theory of income distribution, his evolutionary view of social change suggests an unending process of adjusting means to ends and ends to means, with community serviceability as the standard of value for all economic activity.

As an economic historian and theorist of growth, Veblen is best known for his 'institutionalism', a term coined by Walton Hamilton during the First World War. In one sense the term is misleading because it was existing institutions which Veblen criticized because of their inhibitive impact on technological change. In his theory of cultural lag, he develops the idea that institutions are inhibitory and backward-looking, whereas science and technology are dynamic and orientated towards change. The question at any point in time is whether institutions are sufficiently malleable to permit efficient exploitation of existing technological potential. As the tool continuum evolves, it may become more or less absorptive of cultural cross-fertilization processes which bring together more and different tools, making possible new technologies. Veblen thus explains the economic history of the West by linking cultural anthropology and social history with changes in the technoeconomic base; the main variables in his explanation are the degree of institutional rigidity and the force exerted on it by technology.

Veblen's theory of economic growth is closely linked with his ideas regarding economic waste. The rate of economic growth cannot be maximized if all output is not serviceable and if efficiency is sacrificed to pecuniary interests. The rate of maximum growth is thus governed by technological advance which controls the size of the nation's economic surplus, although this rate is also a matter of the disposition of the surplus between serviceable and non-serviceable uses. In short, Veblen incorporates a theory of waste – that is, unproductive consumption, investment and labour – within his theory of social change. This permits him to show the conditions under which economic growth will stagnate and, also, the conditions under which economic growth will not be synonymous with the economic welfare of the community. The concept of economic efficiency is thus clarified and linked with the processes of social change and non-invidious economic growth.

In 1914 Veblen published *The Instinct of Workmanship* which he believed was his only important book. It can profitably be read as a sequel to *The Theory of the Leisure Class*. Whereas the latter focused on emulatory consumption and display, the former outlined the aesthetic and moral aspects as well as the economic significance of work. Veblen also discarded the instinct psychology and racism which influenced his early work. This he accomplished by defining 'instinct' as purposive, learned behaviour and by asserting that all Europeans were racial hybrids with little to differentiate them in terms of their natural endowments. Veblen's massive erudition was also evident in his further development of the phases through which he believed humanity has evolved, including the savage, barbarian, handicraft and industrial stages. What separates these stages from each other, in addition to the level of economic development they have reached, is the degree to which the predatory instincts have contaminated the peaceful or non-predatory traits; in short, the extent to which the sporting and pecuniary instincts have influenced the instincts of idle curiosity, parenthood and workmanship.

Three of Veblen's last books *The Vested Interests and the State of the Industrial Arts*, *The Engineers and the Price System* and *Absentee Ownership* focus on the predation and waste of the corporate capitalist order. Writing in a more polemical style than before, Veblen endorsed the dispossession of absentee owners and business-minded executives from the American corporation. He also recommended, perhaps tongue-in-cheek, that engineers and technicians form an alliance with workers and run enterprises themselves. At this point in his career Veblen interacted for a short time with politically progressive engineers, emphasizing the role they might play in the establishment of an industrial republic. But the many allegations by his critics that Veblen was a technocratic elitist who wanted to establish an autocracy dominated by engineers and technicians exaggerate this element in his thought.

It was inevitable in his role as a dissenting economist that Veblen would favour large-scale changes in the capitalist order, although it was unusual for him to make serious policy recommendations. What distinguished him from other radicals was his view of the means that were available to make these changes. Orthodox Marxists still put their faith in a proletariat, whether it was revolutionary or not, but Veblen was sceptical of this labour metaphysic. Nevertheless, he persisted in his search for a social change agent, a political technology and a vehicle for structural change. Early in his career the American proletariat and Bellamyite socialism attracted his attention in these regards. After them, anarcho-syndicalism in the form of 'the Industrial Workers of the

World' aroused his sympathies and, of course, later he endorsed (tongue-in-cheek) progressive engineers and technicians as the wave of the future. Ultimately, however, he retreated into pessimism as regards the American scene, believing 'imbecile institutions' to be dominant.

However, his own analysis of the social psychology of classes makes uncertain the outcome of industrial civilization. On the one hand, the machine process has an emancipatory impact on the psyche of industrial workers which turns them against social convention and presumably in favour of socialism; on the other hand, status emulation infected the working class and served as a social bonding agent to offset the class mentality and conflict induced by the machine process. Status emulation was in turn reinforced by patriotism, as Veblen indicated in *The Nature of Peace*. Would the machine process triumph and turn the working class against capitalism as suggested in *The Theory of Business Enterprise*, or would emulatory consumption reinforced by patriotism triumph? In the final analysis, despite his pessimism, Veblen did not know or at least he did not say.

Estimates of Veblen's creative contribution as a dissenting economist vary greatly depending on the political and social philosophy of the critic. Most neoclassical economists who are politically conservative find little merit in his work because they see themselves correctly, both as economists and consumers, as the objects of his satire. Liberals react differently to Veblen depending on how far left they are in the political spectrum. To illustrate, those still partly under the influence of classical liberalism find little of value other than his humour, while collectivist liberals often respect both his satire and social theory. However, it is on the radical left that Veblen's theory and doctrine meet with greatest approval, although Marxists like Paul Baran and Theodor Adorno have been very critical.

The creation of the Association for Evolutionary Economics and the publication of its organ the *Journal of Economic Issues* since 1966 have provided a forum for the study of Veblen and his ideas; more recently the Association for Institutional Thought (1979) and the European Association for Evolutionary Political Economy (1988) provide evidence of the continued growth of a dissenting tradition with Veblenian roots. Veblen's theoretical and doctrinal arsenal as a dissenter from the neoclassical paradigm is thus more widely accessible to a new generation of economists in search of a viable alternative to the neoclassical paradigm.

Veblen's Major Writings

(1899), *The Theory of the Leisure Class*, New York: Macmillan.
(1904), *The Theory of Business Enterprise*, New York: Charles Scribner's Sons.
(1914), *The Instinct of Workmanship*, New York: B.W. Huebsch.
(1917), *The Nature of Peace*, New York: Macmillan.
(1919a), *The Place of Science in Modern Civilisation*, New York: B.W. Huebsch.

(1919b), *The Vested Interests and the State of Industrial Acts*, New York: B.W. Huebsch.

(1921), *The Engineers and the Price System*, Harcourt Brace and World.

(1923), *Absentee Ownership*, New York: B.W. Huebsch.

Other References

Dente, L.A. (1977), *Veblen's Theory of Social Change*, Salem, Mass:Arno Press.

Dorfman, J. (1934), *Thorstein Veblen and his America*, New York: Viking Press.

Edgell, S. and Tilman, R. (1989), 'The Intellectual Antecedents of Thorstein Veblen: A Reappraisal', *Journal of Economic Issues*, **23**.

Leibenstein, H. (1950), 'Bandwagon, Snob, and Veblen Effects in the Theory of Consumer's Demand', *Quarterly Journal of Economics*, **64**.

Tilman, R. (1972), 'Veblen's Ideal Political Economy and its Critics', *American Journal of Economics and Sociology*, **31**.

Tilman, R. (1973), 'Thorstein Veblen: Incrementalist and Utopian', *American Journal of Economics and Sociology*, **32**.

Sidney WEINTRAUB
(1914–1983)

Johan Deprez and William Milberg

... authority has ever been the great opponent of truth. A despotic calm is usually the triumph of error. In the republic of the sciences sedition and even anarchy are beneficial in the long run to the greatest happiness of the greatest number.

– W.S. Jevons (1871, pp. 275–6)

Sidney Weintraub once described himself as a 'Jevonian seditionist' who 'often railed in mutiny at the Establishment...to enhance the economy bounty and to iron out its division' (see 1985). Weintraub was a dissenting economist in the most appropriate sense – a person who sought truth and explanations independent of the prevailing intellectual and political winds. He combined a keen pragmatism towards economic theory and policy with an idealism aimed at making life better for all. Speaking about those believers in the Phillips curve who called for an increase in unemployment to reduce our inflation ills, Weintraub insisted that these economists be the first to give up their jobs!

Most important, Weintraub developed and promoted an interpretation of Keynes that had an explicit supply side, a variable price level and a macroeconomic theory of income distribution – all this at a time when classical Keynesianism lacked any meaningful discussion of these components. This line of thought has been labelled 'Fundamentalist Keynesianism' (Coddington, 1976); Weintraub's almost solitary and unfashionable adherence to this view led Paul Samuelson (1964) to label him a 'lone wolf'. Yet this approach provided the theoretical underpinnings for Weintraub's wage-cost mark-up theory of inflation, which he discussed well before inflation became such a pervasive problem in industrialized countries, and allowed him to propose his well-known tax-based incomes policy as a way of fighting inflation without creating unemployment.

Sidney Weintraub was born in Brooklyn on 28 April 1914 and died on 19 June 1983. The realization that he lacked the skills to pursue his first love – baseball – as a profession, together with his mother's objections to such an endeavour, eventually led Weintraub to his second career – economics. His early studies were carried out at New York University (NYU) where, according to Weintraub, 'the courses were ... too easy (b)ut they freed me to live in the library' (1985). The major influences on Weintraub at NYU were Herbert B. Dorau, Marcus Nadler and Thomas F.P. McManus.

At the urging of McManus, Weintraub attended the London School of Economics from October 1938 until May 1939 where he attended the lectures of Robbins, Hayek, Kaldor, Durbin and others. The London-Oxford-Cambridge seminar series brought him into contact with many of the graduate students of his generation who were in England at the time. It is interesting to note that Weintraub had begun to translate Pareto's *Manual of Politi-*

cal Economy when, with 122 pages completed, Lionel Robbins persuaded him to stop the project. An English version did not appear until Ann Schweir's translation was published in 1971.

Weintraub received his Ph.D. from NYU in 1941 with a dissertation entitled 'Monopoly and the Economic System'. During the Second World War he worked for a variety of government agencies, including the Treasury, the Office of Price Administration and the Federal Reserve Bank of New York. The military service that he desired – and performed for almost three years – included participation in the Battle of the Bulge and coincided with the turning of the tide in favour of the allies. After returning to the US, Weintraub held a variety of academic jobs until he joined the economics faculty at the University of Pennsylvania in 1950. Except for short teaching stays at a variety of universities – the University of Waterloo (Canada) being possibly the most important – he remained at Penn until his death.

During his lifetime Weintraub wrote or edited 18 books, published about 100 professional articles and about 200 or more 'popular' pieces. He lectured internationally and in 1972–73 wrote a weekly column for the *Philadelphia Bulletin*. Weintraub was the major driving force in the founding of the *Journal of Post Keynesian Economics* in 1979 and he served, until his death, as its co-editor with his former student Paul Davidson.

His dissertation and work in microeconomics led to three articles in one year in the 'major' journals (1942a, 1942b, 1942c), another in 1946 and in 1949 to his first book *Price Theory*. This book stands out for two reasons. First, Weintraub's understanding of Keynes had led him to the realization of the incompatibility of Keynesian macroeconomics with the marginal productivity theory of distribution. Thus his microeconomics books leave out any discussion of the latter. Second, the last part of this book is devoted to dealing with unconventional ideas related to dynamics such as anticipations and uncertainty, subjective and objective demand and cost curves, imperfect equilibrium adaptations, multiple-period anticipations, clock-time sequences and path analysis. To this day such topics are largely ignored in microeconomics textbooks. The failure of microeconomists to pursue these themes has prevented the development of a microeconomic theory consistent with the monetary production economy described by Keynes (cf Davidson, 1985).

Keynes's macroeconomic model of the *The General Theory* and after is one in which 'the volume of employment is given by the point of intersection between the aggregate demand function and the aggregate supply function' (Keynes, 1936, p.25). Just as classical economists had, on the basis of Say's Law, virtually ignored demand considerations, classical Keynesians tended to ignore supply factors. One of the few Keynesians to stay true to Keynes's original formulation, Weintraub included an explicit supply side in his model. This omission in classical Keynesian models, both in their 45-degree line

'Keynesian cross' and in IS-LM variants, prevented the adequate treatment of price changes and income distribution. This led Weintraub to argue for an abandonment of these models well before others began to question them (1958, 1961). He attacked the 45-degree line model for its logical inconsistency. And he rejected the IS-LM model ultimately because it lacked a theory of the price level.

Weintraub criticized the 45-degree line model for a number of reasons, including (i) the view that the economy could either experience inflation or unemployment and that fiscal policy could control each; (ii) its inclusion of inflationary and deflationary gaps even though the model was set up in real terms to exclude price and money wage elements; (iii) its ignoring of Keynes's 'animal spirits' and uncertainty in favour of accelerator notions of investment depending mechanistically on past values of output or profits; (iv) its assumption of a purely exogenous quantity of money; and, (v) a general lack of microeconomic foundations and consideration of the distribution of income. Weintraub argued that while the IS-LM model solved the logical problem of the 45-degree line model, it still excluded a price theory and a role for money wages. The model also suffers from critiques (iii), (iv) and (v). The Phillips Curve is an *ad hoc* addition that finally puts the price level into these classical Keynesian models.

Weintraub's development of the aggregate supply and aggregate demand model culminated in his 1958 book, *An Approach to the Theory of Income Distribution*. These works adopt Keynes's two fundamental units: money-units and labour units. Aggregate supply is derived from the ordinary Marshallian micro-supply function with only limited modifications like user costs. The aggregation across industries is in money-units and presented with respect to labour-units. The aggregate supply value at any employment level then implies a particular composition of output between industries. Just as at the firm level, the different levels of production and employment are associated with particular unit-supply prices and aggregate versions of the different cost components like the wage bill and fixed payments.

Because every employment level has a different income amount associated with it, there is a different microeconomic demand curve appropriate for each output level. The demand-outlay function is the locus of demand prices that is consistent with each output level and the income level that each output level generates. The demand values at each output and employment level determine the aggregate demand function. Hence the aggregate demand curve, like the aggregate supply curve, has embodied in it variable unit prices. The intersection between the two curves that specifies the point of effective demand determines simultaneously the quantities of output and employment and unit prices – a significant improvement over the 'fix-price' classical Keynesian models.

Weintraub's model allows for the incorporation of different technological and cost structures, different specifications of the expectations of firms and different market structures. For example, Weintraub extended the basic approach to deal directly with the case of monopoly (1958, Chapter 4). The model also provides for the macrofoundations of the analysis of the labour market and the distribution of income. Given its explicit microfoundations and its numerous possible extensions, the model met the unfortunate fate of being largely ignored or severely criticized by orthodox Keynesians.

Weintraub's extension of this model into growth theory is contained in his underappreciated 1966 book, *A Keynesian Theory of Employment Growth and Income Distribution*. Growth theory has been dominated by the Harrod and Cambridge traditions, both of which take the steady-state as a starting point. The Weintraub approach to growth is one of shifting aggregate demand and aggregate supply curves where these steady-states are nothing but very special cases. Essentially this is an articulation of Keynes's shifting equilibrium model (Keynes, 1936) applied to a variety of growth problems, including nonlinear growth paths.

Weintraub's sharp criticism of the marginal productivity theory of distribution in *Approach* (1958) occurred about the time the Cambridge Keynesians were starting to attack the same concepts. But while Joan Robinson, Nicholas Kaldor and others engaged Cambridge (US) classical Keynesians in capital theory debates, Weintraub remained aloof from this discussion, moving instead to an analysis of the importance of money wages and their relation to price changes.

The use of Keynes's aggregate demand and aggregate supply model allowed Weintraub to address price dynamics directly as part of the same processes that determine output and employment. Using the AS = AD accounting definition:

$$Y = PQ = kwN \qquad (1)$$

where Y is national income, P is the aggregate price level, Q is real output, k is the average mark-up over labour costs by firms, w is the nominal wage and N the level of employment. Solving for P gives Weintraub's well-known wage-cost mark-up (WCM) equation:

$$P = kw/A \qquad (2)$$

where A = Q/N = average labour productivity. Weintraub based the WCM theory of inflation on this simple expression and offered it as an alternative to the quantity theory of money which is based on the equation of exchange. Using empirical evidence and theoretical arguments, Weintraub saw k as a 'magical constant' which had varied little in US history (cf. Weintraub, 1978, pp. 77–84). The constancy of the mark-up implies that the cause of inflation is money-wage growth in excess of productivity growth. Weintraub contrasted this model favourably with the monetarist approach. The monetarist view is 'muddled' since, without assuming full employment, it is unable to say anything about the relative impact of a money supply change on output and prices. Moreover, the WCM model assumes an exogenously determined money wage and thus flies in the face of the Phillips curve trade-off between (wage) inflation and unemployment. The Phillips curve, in Weintraub's view, is an *ad hoc* construction required to save the price-theoryless IS-LM model, but completely inadequate to explain the stagflation experience (recession and inflation simultaneously) in the US in the 1970s (and perhaps again in the 1990s). Appeals to a shifting Phillips curve simply lay bare the ad hocery of the original concept.

Weintraub's inflation theory was vehemently attacked by orthodox Keynesians, although some eventually accepted his policy recommendations. Sympathetic critiques of the WCM inflation theory have been twofold. First, the constancy of k does not imply that the inflationary process is necessarily initiated by wage increases. It may be started by factors that determine k, such as capital intensity, depreciation charges, monopoly power, market conditions and social and collective bargaining power. In this case wage changes are a reaction. Second, the constancy of k itself has been put into question; moreover, even slight changes in k may reflect large changes in the non-wage components of costs (Rothschild, 1985, p. 583).

Weintraub's inflation theory led him naturally to the formulation of the now-famous 'Tax-Based Incomes Policy' (TIP) for controlling inflation. Early in his career, he established the view that the control of money wages is essential for maintaining a stable price level. When, in 1959, he put forth his inflation theory, Weintraub recommended a 'watchtower approach' whereby a research agency would collect data on the most important wage agreements upon which Congress could act to control inflationary tendencies. Walter Heller, chief economic adviser to President Kennedy, was likely influenced by this idea. The first version of TIP was published by Weintraub in 1971 in *Lloyd's Bank Review*. Later in the same year Henry Wallich, a member of the Board of Governors of the Federal Reserve System, and Weintraub laid out the policy in greater detail. The basic idea is that given the constancy of k, it is the wage rate which needs to be controlled. To curb excessive wage increases an additional tax is imposed on corporate profits if any corporation grants average annual wage increases in excess of some norm. The TIP would not disrupt the market mechanism in that it changes the incentive structure for firms without any direct controls, and it is easy to implement within existing institutions for tax collection. Since 1971 there have been further developments of Weintraub's proposal, including a 'market-based anti-inflation policy' (MAP) whereby inflation is fought by creating a market for the right to raise prices, and a 'value added tax-based incomes policy' (VATIP) according to which a value added tax is used instead of a tax on corporate profits. The idea of a TIP gained popularity in the Carter administration in the inflationary period of the late 1970s. Had President Carter been re-elected in 1980, a TIP would likely have been implemented. Instead, President Reagan imposed a policy of monetary restraint, recession and regressive redistribution of income and wealth, precisely the outcome Weintraub had spent his career struggling against (see 1981–82).

Weintraub's Keynesianism focused on the real exchange economy. The incorporation of money prices and money costs in the determination of output and employment is key to a monetary, production economy. This focus, in conjunction with the WCM theory, formed the basis of his critique of monetarism. If inflation comes from money wage changes, then changes in the money stock will neither cause nor cure inflation (see 1973). The dependence of the money stock on the needs of production and circulation makes the amount of money at least partially endogenous and raises the importance of a variety of near-monies for transactions purposes, in contrast to the usual textbook presentations (1958). Liquidity constraints and preferences are seen as crucial to the production and investment decisions of firms. This follows Keynes's monetary theory, and has been extended by a number of people including Paul Davidson. Armed with his views on money and inflation, Weintraub was able to explain America's stagflation woes. Inflation follows the WCM formula, and insufficient money growth leads liquidity-constrained firms to cut production and employment.

The same framework used for the WCM also provided a theory of income distribution, the focus of Weintraub's last theoretical writings (1979, 1982), a number of debates in the *Journal of Post Keynesian Economics*, as well as a significant number of works by other economists extending or empirically testing Weintraub's model. By definition:

$$W/Y = (wN)/(PQ) \qquad (3)$$

where $W = wN$ = the total wage bill and thus W/Y is labour's share of total income. Substituting (2) into (3):

$$W/Y = (w/A)/P = 1/k. \qquad (4)$$

The constancy of k thus assures a constant wage share-out of income. Weintraub then generalized the framework to allow for the non-constancy of k, that is a varying degree of monopoly (to use the Kaleckian term to which k is so often compared), and to allow for a variation in consumption propensities out of labour and capital income. In so doing, he tried to bring together the complementary work of Kalecki and Kaldor (see Rothschild, 1985).

In his drive to understand the world and change it for the better, Weintraub left us with a very important interpretation of Keynes. He provided an aggregate supply and aggregate demand model which contains particular microfoundations and a powerful explanation of inflation. His early critique of economic policy based on a rejection of the neoclassical synthesis and the Phillips curve forms one of the building blocks of US post-Keynesian thought. His alternative model of growth and distribution provides a rigorous underpinning for policies which can deal with inflation and unemployment simultaneously. Such policies have become integral to the post-Keynesian tradition in the US; in the light of his contributions, Weintraub could be considered the founder of this tradition. Finally, his work has been extended in a number of directions by his students, including Paul Davidson, Eugene Smolensky, Eileen Appelbaum, John Hotson, Ingrid Rima and Ronald Bodkin, and in turn by their students. Weintraub's son, E. Roy Weintraub, also joined the economics profession, but has been mainstream despite his gene pool. The influence of Sidney Weintraub thus spans across economic theory into issues of economic policy and, with his work as founding co-editor of the *Journal of Post Keynesian Economics*, makes him a leading force in the development of alternatives to orthodox economic thought in the United States.

Weintraub's Major Writings

(1942a), 'Monopoly Equilibrium and Anticipated Demand', *Journal of Political Economy*, **50**.
(1942b), 'The Classification of Market Positions: A Comment', *Quarterly Journal of Economics*, **56**.
(1942c), 'The Foundations of the Demand Curve', *American Economic Review*, **32**.
(1946), 'Monopoly Pricing and Unemployment', *Quarterly Journal of Economics*, November.
(1949), *Price Theory*, London: Pitman. (Modified for an undergraduate audience and reprinted in 1964 under the title *Intermediate Price Theory*, Philadelphia: Chilton.)
(1958), *An Approach to the Theory of Income Distribution*, Philadelphia: Chilton.
(1959), *A General Theory of the Price Level, Output, Income Distribution and Economic Growth*, Philadelphia: Chilton.
(1961), *Classical Keynesianism, Monetary Theory and the Price Level*, Philadelphia: Chilton.
(1966), *A Keynesian Theory of Employment Growth and Income Distribution*, Philadelphia: Clifton.
(1971), 'An Incomes Policy to Stop Inflation', *Lloyd's Bank Review*, **99**, January.
(1973), 'Money as Cause and Effect' (with Paul Davidson), *Economic Journal*, **83**.
(1978), *Capitalism's Inflation and Unemployment Crisis: Beyond Monetarism and Keynesianism*, Reading, Mass: Addison-Wesley Publishing.
(1979), 'Generalizing Kalecki and Simplifying Macroeconomics', *Journal of Post Keynesian Economics*, **1**.
(1981), 'An Eclectic Theory of Income Shares', *Journal of Post Keynesian Economics*, **4**.
(1981–82), 'Keynesian Demand Serendipity in Supply-Side Economics', *Journal of Post Keynesian Economics*, **4**.
(1985), 'A Jevonian Seditionist: A Mutiny to Enhance the Economic Bounty', *Journal of Post Keynesian Economics*, **7**.

Other References

Coddington, A. (1976), 'Keynesian Economics: The Search for First Principles', *Journal of Economic Literature*, **14**.

Davidson, P. (1985), 'Sidney Weintraub – An Economist of the Real World', *Journal of Post Keynesian Economics*, **7**.

Keynes, J.M. (1964), *The General Theory of Employment, Interest and Money*, New York: Harcourt Brace Jovanovich. Originally published in 1936.

Rothschild, K. (1985), 'Some Notes on Weintraub's Eclectic Theory of Income Shares', *Journal of Post Keynesian Economics*, **7**, Summer.

Samuelson, P.A. (1964), 'A Brief Survey of Post Keynesian Developments' in Lekachman R. (ed), *Keynes' General Theory: Reports of Three Decades*, New York: St Martins.

Thomas E. WEISSKOPF (born 1940)

Thomas Weisskopf was born in 1940 in the United States to immigrant Viennese-Jewish and Danish-Lutheran parents. He was raised in the environs of Boston and studied at Harvard University (where he received his B.A. in Economics in 1961) and the Massachusetts Institute of Technology (where he attained his Ph.D. in Economics in 1966).

Although initially he concentrated on mathematics and physics, his interests as an undergraduate student soon shifted to the social sciences in general, and to Third World economic development in particular. Following his graduation from Harvard in 1961, he took advantage of an opportunity to spend a year at the Indian Statistical Institute (in Calcutta) as a teacher of economics to undergraduate students from all over India. During this year he acquainted himself directly with problems of Indian economic development and pursued a particular interest in techniques of economic planning.

Returning from India to begin his graduate studies at MIT, Weisskopf sought to master the analytical tools of the discipline of economics as taught by such prominent mainstream North American economists as Paul Samuelson and Robert Solow. Not yet a dissenter in any fundamental respect, his primary objective was to learn how to apply quantitative economic methods to problems of Third World economic development. After spending another year in India in 1964–65, this time on a doctoral research fellowship at the New Delhi branch of the Indian Statistical Institute, he completed his Ph.D. dissertation on 'A Programming Model for Import Substitution in India' in 1966.

More interested at first in working in the 'real world' than in academia, Weisskopf was intending to accept an offer to join the staff of the US Agency for International Development in New Delhi as a research economist. Just before this assignment was about to begin, however, he decided to turn down the offer – in order to disassociate himself from the US government which by then had escalated its involvement in Vietnam into a full-fledged war. As it turned out, he was nonetheless able to work in India for the next two years;

after his rejection of the USAID job, he was offered a two-year visiting professorship at the New Delhi branch of the Indian Statistical Institute. From 1966 to 1968 he worked at the Institute, teaching in its graduate economics programme and carrying out research both on problems of Indian national economic planning and on the operation of the irrigation and power system associated with the massive North Indian Bhakra-Nangal dam.

It was during this two-year stay in India that Weisskopf began to nurture serious doubts about the relevance of mainstream economics to the issues with which he was most concerned. Committed to the vision of a 'socialistic pattern of society' that Jawaharlal Nehru had articulated for independent India, and believing in the constructive role that a technically skilled economist could play in achieving that vision, Weisskopf became increasingly disillusioned by the way in which the best economic ideas and advice could be frustrated and rendered irrelevant by the structure of real power and influence in a society. This led him to look for a more broad-ranging political-economic approach to understanding problems of economic development as an alternative to the relatively narrow training he had received in mainstream economics. For the first time he began to acquaint himself with the work of Karl Marx and such contemporary dissident economists as Michal Kalecki, Paul Baran and Paul Sweezy, as well as numerous Indian nationalist and Marxist social scientists.

Returning to the US in 1968 to take up an appointment as assistant professor at Harvard, Weisskopf found that his evolving views on politics and economics were completely in harmony with those of a growing number of young North American economists associated with the 'New Left' movement of the time. Joining his friend and colleague Samuel Bowles, as well as numerous dissenting Harvard economics graduate students, he participated in an informal seminar on 'radical political economy' whose primary purpose was to develop a new undergraduate course in the social sciences that would provide a radical alternative to the standard fare on offer. The seminar participants offered this course (collectively) for the first time in 1969 under the title 'The Capitalist Economy: Conflict and Power'.

In the autumn of 1968 Weisskopf joined a group of like-minded young economists – most of them from Harvard, MIT and the University of Michigan – in founding the Union for Radical Political Economics (URPE). This was designed to provide an institutional foundation for the development of a dissident form of economics in North America – one which would challenge, from a broadly-defined Marxian perspective, the contemporary orthodoxy in the discipline as well as the capitalist political and economic environment in which it was situated. URPE was one of many dissident organizations formed to challenge mainstream academia during the height of the New Left movement in the late 1960s and early 1970s; it is one of the few to have survived and maintained to the present day its peak membership (about 2000), regular semi-annual meetings and the publication of a quarterly journal (the *Review of Radical Political Economics*).

During the four years he spent as an assistant professor at Harvard (1968–72), most of Weisskopf's research and writing reflected a broadly-defined Marxian political-economic approach to the analysis of imperialism and underdevelopment in the Third World. In an early article (1972a), he sought to develop a new and broader dependency-theory framework for analysing Third World development, examining how capitalist economic institutions tend to bias the pattern of development in Third World societies in ways that lead, at best, to a dependent, inegalitarian and undemocratic form of economic growth. He then applied the same kind of analysis to the case of independent India (1973). He also carried out and published econometric research on alternative 'two-gap' constraints on economic growth and on the impact of foreign capital inflows on domestic saving in Third World nations. His article on the latter issue showed that foreign capital inflows tended to depress domestic saving rates (see 1972b).

Having participated for several years in the collective teaching of the new course, 'The Capitalist Economy: Conflict and Power', Weisskopf collaborated with two of his colleagues – Richard Edwards and Michael Reich – in preparing a book to present the main issues raised in the course. The result, *The Capitalist System: A Radical Analysis of American Society* (1972c) included contributed articles by the three author-editors, as well as reprinted articles by many other radical political economists. Widely used for undergraduate teaching of political economy in the US, it has twice been extensively revised (in 1978 and 1986).

In 1972 Weisskopf was offered a tenured position as associate professor of economics at the University of Michigan, partly as a consequence of student demands that a radical political economist be hired to teach in the graduate programme there. Accepting the appointment, he proceeded to establish (with his colleague, Daniel Fusfeld) a graduate field of specialization in the area of political economy. Since 1972 Weisskopf has remained at the University of Michigan, where he is now a full professor, dividing his time between the Economics Department and the Social Science Program of the Residential College (an innovative undergraduate liberal arts college within the University of Michigan).

During his initial years at Michigan, Weisskopf continued to carry out research and publish papers dealing with development and underdevelopment in the Third World, focusing *inter alia* on contrasting patterns of development in India and the People's Republic of China. But as the US and indeed the world capitalist economy began to experience increasing symptoms of crisis in the 1970s, his teaching and research interests shifted to the macroeconomic problems of the advanced capitalist economies. In particular, he began to seek ways to develop and apply Marxian crisis theory to such contemporary macroeconomic problems in the US as rising unemployment and inflation and falling profitability and productivity growth.

Weisskopf's early work in this area sought to distinguish between three different variants of Marxian crisis theory – the orthodox theory of 'the tendency of the rate of profit to fall' (due to a rising organic composition of capital); the theory of underconsumption (or, more generally, realization failure); and the theory of the depletion of the reserve army of labour (leading to a 'wage squeeze on profits') – each of which was a possible source of declining profitability and consequent economic crisis. Having developed an overall framework for addressing these theoretical distinctions in an earlier article, he applied the framework to the empirical analysis of profitability trends in the post-World War II US economy (see 1979). He found that the third of the three variants of Marxian crisis theory was the most relevant to the post-war US situation in explaining both long-run (secular) and short-run (cyclical) profitability declines and crisis tendencies.

In the early 1980s, as the world economic crisis reached its nadir, Weisskopf began a long-term research collaboration with Samuel Bowles and David Gordon, with the aims of applying contemporary radical political economics to the study of the continuing US economic crisis and of developing a democratic and egalitarian alternative economic strategy to overcome the crisis. This collaborative research resulted in a book, *Beyond the Waste Land* (1983a), subsequently published also in British, French and Japanese editions, as well as numerous more technical articles on key elements of the analytical underpinning of the book (for instance, 1983b and 1986).

In their joint work, Bowles, Gordon and Weisskopf place the post-war experience of boom and crisis in the US economy into the broader historical context of 'long swings' differentiated from one another by differing 'social structures of accumulation' (SSAs). Each SSA is characterized by a set of social/political/economic institutions that govern relations between the capitalist class and other relevant classes and economic actors. Each SSA is characterized, first, by the success of these institutions in assuring an environment favourable to capitalist profitability and accumulation (in the initial boom period) and, then, by internal contradictions leading to the erosion of the same institutions (in the subsequent crisis period). According to this analysis, the post-World War II SSA in the US was successful in promoting capitalist prosperity through the late 1960s, but then gave way to a series of contradictions that generated the economic crisis of the 1970s and 1980s – from which the US economy has yet to recover in any fundamental way.

More recently Weisskopf has undertaken to extend and apply some aspects of his joint work with Bowles and Gordon in a comparative international context, analysing, for example, how different kinds of social and political relations between capital and labour affect workplace behaviour and labour productivity in different advanced capitalist economies. He has found that the 'worker discipline effect', whereby high unemployment raises productivity, is far more evident in countries (such as the US) in which capital-labour relations tend to be highly antagonistic than in countries (such as Sweden) in which capital-labour relations have been more cooperative (see 1987). In joint work with Francis Green, he has made a similar finding with respect to differences in the worker discipline effect in 'secondary industries' – with relatively low unionization, low wages and little job security, and thus presumably more antagonistic capital-labour relations – as distinct from 'primary industries' which have the opposite characteristics (see 1990a).

Most recently, Weisskopf has been working with S. Bowles and D. Gordon on an updated and much revised version of their joint book now entitled *After the Waste Land: A Democratic Economy for the Year 2000*. This book goes beyond the earlier one in addressing the contradictions and deleterious impact of 'Reaganomics' on the US economy in the 1980s, and in conceptualizing the potential economic as well as political benefits of a more democratic and egalitarian economy.

Finally, stimulated by the peaceful revolutions of 1989 in the 'actually existing socialist societies' of Eastern Europe and the continuing process of reform both there and in the Soviet Union, Weisskopf has once again begun to shift the primary focus of his teaching and research interests – this time to an exploration of the meaning of 'socialism' as a relevant alternative to capitalism in the contemporary world.

Weisskopf's Major Writings

(1972a), 'Capitalism, Underdevelopment and the Future of the Poor Countries', in J. Bhagwati (ed), *Economics and World Order*, Macmillan. Reprinted in the *Review of Radical Political Economics*, **4**, 1972; German translation in Dieter Senghaas (ed), *Imperialismus und Strukturelle Gewalt: Analysen uber Abhangige Reproduktion*, Frankfurt: Suhrkamp Verlag, 1974.

(1972b), 'The Impact of Foreign Capital Inflow on Domestic Savings in Underdeveloped Countries', *The Journal of International Economics*, **2**, February.

(1972c), *The Capitalist System: A Radical Analysis of Contemporary American Society* (with R. Edwards and M. Reich), Englewood Cliffs: Prentice-Hall. 2nd edition 1978; 3rd edition 1986.

(1972d), 'An Econometric Test of Alternative Constraints on the Growth of Underdeveloped Countries', *Review of Economics and Statistics*, **54**(1), February.

(1973), 'Dependence and Imperialism in India', *Review of Radical Political Economics*, **5**. Reprinted in M. Selden (ed), *Remaking Asia: Essays on the American Uses of Power*, New York: Pantheon.

(1975), 'China and India: Contrasting Experiences in Economic Development', *American Economic Review*, **65**(2), May.

(1977), 'The Persistence of Poverty in India: A Political Economic Analysis', *Bulletin of Concerned Asian Scholars*, **9**(1), January–March.

(1979), 'Marxian Crisis Theory and the Rate of Profit in the Postwar U.S. Economy', *Cambridge Journal of Economics*, **3**. Reprinted in J.E. King (ed), *Marxian Economics*, Aldershot: Edward Elgar, 1990.

(1983a), *Beyond the Waste Land: A Democratic Alternative to Economic Decline* (with S. Bowles and D.M. Gordon), Doubleday. Paperback edition, Anchor Press, 1984; British edition, Verso Press 1985; French edition, *L'Economie du Gaspillage: La Crise Americaine et les Politiques Reaganiennes*, Editions La Decouverte, 1986; Japanese edition, Toyo Kezai Shiposha, The Oriental Economist, 1986.

(1983b), 'Hearts and Minds: A Social Model of US Productivity Growth' (with S. Bowles and D. Gordon), *Brookings Papers on Economic Activity*, 2.

(1986), 'Power and Profits: The Social Structure of Accumulation and the Profitability of the Postwar U.S. Economy' (with S. Bowles and D. Gordon), *Review of Radical Political Economics*, **18**.

(1987), 'The Effect of Unemployment on Productivity: An International Comparative Analysis', *International Review of Applied Economics*, **1**.

(1989), 'Business Ascendancy and Economic Impasse: A Structural Retrospective on Conservative Economics, 1979–87' (with S. Bowles and D.M. Gordon), *Journal of Economic Perspectives*, 3(1), Winter.

(1990a), 'The Worker Discipline Effect: A Disaggregative Analysis' (with F. Green), *The Review of Economics and Statistics*, **72**.

(1990b), *After the Waste Land: A Democratic Economics for the Year 2000* (with S. Bowles and D.M. Gordon), New York: M.E. Sharpe.

E.L. (Ted) WHEELWRIGHT (born 1921)

Born into the industrial working class in Sheffield in 1921, E.L. (Ted) Wheelwright, son of a semi-skilled steelworker, left school early during the depression years, to supplement the family's unemployment pay with the salary of a bank clerk. War broke out when he was 18, and in 1941 he joined the RAF, becoming a navigator in Bomber Command; he was awarded the DFC in 1943, and demobilized in 1946 with the rank of Squadron Leader.

Wheelwright sought further education; he wanted to know why his father had been out of work the whole time he was in high school, what were the causes of the war, and why there had been money readily available to train him in the arcane skills of navigating night bombers over Europe, but none to finance his transition from school to university.

Fortunately he was able to participate in the post-war education scheme which paid ex-service persons a living wage whilst studying for a degree, being accepted as an arts degree candidate (majoring in economics and political science) at the University of St Andrews, which gave such students top priority. Hence his first economic lesson was learned from practice rather than theory: public money is much more likely to be available for war-related projects than for peace-time ones.

The late 1940s was an exciting time to be an undergraduate at such a university, full of mature students, mostly striving to ensure a brave new world. Not only had many seen war service all over the globe, but there was a political struggle going on in Europe before their eyes, as American power and money suppressed incipient socialism, while in Asia, communist armies were marching to victory. Power *was* growing out of the barrel of a gun, but it was also being bought with money. This lesson did not appear in the textbooks they studied; the real world imposed itself on the fantasies of perfect competition, the invisible hand and market forces in a way that perhaps no other generation had experienced. Some decided that the invisible hand was inside an iron glove.

This was a perfect breeding ground for dissenting economists; what was in the textbooks of economics and politics did not square with what was happening in the real world. At least politics had its *Prince*, by Machiavelli, which was on the reading list, but *Capital*, by Marx, was not; he was taboo. Here was another lesson from practice: academic objectivity is in the eye of the beholder.

However, in such an environment, conservative professors did not have it all their own way; for instance, dissent in the department of economics ensured that *both* Hayek's *Road to Serfdom* and Finer's *Road to Reaction* were studied. Such dissent was also fostered by the fact that there was no economics degree as such. At least one other discipline had to be taken for honours, the implication being that economics, studied *per se*, stultified the mind, an implication Wheelwright found to be verified later, particularly when economics degenerated into the 'imperialism of the social sciences'.

Wheelwright took a first in economics and political science at St Andrews, and obtained an assistant lectureship at the University of Bristol in 1949. He found the 'imperialism of economics' further advanced in British provincial universities, where it was possible to obtain degrees in economics and commerce. Theory was paramount, and social and political contexts played down. Perhaps the greatest initial impression was the predominantly middle-class nature of the university; people from working-class backgrounds seemed to be rather rare and the process of osmosis diluted their contribution. A curious exception at Bristol was H.D. Dickinson, a contemporary of Maurice Dobb at Cambridge, who was a socialist sprung from the middle class, a genuine scholar of the old school who, besides being an economist, was a mathematician who could handle the transformation problem and an historian who could cope with the history of capitalism.

Dickinson made a big impression on Wheelwright, who thought his books, *The Economics of Socialism* and *Institutional Revenue*, were the clearest expositions of economic theories and their social and political implications that he had read. These, of course, reflected some of the interests of the 1930s, particularly whether a socialist economy could act rationally – in economic terms – and what that meant. It is interesting to reflect, in today's climate, that Dickinson was adamant that the price mechanism was a most important discovery (ranking with the invention of the alphabet) and essential for an appropriate allocation of resources – *given a reasonably egalitarian distribution of incomes.*

At Bristol, Wheelwright continued to be disillusioned with much of economic theory; Keynes was beginning to be 'bastardized', as Joan Robinson was later to call it, so that he was pleased to be allocated lectures on industrial organization. There, at least, he felt he could concentrate on the institutions he thought were the main actors on the economic stage: big companies, big unions and big government. He began research on industrial relations and on the ownership and control of large corporations, but the Cold War had begun, followed by the hot war in Korea. Britain under a Labour government had begun to rearm and to cut expenditure on health services and education to help pay for it. So much for the brave new world.

The future of British universities appeared bleak, as did that of the British economy in the long term. Wheelwright did not have tenure and decided to emigrate. In 1952 he made a successful application for a lectureship with tenure at the University of Sydney, where he stayed until his retirement as Associate Professor in 1986 (having been refused a full professorship on six occasions). At that time young lecturers were encouraged to research whatever subject they were interested in and prepared to work on; in his case, this was international economics and the Australian economy. An application for funding to investigate the ownership and control of Australian companies was successful; after four years' work a book of the same title was published (1957).

His discovery of a heavy concentration of shares in a few hands meant that power was being focused and wielded by a small directing group representing family owners, financial institutions and foreign investors. Here was evidence of the concentration and 'depersonalization' of capital in Australia which, mainly because of its relative smallness and immaturity, had not yet developed to quite the same extent as in Britain or the US. However, there was one significant difference: of the 100 largest companies examined, over one-sixth were controlled by foreign interests, mainly British and American; these were in highly concentrated sectors and growing faster than Australian companies. There was not much 'people's capitalism' here.

Although this was dissent from conventional wisdom, it surprisingly led to a sabbatical year financed by a Fellowship from the Rockefeller Foundation. Spent initially at Harvard and later in Asia, its purpose was to investigate the consequences of growing foreign ownership and control of economic systems. Hence 1958 was very influential for Wheelwright's future development. He encountered the tail-end of McCarthyism at Harvard, leavened by Galbraith, whose *Affluent Society* was published in that year. In seminars, Galbraith used to relate what appeared later in his writings:

A powerful tendency in modern political economy is for the voice of the affluent, and that of the business spokesmen in particular, to be mistaken for the voice of the masses. ...Unless economists understand that our subject is intrinsically contentious – that what is good for the poorest of our people is best for economic performance – our economic policy will be a failure
('Economists: Why They Have Failed Us', *National Times*, 30 January 1978).

Particularly strong impressions were made during contacts with Paul Sweezy and Leo Huberman of *Monthly Review*, and with Paul Baran of Stanford University, whose *Political Economy of Growth* inspired Wheelwright to dissent from orthodox paradigms of economic growth. This experience set directions for future research on the role of foreign investment in a new imperialism of economic development.

The rest of the sabbatical provided immense benefits for the young dissenting scholar. In India he became involved in debates at the Delhi School of Economics over the question of foreign investment. And in Jakarta (Indonesia), Wheelwright first met American 'economic advisers', known in those days as the 'Berkeley Mafia', precursors of 'Los Chicago Boys' in Chile. Here were the Trojan horses of 'value free' economics, maximizing assent to orthodoxy and minimizing dissent from it, in the tradition of economics being 'the nicely calculated lore of less or more'.

Tenure was very important for dissenters, as Wheelwright discovered when he tried to move from Sydney to the Australian National University in Canberra to concentrate on economic development. He was allowed to spend a year there as Visiting Fellow, and produced a book on Malaysia (showing how decolonization had been delayed to ensure maximum security for British capital, how state power was used to create a new middle class of a particular ethnic origin, and how foreign investment was fostered to offset the power of indigenous capitalists). However, the only positions offered were non-tenurable, and it was clear that to achieve more it would be necessary to toe the orthodox line being set in a framework of Ford Foundation research money, conservative governments, bureaucrats and senior academics, in a company town in which the company was the federal government.

Consequently, Wheelwright returned to his tenured position at Sydney and began research on the foreign ownership and control of the Australian economy. The initial result was a book published in 1965, co-authored with a radical economic historian who could not obtain university employment and had to resort to journalism. It was a polemical book, written for a popular audience and naturally sneered at by most academics. But first in the field, it dissented from the orthodox position that uncontrolled foreign investment was the best way of 'developing' Australia.

The Highest Bidder documented the increasing foreign ownership and control of key sectors of the economy – especially American – and argued that economic domination led to political, cultural and ideological subservience. A form of economic nationalism was advocated which, given current Australian political realities, could not be socialist; it would have to be state capitalist, with some reliance on publicly-owned enterprise. The book suggested that the US was the residuary legatee of British imperialism and, if nothing was done, Australia would end up a neo-colony of the US, helping to fight its wars (as had been the case with Britain). It noted that the Australian Prime Minister of the day, who instituted military conscription for Vietnam, described America's intervention there as 'the greatest act of moral courage since Britain stood alone in World War II'.

The book was largely ignored by academics, but it had an impact on Labor politicians and eventually on the short-lived Whitlam government (1972–75). It tried to establish a kind of economic nationalism, proposing a screening system for foreign investment as well as national ownership and control of key sectors such as energy production and distribution. This government was brought down, as has been well documented, by an alliance between sectors of domestic enterprise, foreign corporations, local intelligence services and the CIA. (Wheelwright was on two government committees of enquiry at that time, and can testify to the power of the foreign investment and 'defence' lobbies.)

However, well before this he had had experience of foreign *coups d'état* which were related to foreign investment and imperialism. Although largely ignored by the Australian academic establishment, Wheelwright's dissenting views attracted attention in other parts of the world, especially Latin America. In the mid-1960s he was invited to Argentina to co-author a comparison of Australian and Argentine economic development, with special reference to foreign investment. This work ceased abruptly when in mid-1966 he awoke to find guns and tanks and soldiers in the street outside his apartment in Buenos Aires. He thought it prudent to leave promptly and quietly; the work was never finished for obvious reasons.

Similarly, in the early 1970s Wheelwright was invited to Chile to make a comparison of foreign investment there with that in Australia. This work was not published either, because of the chaos induced by opponents of the Allende regime. 'Los Chicago Boys' were hard at work, the code-name for their machinations to bring down that regime being 'Operation Jakarta'. He decided that equilibrium occurred there only at the point of a bayonet.

Some of Wheelwright's conclusions were published in his collected essays, *Radical Political Economy* (1974). It was clear that Fidel Castro had cast a large shadow over Latin America: any nationalistic attempts to reduce economic dependence on the US were seen as subversive, especially if associated with trade unions or workers' parties. The ruling classes, the oligarchs, had retained control of the armed forces as their praetorian guards, and let them loose on the populace whenever they felt threatened, usually with the connivance of the imperial power. This had to be seen as a form of fascism, different in some respects from the European manifestation, but just as vicious. Chomsky called it 'sub-fascism'; its essential ingredients were denationalized neo-fascist elites, with a weak internal base of comprador and conservative business interests; strong external support (economic and military) having a dogmatic adherence to free enterprise; and an open door to foreign investment as the road to prosperity.

Australia appeared to be different: its landed oligarchy had to contend with trade unions and parliamentary democracy much earlier; industrialization came sooner, partly as a result of participation in Britain's wars; and basic wage and social security systems had reduced the income inequalities of pastoral capitalism, especially in the 1940s and 1950s. But by the 1970s the Chomsky criteria were beginning to apply to Australia, and in the preface to his *Capitalism, Socialism or Barbarism? The Australian Predicament* (1978), Wheelwright wrote:

> Australian capitalism is in crisis, as it twists and turns to try to accommodate itself to the gyrations of world capitalism; it is unlikely to adopt a form of independent socialism which could extricate itself from its predicament; there is a danger of barbarism emerging in the form of an Australian species of the genus, fascism. In the process, the nation is likely to disintegrate, caught in the vortex between two imperialisms, American and Japanese.

A decade earlier he had the opportunity to witness a socialist economy in crisis, spending two months in China in the early phases of the Cultural Revolution in late 1966. He arranged for a colleague to visit in 1968, and in 1970 they co-authored *The Chinese Road to Socialism*, which was published in New York and translated into five languages. Joan Robinson said in her Foreword:

> The authors of this book know the right questions to ask. ...Political economy cannot be understood without considering ideology and morality. They emphasise the moral element in Chinese socialism. ...Our authors understand orthodox economics. They understand it well enough to see through it. For two centuries we have been following Adam Smith's doctrine that the individual's pursuit of self-interest is the foundation of national prosperity. China...has set out to prove the opposite. But it does not expect such a profound reversal to be easily achieved.

In 1966 Mao had insisted that 'if things are not properly handled it is possible for a capitalist restoration to take place at any time'. In March 1976 he said, 'A socialist revolution is being conducted without knowing where the bourgeoisie are. They are in the Communist Party. They are the party leaders taking the capitalist line. They have always been following this line.'

In November 1976, Wheelwright quoted this dictum of Mao, noting that what was then called the 'big right deviationist wind' of Deng Xiaoping was already putting economics instead of politics in command – advocating material incentives to mobilize the enthusiasm of workers and peasants, as well as reliance on specialists to run factories and academic institutions and on the importation of foreign technology to speed up economic development. However, Wheelwright argued that the time bomb Mao left to the nation could not be defused; that it would 'tick away amongst the present gerontocracy and explode when a new and younger generation comes to power'. He concluded by quoting vintage Mao, very relevant to the 1990s:

> Those of you who do not allow people to speak, who think you are tigers, and that nobody will dare to touch your arse, will fail. People will talk anyway. You think that nobody will really dare to touch the arse of tigers like you? They damn well will!

Wheelwright retired from formal academic life in 1986, but his last decade therein was eventful and productive. In 1975, as a result of receiving research funds from private and public sources, he founded the Transnational Corporations Research Project which has published 20 books and over 70 research papers on various aspects of transnational capitalism, with special reference to Australia, South East Asia and the Pacific. He edited *Consumers, Transnational Corporations and Development*, which attempted to integrate the relationships between transnational corporations, economic development and the interests of consumers. Its main theme was the use and abuse of power by such corporations, and the response of new citizen networks and social action groups pressing for a new paradigm of development – more open, participatory, equitable and ecological. It doubted if any real contribution was being made by such corporations to much of the developing world, especially the poorest sectors thereof.

New courses in political economy began at the University of Sydney in 1975 as the result of a long struggle by staff and students, in which Wheelwright played a key role. For this course he co-edited two volumes of *Readings in Political Economy* designed to provide alternative approaches to the analysis of capitalist systems, as well as offering perspectives on socialist systems. For eight years Wheelwright gave the introductory lectures to these courses (which were attended by over 300 students before being abolished by the academic counter-revolution). He also co-edited five volumes of *Essays in the Political Economy of Australian Capitalism* which were designed to provide the essential ingredients for a basic Marxist history (for the first volume, see 1988).

Further co-authored work on the foreign ownership and control of the Australian economy was published under the title of *Australia: A Client State* in 1982, and translated into Japanese in 1986. It argued that dependence on foreign capital and technology had reached such a stage in Australia that the *state itself* had become a client of international capital. This meant an effective loss of any real independence, an emasculation of democracy and further integration into transnational capitalism, permitting only those policies acceptable to foreign investors to be pursued. The following year a Labor government was elected which de-regulated the-financial system, floated the Australian dollar and exposed the entire system to far more foreign penetration than its predecessors, quadrupling the foreign debt in six years and depreciating the Australian dollar by 30%. In 1986 the Labor Treasurer declared that Australia was in danger of becoming a 'banana republic'.

The Japanese connection continued in the late 1980s when Wheelwright's Transnational Project reached a three-year research agreement with Professor Shigeto Tsuru of the Meiji Gakuin University. The countries of Asia were coming to be the dominant investors in Australia and its major trading partners, particularly Japan. In 1989 he co-authored, with a young trade unionist, *The Third Wave: Australia and Asian Capitalism,* which argued that the first wave of foreign investment in Australia had been British, the second American, and the third Asian, especially Japanese. This was the first time that the dominant forces of capitalism in the region were no longer of European or Anglo-Saxon origin. This new wave was much more focused and coordinated than previous ones; the political, social and moral traditions of the investing countries were different, and the language and cultural barriers more difficult to surmount. Consequently, Australia faced both a crisis of identity and of political alignments, and a new economic integration. The book attempted to point out what this meant for the working people of Australia, and argued for more and stronger links with Asian trade unions and similar organizations.

This book was the high-water mark of Wheelwright's dissent, the first edition being sold out in six weeks. Emphasizing as it did the dangers to working people of the accelerating internationalization of capitalism, it appealed especially to trade union and labour circles. Its message was that, ironically, the *capitalists* of the world had taken Marx's advice to unite and that Australian workers were particularly vulnerable. The most pleasing aspect was its translation into Japanese, for which edition Wheelwright wrote a special Foreword. Wheelwright believes it is vital for Asian economists to dissent from the orthodox doctrine that is still being used to justify the exploitation of the world and its people.

Wheelwright's Major Writings

(1957), *Ownership and Control of Australian Companies*, Sydney: Law Book Company.
(1965a), *Industrialization in Malaysia*, Melbourne: Melbourne University Press.
(1965b), *The Highest Bidder* (with Brian Fitzpatrick), Melbourne: Lansdowne Press.

(1970), *The Chinese Road to Socialism* (with Bruce McFarlane), New York: Monthly Review Press.

(1974), *Radical Political Economy*, Sydney: ANZ Book Company.

(1975–83), *Essays in the Political Economy of Australian Capitalism* (with Ken Buckley), Volumes 1–5, Sydney: ANZ Book Company.

(1978), *Capitalism, Socialism or Barbarism? The Australian Predicament*, Sydney: ANZ Book Company.

(1982), *Australia: A Client State* (with Greg Crough), Melbourne: Penguin.

(1986), *Consumers, Transnational Corporations and Development*, Transnational Corporations Research Project, University of Sydney.

(1988), *No Paradise for Workers* (with Kent Buckley), Oxford: Oxford University Press.

(1989), *The Third Wave: Australia and Asian Capitalism* (with Abe David), Sydney: Left Book Club; reprinted 1990.

TO BE
DISPOSED
BY
AUTHORITY